WHAT IS THIS BABBLER TRYING TO SAY?

WHAT IS THIS BABBLER TRYING TO SAY?

Essays on Biblical Interpretation

MICHAEL S. MOORE

☙PICKWICK *Publications* · Eugene, Oregon

WHAT IS THIS BABBLER TRYING TO SAY?
Essays on Biblical Interpretation

Copyright © 2016 Michael S. Moore. All rights reserved. Except for brief quotations in critical publications or reviews, no part of this book may be reproduced in any manner without prior written permission from the publisher. Write: Permissions, Wipf and Stock Publishers, 199 W. 8th Ave., Suite 3, Eugene, OR 97401.

Pickwick Publications
An Imprint of Wipf and Stock Publishers
199 W. 8th Ave., Suite 3
Eugene, OR 97401

www.wipfandstock.com

PAPERBACK ISBN 13: 978-1-4982-0852-9
HARDCOVER ISBN 13: 978-1-4982-0854-3

Cataloguing-in-Publication Data

Moore, Michael S.

What is this babbler trying to say? : essays on biblical interpretation / Michael S. Moore

xx + 348 p. ; 23 cm. Includes bibliographical references and index.

ISBN: 978-1-4982-0854-3 (paperback) | ISBN: 978-1-4982-0854-3 (hardback)

1. Bible. Old Testament—Criticism, interpretation, etc. I. Title.

BS1171.3 M66 2016

Manufactured in the U.S.A.   03/02/2016

This book is dedicated to the memory of my dear mother,
Marjorie Lee Moore.

CONTENTS

Preface | ix
Abbreviations | xi

PART 1: TORAH
1 Another Look at Balaam | 3
2 Balaam the "Prophet"? | 20
3 Role Preemption in the Israelite Priesthood | 25

PART 2: PROPHECY AND APOCALYPTIC
4 Yahweh's Day | 45
5 Jeremiah's Progressive Paradox | 58
6 Jeremiah's Identity Crisis | 81
7 The Laments in Jeremiah and 1QH: Mapping the Metaphorical Trajectories | 94
8 Jehu's Coronation and Purge of Israel | 122
9 Big Dreams and Broken Promises: Solomon's Treaty with Hiram | 140
10 Searching In Sheba: The Desire for "Biblical Literacy" | 156
11 Resurrection and Immortality: Two Motifs Navigating Confluent Theological Streams in Daniel 12:1–4 | 166

PART 3: WISDOM AND OTHER WRITINGS
12 Ruth the Moabite and the Blessing of Foreigners | 183
13 To King or Not To King: A Canonical-Historical Approach to Ruth | 197
14 Job's Texts of Terror | 212
15 Human Suffering in Lamentations | 226
16 Bathsheba's Silence | 245

17 "Wise Women" or "Wisdom Woman?" A Biblical Study of
   Gender Roles | 256

Bibliography | 269

PREFACE

ONE OF THE MOST creative biblical interpreters of all time once had a group of philosophers, after listening to him speak his mind publicly, disdainfully ask, "What is this babbler trying to say?" (Acts 17:18). The word translated "babbler" in most English translations of this ancient Greek text is σπερμολόγος, a composite word composed of two shorter ones: σπέρμα ("seed") + λέγω ("to pick up"). On the page it looks pretty straightforward. These folks call Saul of Tarsus a "seed-picker." Spinning the word positively, we might suggest that they see him as someone gifted at, say, "picking up" the "seeds" of "great ideas" and "planting" them in the fertile minds of eager students. Perhaps they think of him as a college lecturer or high school teacher. Like a lot of ancient terms, however, what this one *actually* means is something far different from what it looks like on the page.

Dionysius of Halicarnassus tells the story of a man named Postumius, a patrician sent by Rome to serve as ambassador to the bustling port city of Tarantus in southeastern Italy (where the "sole" meets the "heel"). After delivering a get-acquainted speech to his new neighbors, he soon finds himself accosted by a man named Philonides, whom Dionysius calls a "σπερμολόγος," describing him in no uncertain terms as a drunk and a scoundrel. So, when the Stoics and Epicureans use the same word in Athens, doubtless this is more the type of "babbler" they have in mind.

Engagement with these two encounters yields two reflections. *First*, it seems prudent here at the outset of *this* book to advise readers picking up *these* "seeds" (i.e., the essays published here) to gauge their expectations accordingly. Though revised and updated, these studies span several decades, countries, and institutions of higher learning. Some of the ideas here have certainly changed over the years, but many have basically remained the same. *Second*, like Postumius and Paul, perhaps it also seems appropriate to caution *this* biblical interpreter (me) to gauge *my* expectations. If the folks in ancient Athens respond to Paul's words by calling *him* a "babbler," what sort of reaction should I realistically expect from colleagues and critics and students and friends and anyone else picking up *these* words?

Let's see, shall we?

ABBREVIATIONS

ABD	*Anchor Bible Dictionary.* 6 vols. Edited by David Noel Freedman. New York: Doubleday, 1992
ABL	*Assyrian and Babylonian Letters* (Harper)
ad loc.	to the place (Lat)
AfO	*Archiv für Orientforschung*
AGH	*Die akkadische Gebetsserie "Handerhebung"* (Ebeling)
Aḥiq	*Aḥiqar* (CAP 210)
AHw	*Akkadisches Handwörterbuch.* 3 vols. Edited by Wolfram von Soden. Wiesbaden: Harrassowitz, 1961
A.J.	*Antiquities of the Jews*
AJBI	*Annual of the Japanese Biblical Institute*
AJSL	*American Journal of Semitic Languages and Literature*
Akk	Akkadian
ANE	Ancient Near Eastern
ANET	*Ancient Near Eastern Texts Relating to the Old Testament.* 3rd ed. Edited by James B. Pritchard. Princeton: Princeton University Press, 1969
a posteriori	knowledge dependent on experience or empirical evidence (Lat)
a priori	knowledge independent of experience or empirical evidence (Lat)
Aq	Aquila
Ar.	Aristophanes
Aram	Aramaic
ARM	*Archives royales de Mari* (Parrot & Dossin)
art.	article

AT	*The Alalaḫ Tablets* (Wiseman)
BA	*Biblical Archaeologist*
BAR	*Biblical Archaeology Review*
BASOR	*Bulletin of the American Schools of Oriental Research*
BBR	*Beiträge zur Kenntnis des babylonischen Religion* (Zimmern)
BHS	*Biblia Hebraica Stuttgartensia*. Edited by K. Elliger & W. Rudolph. Stuttgart, 1983
Bib	*Biblica*
BibInt	*Biblical Interpretation*
BuBR	*Bulletin for Biblical Research*
BJS	*British Journal of Sociology*
BMS	*Babylonian Magic and Sorcery* (King)
BR	*Biblical Research*
BSac	*Bibliotheca Sacra*
BSOAS	*Bulletin of the School of Oriental and African Studies*
BTB	*Biblical Theology Bulletin*
BZ	*Biblische Zeitschrift*
CA	*Current Anthropology*
CAD	*Chicago Assyrian Dictionary*. 20 vols. Edited by Martha T. Roth *et al*. Chicago: Oriental Institute of the University of Chicago, 1921–2011
CANE	*Civilizations of the Ancient Near East*. Edited by Jack M. Sasson. Peabody, MA: Hendrickson, 2000
CAP	*Aramaic Papyri of the Fifth Century B.C.* Edited by A. E. Cowley. Oxford: Clarendon, 1923
CAT	*The Cuneiform Alphabetic Texts from Ugarit, Ras Ibn Hani and Other Places*. Edited by Manfred Dietrich *et al*. Münster: Ugarit, 1995
CBQ	*The Catholic Biblical Quarterly*
CD	*Damascus Document*
CEJ	*Christian Education Journal*
cf.	compare
CH	*Codex Hammurabi*
CML	*Canaanite Myths and Legends*. Edited by J. C. L. Gibson. Edinburgh: T. & T. Clark, 1977

contra	against (Lat)
CTH	*Catalogue des textes hittites*. Edited by E. Laroche. Paris: Klincksieck, 1971
d	determinative for the deity (Sum DINGIR)
D	doubled (i.e., the intensive form of semitic verbs)
DA	*Deir ʿAllā texts* (Hoftijzer & van der Kooij)
DDD	*Dictionary of Deities and Demons in the Bible*. Edited by Karel van der Toorn *et al.* Leiden: Brill, 1999
DH	deuteronomistic historian
DN	divine name
DNWSI	*Dictionary of North-West Semitic Inscriptions*. Edited by J. Hoftijzer and K. Jongeling. Leiden: Brill, 1995.
DOTPr	*Dictionary of the Old Testament Prophets*. Edited by Mark Boda & J. Gordon McConville. Downers Grove, IL: IVP Academic, 2012
DSD	*Dead Sea Discoveries*
Dtr	deuteronomistic (revision/editor)
DtrH	Deuteronomistic History (Joshua-Kings)
DTT	*Dansk teologisk tidsskrift*
DTTML	*Dictionary of the Targumim, Talmud, and Midrashic Literature*. Compiled and edited by Marcus Jastrow. New York: Chorob, 1926.
EA	*Die El Amarna Tafeln* (Knudtzon)
ECB	*Eerdmans Commentary on the Bible*. Edited by James D. G. Dunn & John W. Rogerson. Grand Rapids: Eerdmans, 2003
EDB	*Eerdmans Dictionary of the Bible*. Edited by David Noel Freedman. Grand Rapids: Eerdmans, 2000
EDSS	*Encyclopedia of the Dead Sea Scrolls*. 2 vols. Edited by Lawrence H. Schiffman. New York: Oxford University Press, 2000
Ee	*Enûma Eliš*
e.g.	for example
EgT	*Eglise et Théologie*
EI	*Eretz Israel*
Emar	*Emar* (Arnaud)

EOHJ	*Encyclopedia of the Historical Jesus*. Edited by Craig A. Evans. New York: Routledge, 2008
ER	*The Encyclopedia of Religion*. 16 vols. Edited by Mircea Eliade. New York: MacMillan, 1987
Erra	*The Epic of Erra* (Cagni)
esp.	especially
ET	English translation
et al.	and others (Lat)
EvT	*Evangelische Theologie*
ExpTim	*Expository Times*
f.	feminine
FH	*Fides et Historia*
frag.	fragment
FS	*Festschrift* (anthology of essays dedicated to a senior scholar)
FT	*Fragment Targums* (Klein)
GCA	*Gratz College Annual*
GE	Gilgamesh Epic
GKC	*Gesenius' Hebrew Grammar*. Edited by E. Kautzsch. Trans. by A. E. Cowley. Oxford: Oxford University Press, 1910
GN	geographic name
GNT	Greek New Testament
HAL	*Hebräisches und aramäisches Lexikon zum Alten Testament*. 5 vols. Edited by Ludwig Koehler *et al*. Leiden: Brill, 1967–95
Heb	Hebrew
Hit	Hittite
HS	*Hebrew Studies*
HT	*Hethitisches Totenrituale* (Otten)
HTR	*Harvard Theological Review*
HUCA	*Hebrew Union College Annual*
HUSLA	*Hebrew University Studies in Literature and the Arts*
Ibid.	same source as that cited in preceding footnote (Lat)
IDB	*Interpreters Dictionary of the Bible*. 5 volumes. Edited by George A. Buttrick. Nashville: Abingdon, 1966
Idr	*The Statue of Idri-mi* (Smith)

i.e.	that is
IEJ	*Israel Exploration Journal*
Int	*Interpretation*
ipf.	imperfect
ipv.	imperative
JANESCU	*Journal of the Ancient Near Eastern Society of Columbia University*
JAOS	*Journal of the American Oriental Society*
JBL	*Journal of Biblical Literature*
JCS	*Journal of Cuneiform Studies*
JHS	*Journal of Hebrew Scriptures*
JJS	*Journal of Jewish Studies*
JL	Jeremiah's laments
JNES	*Journal of Near Eastern Studies*
Jos.	Josephus
JPC	*Journal of Pastoral Counseling*
JRT	*Journal of Religious Thought*
JSJ	*Journal for the Study of Judaism in the Persian, Hellenistic and Roman Periods*
JSOT	*Journal for the Study of the Old Testament*
JSS	*Journal of Semitic Studies*
JTS	*Journal of Theological Studies*
KAI	*Kanaanäische und aramäische Inschriften* (Donner & Röllig)
KAR	*Keilschrifttexte aus Assur religiösen Inhalts*. Edited by E. Ebeling. Leipzig, 1923
KBo	*Keilschrifttexte aus Boğazköy*
KS	Kurkh Stele (Grayson)
KUB	*Keitschrifturkunden aus Boğazköy*
LAB	Ps.-Philo's *Liber Antiquitatum Biblicarum* (Harrington)
Lane	*An Arabic-English Lexicon*. Edited by Edward William Lane. Edinburgh: Williams and Norgate, 1863
Lat	Latin
LB	Late Babylonian
Leitwort	key-word
lit.	literally

LSJ	*A Greek-English Lexicon.* Edited by H. G. Liddell, R. Scott, and H. S. Jones. Oxford: Oxford University Press, 1996
Lu	Luwian
Lud	*Ludlul bēl nēmeqi.* Edited by A. Annus and A. Lenzi. Helsinki: The Neo-Assyrian Text Corpus Project, 2010
LW	Martin Luther. *Luther's Works.* St. Louis & Philadelphia: Concordia & Fortress, 1956
m.	masculine
Maq	*Maqlû* (Meier)
MDB	*Mercer Dictionary of the Bible.* Edited by Watson E. Mills. Macon, GA: Mercer University Press, 1990
mid.	middle (voice)
MIO	*Mitteilungen des Instituts für Orientforschung*
MT	Masoretic Text
N.B.	nota bene ("note well," Lat)
NIV	New International Version
NRSV	New Revised Standard Version
NTS	*New Testament Studies*
Nub.	*Nubes* ("Clouds")
OAN	Oracles Against the Nations
OB	Old Babylonian
OG	Old Greek
OL	Old Latin
op. cit.	in the work cited (Lat)
Or	*Orientalia*
OT	Old Testament
OTWSA	*Ou-Testamentiese Werkgemeenskap in Suider-Afrika*
P	the priestly (editorial) stratum of Torah
p.	person
pace	with all due respect for (Lat)
passim	throughout (Lat)
PBS	Publications of the Babylonian Section, University Museum, University of Pennsyvania
pf.	perfect
Ph	Phoenician
pl.	plural

PN	proper name
pres.	present (tense)
PSB	*Princeton Seminary Bulletin*
PSD	*The Compendious Syriac Dictionary, founded upon the Thesaurus Syriacus of R. Payne Smith*. Edited by J. Payne Smith. Oxford: Clarendon, 1903
Q	Qur'an
qal waḥomer	"from minor to major"
RA	*Revue d'Assyriologie*
Racc	*Rituels accadiens* (Thureau-Dangin)
RB	*Revue biblique*
RBL	*Review of Biblical Literature*
RelEd	*Religious Education*
ResQ	*Restoration Quarterly*
RevQ	*Revue de Qumran*
rev.	revised
RHA	*Revue hittite et asianique*
RHPR	*Revue d'histoire et de philosophie religieuses*
RlA	*Reallexicon der Assyriologie*. Edited by Erich Ebeling, et al. Berlin: 1928-
RN	royal name
RPL	*Revue philosophique de Louvain*
RS	*Ras Shamra* (field numbers of excavated tablets)
RSR	*Recherches de science religieuse*
šā	šumma ālu (Nötscher)
SAA	*State Archives of Assyria*
Sam	Samaritan Pentateuch (von Gall)
SBL	Society of Biblical Literature
SBLSP	*Society of Biblical Literature Seminar Papers*
Sem	*Semeia*
sg.	singular
SJOT	*Scandinavian Journal of the Old Testament*
SSI	*Textbook of Syrian Semitic Inscriptions*. Edited by J. C. L. Gibson. 3 vols. Oxford: Clarendon, 1971, 1975, 1982
ST	*Studia Theologica*

suff.	suffix
Sum	*Sumerian*
Šur	*Šurpu* (Reiner)
s.v.	*sub verbo* ("see under")
Syh	Syro-hexaplaric translation of OG
Sym	Symmachus
Tanak	The Hebrew Bible
TDOT	*Theological Dictionary of the Old Testament.* 14 vols. Edited by G. Johannes Botterweck et al. Grand Rapids: Eerdmans, 1978–2004
Tg. Esth.	*Targum Esther* (Grossfeld)
Tg. Neof.	*Targum Neofiti* (Diez Macho)
Tg. Onk.	*Targum Onkelos* (Drazin and Wagner)
Tg. Ps.-J.	*Targum Pseudo-Jonathan* (Clarke et al.)
Th	Theodotian
TJob	*Testament of Job*
trans.	translated/translator
TS	*Theological Studies*
TSol	*Testament of Solomon*
TT	*Theologisch Tijdschrift*
TuL	*Tod und Leben* (Ebeling)
TynBul	*Tyndale Bulletin*
TZ	*Theologische Zeitschrift*
UET	Ur Excavations, Texts
UF	*Ugarit Forschungen*
Ug	Ugaritic
Ugar	*Ugaritica* (Nougayrol et al.)
UNP	*Ugaritic Narrative Poetry.* Edited by Simon B. Parker. Atlanta: Scholars, 1997
USQR	*Union Seminary Quarterly Review*
UT	*Ugaritic Textbook.* 3 vols. Edited by Cyrus Gordon. Rome: Pontificium Institutum Biblicum, 1965
v(v).	verse(s)
VBoT	*Verstreute Boghazöi-Texte* (Goetze)
Vg	Vulgate

viz.	namely
VT	*Vetus Testamentum*
VTSup	*Vetus Testamentum Supplements*
WA	Martin Luther. *D. Martin Luthers Werke*. Weimarer Ausgabe. 127 Vols. Weimar: Böhlau, 1893
WCA	*A Dictionary of Modern Written Arabic*. Edited by Hans Wehr and Milton Cowan. Ithaca, NY: Cornell University Press, 1966
WTJ	*Westminster Theological Journal*
WVDOG	*Wissenschaftliche Veröffentlichungen der Deutschen Orient-Gesellschaft*
WW	*Word & World*
ZA	*Zeitschrift für Assyriologie und vorderasiatische Archäologie*
ZÄS	*Zeitschrift für ägyptische Sprache und Altertumskunde*
ZAW	*Zeitschrift für die alttestamentliche Wissenschaft*
ZDPV	*Zeitschrift des deutschen Palästina-Vereins*

PART 1: TORAH

1

ANOTHER LOOK AT BALAAM*

BALAAM BEN BEOR IS a multidimensional figure, whether we examine his activity in the Hebrew Bible, in Second Temple Judaism, or on the plaster inscription from Tell Deir ʿAllā.[1] Within the Balaam cycle in Tanak (Num 22–24) the text depicts him as Yahweh's "obedient servant."[2] Yet within this cycle he also behaves as a bungling buffoon in a satirical "burlesque,"[3] a blind "seer" unable to "see" Yahweh's angel standing directly in his path. Micah of Moresheth preserves a memory of him acting as Moab's antagonist (Mic 6:3–5), but most Tanak sources depict him as Israel's quintessential antagonist.[4]

This polarized response to Balaam hardens in several Second Temple texts. Ps.-Philo, for example, continues to portray him as God's faithful "servant" (Lat *servum tuum*)[5] while an anonymous rabbinic commentator

---

* Revised from a paper first read to the Hebrew and Cognate Literature Section of the SBL on Nov 20, 1989 in Anaheim, California, subsequently published in *RB* 97 (1990) 359–78.

1. Discovered in 1967 at the Zerqa river in Jordan (see Hoftijzer & van der Kooij, *Deir ʿAllā*). Excavated by a Dutch team of archaeologists led by H. J. Franken, this reconstructed plaster inscription now sits on display in the National Museum of Jordan in Amman.

2. Num 22:1–21, 36–41; 23:1–24:25.

3. Num 22:22–35; Rofé, *Blʿm*, 51 (ברלסקה).

4. Num 31:8, 16; Josh 13:21–22; 24:9–10; Deut 23:4–7; Neh 13:1–2. See Moore, *Balaam*, 1–11.

5. *LAB* 18.4.

calls him "a prophet greater than Moses."[6] Contradicting these portrayals, however, the Fragment Targums,[7] Talmud,[8] and Greek New Testament[9] all portray him as "Balaam the Wicked."[10] Recognizing the danger posed by such lopsided polarization, Josephus cautiously suggests that readers go back to Tanak and examine it carefully before making up their minds about Balaam.[11]

The Deir ʿAllā texts give us more information. Here Balaam appears as a "seer of the gods" (ḥzn ʾlhn) on the first line of Combination 1,[12] an envoy allegedly chosen by a divine council to convey a doomsday oracle to a local populace. Combination 2, however, though more fragmentary, depicts him in categories more congruent with the occultic activity alluded to in Num

---

6. *Sifrê Deut* 34.10, cited in Rofé, *Blʿm*, 28. The desire to "nabi-ize" Balaam—i.e., turn him into a Yahwistic "prophet"—has a long history among those tradents who find his multiplicity of roles socially, culturally, and religiously disturbing (e.g., Josephus, *A. J.* 4.104; see discussion in Moore, "Balaam," 104). Anthonioz succinctly explains (*Prophétisme*, 13–14): "The generalization of the term 'prophet' . . . is driven by a certain uniformity of presentation with regard to different types of personnel connected to divine revelation (diviners, seers, visionaries, men of God, prophets), resulting in a redefined prophetic ideal in which the social aspects, practices, techniques, and rituals of ancient prophecy become 'hidden' (*occulté*)."

7. בלעם רשיעא (*FTNum* 22.30); בלעם הרשע (*b. Taʿan.* 20a; *Num. Rab.* 20.14).

8. *b. Sanh.* 106b. Arguing over whether or not Job might be Israelite, some rabbis list him alongside Balaam as one of שבעה נביאים נתנבאו לאומות ("seven prophets who prophesy to the nations"), the other five being Eliphaz, Bildad, Zophar, Elihu, and Balaam's father (*b. B. Bat.* 15b).

9. 2 Pet 2:16 warns readers not to be like Balaam, described here as a "prophet" (προφήτης) prone to "madness" (παραφρονία // παρανοία in Ar. *Nub.* 845). Similarly lopsided portrayals occur in Jude 11 and Rev 2:14.

10. Qurʾan contains no explicit reference to Balaam, but most readers take Q 7.175–76 to be a depiction parallel to that found in *b. B. Bat.* 15b: "Recite against them (i.e., the Jews) the story of him (Balaam) to whom we brought our signs. But he separated himself from them, Satan followed him, and he became 'one of the faithless' (من الغاوين)."

11. Josephus, *A. J.* 4.158.

12. DA 1.1 (written in red ink). Levine transliterates and translates *DA* Combinations 1 and 2 (*Numbers*, 243–63), as does Hackett (*Deir ʿAllā*, 25–30), Hoftijzer & van der Kooij (*Deir ʿAllā*), and Caquot & Lemaire ("Deir ʿAllā," 189–208)

31:16.¹³ Whatever the interpretive possibilities,¹⁴ the *DA* discovery removes all doubt about the existence of a non-Hebrew Balaam tradition in Iron Age Transjordan among a people evidently non-Yahwistic and probably non-Israelite.

Yet in spite of this new evidence several studies of this ancient Near Eastern specialist continue to construct his multidimensionality within bipolar parameters first proposed by nineteenth-century literary critics to explain, prior to the great archaeological discoveries of the twentieth century, the character and development of Torah. Within this framework Balaam is either a "blesser" or a "curser," but these are the only options.¹⁵ The vestigial "2-source" hypothesis underlying this polarized framework has been and continues to be contested. Some angrily rail at it;¹⁶ others try to work within its bipolar parameters (often without presuming the existence of independent literary "documents");¹⁷ and still others ignore it.¹⁸ Few attempt to engage seriously the sociohistorical context out of which the Balaam traditions originate.¹⁹

The question raised here is therefore simple. Is Balaam *only* a "curser"/"blesser," or is the nineteenth-century bipolar approach to the Balaam traditions inadequate and outdated? Without denying that Tanak

---

13. The telling line here, למסר מעל ביהוה ("to break faith with Yhwh") . . . בדבר בלעם ("at Balaam's word") cross-references the portrait in Num 22–24 with the occult ritual in 25:3 where יצמד ישראל לבעל פעור ("Israel yokes itself to the Ba'al of Peor"). Based on the parallel between פעור and Ph *p'r* // Lu *pa-ḫa-r[a]* in the Karatepe bilingual inscription (*KAI* 26A.6), Mendenhall plausibly suggests a North Syrian/Anatolian origin for the Ba'al Peor cult, translating בעל פעור as "Lord of Fire" (Hit *paḫḫuwar*, "fire"; *Tenth*, 109). Pope views the Ba'al Peor cult as a Transjordanian example of מרזח (Amos 6:7; Jer 16:5), however it may have been planted there (*Song*, 217).

14. See opinions listed in Moore, "Balaam," 101–106.

15. Wellhausen, *Composition*, 109–16; 347–53; Mowinckel, "Bil'amsage," 233–71; Noth, *Pentateuchal*, 78.

16. Kuenen, "Bileam,", 497–540; Rudolph, *"Elohist,"* 97–128; Buber, *Kingship*, 210–14. Among more recent critics of the "2-source" hypothesis, special mention goes to Gross (*Bileam*) and Rofé (*Bl'm*).

17. Schmidt, "Bileamüberlieferung," 234–61; Donner, "Pseudopropheta," 112–23; Müller, "Dēr 'Allā," 56–67; "Bileamsprüche," 214–44.

18. Kalisch, *Balaam*; Albright, "Balaam"; Liver, "Balaam"; von Pákozdy, "Bileam-Perikope"; Coppens, "Bileam"; Vetter, *Seherspruch*; Rost, "Bileam."

19. *Exceptions:* Prior to the discovery of *DA*, a few scholars compare Balaam's behavior with that of other specialists. Ignaz Goldziher, e.g., compares Balaam's משלים ("oracles," Num 23:7, 18; 24:3, 15) with a species of Arabic poetry called هجإ ("satirical lampoon"; *Philologie*, 41–44; see van Gelder, *Hijā*, 1–12), while Samuel Daiches ("Balaam") and René Largement look for parallels in the Mesopotamian literature ("Bile'am"). Since the discovery of *DA*, however, some have begun to wonder whether a holistic understanding of Balaam is even possible; see Kaufman (Review); Knauf (Review); and Halpern (Review).

editors largely succeed in corralling the Balaam traditions within enclosures structured by the "blessing-curse" polarity,[20] perpetuation of this nineteenth-century approach practically guarantees that the multidimensional roles enacted by this specialist will remain hidden from view. Better to switch methodological gears and re-examine the Balaam traditions from a perspective informed by selected anthropological studies of religion,[21] especially the adaptable variables generated by contemporary role theorists.[22] Such an approach has already helped us see deeper into the inner workings of the priestly (Israelite) cult[23] and (Hebrew) prophecy,[24] so the likelihood seems strong that a similar approach to the Balaam traditions will produce similar results—assuming, of course, that all the known literary portrayals of this specialist are rooted in actual praxis.[25]

PLOTTING ROLES ON A MAGIC-RELIGION CONTINUUM

Anthropologist Annemarie de Waal Malefijt argues convincingly that it's impossible to draw neat, static distinctions between "magic" and "religion" in any given culture, but that some distinction between the two is necessary if comparative analysis is to proceed.[26] Thus it can be helpful (in certain cases) to visualize "magic" as "manipulative" and "religion" as "supplicative"

   20. Halpern's self-admittedly "crass" description of this agenda as a process whereby "pentateuchal narrators loot and uproot Balaam," then "mill and plane him" into "decorative paneling in a two-dimensional depiction of pre-monarchic antiquity" unnecessarily denigrates this theology ("Deir `Allā," 119). Wilson's discussion is less flippantly polemical (*Prophecy*, 147–50).
   21. De Waal Malefijt, *Religion*, 228–45; Banton, *Religion*; Morris, *Religion*.
   22. Harnisch, "Role Theory"; Biddle, *Role Theory*; Turner, *Role Theory*; Sarbin & Allen, "Role Theory"; Goodenough, "'Status' and 'Role'"; Keesing, "Role Analysis"; Popitz, *Theorie*.
   23. Mary Douglas' influence (*Purity*) is pervasive in the work of Gottwald (*Hebrew Bible*, 473–78), Hendel ("Aniconic"), and other students of Hebrew cult.
   24. Wilson (*Prophecy*) is heavily influenced by the theories of Lewis (*Ecstatic*), and Petersen (*Roles*) follows the theoretical path carved out by Sarbin & Allen ("Role Theory"), as do I in my dissertation (*Balaam*, 110–22). Buss obliquely explains some of the more obvious cognitions championed by role theorists ("Prophecy," 3), and Morris (*Religion*, 231–33) critically analyzes the strengths and weaknesses of Douglas (*Purity*) and Lewis (*Ecstatic*).
   25. For some readers this is an untenable presumption, but "in the area of literary techniques the evidence from the literate neighbors of ancient Israel is not only relevant . . . but also enjoys a scholarly consensus based on a maximum of facts and a minimum of theories" (Hallo, "Cuneiform," 12–13).
   26. De Waal Malefijt, *Religion*, 14–15.

(with Frazer),[27] or "magic" as "utilitarian" and "religion" as "celebratory" (with Malinowski),[28] or "magic" as "individual" and "religion" as "communal" (with Durkheim).[29] None of these distinctions is absolute, of course, but all can be helpful as long as "the boundary between magical formula and supplications remains fluid."[30] Magic and religion are not static categories, nor is it helpful to conceptualize them via "ideal types,"[31] or worse, pretend that no boundaries exist between them at all.[32] Magic and religion are best viewed as opposite poles on a dynamic continuum upon which the roles of any given "magico-religious" specialist can be defined and plotted.[33]

ANCIENT NEAR EASTERN MAGICO-RELIGIOUS SPECIALISTS

Most ancient Near Eastern magico-religious specialists enact pluralistic roles on variegated overlapping spectrums within the magic-religion continuum. Etymological analyses of *titles* thus do little to help us understand the sociological phenomenon of *role enactment*.[34] Both *bārû* and *šā'ilu* specialists, for example, enact roles as "dream-interpreters" in Mesopotamia.[35] This label describes one of several roles enacted by the *bārû*, but for all intents and purposes sums up the totality of the *šā'ilu*'s societal function. In fact, even though the Akkadian noun *bārû* philologically derives from the verb *barû* ("to look upon, inspect," *CAD* B.115), the *bārû*-"priest"[36] in

27. Frazer, *Bough*, 56–69 (critiqued by Morris, *Religion*, 103–6).
28. Malinowski, *Magic*, 390–98 (critiqued by Morris, *Religion*, 144–51).
29. Durkheim, *Elementary*, 60 (critiqued by Morris, *Religion*, 106–22).
30. Weber, *Sociology*, 26.
31. Fischoff, "Preface," xxxiii.

32. Cryer's *avant-garde* attempt to eradicate all boundaries between magic and religion is hardly convincing (*Divination*, 70–95), nor are the attempts of Kitz ("Prophecy," 22–42) and Jeffers (*Magic*, 1–4). More persuasive are the careful analyses of Grabbe (*Specialists*, 250–51), de Tarragon ("Witchcraft," 2071), and Nissinen (*Prophets*, 1–6)

33. Garr's judicious use of "continuum" significantly advances our understanding of Syro-Palestinian linguistics beyond Bergstrasser, Harris, and Rabin (*Dialect*, 205–40), and Anthonioz' attempt to catalogue all divinatory activity into three simple categories—divination by natural elements, divination by animals, divination by humans—is too heuristic (*Prophétisme*, 22–27).

34. Moore, *Balaam*, 111–13.

35. For *bārû*, the couplet preserved on an Assyrian tablet published by Weidner ("Tagen," 5.9) reads *ba-ru-tum ip-pu-šu šu-na-ti i-ta-nam-ma-r[u]*, "he performs divination; he experiences dreams." For *šā'ilu*, note the texts cited in Oppenheim (*Dreambook*, 221–25) and Renger ("Priestertum," 217–18).

36. That there seems to be no generic Akk term for "priest" (Renger, "Priestertum,"

8   PART 1: TORAH

Mesopotamia is much more than mere "diviner." In point of fact he enacts several roles, all clustering around the "religion" pole of the magic-religion continuum. Following R. K. Merton's lead, we designate this cluster of roles a "diviner-seer" *role-set*.[37] The dominant roles within the *bārû* role-set thus include "diviner," (including "libanomantic" [smoke-diviner],[38] "lecanomantic" [oil-diviner],[39] "rhabdomantic" [rod-diviner],[40] "ornithomantic" [bird-diviner],[41] "extispicist" [entrails-diviner],[42] "oneiromantic" [dream-diviner],[43] and "oracle-reciter").[44]

Clustered around the "magic" pole of the continuum, however, stand the variegated roles enacted by the *āšipu*-priest, premier among which stand the roles of "exorcist,"[45] "purification-priest,"[46] "healer,"[47] and "sorcerer."[48] Distinguishable from the "diviner/seer" role-set on the other end of the continuum, the "exorcist" role-set encompasses a fascinating range of behavior well supported by now-extensive primary data.[49]

---

110) does not prohibit analysis of this *social role* in ancient Mesopotamia.

37. Merton, "Role-Set."

38. *CAD* B.122; Gurney, "Babylonians," 152–53.

39. *BBR* 79–82.21–2. *Bārû*-priests divine by oil (Gen 44:14–17) to determine whether enemies can be fended off, whether cities can be seized, and whether curses can be formulated for pronouncement by *āšipu*-priests enacting roles as "sorcerers" (see Gurney, "Babylonians," 152).

40. *TuL* 74.4; *HT* 32.9–14; *CAT* 1.16.6.8; see Moore, *Balaam*, 52–3.

41. *BBR* 1–20.8; Nougayrol, "Oiseau," 23.7–16. *Bārû*-priests use birds for divination purposes, but Akk texts are unclear about specific techniques, especially when compared with the Hittite texts (e.g., *KUB* 18.5.12; 22.15.1.1–14; Haas & Wilhelm, *Riten*, 139–42).

42. Aro, "Extispicy," 109–17; Starr, *Diviner*.

43. Weidner, "Tagen," 5; Mouton, *Rêves*. Oppenheim thinks that though *bārû* participate in this type of divination, dream interpreters as a "class" usually come from lower positions in the religious hierarchy (*Dreambook*, 221).

44. Knudtzon, *Gebete*, 7–62.

45. Zimmern, "Keilschrifttexte," 206–13; Geller, "Incipits," 242–54.

46. Laessøe, *Studies*.

47. Labat, *Traité*; Ritter, "Medicine"; Geller, *Medicine*.

48. The second tablet of *Maqlû* shows the *āšipu*-priest asking the Seven Wise Men of Eridu (a) to protect his client from the magical power of the *kaššaptu*-sorceress (*Maq* 2.124; *CAD* K.291–92; cf. מכשפה, Exod 22:17; מכשף, Deut 18:10), and (b) that she be pursued by *šēdu* demons (*Maq* 2.210; see Moore, "Terror," 662–63). In *bît rimki* an *āšipu* curses her via a familiar bipolar formula: *[ši-]i li-mut-ma ana-ku lu-bu-lu[t]* ("May she die, and may I live," Laessøe, 47.7; note also ארור ואררריך ברוך מברכיך in Num 24:9, "Blessed are those who bless you, and cursed are those who curse you").

49. Starr, *Diviner*; Mayer, *Gebetsbeschwörungen*; Geller, *Medicine*.

In Anatolia, however, the evidence generates a different picture. Whereas roles on opposite ends of the magic-religion continuum tend to be enacted by separate specialists in Mesopotamia, complementary roles overlapping the spheres of both magic and religion in Anatolia/North Syria are often enacted by the same specialist. The "old woman" (^{SAL}ŠU.GI, Hit ḫašawaš),[50] for example, is a remarkably diverse specialist who enacts a wide range of roles in the Boğazköy texts, including at least those of "diviner"[51] and "oracle-reciter"[52] near the religion pole, and "exorcist,"[53] purification-priest,"[54] "incantation-reciter,"[55] and "sorceress"[56] at the magic pole. Another example is the "augur" (^{LÚ}MUŠEN.DÙ),[57] a specialist who, like the "old woman," enacts both "magical" and "religious" roles.[58]

In Syria-Palestine we lack the sort of raw evidence like that attested in Mesopotamia and Anatolia, but we do have indirect evidence from Ugaritic, Phoenician, and Aramaic texts for identifying divinatory and exorcistic role-sets. From the evidence available it is possible to postulate that various Syro-Palestinian specialists enact roles as "ornithomantics"

---

50. Goetze, *Kleinasien*, 149.

51. Gurney (*Hittite*, 42–44); Vieyra ("Hittite," 110–15); Kammenhuber (*Hethitern*, 9–13, 27–8). Goetze (*Kleinasien*, 149) links the ^{SAL}ŠU.GI primarily with the KIN-oracle (an Anatolian form of cleromancy), but notes that she also practices augury via "bird" (MUŠEN) and "snake" (MUŠ) omens.

52. Vieyra, *Sorcier*, 111.

53. One North Syrian ^{SAL}ŠU.GI exorcises demons called "the thing which sticks to the mouth (*dam-me-in-ku-wa-ar*), "the evil eye" (IGI$^{ḪI-A}$), "the fear of the lion," and "the terror before the snake" (see texts in Haas & Thiel, *Allaituraḫḫi*, 104, 146; Moore, "Terror," 662–63).

54. Maštikka, another ^{SAL}ŠU.GI from North Syria, uses homeopathic ritual to cleanse impurity from a family in conflict (Rost, "Ritual," 345–79; see Gurney, *Hittite*, 52–58; Vieyra, "Hittite," 110–12; *ANET* 350–51).

55. The ^{SAL}ŠU.GI, for example, manipulates the *šalliš waštaiš* ritual ("great passing away"), with its repeated incantations to the sun deity, to save her client from damnation (*HT* 58.3–60.7; 66.1–68.36; see Bryce, *Hittite*, 142–43).

56. In one text a ^{SAL}ŠU.GI entices a city's gods to abandon it so her client (the king) can curse it directly (*KUB* 7.60, cited in Haas & Wilhelm, *Riten*, 234–3; see Friedrich, *Elementarbuch* 2.42–43).

57. The title of this specialist (^{LÚ}MUŠEN.DÙ) suggests a core occupation with birds as a "fowler" (Akk *ušandû*), and one text shows a ^{SAL}ŠU.GI conducting a purification ritual alongside a ^{LÚ}MUŠEN.DÙ named Ḫuwarlu (*KBo* 4.2, cited in Ünal, "Augures," 31); see Gurney ("Hittites," 155) and Collins ("Ḫuwarlu").

58. *KUB* 18.5.4 reads, "An *alliya*-bird came back up from behind the river flying low, and settled in a poplar tree. While we watched it, another *alliya*-bird attacked it"; see Ünal ("Augures," 46–47); Haas (*Orakel*, 27–47); Mouton & Rutherford ("Augury," 329–44).

(bird-diviners),⁵⁹ "cleromantics" (lot-diviners),⁶⁰ "oneiromantics" (dream-diviners),⁶¹ "lecanomantics" (oil-diviners),⁶² "rhabdomantics" (rod-diviners),⁶³ "necromantics" (underworld-diviners),⁶⁴ "sacrificial-priests,"⁶⁵

59. Idri-mi "looks into lambs" (*pu-ḫā-dē ab-ri-ma*) and "releases birds" (*iṣṣūrē u-za-ki*) to divine the will of Adad (*Idr* 28–29), and one of the Amarna letters preserves a request from a Cypriot king for a "man who inquires by eagles" (^LÚ*ša-i-li naš-rē, EA* 35.26). A ^LÚMUŠEN.DÙ appears at Alalaḫ (Akk *ušandû*, "fowler," *AT* 281), and Daniel's lament over Aqhat likely reflects an ornithomantic context, though this is disputed (*CAT* 1.19.3.2–4, 10, 24, 32–33, 38; see Haldar, *Prophets*, 80).

60. Iwry thinks that the twelfth-to-tenth-century bronze arrowheads found in Lebanon and points south are used in cleromantic praxis ("Belomancy," 27–34) over Milik's objection ("Arrowhead," 3–6), but with Cross' tepid approval ("Alphabet," 8–24). Hebrew cleromancy is best represented by the אורים ותמים ("Urim and Thummim," Exod 28:30); see Caquot ("Divination," 87); Huffmon ("Divination," 355–59); van Dam (*Urim*).

61. Kirta learns of his son's birth in a dream (*CAT* 1.15.3.46–51), and a נביא or a מלך can receive a vision (מראה) or a dream (חלום, Num 12:6; 1 Kings 3:4–5); see Cryer (*Divination*, 267–72); Oppenheim (*Dreambook*); Gnuse (*Dreams*, 34–128); Alexander ("Dreambook"); Noegel ("Dreams"); Mouton (*Rêves*).

62. Caquot ("Divination," 104); Noegel ("Religion," 30); Anor (*Omens*).

63. The מטה האלהים ("rod of God," Exod 4:20) carried by Moses parallels the ^iṣerina n[a-ra]m ilani rabuti ("cedar rod of the great gods") of the *bārû*-priest (*BBR* 24.9) and the *ḫultuppû* ("magic rod") of the *āšipu*-priest (*BBR* 26.1.20). The envoy sent by El to heal Kirta (*Šaʿtiqat*) taps the king on the head with a *ḫṭ* ("magic rod," *CAT* 1.16.6.8), and Hosea inveighs against Canaanite forms of rhabdomancy in eighth-century Israel (מקל, "divining rod," Hos 4:12).

64. Finkel ("Necromancy"); Tropper (*Nekromantie*); Kleiner (*Wahrsagung*); Schmidt (*Necromancy*).

65. On one occasion a ראה-"seer" enacts a role as "sacrificial-priest" over a gathering of קראים ("invited guests") serviced by a טבח ("butcher") at a במה ("high place," 1 Sam 9:12–24). The socioreligious equation in 1 Sam 9:9 (נביא > ראה) redactorally removes the "objectionable" elements of ראה-seer praxis for the theological benefit of later readers; see Lindblom (*Prophecy*, 83–104); Wilson (*Prophecy*, 139); Petersen (*Roles*, 38–40).

and "oracle-reciters"[66] toward the "religion" end of the continuum, and roles as "exorcists"[67] and "sorcerers"[68] on the "magic" end.

PLOTTING BALAAM'S ROLES ON A MAGIC-RELIGION CONTINUUM

In light of all this evidence, therefore, we should not be surprised to see a specialist like Balaam enacting a variety of roles on both ends of the magic-religion continuum. *DA* 1.1 designates him a *ḥzh 'lhn* ("seer of the gods"), unpacking this title to describe the roles enacted by "oneiromantics"[69] and "oracle-reciters"[70] in the first paragraph of Combination 1 (roles also en-

66. Both *ḥzyn* ("seers") and *ʿddn* ("soothsayers") serve the Aramean king Zakkur at Hamath (*KAI* 202.12–14), the latter parallel to Ug *ʿdd* ("herald," *CAT* 1.4.7.46) and OB *āpilu* ("answerer," *ARM* 9.22.14; 13.23.6; *CAD* A/2.170); see Huffmon ("Prophecy," 5.478); and Malamat ("Mari," 211–14). Whether fully Yahwist or quasi-Canaanite, Gad the חזה-seer shuttles דברים ("words") back and forth between David and Yahweh (2 Sam 24:13; see Haag, "Gad," 141–42).

67. At Ugarit a *mlḫs* ("incantation-reciter," see מלחש, "whisperer," Ps 58:6) charms snakes by magical means and conducts *namburbi*-type apotropaic rituals (*CAT* 1.100.5; Caplice, *Namburbi*). Canaanite exorcists call on their "great gods" to protect them from darker deities; e.g., [x]b/dt bʿl ḥẓ ršp ("[May] Baʿal [stop] the arrow of Rešeph," *CAT* 1.82.3 // רשף, "plague," Hab 3:5); see de Moor & Sprank ("Demons"); Münnich (Resheph, 124-69).

68. Hebrew preachers warn their congregations against all types of sorcerers: מכשף ("sorcerer"; Akk ᴸᵁ*kaššāpu*, Deut 18:10; Dan 2:2); מעונן ("conjurer," Deut 18:10; Lev 19:26); מנחש ("[snake-]charmer," Deut 18:10; Ezek 16:36); חובר ("enchanter/binder," Deut 18:11; Ps 58:6; Isa 47:9, 12); מלחש ("whisperer," Ps 58:6; Isa 3:3; Jer 8:17); חכם חרשים ("craftsman of [homeopathic] images," Isa 3:3; Ug *ḥrš*, *CAT* 1.16.5.26; Syr ܚܪܫܐ; "Simon the sorcerer," *PSD* 159); חרטם ("engraver," Dan 2:2, 10, 27; 4:4); אשף ("sorcerer," Dan 2:2, 10, 27; 4:4; Akk *āšipu*).

69. Like the dreams of Gudea (Edzard, *Gudea*, 69–71) and Addu-dūri (Noort, *Mari*, 27), Balaam's nocturnal vision/audition may well be the result of provoked incubation, an ANE phenomenon widely attested (see Kim, *Incubation*, 27–60). De Vaulx sees incubation in Num 22:8–20 (*Nombres*, 256), but the text is silent as to whether Balaam's nocturnal experience takes place in a recognized sanctuary, or whether an icon/deity stands close by, or whether he might be dreaming—the customary requirements for most incubations (Caquot, "Songes," 110–11).

70. The role enacted by *DA* Balaam appears to correspond closely with that enacted by other "divine council" messengers (Jer 23:8; Job 15:8). Having witnessed the council's decision, he "announces" it (*ḥwh*; N.B. אחוך in Job 15:17 replicates the D pf. 1 sg + 2 m. suff. in *'ḥwkm*, *DA* 1.5) to its intended recipient (presumably "his people," *ʿmh*, *DA* 1.4), introducing his announcement with a stereotypical oracular epithet, *lkw rʾw pʿlt 'lhn* ("Come see the works of the gods," *DA* 1.5; see Ps 66:5). Following Robinson ("Council") and Cross ("Council"), Mullen argues for a type of "prophecy" where "the prophet is the herald of the divine council" (מי עמד בסוד, "Who has stood in the Council?" Jer 23:18), even suggesting, on the basis of Nathan's nocturnal experience (2 Sam

acted in Num 22–24).⁷¹ Moreover, since the roles just mentioned cluster around the "religion" pole, the mention of "birds" and "rods" in *DA* 1.7–9 doubtless reflects the presence of a complementary role-set much like that enacted within other "diviner/seer" role-sets; viz., "ornithomantic,"⁷² and "rhabdomantic."⁷³ The North Syrian warlord Idri-mi, for example, enacts complementary roles as "ornithomantic"/"extispicist,"⁷⁴ while the Hebrew patriarchs Jacob and Joseph also enact complementary divinatory roles. According to Tanak tradition Joseph practices "oneiromancy" as well as "lecanomancy,"⁷⁵ while Jacob engages in both "oneiromancy" and "rhabdomancy."⁷⁶ In the ancient Near East it's not unusual for one kind of divination to be validated by another. In fact, clients often demand multiple divinatory inquiries so that they might more exactly clarify the divine will before going in this or that spiritual direction.⁷⁷ Is it impossible for Jewish

---

7:4–5), an oneiromantic praxis (*Council*, 216–26).

71. Micah of Moresheth depicts Balaam as an "oracle-reciter" in the historical résumé of Yahweh's covenant lawsuit; i.e., Balaam "responds" (ענה) to Balak's provocative "counsel" (יעץ) so that Judah might "know Yahweh's righteous plans" (דעת צדקות יהוה, Mic 6:5).

72. *DA* 1.7–9, though fragmentary, lists several types of violent behavior between differing bird species. If a falcon kills a raven, e.g., this means that his client will conquer his enemy (šā 79.35). If a raven kills a falcon, however, this means that his client will be conquered by his enemy (šā 79.36). The twist in *DA* is that in addition to prey "reproaching" predator (ḥrpt, *DA* 1.7–8), even non-violent birds like the "swallow attack the dove" (drr nšrt ywn, *DA* 1.8–9; see Moore, *Balaam*, 70).

73. The text is fragmentary, but *DA* 1.9 preserves a word-pair (mṭh//ḥṭr) quite similar to the one featured in a well-known Canaanite myth about El's ability to spawn healthy offspring through the manipulation of his "rod" (mṭ//ḥṭ, *CAT* 1.23.33–37, 39–46), evidence of a rhabdomantic praxis like that underlying other texts alluding to sexual potency (e.g., *TuL* 74.5–6; Num 17:23). Satirizing Balaam, Talmud accuses him of קוסם באמתו ("divining with his penis," *b. Sanh.* 105a), raucously ridiculing his (in)ability to use *his* "rod."

74. *Idr* 28–29.

75. Joseph is a פותר חלומות (lit., "unraveler of dreams," Gen 40:8; 41:13; cf. *Akk ša musi ippušanima ša kal ūmu apašaršinati*, "the nocturnal bindings [of the sorceresses] I 'unravel' [*pašāru*] the next day," *Maq* 4.110–11) who possesses a cup והוא נחש ינחש בו "from which he (drinks . . . and) practices divination" (Gen 44:4–5).

76. Just like *DA* Balaam (according to our analysis). Older "2-source" critics generally fail to find any connection between Jacob's oneiromantic (Gen 31:10–12) and rhabdomantic (30:37–42) activities, but from a role theory perspective what he does is quite clear. He enacts complementary roles within a "diviner/seer" role-set.

77. In Anatolia, e.g., Muwattili asks the storm-god Telepinu to confirm a ᴳᴵˢHUR-oracle (wood engraving) via a dream (*KUB* 24.3.2.42; see Kammenhuber, *Orakelpraxis*, 24), and the success of a fertility ritual is oneiromantically confirmed (*KUB* 7.5.4.1–10; see Beckman, *Birth*, 170–71). Neither Saul nor Muršili II are slow to consult prophets, oneiromantics, cleromantics, nor in Saul's case, necromantics (1 Sam 28:6–7; *KUB*

observers to understand this socioreligious behavior? No. Philo of Alexandria, for example, sees Balaam not simply as a "curser"/"blesser," but as a "man famous for divination, initiated into divination in all its forms,"[78] especially "augury" (οἰωνοσκοπία)[79] and "dream interpretation" (ὀνείρατα διηγούμενος),[80] while Ps.-Philo sees him enacting the roles of "dream interpreter" (*interpretem somniorum*)[81] and "sacrificial priest."[82]

Plotting Balaam's "religious" roles is a less difficult task than identifying his darker "magical" roles. Two factors combine to exacerbate this. *First*, overt reference to magic and the occult is a delicate matter in Tanak, not least in the Balaam traditions. The social, cultural, political, and religious factors responsible for triggering this Hebrew allergy are well known and need no rehearsal here.[83] Balaam's darker side occasionally peeks through a few biblical texts *outside* the Balaam cycle (e.g., Num 31:16),[84] but in Num 22–24 one gets the distinct impression that Yahwistic editors have carefully expunged it of all "objectionable" elements.[85] *Second*, the text surviving on *DA* 2 is much more fragmentary than that found on *DA* 1, thereby unavoidably rendering Combination 2 susceptible to more types of interpretation.[86]

24.1–4).

78. Philo, *Moses* 1.264.

79. Lit., "bird-gazing."

80. Philo, *Moses* 1.268.

81. Apparently *LAB* 18.2 follows Vg (*ariolum*) in rendering פתורה in Num 22:5 not as a proper name (OG, Syr), but as "the interpreter" (i.e., as an articulated Aramaic noun).

82. *Cum offeras Deo holocaustamata reconciliabitur Deus hominibus* ("When you offer holocausts to God you reconcile God to men," *LAB* 18.7). Whether either observer is aware of the roles enacted in *DA* is tantalizing, but unanswerable.

83. See Trachtenberg (*Magic*); Bohak (*Magic*, 8–69); Schmid ("Magic," 243–62); Schmitt (*Magie*, 1–66). Caquot ("Divination," 84, 100) subdivides Tanak divinatory material into three categories: "official," "licit," and "illicit," suggesting that the incantation chanted by the בעלת אוב in 1 Sam 28 is editorially removed because of its "illicit" character. We *cannot* say, with Eichrodt (*Theology*, 2.180), that "ancient Israel knows nothing of a world of evil spirits" because such statements are historically ridiculous (see Anderson's devastating critique in *Sacrifices*, 3–14). But we *can* say, with Levine (*Presence*, 91), that "in the ancient Israelite mentality the reality of anti-God forces is present, and is inculcated by means of stringent ritual codes."

84. Rab Yoḥanan posits that even Balaam's blessings begin as curses before eventually "reverting to the curse" (חזרו לקללה, *b. Sanh.* 105b).

85. Daiches ("Balaam," 69) sees Balaam engaging in magical praxis in Tanak, but only in a "veiled way."

86. Hoftijzer & van der Kooij (*Deir ʿAllā*, 270–82) read *DA* 2 as a series of curses threatening impending doom, apparently transferring the "sorcerer" role enacted in the biblical tradition to the *DA* tradition, interpreting *DA* 2 accordingly. Hackett (*Balaam*, 80–89) reads it as a liturgy for a child sacrifice ritual. Levine ("Deir ʿAllā," 196) reads it

Yet too many clues exist here to designate this text simply and only as historical or even mythological narrative. It is extremely difficult, from an anthropological point of view, to deny the prospect that *DA* 2 preserves a typical purification ritual.[87] Several of these clues might be listed, but two are particularly telling. *First*, the *beginning* (*DA* 2.5) focuses on the "preparation" (*kl*) of "foliage" (*rṭb*) within a (magical) "circle" (*mdr*)—all elements found at the beginning of ritual series like the Assyrian series *Šurpu*.[88] *Second*, the red-inked *ending* (*DA* 2.17) focuses on "making known" (*ldʿt*) the preceding material. What makes this detail significant is that priestly colophons concluding ritual texts usually emphasize a "professional" desire to keep incantational material "secret"; i.e., away from the eyes of "the unknowing." E.g., "Secret (Akk *pirištu*)[89] of the great gods. Let the 'knowing' (*mudû*) show it to the 'knowing' (*mudâ*); the 'unknowing' (*lā mudû*) shall not view it."[90]

The key to interpreting these texts is, again, anthropological. Whenever we try to understand the behavior of magico-religious specialists like Balaam apart from some understanding of "good"-vs.-"evil" magic,[91] we quickly fall into the flytrap of cultural illiteracy which ensnares the pioneer comparativist Samuel Daiches, who writes in 1909: "I think there exists evidence which goes to prove that Balaam is a sorcerer, pure and simple."[92] This assessment comes from a gifted interpreter trying to make sense of a difficult Hebrew tradition by means of then newly-discovered Mesopotamian texts. But it fails miserably because (a) it does not recognize the clear anthropological differences in the Assyrian ritual texts between the

---

as a text consigning Balaam's corpse to Sheol, where it eternally "moans" (*'nḥ*, *DA* 2.12). Caquot & Lemaire ("Deir ʿAllā," 203) shy away from a necromantic interpretation, translating *byt lyʿl hlk wlyʿl ḥtn* as "house for the use of the traveler and the bridegroom (*DA* 2.7). Rofé (*Blʿm*, 68) builds on their reading, imagining this line referring to a house of sacred prostitution from which come the Midianite ladies seducing Israel's young men into polytheistic idolatry at Baʿal Peor.

87. Practically everyone familiar with the language of this text agrees with this observation.

88. *Šur* 1.1–3.

89. N.B. the phrase *tāmīt pi-riš-ti bārûti* ("oracle [revealing] the secret of divination," *BBR* 1–20.18). See סתב ("secret") in Dan 8:26.

90. *TuL* 7.26. Lenzi explains the political rationale for this secrecy: "The task of maintaining the king's secrets is a genuine and widespread concern among Mesopotamian elites" (*Secrecy*, 377). The twist at Deir ʿAllā is that the Transjordanian scribe responsible for this "secret inscription" posts it on a plaster billboard for public display—perhaps because there is no monarchical bureaucracy to stop him (see Moore, "King," 27–41).

91. Eliade, *Shamanism*, 184–89.

92. Daiches, "Balaam," 60.

roles enacted by *bārû*-priests and those enacted by *āšipu*-priests; and (b) it does not recognize the sociological distinctions between "good"-vs.-"evil" magicians. "Sorcerers" and "exorcists" both curse, but for very different reasons.[93] A "sorcerer" is an "evil" magician seeking to *invade* the established order, while an "exorcist" is a "good" magician seeking to *protect* it.[94] "Sorcerers" leave no written legacies of their activities because the activities themselves are illegal.[95] "Exorcists," on the other hand, are often happy to leave extensive written evidence of their work. Thus whenever an exorcist, after exhausting every other means of apotropaic purification possible, takes on the dangerous task of cursing a client's enemy, it is always to *protect*, never to *invade*.[96] Tanak often labels Balaam an "evil" magician, but such a role-label is not surprising when it is the only one available in cultures (like Israel) where any and all things "magical" are against the law.[97] In the Bible, theology is more important than anthropology, even though, as *DA* so glaringly reminds us, magico-religious specialists can and do enact roles as "sorcerers." Like the North Syrian "old woman" Allaiturah̬(h̬)i, who with her royal client curses an enemy city after first making sure its protective gods have been drawn away from protecting it,[98] so Balaam ben Beor ritually attempts—but repeatedly fails—to curse a foreign enemy threatening the borders of *his* client, Moab.[99] Tanak makes it clear that this role is protective, not invasive, when Balak, having asked Balaam to "curse" (קלל) his enemy,

---

93. Lewis, *Ecstatic*, 122.

94. Copenhaver, "Magic," 278.

95. Laws against sorcery appear in Anatolian (*ANET* 195.170), Babylonian (*ANET* 166.2), Assyrian (*ANET* 184.A.47), and Hebrew lawcodes (Exod 22:18; Deut 18:10). Whereas the first law against false accusation in Hammurabi's lawcode condemns the false accusation of murder, the second condemns the false accusation of sorcery (*CH* 5.33–56).

96. Brown, "Sorcery," 124.

97. Deut 18:10. Blenkinsopp (*History*, 189–90) speaks of "the major emphasis (within Israel) on prophecy as a native Israelite phenomenon, contrasted with the different forms of divination and mediation practiced among the nations," an emphasis usually associated with a Yahwistic agenda designed "to bring prophecy within an institutional grid, and thus to define and limit the scope of prophetic authority."

98. *KUB* 7.60.

99. Num 23:11. *Why* he fails to curse Israel, of course, is the reason for preserving the Torah Balaam tradition.

concurrently demands that he "drive out" (גרש)¹⁰⁰ the invader threatening to violate his border.¹⁰¹

Yet "exorcist" does not appear to be the primary role enacted by Balaam, neither in Tanak nor at Deir ʿAllā. Though hidden beneath layers of Yahwistic veneer in Tanak and dingy plaster fragments at Deir ʿAllā, the evidence rather suggests that his primary role is "purification-priest." Purification-priests protect and purify their clients from evil through various kinds of homeopathic rituals. When Tanak Balaam *attempts* (!) to summon the אלהים via a ritual involving seven altars,¹⁰² he tries to enact a "purification-priest" role parallel to that enacted by the *āšipu*-priest in the neo-Assyrian *bît rimki* ("wash-house") ritual.¹⁰³ Several interpreters see a similar purification ritual in DA 2,¹⁰⁴ but most of these readings rely on linguistic analyses of a single term repeated three times, the root *nqr*. Originally meaning "sapling," this

---

100. *Tg. Onq.* translates Heb גרש in Num 22:6 with Aram תרך, then uses this same verb to translate Heb זעם in 23:7, the first "Balaam oracle": תריך לי ישראל "Drive Israel out for me!" Is this an indication that the translator understands Balaam's commission to be fundamentally exorcistic? N.B. the similar use of this Canaanite verb on the lips of another Moabite sheikh: "Kemoš 'drove him (the Israelite king) out' for me" (*ygrš*, *KAI* 181.19, the "Moabite Stone").

101. Num 22:6. The *raison d'être* of all exorcists is to "drive out" evil (Parrinder, "Exorcism," 225), and Reiner ("Magie," 78) reminds us that apotropaic purification from *portended* evil (Akk *namburbi*) is just as much an exorcistic phenomenon. Thus the charms, talismans, portal plaques, and protective amulets found all over the ANE illustrate the phenomenon of exorcism-by-proxy, a form of "demon insurance."

102. Prior to the discovery of DA 1.1 (*wyʾtw ʾlwh ʾlhn blylth*, "and the gods came to him in the night"), von Pákozdy ("Bileam," 169) already understands that אלהים in Num 22 denotes "den Wahrsage- und Zauberdämon des Bileam." Tanak tradition itself is ambiguous about Balaam's attempt לקראת נחשים "to invite daemonic powers" (Num 24:1) onto the seven altars prepared for them at Bamoth Baʿal, Sade Ṣophim and Baʿal Peor (Num 22:41; 23:14; 23:28), and while this is not the only passage where theologians wrestle with the sg.-pl. ambiguities built into the pl. term אלהים ("G/god[s]"), the depth of interreligious interface embedded in this text certainly makes it one of the most difficult to Yahwicize. Hamilton's (*Balaam*, 705) presumption that I misunderstand—or worse, dismiss—the rationale behind this Yahwicization process thus completely misses the anthropological point.

103. Laessøe (*bît rimki*); Moore ("Priesthood," 318–21). Both diviners and exorcists "summon the gods" in ANE ritual, but for entirely different reasons. *Bārū*-priests "summon the gods" into their sacrifices in order to read divine *tamītu*-answers to their prayer-petitions; e.g., "invite the great gods via cedar resin" (cited in Starr, *Diviner*, 37). *Āšipū*-priests, on the other hand, "summon the gods" into their sacrifices in order to manipulate them via homeopathic sleight-of-hand; e.g., "Come to the bread and water of him who worships you" (*KAR* 25.2.22).

104. See especially P. K. McCarter (cited in Hackett, *Balaam*, 80–89), Hackett (*Balaam*, 80–89), and Levine ("Deir ʿAllā," 201).

term can figuratively refer to "royal scion,"[105] and may even refer here to a royal scion who is sacrificed to a Transjordanian deity.[106] But this is terribly hypothetical.[107] Rather than hypothesizing yet another linguistic history for this key term, the following paragraph briefly analyzes how it fits within the larger ritual sequence presented on DA 2.

(1) The first appearance of *nqr* occurs near the beginning of DA 2 in what appears to be a context of *preparation*[108] (N.B. the telltale mention of "foliage"[109] and "[magic] circle").[110] As in the purification rituals alluded to in the Tanak Balaam cycle (and indeed, rituals everywhere), preparation is always the first order of business.[111]

(2) The second appearance of *nqr* occurs within a context of *transference*. The "moaning" (*n'nh*)[112] of the *nqr* "in his/its heart" (*blbbh*) occurs

---

105. נצר, Isa 11:1.

106. Failing to stop the invasion of his country by conventional military means, another Moabite king (Mesha) publicly sacrifices his son to Kemoš in a last-ditch maneuver to save the city (2 Kings 3:27; see Moore, *Faith*, 308-9).

107. Hoftijzer (*Deir 'Allā*, 237) reads *nqr* as a passive participle ("the one bored out"; i.e., "blinded," Judg 16:21), but Caquot & Lemaire ("Deir 'Allā," 202) read the middle radical *q* as a grapheme for *ṣ* as in other Aramaic texts (e.g., *'rq*, "earth," in *KAI* 202B.26; 216.4; 222A.26, 28). Opinions are divided over whether the graphemes for the interdentals derive from dialectical influence ("Canaanisms") or instead represent the proto-Semitic interdentals, following upon the adoption of an alphabet (Phoenician) which lacks graphemes for them (see Moscati, *Grammar*, 29-30).

108. Reading *kl* in DA 2.5 as "prepare" (Hackett, *Balaam*, 58). One of the *āšipu*'s roles is to "consecrate the prepared place" (*kul-la-ta tu-qad-daš*, BBR 52.2; von Soden translates "Lehmterrasse," AHw 502) and "prepare the house of the *rābiṣu*-demon" (*bīt rābiṣi u-kal*, TuL 17:20).

109. For *rtb* ("foliage," DA 2.5) N.B. the GIŠ.MEŠ*kar-tu-ti* ("trimmed reeds") laid out on the *nappaṭu* (clay brazier) at the beginning of *Šurpu* (Šur 1.2).

110. The *mdr* (DA 2.5) has analogues in the מדורה (Isa 30:33; Ezek 24:9), the Mesopotamian *abru*-pyre (BBR 26.2.25) and *nappaṭu/ḫuluppaqu* brazier (Šur 1.2; Maq 9.22), and the Anatolian *ukturi* (HT 66.1, 10, 20). The root of the Heb analogue (דור) can mean "ball" in the nominative (Isa 22:18) or "to encircle, heap up" in the verbal form (Ezek 24:5), so N.B. the *āšipu*'s magical "sphere of activity" (*zi-sur-ra-a*) at the beginning of *Šurpu* (Šur 1.3; see also TuL 117.3).

111. Moore, "Priesthood," 319-21. Again, well before the discovery of DA, interpreters of the Balaam cycle recognize parallels from Mesopotamian religious texts. Gray, e.g., sees Balaam's seven altars as a clear reference to the Sibitti (*Numbers*, 342), and Mowinckel ("Bil'amsage," 260) hypothesizes late Assyrian influence, albeit as something reflected only by "the Elohist," while de Vaulx (*Nombres*, 274-75) sees Mesopotamian influence only as "background noise."

112. Several texts allude to "moaning" in the course of exorcistic ritual praxis. In a complex ritual to purify a defiled temple, for example, several magico-religious specialists participate in specific, complementary activities. Alongside a *bārû*-priest and a *kalû*-priest, a *zammaru*-singer "moans loudly" (*in-ḫa in-ni-iḫ*, Racc 44.1-5). Elsewhere

alongside some group (simultaneously?) "moaning in their heart" (*blbbm n'nḥ*).¹¹³ This "moaning" ritual appears to preserve the moment in the ritual when the conducting priest homeopathically transfers the evil distressing his client onto an (in)animate image (Lev 16:21!).¹¹⁴ Homeopathic magic cannot proceed without faith in the possibility, viability, and effectuality of this spiritual transference.

(3) The final appearance of *nqr* occurs within a context of *destruction* in which "the heart of the *nqr* dies out" (*lbb nqr šhh*).¹¹⁵ Once the purification-priest successfully transfers the evil to an (in)animate image, it can be harmlessly destroyed. Animate images are killed. Inanimate images are burned, dissolved, washed clean, or otherwise dispatched. The goal of every purification ritual is always the same: to drive evil away from one's client as far as possible.¹¹⁶

In short, DA 2 appears to preserve a rather standardized purification ritual memorializing the standardized sequence of *preparation, transferral,* and *destruction*. Balaam receives an oneiromantic message of impending doom from the Unseen World, a message he confirms (or has confirmed) through ornithomantic and perhaps also rhabdomantic omens. Having thus identified the evil threatening his clients, he homeopathically transfers it away from them to an (in)animate image which he then destroys (or has destroyed).

CONCLUSION

In other words, Balaam essentially enacts the same range of roles at Deir 'Allā as he does in the Bible. Both texts show that these roles noticeably overlap opposing spheres of the magic-religion continuum. Much like the Anatolian/North Syrian "old woman" Balaam enacts complementary "diviner/seer" and "exorcist" role-sets, a conclusion strongly resonant with George Mendenhall's theory of an Anatolian origin for the Ba'al Peor cult as

---

an *āšipu*-priest begins a purification ritual for the king with "moaning" (*uš-ta-ni-iḫ*, BBR 26.1.11), and an exorcist's client alludes to "my heart" (*lib-bi-ia*) full of tears and "moaning" (*ta-ni-ḫi*, AGH 132.47). Ritualistic "moaning" is an integral part of exorcistic praxis.

113. DA 2.12. Hackett suggests several philological/syntactic possibilities, but that these phrases stand in parallel is not seriously disputed.

114. Milgrom, *Leviticus*, 42–43; Schmitt, *Magie*.

115. DA 2.14, reading *šhh* as a variant of *šh'*. In *Tg. Isa* 37.26, שׁאה refers to the post-war "desolation" of cities, but N.B. that ܢܰܚ can explicitly refer to the "dying out of a fire," as in the expression ܢܰܚ ܢܽܘܪܐ "the fire dies out" (*PSD* 561).

116. Vyse, *Magic*, 8–9.

well as Al Wolters' theory that the Deir ʿAllā tradition originates in North Syria before being transplanted to Transjordan via the Assyrian conquest.[117]

The comparative anthropological approach to the Balaam traditions is attractive because instead of hypothesizing literary sources underneath the text it seeks rather to examine the actual roles enacted by other magico-religious specialists in the ancient Near East. Source-critical attempts to interpret these traditions are at an impasse because they cannot sufficiently explain why the specialist responsible for contacting the divine realm in Num 22:8–20 also participates in what looks to be a magical purification ritual at Bamath Baʾal, Sade Ṣophim and Baʾal Peor. Nor do they help us make sense of the *šdyn* oracle in *DA* 1 as well as the "moaning" ritual in *DA* 2.[118] Ultimately this approach fails because it cannot correlate all the known facts about Balaam into an identifiable whole.

---

117. Mendenhall (*Tenth*, 109); Wolters ("Balaamites," 101–13).
118. Levine (*Numbers*, 241–75); Moore ("Terror," 662–66).

2

BALAAM THE "PROPHET?"*

MEINDERT DIJKSTRA, A DUTCH scholar from the University of Utrecht, advances several proposals about the Balaam traditions which not only fail to advance, but unfortunately damage and hold back our understanding of these fascinating texts.[1] First, he argues, "neither OT tradition nor recent biblical exegesis know what to make of Balaam."[2] Second, he perpetuates the populist strategy of reducing every role enacted by this ancient Near Eastern magico-religious specialist down to one single, "safe" role, subjectively defining it via the nebulous term "prophecy."[3] Third, in support of these positions, he argues that the Deir ʿAllā texts contain "the first clear extrabiblical example of a prophet proclaiming doom to his own people."[4] Each of these presumptions needs to be critically examined.

---

* Revised from a paper first published in *ResQ* 39 (1997) 101–6.

1. Meindert Dijkstra, "Is Balaam Also Among the Prophets?" *JBL* 114 (1995) 43–64; trans. and rev. by J. G. Rigg from a Dutch article originally published in *Gereformeerd Theologisch Tijdschrift* 90 (1990) 159–85.

2. Dijkstra, "Balaam," 43 (citing my dissertation as an example of this ignorance).

3. According to Dijkstra, Balaam "has the dubious honor of being the first OT prophet to be dug up in the land of the Bible" ("Balaam," 43). Recent discussions of the disputed dynamics and contours of "prophecy" appear in Moore (*Pressure*, 237–48), Stökl (*Prophecy*, 1–28), and Anthonioz (*Prophétisme*, 9–17).

4. Dijkstra, "Balaam," 44. See Müller ("Bileamsprüche," 214–44) and Blum ("Deir ʿAllā," 573–601).

METHODOLOGICAL PROBLEMS

First, the fact that Tanak writers interpret the Balaam traditions along variegated, even contradictory paths sometimes, however unexpected or unsettling, does not mean that no one knows what to "make" of him.[5] More accurate is it to say that serious interpreters of these Syro-Palestinian traditions—both ancient as well as (post)modern—simply refuse to flatten them into two-dimensional cartoons.[6] Or, to put it another way, serious readers know precisely what to "make" of various *strands* of the Balaam tradition trajectory.[7] Veteran Bible readers know that Tanak writers can and do interpret various traditions from various angles because the Bible is a "book quite full of itself."[8] One well-known example is the "wilderness-wandering" tradition in *Exodus-Numbers*.[9] Where one prophet views Israel's desert experience as a time of adolescent rebellion (Ezek 20:33–38), another remembers it as a time of prenuptial bliss (Jer 2:2).[10] The spectrum of interpretive angles on the Babylonian exile experience is particularly wide.

> For Lamentations, the exile is especially the result of placing false trust in the security of Jerusalem; for the Deuteronomistic History, of ignoring the fundamental Deuteronomic requirement that Yahweh be worshiped exclusively at the shrine he would choose; for Ezekiel, of the unfaithfulness of the temple worship itself; for Jeremiah, of the people's political, social, and moral waywardness, as well as the unfaithfulness of their worship.[11]

Other examples orbit around what we might call the "assimilation-resistance polarity." That is, where Jeremiah encourages Hebrew-Babylonian intermarriage (Jer 29:6), Ezra strongly condemns it (Ezra 9–10).[12] Where

---

5. Gunkel's question is prescient: "Is the Old Testament a system in which there can be no contradiction, or does it not contain a varied plenitude of records of a great religio-historical process in which there have actually been all sorts of different positions?" (*Israel*, 20).

6. Halpern ("Dialect," 119) satirizes approaches to the Balaam traditions which presume them to be "decorative paneling in a two-dimensional depiction of pre-monarchic antiquity."

7. See Moore, *Balaam*, 110–22. "Trajectory" has been and still is a fruitful metaphor for describing the dynamics contributing to the growth and development of ancient literary tradition (see Robinson & Koester, *Trajectories*).

8. Sanders, "Intertextuality," 35; see Noth, *History*, 58.

9. von Rad, *Theology*, 1.280–89.

10. DeRoche ("Wilderness," 364–76); Zimmermann ("Nuptial," 153–83).

11. Goldingay, *Diversity*, 7.

12. S. J. D. Cohen cites the parallel between Pericles' citizenship law in 450 BCE and

the prophet Nahum advocates destroying the Assyrians, the book of Jonah champions their salvation.[13] Seasoned readers instinctively know that the deeper, more complex Tanak traditions cannot be adequately deciphered apart from methodological approaches intentionally designed to pay attention to the polyphonic dynamics churning within the texts themselves.[14] How else can we "make sense" of the fact that where one writer sees Balaam as a "prophet,"[15] another sees him as a "sorcerer,"[16] and still another as a "seer/diviner?"[17] Instead of simply choosing one role-label over all the others, does it not seem wiser to pay attention to the context and criteria responsible for generating each role-label?

Standing firmly within the Eurocentric academic tradition,[18] Dijkstra patently ignores this question, insisting that since every Balaam tradition radiates some degree of conflict (both in Tanak and in *DA*), all attempts to make sense of these texts are somehow destined to fail. To me, this is an exegesis of despair based on two faulty presumptions. First, Dijkstra fails to mention, much less engage the unresolved problem of methodological direction in contemporary studies of the Pentateuch.[19] His bipolar approach therefore fosters an inchoate strategy for interpreting *any* "great text,"[20] not

---

its consequences (Aristotle, *Ath. Pol.* 26.3) alongside the mass divorce of foreigners in Ezra as examples of "the matrilineal principle" (*Jewishness*, 267–68). Fried, however, suggests (a) that because the group complaining to Ezra is specifically called השרים (lit., "the leaders," Ezra 9:1), this implies that they are, in fact, ranking political officials of the Persian empire, and (b) that the prevalence of marriages between Judeans and the families of Sanballat and Tobiah "may be seen by (these) Persian officials as threatening to create a power base and source of wealth independent of the king" (*Ezra* 26–27). Thus the mass divorce in Ezra 10 probably has more to do with socioeconomic than ethnoreligious concerns.

13. As Gaines puts it, the book of Jonah "reiterates . . . the essential lesson that no one should begrudge or try to control God's love, mercy, and forgiveness to all the peoples of the earth" (*Forgiveness*, 124).

14. Bakhtin (*Dostoevsky*, 122–24); Newsom ("Polyphonic," 3–31); Talmon ("Method," 320–56). As Bloch puts it, Hebrew writers continue to interpret Tanak texts from a variety of perspectives, "often with remarkable freedom of content" (*Drehbühnen*, vii).

15. Num 24:4 (שמע אמרי אל, "the one who hears the words of El"; see Mic 6:5, ענה, "the answerer"). Never does any Tanak tradent explicitly call Balaam a נביא-"prophet" (see Stökl, *Prophecy*, 157–204).

16. Josh 13:22 (הקוסם, "the diviner").

17. *DA* 1.1 (ḥzh, "seer").

18. See, e.g., Wellhausen (*Composition*); Noth (*History*); Friedman (*Bible*); and Baden (*Composition*).

19. See, e.g., Rendtorff (*Problem*); Blum (*Pentateuch*); Kratz (*Composition*); and Carr (*Formation*).

20. Reiner ("Literatur") includes as "great literature" the following categories: myths, epics, autobiographies, propaganda, poetry (including hymns and prayers), love lyrics,

just the Balaam traditions. *Second* (and consequently), Dijkstra ignores every other approach to understanding this material other than the one he inherits. Nowhere, for example, is serious consideration given to reading the Balaam traditions against an intertextual backdrop thoroughly informed by a contemporary corpus of other ancient Near Eastern texts. This is unfortunate, because when viewed intertextually the Balaam traditions come alive and begin to make very good (not perfect, but good) "sense."[21] Simply to compare the Deir ʿAllā fragments against a backdrop of Hebrew prophetic texts,[22] while appreciated, does not begin to take seriously the task of comparative intertextual analysis, and readers who fail to locate these traditions within some sort of recognizable socioliterary matrix will continue to be unsettled, confounded and perplexed about them—often (like Dijkstra) to the point of exegetical despair.

ANTHROPOLOGICAL CONSIDERATIONS

The suggestion that Balaam is a merely and only a "prophet" cannot be sustained from the evidence at hand. In point of fact, to label this specialist a "prophet" is to make an *anthropological* decision, not an historical or literary or theological one.[23] One would hope that such a decision would sufficiently sensitize the decision-maker to the basic anthropological contours of the cultures among whom magico-religious specialists like Balaam live and work. Not so in Dijkstra's analysis. Instead it simply stigmatizes the character of Balaam by reducing everything he does to a single area of activity, placing him underneath the role-label of "prophet" without doing any of the research necessary to validate such a decision.[24] The question I would therefore raise to approaches like this (and Dijkstra's is fairly typical) is simple: Why should we continue to entertain the role-label of "prophet" when describing Balaam or any other ancient character when the methodology used to interpret his behavior does not come from a perspective designed to analyze, catalogue and understand role-labels? Where, in other words, is the hard evidence needed to justify such an anthropological claim?

---

laments, elegies, wisdom (both philosophical and didactic), satirical/humorous, and prose texts of elevated stature. Foster ("Literature") basically agrees with this taxonomy.

21. Readers sensitive to this approach prior to the discovery of *DA* include Goldziher (*Philologie*, 41–44); Daiches ("Balaam," 60–70); and Largement ("Bileʿam," 39).

22. Dijkstra, "Balaam," 60–61.

23. Moore, *Balaam*, 11–19.

24. The dynamic behind this is simple: "In restricted role-sets the partners are satisfied with a restrictive vocabulary" (Rothbell, "Housewife," 27, citing Ruth Laub Coser).

Apparently Dijkstra is blissfully unaware of the fact that the desire to "nabi-ize" ("prophet-ize") Balaam has a long history, particularly among those Hebrews who find his multiplicity of roles socially, culturally and religiously disturbing.[25] Dijkstra not only neglects to read these traditions intertextually, he suggests no theoretical framework for analyzing Balaam's magico-religious behavior in a way designed to "make sense."

PERPETUATING A FALLACY

In light of all this, it's not surprising to see approaches like Dijkstra's simply run aground,[26] limited as they are to narrow options like the influence *DA* might have on Tanak or the influence each might have on the other, not to mention the much broader (and more difficult) question of common influences.[27] Like many of his colleagues and predecessors, Dijkstra simply reads the Balaam traditions through a literary prism designed to segregate artificially the "positive" from the "negative." Thus any "doom-oracle" against one of Israel's enemies (Balaam's *DA* audience), must automatically be perceived in Israel as an "oracle of salvation." To this way of thinking *DA* thus neatly "proves" why the portrayal in Num 22–24 is essentially "positive," while the portrayal in Num 31:16 is essentially "negative." It's because the Hebrew editors responsible for transmitting the Balaam traditions (a) know about the *DA* tradition (a huge, unattested assumption), and this motivates them to (b) insert Israel's name into the "literary slot" originally designed for the audience of the *DA* "doom oracle."

One may choose to agree or disagree over whether comparative anthropological or bipolar literary approaches best enhance the task of analysis, yet in the final analysis any serious approach to interpreting the Balaam traditions must engage them via a comprehensive, controlled, systematic methodology based on intertextual analysis of all relevant, contemporary Near Eastern texts.

---

25. Dijkstra, "Balaam," 60–61. The effort to domesticate Balaam by "nabi-izing" him begins as early as the Targums. Where MT Num 23:7 describes his activity via the semantically broad term משלו ("his oracle," see Eissfeldt, *Maschal*, 20, 28, 30, 45–71), both *Tg. Neof.* and *Tg. Ps.-J.* read מתל נבות[י]ה ("the *mašal* of his prophecy").

26. Dijkstra's uncertainty over whether or not to label Balaam a "prophet" ("Balaam," 64) is well taken, but not surprising, given his faulty presumptions.

27. Schmitt (*Israel*, 14) offers a thoughtful analysis of these options.

3

ROLE PREEMPTION IN THE ISRAELITE PRIESTHOOD*

BIBLICAL SCHOLARS HAVE LONG struggled with the problem of understanding the character and development of the Israelite priesthood.[1] At least four major hurdles, however, stand in the way of progress.

(1) Many interpreters, particularly those schooled in the Western "intellectualist" tradition, still harbor deep bias against ritual and ritual studies.[2] Pejorative terms like "preliterate," "irrationalist," and "primitivist," though less common than they used to be, still dot the landscape of their analyses,[3] exemplifying little more than the prejudices of an entrenched mindset mired in the quicksand of reductionist interpretation, ideological reaction-formation, and institutionalized classism.[4]

---

* Revised from a paper first read to the Hebrew and Cognate Literature section of the SBL on Nov 22, 1993 in Washington, DC, subsequently published in *VT* 46 (1996) 316–29.

1. Blenkinsopp's opinion is blunt, but correct: "The history of the Israelite priesthood remains very obscure" (*Pentateuch*, 153).

2. Tylor (*Primitive*, 101–44), Lévy-Bruhl (*Primitive*, 503–22), Spencer (*Sociology*), and Radcliffe-Brown (*Primitive*, 1–27) are perhaps the best known representatives of this school.

3. Modified cognitive approaches continue on in the work of Atran (*Gods*, 13–15), Guthrie ("Religion," 177–204), Lewis-Williams & Dowson ("Entoptic," 201–45), and Luhrmann (*Witch*, 3–41).

4. Heschel documents an extremist example of this mindset (*Aryan*, 1–25). Cornell simplistically argues that Islam "generalizes the priesthood by abolishing the hierarchy and making every believer a priest" (*Voices*, 14), but the fact remains that Qur'an, like many of the rabbinic texts, tends to avoid the term "priest" (كاهن). See Wheeler (*Moses*,

(2) Priestly ritual is technical, cryptic, mysterious, and inherently difficult to interpret.[5] Hebrew priestly texts are, if anything, even more mysterious than their ancient Near Eastern counterparts, due largely to the socioliterary framework in which they now sit.[6]

(3) A vast corpus of ancient Near Eastern priestly literature has come to light in the past century or so,[7] and new discoveries are not infrequent.[8] Relatively few interpreters, however, engage this literature from a holistic perspective informed by a critical understanding of social anthropology.[9]

(4) Generally speaking, previous study of the Israelite priesthood, when divorced from holistic interdisciplinary analysis, suffers greatly from the slings and arrows of methodological uncertainty,[10] ideological bias,[11] and reactionary sophism.[12]

The present state of affairs may be summarized by two broad appraisals: (a) many still feel the priesthood of ancient Israel to be something quite unique, yet (b) consensus remains elusive over exactly how to define this

---

57).

5. The classic study of Mesopotamian priesthood is by Renger ("Priestertum"), the classic study of Hittite priests is by Sturtevant ("Hittite"), and Cody surveys the peculiarities of the Hebrew priesthood ("Priesthood").

6. Wellhausen (*Geschichte*, 125–74); Gorman ("Ritual," 13–36); Klingbeil (*Ritual*, 226–41). "Temple priesthoods are indispensable to political order, but the relationship between rulers and priests is often rocky," esp. when politicians perceive themselves to be "privileged deputies of the gods" (Gottwald, *Politics*, 146).

7. Roberts, "Environment," 92.

8. See, e.g., Arnaud (*Emar*); Fleming (*Installation*); Hoftijzer & van der Kooij (*Deir ʿAllā*); Levine (*Numbers*, 241–75); Renger ("Priestertum"); Klinger (*Kultschicht*); and Wright (*Impurity*).

9. Exceptions: Douglas (*Wilderness*); Milgrom (*Leviticus*); Gorman (*Ideology*); Haran (*Temple*); Levine (*Presence*); Olyan (*Inequality*). Cryer justifiably criticizes those who gravitate to sociology "as a magic wand to make the biblical and other ancient texts intelligible" (*Divination*, 14).

10. "Due to the scholarship of the past few decades, a post-exilic date for P can no longer be merely assumed. Even if one disagrees with the arguments of Haran, Kaufmann and Milgrom, biblical scholars must consider—at the very least—the possibility of a date for P which is earlier than that proposed by Wellhausen. In the wake of discussion of the term 'sons of Aaron' by scholars like Cody, Haran and Cross, and the suggestion that Chronicles may preserve some reliable traditions, Wellhausen's view that 'sons of Aaron' is an artificial creation must also be questioned" (O'Brien, *Priest*, 23). See Knohl (*Sanctuary*).

11. Blenkinsopp (*Pentateuch*, 11–12) justifiably labels Wellhausen a "Hegelian" in the sense that Wellhausen, like Hegel, believes ideas to have "an almost hypostatic character."

12. See Curtiss (*Priests*, 153–67); Abba ("Priests," 887–89); Rooker (*Leviticus*, 139–66).

"uniqueness." Many questions remain. How is the genius of the Israelite priesthood to be defined? How does it develop over time? What sort of methodological approach best helps explain this development?

The present essay presumes that any approach disregarding or even marginalizing the decipherment of priestly texts is *a priori* inadequate.[13] On the contrary, only careful comparison of Hebrew ritual texts alongside the ritual texts of other ancient Near Eastern cults can help us discern that which is unique from that which is not in the cryptic world of Hebrew ritual. And only after squarely and responsibly engaging this context can the way be cleared to ask deeper, more focused questions about the character and development of the Israelite priesthood.[14] This seems a prudent enough methodology even though comparative analysis, like any other approach, suffers its own set of risks.[15] Examination of Hebrew purification ritual in its socioliterary context is a valid, if generally neglected, enterprise,[16] but one which quickly loses its way whenever it fails to adhere to a methodology perceptive enough to identify similarities, yet sensible enough to point out dissimilarities.[17]

The following analysis will (a) compare and contrast two Akkadian purification rituals and (b) examine the roles enacted by Micah's priest (Judg 17–18)[18] alongside those enacted by Aaron and his sons (Lev 8–9).[19] After this it will attempt (c) to weigh the results of this study alongside those of previous studies, and (d) offer some suggestions for future research.

---

13. Esp. hypothetical approaches almost exclusively limited to Tanak texts (e.g., Wellhausen, *Geschichte*, 125–74).

14. "In the early stages of research on the Bible, there was less material evidence to go on, so our forerunners' arguments were more theoretical. As is commonly pointed out, the nineteenth-century models of the Bible's formation reflect the dominant theories of the day about social evolution. But more secure forms of evidence have arisen in recent decades" (Friedman, "Method," 3).

15. Kunin (*Incest*, 11–48) shows a keen awareness of these risks; e.g., radical ahistoricism, overemphasis on language-patterning, and hyper-binomialism, just to name a few. Odell expands: "Turner and van Gennep's theories of liminality and ritual process are applied to narrative studies in the Hebrew Bible, but only with limited success. Central to the problem is the extent to which an anthropological theory about behaviors of living communities can be applied to the interpretation of narrative texts" ("Ezekiel," 237). The present study sidesteps this problem by engaging only *ritual* texts.

16. Previous studies include Sabourin (*Priesthood*) and Schulz (*Leviten*), though neither examines the Hebrew priesthood from a role theory perspective.

17. A classic example of this "lostness" occurs in the work of Friedrich Delitzsch (critiqued by Gunkel, *Babylon*).

18. See Moore, *Ruth*, 293–308.

19. See Klingbeil, *Ordination*.

AKKADIAN PURIFICATORY RITUAL

Purifying Aššur's High Priest

One of the texts best exemplifying Akkadian purificatory praxis is the "wash-house" (Akk *bît rimki*), a lustration ritual identifiable from tablets found in Aššurbanipal's library at Tell Kouyunjik (ancient Nineveh).[20] Its purpose, like that of other Assyrian lustration rituals, is to "purify" (*kapāru*) an ordinand for religious service, in this case the "king" of Assyria (*šarru*).[21] Without it, Assyria's priest-king remains unclean and defiled, and therefore unfit to perform his duties as Aššur's high priest.[22]

The ritual begins at night in a temple courtyard with an elaborate invocation to the Sibitti, that dangerous gang-of-seven daemons roaming "to-and-fro"[23] in the *Erra Epic* and elsewhere in Middle Eastern myth.[24] Attendants prepare for their arrival by laying out seven incense stands, seven food-laden tables, and seven temporary huts, all in the hope of attracting them away from the wash-house where the ordinand is about to be consecrated. Prophylactically sealing the "door to the outside"[25] with "blood,"[26] an *āšipu*-priest prepares to escort the king from the security of his royal palace to the door of the first hut.

As dawn breaks (and Šamaš makes his appearance),[27] the ordinand enters the first hut of *bît rimki* and while proceeding through each hut engages the *āšipu*-priest in a series of antiphonal incantations. The *āšipu*-priest chants a prayer to Šamaš and the ordinand responds with the requisite formulaic incantation, after which the two team up to perform the expected

---

20. Laessøe, *bît rimki* (lit., "house of washing"); see Robson, "Libraries," 41–45.

21. *šarra tu-kap-par*, "you shall purify the king" (*BBR* 26.1.19; 26.2.2). Laessøe (*bît rimki*) and Reiner (*bît rimki*) offer improved readings of this ritual text. Von Weiher transliterates the LB version from Uruk (*Uruk*, 61–69, 95–99) and Scurlock ("*bît rimki*") identifies the incantation programmed for the all-important seventh "hut."

22. Van Driel, *Aššur*, 170. De Tarragon believes that Canaanite kings also double as high priests (*Ugarit*, 78–96; see also Sapin, *Syrie*, 180–81).

23. Job 1:7 (משוט). N.B. the seven פקדות ("executioners") in Ezek 9, each with כלי משחתו ("his weapon of destruction"). See Bodi, *Ezekiel*, 95–110.

24. *Erra* 1.23–44; see Geller (*Medicine*, 146–49) and Scurlock (*Medicine*, 361–645).

25. Akk *bābu kamû* (*BBR* 26.3.19; see George, *Topographical*, 421–22).

26. Attendants smear "sheep blood" (Akk *dāmi urīzi, BBR* 26.3.20) on the left and right side of the palace door, probably on the "doorjamb," according to Zimmern's restoration (Akk *askuppāti, BBR* 26.3.20–21). N.B. the anthropologically similar prophylactic ritual at Passover involving the smearing of blood on the משקוף ("lintel") and מזוזות ("doorposts," Exod 12:22).

27. Šamaš is the Mesopotamian sun-god (Lipiński, "Shemesh," 764–68).

homeopathic ritual.²⁸ This routine repeats itself through each of the seven huts until the king emerges, purified from defilement and ready to take on his priestly duties.

Though late and attested only for Assyrian kings, *bît rimki* represents a complex purification ceremony incorporating several of the cleansing mechanisms, sacrificial animals, patron deities, and incantational formulae seen elsewhere in isolation, but here fused together into one hybrid complex.²⁹

Purifying Hadad's "Wife"

Due to the accident of archaeological discovery, the study of Syro-Canaanite religion tends to focus on information discovered on the cuneiform tablets from Tell Ras Shamra on the coast of modern-day Syria (ancient Ugarit).³⁰ These Ugaritic texts have so far shed much more light on Syro-Canaanite myth than Syro-Canaanite ritual.³¹ More recent excavations at Tell Meskene (ancient Emar), however, a river-town on the great bend of the Euphrates,³² are proving to be more revealing, having yielded so far over two hundred fragments of ritual texts from the library of a ᴸᵁ́HAL-diviner.³³ One of these texts, catalogued by the excavator as *Emar* 369,³⁴ preserves a priestly ordination ritual laid out in four stages:

(1) *Selection.* This text preserves a ritual in which a candidate for Hadad's "wife"/priestess³⁵ undergoes, like the priest-king in *bît rimki*, a rite of purification to prepare her for temple service:³⁶

---

28. Laessøe (*bît rimki*, 128–93). See Abusch (*Witchcraft*, 118); Oshima (*Prayers*, 329).

29. "The purpose of *bît rimki* is to transfer evils... from the king to a whole series of unjust persecutors, usually by polluting their figurines with wash water or spittle... in the course of the performance of which each persecutor gets his just deserts" (Scurlock, "*bît rimki*," 203).

30. Yon, *Ugarit*, 18–26.

31. Levine, "Ugarit," 467–75.

32. Located approx. 100 km SE of Aleppo, this border-town often changes hands at the turn of the 1st millennium BCE between opposing Assyro-Babylonian and Syro-Anatolian bureaucracies (see Finet, "Emar," 27–48; Goodnick-Westenholz, "Emar," 145–68).

33. Akk *barû*.

34. Dietrich, "Einsetzungsritual," 47–100.

35. This ritual "seems to play a mediating role in the uneasy moment of equating the storm-god's divine consort, Ḫebat, with the human consort" (Rutz, *Emar*, 145).

36. Distinguishing between divine and sacred marriage (with Renger, "Hochzeit,"

"Tablet of rites"[37] for the NIN.DINGIR[38] of ᵈIM[39] of Emar. When the sons of Emar elevate the NIN.DINGIR to ᵈIM, the sons of Emar will take the lots[40] from the temple of ᵈNIN.URTA[41] and manipulate them before ᵈIM. The daughter of any son of Emar may be identified.[42]

The candidate having thus been cleromantically chosen, the sons of Emar reimburse the officiating priest and personnel of the ᵈNIN.URTA temple for their trouble.

(2) *Consecration.* Next comes a procession to the storm-god's "house," complete with singers, attendants, and the "divine weapon," a mysterious object carried by the ordinand's father.[43] Arriving at the "opening of the courtyard gate,"[44] attendants shave the ordinand's head[45] and the ᴸᵁHAL conducts an "honors-ceremony."[46] Sensitive to the desires of the storm-god and his divine colleagues, attendants lay out tables of food for all the invited deities and dignitaries,[47] the menu including beer, wine, mutton, bread and

---

255), Marsman reminds us that ordination is the doorway to both male and female "temple priests" (Akk *ēn/tu*) becoming "consorts/spouses" of the deities to whom they devote their lives (*Women*, 490–95).

37. Akk *ṭup-pu par-ṣi* (see *BWL* 60.101; *KBo* 1.7.24).

38. That is, the ordinand in need of purification (Schwemer, *Wettergottgestalten*, 551–58).

39. The constant cultural interface of Hittite, NW Semitic, and Mesopotamian peoples at Emar leads Fleming to suggest that the logogram ᵈIM may refer to the storm-gods Teššub, Ba'al and/or Hadad (*Installation*, 71).

40. Akk *pu-re-[e]* (Emar 369.2; see *CAD* P.528 // פור, *HAL* 870), strengthened by the use of *leqû* in the next line ("to handle, manipulate," *CAD* L.136).

41. Rooted in the cultic tradition from Nippur (Uehlinger, "Nimrod," 627–28), the deity Ninurta appears to "represent the 'citizen' power of Emar" (Feliu, *Dagan*, 236).

42. Emar 369.2–3.

43. Sum ᴳᴵˢTUKUL.DINGIR (*Emar* 369.7, replaced by Akk *ḫaṣṣinu* in lines 45, 46 and 63, meaning "axe"). Against the cautions of Dietrich and Fleming, Smith sees the ᴳᴵˢTUKUL.DINGIR as more than a mere symbol of Hadad's power (*Ba'al*, 339).

44. Akk *a-na pí-i* KÁ *ša ta-ar-ba-ṣi* (*Emar* 369.9). Sacred boundaries like temple portals cannot be violated without incurring significant divine wrath. See Wightman (*Spaces*, 49–61); Hundley (*Dwellings*, 131–38); Heinrich (*Tempel*, 149–50, 163–64).

45. Olyan, "Shaving," 611–22. Qur'an also combines حلق ("[head]-shaving") with ستيسر ("sacrifice," Q 2.196).

46. Akk *kubadu* (Heb כבד) may involve a "final goodbye" to her family since after her father carries the "divine weapon" in the first procession, she herself carries it in the final procession (see *CAD* K.17–18).

47. Including the previous NIN.DINGIR of Emar, the NIN.DINGIR of Šumi, the *maṣ'artu*-priestess (*Emar* 370.26, 29), and two political envoys (*Emar* 369.16–17).

beef. Then, just before sunset, the ordinand's head is anointed with oil and she returns to her family's house.

(3) *Installation.* The next day she returns to the temple of the storm-god to participate in yet another "honors ceremony." As in the *bît rimki* ritual from Nineveh, the ordinand here proceeds carefully through a series of seven temporary huts so that she might experience complete purification, after which she emerges as Emar's new NIN.DINGIR. Celebrating this new status, attendants give her a set of earrings and a golden bracelet before returning her back to her family for one last night.

(4) *Consummation.* The final day of the ritual sees the newly ordained priestess leave her family home for the last time, "her head covered as a bride by a colorful sash."[48] Then, after participating in more sacrifices to yet more deities, a female attendant washes her feet, clothes her in a new robe, and ushers her into the bedroom specially prepared for her in Hadad's temple.[49]

COMPARISON WITH HEBREW RITUAL

Similarities

Hebrew ordination ritual is both similar and dissimilar to these two rituals. Torah scholars are more familiar with the ritual in Lev 8–9, of course,[50] but since so many scholars dispute its authenticity, comparative synchronic analysis often surrenders to the demons of diachronic doubt.[51] Questions about historicality, however, do not exempt this or any other Hebrew text from comparative anthropological analysis.[52] Thus intertextual comparison of the ritual in Lev 8–9 alongside the lustration ritual of *bît rimki* surfaces the following similarities:

---

48. *Emar* 369.61. These four stages take ten days to complete.

49. Whether her "sacred marriage" (ἱερὸς γάμος) to the storm-god is literally or figuratively consummated is, and probably always will be, a matter of dispute (see Marsman, *Women*, 490–95).

50. Milgrom and Levine see the description in Lev 8–9 as dependent upon Exod 29, but this is disputed; see Milgrom (*Leviticus*, 545–49); Levine ("Tabernacle," 311); and Elliger (*Leviticus*, 113–14).

51. Gerstenberger (*Persian*, 174) speaks for many when he attributes Exod 6–Lev 9 to "creative priests of the late period." Another European reader, however, suggests that Tanak be read as a "diachronically reflective synchrony" (Markter, *Transformationen*, 57).

52. Perdue (*Collapse*, 7–11); Esler & Hagedorn ("Analysis," 15–32); Klingbeil (*Ordination*, 32–39).

- Both rituals retain an antiphonal structure involving tandem specialists;[53]
- Both employ the traditional cleansing agents of blood, water and fire;[54]
- Both employ ritual washing, anointing, and clothing;[55]
- Both employ animal sacrifice;[56]
- Both feature the ingestion of foodstuffs;[57]
- Both focus on the number "seven";[58]
- Both manage the purification process via temporary "huts";[59] and
- Both define the purification process via the root *kpr*.[60]

Juxtaposing Lev 8–9 alongside *Emar* 369, moreover, surfaces the following parallels:

- Both employ ritual washing, anointing, and clothing;
- Both make extensive use of foodstuffs;
- Both rely on "priestly attendants";
- Both rely on "temporary huts";
- Both ordinands have their bodies symbolically altered;[61]

---

53. Moses consecrates Aaron // the *āšipu*-priest consecrates Aššurbanipal. Structurally, this is probably the most significant parallel.

54. A critical detail apparently never fully comprehended by Nadab and Abihu (Lev 10:1–3).

55. "The implication of anointing as a sacred rite is that the anointed one receives divine sanction and that his person is inviolable" (Milgrom, *Leviticus*, 553).

56. Schiffman ("Temple," 255–72) discusses how the Temple Scroll (11Q19) engages and elaborates on each one of these sacrifices.

57. Granted, Torah does not show the ordinand and his party sitting down to a full meal, but (a) Aaron and his sons do "boil the meat at the door to the tent of meeting and eat it there" (Lev 8:31), and (b) Moses sets cakes and breads on sacrificed portions of the איל המלאים ("ram of ordination," Lev 8:22, NRSV) so that he might offer it to Yahweh as a תנופה ("wave-offering," Lev 8:22–27). In Lev 8:27 "he shall wave" (וינף, i.e., the officiating priest Moses), but in the Temple Scroll "they shall wave" (וניפו, i.e., the newly ordained priests, 11Q19.15.11).

58. "There can hardly be any doubt that the symbolic significance of numbers like three, ten, twelve, and their multiples is surpassed by 'seven,' rightfully having been called the sacred number *par excellence*" (Warning, *Artistry*, 28).

59. Koch, "אהל," 118–30.

60. Akk *kapāru* (*CAD* K.178–80); Heb כפר (*HAL* 470); Syr ܚܦܐ (*PSD* 223); Arab كفر (Lane 2620; see Levine, *Presence*, 123–27; Milgrom, *Leviticus*, 1079–84; Kiuchi, *Purification*, 87–109).

61. The ᵈNIN.DINGIR has her head "shaven" (*gal-lu-bu*, *Emar* 369.7); Aaron has blood "put" (נתן) on his right earlobe, right thumb, and right big toe (Lev 8:23).

- Both rituals feature the roots *kdš* and *kbd*.

Any one of these similarities might (and should) be explored in more detail. The point here is simply that the ordination rituals from Emar, Nineveh, and Israel all follow the same *sequential pattern*:[62]

(1) *Selection*. At Emar, *selection* of the candidate occurs via cleromancy (divination by lot-casting),[63] and Aaron's priestly ministry validates the use of binomial cleromancy for ascertaining, when necessary, the deity's will.[64] Tanak omits the divinatory option *per se*; instead Yahweh commands Moses to "Take Aaron and his sons . . . ."[65]

(2) *Consecration*. Tandem priestly activities appear in Tanak's depiction of Aaron's ordination: משח ("to anoint") and קדש ("to consecrate"). The first of these terms blooms over a rather wide semantic field in biblical Hebrew, especially in the prophetic/apocalyptic texts,[66] while the second philologically parallels a major *Leitwort* at Emar.[67] That is, just as Moses anoints Aaron with fine oil and "consecrates" (קדש) him for service,[68] so also the sons of Emar anoint[69] and consecrate[70] the NIN.DINGIR. Since Near Eastern scribes portray consecration as something of a "rite of passage" from one plane of existence to another, ritual consecration often takes several days to complete. Why? Because (as Edmund Leach observes) it takes

---

62. Following Lévi-Strauss (*Anthropology*, 31–54) and Leach (*Culture*, 78), Kunin emphasizes the importance of recognizing underlying structural patterns in mythical/ritual texts (*Incest*, 17).

63. Fleming (*Emar*, 175); Moore (*Balaam*, 48–50). See فكان, "lots" (Q 37.141).

64. I.e., via the אורים ותמים ("Urim and Thummim") stored in the אפד ("ephod") behind the חשן ("breastplate," Lev 8:7–8). Kitz ("Plural," 402–5) shows that strong affinities exist between the אורים ותמים and the Hittite KIN-oracle, as attested on texts like *KUB* 5.1, and Kaufmann (*Religion*) argues that "the absence of priestly sanctums such as the ark, the Urim and Thummim, and the anointing of oil in the postexilic age speaks eloquently for their antiquity" (Milgrom, "Numbers," 1150).

65. Lev 8:1–2. "Leviticus 8 is the *implementation of God's vision* for a priesthood, a vision that has hovered over and shaped the priestly story line of the Torah since Exodus 29" (Balentine, *Leviticus*, 70).

66. Roberts, "Messianic," 39–51.

67. Akk *qadāšu* (*Emar* 369.6, 13, 21–22).

68. Lev 8:10–13.

69. Akk *tabāku* ("to pour out," *Emar* 369.21) is not an exact cognate of Heb משח, but these terms engage the same semantic field. The verb in 369.4 is altogether different (Akk *šakānu*, "to put/place"; see Fleming, *Emar*, 176).

70. *Emar* 369.2–21. Fleming argues that the cognate root *qdš* can mean "to treat as holy" in both Tanak and the Emar texts, while its use in the D conjugation can mean "to purify/consecrate/make holy" (*Emar*, 162). The point here, however, is not philological, but literary/structural; viz., that "holiness" appears *in tandem* with "anointing" in both Assyrian and Hebrew ordination rituals.

time for an ordinand to travel from an initiatory stage of selection through a dangerous marginal stage of potential abandonment to a final stage of re-acceptance into the community.[71] Something can always go wrong on the path of this journey.[72]

(3) *Installation.* Immediately following the consecration ceremony, similar installation rites occur. At Emar the candidate takes the "divine weapon" from her father and carries it to her installation ceremony.[73] In Israel, Aaron takes the weapon[74] out of Moses' hand and "slaughters" his first calf.[75] Both rituals highlight the moment of change in *status* when each ordinand performs his/her first official priestly task.[76]

(4) *Consummation.* Consummation occurs when the attendants bring all the sacrificial offerings and assorted foodstuffs before the deity and seek his blessing, often within the context of a communal meal.[77]

Dissimilarities

Comparative analysis of these texts shows that priestly ordination in the Hebrew context diverges significantly from the Assyrian context at several points:

(1) Hebrew ritual never presumes the presence, much less the activity, of multiple deities,[78] nor does it attempt to depict God via humanoid images, behaviors, or relationships.[79]

---

71. Leach, *Culture*, 78.
72. Eliade, *Shamanism*, 164–68.
73. *Emar* 369.31.
74. Perhaps a מאכלת like that used by Abraham to "slaughter" (שחט) his son on Mt. Moriah (Gen 22:10; see also Judg 19:29).
75. שחט, "to slaughter" (Lev 9:8). See Ug *šḥṭ* (*CAT* 1.18.4.24); Aram *šḥṭ* (*KAI* 222A.32); Syr ܫܚܛ ("to harm, mar, abuse," *PSD* 570); Arab سحط ("to slaughter").
76. "Status, as used here, moves in two directions. First, it refers to a person's standing within society. This may be understood in institutional terms (e.g., the priesthood), but may also be understood, in the Priestly traditions, in terms of the categories of purity and pollution" (Gorman, *Ideology*, 10).
77. In Israel, the ordination ritual concludes when Moses and Aaron exit the אהל מועד ("tent of meeting") and the כבוד יהוה ("glory of Yahweh") reveals itself "to all the people" (אל כל העם, Lev 9:22–24).
78. This is not to argue against עזאזל as the proper name "Azazel" in Lev 16:26, nor is it to challenge Smith's (*Memoirs*, 87) insistence that "to understand biblical monotheism better, we must understand the polytheism of early Israel as well as the polytheism of its cultural antecedents."
79. Hendel, "Aniconic," 365–82; Walker & Dick, *Induction*, 4–31. This point cannot be overemphasized to readers living in victimology cultures where eternity is imagined

(2) Assyrian candidates progress through a symbolic number (usually seven) of specially built temporary huts over a period of several days,[80] while Hebrew candidates spend seven days in the same "hut"—the אהל מועד ("tent of meeting").[81]

(3) The community at large plays a significant role in the Hebrew ordination ritual while the Assyrians limit congregational participation to professional specialists working behind closed doors.[82]

(4) Hebrew ordination ritual serves "not only to pass Aaron and his sons into their status as priests," but also "to establish the institution of the priesthood" itself,[83] a trait hardly echoed in Assyrian ordination ritual.

(5) Where Hebrew and Assyrian priests focus on *purification* as the primary function of cultic ordination,[84] Hebrew priests add another component conspicuously missing from the Assyrian texts: *endowment*.[85] The Temple Scroll underlines this when, alongside the idiom מלא יד ("fill the hand"),[86] it portrays priestly ordination via the expansive phrase מלא על נפש ("fill up the soul").[87]

---

solely in categories limited to and dictated by temporal human experience. See Olfman (*Childhood*); Rich (*Offenders*); Frymer-Kensky (*Goddesses*); Ruether (*Goddesses*); Hayter (*Abuse*, 18) and Moore ("Women").

80. In *Emar* 369.33–34 these "huts" include the *bît tukli* (where a lamb is presented to the god Adammatera; see Fleming, *Time*, 163–64) and the *bît Gadda* (where a lamb is presented to Hadad; see Nunn, "Widerspruch," 133).

81. Yet N.B. the seven-day festival of סכות ("Sukkot"—i.e., "huts/booths/tabernacles," Lev 23:34). See Weyde (*Festivals*, 113–30).

82. Lenzi (*Secrecy*, 27, 41–45, 55–63) documents how professional Mesopotamian diviners carve out roles for themselves as conveyors of secret information as they shuttle between royal and divine councils (see Jer 23:18).

83. Gorman, *Ideology*, 103.

84. Predominantly through parallel use of the root *kpr*. In Q 22.37 God graciously provides livestock for food, but animal meat and animal blood "do not reach Alla" (لن ينال الاة).

85. See *HAL* 552–53.

86. The D idiom is מלא יד, "fill the hand" (Lev 7:37; 8:33). N.B. that both components occur together in the ritual for *yôm kippur*: כפר ("to cover/atone") and מלא יד ("to fill the hand/endow," Lev 16:32; see Snijders, "מלא‎," 301–6).

87. 11Q19.15.14. Milgrom translates "complete their ordination," but this ignores the obvious implications indicated by the change of noun (*Leviticus*, 560; see Schiffman, "Temple," 263–65). Nazarene writers continue to reflect on this "endowment" component when Luke, for example, balances ἄφεσιν τῶν ἁμαρτιῶν ("remission of sins") with δωρεὰν τοῦ ἁγίου πνεύματος ("endowment of the Holy Spirit," Acts 2:38). Conradie (*Re-Creation*) surveys exponents of this "both-and" mentality among several Christian thinkers.

(6) Blood ritual is not unknown outside of Tanak,[88] but where Assyrian ordination ritual barely mentions it, blood is by far the predominant cleansing agent in Hebrew ritual.[89]

ROLE PREEMPTION IN THE ISRAELITE PRIESTHOOD

Eurocentric Philosophies of History

Hopefully this brief analysis shows the potential of synoptic synchronic comparison over against nineteenth-century European approaches to the history of the Israelite priesthood. Julius Wellhausen, for example, argues that the tradition about the Levitical priest in Micah's shrine (Judg 17) *must* reflect a primitive era characterized by oracular divination, oneness with nature, decentralized government, and a general atmosphere of non-institutionalism.[90] The ordination of Aaron in Leviticus, on the other hand, *must* reflect a post-exilic portrayal of an "Aaronid victory" over all other priestly houses.[91]

This philosophy of history, however, suffers from at least two glaring weaknesses. First, it does not examine the Israelite priesthood alongside other, contemporary priesthoods. Wellhausen cannot be faulted for this because in his era the Assyrian tablets examined in the present essay still lay underground. Cross-culturally reading Tanak against pre-Islamic Arabic literature (texts which inform us very little about ancient ritual),[92] he produces a brilliantly insightful analysis of the texts at his disposal, but today most interpreters recognize that the paucity of comparative data at his disposal forces him to draw conclusions more dependent upon hypothetical reconstruction than intertextual analysis, and further, that the philosophy

---

88. In addition to *BBR* 26, note the Anatolian references cited by Feder (*Blood*, 209–10) and Beckman ("Blood," 95–102) *contra* the myopic claims of Walton *et al.* (*Background*, 120).

89. Gilders (*Blood*, 85–108); De Troyer ("Blood," 45–64); Biale (*Blood*).

90. Contrasting Eli's priesthood at Shiloh (1 Sam 1–3) with the Levite's priesthood at Micah's shrine (Judg 17:1–13), Wellhausen (*Geschichte*, 134) even suggests that "der letztere Fall stellt vermutlich eher die Regel dar als der erste" ("the latter case rather than the first probably represents the rule").

91. Cross ("Houses," 195–215) sees two rival priestly families in Israel: the Aaronids (represented by Zadok, whom he traces to the Hebronite clan descended from Aaron) and the Mushites (represented by Abiathar, whom he traces to the Shilonite house of Eli descended from Moses), agreeing with Wellhausen that the Aaronids eventually become the dominant priestly family.

92. One of Wellhausen's most enduring accomplishments is his *Reste Arabischen Heidentums* ("Remnants of Arabic Heathenism"), first published in 1887.

of history upon which he relies to "fill in the gaps" depends more on nineteenth-century Hegelian ideology than ancient Near Eastern history.[93]

Second, Wellhausen's reconstruction of the Israelite priesthood rests on a hopelessly naïve view of history itself because it rests on the presumption that history always progresses from the "primitive" to the "complex," that ethical ideas are always more progressive than "primitivist" ritual, and that human cultures never revert "backward," only evolve "forward." Few, if any, historians would accept such a view today. The horrors generated by two genocidal world wars have conclusively proven, if nothing else, that human cultures, individuals, and institutions can be radically self-centered, irrationally dysfunctional, and rapaciously greedy.[94]

Role Theory

Yet contemporary biblical scholarship, for all its paradigm shifts and new approaches, has yet to replace the nineteenth-century European paradigm with something else.[95] Comparative approaches may not be the sole answer, but at least they try to listen more sensitively to more constituent voices. The fact remains that we have much more empirical evidence to work with today than Wellhausen did in his day, and we know much more about ancient Near Eastern ritual now than Wellhausen did then. The question is not whether, but *how* to engage this evidence. Role theory can be of great help here because this academic discipline offers a coherent, proven method for interpreting sociological data within a defensible theoretical grid;[96] i.e., one completely "purified" from ideological notions about "inevitable progress."[97]

---

93. Blenkinsopp (*Pentateuch*, 11–12); Buchwalter ("Eurocentric," 87–110).

94. Moore, *WealthWatch*, 18–19. Parekh " ("Race," 111–34) documents how Hegel violates his own claim to impartiality via comments which today would be be put in the category of "racial profiling."

95. Yet see Kuenen (*Pentateuch*), Kaufmann (*Religion*), Rendtorff (*Pentateuch*), and Carr (*Formation*).

96. Role theory is an academic sub-discipline within social psychology. "Role enactment" describes the number of roles enacted within a given "role-set." "Role strain" occurs when the "role expectations" within different segments of an audience or between different audiences become measurably dissonant. "Role preemption" occurs when any one role within an actor's role-set preempts all other roles (Sarbin & Allen, "Role," 489–91). Tanak applications appear in Petersen (*Roles*) and Moore (*Balaam*).

97. Hegel, "Systemfragment," 343–51. Von Ranke's response to Hegel is to document events empirically in order to depict history *wie es eigentlich gewesen* ("as it actually was," *Geschichten*, vii).

Role Theory Analysis of the Israelite Priesthood

One of Wellhausen's typical arguments is that the roles enacted by Micah's priest (Judg 17–18) are more "primitive" than those enacted by Aaron and his sons (Lev 8–9); thus these texts *must* reflect an earlier historical era. He holds firmly to this opinion, even though Tanak places Aaron's story well before that of Micah's Levite. Role theory, however, raises a whole different set of questions to these texts.

Role Enactment

First, the Danite gang responsible for capturing Micah's priest commands him to שאל נא באלהים ("Inquire of the gods!"),[98] thereby implying that this magico-religious specialist enacts a "diviner-seer" role-set in Iron Age Ephraim.[99] The text does not specify what type of divination this might be, but that this is indeed divination—not prophecy or some other form of divine-human communication[100]—is not up for dispute.[101] Thus Micah's Levite enacts a role-set quite similar to that of Aaron, the Hebrew priest who keeps אורים ותמים in his חשן ("breastplate").[102] The fact that the Danites also call Micah's Levite אב and כהן tells us little about other roles in his role-set, yet the technical idiom used to describe his "ordination," מלא יד ("fill the hand"), is identical to that used to describe Aaron's.[103]

Role Expectations

Second, the cultic icons in Micah's בית אלהים include פסל ומסכה ("sculpted metal image"),[104] אפד ("ephod"),[105] and תרפים ("teraphim").[106] Since Mi-

---

98. The term אלהים refers to "gods" (pl.) instead of "God" (sg.) because the verb in Micah's statement to the Danites, את־אלהי . . . לקחתם ("My gods . . . you have taken *them*," Judg 18:24), has appended to it a 3 m. pl. pronominal suffix.

99. Moore, *Balaam*, 12–19, 27–28, 32, 42–44, 47–55.

100. Anthonioz, *Prophétisme*, 13–14.

101. Huffmon, "Divination," 355–59.

102. Kitz, "Plural," 401–10.

103. Judg 17:12; Lev 8:33; see *HAL* 552–53.

104. Granted, פסל ומסכה appears as a tandem pair in Deut 27:15 and Nah 1:14 ("carved image and molten image"), but here it references a singular entity, since the verb עשה has appended to it a 3 m. sg. suffix (ויעשהו, "and he made *it*," Judg 17:3).

105. Meyers, "Ephod," 550–51.

106. Lewis calls the תרפים "ancestor figurines which function in necromantic

cah explicitly associates these icons with אלהים in his discussion with the Danites, אלהים doubtless references here the world of chthonic "daemons"— those mysterious beings which animate the earliest layers of the Balaam traditions,[107] Job dialogues,[108] and Hebrew ancestor stories.[109] Granted, the evidence for this is only sparsely preserved (and deliberately muted),[110] but there seems to be enough to conclude, at least tentatively, that the role-set enacted by Micah's priest leans more to the "magic" pole of the magic-religion continuum than Aaron's.[111]

Role Complexity

Third, Aaron enacts a role-set which appears to be more complex than that enacted by Micah's Levite. Like their Assyrian counterparts, these Hebrew priests serve their congregations by means of temporary structures. The Levite serves in a בית אלהים ("house of gods," probably a household shrine)[112] while Aaron's ordination takes place in a אהל מועד ("tent of meeting"—the most mobile of all Hebrew shrines).[113] Viewing this contrast against the backdrop of the urban *bît rimki* from Nineveh and the provincial ordination ceremony from Emar only strengthens the likelihood of this possibility.[114]

Role Preemption

The point is this. *None* of these observations necessarily imply that the details associated with Aaron's ordination *must* be the product of later priestly

---

practices in particular as well as divinatory practices in general" ("Teraphim," 849).

107. Von Pákozdy ("Bileam," 161–76); Moore (*Balaam*, 99).

108. Moore, "Terror," 664–65.

109. "The biblical תרפים/אלהים correspond, in so far as Genesis 31 is concerned, with Nuzi *ilāni* (Akk 'gods') in their intimate role in regard to family law" (Draffkorn-Kilmer, "*Ilāni/Elohim*" 222).

110. Smith speaks of "the editing of later monotheists" (*Origins*, 155).

111. My understanding of the relationship between magic and religion is discussed in the previous chapter of the present book.

112. Lewis, "Teraphim," 849.

113. Tanak references three Yahwistic sanctuaries: אהל מועד ("tent of meeting"); משכן ("dwelling"; Akk *maškanu*; Ug *mšknt*; // אהל , Num 24:5); היכל ("temple"; Sum É-GAL, "palace"; Akk *ekallu*, "palace"; Ug *hkl*, "palace"). Whether these structures chronologically succeed or overlap each other is impossible to ascertain from the data available (*pace* Friedmann, "Tabernacle," 292).

114. Construction of a clearer picture necessitates the discovery and analysis of more ordination texts than presently at our disposal.

imagination, as Wellhausen's academic descendants continue to insist.[115] It may well be earlier, as Kaufmann and his students argue.[116] All we can say is that the roles enacted by Micah's Levite seem to occur at a time of weak resistance to non-Yahwistic influence, at least in the hill country of Ephraim, a time when "official" Yahwism is preempted by religious views and practices more open to Canaanite variability. What we can say with relative certainty is that history is more volatile and complex than many readers will allow.[117] Civilizations rise and fall; nations elevate and disintegrate; cultures evolve and devolve. And so do the social institutions which make them up, including those we call "priesthoods." The role-sets enacted within these institutions are never static, but always dynamic, constantly responding to pressures both internal as well as external.[118] Only the most mindless Hegelian would insist that the simpler, more "primitive" institution must always precede the more "developed" one.[119]

The better question to ask is whether the history of the Israelite priesthood might contain a block of chapters in which the roles enacted by Hebrew priests oscillate back-and-forth between opposing poles on magic-religion as well as generalization-specialization continuums.[120] As Israel resists, then assimilates, then resists the cultic habits of its neighbors *ad infinitum*, so apparently roll in, then roll out, then roll back in the ideologies, practices and cultic appurtenances of its alternately Yahwicizing, then Canaanizing, then re-Yahwicizing priesthood(s). Role theory, particularly the variable of role preemption, helps us understand the dynamics of this process in a more holistic way.

SUGGESTIONS FOR FUTURE RESEARCH

Comparative intertextual analysis can help us understand the basic character and development of the Israelite priesthood, yet the present essay only scratches the surface of what needs to be done.

115. Gerstenberger (*Persian*, 177), for example, suggests that the "clerical discord" in Lev 10 reflects "a profound cultic, theological division in the postexilic community."

116. Kaufmann (*Golah*, 110–68); Milgrom (*Leviticus*, 493–569).

117. Moore & Kelle, *History*, 1–4.

118. "The two fields are not fundamentally different: History cannot do without alluding to recurrent causal sequences even though it has the tendency to take them for granted, and the natural sciences cannot do without concrete individual initial conditions when explaining an outcome, although they are inclined to make them 'disappear' behind general laws" (Heidelberger, "Causality," 243).

119. McCumber tries to salvage Hegel's philosophy of history ("Logics," 69–86), even after von Ranke basically demolishes it (see Beiser, "Hegel," 332–50).

120. Sarbin & Allen, "Role," 488–93.

(1) *Content.* The constant flow of data from Middle Eastern excavations is constantly changing our understanding of priestly ritual—sometimes unexpectedly,[121] sometimes dramatically.[122] The upside of this is a larger corpus of evidence with which to work. The downside is the increasing possibility that some of us may "get lost in the forest" (non-Israelite ritual) while looking for the "trees" (Israelite ritual).[123]

(2) *Method.* Role theory can help mitigate this danger, but this is not the only theoretical model through which these ancient texts can be viewed. Analogical language models,[124] symbolic language models,[125] ritualization models,[126] indexical approaches[127]—each of these approaches offers something exegetically helpful.

(3) *Theory.* In this pluralistic age it seems more than a little foolish to expect one overarching theory to dominate discussion about this or any other aspect of ancient Near Eastern study.[128] Perhaps it's therefore time to consult the "complexity" theorists[129] and start rethinking how we define the "practice of religion" so that additional research can more easily "qualify or falsify (our thinking) about the relationship between Israelite and non-Israelite cultures."[130]

---

121. Arnaud, *Emar*.

122. Discovery of the ritual text at Tell Deir ʿAllā (Combination 2), for example, reframes everything previously known about the character and activity of Balaam ben Beor.

123. Moore & Kelle, *History*, 466–75.

124. Rappaport, *Ritual*, 30.

125. Klawans, *Purity*, 6–10.

126. Bell, *Ritual*, 74.

127. Gilders, *Blood*, 5–8.

128. Indeed, as Zevit observes (*Religions*, 1), "the study of ancient Israelite religion (itself) is in a quandary. Intellectual certainty that the flood of philological, historical, and archaeological research initiated since the 1950s would provide an adequate description has dissipated.... Much contemporary discussion either repackages the same old thing for new consumers or savagely attacks the same old thing."

129. Waldrop (*Emerging*, 12–13) defines "complexity theory" as "the first rigorous alternative to the kind of linear, reductionist thinking that has dominated science since the time of Newton, and that has now gone about as far as it can go in addressing the problems of the modern world." Zevit tries to reimagine the character and development of Israelite religion through lenses ground by the tenets of "complexity theory" (*Religions*, 646).

130. Zevit, *Religions*, 118–19. Smith-Christopher ("Reading," 62) argues that "the reality of extensive and exciting discussion and debate in biblical studies does not mean that the field is wandering aimlessly ... Appearances, especially in the contemporary world, can be deceiving."

PART 2: PROPHECY AND APOCALYPTIC

4

YAHWEH'S DAY*

ZEPHANIAH'S PROPHECY PRESERVES ONE of the clearest expressions of perhaps the most characteristic of all prophetic motifs, the "Day of the LORD."[1] Following several warnings threatening to "sweep away" (סוּף) all things "foreign" from the streets of Jerusalem,[2] the tone shifts in verse seven away from "prophetic judgment" to "priestly purification":

> Be silent[3] before my lord Yahweh, for Yahweh's day is near.[4]

* Revised from an essay first published in *ResQ* 29 (1987) 193-208.

1. Heb יום יהוה ("day of Yahweh"). "Zephaniah gives a rich picture of the Day of Yahweh. He is the prophet who speaks in the most concentrated manner about the Day" (Kapelrud, *Zephaniah*, 80). "Zephaniah's prophecy certainly belongs to the most important material at our disposal concerning the concept of the Day of Yahweh" (von Rad, "Yahweh," 102). See Cathcart ("Day," 84-85), Hiers ("Day," 82-83), Barker ("Day," 132-43), and Udoekpo (*Zephaniah*, 43-80).

2. Zeph 1:2-6. N.B. נכרי ("foreign") in Zeph 1:8 (see Moore, "Foreigners," 203-17).

3. Keller emphasizes the liturgical use of הס not only here, but in Zech 2:17 and Neh 8:1 (*Sophonie*, 190-91). Sabottka (*Zephanjah*, 31-32) draws semantic parallels between הס ("Be silent!") and *favete linguis* in Latin liturgical texts (Horace, *Carm*. 3.1.2; Ovid, *Metam*. 15.678; Virgil, *Aen*. 5.77), each intended to invoke reverence before the gods.

4. Elliger suggests an original cultic formula later modified by addition of the term יום ("day," *Zephanjah*, 63), a suggestion which, if correct, challenges von Rad's attempt to anchor the entire expression כי קרוב יום יהוה ("for Yahweh's day is near") in purely Yahwistic tradition ("Yahweh," 108). Kapelrud (*Zephaniah*, 61) suggests that the "nearness" motif depends upon prior usage of קרוב in Isa 13:6, but if the oracle against Babylon in Isa 13 is exilic (Eissfeldt, *Introduction*, 319-20), this is impossible. Following Bourke ("Jahvé," 191-212) and Černý (*Day*, 10-17), Keller (*Sophonie*, 191) interprets Yahweh's "day" as Yahweh's "theophany," defining "theophany" as a two-sided

Indeed, Yahweh has prepared a[5] sacrificial feast;[6] he has consecrated his guests.[7] On the day of Yahweh's sacrifice I will heap punishment upon[8] the officials,[9] the king's children, and all who clothe themselves in foreign attire.[10] On that day I will punish all

---

phenomenon: Yahweh's holiness (a) consumes everything "foreign" (Zeph 1:14–18), and (b) extends life to all survivors (3:14–20).

5. OG reads αὐτοῦ ("his").

6. In order to maintain the purity of his "theophanic" interpretation Weiss ("Day," 31–32) tries to eliminate all traces of "holy war" from the terms חרב ("sword") and חרם ("devoted things") in Jer 46:10 and Isa 34:2–6. Defining זבח in these passages as the "communion meal" to which Yahweh invites his guests, Weiss argues that Jeremiah and Isaiah engage the term from a "theophanic" perspective. Sabottka (*Zephanja*, 33–34) and Keller (*Sophonie*, 191–92) concur, the latter imagining this "sacrifice" having two components: (a) the sacrifice of an animal, followed by (b) the feast convened to consume it, associating the causative verbs bracketing זבח (הכין, "to prepare," and הקדיש, "to consecrate") with the union of sacrifice + sacrificial meal at Baʿal's victory feast in Canaanite myth (*CAT* 1.3.1.2–11).

7. הקדיש (lit., "to make holy," Zeph 1:7). Von Rad (*War*, 41–50) hangs a great deal of weight on the "holy" (קדש) in "holy war," viewing it as an old, essentially cultic phenomenon later stripped of all cultic associations by zealous prophetic tradents. Seeking to refute von Rad, Weiss tries to dissociate קדש from the conduct of war by presuming its usage to be largely metaphorical ("Day," 32). This, however, strangely contradicts his intention to interpret זבח as a sacral term rooted in the cult, not to mention his failure to cite a single instance in which the causative form of קדש is indeed "metaphorical." Since so much of his hypothesis rests on this point, it's difficult to avoid concluding that the motive driving Weiss' analysis, like that behind Fohrer's (*History*, 89–94), is his ideological distaste for von Rad's *heilsgeschichtliche* approach generally. Miller ("Divine," 100–101) attempts to mediate, positing that "the divine council participates as a cosmic or heavenly army in the eschatological wars of Yahweh, those military activities associated with the Day of Yahweh, and that these conflicts (or conflict?) enjoy a joint participation of human or earthly forces and divine or heavenly armies." In other words, the later prophets eschatologize the "day" to include cosmic "consecrated guests" as well as the nations around Judah. Sabottka applies Miller's hybrid thesis directly to Zeph. 1:7, even while admitting that the ambivalent language in this passage remains problematic (*Zephanja*, 35). Rudolph (*Zephanja*, 266) thinks that Zephaniah intentionally transforms a well-known Israelite dream—eschatological participation in a communion meal consisting of enemy carcasses—into a nightmare.

8. While פקד simply means "to visit" (1 Sam 17:18; Isa 26:16), the phrase here, אפקדתי על ("I will heap punishment upon") appears three times in these few verses, leaving little doubt as to what kind of "visit" the prophet has in mind. McCarter ("Temper," 87–88) argues that because so many Ugaritic myths equate divine anger with divine "sickness," perhaps Yahweh's anger can sometimes be viewed as "a hypostatic or quasi-independent entity" which, in spite of his "beneficent regard for people, can be provoked into destructive activity by certain forbidden human activities, especially . . . cultic violations."

9. In Ezra 9:1 Fried reads שׂרים (Zeph 1:8) as Persian government "officials" (*Ezra*, 24).

10. From Zephaniah's perspective these three groups see themselves as "entitled,"

who leap over the threshold[11] to instill violence and fraud into their master's house ... The great day of Yahweh is near—near and hastening fast. The noise on that day will be unbearable,[12] (like that of) a warrior screaming for help. It will be a day of wrath, a day of anguish and distress, a day of ruin and devastation, a day of darkness and gloom, a day of clouds and fog, a day of trumpet blast and battle cry.[13]

As the foregoing notes begin to indicate, considerable debate hovers over how, exactly, to define the origin and development of this quintessentially prophetic motif.[14] The purpose of this short essay is twofold: (a) to examine and critique the major voices contributing to this debate, and (b) to advance a holistic interpretation strategy.

HISTORY-OF-TRADITION APPROACHES

Well before the study of Hebrew tradition-history reaches its zenith,[15] *Alttestamentler* Ernst Sellin identifies Yahweh's "day" by situating Israel's messianic hope on a tradition trajectory tracing its beginning to the "day" of Yahweh's revelation to Moses on Sinai.[16] Fifty years later Charles Fensham stretches this insight into an argument, positioning this "Sinai day" within

---

not "blessed" (see Brueggemann, *Memory*, 19–27).

11. The term מפתן ("threshold," Zeph 1:9) appears elsewhere in another cultic context (מפתן דגון, "threshold of Dagon," 1 Sam 5:5), and OG's translation (πρόπυλα, "gates") appears in Herakles' "resurrection" speech by Euripides (*Herc. fur.* 523). Thresholds are tricky things in antiquity because the ancients perceive them to mark the boundaries between "in/out," "safety/danger," and "sacred/secular" (Eliade, *Sacred*, 25). Where the wise treat them with respect, the foolish ignore, disregard and make them blurry. See Roberts (*Zephaniah*, 179), and the fascinating list of examples collected by Frazer (*Folk-lore*, 3.1–18).

12. "Unbearable" seems a more appropriate translation of MT מר than "bitter," at least when describing קול ("noise," Zeph 1:14), esp. since OG reads πικρὰ καὶ σκληρά ("bitter and hard").

13. Zeph 1:7–16. Comparable military images orbit the "day of Yahweh" motif in Isa 13:6–13.

14. Working within categories developed by Talmon ("Motifs," 151), Fields defines a "motif" as an "encapsulation of a basic principle or societal experience with which the authors of narratives are concerned" (*Sodom*, 20). Hendel elaborates: "motifs" are "essential semantic units of biblical narrative ... To elucidate them adequately requires knowledge of language, literary and religious traditions, and cultural context, as well as an eye for intertextuality and the nuances of literary style" (*Sodom*, 127).

15. See the seminal *résumé* of Childs (*Crisis*, 65–72) and the responses of Smart (*Past*, 22–23) and Barr ("Biblical," 3–19).

16. Sellin, *Prophetismus*, 148–51.

the distinctive parameters of Hebrew covenant theology, secondarily aligning it with what he calls the "covenantal act" of animal sacrifice.[17] To Mowinckel's attempt to situate the "day" within the "festal cult at the New Year festival,"[18] Fensham responds by insisting that the "day" of Yahweh's Sinai revelation is not only more ancient, but more credible, given the fact that no "annual enthronement ritual"[19] can be attested *in Israel*,[20] and that even if it could be, would represent only one small segment of Judahite society—the monarchy.[21] Few find this "covenant" thesis convincing, however. After all, as Weiss keenly observes, how is it that "Yahweh's day" does not figure in any form whatsoever in extra-prophetic literature? If it is indeed rooted in Torah covenant tradition, as Fensham argues, then why does the יום יהוה motif not appear in the Sinai episode (Exod 19–23) or the covenant renewal narratives (Exod 34; Josh 24)?[22]

More widely accepted is the tradition-historical thesis of Gerhard von Rad, who writes that

> the Day of Yahweh encompasses a pure act of war. . . . There is no support whatsoever . . . for the supposition that the enthronement of Yahweh, too, belongs to the Day of Yahweh.[23]

The great strength of this position is its careful attention to a clear methodology. The great weakness is its close-minded dismissal of all other approaches. Prior to von Rad, few scholars (with the obvious exception of Mowinckel) seriously attempt to reconstruct the *Sitz im Leben* of this motif.[24] Yet not only does von Rad significantly restrict the number of potential *Sitzen im Leben*, he insists that the canons of form- and tradition-criticism (which, after all, he helps to hammer out) be employed. *Result:* For von Rad the יום יהוה motif stands "in the centre of an entire circle of ideas" from which it cannot be extricated.

---

17. Fensham, "Day," 90–97.

18. Mowinckel, *Cometh*, 132.

19. Bidmead sensitively explains how and why ANE priesthoods use New Year festivals to establish, legitimate and maintain monarchical power (*Akītu*, 39–41).

20. Bidmead's skepticism is understandable, if a bit draconian (*Akītu*, 29–32).

21. Fensham, "Day," 97. Gottwald weighs the pros and cons of whether or not the monarchy is progressive or regressive (*Introduction*, 167–74).

22. Weiss, "Day," 41.

23. Von Rad, "Day," 98.

24. Most studies from this era focus on the question of prophetic eschatology. Gressmann (*Eschatologie*, 143–45), e.g., theorizes that the Hebrew prophets assume in their hearers some awareness of a "popular eschatology."

This "circle of ideas," of course, is his hypothetical reconstruction of the Israelite "holy war," an institution he feels to be an indigenously Yahwistic phenomenon, and the location of which he posits in what scholars used to call the "Israelite League."[25] Few find this hypothesis acceptable today, however, because (a) its connection to Greek "amphictyonic leagues"[26] is too speculative, and (b) its dependence on the canons of the *Heilsgeschichte* school is too parochial.[27] Yet if nothing else, von Rad's work stimulates more critical reflection on the יום יהוה motif than any other study.

COMPARATIVE INTERTEXTUAL APPROACHES

Von Rad's 1951 study is a measured response, in part, to the influential work of one of Hermann Gunkel's brightest students, the Norwegian scholar Sigmund Mowinckel. Focusing on the use of יום יהוה in the book of Amos (commonly thought to be the earliest source),[28] Mowinckel builds on the work of Hoffman,[29] Volz,[30] and Hölscher[31] to argue (a) that Israel, like most other ANE monarchies, regularly empowers itself via an annual "day of enthronement";[32] (b) that Israel's priesthood, like all other ANE priesthoods,

---

25. Schunk ("Strukturlinien," 328–30) modifies von Rad's "holy war" thesis to include two stages of development, one historical (pre-eschatological) and the other eschatological. Wolff more clearly articulates this "two-stage" hypothesis (*Joel*, 34).

26. Noth, *Stämme* (see Demosthenes, *De pace* 5.19; Strabo, 8.6.14). As Lemche ("Amphictyony," 48) points out, the oldest Greek ἀμφικτυονία dates back only as far as the eighth century BCE—not, as Noth suggests, the 11th century. Thus "objections to Noth's thesis are overwhelming" because "the full Greek model does not exist until three or four centuries after the Israelite tribal period" (Weir, "Amphictyony," 27).

27. Von Rad, *Theology* 2.177. The most serious attacks come from Weippert ("Heiliger," 460–93) and Smend (*Jahwekrieg*, 20–32), who insist on relocating the emergence of the Israelite "holy war" not to a post-Mosaic "Israelite league," but to the late premonarchical era. See Childs (*Testaments*, 16–18), Barr (*Interpretation*, 26–27), Robinson ("Historicality," 124–28), and Hopkins ("Promise," 190–93).

28. "Commentators generally agree that in Amos' time 'the Day of Yahweh' is popularly thought to mean the time when Yahweh will vindicate Israel by defeating its enemies ... In contrast, Amos warns his Israelite hearers that 'the Day of Yahweh' will not be what they want" (Hiers, "Day," 82).

29. Hoffman, *Amos*, 112.

30. Volz, *Neujahrsfest*.

31. Hölscher, *Eschatologie*, 1–16. "If the assumption that the idea of the 'Day of Yahweh' belongs within the ritual of public lament is correct, this opens the possibility of a connection between vv. 16–17, which depict a public lament, and the pronouncement on יום יהוה in vv. 18–20" (Barstad, *Amos*, 110).

32. Linguistically the key parallel is the climactic moment in Babylonian coronation ceremonies when the high priest announces ^{d}*marūtuk-ma šarru* ("Marduk is king," *Ee*

conducts these empowerment rituals for the king every רוש השנה ("New Year's Day");³³ therefore (c) Israel's priestly cult is the most likely source responsible for generating the יום יהוה motif. *Conclusion:* The original יום יהוה is the day of Yahweh's ritual enthronement, the annual feast-day when Yahweh (re)conquers the forces of chaos,³⁴ (re)establishing שלום ("peace") on earth for succeeding generations.³⁵

Von Rad rejects this argument on two fronts. *First,* the lack of empirical evidence for a Hebrew "day of enthronement" cannot be over-emphasized, whether it occurs on רוש השנה or any other day. The unavoidable fact of the matter is that Tanak is conspicuously silent on this point.³⁶ *Second,* to Mowinckel's reliance on non-Hebraic mythical imagery, von Rad instead proposes an extension and elaboration in the late preexilic period (an era fraught with political danger and intrigue) of a fundamentally Yahwistic tradition-complex (the "holy war") to explain the rise of the יום יהוה motif in Amos, Isaiah, Zephaniah and other prophets.³⁷ While some find his frame of reference too narrow,³⁸ others find it most attractive. Drawing from the OB Mari texts often designated "prophetic,"³⁹ for example, Jean-Georges

---

4.28). Mowinckel (*Psalmenstudien* 83–85) sees an "obvious" parallel in the Psalter with the phrase מלך יהוה ("Yahweh is king"; see Pss 93:1; 96:10; 97:1). Both Volz (*Neujahrsfest,* 12–14) and Mowinckel theorize that an original Hebrew *Neujahrsfest* assimilates early into the Hebrew חג הסכות ("feast of booths," Deut 16:13).

33. Bidmead, *Akītu,* 39–41. Mowinckel (*Psalmenstudien,* 211–314) arrives at these conclusions via an inductive study of the royal psalms (Pss 47, 93, 95, 96, 97, 98, 99, 100) plus other psalms resonating with their distinctive vocabulary (Pss 8, 15, 24, 29, 33, 46, 48, 50, 66A, 75, 76, 81, 82, 84, 87, 114, 118, 132, 149, and Exod 15:1–18). Roberts critiques the impact of Mowinckel's work on subsequent Tanak scholarship ("Enthronement," 97–115).

34. The model upon which Mowinckel relies, of course, is Marduk's conquest of Tiamat in the Babylonian Creation Myth (*enūma eliš*), particularly *Ee* tablet 4 (see Lambert, *Creation,* 86–95).

35. The opposite of a "day of empowering" would be a "day of cursing," like the one for which Job so painfully pleads (Job 3:1–10; see Jacobsen & Nielsen, "Day," 187–204). "The element of the priestly worldview that holds together priestly creation theology and priestly ritual is the desire to bring order to human existence" (Gorman, *Ritual,* 39).

36. Gruenwald argues (a) that there can be no mythical meaning without ritual "activity" (תעשה), (b) that the latter always precedes the former; thus (c) one cannot be discussed apart from the other (*Rituals,* 1–39).

37. Von Rad, "Day," 105–8. Ringgren offers a fuller discussion of comparative approaches ("Impact," 31–46), as do Roberts ("Environment," 75–121), Sparks (*Word,* 57–72), and Niehaus (*Ancient,* 1–33).

38. Examining several Hittite, Egyptian, Sumerian, and Akkadian texts, Stuart argues that many ancients believe in the notion that a great king can win a difficult battle in a single day—and that Yahweh's "day" is most likely *this* "day" ("Sovereign," 159–64).

39. Nissinen, *Prophets,* 13–78.

Heintz tries to make a case for a similar "holy war" ideology in eighteenth-century Syria.[40] Disagreeing with von Rad's decision to restrict analysis of the יום יהוה motif only to Tanak texts, Heintz seeks to buttress *his* "holy war" thesis by isolating the OB phrase *ūmūšū qerbū* ("his days are near") in *ARM* 10.6.8´ as a forerunner/ parallel of the Heb phrase כי קרוב יום יהוה ("for Yahweh's day is near"),[41] positing behind each phrase a "stereotypical battle-cry."[42]

As evidence for this parallel, Heintz closely inspects one of the OB letters from the queen of Mari (Šibtu) to her royal husband (King Zimri-Lim) in which she warns him to beware an unnamed enemy busily fomenting plots against him:

> This man plots many things against this country, but he will not succeed. My lord will see what the god will do to this man. You will capture him; you will stand over him. His day(s) is/are near (*u-mu-šu qé-er-bu*).[43] He will not survive.[44]

Parallels between the יום יהוה texts and this alleged battle cry sent from an OB deity (Annunitum)[45] to a Babylonian queen through the mouth of a "cultic functionary" (*assinnu*),[46] however, are problematic on several fronts. *First*, the dates are much too far apart, bringing to mind Samuel Terrien's criticism of Mitchell Dahood's grammatical reinterpretation of the first millennium Psalter through the linguistic lenses provided by second millennium Ugaritic poetry,[47] a dubious process he likens to a "Patagonian translator in 2968 ... (attempting) to elucidate Shakespearean vocabulary and syntax in the light of the Beowulf epic."[48] Similarly, how can any precise correspondence between two "stereotypical" battle-cries be justified without accounting for the 1,000 years of linguistic evolution which separate them?

Second, there are serious grammatical incongruities. If this is indeed a "stereotypical" expression, then why is the OB usage plural and not the

40. Heintz, "Oracles," 112–38.

41. Isa 13:6; Zeph 1:7; Joel 1:15; 4:14; Ob 15.

42. Heintz, "Origines," 528–40.

43. Heimpel (*Mari*, 260), Heintz ("Origines," 528–40) and Nissinen (*Prophets*, 46) all read "days." Roberts reads "day" ("Mari," 191).

44. *ARM* 10.6.3´-8´.

45. Annunitum is as an epithet for the war-goddess Inanna, as in the epithetical phrase *Inanna an-nu-ni-tum* ("Inanna is the skirmish," *PBS* 5.36.4´; *UET* 1.276.1–2).

46. Roberts translates OB *assinnu* as "cult-homosexual" ("Mari," 189), but the editors of *CAD* find "no specific evidence" for this translation (*CAD* A/2.341).

47. Dahood, *Psalms* (see Moore, *Psalms*, 38).

48. Terrien, *Psalms*, 391.

Hebrew? Heintz tries to anticipate this objection by positing a complicated hypothesis for the development of a phrase originally reading, "(the end of) the days (of the enemy) is near."[49] This provides a singular subject and predicate, but one would think that a "stereotypical battle cry" would not only be empirically attested, but plentifully so.[50] *Third*, and most importantly, if the phrase כי קרוב יום יהוה ("for Yahweh's day is near") is truly a תרוע ("war-cry"), as von Rad repeatedly claims[51] and Heintz appears to concede, then why is there still lacking any empirical evidence, either from OB or Hebrew sources, of its being employed by actual troops in actual battles? *Conclusion:* Von Rad and Heintz make a good case for seeing "day" phraseology on the lips of Hebrew prophets and Syrian cult functionaries, but the presumption that an original תרוע formula lies behind the יום יהוה motif must be critically treated like any other hypothesis.[52]

THEOPHANIC APPROACHES

What do the following elements have in common: a summons, a "consecration," a panic, a "ban," a change in the heavens, darkness, thunder, and earthquake? Von Rad views all these elements as essential components of Israelite "holy war."[53] Without overly discounting this possibility, others point to what they believe to be much wider *Traditionskreis* ("circle of tradition"), one allegedly more primitive than that posited by von Rad. Actually, the word *Traditionskreis* is misleading. A more appropriate term for this methodological approach would be *Begriffsuntersuchung* ("concept investigation"). Readers who feel restricted by von Rad's approach, yet who feel that the origin of the יום יהוה motif should be firmly anchored in Tanak itself, hypothesize a much looser reconstruction of its *Sitz im Leben* by reexamining every Tanak passage in which the motif appears and asking whether another *Sitz im Leben* besides "holy war" might be possible. The result is an

---

49. Heintz, "Origines," 533.
50. See Christensen, *War*, 54–62.
51. Von Rad, "Day," 108.
52. Rudolph finds the whole attempt to posit a foreign literary expression as stereotypical to Hebrew prophetic discourse more than a little puzzling, asking, "How should the prophet otherwise express himself when he believes that Yahweh's day is near?" (*Zephanja*, 267). Critical of facile comparisons between Israel and Babylon, Noort nevertheless finds Heintz's "holy war" thesis quite plausible (*Mari*, 2). Moran, on the other hand, identifies the OB phrase *u-mu-šu qé-er-bu* (*ARM* 10.6.8´) simply as a protasis to which a concluding apodosis like *i-ba-al-lu-uṭ* ("he will get well") regularly occurs in Akkadian incantation texts ("Mari," 37).
53. Von Rad, *War*, 94–114.

attempt to situate the origin of the יום יהוה motif in Hebrew traditions about *theophany*.[54] Meir Weiss,[55] following Jörg Jeremias,[56] who in turn reflects the influence of Ladislav Černy,[57] is a leading exponent of this hypothesis. Reacting to von Rad, Weiss argues that

> the Day of the Lord motif-complex does not hark back to an ancient "holy war" tradition, but has its roots in the ancient motif-complex of the theophany descriptions. It is in this sphere that Amos ... stumbles on the designation יום ה'.

To support this hypothesis Weiss *first* observes that several Tanak passages allude to war without mentioning Yahweh's "day." Therefore they cannot, in his opinion, be inextricably bound to the tradition-complex of "holy war." *Second*, of the ten elements listed by von Rad as "constitutive" of the יום יהוה prophecies,[58] six appear in Isa 13 and Joel 2—comparatively late texts.[59] Accepting Wolff's argument that Joel 2 parallels Isa 13, Weiss finds it disconcerting that von Rad locates the majority of his "constitutive" elements within such late sources. *Third*, relying heavily on Jeremias, Weiss proposes that all these elements appear in theophany descriptions Jeremias holds to be quite ancient, even though many are not expressly linked to the יום יהוה motif. Building on these assertions, Weiss thus attempts to dissociate each of the יום יהוה passages from the institution of "holy war."[60]

Without commenting in detail on the efficacy of these dissociations, Weiss' presumptions stand in need of critique. *First*, Von Rad's critique of Černy still holds. *Begriffsuntersuchunglich* approaches tend to rely on "too many ideas whose connection with the Day of Yahweh still remains to be proved."[61] Weiss argues from silence when he observes that the phrase יום יהוה does not explicitly appear in many Tanak texts alluding to war, and that because of this absence many, if not all of von Rad's "holy war" elements must therefore be reimagined from a more compelling perspective. Yet this *argumentum ab silentio* does not at all prove that the יום יהוה motif and the theophany tradition-complex are somehow "bound together." Since he

---

54. See Barr ("Theophany"), Hiebert ("Theophany"), Jeremias (*Theophanie*), Cross ("Yahweh"), and Savran (*Encountering*).

55. Weiss, "Day," 60.

56. Jeremias, *Theophanie*, 78–89.

57. Černy, *Day*, 74–102.

58. The list above is somewhat telescoped.

59. Wolff, *Joel*, 7–8.

60. Isa 13:6–22; 22:1–14; 34:1–17; Jer 46:1–12; Ezek 7:1–27; 30:1–9; Joel 1, 2, 3, 4; Obadiah; Zeph 1:7–2:4; Zech 14.

61. Von Rad, "Day," 97.

concedes as much in his conclusions,⁶² one can only wonder why he spends so much time trying to link Yahweh's "day" to Yahweh's "theophany." *Second*, Weiss' suggestion (which he concedes to be unprovable) that Amos coins the יום יהוה concept more or less "from scratch" to an audience unfamiliar with it seriously ignores the literary structure of the book of Amos. To support this opinion he cites the highly controversial statements of older scholars opting for radically simplistic dichotomies between Hebrew and Hellenistic notions of "time," arguing that when Amos' pan-Hebraic audience hears him employ the יום יהוה motif, "the time of the action, which for us is the principal thing, (is) of no importance to the Hebrew."⁶³ Not only do contemporary Semitic philologists condemn this whole approach to comparative semantics,⁶⁴ but the discipline of sociolinguistics makes it very clear that human speech communitities are rarely, if ever, homogeneously monolingual/monocultural.⁶⁵ Thus any theory that ancient Hebrews *must* interpret the word יום as a "neutral" notion possessing no connotations of "time" and only connotations of "occurrence" (in Weiss' application, the "theophanic" occurrence) is questionable, to say the least.⁶⁶

POLYMORPHIC APPROACHES

Frank Moore Cross proposes a much more attractive solution to the problem of defining the יום יהוה motif, spinning it off from his larger thesis on the syncretistic socioliterary relationship between Canaanite myth and Hebrew epic.⁶⁷ For Cross, the motif of Yahweh as a "divine warrior" finds traditional moorings both in Exodus conquest traditions about Yahweh Ṣebaoth's march from Sinai to Jerusalem (Exod 15:1–19 ; Deut 33:2–3; Judg 5:4–5)⁶⁸ as well as Jerusalem cult traditions in which the "divine warrior" repeatedly (re)conquers the forces of chaos (Pss 24:7–10; 132:1–18).⁶⁹ Presuming that early Hebrew scribes ritually preserve the conquest/exodus traditions in the so-called "Gilgal cultus,"⁷⁰ he bases his reconstruction of this cul-

---

62. Weiss, "Day," 60.
63. Weiss, "Day," 64 (citing Pedersen, *Israel*, 120) alluding to Boman (*Hebrew*, 139).
64. Barr, *Semantics*, 21–22.
65. Sebba, "Bilingualism," 450–53.
66. Wolff rejects on form-critical grounds any suggestion that Amos invents the יום יהוה motif (*Joel*, 255).
67. Cross, "Warrior," 91–111.
68. N.B. the depiction of Yahweh in Exod 15:3 as איש מלחמה ("man of war").
69. Cross, "Warrior," 91–99.
70. Kraus, "Gilgal," 181–99; Soggin, "Gilgal," 263–77.

tus on a traditio-historical reading of the events sung about in the ancient "victory hymn" over Egypt (Exod 15), particularly as it is regularly reenacted at Gilgal (Josh 3–5).[71] Only later does a northern prophet-historian (DH)[72] rework these old traditions, even as southern, monarchical scribes mythologize them through a process designed to give the "divine warrior" motif more "cosmic depth."[73] The ideology of "holy war," thus saturated with cosmic elements in its earliest stage of development,[74] effectively bridges the gap between these two tradition-complexes.[75] Numerous prophetic texts attest this in the way exodus/conquest motifs interface and interweave with those about cosmic warfare, leading Cross to conclude that

> the Day of Yahweh is the day of victory in holy warfare; it is also the day of Yahweh's festival, when the ritual conquest is reenacted in the procession of the Ark, the procession of the King of glory to the temple.[76]

Instead of von Rad and Mowinckel being locked in opposition, Cross proposes (whether or not one accepts his prosodic presumptions)[77] that the tension between these "opposing" positions is more creative than competitive.

Hans Walter Wolff's approach is somewhat less comprehensive, yet nonetheless pervasive in its attempt to explain the paradoxical blessing/curse character of Yahweh's Day, particularly as the motif flows through the proto-apocalyptic texts of Joel and Zech 14.[78] He accepts, with von Rad and Cross, the ancient character of the "holy war" conquest traditions as the most likely crucible for the יום יהוה motif, but at the same time he refuses to dismiss out of hand the "theophany" hypotheses of Černy and Weiss. To explain the ambivalent blessing/curse disposition displayed by the motif in late prophetic/early apocalyptic texts, however, Wolff posits a rather in-

---

71. Cross, "Warrior," 103–5.

72. Cross posits two editions of DH, one pre-exilic, the other exilic ("History," 278–89).

73. So successful is this process that these texts naturally attract the attention of later apocalypticists writing for audiences experiencing "the decline and transformation of prophecy (and) the recrudescence of mythic themes, stemming in part from decadent royal ideologies and from archaic lore preserved in the wisdom schools" (Cross, "Apocalyptic," 343).

74. It is important to note that von Rad views war in antiquity as "a religious and specifically cultic event" (*War*, 7).

75. See Brueggemann, "Priests," 3–14.

76. Cross, "Warrior," 111.

77. Petersen insightfully observes that *metri causa* arguments (like those employed by Cross and his students) often lead to "risky" results (*Poetry*, 18).

78. Wolff, *Joel*, 33–34.

volved tradition-history. *First*, he observes that the earliest "day" traditions appear predominantly in old prophetic oracles against the nations—e.g., Midian, Isa 9:3 (see Judg 7) and Rephaim, Isa 28:21 (see 2 Sam 5:20–25).[79] *Second*, reflecting upon the fall of Jerusalem (587 BCE), he observes that some eventually come to realize that the "day" not only comes for the nations, but for Judah as well.[80] *Third*, this realization leads to an "eschatological shift" in thinking strong enough to shape the forms and functions of late pre-exilic texts like Amos 5:18–20, Isa 2:6–22, and Zeph 1:7–2:14. *Fourth*, as time passes, various Hebrew writers modify and refocus the יום יהוה motif for later audiences, re-directing it toward the nations in proto-apocalyptic texts like Zech 15, Ezek 38–39, and Joel 1–4, thereby transforming it into a paradoxical symbol for blessing the righteous while simultaneously punishing the wicked, regardless of ethnic/national origin.[81]

CONCLUSIONS

When Zephaniah comes to the יום יהוה motif he evidently sees in it a powerful literary weapon able to penetrate the heart of Jerusalem, piercing through its addictions and cutting out its sins. Whether or not contemporary interpreters fully understand its form and function,[82] the residents of Judah learn from Zephaniah that Yahweh plans to use the thing to which

---

79. Christensen, *War*, 71–72.

80. Lam 1:12; 2:1, 21, 22; Ezek 13:5; 34:12.

81. Wolff, *Joel*, 34. Everson ("Days," 329–37) basically adopts Wolff's explanation, but Fohrer (*History*, 186) suggests that corrosion of the belief in Israel's unique election (through the prophetic attacks of Amos, Hosea, and Micah) is the primary factor leading to Israel's becoming the key nation called to account before a universal forum of nations. Kapelrud's proposal (*Zephaniah*, 86–87) relies heavily on Mowinckel's hypothesis; i.e., that Zephaniah's employment of יום יהוה betrays a "pattern that has its origin in Assyrian-Babylonian ideology of the great god determining the fate of men at the great annual festival." Sabottka (*Zephanja*, 31) thinks that Zephaniah's message is a sociocultural blend of liturgical and "holy war" traditions, but Heintz ("Origines, 540) advances perhaps the most comprehensive polymorphic synthesis: "The day of God's victory, the festival day of triumph, the curses proclaimed against the enemy—all of the aspects of this theophanic moment of divine sovereignty . . . are themselves integrated into this important theological theme of the 'Day of Yahweh,' plunging their roots into the ancient ideology of the "holy war," as it is proclaimed by a prophetic line whose antecedents are already prefigured at Mari . . . (viz.,) the preaching of Israel's prophets."

82. Several critics explore the form-critical connections linking יום יהוה ("Yahweh's day"), ביום ההוא ("on that day"), and even בעת ההיא ("at that time") in Zeph 1:7–15. Munch (*Expression*, 17–18) thinks that the phrase ביום ההוא holds little in common with יום יהוה, and that it operates primarily as "an editorial connective formula." Others disagree; see Rudolph (*Zephanja*, 264), Krinetzki (*Zefanjastudien*, 32–39), and Irsigler (*Jahwetag*, 128, 168–69, 200–201).

they seem most addicted—foreign power—and discipline them with it on the "day" of his "visitation." This warning, polymorphically blended together from several sources, forces Jerusalem to figure out some kind of response. Whether this or that response is loudest (pitting "priest" against prophet"; "northerner" against "southerner") is in the final analysis irrelevant. What *is* relevant is that by the time of the Latter Prophets (eighth to seventh centuries BCE), many older traditions have long since become assimilated into newer, more composite tradition-complexes.[83] Thus it seems foolish to speculate whether holy war traditions, theophany traditions, covenant traditions, or cultic ritual traditions dominate Zephaniah's thinking. To ignore the polymorphic character of the יום יהוה motif is to engineer interpretational failure because ultimately this is the type of motif which transcends not only the Testaments,[84] but literary-historical categories in general. Yahweh's Day was/is/will be fearful/wonderful, hideous/beautiful, and bellicose/peaceful not because no one knows what it means, but because its origin comes from an "irascible, elusive, polyvalent Subject" much greater than *any* isolated perspective.[85]

---

83. Recent research on the Book of the Twelve focuses on "the numerous thematic and terminological connections" linking these prophetic scrolls together at a deep intertextual level, themes like "the critique of specific cultic and social abuses, the announcement of Yahweh's Day, various judgments against the nations, and the expectation of a journey to Zion for the peoples of the world" (Wöhrle, *Zwölfprophetenbuches*, 1).

84. Snyder ("Delay," 19-35) appears to understand this in his approach to one of the greatest cruxes in Christian scholarship; viz., how to define, with some measure of consistency, the sayings in GNT about the delay of the παρουσία (lit., "the appearing"; see Matt 24:27, 37, 39). Snyder's response to this "problem" is that there is no way to document from the GNT a growing sense of frustration in the primitive Christian community over the "delay" of the παρουσία because (a) the Nazarenes understand the יום יהוה motif in Habakkuk, Ezekiel, Isaiah, and Amos to be ambivalent and paradoxical (see Acts 1:6-7), and (b) that its pronouncement is an effective device used by prophets in both Testaments to effect attitudinal change. Snyder speaks, however, to a scholarly community basically convinced (a) that "the delay" is a critical problem in the early church, and (b) that the author of Luke-Acts feels compelled to de-eschatologize it before the eyes of a cosmopolitan, hellenized public (e.g., Conzelmann, *Luke*, 98-136).

85. Brueggemann, *Exuberant*, 6. See Terrien, *Elusive*, 227-77.

5

JEREMIAH'S PROGRESSIVE PARADOX*

> The deepest, the only theme of human history . . . is the conflict of skepticism with faith.[1]

IN THE LATE 1950S Franklin Baumer's students publish a *Festschrift* in his honor sensitive to his understanding of the faith-scepticism polarity,[2] discovering in the process of re-reading his work how much it shapes their own, especially his groundbreaking *Religion and the Rise of Scepticism*.[3] Decades later, James Crenshaw gravitates to this same discussion when introducing *his* students to the faith-scepticism polarity, especially as it impacts the character and shape of Tanak. Neither teacher stands alone. Baumer is certainly not the first to grasp the power of skepticism on the practice of religion, nor is Crenshaw the first to puzzle over the origins of the skepticism bubbling deep inside the diatribes of Qohelet[4] and the קינה-

---

* Revised from an essay first published in *RB* 93 (1986) 386–414.

1. Goethe, *Wisdom*, 72 (cited in Baumer, *Religion*, 3).
2. Wagar, "Introduction," 1.
3. New York: Harcourt, Brace, 1960.
4. Galling, "Kohelet," 276–99; Lauha, *Kohelet*, 17–19. Schmid (*Wesen*, 199) insists that the "crisis" in Israelite wisdom must first be taken into account before comparing the theological positions of "prophets" and "wise men" à la McKane (*Prophets*). Jeremiah's interaction with the חכמים is doubly ambiguous because little empirical evidence exists upon which to determine where the חכמים might stand at any given time on the

dirges of Lamentations (just to cite two obvious examples).⁵ Efforts to locate the origins of this skepticism in the minds of Graeco-Persian thinkers, however, continue to be disputed. Many hold this foreign *Sitz im Leben* to be most influential, but others reject the notion that pre-exilic Hebrews are somehow immune to this basic human dilemma.⁶ Prof. Crenshaw's determination to situate the origins of חכמה ("wisdom") within the wellsprings of indigenous Hebrew thought takes very seriously the countermeasuring influence of a healthy Israelite skepticism over against the "radical excesses" of extremist Yahwism. In fact, the influence חכמה exercises against these "radical excesses" is probably the primary reason for its eventual occlusion at the hands of wary deuteronomistic and apocalyptic editors.⁷

This argument has merit, if only to shine a brighter light on the pervasiveness of the faith-scepticism polarity in Israel *before* Jerusalem's destruction in 587 BCE. *Questions:* Is the faith-scepticism polarity *only* a problem for intellectuals, as von Rad contends,⁸ or does it affect other groups as well? Does the stimulus generated by repetitive sociopolitical crisis serve as nursemaid or as midwife to an already ingrained *habit* of doubt?⁹ Most importantly for the present essay, how should non-deuteronomistic,¹⁰ sapientially-colored texts like Jer 8:8-9; 9:22-23; and 18:18 be interpreted—from a post-exilic perspective, or from a pre-exilic perspective much closer to the prophet's own sphere of reference?¹¹

With regard to the prophets, only the most naive reader would assume that every Hebrew prophet always clings to an unquestioned faith in Yahweh and his directives. Habakkuk, for example, raises pointed questions to Yahweh about his "silence" (חרש, 1:13) in the face of "obvious" injustice, nor does he appear the least bit hesitant to challenge the answers he receives

---

faith-doubt continuum.

5. קינה means "funeral song, dirge, lament" (2 Chron 35:25). Sherwood (*Afterlives*, 220) observes that recent biblical scholarship has "the theologically less congenial books (such as Lamentations and the Wisdom books) coming out of the closet ... confronting the reader with a deity who makes life crooked, who wraps himself in clouds so no prayers can break through, or who 'answers' Job's suffering with a parade of freak animals that seem (mis)designed to demonstrate the baffling 'dysteleology' of creation."

6. See Gerstenberger, *Wesen*, 110-12.

7. Crenshaw, *Wisdom*, 229-50 (see Moore, *Wisdom*, 185-88).

8. Von Rad, *Wisdom*, 237-39.

9. Audet, "Sagesse," 355-57.

10. See Duhm (*Jeremia*), Mowinckel (*Jeremia*), and Holladay (*Jeremiah*).

11. Laberge ("Jérémie") and Davidson (*Doubt*) pursue questions similar to these (see Shields, *Wisdom*, 1-6; and Moore, *Pressure*, 269-99).

(unlike, say, Job).[12] Yet no other Nevi'im text, as Norbert Ittmann painstakingly points out, so poignantly and painfully displays the dynamics of the faith-scepticism polarity like Jeremiah's laments (JL).[13] In fact, in spite of a few formal similarities (such as the use of divine-human dialogue, the use of "I"-language, and the pervasiveness of hostile enemies, or worse, hypocritical indifference),[14] JL represents a fundamental break from traditional Mosaic prophecy.[15] Elsewhere in the book of Jeremiah, even when divine wrath breaks through the prophet's consciousness to reveal the horrifying possibilities "on the other side," JL's repeated threat of filing a ריב-lawsuit against Yahweh still shocks and astounds readers.[16] Whether the aforementioned Jeremiah texts indicate a "gradual knowledge about unconditional judgment," or perhaps even a "forerunner" to JL itself,[17] the prophet's decision to sue God is not easily explained.[18] For all intents and purposes, then, von Rad's 1936 assessment of JL still holds true:

> Jeremiah, via the peculiar words of his Confessions, has abandoned his prophetic office.... The direction of his words is not from above to below, but from below to above, and that to which he bears witness is not primarily a word of God, but his inner problems, his suffering, and his doubting.[19]

---

12. Hab 1:2–4. See Haak (*Habakkuk*, 17–19) and Andersen (*Habakkuk*, 346–47).

13. Ittmann, *Konfessionen*, 22–23. Jeremiah's "laments" (sometimes called "confessions" because of the influence of Augustine's *Confessions*) include the material in Jer 11:18–12:6; 15:10–21; 17:14–18; 18:18–23; and 20:7–18, and stand at the center of an extensive secondary literature. See von Rad ("Konfessionen"), Behler (*Jérémie*), Mihalic ("Confessions"), Reventlow (*Jeremia*), Culley ("Confessions"), Donner ("Confessions"), Mottu (*Jérémie*), Diamond (*Confessions*), Crenshaw ("Confessions"), Dong (*Jeremiabuch*), Polk (*Jeremiah*), O'Connor (*Confessions*), and Smith (*Laments*).

14. Hab 1; Isa 8:16–18; Mic 1:8; 7:1–4; Ezek 33:30–33.

15. I.e., as defined in Deut 18:9–22 (see Schmitt, "Prophecy," 482–89).

16. Jer 11:20; 12:1; 15:10; 20:12 (repetition of 11:20; see Gunkel, *Psalmen*, 364–65). In 18:19 MT (followed by Aq and Sym) reads יריבי ("my adversaries"), but OG reads δικαιώματός μου, an obvious translation of ריבי ("my lawsuit"; see Wimmer, "Sociology," 402). Hubmann's attempt ("Konfessionen," 281–82) to preserve MT יריבי is problematic precisely because it cannot account for the repetition of ריב throughout JL.

17. Ittmann, *Konfessionen*, 34–35.

18. Prophetic figures warn kings in OB oracles (e.g., *ARM* 10.4.35; 10.50.23–26), and Ipu-Wer admonishes Pharaoh for allowing chaos to displace order (*ANET* 443), but prophetic lawsuits against deities are nowhere to be found. Thompson delimits JL to the private sphere (*Jeremiah*, 91), but should JL be crafted for public pronouncement, as Wimmer suggests ("Sociology," 406), then this peculiarity would be even more striking.

19. Von Rad, "Konfessionen," 267.

Put simply, JL is a living literary laboratory within which to test the applicability of Goethe's dictum to the character and development of Hebrew prophecy.[20] The question provoking the present essay is deceptively simple. What force(s), person(s), event(s), or combination of factors leads Jeremiah to break with prophetic tradition, enough to (a) accuse the deity of "deceiving" him (פתה),[21] and (b) file against him a "lawsuit" (ריב)?[22]

PRIESTS, PROPHETS, AND PROFESSORS

Jer 18:18 lists three groups hostile to Jeremiah and his mission: the כהנים ("priests"), the חכמים ("wise men"/"professors"), and the נביאים ("prophets").[23] Each plays a role in attacking the prophet from Anathoth, and many readers theorize over which group is the most lethal. Instead of taking the usual Continental tack of analyzing the laments in the Psalter from a form-critical perspective, then comparing the results with JL,[24] Norbert Ittmann focuses instead on how the laments in Jer 11, 12 and 18 articulate this "hostility" motif, his goal being to avoid the "too-generalized reflections and ... imprecise suppositions" often used to identify the contours of JL's socioliterary context.[25] Of course, to those readers uninterested in JL's socioliterary context Ittmann's approach will appear little more than a waste of time.[26] But to those grown tired of constant reductionist attempts

---

20. Questions about how JL helps shape the larger context of Jer 11–20, while important, are not the focus of the present essay (see instead Smith, *Jeremiah*; Biddle, *Jeremiah*; and Plant, *Jeremiah*).

21. Jer 20:7. Clines and Gunn try to soften פתה to mean "persuade" ("Persuade," 20–27), but Balentine rightly resists (*Prayer*, 165).

22. See Huffmon, "Lawsuit," 285–95; Limburg, "Lawsuit," 291–304.

23. Alluded to most clearly in Jer 29:31, "false prophecy" is a major problem in Hebrew history; see Meyer (*Jeremia*, 98); Nicholson ("Prophets," 155–56); Brettler ("Amos," 108–10); and Hofman (*Propheten*).

24. Baumgartner, *Jeremia*, 1–14.

25. Ittmann, *Konfessionen*, 82. Ahuis (*Gerichtsprophet*, 24–26) identifies three stages in the "messenger-sending process": the commissioning, the execution, and the reporting-back, positing a form-critical bond between the "commissioning" in Jer 16:5–7 and the "reporting-back" in 15:10, 17–20. Berridge finds this reconstruction to be more than a little "excessive" (*Gerichtsprophet*, 453).

26. Pohlmann dates JL to the post-exilic period (*Jeremiabuch*, 3–25), and Bultmann doubts whether there is "enough evidence ... to confirm or deny the possibility that Jeremiah may have shared these first-person singular compositions in an oral or written form" ("Jeremiah," 83).

to sculpt greater relevance for JL *after* 587 BCE than *before* it,[27] Ittmann's thesis is quite refreshing:

- *First*, he argues, the laments in chapters 11, 12, and 18 seem older than those in 15, 17 and 20 because they appear to resonate more loudly with the Hebrew psalms of lament, both with regard to overall world-view as well as literary structure (description of situation; statement of trust; divine reaction, confession of hope, etc.).[28] Structural changes occur in chapters 15 and 20 because Jeremiah needs to accommodate a rapidly growing, ever-pressing concern: the as-yet-unexplained success of his "enemies."[29]

- *Second*, this "breakdown" of the lament-form in chapters 15 and 20 (or "innovative transformation," depending on one's point of view) *has* to occur because the older lament forms are unable to channel the virulent skepticism now erupting in Jeremiah's heart. Indeed, this "new uncertainty" in his life "needs a new strongly-stated form able to carry the load."[30]

- *Third*, identification of the "enemy" as רשעים ("wicked") and בגדים ("treacherous"), i.e., as individuals for whom Yahweh is "near to their mouths yet far from their hearts,"[31] implies that the "original" enemies of Jeremiah are most likely the (cult) prophets.[32] Only later, in the "transformed" laments of chapters 15 and 20, does the notion of a larger, more pervasive enemy begin to coalesce: "Only on the basis of a broad polemic against the prophets does he (Jeremiah) recognize the people as his true enemy."[33]

What can be said in response to this hypothesis?

- *First*, Ittmann's investigation of Jeremiah's conflict with the "prophets" hardly exhausts Jeremiah's possible "enemies" because it fails to take seriously the three-pronged attack in Jer 18:18. Yet on this point Ittmann hardly stands alone. Franz Hubmann, writing in one of the most exhaustive

---

27. Carr (*Formation*, 222) states the problem clearly: "Given the manuscript documentation for various additions to Ezekiel and Jeremiah well into the Hellenistic period, we can suppose that some of these additions may have been added earlier, but there is little to allow us to locate specific additions in the Persian period."

28. Westermann, *Praise*, 165–213.

29. Ittmann thinks he sees the insertion of a lament-cry in 15:10–12 and the rearrangement of "typical" lament structure in 20:7–18.

30. Ittmann, *Konfessionen*, 78.

31. Jer 12:1–2.

32. See Mowinckel, *Psalmenstudien* 3.1–29; Wilson, *Prophecy*, 306. Hilber (*Prophecy*, 37) thinks that "evidence is not sufficient to identify with certainty the functionaries responsible for prophetic mediation in the cult, assuming such takes place," and that "probably both priestly officials and non-priestly functionaries prophesy."

33. Ittmann, *Konfessionen*, 154.

examinations of JL ever published, singles out the כהנים and the נביאים in 18:18 without saying much about the חכמים at all,[34] mainly because Tanak says more about the other two groups. Ittmann's strategy is particularly problematic because he makes the three-pronged attack in 18:18 the starting point of his investigation.

- *Second*, should more credence be given to all three *groups*, the question then arises as to which of these three *conflicts* most likely sets the stage for the questions belabored in JL—Jeremiah vs. the כהנים? Jeremiah vs. the נביאים? Or Jeremiah vs. the חכמים?

- *Third*, interpretation focusing on only one (or two) of these conflicts must be said to run the risk of being "reductionistic." Even if one speculates a *qal waḥomer* leap in the prophet's thinking from "prophets" to "population at large" (as Ittmann suggests),[35] this still implies that Jeremiah's other conflicts contribute little to his skepticism.

- *Fourth*, Ittmann dismisses the psychological approaches of Skinner, Volz and Rudolph because they fail (in his opinion) to take the historical context seriously,[36] thereby isolating Jeremiah as the founder of "personal religion" in the tradition of Wellhausen.[37] But this may well be an overreaction. True, the schizoid disjunction which takes place whenever readers segregate Jeremiah "the man" from Jeremiah "the prophet" often *does* lean more heavily on the first person than the second. But should this exegetical excess be used as a pretext to exclude *all* internal factors? Surely the goal of balanced interpretation is to take both *internal* as well as *external* factors into careful consideration, regardless of how better attested one proves to be *vis-à-vis* the other.[38]

Norbert Ittmann's study is an eloquent attempt to defend JL from what he perceives to be a host of capricious hypotheses persistently seeking to divorce it from its original context. In this he basically agrees with von Rad that "the Confessions belong at the center of every interpretation of the

---

34. Hubmann, "Konfessionen," 279. Long ("Conflict," 45) posits the conflict, on broader sociological grounds, to be between "autonomist" and "coexistent" forces.

35. Ittmann (*Konfessionen*, 122), though it must be noted that Ittmann *does* recognize the priests and political advisors as groups hostile to Jeremiah and his message.

36. Skinner (*Prophecy*, 201–30), Volz (*Jeremia*, 301), Rudolph (*Jeremia*, 4–9).

37. "His (Jeremiah's) book contains not merely his speeches and oracles, but confessions every now and then about his suffering and doubts" (Wellhausen, *Geschichte*, 140). Hubmann ("Konfessionen," 273) credits Heinrich Ewald as the first "modern" scholar to interpret the material in JL as "personal overflowings" (Ewald, *Jeremja*, 8).

38. See Kille, *Criticism*, 1–38.

book of Jeremiah."³⁹ The purpose of the present essay, however, is to identify the primary factor(s) responsible for generating Jeremiah's skepticism.⁴⁰ Ittmann makes a good start toward understanding the dynamic complexity of this process by carefully examining the impact of the role(s) enacted by the (cultic) נביאים, but attention should also be given to his other opponents, particularly Jerusalem's חכמים ("sages/professors"). Can a developmental trajectory of *this* relationship be reconstructed from the evidence at hand?

PLOTTING A TRAJECTORY

The root חכם appears seventeen times in the book of Jeremiah, always in the nominal form. Most agree that the occurrences in 4:22 and 9:16 come from the prophet himself, but agreement on the authenticity of the material in 8:8–9, 9:22–23, and 18:18 remains elusive,⁴¹ though rarely are these texts attributed to a Dtr editor.⁴² In point of fact only 8:8–9, 9:22–23 and 18:18 employ masculine singular and plural forms in contexts of social conflict in Jeremiah. That is, these are the only non-Dtr passages in the book which allude to the complex relationship between Jeremiah and the חכמים. Thus it seems more than a little problematic to dismiss these texts as "post-exilic" simply and only because of their sapiential character. On the contrary, careful exegesis sensitive to this character may be the only way to outline the contours of the relationship between Jeremiah and the Judahite intelligentsia, particularly since, as Crenshaw and others have shown, no convincing rationale exists for situating the *origin* of these texts in late Graeco-Persian sources.

---

39. Von Rad, *Theology* 2.204. The last sentence of Ittmann's dissertation goes one step further: "Only the Confessions open up the access-way to a proper interpretation of Jeremiah" (*Konfessionen*, 199).

40. נביא לגוים נתתיך, "I give you (to be) a prophet to the nations" (Jer 1:5).

41. Thiel (*Jeremia*, 217), e.g., doubts the historicality of Jer 18:18. Sapiential references in the OAN (49:7; 50:35; 51:57), the comparison between Yahweh and the חכמי הגוים ("international professors," 10:7), and the question voiced in 9:11 are usually interpreted as coming from a later source.

42. That is, Mowinckel's Source "C." According to his typology source "A" comes from the historical prophet; source "B" from Baruch and/or another close assistant; source "C" is sermonic prose from a later writer using Dtr vocabulary and style; and source "D," from a Persian source, includes the material gathered up into the Book of Consolation (Jer 30–31). See Mowinckel (*Komposition.*) and Holladay ("Jeremiah," 402–8).

Jer 8:8-9

This passage consists of three sections framed underneath the rubric of the prophetic commission formula כה אמר יהוה ("thus says Yahweh").[43] The first begins and ends with a rhetorical question, as does the third. Saturated with animal imagery, the second section contrasts the "knowledge" of dumb animals with the "ignorance" of Jerusalem's intelligentsia. Five rhetorical questions knit all three sections together, and since the subsequent section in 8:10b-12 doubles the material in MT 6:13-15 (absent in OG),[44] 8:4-9 looks to be demarcated by clear boundaries. Further, Jeremiah often uses לכן ("therefore") to signal Yahweh's response to laundry lists of specific *sins* as well as specific sinful *groups*.[45] After לכן in 8:10 the subsequent threat of giving wives and fields to others repeats verbatim the material in 6:12, a fact which helps explain the attraction of 8:10b-12 to the diatribe in 8:4-9 as well as the attraction of 6:13-15 to the oracle in 6:9-12. In short, this diatribe consists of an introductory commissioning formula followed by three well-defined sections: 8:4a-6b (section one); 8:6c-7 (section two); and 8:8-9 (section three).

Section One

ואמרת אלהם כה אמר יהוה	You shall say to them, "Thus says Yahweh:
היפלו ולא יקומו	Do (people) fall down and not get back up?
אם ישוב ולא ישוב	If they wander off, do they not return?
מדוע שובבה העם הזה ירשלם	Why does this people (Jerusalem) wander off
משובה נצח	on endless walkabout?
החזיקו בתרמית	Why do they cling to deceit?
מאנו לשוב	Why do they refuse to change?
הקשבתי ואשמע	I have listened and paid close attention,
לוא כן דברו	(but) they do not speak what is right.
אין איש נחם על רעתו	No one regrets their wickedness,

---

43. "The commission formula ... which frequently introduces prophetic speech in the OT, is often a more complete form of the messenger formula" (Aune, *Prophecy*, 90).

44. "The question of doublets in Jeremiah is bound up with the much wider problem of the relationship of the LXX and the MT" (Jellicoe, *Septuagint*, 21).

45. E.g., כהנים ("priests"), תפשי התורה ("torah handlers"), רעים ("shepherd-leaders"), and נביאים ("prophets," Jer 2:8-9; 5:13-14; 14:14-15); נביא ("prophet") and כהן ("priest," 6:13-15); צפים ("sentinels," 6:17-18); אנשי ענתות ("men of Anathoth," 11:21-22); רדפים ("persecutors") and משחקים ("merrymakers," 15:15-19); נביא ("prophet"), כהן ("priest"), and עם ("people," 23:34-38).

לאמר מה עשיתי   saying, 'What have I done?'

Section Two

כלה שב במרוצתם	Everyone reverts to their own course
כסוס שוטף במלחמה	like a horse plunging headlong into battle.
גם חסידה בשמים ידעה מועדיה	The stork in the heavens knows its migration schedule,
ותר וסיס ועגור שמרו את עת באנה	as do the turtledove, swallow and crane.
ועמי לא ידע את משפט יהוה	But my people know nothing of Yahweh's justice.

Section Three

איכה תאמרו חכמים אנחנו	How can you say, 'We are wise men
ותורת יהוה אתנו	and Yahweh's Torah is with us?'
אכן הנה לשקר עשה	when in fact the false pen of the
עט שקר ספרים	scribes twists it into a lie?
הבישו חכמים חתו וילכדו	The wise men are ashamed, shattered, and convicted.
הנה בדבר־יהוה מאסו	Since they reject *Yahweh's* word, what 'wisdom'
וחכמת מה להם	do *they* have?"

נצחת—Since נצח connotes "endless endurance" in JL,[46] "endless" seems an appropriate English translation here.

איכה—Though often used as an exclamatory adverb followed by a pf. verb,[47] Jeremiah shows a particular fondness for interrogative usage, often using 2 ipf. אמר followed by a quotation (often signified in OG by ὅτι recitative): e.g., Jer 2:23: איך תאמרי לא נטמאתי ("How can you say, 'I am not defiled?'").[48] More noteworthy is the way in which איך תאמרו precedes a quotation explicitly singling out the חכמים in Isa 19:11, a passage showing striking similarities to this text in Jeremiah (איך תאמרו ... בן חכמים אני, "How can you say, 'I am a son of wise men?'").[49] Both Isaiah and Jeremiah like to employ this

---

46. Jer 15:18.
47. *GKC* §148a.
48. See also Judg 16:15; Ps 11:1; and Gen 26:9.
49. See also Jer 48:14a: איך תאמרו גברים אנחנו ("How can you say, 'We are mighty

exclamatory adverb interrogatively, adapting it to the rhetorical question format so characteristic of the sapiential literature,⁵⁰ ingeniously using one of the forms most familiar to the חכמים when critiquing them. The primary difference between the two is that Isaiah uses this form to satirize the חכמים in Egypt while Jeremiah uses it to satirize the חכמים in Jerusalem.

תאמרו—ὅτι recitative does not occur in OG Jer 2:23, 48:14 or Isa 19:11, indicating perhaps the OG's intention here to make sure that the reader notes the presence of direct discourse. Cyril of Alexandria's (d. 444 CE) insertion of ὧς ("thus") seems to affirm this intentionality.

לשקר—The first word of MT 8:8b, אכן, is often contrastive in Nevi'im, especially after אמר.⁵¹ Nevertheless in Jer 3:23 אכן appears alongside לשקר in a non-contrastive, yet asseverative manner, just like the construction here. OG Jer 3:20 and 23 attempts to bring out this nuance (πλὴν ὡς in 3:20; ὄντως in 3:23), yet some sort of asseverative adverb is missing in OG 8:8b. In fact, something is amiss with the text of Jer 8:8b. MT is metrically awkward, but more importantly the finite verb in OG is γίγνομαι. Never, however, are the finite forms of עשה in Jeremiah ever translated with something other than ποιέω. Consequently the usage of γίγνομαι here seems curiously inapt, as if OG is reading a text devoid of עשה or any other finite verb, thereby implying the existence of an underlying Hebrew text⁵² consisting of three verbless clauses, each designed to contrast sharply with the finite forms חתו, הבישו, and ילכדו in 8:9a. N.B. the balanced arrangement of these verbless clauses, the assonance between אנחנו and אתנו, the inclusio-like balance between חכמים and ספרים, the wordplay on שקר, and the repetitive 3-syllable meter throughout. Apparently OG inserts γίγνομαι here without giving much thought to this symmetry, only "smoother" verbal flow. Further, since לשקר appears to function adverbially in other Jeremianic oracles,⁵³ perhaps the linkage between אכן and לשקר in these passages⁵⁴ accounts for the presence of אכן הנה לשקר in MT 8:8b.⁵⁵

ספרים—Because of the textual and linguistic reasons just given, these three verbless clauses should probably be viewed together as conjugal elements of

---

men?'").

50. Kuntz, "Wisdom," 191.

51. See Isa 49:4b; 53:4; Zeph 3:7c; Jer 3:20.

52. See Janzen (*Jeremiah*, 1–9); Soderlund (*Jeremiah*, 199); and Lundbom (*Jeremiah*, 1–45).

53. Jer 3:23; 5:2; 7:9 (Temple sermon).

54. Jer 3:23 (אכן twice); 5:2 (reading with several Syr mss).

55. Aq and Theod apparently read לקן.

one quotation through which Jeremiah satirically highlights the intellectual arrogance of those חכמים who dare to assert that Torah cannot be "correctly" interpreted apart from their direction, even though he would probably agree with their reasons for lamenting its shameful history of treatment at the hands of the כהנים.

הבישו . . . חתו וילכדו—These three finite verbs are frequent friends in Jeremiah, occurring in the word-pairs[56] חתת//בוש and חתת//לכד as well as the triad לכד//חתת//בוש.[57] The word-pair חתת//בוש occurs in 17:18 (in JL) in a context going all the way back to Jeremiah's call,[58] while חתת//לכד occurs in 8:9 and 51:56, an oracle against Babylon threatening Babylon's גברים with the same word-pair as the one launched here against the חכמים. Something interesting happens in the Greek tradition, though, with regard to the semantic preferences of the translators. OG, for example, almost always renders בוש with some form of αἰσχύνομαι,[59] while the OG translation for חתת most often gravitates to the term πτοέω.[60] For לכד, however, we find two Greek terms rather equally distributed: λαμβάνω[61] and ἁλίσκομαι,[62] the latter always gravitating to לכד when conjoined with בוש and חתת. Since ἁλίσκομαι often carries legal connotations,[63] the English term "convicted" thus seems to capture the nuance intended by לכד better than "captured" or "trapped."

יהוה—The divine name is set off metrically for emphasis.

וחכמת—Absence of the *nomen rectum* in this construct phrase is puzzling. Only twice elsewhere in Tanak does such a phenomenon occur with חכמת, and both warrant reading something else besides MT.[64] Rudolph suggests an original חכמתם here, the 3 m. p. suffix falling off through haplography,[65] but this is pure speculation. Perhaps the writer, in his desire to demarcate the section with a rhetorical question, simply inverts the usual word order.[66] This does not explain, however, the occurrence of חכמת in the *status*

---

56. Watters, *Poetry*, 133–35; and Watson, *Poetry*, 128–43.
57. See Jer 8:9; 48:1; 50:2.
58. See חתת in Jer 1:17.
59. See Jer 17:18; 10:14; 50:2; *et al.*
60. See Jer 1:17; 17:18; 50:2 (Aq, Syh); 51:56.
61. See Jer 38:28; 48:41.
62. See Jer 50:9, 24; 51:31, 41, 56.
63. *LSJ* 66.
64. See Isa 33:6 and Dan 1:20.
65. *BHS* 798.
66. That is, interrogative pronoun + noun > noun + interrogative pronoun.

constructus without a *nomen rectum*. Based on parallels with other Nevi'im texts,[67] the possibility exists that an original *nomen rectum* falls out via ellipsis, whether for metrical reasons or because the poet's audience well understands its meaning, yet deliberately omits it to heighten poetic suspense. There is another possibility, however. The original reading may be influenced by the Aramaic term חכמתה, as in the Zinjirli Inscription,[68] in material exercising influence on the appearance of צדקה and חכם in Jer 9:22–23 (see below). When adapted for use here, however, the original Aram 3 m s suffix falls off, replaced by the Heb 3 m s suffix.[69] The similarity between מת—and the subsequent interrogative מה, however, provokes an early copyist to drop it altogether (homoioteleuton).[70]

Not all are willing to see the חכמים as a distinct group in pre-exilic Judah, nor this passage as Jeremiah's response to their perversion of Torah. Mowinckel, for example, denies the possibility, in spite of Lindblom's arguments,[71] that any such "classes of the intelligentsia" exist in pre-exilic Judah, much less challenge Jeremiah's proclamation of דבר־יהוה.[72] Rudolph merely identifies חכמים and ספרים as synonymous epithets of כהנים,[73] but this presumes that כהנים and תפשי התורה in Jer 2:8 must also be synonymous rather than separate referents for separate groups alongside ראים ("seers") and נביאים ("prophets"). Since ראים and נביאים never appear as a word-pair in Jeremiah, however, this casts considerable doubt on Rudolph's suggestion. It therefore seems more likely that all four groups in Jer 2:8 have their own identifying referents, each being a "sinful group" situated in yet another laundry list followed by לכן (v. 9). Unfortunately, expositors following Rudolph's lead tend to focus on the כהנים and the "difficult problem of book religion,"[74] thereby obscuring the point of the passage; i.e., that even though ספרים *have* done a miserable job interpreting Torah, it is ludicrous to imagine that חכמים can do any better. By asserting their "superiority" over ספרים, the חכמים only condemn themselves, in the prophet's mind, because of their incredible intellectual arrogance. These professors are not interested in *Yahweh's* wisdom, only the international *Wissenschaft* of the גוים ("nations").

---

67. See 1 Kings 5:10, 14; 10:4; Isa 29:14.
68. *KAI* 215.11.
69. As in Jer 9:22.
70. See the critical commentaries for other possibilities.
71. Lindblom, "Wisdom," 195–96.
72. Mowinckel, "Wisdom," 206.
73. Rudolph, *Jeremia*, 61.
74. Weiser, *Jeremia*, 72.

Jer 9:22–23 (ET 9:23–24)

This pericope breaks down into two sections, one a triad of negative jussive statements orbiting around the verb הלל, the other a positive jussive statement followed by an imperative command framing a triad of nouns describing Yahweh's basic character, all of which the writer situates under the messenger formula rubrics כה אמר יהוה and נאם יהוה.

Section One

כה אמר יהוה	Thus says Yahweh:
אל יתהלל חכם בחכמתו	"Let not the wise man boast in his wisdom!
ואל יתהלל הגבור בגבורתו	Let not the warrior boast in his strength!
אל־יתהלל עשיר בעשרו	Let not the rich man boast in his riches!

Section Two

כי־אם בזות יתהלל מתהלל	Rather, let the boaster boast in this:
הסכל וידע אותי	Investigate and understand who *I* am!
כי אני יהוה	For *I* am *Yahweh*,
עשה חסד משפט וצדקה בארץ	The one who makes faithfulness, justice, and loyalty on the earth.
כי באלה חפצתי	For it is in *these* things that I take delight."
נאם יהוה	[says Yahweh]

אל־יתהלל—OG consistently reads יתהלל with καυχάσθω, parsed here as pres. mid. ipv. 3 m. sg. (deponent) of καυχάομαι. Jussive הלל recurs in Ahab's blustery response to Benhadad in his recitation of the proverb, "Let not the one putting on his armor boast like the one removing it."[75] Yet a closer parallel occurs in Jer 4:1–2: both texts refer to Yahweh's משפט and צדקה, while חסד in 9:23 finds a parallel in 4:2 via the term אמת.[76] In Ps 49:7 (a wisdom psalm similar to Ps 73), the psalmist uses הלל to question his own courage before men who trust in their material wealth and "boast in the abundance of their riches."[77]

---

75. אל־יתהלל חגר כמפתח (1 Kings 20:11).
76. Both 4:1 and 8:4–5 feature word-plays on the term שוב.
77. ברב עשרם יתהלל (Ps 49:7, ET 49:6). See Moore, "Resurrection," 28–29.

גבור—On the basis of other lists in Jeremiah,[78] and especially the recurrence of גבור in JL (20:11), "warrior" seems the better English translation.

גברתו—The motivation driving the Uruk elders' warning to the hero Gilgamesh ("Trust not, Gilgamesh, in all your own strength")[79] parallels this prophetic warning in the broad sense that both traditions appeal to deity for strength before great challenges. Where Enkidu becomes Gilgamesh's "strength," however, Yahweh is the faithful Israelite's true גבור.[80]

עשרו—Just as גבורים are warned to beware the limitations of their "strength," so sapiential traditions of warning directed to the rich are not uncommon. N. B., for example, the stern warning preserved in the scroll of proverbial sayings attributed to the sage Aḥiqar: "Let not the rich man say, 'In my riches I am glorious.'"[81] N.B. four parallels between Aḥiqar and Jeremiah: both texts employ the jussive; both begin with the negative particle אל; both employ nominal forms of the root עש/תר; and both prefix the preposition ב before the second of these nominal forms. The only major difference, besides the choice of verbs, is the substance of the quotation itself. According to Hoftijzer and Jongeling, the root הדר appears only one time in the corpus of Aramaic inscriptions at their disposal:[82] "Glorious is the king to see, like Šamaš, and precious is his sovereignty."[83] So, since the parallel terms in this proverb are שפיר//יקיר and מלך//הרד, "sovereignty" seems the most semantically appropriate translation, even though it stands rather close to the edge of its root meaning. This may not be unusual, however; this root occurs alongside the Ug cognate hdr in the Canaanite legend of Kirta: "Kirta awoke, and it was a dream; the servant of El, and it was a 'majestic experience.'"[84] Gordon explains the ḥlm//hdr parallel via the following equation: *divine majesty=theophany=dream*,[85] an equation Cross finds most helpful in explaining the functional definition of Heb הדרת in Ps 29:2.[86] Of

---

78. Jer 50:36; 51:57. See Overholt, "Jeremiah," 266.

79. In this text (GE 3.2) the Uruk elders warn Gilgamesh not to invade the Cedar Forest by relying on his own *gimru*, an Akk term usually translated "strength," but which in some contexts can mean "financial resources" (see CAD G.77–78), a nuance captured in Jeremiah by the persistent association of גבר ("strength") with עשר ("riches").

80. Jer 14:9; 20:11; 32:18. See Moore, *WealthWatch*, 31–44.

81. אל יאמר עתרא בעתרי הדיר אנה (Aḥiq 13.207).

82. DNWSI 270.

83. שפיר מלך למחזה כשמש ויקיר הדרה (Aḥiq 7.108, following Cowley's trans. of הדר as "sovereignty," CAP 223).

84. krt yḥṭ wḥlm ʿbd îl whdrt (CAT 1.14.3.154–55).

85. UT 19.752.

86. Cross, "Canaanite," 19–21, accepted by Dahood, *Psalms* 1.176.

course, Heb הדר occurs some forty times in Tanak, seventeen of which stand in direct descriptions of Yahweh, six in descriptions of the king, and two in depictions of Jerusalem.[87] In other words, the vast majority of occurrences hovers suggestively over the parapets of the Jerusalem temple on Mt. Zion. Coupling this with the fact that (a) two out of three known extra-biblical occurrences occur within contexts of "dynastic kingship," and (b) Jer 9:22 formally and substantively parallels Aḥiq 13.20, it seems safe to suggest that this proverb finds its deepest roots in the pluralistic world of international wisdom.[88] This further suggests that Jeremiah the prophet knows enough about this world to adapt its language to his own defense against the intellectual attacks of the חכמים. Thus it hardly seems necessary to relegate this passage to post-exilic hands simply because it betrays the telltale marks of Wisdom.

כי־אם—OG reads ἀλλ' ἤ, but other witnesses read ἀλλ or ἀλλά for MT כי־אם.

השכל וידע—Reading השכל and ידע as emphatic imperatives following a finite ipf. verb, as in Jer 2:2,[89] note the oscillation (as in Jer 8:8–9) between finite clauses and verbless/non-finite clauses:

- Jer 8:8—three verbless clauses (according to reconstruction above of OG *Vorlage*);
- Jer 8:9a—three finite verbs;
- Jer 9:22—three finite verbs (jussives);
- Jer 9:23b—three non-finite forms (infinitive absolute employed twice, followed by active participle).[90]

In 8:8–9 this syntactic oscillation helps contrast the passivity of human wisdom with the dynamic immediacy of דבר־יהוה. Here it helps highlight the difference between Yahweh's timeless qualities and the frenetic boasting of עשרים, חכמים, גבורים.

אותי . . . אני—Jeremiah twice emphasizes the uniqueness of Yahweh by referring to him in the 1st person—once via the direct object particle, then again via the 1st sg. personal pronoun.

---

87. Yahweh's *majesty*—Isa 2:10, 19, 21; 35:2; 63:1; 1 Chron 16:27, 29; 2 Chron 20:21; Pss 29:2, 4; 90:16; 96:6, 9; 104:1; 111:3; 145:5, 12. Yahweh's *king*—Pss 21:6; 45:4, 5; 110:3; Prov 14:28; 25:6. Yahweh's *city*—Isa 5:14; Lam 1:6.

88. See 1 Kings 3–11 (Moore, *Pressure*, 191–98).

89. See *GKC* §113bb.

90. N.B. that OG also reads חפצתי as a nominative form (τὸ θέλημά μου).

חסד משפט וצדקה—the use of משפט and צדקה further links this material to the Jerusalem cult, since these terms most persistently interface with the Zion traditions.[91] Note also the phrase on the eighth-century Pannamuwa inscription at Zinjirli: "In his (i.e., Pannamuwa's) wisdom and in his loyalty he grasped the skirt of his lord, the king of Assyria."[92] This inscription, as Donner points out,[93] situates the term צדק within a specific political context shaped by the lord-vassal relationship.[94] In light of the lord-vassal relationship underlying the commands to exercise צדקה elsewhere in Jeremiah,[95] "loyalty" seems the best English translation.

חפצתי—Finally, חפץ is another dominant term in the Zion traditions of the Jerusalem cult, often linked explicitly to the king who "takes delight,"[96] or to Yahweh, who "takes delight" in the behavior of the king.[97] The prophets use this term to describe Yahweh's persistent attempt to call back his people to that in which he truly "delights,"[98] particularly in the Isaianic traditions.[99]

Not unexpectedly, agreement on the authenticity of this passage remains elusive. Volz questions it because the "knowledge of God" cannot refer, in his opinion, to a practical relationship, but instead must be intended in an abstract sense, and therefore from a hand much later than Jeremiah's (!).[100] Noting the absence of a copula in the warning to the עשרים, Schreiner follows the lead of Rothstein and assigns the third warning to a later redactor while maintaining the authenticity of the previous two warnings.[101] Kutsch's otherwise lucid formal analysis presumes a lengthy tradition-history behind the proverbial language in Jer 9:22–23,[102] but without even entertaining the *possibility* that Jeremiah might have something to say to the חכמים of his day, or that he might be at all acquainted with the sapientially-influenced language of the Jerusalem cult tradition. Unsurprisingly, Rudolph, Bright

---

91. Roberts, "Zion," 331–47; Ollenburger, Zion, 129–30.
92. בחמתה ובצדקה פי אחז בכנף מראה מלך אשור (KAI 215.11, 19).
93. KAI vol. 2, p. 227.
94. N.B. the stereotypical phrase אחז בכנף ("grasp the skirt"; see Rosenthal, "Sefire," 28–29).
95. Jer 22:3, 15; 23:5.
96. 1 Sam 18:22.
97. 1 Kings 10:9; Ps 22:9; 2 Sam 22:20 (Ps 18:20).
98. Hos 6:6; Mic 7:18; Isa 1:11; Mal 2:17 (see Botterweck, "חפץ," 92–106).
99. Isa 55:11; 56:4; 65:12; 66:4 (see Baltzer, *Deutero-Isaiah*, 444).
100. Volz, *Studien*, 78.
101. Schreiner, "Hintergrund," 530–42; Rothstein, *Jeremia*, 751.
102. Kutsch, "Weisheitsspruch," 179: "The taking over and reformulation of the saying most likely does not go back to the prophet Jeremiah."

and Hyatt all reject Volz's analysis as eisegetical projection floating over biased presumption about the origins of חכמה.[103] The analysis offered here not only suggests an organic connection between Jer 8:8–9 and 9:22–23, but also an organic connection between these texts and JL.

Jer 18:18

Jer 18:18–23 consists of a brief prose introduction followed by a poetic section designed to raise before Yahweh the agonizing question in v. 20. The introductory prose in v. 18 resonates loudly with the two sapiential passages just analyzed while the thematic content resonates with that which follows.

ויאמרו לכו ונחשבה על ירמיהו מחשבות	And they said, "Come, let's devise plots against Jeremiah
כי לא תאבד תורה מכהן	so that Torah might not perish from priest,
ועצה מחכם	nor counsel from wise man,
ודבר מנביא	nor word from prophet."
לכו ונכהו בלשון	"Come, let's strike him with the tongue
ואל נקשיבה אל כל דבריו	and listen no longer to any of his words!"

מכהן—The term תורה appears eleven times in Jeremiah. Of this number only three occurrences are expressly "class conscious": Jer 2:8; 8:8; and 18:18.[104] The juxtaposition of תופשי התורה with כהנים in 2:8 leads Rudolph to reject Hyatt's attempt to define תופשי התורה as a group separate and distinct from כהנים,[105] but careful attention to the way in which Tanak manipulates the root תפש lends greater support to Hyatt's view than Rudolph's.[106] Most of its sixty-one occurrences denote the "grasping" of something in a literal sense, such as sword, bow, or household tool. Very few allude to the "grasping" or "(mis-)handling" of an abstract idea. Besides here, the only other clear example of this occurs in the book of Proverbs: "Lest I be sated and disavow (you) and say, 'Who is Yahweh?,' and lest I be deprived and steal and 'mishandle' the name of my God."[107] N.B. the similarities with Jer 2:8: (a) *similar question*—"Where is Yahweh?"// "Who is Yahweh?" and (b) *similar perpetrators*—"those who mishandle Torah"//"those who mishandle Ha-Shem."

---

103. Rudolph, *Jeremia*, 69: "The genuineness of the oracle is not to be disputed." See Bright (*Jeremiah*, 79); Hyatt (*Jeremiah*, 893–94).

104. Other appearances occur in Jer 6:19; 9:12; 16:11; 26:4; 31:33; 32:23; 44:10, 23.

105. Rudolph, *Jeremia*, 16.

106. Hyatt, "Jeremiah," 385–87.

107. פן אשבע וכחשתי ואמרתי מי יהוה ופן אורש וגנבתי ותפשתי שם אלהי (Prov 30:9).

Early traditions about the priesthood show that the teaching of Torah receives a very high priority, particularly the need to emphasize its moral and ethical components. Later traditions show this vibrant ethical perspective shunted aside, replaced in many cases by lifeless formalism.[108] The תופשׂי התורה may be synonymous with the כהנים in Jer 2:8 (Rudolph), but the possibility needs to be considered (based on the remarkable parallels between Jer 2:8 and Prov 30:9, as well as the interpretation of Jer 8:8 above) that תופשׂי התורה in Jer 2:8 refers to those Judahites who have become thoroughly dismayed by the priesthood's lifeless interpretation of Torah, yet whose own treatment offers little hope for improvement (Jer 8:8). To the priesthood's policy of hyper-externalization, the תופשׂי התורה look to be guilty of hyper-intellectualization. Both are inadequate in Jeremiah's eyes. His detractors therefore demand that he shut up and go away, fearful that his criticism of their behavior might somehow, in a sad case of overstatement, cause the traditional priestly task of Torah interpretation to "perish" (אבד).

מנביא—Jeremiah's detractors feel that the best course to follow, even in light of the impending Babylonian invasion, is the *status quo*, not repentance before Yahweh. That is, they think that all segments of Jerusalemite society should go on doing what they traditionally do. Their reactionary attempt to reassign Torah to the כהנים, counsel to the חכמים, and דבר-proclamation to the cultic נביאים represents, if nothing else, a conservative decision to "eliminate the riff-raff" and maintain power at all costs over a broken society threatened by internal infection as well as external destruction. Hiding behind a traditional triadic list of magico-religious specialties,[109] Jeremiah's enemies want to continue operating by blind faith in the religious *process*, even in the face of Jeremiah's attempts to point them to a divine *person*.[110]

נכהו בלשׁון—Hebrew expressions using לשׁון can be highly idiomatic,[111] but it's difficult to find anything quite like this phrase anywhere else in Tanak. Extra-biblically, however, a similar idiomatic expression for "slander" occurs in the Aramaic phrase שׁלח לשׁן (lit., "send the tongue") in the Sefire

---

108. 1 Chron 16:40; 2 Chron 8:13; 23:18; 30:5 (see von Rad, *Theology*, 1.352; Schweitzer, *Utopia*, 170–71).

109. Even on the "day of Yahweh's wrath" (Ezek 7:19), Jerusalem will seek חזון מנביא ("vision from prophet"), fearful that תורה תאבד מכהן ("Torah will perish from priest") and עצה מזקנים ("counsel from elders," Ezek 7:26). Earlier Hittite tablets show Mursili II begging his gods to address his crisis-situation, whether by "man of God" (i.e., "prophet"), ˢᴬᴸŠU.GI ("old woman"/"priestess"), or "dream-interpreter" (see Singer, *Prayers*, 52).

110. Jer 7:3–7.

111. E.g., אישׁ לשׁון (lit., "man of [the] tongue," Ps 140:12 [ET 140:11]); בעל הלשׁון (lit., "lord of the tongue," Qoh 10:11).

inscription.[112] "Strike with the tongue" may not be an exact parallel to "send the tongue,"[113] but there does appear to be enough idiomatic similarity here to question the Syr translation ܒܠܫܢܢ ("with *our* tongue"). Once again, Jeremiah looks to be taking a recognized sapiential idiom and turning it back on his detractors, even those angry enough to flaunt a universally recognized moral code (prohibition against slander) to justify silencing him.

ואל נקשיבה אל כל דבריו—The textual dilemma here is whether to keep (MT) or dispense with (OG) the negative particle. Bright admits that both readings are attractive,[114] while Hubmann opts for the OG reading.[115] Nevertheless, the text of 4QJer[a] 18:18 retains the negative particle, and if the similarly-constructed statement in Jer 6:19 has a say, the evidence in MT clearly outweighs that in OG.

What is significant about this text? *First*, with regard to *form*, N.B. the now-familiar use of אמר followed by a quotation (the same construction found at the beginning of 8:8a). Instead of interrogative usage featuring אמר in the 2nd person, however, the text here grafts in the ipv. לכו plus the 1st pl. cohortative, a construction occurring only eleven times in Tanak. Nine of these instances occur in Nevi'im while the rest occur in contexts alluding to the act of "coming into" Yahweh's holy presence, represented either by Mt. Zion or some synonym.[116] Hosea appears to be using this construction to satirize Ephraim's "piety,"[117] while Nehemiah uses it to revive interest in rebuilding the walls of Zion.[118] Extrabiblically, Aḥiqar uses it in a conversation between a leopard and a goat illustrating the principle, "Nothing happens without divine help": "The leopard answered and said to the goat, 'Come, I will cover you with my hide!'"[119] The construction pops up again in Jeremiah's warning to Moab about the tenacity of *her* enemies: "Come, let's cut her (Moab) off from (being a) nation!"[120]

Second, with regard to *substance*, N.B. the use of חשב throughout Jer 18:

---

112. *KAI* 224.17–21.
113. The closest Tanak parallel is האריך לשון (lit., "make long the tongue," Isa 57:4).
114. Bright, *Jeremiah*, 124.
115. Hubmann, "Konfessionen," 279.
116. Isa 2:3, 5; 30:21; Mic 4:2 (See Moore, "Presence," 166–70).
117. לכו ונשובה אל־יהוה, "Come, let's return to Yahweh" (Hos 6:1).
118. לכו ונבנה את־חומת ירשלם, "Come, let's (re)build the wall of Jerusalem" (Neh 2:17).
119. ענה נמרא ואמר לענזא אתי ואכסנכי משכי (*Aḥiq* 8.118).
120. לכו ונכרתינה מגוי (Jer 48:2).

- 18:8—If the nation repents, Yahweh will repent of the evil he "plans" (חשב) against it;
- 18:11—Like a potter shaping evil, Yahweh is "devising a plan" (חשב מחשבה);
- 18:12—The people respond, "No, we will follow "our own plans" (מחשבותינו)
- 18:18, "let us devise plans" (נחשבה ... מחשבות).

Taking this context into consideration, it's difficult to avoid the conclusion that one of the primary reasons for Jeremiah's soliloquy in 18:18–23 is to voice the growing fear that Yahweh has somehow reneged on *his* "plans."[121] Can 18:18 *really* be a later insertion? Or is it not part of the warp and woof of Jeremiah's motivation for crying out in the first place?

QUESTIONS AND CONCLUSIONS

Is Ittmann correct in his assertion that Jeremiah's turbulent relationship with the (cult) prophets is *the* factor responsible for the process eventually leading to the creation of JL? If the answer to this question is "no," then what other confrontational experiences more adequately explain the profound skepticism embedded in the agonizing questions scattered throughout JL? Well, the answer to the first of these questions cannot be an unqualified "yes." Although Ittmann has shown that the conflict between Jeremiah and נביאים plays a significant role in the growth of JL, he has not demonstrated that this conflict is the only one. The evidence gathered above points strongly to the likelihood that his relationship with חכמים plays a much more significant role in the development of his skepticism. Moreover, this same evidence tends to identify the *Sitz im Leben* of these חכמים with those circles within the Jerusalem cult tradition most receptive to the tenets of international Wisdom. The evidence for this may now be summarized as follows:

- *wisdom psalms and proverbs* (Jer 9:22//Ps 49:7; Jer 2:8//Prov 30:9);
- *Isaianic mediation* (Jer 8:8a//Isa 19:11; Jer 8:9b//Isa 5:24);
- *Leitwörter* (תפש, הדר, חפץ, צדקה, משפט);
- *intertextual parallels* (Jer 8:9; 9:23//*KAI* 215.11; Jer 9:22//*Aḥiq* 13.207; Jer 18:18//*KAI* 224.17–21);
- *intratextual parallels* (Jer 8:8–9//9:22–23 [triad of verbless clauses//triad of finite verbs]; Jer 8:8//18:18 [אמר followed by quotation of "enemy"]; Jer 9:22–23//18:18 [listing of societal "classes"]);

121. I.e., אתך אני להצלך, "I am with you to deliver you" (Jer 1:8).

- *intra-Jeremianic parallels with JL* (8:8-9//17:18 [בוש//חתת]; 8:8-9//12:4 [אמר followed by quotation]; 8:8-9//18:22 [לכד]; 8:8-9//17:17 [מחתה]; 8:8-9//20:11 [בוש]; 8:8-9//20:18 [בושת]; 9:22-23//11:20 [שפט צדק]; 9:22-23//12:1 & 20:12 [צדיק]; 9:22-23//12:1 [משפטים]; 9:22-23//20:11 [גבור]; 18:18//11:19 [חשב + cognate accusative]; 18:18//18:23 [עצה]; 18:18//12:2 & 15:19 [פה/לשון]; 18:18//12:4 [אמר followed by quotation]; 18:18//12:6 [לשון/ "speaking fair words"]; 18:18//18:19 [catchword קשב]).

The answer to the second question is a bit more complex, and all that can be offered here are reflections designed to complement the results of previous research. In Jer 8:8–9 Jeremiah holds up the חכמים for public ridicule because they arrogantly presuppose that their hyper-intellectual approach to Torah interpretation is inherently superior. The form housing this rebuke is thoroughly prophetic,[122] yet heavily sprinkled with sapiential ornamentation. Jeremiah joins with the חכמים in their assessment of the ספרים, but not without cautiously distancing himself from both groups.

Yet the material in 9:22–23 shows movement toward adapting a sapiential (proverbial) form for a "prophetic" purpose. The proverbial saying embedded here radiates a terminology betraying strong linkages to the semantic spheres in which international diplomats operate, not to mention several other motifs quite at home in the corridors of the Jerusalem cult, rather than, say, the Mosaic covenant terminology so revered in Ephraim and Anathoth. In this way Jeremiah transforms the forms and contents of both northern and southern tradition-complexes into relevant messages tailored to the needs of *all* his contemporaries, including the Jerusalemite חכמים. Such usage implies that Jeremiah is quite aware of the linguistic forms and traditions peculiar to this "academic" segment of Judahite society, even secure enough in his understanding to use these motifs in his preaching.

In JL, however, the prophet begins to engage much more than just the peculiar forms and terminology of the חכמים. Now he begins to tap into their ideological concerns about human suffering in order to express more adequately the depth of his anguish. The skeptical question Jeremiah the prophet now dares to raise ("Is evil a recompense for good?"),[123] pronounced in the midst of deep inner pain, well illustrates the radicality of his transformation. Without denying its formal infinities to individual laments in the Psalter, this rare D passive usage of שלם finds its closest ideational affinity in the book of Proverbs.[124] In short, Jeremiah finds himself being passively pulled, in spite of his former reservations, deeper and deeper into the

---

122. כה אמר יהוה (Jer 8:4).
123. הישלם תחת טובה רעה (Jer 18:20).
124. Prov 11:31 and 13:13.

wise man's ideological world, driven by his need to find a way to express his own suffering. With his חכמים "brothers" Jeremiah even begins to question the simplistic assurances laid down in the "old wisdom" proverbs just cited as he dares to ask (with them) why innocent persons (like himself) must suffer along with the guilty.[125]

The corollary question, of course, almost always immediately follows in discussions about innocent suffering: "Why does the way of the wicked prosper?"[126] Not coincidentally, this is the very question raised at the beginning of JL. Here one begins to see more overt similarities to the book of Proverbs as well as the book of Job. Traces of Job's antiphonal human-lament-followed-by-divine-response format suddenly surface in the sapiential divine response in 12:5 to the desperate scepticism in 12:1–4.[127] The next question in JL ("Where is the word of Yahweh?")[128] sounds much like the question Jeremiah satirically puts into the mouth of his "enemies" in chapter 2 (viz., "Where is Yahweh?").[129] Boldly Jeremiah demands from Yahweh that those who mock him with such questions be "put to shame" (בוש) and "dismayed" (חתת),[130] using the same word-pair here which appears earlier in the oracle satirizing the חכמים and their intentions.[131] Yet the pain deepens: "Why is my pain unceasing, my wound incurable, refusing to be healed?"[132] To this question Yahweh patiently directs another Joban response, pointedly reminding Jeremiah of his original prophetic call, yet one gets the distinct impression that little of this conversation can satisfy the prophet's now thoroughly sceptical heart.[133]

Jeremiah thus progresses deeper and deeper into a world from which many preachers do not escape. What begins as a vigorous attempt to refute the ideology of his more sceptical colleagues now slowly entices him, under intense internal and external pressure bearing down on him from all sides, to begin doubting both his faith in Yahweh's justice as well as his desire to

---

125. On the "old wisdom"-vs.-"new wisdom" polarity, see von Rad, *Theology*, 1.425.

126. מדוע דרך רשעים צלחה (Jer 12:1).

127. Are the "running" (Jer 12:5) and "warrior" (20:11) motifs only coincidentally reflected in Job 16:14? (See Maier, *Jeremia*, 48–135).

128. איה דבר יהוה (Jer 17:15).

129. איה יהוה (Jer 2:8).

130. Jer 17:18.

131. Jer 8:9.

132. למה היה כאבי נצח ומכתי אנושה מאנה הרפא (Jer 15:18; see Job 16:16).

133. Where Diamond sees a major part of JL dominated by the prophet's "mis-interpretation of (his) mission" (*Confessions*, 142), the present essay prefers to describe this process as the gradual development of a "progressive paradox" in the prophet's thinking triggered by his history of confrontation with the חכמים.

serve such a deity. The intelligentsia's arguments even lead him to wonder whether Yahweh might be "deceiving" him, provoking him to lament the day of his birth in language identical to that found in Job.[134] Yet he cannot stop warning his people of the Shoah about to explode because he knows that Yahweh's word will torment him even more if he stops speaking, "like a fire shut up in my bones."[135] He thus finds himself locked in the jaws of a progressive paradox—unable to keep silent, yet unable to speak the word which brings him nothing but scorn and derision.

In short, there appears to be a reasonable amount of evidence embedded in the confrontations between Jeremiah and Jerusalem's חכמים to conclude that the results of these confrontations gradually lead Jeremiah into a progressive paradox from which it almost appears he will not escape. As the years go by and the burden of his personal torment increases, he feels drawn to the surface questions of the חכמים, even though the prophetic *persona* inside of him knows that their superficial answers can never measure up to the clarity, immediacy, and singular purity of Yahweh's word.

---

134. Particularly noteworthy is the Jer 20:14–18//Job 3:1–12 parallel (see discussion in Huey, *Jeremiah*, 194).

135. Jer 20:9.

6

JEREMIAH'S IDENTITY CRISIS*

HE HAD US IN the palm of his hand. From opening illustration to final application he never lost our attention—not once. We were spellbound, inspired, convicted by his message. He encouraged us. He challenged us. He did what all good preachers do—he brought us closer to God. Only about twenty or so people showed up that night, but it mattered little to him. To us it was just another banquet for graduating seniors in our church's youth group. To him it was much, much more. It was another chance to *preach*, another chance to invite people to *come home*. His message was a sparkling jewel, carefully polished . . . an awesome revelation, dramatically unveiled . . . a sharp scalpel, surgically precise . . . a healing poultice, lovingly applied.

What he said was as deeply biblical as it was refreshingly relevant—as familiar with ancient scripture as with contemporary developments in the Middle East; as knowledgeable about the moral fiber of Torah as the upcoming presidential election. Though young in years, he had already mastered that most difficult of homiletical disciplines—how to stand before the Lord and wait . . . before daring to speak a word from the King.

His was a spirit surrendered to the Holy One, an intellect devoted to the Word, a ministry captured by the Cross, a life transformed by the Resurrection.

Until he burned out.

---

* Revised from a paper read to the 11th annual Christian Scholar's Conference on July 19, 1991 at David Lipscomb University in Nashville, Tennessee, subsequently published in *ResQ* 34 (1992) 135–49.

Family, congregation, colleagues, friends—we all ignored the warning signs: how beaten down by the grind he was, how weary of the criticism, how hungry for a vision, how desperate for support, how pathetically lonely he had become. Asked to explain what happened, all he could say in response was, "I have no more Sundays left in me." Sundays had become for him, in the words of Ernest Campbell, "an endless line of telephone poles rushing past the window of life's train . . . until one looks no different from the other."[1]

He just burned out.

I wish I knew what happened, exactly. The last I heard, he had divorced his wife, pulled away from his children, and become (of all things) a marriage-and-family therapist. I wrote him a letter a few years ago, trying to reconnect, but have yet to receive a reply. No words have passed between us for years now, and we used to be trenchmates in the Kingdom together.

Why rehearse stories like this one today? Because *first*, this is not the first pastor ever to burn out, nor is it likely to be the last. Too many of us know of situations like this. We call them "horror stories," and often share them with each other in the corridors and back rooms of conferences like this one. Pastoral burnout is a serious problem in the Church today—another symptom, no doubt, of the wholesale secularization now crippling the North American Church.[2] *Second*, for every burned-out pastor there's a hurting congregation out there struggling to pick up the pieces and move on. No matter how autonomous we think we are, this is the kind of tragedy which affects all of us, sooner or later. One elder, struggling for words, recently confided to me that no other event in his memory had so drained his spirit and that of his flock as the tawdry spectacle of watching their pastor crash and burn. Could this be one of the most debilitating, most commonplace, yet least discussed problems in the Church today?

Charles Wickman thinks so. That's why he wrote *Pastors at Risk: Protecting Your Future, Guarding Your Present*. Chapter titles include the following:

- "Bummed Out, but Not Burned Out,"
- "Can We Talk? Isolation and Loneliness,"
- "A Spouse Ready to Quit,"
- "So What Do They Want Anyway? Multiple Expectations," and

1. Cited in Long, *Witness*, 20.

2. On the phenomenon of secularization the literature is vast. For a sampler, see Gogarten (*Säkularisierung*); Taubmann (*Gogarten*); Baumer (*Religion*); Wagar (*Secular*); Brown & Snape (*Secularisation*); Eberstadt (*Secularization*); Swatos & Olson (*Secularization*); Joas & Wiegandt (*Secularization*).

- "Burnout—Is the Church Responsible at All?"³

Packed with common sense and sage advice, this little handbook not only recognizes the multidimensional complexities embedded in the problem of pastoral burnout, it also dares to propose some creative solutions. Others are writing about it, too. Complementing Wickman's work, Arthur Gross Schaeffer and Steve Jacobsen focus on external concerns, identifying what they feel to be the most common characteristics of restless congregations unable or unwilling to keep covenant with their pastors. Chapter titles include:

- *Unrealistic Expectations* ("Can't You Meet Our Every Need?");
- *Role Conflict* ("Be a Strong Moral Leader, but Don't Offend Anyone Who Might Leave and Hurt the Budget");
- *Role Conflict* ("Promote Personal Balance for Others, but Work Yourself to Death");
- *Vocational Boundaries* ("So, You Really Expect Me to be at *Every* Committee Meeting?");
- *Conflict Between Vision and Reality* ("It Sounds Like You've Become Disillusioned");
- *Public/Private Boundaries* ("Why Are They Looking at My Shopping Cart?").⁴

Then there are the ideological analyses. Richard Porter inherits a church whose pastor burns out and leaves, and discovers in the process of leading them through the grief process that several members have given in to the temptation to turn away from belief in a fully incarnate God to one "safely detached" from the cares of life.⁵ Hauerwas and Willimon attack the problem head-on in their classic exposé, *Resident Aliens*:

> Why do people, having once put their hands to the plow, look back, fall back, drop out, and burn out from the church? Scores of commentators on ministerial malaise urge pastors to strengthen their ego, take a day off, take up a hobby, stand up to the board and tell them where to get off. These would-be defenders of the clergy all seem to assume that the problem in ministry is primarily a problem of improper psychological disposition in the clergy or unrealistic demands by the church,

---

3. Wickman, *Pastors*, 1–8. See also Rediger, *Scandals*, 139–204.

4. Gross Schaefer & Jacobsen, "Burnout," 20–30. Rayburn *et al.* target some of the demographic variables associated with pastoral stress ("Professionals," 1–71), and Gaddy (*Siege*) writes from the perspective of a burnout survivor.

5. Porter, "Fallen," 42–57.

and so on . . . .. In our opinion such solutions only waltz around the symptoms rather than get to the source of the problem. The pastoral ministry is too adventuresome and demanding to be sustained by trivial, psychological self-improvement advice. What pastors, as well as the laity they serve, need is a theological rationale for ministry which is so cosmic, so eschatological and therefore countercultural, that they are enabled to keep at Christian ministry in a world determined to live as if God were dead. Anything less misreads both the scandal of the gospel and the corruption of our culture.[6]

Pastoral burnout is not new. It's as old as the call to ministry itself. What *is* new is the degree to which such patently secular "solutions" are so readily proposed and accepted in response to it. Pastors quit their jobs, "experts" argue, because they feel professionally unfulfilled, economically disadvantaged, emotionally battered, and/or physically unable to do everything expected of them. Doubtless these things do wear out pastors, but are these the *primary* factors? Put another way, can the social sciences *alone* explain it?[7] The thesis of this essay is that pastoral burnout not only impacts the lives of prophets in the Bible, but that the God of Israel has something quite intelligible to say about it. My first presumption is that an adequate understanding of the identification process in Tanak is absolutely indispensable for successfully dealing with the problem of pastoral burnout today. Put bluntly, neither pastoral burnout nor pastoral rebirth can be adequately understood apart from a clear examination of the germane texts addressing the problem, premier among which stands the book of Jeremiah.

Because of space restrictions, the focus here is limited only to *sections* of Jeremiah, particularly the laments in chapters 11–20 (hereafter JL).[8] Whether this prophet actually *succumbs* to pastoral burnout is another question altogether, a bandwagon upon which several theories keep riding with little or no evidence. We simply presume (second major presumption) that Jeremiah keenly understands the dynamics of the problem. Moreover, the problems facing Jeremiah are multidimensional. *Externally*, he faces opposition from several Judahite groups, all claiming to represent Yahweh, yet all conspicuously unable to address (or even explain) the reason(s) for Judah's international problems (primarily with the Babylonians, but also with the Egyptians and Transjordanians). Instead, they just spend their time scapegoating Jeremiah for stubbornly refusing to stop preaching Yahweh's

---

6. Hauerwas & Willimon, *Aliens*, 87.

7. Berger criticizes lay leaders who spend more time doing amateur sociology than their mission ("Gospels," 1–14).

8. Jer 11:18—12:6; 15:10–21; 17:14–18; 18:18–23; 20:7–18.

word.⁹ *Internally* he has to face the familiar demons of doubt and despair always afflicting religious leaders, regardless of social status, psychological profile, economic situation, or ideological identity.¹⁰

The major difficulty with such examination, of course, is that few Tanak characters ever come drawn in such a way that their innermost thoughts are laid bare for all to see. Contemporary writers operate in exactly the opposite way, depicting characters as intimately as possible via techniques Stanley Hopper calls "inscaping."¹¹ Ancient Hebrew writers, however, rarely "inscape" their characters. Words and actions can weave in and through Tanak character profiles, but seldom are we permitted the luxury of reading anyone's innermost thoughts.¹²

Jeremiah appears to be the exception which proves the rule. The tradition preserving his memory is deliberately, eloquently, even passionately "inscaped," primarily in JL but also occasionally in his more outwardly directed oracles. From the texts at hand the depiction handed down is that of a vulnerable, introverted young man struggling to communicate an unpopular message to an arrogantly resistant audience.¹³ *Questions:* What are some of the major factors responsible for Jeremiah's "pain?"¹⁴ How does Yahweh respond? Is this response still valid?

---

9. דבר יהוה (see Jer 8:8–9; 9:22–23; 11:21; 15:15; 18:18; 20:1–6; 23:9–22; 26:10–11).
10. Witte ("Profession," 168–80); Nauta ("Flight," 211–23).
11. Hopper, "Sonnets," 63.
12. Alter, "Reticence," 114–30.

13. Contemporary debate on JL is complex and unresolved. Some presume that the laments preserve the private words of the historical Jeremiah (Skinner, *Prophecy*, 202; von Rad, "Konfessionen," 265–76; Clements, *Jeremiah*, 108). Others accept them as the authentic words of Jeremiah, but that the first-person "I" is representatively spoken on Judah's behalf (Reventlow, *Jeremia*). Many interpret JL as a thickly-layered tradition ultimately rooted in historical reality, but now creatively restructured to apply to later circumstances (Gerstenberger, "Jeremiah," 393–408; Carroll, *Chaos*, 107–35). Some read them simply as great literature, abandoning historical methods altogether (Polk, *Persona*).

14. Jer 15:18 reads "Why is my 'pain' (כאב) unceasing?"; see Moore, "Wounds," 313–24. Eichler (*Jeremia*, 200) sees Jeremiah's crisis comprising two elements: (a) the potential of outright rejection in response to his message; and (b) the potential of opposition and persecution in response to delayed fulfillment of his message.

FACTORS RESPONSIBLE FOR JEREMIAH'S CRISIS

External Factors

Murray Polner tells the story of a young American rabbi called to console survivors recently liberated from the Nazi deathcamps.[15] Shocked and appalled by what he sees, the only thing he can think to say in response is, "Observe the Sabbath." Some of those overhearing this react negatively, feeling it to be cold and unfeeling. Few can see what he wants to accomplish. Sabbath observance is a historically proven way to help suffering survivors rebuild their lives. To quote Abraham Heschel, "the Sabbath comes like a caress, wiping away fear, sorrow and somber memories."[16] War has a way of reducing platitudes to ashes and stripping down cultures to their essential components. Perhaps this is why God allows it. Such is the case for those imprisoned in Nazi deathcamps as well as those violently dragged from their homes by the Babylonians in ancient Judah.[17] In fact, the threat of military invasion stands behind everything Jeremiah says and does, from the "foe from the north" oracles at the front of the book to the anti-Babylonian oracles at the back.[18] Dangers like this often motivate prophets like Jeremiah to challenge people to face their fears, especially when they become embedded in their leaders. Micah, for example, castigates the rulers, prophets, seers, diviners, and priests for lying, extorting, and corrupting Judah during the Assyrian crisis.[19] Ezekiel foresees a time when war-torn survivors will seek visions from their prophets, Torah instruction from their priests, and counsel from their elders, but receive nothing but a mourning king accompanied by a whiny crown prince.[20]

Jeremiah perfects the use of such indictment-lists. He brands the priests, Torah handlers, rulers, and prophets as apostates and liars (Jer 2:8). He indicts the king, princes, priests, and prophets for refusing to renounce

---

15. Polner, *Rabbi*, 212–13.
16. Heschel, *Sabbath*, 2.
17. See Ezek. 1:1; 3:15, 23; 10:15, 20, 22.
18. Jer 1:14; 51:1–14.
19. Mic 3:5–12 (see Childs, *Assyrian*, 66, 93). On the exchange of משפט ("justice") for שחד ("bribe") in 3:11, see Moore, *WealthWatch*, 45–47, 51–52, 82–83, 155, 175, 182, 200, 213–15, 226–28.
20. Ezek 7:26–27 (reading ילבש שממה as "clothed [in] terror"; i.e., אבל // שמם). Poser (*Trauma*, 5) reads Ezekiel as a "literary work written about the individual and collective experience of the war and deportations associated with the catastrophe of the Exile in Judah," and Markter reads it to investigate "whether and under what circumstances a renewing of the heart is possible" (*Ezekiel*, 57–58).

corruption (4:9).²¹ He warns kings, princes, priests, and prophets that their blood will soon be smeared on the ground like dung (8:1). He announces to kings, priests, and prophets that Yahweh will first inebriate them, then "smash" them to pieces (13:13-14).²² He drafts a caustic letter to the elders, priests, and prophets exiled to Babylon (29:1-23).²³ He reminds Judah's princes, eunuchs, and priests that the penalty for breaking covenant with Yahweh will certainly mirror the judgment template to which their ancestors pledged allegiance (34:19).²⁴ Perhaps the most famous of these lists occurs in Jer 18:18, where Jeremiah satirizes the bitter accusations of three hostile groups in a style which can only be called "Jeremianic."²⁵ Observing its occurrence in Jeremiah over one hundred times, Thomas Overholt calls this the "citation of the opponents" formula.²⁶ These particular three groups—the prophets, priests, and professors—stand among Jeremiah's most vocal opponents.²⁷ Commentators argue over how coherent or self-aware they might be (of themselves or one another),²⁸ but the fact remains that the listing of opposition groups in clusters of three or more is a hallmark of Jeremianic style.

Question: Why are these three groups so angry? *Answer:* The *prophets* are angry because Jeremiah accuses them of lying, dreaming empty dreams, grasping for power, failing to provide a moral example, profaning the temple, committing adultery, extending false hope to the impenitent, and general worthlessness.²⁹ By far their greatest flaw is that no one ever

21. On contemporary questions and concerns about corruption, see Glazer & Glazer (*Whistleblowers*, 97-132), Elliott (*Corruption*, 1-6), and Moore (*WealthWatch*, 88-89, 225-26).

22. The OB cognate of נפץ in v. 14 (here trans. "smash") sometimes denotes the "smashing" of barley and malt in the brewing of beer (*napāṣu*, *CAD* N/1.287), a nuance which, if intended, cleverly illuminates the "drunkenness" motif.

23. Leuchter thinks it highly "likely that Jeremiah 29 is composed well before the relevant passages in chapters 50-51" (*Polemics*, 48).

24. Deut 27-28. Other groups find honorable mention: the shepherds who destroy and scatter (Jer 2:9; 23:1-4); the intellectually gifted Torah handlers who squander their gifts (2:8); the military officers who go on fighting long after Jerusalem has fallen (43:2); and the scribes who delight in thinking up new ways to twist Torah (8:8).

25. Jemielity sees Jeremiah "projecting himself into the mindset of those seeking his harm" (*Satire*, 180; see Moore, "Paradox," 406-10).

26. Overholt, "Audience," 262-73; see Gordis, *Poets*, 104-59.

27. In fact, the list in 18:18 seems intentionally designed to reflect the three divisions of Tanak, the כהנים ("priests") with Torah, the נביאים ("prophets") with Nevi'im, and the חכמים ("wise men") with Ketuvim.

28. See Mowinckel ("Wisdom," 206), von Rad (*Wisdom*, 15-23), Whybray (*Intellectual*, 21-24), Harding ("Goddess," 216), and Lange ("Prophecy," 185-86).

29. Jer 23:9-32.

changes under their preaching.³⁰ No one repents of anything they have done; indeed, no one is even asked to do so. To the prophets, therefore, Jeremiah is a troublesome whistleblower who threatens the comfortable security of their well-established bureaucracy.³¹ Chapter 28 memorializes this prophet-vs.-prophet conflict with the story of Hananiah-vs.-Jeremiah.³² The *priests* hate Jeremiah because he accuses them of ignorance, apathy, falsehood, arrogance, ruthlessness, shallowness, and Torah-peddling.³³ As with the prophet-vs.-prophet conflict, the prophet-vs.-priest conflict also comes with an illustrative story: the story of Pašḥur-vs.-Jeremiah.³⁴ The conflict between Jeremiah and the *wise men*, however, comes with no illustrative story, nor is this opposition group singled out as often as the priests and prophets. Yet this conflict is the one which best explains the structure and contents of the tortured questions scattered throughout JL.³⁵

In short, the external factors responsible for Jeremiah's identity crisis arise ultimately from the international pressures driven by the threat of Babylonian invasion, and penultimately by Judah's dismally inappropriate response to it. Jeremiah singles out the prophets, priests, and professors for special critique because each important group, rather than doing their jobs in the midst of this crisis, cravenly abandon their posts, leading Judah *away from* the divine Presence, not *toward* it.³⁶

Internal Factors

Jeremiah views this international crisis as an opportunity for Judah to renew its commitment to the Mosaic covenant. Not so his detractors. They rather see it as a way to ensure the accomplishment of their own, self-centered agendas. Thus plots thicken, egos flare, gossip corrodes, and reputations are

---

30. ואם עמדו בסודי וישמעו דברי את עמי וישבום מדרכם הרע, "But if they had stood in my council they would have caused my people to hear my words, and turned them from their evil path" (Jer 23:22).

31. For contemporary parallels, see Alford (*Whistleblowers*, 1–16) and Cohn (*Whistleblower*, xi-xix).

32. See Clements (*Jeremiah*, 166–69); and Lalleman (*Jeremiah*, 215–17).

33. Jer 2:8; 5:31; 6:13; 8:10; 14:18; 20:1–3; 27:16–22; 29:26.

34. Jer 20:1–6. Stulman compares Pašḥur with Amaziah (Amos 7:10–17) because both priests see themselves called to neutralize the disruptions caused by "anti-establishment rhetoric" (*Jeremiah*, 176).

35. Moore, "Paradox," 410–14.

36. See Blank ("Prayer," 331–32); Terrien (*Presence*, 253–56); Moore ("Presence," 168).

dragged through the mud.³⁷ Months, perhaps even years of this muckraking eventually turn Jeremiah inward, to the only place he feels he has left to pour out his pain. Amazingly JL inscapes these emotions for us in language delicately tinged with anger and regret. Norbert Ittmann makes a strong case for interpreting this language from a developmental perspective grounded in a pre-exilic context.³⁸ While not the first, his is one of the very few attempts to visualize Jeremiah's identity crisis from a sociohistorical perspective, singling out his conflict with the prophets as the major contributing factor. In a 1986 essay I agree with him that JL indeed sits atop a recognizable history of development, but disagree with his decision to anoint the prophet-vs.-prophet conflict as the only sociohistorical factor contributing to it.³⁹ To avoid reductionism we must pay attention to each and every oppositional group, especially the "wise men." Why? Because no other conflict best explains the radically skeptical questions preserved in JL.

Jeremiah's oracles in chapters 8 and 9 masterfully retool several sapiential language-forms in order to satirize more effectively the thoughts and intentions of these "wise men."⁴⁰ Yet JL goes deeper, mining not only the peculiarities of their rhetoric, but probing deeply into the foundations of their ideology, portrayed here as an exhausted, cutthroat philosophy in which "the unfathomableness of the conduct of individual lives presents more and more difficult problems for faith."⁴¹ *Examples*: The question raised in 18:20, "Is evil a reward for good?" overtly challenges, alongside Job and Qoheleth, the "old wisdom" in which the righteous are always rewarded and the wicked always punished.⁴² The question in 12:1, "Why does the way of the wicked prosper?" addresses the vexing problem of socioeconomic inequality.⁴³ The remainder of the rhetorical questions in JL look more at home in the book of Job than in Nevi'im.⁴⁴ In 17:15, for example, the question "Where is the word of Yahweh?" articulates a level of skepticism against which Judah is constantly warned, at least by older sages. In 15:18, the prophet agonizes,

37. In Jeremiah's case, quite literally (Jer 38:6).
38. Ittmann, *Konfessionen*.
39. Moore, "Paradox," 392–93; Ittmann, *Konfessionen*, 73–75.
40. Ibid., 395–405.
41. Von Rad, *Wisdom*, 206.
42. See Schmid (*Weisheit*, 34) and Murphy ("Sirach," 31–40).

43. "A century or so after Amos and Isaiah, just prior to the Babylonian destruction of the monarchy and its temple in Jerusalem, the prophet Jeremiah again pronounces God's condemnation of the monarchy on the basis of covenant principles" (Horsley, *Economics*, 74).

44. "In both Jeremiah and Job the problem of theodicy is raised because there is 'punishment' for which there is no identifiable sin" (Brueggemann, *Jeremiah*, 147).

"Why is my pain unceasing, my wound incurable?" a question for which the divine response, as in the whirlwind speeches at the end of Job, overlooks much while satisfying few.[45]

In sum, the internal questions in JL indicate a significant degree of skepticism over the usual problems with which skeptics usually struggle, a struggle more at home in the world of sages and scribes than anywhere else. What begins in Jeremiah as a vigorous attempt to upbraid these intellectuals for their ivory tower arrogance apparently leads the prophet into a deepening intellectual flirtation with their questions, especially those focused on the problem of innocent suffering. Eventually this pushes him up against the boundaries of his Yahwistic faith, even to the point where he accuses Yahweh of "entrapping" him.[46]

YAHWEH'S RESPONSE

Pete Diamond points out that JL breaks down into two separate cycles.[47] Cycle 1 focuses on the nature of Jeremiah's prophetic mission, depicted as a struggle between prophet-vs.-deity in chapters 11–15. Cycle 2 shifts the focus away from prophet-vs.-deity to prophet-vs.-nation in chapters 17–20. Yahweh, in other words, responds to Jeremiah's cries in Cycle 1, but remains conspicuously silent in Cycle 2. Each lament in Cycle 1, moreover, increases in intensity as Jeremiah struggles with the dynamics of his call. In the *first* lament (11:18–23) he complains that the residents of his hometown want to kill him, and Yahweh responds by condemning outright the bullies from his hometown, Anathoth. In the *second* lament (12:1–6) Jeremiah files a "lawsuit" (ריב) against Yahweh for allowing the wicked to prosper.[48] Against this charge, however, Yahweh asks his own question: "If with pedestrians you run and get tired, how will you run with horses?"[49] *Application:* "Your

---

45. Diamond, *Confessions*, 147-76; Schifferdecker ("Whirlwind," iv) argues that the whirlwind speeches in Job 38–42 connect more closely to the dialogues in chapters 3–37 than most readers think, and further, that they "offer a view of creation—and of humanity's place in creation—that is fundamentally different from any other theology of creation in the Bible," viz., that "creation is radically non-anthropocentric."

46. Jer 20:7 (פתה); see Clines & Gunn, "Persuade," 20–27.

47. Diamond, *Confessions*, 260–61.

48. Huffmon, "Lawsuit," 285–95.

49. Peterson's take (*Horses*, 22) on this metaphor is compelling: "Are you going to live cautiously or courageously? I called you to live at your best, to pursue righteousness, to sustain a drive toward excellence. It is easier, I know, to be neurotic. It is easier to be parasitic. It is easier to relax in the embracing arms of The Average. Easier, but not better. Easier, but not more significant. Easier, but not more fulfilling. . . . What is it you really want, Jeremiah? Do you want to shuffle along with *this* crowd? Or do you want

brothers and your father's house—both clamor after and betray you. Never put your trust in them completely, even when their words seem well-intentioned." In the *third* lament (15:10–14) Jeremiah pronounces a woe upon himself because of all the strife and contention he has to face. He wants to give up preaching altogether. All it appears to bring him is heartache. To this Yahweh responds by reminding Jeremiah of his ultimate invincibility; i.e., that his protector is none other than Almighty God. Long after his vindication, he promises, his opponents will still be in a Babylonian prison. Indeed, it's easier to destroy a solid brass wall than to harm one of God's servants. Jeremiah pulls out all the stops in his *fourth* lament (15:15–21), pathetically rehearsing what is left of his self-dignity. Hoping to secure divine approval, he ticks off a laundry-list of complaints: "I have endured reproach; I have 'eaten your words'; I have avoided idle partying; I have endured the pain of constant rejection." Yahweh's response this time, however, is neither cryptic nor indirect. Like the angel confronting Balaam,[50] he warns Jeremiah that the danger looming before him is very real:

> If you repent I will restore you, and you can stand before me. If you learn to distinguish what is precious from what is base, then you can speak for me. Let them turn against you, but do not turn back to join them. They may make war against you, but they will not prevail . . . because I am with you.

In sum, Yahweh employs several arguments to strengthen Jeremiah in the midst of his identity crisis. First, he assures him that all the threats against his life are just that—*threats*. Then he applies reason: "Are you going to preach my word only as long as it costs nothing? What are your goals, Jeremiah? To make friends and influence people? To endear yourself to your nation? Your hometown? Your family? Or is it to serve me? Do you not realize that the *really* difficult times are yet to come? How are you going to handle it when ministry *really* gets tough?" Then he engages Jeremiah's skepticism. "Do you believe," he asks, "that ministry is a privilege or a burden? Remember, I do not need *you*, Jeremiah, you need *me*. Start practicing what you preach. Repent of your sins and I will restore you." Finally, he offers his servant the same assurances Christ offers his servants. "Stop worrying so much about what you think you are giving up. I am always with you. Your job is not to engineer change. Your job is to be faithful to my word, whether or not people conform to it. The suffering you now endure

---

to run with the horses?"

50. Num 22:31–33.

is but a microcosm of my own. Your loneliness is *my* loneliness. When your heart breaks, *my* heart breaks."

CONCLUSION

Tom Long takes a good, hard look at ministry in a thoughtful little book entitled *The Witness of Preaching*. In it he recognizes that some pastors seem ideally suited to their work, giving years of devoted service with little or no emotional distress. Others, however, find ministry a "terrible burden" and struggle hard to be faithful to everything it entails. Jeremiah definitely fits in the latter category. Helmut Thielicke says it well:

> No man will ever come to the truth . . . who has not faced doubt, despair, and shipwreck . . . . He who knows what faith is must have stood beneath the baleful eye of that demonic power against which we fling our faith. Faith is either a struggle or it's nothing.[51]

S. P. Pittman issues a stern warning in 1919:

> Too many "enter the ministry" from sinister motives: for pecuniary advantage, to exploit talent, to gain notoriety . . . to hide sin under a ministerial robe . . . It (is foolish) to say that the ministry of the church of Christ could not be bettered . . . (and) fatal to put forth no effort to make it better.[52]

Karl Barth simply asks, "Who dares, who can preach, knowing what preaching is?"[53]

Discovering what the price of faithful ministry *really* is can be a bone-jarring experience for a young pastor. Ministry is difficult enough when times are good, but it can be enormously stressful when things turn tough: when the economy bottoms out and unemployment hits the congregation like a runaway train; when people lose their savings, then their homes, then their kids; when husbands and wives give up and turn on one another like wild dogs; when everything one tries to do to stop all the carnage is criticized by someone with an ax to grind. Under stress like this even the hardiest pastor may wonder, with Jeremiah, why ministry once seemed to be the "right vocational choice."

---

51. Thielicke, *Nihilism*, 176–77.
52. Pittmann, "Ministry," 828.
53. Barth, "Preaching," 126.

Yet what happens when we try to apply the דבר־יהוה to contemporary life situations? *First*, good pastors, as we all know, are hard to find and expensive to train. But they are even more difficult to keep. We cannot afford to lose a single one of them, yet we do. Does it not seem more than a little foolish, in view of the "impending crisis,"[54] to continue to focus the bulk of our attention on recruiting and training pastors while practically ignoring them when they burn out?[55] Why are we so intent on competing with one another for students and so utterly disinterested in what happens to these disciples once they leave our classrooms? Yahweh promises never to abandon Jeremiah. How do we help incarnate this promise to the Jeremiahs in *our* midst? *Second*, tired pastors experiencing symptoms of burnout cannot afford to ignore the warning signs. Granted, many churches should doubtless do more to help them recover from the distressingly commonplace brutality of contemporary ministry. But like Jeremiah, pastors need to decide where to go and what to do if and when the wisdom of the world starts looking more attractive than Yahweh's wisdom. The book of Jeremiah is preserved, in part, to show us what can happen when the words of "the wise" become confused with the דבר־יהוה. *Application:* Sometimes it's more important to pray than study. Sometimes it's more important to sit quietly with the dying than prepare a powerpoint. Sometimes it's more important to spend time with one's spouse than with anyone or anything else in the world. *Third*, probably the most important lesson Yahweh tries to teach Jeremiah is this: *It's more important to be faithful than successful.* Both Jeremiah and his detractors reverse this, and it costs them dearly. It costs Judah her freedom. It costs Jeremiah his self-confidence. For the twenty-first-century church who knows what the final cost will be?[56]

---

54. 1 Cor 7:26.

55. See Witt, *Replenish*.

56. "The huge irony is that the more the gospel is offered in consumer terms, the more that consumers are disappointed. The gospel is not a consumer product; it doesn't satisfy what we think of as our 'needs.' The life of Jeremiah is not an American 'pursuit of happiness.' It is more like God's pursuit of Jeremiah" (Peterson, *Horses*, 10).

7

THE LAMENTS IN JEREMIAH AND 1QH

Mapping the Metaphorical Trajectories*

CONTEMPORARY BIBLICAL SCHOLARSHIP IS thoroughly aware of the exegetical possibilities generated by the discovery and publication of the ancient scrolls discovered in the Judean desert since 1947.[1] Relatively few students, however, have begun the process of examining the striking intertextual echoes resonating between Jeremiah's laments (JL)[2] and the brooding poetry of the *Hodayot* scroll found in Qumran Cave 1 (1QH).[3] In 1960 Svend

---

* Revised from a paper read to the SBL Qumran section on Nov 20, 2006 in Washington, DC, subsequently published in Goldingay, *Jeremiah*, 228–52.

1. See Collins (*Scrolls*, 185–212); Loader ("Contexts," 27–46); and Elwolde ("Hodayot," 79–100).

2. Jer 11:18–12:6; 15:10–21; 17:14–18; 18:18–23; and 20:7–18.

3. Sukenik (*Scrolls*) first labels these poems הודיות (*hodayot*, "thanksgivings") because of the refrain אודך אדוני ("I give you thanks, Lord," 1QH 4.9, 17; 6.8), but this in no way implies that 1QH, as a "species," lacks any reference to קינה ("lament"). See, e.g., 1QH 19.22, which has an insertion above the line which reads אנחתה בכנור קינה [לכול אבל יג]ו[ן], "I have sighed on the harp of lament for every sorrow of ang[ui]sh" (see also 1QH 17.4; Jer 7:29; 9:9, 19). Burrows (*Scrolls*, 380) sees in 1QH a "type known as the individual psalm of lament . . . combined with the note of thanksgiving in some of the poems," and Puech notes that the contents of 1QH "sometimes take the form of thanksgiving, or praise, or lament, or supplication" ("Hodayot," 367).

Holm-Nielsen lists several examples of what he calls Jeremianic "quotations," noting the "especial use... of the laments" in 1QH, but remains conspicuously silent about the intertextual parallels.[4] Ed Greenstein traces the development of several motifs common to both Jeremiah and Job, including "loneliness and betrayal," "cursing the day of one's birth," "lamenting the prosperity of the wicked," "litigating with God," and "becoming privy to divine conversation," but again, shows little interest in how these motifs impact the Qumran literature.[5]

The following essay puts two questions before these two poetic anthologies: (a) What are the predominant metaphors common to JL and 1QH? and (b) What factors might be responsible for adapting, and in some cases transforming, the metaphors in 1QH *vis-à-vis* those earlier laid down in JL?[6]

JEREMIAH'S LAMENTS

To study JL is to plow a narrow furrow in a large field. Others have plowed this furrow, of course (and this field), and though each new pass uses a different methodological blade, most wind up agreeing with Gerhard von Rad that full comprehension of JL is indeed "central to the interpretation of Jeremiah."[7] What I have discovered from my own pass through this furrow is that Norbert Ittmann is doubtless correct: the conflict between Jeremiah and the Judahite prophets *is* an important factor contributing to JL's socioliterary development.[8] But it's not the only one. Jeremiah's conflict with the חכמים ("wise men") is just as important, if not more so.[9] While Ittmann's focus on the prophet-vs.-prophet conflict partially explains JL's formation, the prophet-vs.-sage conflict is in many ways the only way to explain the overtly sapiential questions driving these gut-wrenching laments.[10] Against this conclusion one might argue that Jeremiah's conflicts with the חכמים in

---

4. Holm-Nielsen, *Hodayot*, 310, 356.
5. Greenstein, "Jeremiah," 98–110.
6. As Schuller & Newsom note, several *Hodayot* editions are presently known (*Hodayot*, 1–11; see also Harkins, "Observations," 233), but in this essay 1QH and 1QH^a are, for all practical purposes, equivalent.
7. Von Rad, *Theology* 2.204. Indeed, Brueggemann sees in this poetry "the most direct, candid, and intimate prayers" in all of Tanak (*Jeremiah*, 114).
8. Ittmann, *Konfessionen*, 73–74.
9. Moore, "Paradox," 390–94.
10. Ibid.

8:8–9 and 9:22–23 occur only in late "Dtr prose,"[11] but three factors combine to derail this conclusion: (a) interpreters since Bernhard Duhm remain deeply divided over what, exactly, constitutes a "Dtr" text;[12] (b) Mowinckel's "Source C," the theory most often cited in support of this position, justifiably stands under intense critical scrutiny today;[13] and (c) the prose in 8:8–9 and 9:22–23 appears to sit atop a recognizably poetic *Vorlage*.[14]

Therefore there seems to be little doubt today that Jeremiah's confrontations with the חכמים are just as impactful as his conflict with the נביאים, *especially* when it comes to calibrating the depth of the "progressive paradox" into which he finds himself inexorably drawn. On the one hand, this sensitive preacher gravitates to the arguments of the חכמים because, comparatively speaking, they seem best able to address the theodical doubts persistently bothering him.[15] On the other hand, Jeremiah of Anathoth is a נביא יהוה ("prophet of Yahweh"), and as such, refuses to engage, much less accept anything which might challenge, undermine, or even marginalize the validity and authority of דבר־יהוה.[16] The text refrains from indicating whether his primary concern is outright rejection of Yahweh's word or merely its delayed fulfillment—two very different concerns.[17] But neither does it tell us how (or whether) he escapes the consequences of failing to resolve the paradox which plagues him. Unlike Job, the book of Jeremiah has no neat and tidy epilogue tacked on at the end. Instead, like the Balaam cycle, it simply trails off, unresolved, with "no conclusion" and "no result."[18]

This essay will presume that Jeremiah (a) passes on a recognizable literary legacy to his scribe Baruch,[19] thereby (b) effectively communicating a written message to audiences far removed from its original context.[20] These

11. Sharp's question (*Jeremiah*, 17) is more pertinent than ever: "By virtue of what criteria does the interpreter term unique aspects of the prose material (in Jeremiah) 'deuteronomistic' rather than 'deutero-Jeremianic,'" especially when the material in question "does not occur in the Dtr literature otherwise?"

12. Duhm takes Jer 8:8–9 and 18:18 to be original (*Jeremia*, xxi–xxiii) and Eissfeldt (*Introduction*, 359) recognizes the משל-type structure of 8:4–9, but openly confesses his uncertainty about originality.

13. Sommer ("Jeremiah," 646–66); Sharp (*Jeremiah*, 13–26).

14. Moore, "Paradox," 395–405. "The rediscovery of the poetry of the prophets is a major contribution of modern scholarship, as is the recognition of the poetic tradition behind the earliest prose narratives" (Freedman, *Poetry*, 1).

15. Crenshaw, "Confessions," 31–56.

16. Moore, "Paradox," 414.

17. Eichler, "Jeremia."

18. Mowinckel, "Bil`amsage," 238.

19. Avigad, "Baruch," 52–56.

20. Van der Toorn ("Prophet," 196); Smith (*Laments*, xvii–xviii).

presumptions are debatable, of course, but so are those which assign whole sections of Jeremiah, on the basis of outdated distinctions between "poetry" and "prose,"[21] to anonymous banks of Persian-era editors.[22] So far, few interpreters are suggesting that someone other than Jeremiah might be responsible for JL,[23] even among those who practice what Arnaldo Momigliano calls a "devaluation of the notion of evidence" replaced by an "over-appreciation of rhetoric and ideology."[24] Some will always wander off into what Kathleen O'Connor justifiably calls a "complication of readings,"[25] yet this does not negate the fact that "the portrait of Jeremiah as a man characterized by inner struggles with himself and with God is as prevalent in those commentaries which assume that the biblical text presents" a composite fictional character "and those which assume the text is transparent."[26]

1QHODAYOT (1QH)

Contemporary research on the *Hodayot* scroll from Cave 1 focuses on a similar set of questions. Textual critics rely on recovered fragments from Cave 4 to help fill in the lacunae pockmarking 1QH, and tradition historians are working hard to reconstruct the trajectory on which it sits. Both are prerequisites for clearing the way toward deeper investigation of the metalinguistic structure of these "strange and fascinating poems."[27] Where the laments in JL spill out onto the page as the *ipsissima verba* of a well-known historical figure, however, none of the poems in 1QH even *claims* a specific author. Nonetheless, many still imagine the Teacher's[28] spirit hovering over

---

21. Kugel, *Poetry*, 127–29, 140–42. "The Hebrews ... do not draw out basic distinctions, such as that between prose and poetry; the two flow into each other, so that we find poetic elements within prose and prosaic elements within poetry" (Avis, *Imagination*, 51).

22. *Contra* Gerstenberger, "Complaints," 393–408.

23. Roberts' critique of Carroll (*Jeremiah*) is prescient: "Carroll points to some real theological difficulties in the book of Jeremiah, but it is not at all clear why these difficulties must stem from the deuteronomistic redactors and not Jeremiah himself. The problem of how to distinguish between a true and false prophet is never satisfactorily resolved in the OT, but to argue that the issue is more important in the exilic period than in the period prior to 587 BCE is absurd" (*Jeremiah*, 127).

24. Momigliano, *Judaism*, 3.

25. O'Connor, *Jeremiah*, bookreviews.org/pdf/3315_3706.pdf.

26. Callaway, "Lamenting," 48.

27. Sanders, *Qumran*, 330; Schuller, *Qumran*, 233–54.

28. I.e., the מורה הצדק ("Teacher of Righteousness," 1QpHab 1.13; 2.2; 5.10; 7.4; 8.3; 9.9–10; 11.5; CD 1.11; 20.32); see VanderKam & Flint, *Scrolls*, 282–84.

these poems, particularly over those which Jeremias calls the *Lehrerlieder* ("Teacher Hymns"):²⁹

- Thanksgiving to God for Salvation (10.5–19);
- Thanksgiving to God for Protection (10.20–30);
- Thanksgiving to God for the Covenant (12.5–13.4);
- Thanksgiving to God for Supporting His People (13.5–19);
- Thanksgiving to God for Rescuing the Penitent (13.20–15.5);
- Thanksgiving to God for Sustaining His People (15.6–25);
- Thanksgiving to God for Making the Poet a Fountain of Blessing (16.4–17.36).

While it is certainly possible that these laments come from the mind (and perhaps the pen) of the מורה הצדק,³⁰ such cannot be proven or disproven from the evidence at hand.³¹ Thus, as with many conundrums, the question of authorship remains cloaked in uncertainty, a conclusion which in turn generates a wide spectrum of opinion. On one end of this spectrum many reject the Teacher's authorship of these poems because they also presume 1QH to be an amalgamation of variegated songs written by different authors at different times for different (predominantly liturgical) occasions.³² On the other hand however, many find it difficult to imagine anyone else producing such intimate poetry *except* someone of recognized stature in the יחד-community, and the best candidate for *that* job remains the מורה הצדק.³³

In his Chicago dissertation Michael C. Douglas argues that 1QH is a carefully edited anthology laid out in two "blocks."³⁴ "Block A," in his opinion, boasts a significantly higher level of linguistic, stylistic, and thematic "coherence" than the remainder of 1QH, which he calls "Block B." Roughly corresponding to the previously labeled *Lehrerlieder*,³⁵ "Block A" is thus more likely, in Douglas' opinion, to be the product of a single poetic mind.

---

29. Jeremias, *Lehrer*, 168–239. Hughes (*Hodayot*, 233) reads some of these hymns (e.g., 1QH 11.6–19 and 11.20–37) as "examples of a sectarian 'class exercise' in poetic interpretation," an opinion she acknowledges to be "fanciful."

30. 1QpHab 7.4.

31. Puech cautiously suggests that, should the Teacher be involved in writing these poems, then he would "no doubt be capable of expressing himself according to various literary approaches, varying his vocabulary whenever necessary" ("Hodayot," 366).

32. Holm-Nielsen (*Hodayot*, 316–20); Hopkins ("Reassessment," 362–64).

33. Bardtke ("Qûmran," 231–33); Abegg ("Heaven," 72–73).

34. Douglas, "Hodayot," 319–50.

35. 1QH 9.1–20.6. See Morawe (*Loblieder*, 37) and Jeremias (*Lehrer*, 312–13).

Reading 1QH against Victor Turner's model of social change,[36] he suggests that since the material in "Block A" details a fierce conflict between the poet and his detractors, this doubtless implies that this poet has already made his views publicly known, and that an opposition group has already begun reacting to them.[37] Thus, because there appears to be a much higher level of hostility permeating the poems in "Block A" over against those in "Block B," Douglas concludes that the מורה הצדק is most likely the author of "Block A."[38]

POETRY AND METAPHOR

In this essay we offer no new hypothesis about authorship, nor do we presume, with a past generation of scholarship, that determining authorship is a prerequisite for determining meaning. But we do presume a simple truth; viz., that poetry is not the end-product of an editorial process. Poetry rather springs from the minds of gifted artists called "poets," and the fact that this needs to be stated at all speaks volumes about the contemporary academic climate. This is not to discount what John Goldingay insightfully calls the "irreducibly metaphorical form" of Tanak's poetic texts,[39] only to recognize the obvious fact that Western readers of this Oriental literature often fail to escape the influence of occidental rationalism. Thus, for example, because the poems in *Hodayot* so totally immerse themselves in biblical metaphors, some label them "derivative" and "epigonic." Robert Alter speaks for many in this regard:

> "Here and there one encounters an interesting image or line, but for the most part the poems are pastiches of biblical poetry, repeatedly taking the urgency of the supplication psalms . . . and coloring it with the crude emotional hues of apocalyptic."[40]

Bonnie Kittel, however, challenges this assessment because too often it displays, in her opinion, an abysmal "lack of understanding of the poetic forms at Qumran." On the contrary, she insists, the poetry in 1QH can more than

---

36. Turner, *Dramas*, 23–59.

37. Turner calls this type of initiatory conflict the "developing social drama" (*Dramas*, 23).

38. Douglas, "Teacher," 239–66. Harkins (*Hodayot*, 20–24) rejects Douglas's results because she (inexplicably) rejects any taxonomy distinguishing *Lehrerlieder* ("teacher hymns") from *Gemeindelieder* ("community hymns").

39. Goldingay, *Models*, 186.

40. Alter, "Scrolls," 39–40, *contra* Chazon ("Scripture," 25–41), Hughes (*Hodayot*, 42–55), and Harkins (*Hodayot*, 17–24).

hold its own alongside any "other poetry of the ancient world."[41] Nevertheless, like many other literary critics of ANE texts, Kittel makes no attempt to engage the metalinguistic structure of these laments. To address JL and 1QH at *this* level demands at least a minimalist understanding of the contemporary metalinguistic discussion about the character and possibilities of metaphorical speech.

Contemporary research into the structure and function of language has long since shifted focus away from the study of metaphor as literary trope to deeper investigation of its cognitive possibilities, and some of this research is beginning to bleed over into the study of ancient texts.[42] To engage these texts from this deeper perspective, however, we must first ask questions about what Janet Soskice calls "that figure of speech whereby we speak about one thing in terms ... suggestive of another"—i.e., *metaphor*.[43] To cut to the chase, what we are now discovering about metaphor is that it can be much more than "literary ornament." Often it can serve as a "means of cognitive mediation" intentionally designed to "create structure in our understanding of life."[44] According to Max Black, in fact, bipolar categories alone cannot correctly define the cognitive possibilities generated by metaphorical speech; i.e., the "literary trope"-vs.-"iconic object" polarity. Instead this needs to be replaced by a tripartite explanatory template consisting of *substitution, comparison,* and *interaction*.[45] For Black, "substitutional" metaphors are simply and only literary tropes designed to enrich speech, what Nelly Stienstra offhandedly calls "a pretty way of saying something that might also have been said literally."[46] "Comparative" metaphors go deeper, but basically remain little more than literary similes, as in the metaphor "TIME IS (like) MONEY."[47]

"Interactive" metaphors, on the other hand, say something about reality which, for all intents and purposes, cannot be stated "literally."[48] The

---

41. Kittel, *Qumran*, 6.

42. See, e.g., Babuts (*Metaphors*, 59–78), Ready (*Simile*, 11–26), and Eagleton (*Theory*, 79–109).

43. Soskice, *Metaphor*, 15. Orton (*Poetry*) and Bautch (*Genre*) take a much different approach.

44. Brown, *Metaphor*, 5 (citing Lakoff & Turner, *Metaphor*, 38).

45. Black, *Models*, 25–47.

46. Stienstra, *Metaphor*, 22.

47. Ricoeur (*Metaphor*, 96–97) credits Black only with "condensing the essential theses of a semantic analysis of metaphor" first tentatively outlined by Richards in the 1930s (*Rhetoric*, 94–96).

48. What Black describes as "interaction," Ricoeur prefers to call "properly semantic" ("Métaphore," 93–112).

metaphor "MAN IS A WOLF," for example, only has meaning when two or more minds share a common information base about wolves and their behavior. Black calls this common information base the "system of associated commonplaces." For metaphors to work, both producer and receiver must share in and know something about the same "system." Otherwise a given metaphor soon becomes "dormant," and eventually "extinct." What makes this particular metaphor work, moreover, has nothing to do with the technical truth about wolves (e.g., that wolves practice sexual abstinence when necessary to protect the young already born), but with the "system of associated commonplaces" readers hold in common about what they *think* they know about wolves. "Hence interactive metaphors cannot be translated into direct language without a loss in cognitive content," or, put more negatively, "the substitution and the comparison theories are hopelessly inadequate to explain what is actually going on" within a given interactive metaphor.[49]

Application: Whatever biblical scholars might think of this discussion,[50] it shows great potential for exploring more thoroughly the character and depth of the metaphors common to JL and 1QH, and encourages us to ask whether the metaphors in these laments simply and only help sufferers *speak* about their suffering ("substitution"), or actually *create a safe place* for poets like Jeremiah and the *Hodayot* poet to suffer ("interactive").

INTERTEXTUAL ANALYSIS

Again, to emphasize the "obvious," poetry does not trickle down piecemeal over time from the minds (and pens) of multiple authors and editors. No, a given poem is rather the product of a given poet. Thus it seems impossible to overemphasize how inappropriate it is to read this ancient poetry from perspectives better suited to the decoding of engineering schematics and architectural blueprints.[51] That the laments in JL and 1QH continue to speak to the hearts and minds of contemporary readers is not all that surprising. All great literature speaks to later generations—indeed, this is what makes it "great."[52] The question is not *how* or *why* the poetry in JL and 1QH

---

49. Black, "Metaphor," 28.

50. See, e.g., Wu, *Metaphoring,* 29–37.

51. "Since some large fraction, perhaps a quarter to a third of Tanak, must be reckoned as poetry or poetic in character, just its bulk would demand serious attention, but its quality and difficulty make it even more important . . . In poetry, the medium and message are inseparably intertwined to produce multiple effects at different levels of discourse, and evoke a whole range of responses: intellectual, emotional, and spiritual" (Freedman, *Poetry,* 1).

52. "The body of texts conventionally thought of as the Bible's 'poetry' shares with

speaks to later audiences, but *how much*. That is, (a) how much do these poems intertextually connect, and (b) what does a clearer comprehension of this connection contribute to interpretation?[53] To engage *these* questions we need to catalogue the primary terms parallel to JL and 1QH and explore their relative level of metaphorical "resonance." Thus the following analysis begins by laying out in alphabetical order the primary nouns, verbs, and idioms allocated to the "system of associated commonplaces" shared by JL and 1QH.

Common Verbs

אבל—"to mourn"

- "how long will the land 'mourn?'" (אבל, Jer 12:4);
- a source of bitterness "for mourning" (לאבל, 1QH 19.19);
- "I have sighed on the harp of lament 'for every sorrow'" (לכול אבל, 1QH 19.22)

בוש—"to be ashamed"

- let my persecutors be "ashamed," but do not let me be "ashamed" (יבוש, Jer 17:18);
- "let them be greatly ashamed" (בושו מאוד, Jer 20:11);
- "you have not covered my face with shame" (לא טחתה בבושת פני, 1QH 12.23);
- "shame is upon my face" (בושת על פנים, 1QH 13.35, enclitic ם?)

בחן—"to test"

- "you are the one who 'tests' the heart"[54] (Jer 11:20; 1QH 14.26; 15.9);
- (Yahweh is) "the one who tests the righteous man" (בחן צדיק, Jer 20:12);
- "you/to 'test'" (לבחון/בחנת, Jer 12:3; 1QH 10.13)

בקש נפש—"to seek a soul" (i.e., "persecute")

---

our own poetry a vitality and directness that prose often lacks" (Kugel, *Poems*, 9–10). On the challenge of defining "great literature" see Reiner ("Literatur," 151–210).

53. See, e.g., Basson (*Metaphors*, 3–4) and Weigel ("Lamentation," 185–204). Like Kittel (*Qumran*, 50), the approach here moves beyond simplistic polarities like "literal-vs.-figurative." Unlike Kittel, however, it attempts to engage the task of intertextual analysis from a metalinguistic perspective.

54. Markter wants to know "whether and under what circumstances a renewing of the heart is (even) possible among exiled Hebrews" (*Ezechiel*, 57–58).

- "those seeking your soul" (מבקשים נפשך, Jer 11:21);
- "they seek my soul" (בקשו נפשי, 1QH 10.21)

גלה—"to reveal";

- "against you I have revealed/filed my lawsuit" (אליך גליתי ריבי, Jer 11:20; see variations in 1QH 5.9; 9.21; 14.4; 19.17; 20.34)

זכר—"to remember"

- "remember me" (זכריני, Jer 15:15; see 18:20, "remember how I stood before you," (זכר עמדי לפניך);
- "I will not remember him" (לא אזכרנו, 20:9);
- (God's) "stylus of remembrance" (חרת זכרון, 1QH 9.2);
- "but when I remembered the power of your hand" (בזוכרי כוח ידכה, 1QH 12.35)

חזק—"to (em)power/(over)power"

- "you have overpowered me" (חזקתני, Jer 20:8);
- "my spirit stands empowered before affliction" (רוחי החזיקה במעמד לפני נגע, 1QH 12.36);
- you (God) have freed the soul of the poor . . . "from the hand of the one stronger than him" (מיד חזק ממנו, 1QH 10.35);
- (your servant) "cannot stand empowered" (לבלתי חזק מעמד, 1QH 13.29)

חשב—"to scheme"

- "they have schemed" (חשבו, Jer 11:19; 1QH 10.32);
- "schemes" (מחשבות, Jer 11.19; 1QH 10.17; 12.14, 19)

חתת—"to be dismayed, terrified"

- "they will be dismayed" (יחתו, Jer 17:18);
- "at their taunts you have not let me become dismayed" (בגדפותם לא חחתיתני, 1QH 10.35)

יבש—"to make dry/wither"

- "how long will the grass of every field wither?" (שבי, Jer 12:4);
- "you (God) have made me a source of streams in a dry place" (נתתני במקור נוזלים ביבשה, 1QH 16.4 // ציה ["desert"])

ידע—"to know/understand"

- "and I understood" (ואדעה, Jer 11:18; 1QH 11.20; 14.6);

- "I knew" (ידעתי, Jer 11:19; 1QH 6.12, 17; 7.15, 25, 28; 9.21; 12.30; 14.6; 17.19; 19.7; 20.11; 21.14; 22.16);
- Yhwh "made it known to me" (הודיעני, Jer 11:18);
- "you (God) know me" (ידעתני, Jer 12:3);
- "you (God) know" (אתה ידעת, Jer 15:15; 17:16; 18:23);
- "know" (ipv. דע, Jer 15:15);
- "a land you (Jeremiah) do not know" (ארץ לא ידעת, Jer 15:14)

ישע—"to save/deliver" (נצל//פדה//עזר//)

- "deliver me that I might be saved" (הושיעני ואושעה, Jer 17:14);
- "in your kindness you save my soul" (בחסדיכה תושיע נפשי, 1QH 10.23);
- "you save the soul(s) of the poor" (תוצל נפש[י] עני, 1QH 13.13);
- "you save me from the zeal of the deceit-mongers" (תצילני מקנאת מליצי כזב, 1QH 10.31);
- "you redeem my soul from the hand of the powerful" (תפד נפשי מיד אדירים, 1QH 10.35);
- "you redeem my soul from the pit" (פדיתה נפשי משחת, 1QH 11.19; see Isa 38:17; Jon 2:6);
- "you rescue my soul" (עזרתה נפשי, 1QH 15.23)

כשל—"to stumble"

- "let them stumble before you" (ויהיו מכשלים לפניך, Jer 18:23);
- "my persecutors will stumble" (רדפי יכשלו, Jer 20:11);
- "stumbling block of their iniquities" (מכשול עוונם, 1QH 12.15);
- prevent your servant "from stumbling over the precepts of your covenant" (מכשול מחוקי בריתך, 1QH 8.23)

לכד/תפש—"to catch"

- "they have dug a pit to catch me" (Jer 18:22, כרו שוחה ללכדני);
- "they are caught in their schemes" (יתפשו במחשבותם, 1QH 12.19)

בוז/לעג—"to mock"

- "everyone mocks me" (כלה לעג לי, Jer 20:7);
- "my hands are against all who mock me" (ידי על כול בוזי, 1QH 12.22)

מות—"to die"

- "you will not die by our hand" (לא תמות בידנו, Jer 11:21);

- the young men "will die by the sword" (ימתו בחרם, Jer 11:22);
- their sons and daughters "will die by famine" (ימתו ברעב, Jer 11:22);
- "ropes of death" (חבלי מות, 1QH 11.28);
- "gates of death" (שערי מות, 1QH 14.24);
- "breakers of death" (משברי מות, 1QH 17.4)

נטע—"to plant"

- "you (Yhwh) plant them" (the wicked) (נטעתם, Jer 12:2);
- "eternal planting" (מטעת עולם, 1QH 14.15; 16.6);
- "planting of truth" (מטעת אמת, 1QH 16.10)

פקד—"to visit/judge"

- "visit me" (פקדני, Jer 15:15);
- "judgment of their retribution" (פקודת שלומם, 1QH 9.17)

פתה—"to persuade/entice/deceive"

- "you enticed me . . . and I was deceived" (פתיתני . . . ואפת, Jer 20:7);
- "perhaps he (Jeremiah) can be deceived" (אולי יפתה, Jer 20:10);
- "the followers of my testimony are enticed" (נצמדי תעודתי פותו, 1QH 14.19);
- "the men of the covenant are deceived by them" (אנשי ברית פותו בם, 1QH 22.8 [bottom])

ראה—"to see"

- "he (God) does not see our future" (לא יראה את־אחריתנו, Jer 12:4);
- the holy shoot "sees, but does not recognize" (ראה בלא הכיר, 1QH 16.13)

ריב—"to charge/file suit"

- "I am a man of contention" (אהיה איש ריב, 1QH 10.14; 13.22, 35; Jer 15:10);
- "against you I file my lawsuit" (אליך גליתי ריבי, Jer 11:20; 1QH 13.30; 17.23);
- "I file a suit against you" (אריב אילך, Jer 12:1);
- "I am appalled to hear your judgments against the mighty heroes, your lawsuits against the army of your saints" (אפחדה בשומעי משפטיכה עם גברי כוח וריבכה עם צבא קדושיכה, 1QH 18.34–35);
- "you file a lawsuit to valid[ate] the just and sen[tence the guilty" (תריב לאצד[י]ק ולר[שיע רשע, 1QH 25.13)

רפא—"to heal"

- "Heal me, O Yahweh, and I shall be healed" (רפאני יהוה וארפא, Jer 17:14);

- "why . . . is my wound incurable, refusing to be healed?" (למה . . . מכתי אנושה מאנה הרפא, Jer 15:18);
- "my disease" has been changed "into et[ernal] healing" (נגיעי למרפא ע[ולם, 1QH 17.24–25)

שוב—"to turn back/away"

- Remember how I stood before you . . . "to turn away your anger from them" (להשיב את־חמתך מהם, Jer 18:20);
- God is "the one who forgives those who turn back from rebellious sin" (הסולח לשבי פשע, 1QH 6.24);
- "do not turn away the face of your servant" (אל תשב פני עבדך, 1QH 8.26)

שמע—"to listen"

- "listen to the voice of my suit" (שמע לקול ריבי, Jer 18:19, reading with OG);
- "in the distress of my soul you did not abandon me, but listened to my cry for help" (בנצרת נפשי לא עזבתני ושועתי שמעתה, 1QH 13.12)

יכח/שפט—"to judge"

- "Yhwh of Hosts judges rightly" (יהוה צבאות שפט צדק, Jer 11:20);
- "you do [not] judge me according to my sinfulness" ([לא] כאשמתי שפטתני, 1QH 13.5–6);
- "you open my ear to the instruction of those who judge justly" (גליתה אוזני למוסר מוכיחי צדק, 1QH 14.4)

שרש—"to take root"

- "they (the wicked) take root" (שרשו, Jer 12:2);
- "its roots (go down) to the abyss" (שרשיו עד תהום, 1QH 14.16);
- "its roots pierce through the hardest rock" (שרשיו בצור חלמיש, 1QH 16.23, lit., the "rock of flint," Deut 8:15);
- the wicked are a "root bearing the fruit of poison and bitterness" (שרוש פורה רוש ולענה, 1QH 12.14);
- the trees of water "make the shoot grow and take root in the eternal greenhouse" (להפריח נצר למטעת עולם להשריש, 1QH 16.6–7)

Common Nouns

כזב(א)—"deceitful"

- deceitful waters which are unreliable" (אכזב מים לא נאמנו, Jer 15:18);

- "you save me from the jealousy of the deceit-envoys" (ותצילני מקנאת מליצי כזב, 1QH 10.31; see 12.9–10);
- "they go to seek you in the mouth of the deceit-prophets" (ויבאו לדורשכה מפי נביאי כזב, 1QH 12.15–16)

אפך—"your (God's) anger"

- "do not let the extent of your anger cause my removal" (אל־לארך אפך תקחני, Jer 15:15; 1QH 5.5);
- "deal with them in the time of your anger" (בעת אפך עשה בהם, Jer 18:23; 1QH 19.8);
- "when the lot of anger (falls upon) the forsaken" (ורוגל אף נעזבים, 1QH 11.27–28)

דבר—"(God's) word"

- "where is the word of Yahweh?" (איה דבר יהוה, Jer 17:15);
- "your words were found and I devoured them" (נמצו דבריך ואכלם, Jer 15:16);
- "your (God's) word does not turn back later" (אחר דברך לא ישוב, 1QH 5.24 [verbatim repetition in 5.25]);
- "they choose not the path of your [heart], nor do they give ear to your word" (לא בחרו בדרך [לב]כה ולא האזינו לדברכה, 1QH 12.17; see 12.35);
- "so as not to transgress your word" (ולוא לעבור על דברך, 1QH 20.24);
- "and not to scatter your word" (ולוא להפרד . . . דברכה, 1QH 25.14)

חמס—"violence"

- "I cry out, 'violence and destruction'" (אזעק חמס ושד, Jer 20:8);
- "from the assembly of futility and the council of violence" (מעדת שוא ומסוד חמס, 1QH 14.5)

חרפה—"reproach"

- "realize how I am treated as a reproach for your sake" (דע שאתי עליך חרפה, Jer 15:15);
- "you set me up as a reproach and a joke among traitors" (ותשימני חרפה וקסל לבוגדים, 1QH 10.9–10);
- "they set me up for contempt and reproach" (וישימוני לבוז וחרפה, 1QH 10.33–34)

ידך—"your (God's) hand/power"

- "I sit alone in the presence of your hand/power" (מפני ידך בדד ישבתי, Jer 15:18);
- "when I remember the strength of your hand with the abundance of your compassion" (ובזוכר יכוח ידכה עם המון רחמיכה, 1QH 12.35–36);
- "in your hand is the judgment of them all" (בידכה משפט כולם, 1QH 13.4);
- "I know that your speech is truth and that justice is in your hand" (ידעתי אמת בפיכה וידכה צדקה, 1QH 19.7);
- "do not pull back your power from the one who strengthens himself in your covenant" (אל תשב ידכה] . . . מ[היות לו מתחזק בבריתכה, 1QH 23.9 [top])

כאיב—"pain"

- "why is my pain . . . incurable?" (למה כאיבי אנושה, Jer 15:18);
- "it is an incurable pain, a wasting disease in the bowels of your servant" (ותהי לכאב אנוש ונגע נמאר בתכמי עבדכה, 1QH 13.28)

לחם—"bread/food"

- "let's destroy the tree with its sap" (נשחיתה עץ בלחמו, Jer 11:19);
- "my food turns into a lawsuit; my drink into heated arguments" (ויהפך לי לחמי לריב ושקוי לבעל מדינים, 1QH 13.35, lit. "into a *baʿal* of arguments")

מחסה/מעוז/מנוס—"refuge"

- "on the day of disaster you are my refuge" (מחסי־אתה ביום רעה, Jer 17:17);
- "I have no fleshly refuge" (מחסי בשר אין לי, 1QH 15.17);
- "I have no refuge" (אין מעוז לי, 1QH 16.27);
- "you, O God, are my refuge" (אתה אל מנוסי, 1QH 17.27)

בעת/מחתה—"terror"

- "do not become a terror to me" (אל־תהיה לי למחתה, Jer 17:17);
- "terrified by (your) just judgments" (נבעתה במצפטי צדק, 1QH 9.23)

מים—"water"

- "you are to me like . . . unfaithful waters" (תהיה כמו . . . מים לא נאמנו, Jer 15:18);
- "like water pouring down a slope" (כמים מוגרים במורד, 1QH 12.34; same idiomatic phrase in Mic 1:4);
- "when my heart melted like water you strengthened my soul in your covenant" (במוס לבי כמים תחזק נפשי בבריתך, 1QH 10.28);

- "my fo[ot] is caught in the ankle-chain; my knee 'dissolves' like water" (רג[לי נלכדה בכבל וילכו כמים ברכי, 1QH 16.34);

סוד—"council"

- "I do not sit in the council of merrymakers" (לא ישבתי בסוד משחקים, Jer 15:17; cf. "I am a taunt-song among criminals," ואני הייתי נגינה בפשעים, 1QH 10.11 // שחוק, Lam 3:14);
- (you have saved me?) "from the assembly of futility and the council of violence" (מעדת שוא ומסוד חמס, 1QH 14.5), to commune with "the men of your (God's) council" (אנשי עצתכה, 14.11);
- "they are a council of futility, a congregation of Belial" (והמה סוד שוא ועדת בליעל, 1QH 10.22);
- "you (do not) cast my lot into a futile congregation, nor do you place my portion among a council of hypocrites (lit., "concealers")" (הפלתו גורלי בעדת שו ובסוד נעלמים לא שמתה חוקי, 1QH 15.34; N.B. verbatim // in 1Q35 frag. 1.9 [=1QH^b] and in 4Q428 frag. 7.1);
- "council of spiri[ts]" (סוד רוחו[ת], 1QH 5.3);
- "eternal council" (סוד עולם, 1QH 11.21)

צפור/עוף—"bird"

- "beast and bird are swept away" (ספתה בהמות ועוף, Jer 12:4);
- "they evict me from my land like a bird from the nest" (ידיחני מארצי כצפור מקנה, 1QH 12.8–9);
- on the "shoot" (נצר) generated by the "trees of life" (עצי חיים) . . . its foliage will be for every winged bird" (דליתו לכל עוף כנף, 1QH 16.6–9)

עץ—"tree"

- "let us destroy the tree" (נשחיתה עץ, Jer 11:19; cf. "to destroy them (i.e.) every moist tree," להתם כול עץ לח, 1QH 11.29)

כבל/פח—"snare"

- "they dig a pit to capture me and lay snares for my feet" (כרו שוחה ללכדני ופחים טמנו לרגלי, Jer 18:22);
- "my foot is caught in the snare" (רגלי נלכדה בכבל, 1QH 16.34);
- "when the traps of the pit open up all the snares of the wicked funnel out" (בהפתח כל פחי שחת ויפרשו כול מצודות, 1QH 11.26)

פניך—"your (God's) face"[55]

---

55. See Moore, "Presence," 166–67.

- "*you* know what comes from my lips—it stands before your face" (אתה ידעת מוצא שפתי נכח פניך היה, Jer 17:16);
- "I entreat your face via the spirit you have given" (ואחלה פניך ברוח אשר נתתה, 1QH 8.19; cf. "did he [Hezekiah] not fear ... and entreat Yahweh's face," הלא ירא . . . ויחל את־פני יהוה, Jer 26:19)

פרי—"fruit"

- "you plant them (the 'wicked'), they take root, they grow, they bear fruit" (נטעתם גם־שרשו ילכו גם־עשו פרי, Jer 12:2);
- "but you, O God, protect its fruit," ואתה אל שכתה בעד פריו, 1QH 16.11; i.e., of the "holy shoot," נצר ק[ו]דש, 16.10; cf. 16.13, 20)

זמה/עצה—"counsel/scheme"

- "you know all their counsel against me for death" (ידעת את כל עצתם עלי למות, Jer 18:23);
- "you, O God, spurn all their Belial schemes, and establish your own counsel" (אתה אל תנאץ כל במחשבותם בליעל ועצתכה היא תקום, 1QH 12.12–13; see // זמות בליעל, 12.13)

צדיק—"just/righteous"

- "you are righteous, O Yahweh" (צדיק אתה יהוה, Jer 12:1 // 1QH 6.15);
- "there is no one righteous with you" (אין צדיק עמכה, 1QH 20.19);
- "Yahweh of Hosts, who tests the righteous" (יהוה צבאות בחן צדק, Jer 20:12);
- "you (God) are the righteous one" (אתה הצדיק, 1QH 4.20 // 8.17);
- "to God Most High belong all the acts of justice" (לאל עליון כול מעשי צדקה, 1QH 12.31)

עול/רשעים—"wicked/evil"

- "why does the way of the wicked prosper?" (מדוע דרך רשעים צלחה, Jer 12:1);
- "on account of the evil of the wicked I am a rumor on the lips of violent men" (ואהיה על עון רשעים דבה בשפת עריצים, 1QH 10.10–11);
- "the congregation of the wicked is roused up against me" (עלי קהלת רשעים תתרגש, 1QH 10.12);
- "the gates of the pit close behind the woman pregnant with evil" (ויסגרו דלתי שחת בעד הרית עול, 1QH 11.18);
- "they disparage me with evil lip" (ויליזו עלי בשפת עול, 1QH 13.24)

שפתי—"my lip"

- "outcry of my lip" (מוצא שפתי, Jer 17.16; cf. "outcry of our lips," מוצא שפתינו, 4Q427 frag. 7, 2.22);
- "you give the tongue's reply to my [un]circumcised lips" (ותתן מענה לשון לע[רול] שפתי, 1QH 10.7);
- "you put thanksgiving in my mouth, praise on my tongue, and my circumcised lips in a place of joy" (ותתן בפי הודות ובלשוני תהלה ומול שפתי במכון רנה, 1QH 19.4–5)

שארית—"remnant"

- "no remnant will be left to them" (ושארית לא תהיה להם, Jer 11:23);
- "there shall be no deliverance for the one inclined toward sin; it will completely trample him, leaving no rem[nant]" (ואין פלט ליצר אשמה לכלה ירמוסו ואין שאר[י]ת, 1QH 14.32; cf. שרית, 26.2; also 4Q427 frag. 7, 2.8; 4Q431 frag. 1, 1.7)

שוחה—"pit"

- "they have dug a pit for my soul" (כרו שוחה לנפשי, Jer 18:20; cf. "they have dug a pit to capture me," כרו שוחה ללכדני, 18:22);
- "you protect me from all the traps of the pit, for vicious men seek my soul" (ותשוך בעדי מכול מוקשי שחת כ[י] עריצים בקשו נפשי, 1QH 10.21);
- "you ransom my soul from the pit" (פדיתה נפשי משחת, 1QH 11.19);
- "she who is impregnated by the snake writhes in pain, for every act of horror stands at the cervix of the pit" (הרית אפעה לחב לנמרץ ומשברי שחת לכול מעשי פלצות, 1QH 11.12);
- "Sheol and Abaddon relentlessly open up all the shafts of the pit to make their voice heard, echoing it through the Deep" (ובהתרגשם יפתחו ש[או]ל וא[בד]ון כ[ו]ל חצי שחת עם מצעדם לתהום ישמיעו קולם, 1QH 11.16–17);
- "but the gates of the pit close on the woman pregnant with evil" (ויסגרו דלתי שחת בעד הרית עול, 1QH 11.18)

נגינה/שחוק—"laughingstock"

- "I am a laughingstock every day; everyone makes fun of me" (הייתי לשחוק כל היום כלה לעג לי, Jer 20:7);
- "I am a joke to transgressors" (ואני הייתי נגינה לפשעים, 1QH 10.11)

שמך—"your (God's) name"

- "your name is proclaimed over me" (נקרא שמך עלי, Jer 15:16);
- "blessings on your name forev[er]" (לשמך הברכה לעול[ם], 1QH 4.20);

- "to praise your name with every mouth" (להלל שמכה בפה כול, 1QH 9.30–31);
- "from their assembly I will bless your name" (מקהלם אברכה שמכה, 1QH 10.30; cf. 19.6, 25)

תהלה—"praise"

- "you (God) are my praise" (תהלתי אתה, Jer 17:14);
- "you put thanksgiving in my mouth and praise on my tongue" (תתן בפי הודות ובלשוני תהלה, 1QH 19.5; cf. "flute of praise," חליל תהלה, 19.23)

Common Idioms

ארך אפך—"indulging your anger"

- "indulging your anger, do not take me away" (אל לארך אפך תקחני, Jer 15:15);
- "[indulgence of] your anger" ([אורך] אפך, 1QH 5.5)

חרפה וקלס—"reproach and scorn"

- "Yahweh's word is a reproach and scorn for me every day" (דבר יהוה לי לחרפה ולקרס כול היום, Jer 20:8);
- "you have set me up as a reproach and scorn for traitors" (ותשימני חרפה וקלס לבוגדים, 1QH 10.9–10; cf. "contempt and reproach," בוז וחרפה, 10.34)

לי לששון ולשמחה—"joy and gladness for me"

- "your word is joy and gladness for me" (דברך לי לששון ולשמחה, Jer 15:16);
- "your reprimand is gladness and joy for me" (תוכחתכה לי לשמחה וששון, 1QH 17.24)

כאש בערת עצר בעצמתי—"like a burning fire locked in my bones" (Jer 20:9; 1QH 16.30)

יום/קץ/עת "(final) day/end/time"[56]

- "consecrate them for the day of slaughter" (ליום הרגה הקדשם, Jer 12:3 // 1QH 7.20);
- "you are my refuge on the day of evil" (מחסי אתה ביום רעה, Jer 17:17; cf. 16:18);
- "I have not craved the day of despair" (יום אנוש לא התאויתי, Jer 16:16);

---

56. Moore, "Day," 193–208.

- "the sword of God will strike quickly at the time of judgment" (תחיש חרב אל בקץ משפט, 1QH 14.29; cf. "time of your judgments," קץ משפטיכה, 6.4);
- "the time of wrath for every Belial" (קץ חרון כול בליעל, 1QH 11.28; cf. "deal with them at the time of your anger," בעת אפך עשה בהם, Jer 18:23);
- "you hide your laws in [me un]til the time of the revealing of your salvation" (ותורתכה חבתה ב]י ע[ד קץ הגלות ישעכה, 1QH 13.11–12);
- "in the time of your glory they will rejoice" (בקץ כבודכה יגילו, 1QH 20.22)

PROMINENT METAPHOR NETWORKS

Although JL and 1QH hold a number of metaphors in common, they appear to cluster in four networks—"planting," "refuge," "communication," and "lawcourt." Each network comes with (a) its own "system of associated commonplaces," and (b) it own mixture of positive/negative construals:

"Planting"

- "water" (≠ "dry up," deceitful brook");
- "take root" (≠ "land mourns");
- "tree";
- "fruit"/"food";
- "remnant"

Within the "system of commonplaces" associated with the metaphor of "planting," both JL and 1QH manipulate a rich network of motifs. Where Jeremiah challenges Yahweh for "planting" (נטע) the wicked, giving them strong "roots" (שרש), and allowing them to produce "fruit" (פרי), 1QH expands and transforms this metaphor considerably. In 1QH, however, it is not the wicked whom God "plants" and roots," but the "righteous"; i.e., those faithful sectarians who

> sprout like a flower of the field forever / to make a "shoot" (נצר)[57] grow in the branches of the "everlasting plantation" (מטעת עולם) / so that it covers all the wo[rld] with its shade / [and] its [crown] (reaches) up to the skies[58] / [and] its "roots" (שרשיו) down to the

---

[57]. Messianic language about the "shoot" (נצר) protruding from "Jesse's stump" (Isa 11:1) is one of the most significant apocalyptic metaphors in the Qumran literature (Collins, *Scepter*, 49–73).

[58]. The "tree of life" metaphor is quite ancient (Giovino, *Tree*, 1–8).

"abyss" (תהום) / All the rivers of Eden [will irrigate its b]ranches / over fathomless [seas].[59]

Alongside these positive construals about "fertility" and "growth," these texts show no hesitation in examining the other side of the spectrum; i.e., the realm of spiritual "dryness" and "desert." Jeremiah, for example, metaphoricalizes this dryness when he speaks of the land as "mourning" (אבל),[60] the grass of every field having completely "dried up" (יבש).[61] The *Hodayot* poet identifies himself as a fountain of water spewing over a "dry" land (יבשה), a hydromantic spring eternally irrigating a "parched land" (בארץ ציה).[62] Where Jeremiah accuses the deity of being a "deceitful brook" (מים אכזב),[63] the *Hodayot* poet depicts himself as a man whose heart "turns to water" and knees to "water (flowing down) a mountain slope."[64]

"Refuge"

- "save" (≠ "terror," "seek a soul," "scheme");
- "heal (≠ "incurable");
- "empower" (≠ "stumble," "be caught," "trap," "snare," "pit");
- (God's) "face" (≠ "turn away," "divine anger");
- "bird";
- "time of God's glory" (≠ "day of judgment," "time of wrath," etc.)

The metaphor of "refuge," like that of "planting," boasts a similar "system of associated commonplaces," both positively and negatively construed. Predominant within this network stands the motif of "salvation" alongside its negative counterpart, "terror."[65] Where Jeremiah pleads with God—"Save me and I shall be saved!"[66]—the poet of *Hodayot* praises God for "saving" him from the "zeal of the mediators of deceit," thereby "redeeming my soul

---

59. 1QH 14.15–17.
60. Jer 12:2.
61. Jer 12:4.
62. 1QH 16.4.
63. Jer 15:18.
64. 1QH 10.28; 12.34. Sharp (*Irony*, 38) traces the "apex" of this metaphorical trajectory to the Garden of Eden tradition.
65. Creach engages parallels in the Psalter (*Refuge*, 1–21) and I engage parallels in and around the book of Job ("Terror," 662–75).
66. Jer 17:14.

from the pit."⁶⁷ Rarely in 1QH will the poet ask for "salvation" (ישע) or "redemption" (פדה) or "help" (עזר). More often than not he simply acknowledges these gifts as gratefully received. In no way, however, does this imply that JL and 1QH present fundamentally different portrayals of God. Where Jeremiah plaintively begs, "Do not become a 'terror' (מחתה) to me,"⁶⁸ the *Hodayot* poet also describes himself as someone quite "terrified" of God's "just judgments."⁶⁹

One of the major polarities within the "refuge" network focuses on "healing"-vs.-"disease." In JL, Jeremiah begs God to "heal me" (רפאני),⁷⁰ even as he acknowledges the "pain" (כאב) in his heart to be profoundly "incurable" (אנושה).⁷¹ In *Hodayot*, however, the poet praises God for turning "my affliction" (נגיעי) into "et[ernal] healing" (מרפא ע[ולם),⁷² even as he twice speaks, using Jeremiah's exact words, of "incurable pain" (כאיב אנוש).⁷³ Indeed, when it comes to pain, few are as methodical as the *Hodayot* poet:

> My disease increases in bitterness / in incurable pain which never stops / (rushing) over me like creatures clamoring for Sheol / for my spirit hides with the dead / and my life sinks into the pit / my restless soul languishes day and night / like a fire burning deep within my bones.⁷⁴

The twist, of course, is that where Jeremiah blames God for his pain, the *Hodayot* poet imagines the source of his pain to be spewing from the "council of Belial."⁷⁵

Another polarity in the "refuge" network focuses on the wide gap between "empowerment" and "entrapment." *Hodayot*, again, is careful not to accuse the deity of anything infelicitous or "inappropriate," but apparently not so the prophet from Anathoth. Where Jeremiah complains that God "overpowers" him (חזק),⁷⁶ the *Hodayot* poet rejoices that "my spirit stands 'empowered'" (החזיקה) . . . before 'affliction' (נגע),"⁷⁷ thankful to be serving a

---

67. 1QH 10.31; 11.19.
68. Jer 17:17.
69. 1QH 9.23 (נבעתה משפטי צדק).
70. Jer 17:14.
71. Jer 15:18. See Moore, "Incurable," 313–24.
72. 1QH 17.24–25.
73. 1QH 13.28; 16.28.
74. 1QH 16.27–30.
75. 1QH 13.26.
76. Jer 20:8.
77. 1QH 12.36.

God genuinely interested in "freeing the soul of the poor . . . 'from the hand of those more powerful than him.'"[78] Where Jeremiah asks God to make his enemies "stumble,"[79] the *Hodayot* poet similarly asks that his enemies be tripped up, wishing the deity to do it by using their own sins against them.[80] Where Jeremiah laments how his enemies constantly "lay snares for my feet,"[81] the 1QH poet despairs of the "snares of corruption"[82] persistently laid out by his enemies to "trap my fo[ot] in the snare."[83]

Underneath all of this lies the ubiquitous motif of "the pit." Where Jeremiah fears his enemies may succeed in casting his "soul" (נפש) into "the pit" (שוחה),[84] the *Hodayot* poet uses the same two terms to thank God for "protecting me from all the traps of the pit,"[85] especially those laid out by "the vicious men who seek my soul."[86] Hammering the point home, he visualizes for his readers all the possibilities—the "shafts of the pit,"[87] "doors of the pit,"[88] and even the "cervix of the pit"[89]—to head off any temptation toward hyper-abstraction. Where Jeremiah reminds God of the "pits" and "traps" of his enemies,[90] the *Hodayot* poet turns the metaphor on its head, depicting the deity as the "divine fowler." Watching his enemies closely, he sees growing

> in their thoughts a "root" (שורש) of poison and wormwood. / With stubborn hearts they inquire. / They look for you (God) among the idols, / place in front of themselves the "stumbling-block" of their offenses. / They look for you in the mouths of lying preachers attracted to delusion. / They speak to the people with stuttering lip and strange tongue to convert (via cheap tricks) all their deeds to folly. / For they have not chosen the path of your heart, / nor have they listened to your word. They

78. 1QH 10.35 (מיד חזק ממנו). Tigchelaar ("Addressees," 69–71) outlines and discusses the "poverty" motif permeating some of the sapiential literature at Qumran.

79. Jer 18:23; 20:11 (כשל in each passage).

80. 1QH 12.15. In an interesting twist, however, the poet also asks God to keep his servant from "stumbling" over "the precepts of your covenant" (1QH 8.23).

81. Jer 18:22 (פחים).

82. 1QH 11.26 (פחי שחת).

83. 1QH 16.34 (רג[לי נלכדה בכבל).

84. Jer 18:20 (which of course they literally do in 38:6).

85. 1QH 10.21 (תשוך בעדי מכול מוקשי שחת).

86. 1QH 10.21 (עריצים בקשו נפשי).

87. 1QH 11.16 (חצי שחת).

88. 1QH 11.18 (דלתי שחת).

89. 1QH 11.12 (משברי שחת).

90. Jer 18:22.

say of the vision of knowledge, "It's uncertain," / and with regard to the path of your heart, "That's not it." / But you, O God, will answer them, powerfully judging them / according to their idols and numerous sins, / so that those who deviate from your covenant / might be "trapped by their own schemes."[91]

In other words, 1QH apocalypticizes JL's "refuge" metaphor-network by transforming Jeremiah's "day"-oracles[92] into the negative construals of "judgment" and "wrath" alongside the positive construals of "salvation" and "glory."[93]

"Communication"

- "lip(s)" ("circumcised" ≠ "uncircumcised");
- "speaking" (≠ "burning fire locked in my bones");
- "voice" (≠ "voice of adversaries");
- "reveal" (≠ "mock");
- "persuade" (≠ "laughingstock," "shame");
- (found) "words" (≠ departing "word");
- "mourn"

Both poets seem highly conscious of their roles as "communicators." Jeremiah's use of the phrase "outcry of my lip,"[94] e.g., finds practically verbatim echoes in the phrase "outcry of our lips" in an older *Hodayot* fragment from Cave 4.[95] Both poets hold to a strong doctrine of "revelation" (גלה), though 1QH focuses on divine revelation and Jeremiah on human revelation.[96] Both lament the negative side of "revelation" as well, i.e., "mockery." Where Jeremiah complains that "everyone mocks me,"[97] the *Hodayot* poet rests in the fact that God helps him stand up against "everyone who mocks

---

91. 1QH 12.14–19 (יתפשׂו במחשבותם).
92. Jer 12:2; 17:16–18. See Moore, "Day," 193–208.
93. 1QH 6.4; 11.28; 13.11–12; 14.29.
94. Jer 17:16 (מוצא שׂפתי).
95. 4Q427 frag. 7, 2.22 (מוצא שׂפתינו).
96. 1QH 5.9; 9.21; 14.4; 19.17; 20.34; Jer 11:20.
97. Jer 20:7 (כלה לעג לי).

me."⁹⁸ Like Saul of Tarsus, the *Hodayot* poet applies the "circumcision-vs.-uncircumcision" polarity to the lips as well as the heart.⁹⁹

"Persuasion" is a key idea in this network, yet where Jeremiah complains about God's brand of "persuasion"/"deception" (פתה, Jer 20:7), the *Hodayot* poet never uses this verb to describe the deity. Instead, he reserves it for "the followers of my testimony" and "the men of the covenant."¹⁰⁰ Since *Hodayot*, as a general rule, *never* criticizes or challenges the deity's motives, this adds significant intertextual weight to the translation of פתה in Jer 20:7 as "deceive" instead of "persuade."¹⁰¹

One of the most characteristic idiomatic parallels linking these poems is the "fire in my bones" metaphor, repeated in Jer 20:9 and 1QH 16.30. Both poets use this idiom to describe pain, but where Jeremiah uses it to describe the personal anguish descending upon him whenever he stops preaching the דבר־יהוה,¹⁰² the *Hodayot* poet uses it to describe the "disease" inside his heart whether he decides to preach or not, concluding in the process that "refuge" in his case lies outside the realm of possibility.¹⁰³ Why? Because true "refuge" cannot be found in this life; i.e., in mere "flesh."¹⁰⁴ Several negative construals reinforce this sense of existential abandonment which, while less pain-filled than JL, still pulsates with pathos.

"Lawcourt"

- (eternal) "council" (≠ "intrigues of Belial," "council of futility," "council of hypocrites," "council of deceit," "council of violence");

---

98. 1QH 12.22 (כול בוז).

99. See 1QH 10:7 (עורול); 19.5 (מול); and Col 2:11 ("in the circumcision of Christ," ἐν τῇ περιτομῇ τοῦ Χριστοῦ). "The removal of the foreskin would imply the proper functioning of the penis, its designated function for fertility. In the same regard, by using the metaphor 'uncircumcised' for other parts of the body, such as the heart (Jer 9:25; Deut 10:16), the lips (Exod 6:12, 30), or the ears (Jer 6:10), biblical writers express the notion that these parts of the body do not function as God intends" (Livesey, *Circumcision*, 54). See Moore, "Maccabees," 1056.

100. 1QH 14.19; 22.8 [bottom].

101. *Contra* Clines & Gunn, "Persuade," 20–27.

102. Glazov (*Bridling*, 360) believes that "by witnessing to the grief, sorrow, and acquiescence of the prophet to suffering, and by understanding that he bears the burden on their behalf, the people are induced to turn and acquiesce to their own suffering . . . in the hope that by bridling their own tongues, they may come through to the opening of their mouths in joyful knowledge of Yhwh."

103. 1QH 16.27, אין מעוז לי ("there is no place of refuge for me").

104. 1QH 15.17, ומחסי בשר אין לי ("there are no fleshly defenses for me").

- "lawsuit";
- "judge";
- "test";
- "know";
- "memory";
- "justice"/"righteousness" (≠ "wickedness")

The "lawcourt" network is by far the most porous of the metaphor-networks common to 1QH and JL, perhaps because it focuses so strongly on positive construal. The major exception is the polarity between the "eternal council"/"council of spirits" vs. the "council of deceit"/"violence"/"futility"/ "hypocrisy"/"Belial." Jeremiah laments his decision not to join the "council of merrymakers" in Judah,[105] but this "council" looks tame compared to the numerous "wicked councils" in 1QH. No doubt the *Hodayot* poet's political prejudices come through most visibly here. One can almost see the reddened faces and hear the angry voices behind this negative imagery.

Elsewhere, however, we find all the usual suspects connected to the world of the "lawcourt."[106] Jeremiah attempts to "file a suit" (אָרִיב) against Yahweh even as he pleads with him to champion "my suit" (רִיבִי) against the enemies plotting to kill him.[107] Like Jeremiah, the *Hodayot* poet recognizes himself to be a "man of contention to the mediators of error,"[108] a "sour[ce] of contention,"[109] an outcast who, by the very food he eats, elicits conflict from his neighbors.[110] Both poets see God as a "judge" able to tell the difference between "justice" and "vengeance,"[111] imagining him to be someone who can and will "test" the heart of the "righteous,"[112] especially if it helps them come to "know" God's "kindness," hope," "forgiveness," justice," "truth," "glory," "power," "spirit," and "wondrous mysteries."[113] Responding

---

105. סוד משחקים (Jer 15:17).

106. Brueggemann builds his entire *magnum opus* around the metaphor of the "lawcourt" (*Theology*, xvi).

107. Jer 12:1; 11:20.

108. 1QH 10.14 (איש ריב למליצי תעות).

109. 1QH 13.22 (מ[דני לריב).

110. 1QH 13.35, "(even) my food causes contention" (לחמי לריב).

111. Jer 11:20; 1QH 13.6.

112. Jer 11:20; 12:3; 1QH 10.13; 14.26; 15.9.

113. Jer 11:18, 19; 12:3; 15:15; 17:16; 18:23; 1QH 6.12, 17; 7.15, 25; 9.21; 12.30; 14.6; 17.9; 19.7; 20.11.

to this, Jeremiah begs God to "remember me,"[114] while the *Hodayot* poet waxes philosophical:

> What can I say which is not (already) known? / Or declare which has not been told? / Everything has been engraved before you / with the "stylus of remembrance."[115]

CONCLUSIONS

This analysis leads to the following tentative conclusions. *First*, a new day is dawning in the study of Second Temple Hebrew poetry. All the hard work put in by the text-critics, literary-critics, and metalinguists is starting to "bear fruit," converging together to "put down roots" in a new "field" of inquiry. Today it is possible for us to examine Hebrew metaphor both as "interactive cognition" as well as "literary trope," and because older form-critical approaches do not engage the texts at this level, interpreters must now decide whether or not it should be used as a supplement, substitute, or surrogate to the other literary-historical approaches in their expository "quiver." To be truly holistic, critical interpretation of ancient texts must now attend at some level to the text's "metalinguistic activity."[116]

Second, of the approximately 75 verb parallels between JL and 1QH, 60 fall within Douglas' "Block A" (80%). Of the approximately 64 noun parallels, 52 fall within Douglas' "Block A" (81%). Of the approximately 20 idiomatic parallels, 10 fall within Douglas' "Block A" (50%). In sum, of the approximately 160 *leitwörtliche* parallels between JL and 1QH, approximately 122 fall within Douglas' "Block A" (77%), a percentage which makes it seem highly likely that if the so-called "Teacher Hymns" ("Block A") are in fact the product of a single poetic mind, as Douglas argues, and the correlation between the *Leitwörten* in JL and 1QH is approximately 80% within "Block A," then JL is also likely to be the product of a single poetic mind.

Third, metalinguistic examination of JL and 1QH confirms and expands the pioneering work of Bonnie Pedrotti Kittel.[117] The *Hodayot* poet does not invent an "association of commonplaces" *ex nihilo*, but creatively adapts and modifies and transforms the metaphors of earlier poets like Jeremiah to meet the needs of later readers. Wider study of Second Temple He-

---

114. Jer 15:15 (זכרני).

115. 1QH 9.23–24 (בחרת זכרון). Influenced by ספר זכרון ("scroll of remembrance") in Mal 3:16, Knibb reads "stela of remembrance" (*Qumran*, 164).

116. Eco, *Limits*, 54.

117. Kittel, *Hymns*.

brew poetry shows that 1QH hardly limits itself to the metaphor-networks metalinguistically framing JL.[118] JL simply holds a prominent place in the poet's creative mind. Moreover, the priestly poet of 1QH, unlike Jeremiah, *never* questions the deity's motives, nor does he ever despair as deeply as the prophet from Anathoth. Like other writers of his era,[119] he simply takes earlier material and adapts it to the needs of a very specific context, dynamically engaging his literary heritage to (a) build new defenses against new enemies, (b) protect covenant brothers from the ravages of "defilement," and (c) reconsecrate the Name against Belial and his devotees.

---

118. See Holm-Nielsen (*Hodayot*, 301–15), Elwolde ("Psalter," 79–100), and Tanzer ("*Hodayot*," 255–78).

119. Schniedewind, *Transition*, 11–22.

8

JEHU'S CORONATION AND PURGE OF ISRAEL*

THE JEHU TRADITION IS surprisingly complex.[1] Many read it through a prophetic lens like the one behind which it first comes into canonical focus,[2] viewing Jehu as a divinely anointed king committed to restoring "Yahweh's ... mastery over Ba`al and the political machine promoting Ba`al worship."[3] Others, however, imagine Jehu as a violence-prone freedom fighter committed to the use of terrorism as a weapon whenever he feels it necessary to advance his political ambitions.[4] The decision to assassinate the royal families of both Judah and Israel thus appears, from this perspective, to be considerably less "reformational" than ruthless, less "righteous" than pitiless, and less "faithful" than fanatical. Processing the violence pervading this tradition, many succumb to the temptation to subordinate the text's internal/ideological concerns to an external, hypothetical reconstruction of its political context,[5] even though "no easy separation," in Gottwald's words,

---

* Revised from a paper read to the SBL Hebrew and Cognate Literature section in Denver, CO in November, 2001, subsequently published in *VT* 53 (2003) 97-114.

1. 2 Kings 9:1-10:31.

2. See Noth (*Studien*, 1-110), O'Brien (*History*, 3-23), and Römer (*History*, 13-27).

3. LaSor, *Survey*, 207. To von Rad, Jehu is simply and only a divinely sanctioned purgation tool (*Theology* 2.28-29), like Assyria (Isa 10:5-7) and Babylon (Hab 3:13-16). Similarly, Provan (*Kings*, 209) argues that Jehu's "mission" is to "purge" Israel and "cleanse" Judah of Canaanite Ba`alism.

4. Ahlström, "Jehu," 47-69.

5. See, e.g., Schulte ("Dynasty," 133-48). Seibert's assessment is well-taken: "Since

"can be made between personal ambition and social, political and religious sentiment" when processing all of the factors responsible for "violent changes of regime."[6]

Where some question the motives behind Jehu's violent behavior, others isolate the "standardized language" shaping both the Jehu and the Ahab narratives in Kings, and conclude from this comparison that no historical annal might possibly lie behind this text, though to arrive at such a conclusion one must, again, push aside all interest in internal/ideological matters and focus exclusively on external concerns.[7] Yet even among those who accept the Jehu story in Kings as in some sense "historically accurate,"[8] significant doubt hovers over whether everything this monarch does to stamp out "false religion" enjoys the approval of Yahweh, his patron deity. Hosea's negative assessment, for example, is quite serious,[9] as is the negative appraisal of Dtr himself.[10] Combined, they make it difficult to avoid the conclusion that Tanak tradents are conspicuously ambivalent about Jehu. Reflecting on this ambivalence, many note that while Dtr bestows the same negative reprimand on Jehu as that which he bestows on every other northern king, he also confers upon him some very high praise:

> Yahweh says, "Because you have performed well, doing what is upright in my eyes, dealing with the house of Ahab according to everything in my heart, your sons will sit on the throne of Israel for four generations."[11]

Observing this to be one of "the strongest endorsements given to any northern monarch," Mullen hyperbolically suggests that this praise represents "an

---

many people do not know what to do with violent texts . . ., they often do nothing with them. While this is understandable, it is not terribly helpful . . . . Violent texts must be confronted honestly and directly" (*Violence*, 4).

6. Gottwald, *Politics*, 76.

7. Hoffman, *Reform*, 99–101. Hanson takes a sociological tack, simplistically arguing that Jehu's behavior perverts the whole "Yahwistic notion of community" (*People*, 147), but Robker's dissertation (*Jehu*) is perhaps the most extreme example of privileging hypothetical redactoral focus over substantive analysis.

8. On the basis of his reading of the Tell Dan Inscription (Athas, *Dan*, 193–94), Schniedewind ("Dan," 83–85) sees Hazael as the person responsible for killing Jehoram and Ahaziah (and their families) *through* Jehu, whom he sees as the Syrian king's vassal.

9. "I will 'punish' (פקד) the 'house of Jehu' (בית יהוא) for the blood of Jezreel" (Hos 1:4).

10. "Jehu was not careful to walk after Yahweh's *torah* . . . and did not turn away from the sins of Jeroboam" (2 Kings 10:31). Of all the theories vying for attention, Cross' 2-layered explanation of Kings' pre-exilic/(post)exilic redactoral history remains the least problematic (see "Kings," 274–89).

11. 2 Kings 10:30.

innovation on the concept of eternal dynasty promised to David." Why? Because Kings "utilizes the stories of the actions of Jehu in fulfillment of the prophetic condemnations of the house of Ahab," thereby "providing the basis for a uniquely designed divine assurance of stability for the Jehu dynasty."[12] At first glance this explanation looks attractive,[13] yet upon careful reflection it again becomes clear that to sustain it one must refrain from seriously engaging the ideological conflicts embedded *within* the text in order to focus solely on matters *outside* it.[14]

In short, few analyses of the Hebrew tradition about Jehu adequately address what I believe to be its essential *raison d'être*: viz., to illustrate a prophetic theology of reform able to sustain a Yahwistic minority community constantly, ruthlessly, and precipitously threatened by Canaanite Baʿalists.[15] *Questions:* Why does the Yahwistic prophet Hosea excoriate the Yahwist king Jehu for doing what the Yahwist prophet Elisha commissions him to do; viz., exterminate the house of Omri?[16] Why does Jehu so fer-

---

12. Mullen, "Jehu," 196-98.

13. "Although Mullen's point may be valid, the literary structure and redactional history of the passage is complicated" (Suriano, "Formulaic," 84).

14. Negative appraisals of Jehu are nothing new. Augustine (*C. mend.* 3), e.g., finds him to be a reprehensible character motivated by the "lust of his own domination." In Talmud, Rab. Joshua ben Levi throws Jehu onto something of a moral compost heap populated by six other "idolatrous kings": Jeroboam, Baasha, Ahab, Pekah, Menahem and Hoshea (*b. Git.* 88a). Talmud, however, is ambiguous. Attempting to explain why Jehu, a righteous man, eventually defaults to Jeroboam's bad example (2 Kings 10:31), one rabbi rather feebly suggests that it is because of his boast in 10:18. Even though the biblical narrator clearly defines this boast as a ruse (10:19), Rab. Abaye argues that since "a covenant is cut with the lips" (ברית כרותה לשפתים) it's still binding, ruse or not (*b. Sanh.* 102a). Aquinas, on the other hand (agreeing with Jerome), views Jehu's ruse as serving a "useful" purpose (*Summa Theologica*, Question 111). Rofé views Jehu's ruse as folkloristic and anecdotal (*Stories*, 72-78), but Cogan & Tadmor justifiably dismiss Rofé's critique as "excessive" (*Kings*, 117).

15. Like von Rad (*Theology* 1.21), Noth (*History*, 246-47) tries to explain the tension in the Jehu tradition by anachronistically distinguishing between Jehu's "religious" and "secular" sides; i.e., that as "reformer" Jehu "acts as champion of the unsullied worship of Yahweh," but as a "politician" he is "bound to abandon the political line" of the Omrides (Noth's explanation for Jehu's submission to Assyria). Herrmann sees him as "perverting the power with which he has been entrusted" (*History*, 222). Bright finds him guilty of "unspeakable brutality, beyond excuse from a moral point of view" (*History*, 251). Unwilling to segregate religion from politics, Wesley characterizes Jehu as a man of "mixed character" ("Catholic," 568).

16. Irvine hypothesizes ("Jezreel," 494-503) that Hos 1:4-5 anticipates two imminent disasters: (a) the fall of Jehu's dynasty, and (b) the territorial reduction of Israel to the hill country south of the Jezreel valley, speculating that (a) Hosea believes Jehu's massacre to be the signal *par excellence* of coming divine judgment, and (b) references it to counter the propaganda generated by the court of Jeroboam II. McComiskey, on

vently attack Canaanite Ba`alism only to submit soon afterwards to Assyrian hegemony?[17] Whether this submission is more religious than political is, of course, debatable,[18] yet the famous "kneeling scene" on the Black Obelisk *does* show him bowing down before Assyrian king Shalmeneser III,[19] an image which, to say the least, fits poorly with the quasi-heroic depiction of him in 2 Kings 9–10.[20]

The following essay will read the Hebrew Jehu cycle from a comparative intertextual perspective alongside the Ba`al-Anat myth preserved in the Ugaritic texts from Ras-Shamra.[21] To anticipate my conclusions, I will argue on the basis of this comparison that the story of Jehu's coronation and purge is most likely a multi-leveled *parody* of a well-known mythopoeic tradition indigenous to the religious environment of 1st millenium Canaan (BCE), and further, that the Hebrew satirist's goal is very specific—to narrate an important chapter in Israelite history from a perspective covertly and cleverly designed to ridicule the religious traditions of Israel's neighbors/enemies.

---

the other hand ("Irony," 93–101), resists seeing any connection between Jehu's coup and divine judgment, suggesting that Hos 1:4 expresses only the irony that Jehu both ascends and descends to power via *blood*.

17. While textual evidence is weak for widespread Assyrian hegemony, the Black Obelisk clearly shows "Jehu son of Omri" (*Ia-ú-a mār Ḫu-um-ri*) kneeling and paying homage to Shalmeneser III (see photo in Kuan, "Jehu," 683).

18. Gottwald (*Introduction*, 345), e.g., presumes from the inscription on the Black Obelisk that Jehu "formally acknowledges Assyrian gods," but McCarter ("Omri," 5–7) wonders whether Shalmaneser might be confusing Jehu with Jehoram, provoking Halpern to suggest ("Omri," 81–85) that this confusion might somehow be due to the Assyrians' attempt to decipher an as-yet-undiscovered Hebrew king-list.

19. Weippert convincingly shows that *Ia-ú-a mār Ḫumri* on the Black Obelisk refers, in fact, to Jehu ("Jehu," 113–18).

20. Is Jehu, as Schneider speculates ("Jehu," 100–107), a biological (but objectionable) "son of Omri," and is this what Shalmaneser means when he calls him *mār Ḫumri* ("son of Omri")? Does he, as Schniedewind suggests, partner with Hazael in a Syro-Israelite coalition designed to eliminate Jehoram and Ahaziah from power ("Revolt," 75–90)? Does the Naboth reference in 2 Kings 9 predate the Naboth story in 1 Kings 21, and is the latter preserved to legitimate, in White's words, the "house of Jehu" ("Naboth," 66–76)? Is Jehu's purge of the house of Omri and the house of Ba`al more than just anti-Samaritan polemic, even though, in Garcia-Treto's opinion ("House," 47–65), Dtr only poorly integrates it into DtrH?

21. *CAT* 1.3.1–3.

PARODY AND PROPHECY

The Jehu cycle begins with Elisha and the Syrian king Hazael waiting to see the fulfillment of Yahweh's commission to Elijah.[22] Nudged by Elisha,[23] Hazael successfully drags the Omrides into a costly border war, thereby corroding the anti-Assyrian coalition hitherto binding Israel to Aram.[24] The Arameans wound Jehoram in battle, however, and this forces the Israelite king to retreat to the village of Jezreel to recover. Taking advantage of the lull in battle, Elisha sends a prophetic emissary to Ramoth-Gilead to anoint Jehu, one of Jehoram's military commanders, "king over Israel," a risky move since Jehoram is still very much Israel's king.[25] Paralleling this daring *political* move, the narrator of the Jehu cycle makes an equally daring *literary* move, continuing the satire of the Mt. Carmel narrative,[26] continued on into the farcical story of the blind Arameans,[27] and reformulated in the story of the Samarian siege.[28] In this last pericope, for example, an unnamed official laments to the Israelite king that Samaria is doomed, despondently voicing doubt over whether deliverance might be possible even if the "windows of heaven" were to "open up and pour down salvation."[29] As Robert LaBarbera has shown, this "windows of heaven" epithet appears elsewhere in an Ugaritic text describing the construction of Ba`al's palace where Ba`al argues with his "chief engineer" (Kothar-wa-Ḥasis) over whether to cut a window

---

22. 1 Kings 19:16, ואת יהוא בן נמשי תמשח למלך על ישראל, "You shall anoint Jehu son of Nimshi as king over Israel." Na`aman ("Aramaic," 99–100) dates the Tel Dan inscription very close to the events it describes (830s BCE), accepting the stela author's claim (probably Hazael) that *he* killed the kings of Israel and Judah, concluding that the Jehu cycle in Kings, composed centuries later, is a rather poorly remembered prophetic legend.

23. 2 Kings 8:7–15 (see Ghantous, *Paradigm*).

24. Earlier this coalition succeeds in stopping the Assyrians at Qarqar, where, according to the Kurkh Stele, Shalmeneser III squares off against *a-ḫa-ab-bu* ^{mat}*sir-'i-la-a-a* ("Ahab the Israelite," *KS* III R 8 ii 92; see Kofoed, *Text*, 168).

25. Only four men in Kings are anointed "king over Israel": Solomon, Jehu, Joash, and Jehoahaz. In each case the anointing ritual signals, in the words of Caquot, "national salvation following a crisis that is insurmountable from a human point of view" (cited in Coppens, *Messianisme*, 228).

26. 1 Kings 18:1–40 (Moore, *Faith*, 97–102). Carroll speaks of the "savage irony" and "mocking parody" of Elijah's comments to the Ba`al prophets ("Humour," 177), and Jagersma ("Könige," 674–76) traces this parody down to specific verbal parallels, suggesting, e.g., that ישׁן ("to sleep") in 1 Kings 18:27 parodies Ba`al's "death sleep" at the hands of Mot (*CAT* 1.5.5–6).

27. 2 Kings 6:1–23 (Moore, *Faith*, 317–22).

28. 2 Kings 6:24–7:20 (Moore, *Faith*, 148–52).

29. 2 Kings 7:2, 19 (ארבות בשמים, "windows in the heavens"; cf. Isa 24:18; Mal 3:10).

in the floor of his new palace.³⁰ This is not an isolated parallel, nor is the use of satire surprising. In fact, LaBarbera makes a convincing case for reading the entire siege story—the episode immediately preceding the Jehu cycle—as a "cleverly constructed satire" aimed at "the ruling elite of the day ... whether they come from Samaria or Damascus."³¹

LaBarbera's intertextual sensitivities are well taken, especially his appreciation of the technique literary critics call "satire."³² Among other readers of ancient literature, Tanak students are keenly aware of its power and significance.³³ Gaster, for example, identifies the Hosea scroll as "a sustained satire on pagan seasonal festivals."³⁴ Marcus engages no less than fourteen examples of it in Tanak,³⁵ and Yee shows how it replicates, like a virus, the anatomies of the literary forms it sets out to subvert.³⁶ Thomas Jemielity, however, in a book-length study, goes well beyond the observation of formal characteristics to investigate the ideological reasons why prophets (and prophetic narrators) gravitate to this literary technique.³⁷ Like the Roman satirists Horace and Juvenal, he argues, Tanak tradents recognize in satire the ability to "deny and subvert the acceptable moral form which complacency imposes on human action."³⁸ Challenging the powerbrokers of their day, Hebrew satirists spotlight not only their corrupt behavior, but also the religious rationales they use to justify it. Sometimes these attacks can be rather vulgar (Ezekiel's preoccupation with excrement and genitalia, for example),³⁹ and sometimes they veer uncomfortably close to "controlled rhetorical chaos."⁴⁰ Yet underneath its "generic instability,"⁴¹ satire can incorporate—unlike other literary techniques—an amazingly wide range of "technique, theme and victim."⁴² Just as Aristophanes parodies Herakles' "descent to the

30. *CAT* 1.4.5.58–7.29 (LaBarbera, "Satire," 648).

31. LaBarbera, "Satire," 637. Lasine's attempt ("Jehoram," 27–53) to refute LaBarbera's careful literary analysis inexplicably presumes that the horrid cannibalism depicted in this text somehow predetermines its choice of literary framework.

32. Griffin (*Satire*, 1–5); Bogel (*Satire*, 1–40); Quintero (*Satire*).

33. Weisman, *Satire*, i–xii.

34. Gaster, *Myth* 2.620.

35. Marcus, *Balaam*.

36. Yee, "Parody," 565–86.

37. Jemielity, *Satire*, 21–49.

38. Ibid., 57.

39. Ezek 4:12; 23:20.

40. Jemielity, *Satire*, 61. Guilhamet speaks of "the characteristic dynamic of satire to deform (literary) structures as part of their transformation" (*Satire*, 165).

41. Bruns, "Satire," 129.

42. Jemielity, *Satire*, 23.

netherworld" in his play *Frogs*,⁴³ so the second chapter of Jonah parodies Inanna's "descent to the netherworld."⁴⁴ And even as Juvenal parodies the magico-religious practices of the Egyptians,⁴⁵ so Torah unflinchingly parodies the practices of magico-religious specialists like Balaam ben Beor.⁴⁶ At the core of satirical parody stand two things: (a) "an object of attack" infused by (b) an injection of "wit or humor founded on fantasy or a sense of the ... absurd."⁴⁷

Parodying the "Coronation"

The "coronation" of Jehu is another case in point, and for several reasons. *First*, the presiding liturgist in this episode is not a great prophet (like Samuel) or an anointed high priest (like Zadok)—only a nameless "son of the prophets."⁴⁸ We have no idea who this person is, and that is precisely the point. The intentionality with which the narrator protects the anonymity of this character wonderfully intensifies the surprise which ensues when, contrary to Elisha's instructions, a mini-sermonette pops out of his mouth. Elisha gives him one line—"This is what Yahweh says: 'I anoint you king over Israel'"—but instead of delivering his line and walking offstage, he starts to elaborate, commanding Jehu to "destroy the house of Ahab" and "avenge the blood of my servants the prophets," predicting that "the dogs will devour Jezebel" and the "house of Ahab" will become like "the house

---

43. Aristophanes, *Ran.* 1–673.

44. Jon 2:1–10 (see Adelman, "Jonah," 211–58). Payne ("Jonah," 131–34) views the book of Jonah as a satire on what prophets are *supposed* to do. Instead of interceding for others, Jonah is always "descending"—to Joppa, into the ship, into the depths of the sea—away from the divine presence. Marcus (*Balaam*, 90) lists Jonah as one of four anti-prophetic satires in Tanak, the other three being Balaam and the donkey (Num 22:21–35), the boys vs. the bald prophet (2 Kings 2:23–25), and the lying prophet (1 Kings 13).

45. Juvenal, *Sat.* 5.15 (see Keane, *Satire*, 68–71).

46. Num 22:22–35. Goldziher (*Philologie*, 41–44) compares the משלים in Num 23–24 to a type of Arabic satire called هجاء (*hijâ*), and Rofé (בלעם, 51) calls the "she-ass" pericope a בורלסקה ("burlesque"). Other Tanak examples include Zophar's second speech (Job 20:1–29; see Holbert, "Zophar," 171–79), Isaiah's "dirge" over Babylon (Isa 14:4–23; cf. Yee, "Parody," 573–82; Shipp, *Dirges*, 43–47), and a few of the oracles in the book of Amos—e.g., Amos 4:16–23 (Gese, "Amos," 74–95) and 5:6, 14–15 (Hunter, *Seek*, 70–85).

47. Frye, *Criticism*, 224.

48. 2 Kings 9:1, אחד מבני הנביאים ("one from the sons of the prophets"; see Lewis, "Prophet," 231–34).

of Jeroboam son of Nebat."[49] In other words, he thoroughly defames Ahab's son Jehoram by associating him with one of Israel's most notorious *Unheilsherrscher*.[50] We *could* read these lines as redactoral embellishment from a creative editor,[51] but in light of the parodies immediately preceding this cycle, the more likely possibility is that this sermonette somehow links to the narrator's larger literary strategy.

Second, most kings are commissioned to *build* things (temples, palaces, armies, economies).[52] This king, however, is prophetically commissioned to "destroy," "avenge" and "devour," and the objects of his destruction are not Israel's enemies, but its leaders. Like a surgeon, he slices into the Israelite body politic to remove all the cancer he can find, even to the point of cutting away the pink tissue around the edges. Whether or not (post)moderns can understand it, appreciate it, or approve of it, this text makes it crystal clear that Yahweh commissions Jehu to *exterminate* the house of Omri, not engage it in ecumenical dialogue.[53]

Third, the narrator of Kings takes delight in satirizing the army's reaction to this secret commission. At first the liturgist sent to anoint the new king receives no respect from Jehu or his colleagues. They even call him a משגה ("madman").[54] After Jehu's secret meeting with him, however, they soon realize what has happened and their ridicule turns to terror.[55]

---

49. 2 Kings 9:1–10 very much resembles Ruth 3:9 in that both feature younger characters nervously ignoring their instructors.

50. Jeroboam is "Israel's historiographical counterpart to Naram-Sin in Mesopotamia's *Unheilsherrscher* ('doomed leader') traditions . . . . In both cases the traditions emphasize the ruler's misfortune or condemnation and focuses on a general calamity that overtakes the dynasty and nation, claiming that all is the result of certain religious offenses on the part of the king" (Evans, "Jeroboam," 114, 124).

51. Schniedewind ("History," 656) sees all mention of Jezebel as later editorial insertion because he thinks that "the strict condemnation of Jezebel, the foreign bride of Ahab, fits into an exilic and post-exilic situation in which the marriage to foreign women threatens the ethnic and religious existence of Israel." Such arguments used to be applied to another foreign woman as well—Ruth the Moabite (see Moore, "Ruth," 296).

52. Grieshammer focuses on Egyptian parallels ("Altes," 163–66), but others see parallels in several Near Eastern cultures (see Ward, "Egyptian," 2.406). Heintz shows the centrality of "anointing" to ANE coronation rituals ("Messianic," 52–66).

53. "There is a real violence in satire, at least when it is at its most aggressive" (Rieger, *Tragedy*, 11).

54. 2 Kings 9:11. Prophets often suffer at the hands of others. Hosea laments their marginalization as "fools" (אויל) and "madmen" (משגה, Hos 9:7). Jeremiah indicts two of the exiled "prophets" for lying and committing adultery, charges against which Shemaiah retorts by calling him a "madman" (משגה, Jer 29:26).

55. Fretheim playfully calls this a "rump coronation" (*Kings*, 168).

Parodying the "Purge"

What happens next is literarily fascinating. Ever since the Ugaritic Baʿal cycle came to light in 1930, students have puzzled over Anat's behavior.[56] Seeking to explain her over-the-top brutality, some tie her myth in with the seasonal Canaanite calendar, supposing Anat's "bloodbath" to be a primitive metaphor for the revival of the land's "vegetative spirit."[57] Others hypothesize behind this myth the participation of Anat devotees in various homeopathic rituals for which this text serves as a blueprint—perhaps an acted-out "combat ritual" designed to provoke Baʿal into sending the autumn rains and ending the sterility of summer.[58]

Whatever the possibilities, it's difficult to ignore the obvious intertextual parallels resonating so loudly between this Ugaritic text and various passages in Tanak.[59] Philip Stern, for example, applies Mark Smith's observations about Anat to Ps 23,[60] highlighting common references to "table among enemies," "destruction of house and valley," and "house of the deity." Peter Craigie, moreover, draws several parallels between the Anat myth and the Song of Deborah:[61]

> (1) Deborah, like Anat, is a leader of warriors; (2) Deborah, like Anat, has a male warrior-assistant;[62] (3) Just as Anat holds the title "mistress of dominion" (Ug *b ʿlt drkt*), so Deborah's soul "dominates" (תדרכי) her enemies;[63] (4) Both traditions describe Anat and Deborah as "maidens" (*rḥm*//רחם);[64] and (5) Deborah, like Anat, commands an "army of stars."[65]

---

56. Lloyd, "Anat," 151. Anat's purge of Baʿal's enemies appears in the larger Baʿal cycle and Ugaritologists disagree over how, exactly, to reconstruct the sequence of tablets on which this text is inscribed. Pardee's reconstruction/translation ("Baʿalu," 241–74), e.g., is quite different from Smith's (*UNP* 87–180).

57. See Dussaud (*Ugarit*, 115–16); Virolleaud ("Anat," 150–73); Gray (*Canaan*, 18–72); and de Moor (*Anthology*, 2–19).

58. See older sources cited by Lloyd ("Anat," 156–57), Mettinger (*Riddle*, 15–53), and Riley ("Purification," 252–55).

59. Gray, "Anat," 315–24.

60. Stern ("Bloodbath," 120–24); Smith (*Early*, 64).

61. Judg 5:1–31. Craigie, "Deborah," 174–81.

62. Yaṭpan is to Anat (*CAT* 1.18.4.6) what Barak is to Deborah (Judg 4:6).

63. *CAT* 1.108.7 // Judg 5:21.

64. *CAT* 1.6.2.27 // Judg 5:30.

65. מן שמים נלחמו הכוכבים ("the stars fought from heaven," Judg 5:20). Craigie ("Deborah," 380) argues that the phrase *[rb]b.nskh.kbkbm* ("[show]ers which the stars pour over her" in *CAT* 1.3.2.41 "describes the ablutions of Anat following the bloodbath ... described earlier.... The stars are a part of the retinue of Anat, and after her orgy of

JEHU'S CORONATION AND PURGE OF ISRAEL 131

For Craigie, there is thus no reason to doubt whether Dtr is aware of this Canaanite tradition,[66] whether or not it reflects the existence of an active Anat *cult*.[67]

With regard to literary structure, however, Lloyd suggests that in the Canaanite myth Anat leads two separate battles because at the root of her behavior lies the primordial desire of ancient conquerors to perfect their battlefield victories through appropriate sacrifices to their patron deities. Citing epigraphic and iconographic evidence from Moab, Egypt, and Canaan, Lloyd argues that conquerors cannot in fact declare total victory until or unless they bring their enemies before (a statue of) their patron deity and ceremonially slaughter them. In other words, their task remains unfinished until "the actions of war are carried out within the microcosm of the temple itself."[68]

Assuming Lloyd's understanding to be correct, the question arises as to whether the Anat tradition not only reflects this "doubling" mentality, but whether the Jehu cycle satirizing it does as well. Just as Anat purges both "field and house," so Jehu purges both "field and house." Just as Anat puts on paint to adorn herself, so Jezebel puts on paint to adorn herself. The following chart lists these and other parallels according to *characterization*, *plot*, and *theme*.

INTERTEXTUAL PARALLELS

Characterization

- CAT 1.3.1–3 // 2 Kings 9–10;
- One purging tool: Anat // One purging tool: Jehu;
- Two "enemies": Gapnu & Ugar // Two enemies: Jehoram & Ahaziah;

---

killing, the stars aid her in her ablutions by pouring rain over her."

66. Day (*Yahweh*, 137–39) questions the authenticity of these parallels, and Dempster ("Deborah," 33–53) prefers to imagine the Ba`al-Anat relationship paralleling the Yahweh-Deborah instead of the Deborah-Barak relationship.

67. "There is little or no evidence that Anat was a goddess in Israel" (Smith, *Early*, 103). Pardee (*Anat*, 506) recognizes the "difficulty" of Anat *worship* because this goddess represents "the dangerous side of young females ... who have not (yet) knuckled under ... to society." Few, however, question the existence of an ongoing Anat *tradition*, nor that this tradition continues well into the 1st millennium. Van der Toorn ("Anat-Yahu," 97), e.g., agrees with those who identify the "Queen of Heaven" as Anat in Jer 44:15–30.

68. Lloyd, "Anat," 160.

- Anat kicks "heads" (*riš*) around like footballs // Jehu stacks seventy "heads" (רושים);
- The "bow" (*qšt*): Anat's signature weapon // The "bow" (קשת): Jehu "fills the hand" with it;
- Anat adorns her eyes with *anhb* ("snail dye") // Jezebel adorns her eyes with פוך ("mascara");
- Anat closes "the gates" // Jezebel looks out a "window";
- Anat wears her enemies' "palms" (*kp*) on her belt // Jezebel's corpse's "palms" (כף) are barely visible;
- Anat's "liver," "heart," "knees" and "fingers" participate in her victory // Jezebel's "skull," "feet" and "hands" are her only remains

Plot

- Two battles: one in the field, one in Anat's "house" (*bht*)[69] // Two battles: one in the field, one in Baʿal's "house" (בית);
- Anat "meets" (*qry*) officials before final battle // Jehu "meets" (קרה) officials before final battle;
- Anat meets enemies at "the foot of the rock" (*bšt ǧr*) // Jehu meets Jehoram at "Naboth's field" (חלקת לנבות);
- Anat shoots "old men" (*šbm*) with her "shafts" (*mṭ*) // Jehu shoots an "arrow" (חצי) through Jehoram's heart;
- Anat fights "between two cities" (*bn qrtm*) // Baʿal's temple has within it a "city" (עיר);
- Anat mocks her enemies // Jezebel mocks her enemies;
- Anat plunges her knees into "blood" (*dm*) // Jezebel's "blood" (דם) spatters

Theme

- Purgation // Justice;
- Priestly power // Prophetic covenant;
- "House" // "House";

---

69. According to Gordon (*UT* 19.463), the form is plural, but the meaning singular (i.e., multiple buildings, one "house").

- Celebration of enemies' defeat // Reward for obedience

CHARACTERIZATION

In light of satire's "generic instability,"[70] it's important to remember that no literary comparison can ever be "certain,"[71] especially when informed scholars cannot agree on matters as basic as tablet placement and narrative sequence. To be sure, some of these parallels seem more convincing than others. Still, one of the first and most obvious parallels in these texts is that each of the main characters enacts a "flat" role as a *purgatorial agent*.[72] In the Canaanite tradition Anat purges both valley and town on behalf of Baʻal, her master and lord. In the Hebrew tradition Jehu purges both town and temple on behalf of Yahweh, his master and lord. In the Canaanite myth Anat "raises her voice" against two low-level deities, Gapnu and Ugar, vigorously defending her brother/spouse Baʻal from (potential) attack.[73] In the Hebrew story Jehu does not bother to converse, he simply exterminates the kings of Israel and Judah (Jehoram and Ahaziah), thereby offering the narrator an opportunity to deflate the exaggerated self-image of these minor kings by paralleling them, however subtly, with Canaanite demigods functioning at the "lowest level of the divine assembly."[74]

Further, each *purgatorial agent* focuses on the "perfection" (Lloyd's term) of their respective purges; i.e., each purges something "outside" (field/wilderness) as well as something "inside" (city/temple). In the Canaanite text Anat does this by kicking her enemies' heads like soccer balls and wearing their palms into battle as war-trophies.[75] In the Hebrew text Jehu stacks up his enemies' heads before Samaria's gate, then forces the inhabitants of Jezreel to stare at them while he delivers an impromptu speech.[76] Further,

---

70. Jemielity, *Satire*, 60–61.

71. Stern, "Bloodbath," 124.

72. Jehu is not like, say, Bathsheba, who starts out "flat" in Samuel (Forster, *Novel*, 103), then becomes more "rounded" in Kings (see Ogden-Bellis, *Helpmates*, 149).

73. Smith doubts whether these demigods should be perceived as "enemies" (Q & A at 2001 SBL meeting).

74. *UNP* 83.

75. Aboriginal North American warriors used to wear victims' scalps into battle as war-trophies (Axelrod, *Wars*, 96).

76. 2 Kings 10:6–10. Teichman ("Writers," 338–50) notes how 1930s concentration camp commanders force prisoners to cremate the bodies of fellow prisoners as a psychological ploy to break their spirits, and Whittaker documents how Khmer Rouge soldiers stack victims' skulls in heaps around Cambodia to elicit the same response (*Conflict*, 36).

since myths are intentionally designed to be fluid and repetitious, several of these parallels easily shift back and forth between similarly "flat" characters, whether the parallel focuses on Anat//Jehu or Anat//Jezebel.[77] Just as Anat mocks her enemies, so Jezebel mocks her enemies, calling Jehu "Zimri" (the infamous assassin-king violently killed by Omri).[78] And while we might speculate as to why Anat adorns herself, Jezebel's motives seem rather obvious. Jezebel paints *her* eyes because Anat paints *her* eyes. Jezebel puts on mascara because she wants to imitate the behavior of her divine heroine.[79] Whether this eye adornment is military (warpaint) or cosmetic (mascara) is never stated, of course, but what *is* obvious is how immediately the Hebrew narrator seizes upon it. Apparently his intention is to satirize this Ba'alist queen on as many levels as possible, even down to the details of her personal *toilette*.[80]

The parody continues on into the description of her grisly death. In the Canaanite myth Anat's liver "swells with laughter" when she "washes her hands in warrior-blood, her fingers in soldier gore."[81] In Kings, however, Jezebel's skull no longer laughs, nor do her hands write falsely accusatory letters, nor do her feet walk any longer on ancestral land stolen away from innocent citizens. Just as Anat sheds *her* enemies' blood, so Jehu sheds *his* enemies' blood. Readers even nominally familiar with the Ba'al-Anat cycle will not miss these parallels.

PLOT

Beyond characterization, however, each plotline structures itself around two battles: one in the "field" and one in the "town." In the Canaanite myth, Anat grows "dissatisfied with fighting in the valley," then "takes herself to

---

77. Characterization fluidity is more pronounced in some cultures than others, but as a general rule, all myths are "characterized by an inter-changeability of roles (masks)" designed "to emphasize the mutuality and fluidity of narrative protagonists" (Meletinsky, *Poetics*, 312). Robker's failure (*Jehu*, 66) to recognize this fluidity shows profound ignorance about how ANE myth actually functions in ANE culture.

78. 1 Kings 16:15–20. Like Jehu, Omri is a military commander who seizes the throne to save Israel from the horrors of political chaos (see Moore, *Faith*, 93–97).

79. Alexander similarly emulates his hero Achilles when he kills the king of Gaza by dragging him behind his chariot until he dies, thereby imitating Achilles' postmortem treatment of Hector in the *Iliad* (see Worthington, *Alexander*, 112).

80. *Contra* Holbert ("Keren-Happuch," 24), who thinks she paints her eyes to "woo the maniacal Jehu." Some preachers go wild with this text, vilifying all women who wear eye-makeup as "seductive Jezebels."

81. CAT 1.3.2.34–35. I am more inclined to agree with Smith (*UNP* 108) *contra* Gibson (*CML* 48) that the preposition in *bdm.dmr* means "in," not "of" or "from."

her palace."[82] There she starts rearranging the furniture and slaughtering opponents until becoming "sated with fighting in the house, with battling between the tables."[83] The same plot sequence occurs in the Jehu narrative *in the same order*. Jehu begins his attack in the plain outside Jezreel, then quickly moves the battle inside, exterminating his enemies inside the "house" of Baʿal.[84] Outside, on the plain, he purges Israel's politico-military establishment. Inside, in the Baʿal temple, he purges Israel's religious establishment.

Further, if Kings *is* playing off this well-known myth, this helps explain the flashbacks and other suspense-building features in the Jehu cycle. In the Canaanite text Anat "meets youths" (*wtqry ğlmm*) before going into battle.[85] In Kings, however, Jehu "meets" (קרה) a whole slew of people: "horsemen," "officials," "elders," "guardians," a "palace administrator," the "mayor," and a puritan leader named Jehonadab ben Rechab.[86] In several of these meetings someone asks Jehu, "Is it peace?" and Jehu responds like a "madman" (שגעון),[87] neutralizing each one of the emissaries sent out to reason with him. Finally, after prolonging the suspense to the breaking point, the narrative finally describes the climactic battle. In the Canaanite tradition Anat engages her enemies "at the foot of the rock" (*bšt ğr*).[88] In Kings, however, the parties square off at the moral epicenter of the prophetic tradition—Naboth's vineyard.[89] Intensifying the irony, the narrator inserts an historical flashback at this very point to explain why Jehoram *has* to die at this very spot; i.e., because this is his mother's "killing field."[90] This is brilliant writing, a powerful mixture of irony, satire, history and theology. Just as Anat picks

---

82. *CAT* 1.3.2.19, 18.

83. *CAT* 1.3.2.29–30. Stern views this to be the strongest parallel between Ps 23 and the Anat myth ("Bloodbath," 121).

84. 2 Kings 10:18–28. Earlier Ahab sets up an *altar* to Baʿal within the Samarian *house* of Baʿal (1 Kings 16:32).

85. *CAT* 1.3.2.4.

86. 2 Kings 10:15 (This character also appears in Jer 35:6–16).

87. 2 Kings 9:20. The same root (שגע) appears in the soldiers' description of the prophet sent to anoint Jehu nine verses earlier (2 Kings 9:11). Olyan argues that the question השלום ("Is it peace?"), repeated five times (2 Kings 9:11, 17, 18, 22, 31) signals one of the main themes of the Jehu cycle; viz., Yahweh's desire to restore שלום to Israel by removing the obstructive evil preventing it ("השלום," 652–68).

88. *CAT* 1.3.2.5. In Smith's opinion, "Anat's 'house' here presupposes a fortified temple located on her sanctuary-mountain" (*UNP*, 167).

89. חלקת נבות היזרעלי, "the inherited property of Naboth the Jezreelite" (2 Kings 9:21).

90. See discussion of the Naboth murder and its consequences in Moore, *Faith*, 37–44.

up her "bow," so Jehu "fills his hand" with the "bow."[91] Just as Anat drives out "old men" with her "shafts" (*mṭ*), so Jehu drives out the final Omride king with a "shaft" (חצי) to the heart.[92] How ironic is it that Jehoram not only faces judgment at the site of his mother's most heinous crime, but that this judgment comes handed down in a brilliantly-written parody of his mother's religion.[93]

THEME

Like all ANE myths, the Baʿal-Anat cycle mythopoeically reflects a major political reality central to all ancient societies—*priestly power*.[94] Which priesthood has it? Which priesthood wants it? Which priesthood is willing to do whatever it takes to acquire it? In times of unrest, ritualized purgation is the mother's milk of priestly politics, and may well be the most lethal weapon in a given priesthood's arsenal. One need only look at the bitter rivalries between the priesthoods of Amun and Akhenaton in Egypt,[95] or the priesthoods of Marduk and Nabonidus in Babylon,[96] or even the less-ritualized-but-no-less-vicious intramural conflicts between the "Teacher of Righteousness" at Qumran and the Jerusalem bureaucrat he calls the "Wicked Priest."[97] Not to see the political realities behind this literature is to segregate *story* from *history*,[98] and not only is this unnecessary, it drastically

---

91. This phrase, מלא יד ("fill the hand," 2 Kings 9:24), is a technical idiom for "to ordain" in Tanak texts focused on priestly ordination (Lev 8:33; Judg 17:12; see *HAL* 552–53), and appears in priestly literature as late as the Temple Scroll (11Q19.15.15–16), after which it eventually fades from view, replaced by סמוך, "to ordain" (*b. Sanh.* 13b, 37a).

92. See the essays published in Grabbe, *Ahab*.

93. The Jehu cycle concludes with a parody of the feast following Jezebel's death. In the Canaanite cycle Baʿal entertains his guests with "a thousand pitchers of wine" (*CAT* 1.3.1.15), but no such excess occurs in Kings. In fact, just the opposite: Jehu teams up with Jehonadab ben Rechab, an individual known for his asceticism (2 Kings 9:34–10:17; Jer 35:1–11).

94. See Renger ("Priestertum"), Himmelfarb (*Priests*), Berman (*Equal*), Horster & Klöckner (*Priests*), Cross ("Priestly"), and Moore ("Priesthood").

95. Murnane, *Amarna*, 31.

96. Tadmor, "Inscriptions," 351–64.

97. 1QpHab 1.13. See VanderKam ("Maccabees," 52–74) and Schiffman ("Origin," 37–48).

98. From Barstad's perspective, the rationale behind this segregationism is not unclear: "The whole question of history, historicity, historical consciousness, historical understanding, historicism and historiography has been radicalized through the work of so-called 'post-modern' theorists" (*History*, 3).

impoverishes our understanding of these texts and these institutions. As Eckhart Otto observes, "the mythical world of the gods is not a peaceful place"[99]—and this, in my opinion, is largely because the priesthoods responsible for creating this religious literature are so brutally violent.[100]

Whether or not the narrator of Kings fully understands the depth of this political reality, the *priestly purgation* theme in the Anat myth loudly resonates in Kings alongside the Dtr theme of *prophetic justice*. Yahweh establishes the contours of this justice at Sinai and Dtr fully exploits it in, for example, the temple dedication speech of Solomon as well as Kings' final programmatic diatribe.[101] When Jezebel murders Naboth and seizes his inheritance she brazenly challenges the covenantal system of justice established by his Hebrew ancestors. So, whatever else this text may be saying, it takes great care to underline the fact that murder and theft are international—not just Hebrew—crimes, and further, that any deity worth its salt is going to outlaw them.[102] Whether Jehu goes too far in administering this law is another, more difficult question. Even the prophets cannot agree on how to answer it. But that *some* kind of justice has to be meted out is non-negotiable. Otherwise Israel's deity is little more than a pious fraud.[103]

Further, each tradition focuses on its respective fundamentals. From the Canaanite perspective the Ba`al-Anat cycle, in Otto's words, "binds together two originally independent myths about the king-god Ba`al's struggle against Chaos by means of a common skeletal theme focused on the construction of Ba`al's palace."[104] From the Hebrew perspective, however, behavior like that of Anat/Jezebel attempts to plunge a dagger into the very heart of Yahwism. *Question*: Where is prophetic justice even *articulated* in the Canaanite religious texts, much less championed? If the parody hypothesis is correct, or even plausible, does it not follow that Dtr parodies his enemies' traditions as harshly as he does because he wants his audience to (a) remember their history (even its goriest chapters), and (b) learn how to distinguish the differences between the context driving Anat's violence vs. the context driving Jehu's violence?

99. Otto, *Krieg*, 14 ("Die mythische Welt der Götter is keine friedvolle").
100. On this all-too-human scribal proclivity see Moore, *WealthWatch*, 26–29.
101. 1 Kings 8:14–53; 2 Kings 17:7–40 (see Moore, *Faith*, 233–37, 290–94).
102. Greengus, "Law," 242–52.
103. This, of course, is how some contemporary interpreters portray Yahweh. E.g., "Yahweh is not a narcissist because he is absolute and self-sufficient; he is a narcissist because he is *not* self-sufficient" (Lasine, *Kings*, 261).
104. Otto, *Krieg*, 14. Virolleaud ("Déesse," 85–102) hypothesizes that the person serving Ba`al in *CAT* 1.3.1 is Mot and that the victims punished by Anat in *CAT* 1.3.2 are Mot's followers, presumably for rebellious disobedience.

Context is never so critical than when interpreting violence.[105] Where Ba'al wants to build a "house" for himself, Yahweh also wants to build a "house"—only Yahweh's house is overtly a place of covenant justice where widows and prostitutes and mothers and lepers and slave girls and returning exiles can experience *real* צדקה and *authentic* שלום.[106] Characters like these are conspicuously missing from the Ugaritic tablets, and Dtr wants his readers to investigate why. By parodying the characters in this Canaanite religious tradition, his intention is to grab the attention of his audience long enough to teach them how to distinguish between competing religious ideologies.

The problem for many (post)modern readers of these stories is either (a) total indifference to matters of literary-historical context, or worse (b) the unconscious decision to impose upon them a foreign, anachronistic context. Jehu commits horrible acts of violence, yes, *but so does Anat*. Simply to blanch at the violence itself does little to enable holistic, rational, balanced interpretation of this or any other ancient text. Should not the behavior of each character be interpreted in its literary-historical context first, *before* trying to make application to a (post)modern, contemporary context? Interpreters unwilling to do this—i.e., take the exegetical task seriously—are never going to understand how, as Jemielity puts it, prophetic parody can be a "savage, unsettling laughter that God and his prophets enjoy" at the expense of their enemies.[107] Whether or not the Jehu cycle is satirical, or whether this or that definition of satire is universally acceptable, *some* explanation of these literary features is preferable to *no* explanation.[108]

Finally, both traditions epitomize their main themes through poetic summaries designed to highlight their respective ideologies. In the Ba'al

---

105. Seibert recognizes the pervasiveness of what he calls "virtuous" violence in Tanak, but then argues forcefully for applying nonviolent reading strategies to these texts (*Violence*, 147–58).

106. 2 Sam 7:11. The polysemantic properties of בית are well known (see Hoffner, "בית," 107–16).

107. Jemielity, *Satire*, 14. Chesterton (*Heretics*, 126) sees three types of parody: (a) parody where the satirist enjoys himself via an "overwhelming and aggressive happiness in his assertion of anger," using language "which is voluble, which is violent, which is indecent, but is not malicious"; (b) parody which is designed to right a wrong, where the satirist is "maddened by the sense of men being maddened"; and (c) parody in which the satirist is "enabled to rise superior to his victim in the only serious sense which superiority can bear, in that of pitying the sinner and respecting the man even while he satirizes both." The Jehu tradition appears to embody all three types of parody, with perhaps the greatest emphasis on (a). This is a very violent text.

108. Jemielity, *Satire*, 12–17 (responding to Carroll, "Humour"). Rolf Knierim, a Nazi death-camp survivor, sums up: "The Old Testament does not call (unjust violence and) violence considered to be just by the same names" (*Theology*, 119).

cycle a newly-coiffed Anat picks up her harp and sings of her devotion to Ba'al through songs highlighting two traditional concerns: (a) the need to preserve Ba'al's family, and (b) the need to eliminate Ba'al's enemies:

> She sings the love of Mightiest Ba'al / the passion of Pidray, daughter of light / the desire of Tallay, daughter of showers / the love of Arṣay, daughter of the wide world. / What enemy rises against Ba'al? / What foe against the cloudrider? / Surely I fought Yam, the Beloved of El / Surely I finished off River, the Great God / Surely I bound Tunnan and destroyed (?) him / I fought the Twisty Serpent / the Potentate with seven heads.[109]

By contrast, the prophetic oracles in Kings focus on (a) Yahweh's determination to keep his promise, and (b) Yahweh's intention to reward Jehu for his obedience:

> Yesterday I saw the blood of Naboth and the blood of his sons, declares Yahweh, and I will surely make you pay for it on this plot of ground, says Yahweh[110].... Because you (Jehu) have done well in accomplishing what is right in my eyes and have done to the house of Ahab all I had in mind to do, your descendants will sit on the throne of Israel to the fourth generation.[111]

SUMMARY AND CONCLUSIONS

In short, comparative intertextual analysis shows that the Jehu cycle is a rather sophisticated parody of a well-known Canaanite myth, the product of a skilled satirist seeking to promote a prophetic theological programme in the midst of a hostile pagan environment. Like the episodes preceding it, this one tells the story of Israel's history not as dry chronicle, but as biting satire aimed squarely at the religious traditions of Israel's enemies. As Gale Yee points out, only two things are necessary for this or any other parody to work: (a) the literature being parodied has to be at least nominally recognizable, and (b) a majority of readers must be able to "make the connections" and "get the joke."[112] Assuming her definition to be on-target, the story of Jehu's coronation and purge may well be one of the most sophisticated "jokes" in the entire Bible.

109. *CAT* 1.3.3.4–8, 38–42.
110. 2 Kings 9:26.
111. 2 Kings 10:30.
112. Yee, "Anatomy," 567.

9

BIG DREAMS AND BROKEN PROMISES

Solomon's Treaty with Hiram*

SEVERAL YEARS AGO AT an SBL meeting in Boston, Prof. Frank Cross read a paper entitled "Reuben, Firstborn of Jacob."[1] Afterward, in the question-answer period, Prof. Gösta Ahlström asked Prof. Cross, in a voice loud enough for everyone to hear, why he continued to labor under "antiquated" notions like "tribal league" and "premonarchic covenant" in his understanding of Syro-Palestinian history. To this not-so-subtle reprimand Cross responded by politely asking his inquisitor why *he* considered every type of evidence "historical" *except* the biblical evidence. Eleven years later Cross fleshed out this response in an essay entitled "Kinship and Covenant in Ancient Israel"[2] in which he summarily rejects (a) the view of Lothar Perlitt that the term ברית ("covenant/ treaty") *must* be a late idea originating in the minds of Hebrew exiles, and (b) that ברית cannot refer to anything "legal," only the "natural obligation" of "inferiors" to "superiors."[3] Instead, Cross insists,

---

* Revised from an essay first read to the SBL Biblical Law section on Nov 24, 2003 in Atlanta, GA, subsequently published in *BuBR* 14 (2004) 205–21.

1. Later published in Cross, "Reuben," 53–70.
2. Cross, "Covenant," 3–22.
3. Barr's critique of the Wellhausenian revisionism championed by Perlitt

"covenant" is a very *old* idea deeply rooted in the sociological fabric of ANE kinship networks. Marshaling a wealth of onomastic, philological, anthropological, and textual evidence, he shows that ANE covenants and treaties hardly depend on the desperate fantasies of imaginative Persian exiles, nor the romantic individualism of European Protestants. Alongside his understanding of Yahweh as Divine Warrior,[4] he thus posits another role enacted by Israel's deity—Divine Kinsman.[5] Simply put,

> the notion of a ברית in the era of early Israel without the mutual bonds of kinship-in-law between Yahweh and Israel, and between the tribes of the league, is not merely unlikely; it runs counter to all we have learned of such societies.[6]

Anticipating resistance to this conclusion, Cross boldly demands from his critics why so many of them continue to marginalize, ignore, and/or misinterpret the ANE evidence. *Answer:* "In the face of new knowledge from the ANE, the history of religion and law, and advances in social anthropology," the persistence of this mentality stands as "testimony not to the soundness of the Wellhausenist synthesis, but to the power and perversity of Paulinist and anti-Judaic dogma, or, in other words, to the survival of stubbornly, often unconsciously held traditions of Christian apologetics in biblical scholarship."[7]

Whether such accusations are plausible or appropriate is not the concern of this essay. We simply rehearse them here to show how volatile contemporary opinion remains about "covenant" and "treaty." Students like Raymond Cohen and Carlo Zaccagnini are independently fleshing out the anthropological implications of this debate,[8] but the goal here is much more modest. The purpose of this essay is to investigate the character and function of the covenant/treaty semantic field encapsulating the Solomon-Hiram encounter in Kings,[9] particularly as this field operates within the Amarna correspondence.[10] *Questions:* (a) How do the *Leitwörte* associated with international treaty-making function in the Amarna correspondence?

(*Bundestheologie*) and Kutsch (*Verheissung*) is well taken: "With all the will in the world it is a little hard to believe that the covenant of Yahweh with Israel becomes significant only so late" ("Covenant," 37–38).

4. Cross, "Warrior," 91–111.
5. Cross, *Canon*, 6.
6. Cross, *Canon*, 17.
7. Ibid., 16.
8. Cohen ("Diplomacy," 11–28); Zaccagnini (*Scambo*, 108–17).
9. 1 Kings 5:15–32 (ET 5:1–18). See Whitelam, "Hiram," 203–4.
10. Na`aman, "Amarna," 171–84.

(b) How might a study of these *Leitwörte* illuminate the character and contours of the ברית between Tyre and Jerusalem?[11]

The limitations of this study are several: (a) I am not a seasoned cuneiformist; (b) I have not examined the tablets themselves; and (c) I have not consulted the work of every specialist on every Amarna text, only the studies of Cord Kühne, Nadav Na'aman, Ronald Youngblood, Jean Bottéro, Richard Hess, and Anson Rainey (among several others).[12] Like most studies of the Amarna texts, this one relies on the transliterations and translations of Knudtzon and Moran (whose translations, of course, thoroughly engage many of the studies just mentioned). The engine driving this study is an increasing frustration with all the old arguments claiming the ability, on the basis of alleged "stock phrases" and "stock vocabulary," to chart the origin and development of sociopolitical institutions like "treaties" with any sort of intellectual precision.[13] Many remain divided over whether the Hebrew term ברית refers to a preexilic idea *rooted* in Israel's past or a postexilic idea *reformulating* Israel's past (as if these two options are mutually exclusive). Yet among the wealth of evidence now at our disposal, the Amarna texts alone make it clear that the *language* of the ברית-treaty between Hiram and Solomon clearly stands within a definable network of *Leitwörter* animating an identifiable semantic grid.[14] William Moran refers to this grid as "the terminology of international relations" possessing its own "juridical vocabulary."[15] Saul Olyan refers to it as "the technical rhetoric of covenanting."[16] Michael Barré more broadly calls it a "literary genre,"[17] while Dennis McCarthy refers to it more specifically as "the treaty genre."[18] Raymond Westbrook argues for a multiplicity of interconnections between the individual components of this grid and the political realities to which they refer,[19] even though William Murnane questions the existence of actual

---

11. ויהי שלום בין חירם ובין שלמה ויכרתו ברית שניהם ("And there was peace between Hiram and Solomon, and the two of them cut a covenant" (1 Kings 5:24 [ET 5:12]).

12. Kühne (*Amarna*); Na'aman ("Amarna"); Youngblood ("Amarna"); Bottéro (*Ḫabiru*); Hess (*Amarna*); Rainey (*Amarna*); Moran (*Amarna*). I have not mastered Rainey's 4-volume *Canaanite in the Amarna Tablets*.

13. E.g., Kutsch (*Verheissung*); Perlitt (*Bundestheologie*); see discussion in Barr, "Covenant," 23-38.

14. Fensham, "Alalakh," 59-60; and "Tyrians," 71-87; Priest, "Brothers," 400-406.

15. Moran, *Amarna*, xxiv and "Love," 80.

16. Olyan, "Honor," 202.

17. Barré, "Treaties," 656. Newsom ("Polyphonic," 11-15) offers a prescient discussion of "genre" and "genre criticism."

18. McCarthy, *Treaty*, x.

19. Westbrook, "Amarna," 38.

treaties behind this language, particularly in the vassal correspondence.[20] A few see this language to be rather "artificial" because, as Samuel Meier recognizes, "brothers who constantly must be reminded that they are brothers are not good brothers."[21]

Yet however defined, most informed readers recognize there to be an identifiable semantic field orbiting around the concept of treaty-making in the ANE, and further, that its various components are well-documented at sites like Ebla, Boğazköy, Mari, Alalakh, Sefîre, Nineveh, Ugarit, and Amarna. A sampling of these *Leitwörter* from Amarna includes at least the following terms:

- *adê* → *a-di-e . . . tu-še-pi-šu-šú-nu-tu*, "You made them . . . take the loyalty oath (*ABL* 539.21);[22]

- *aḫḫûtu* → [*i-na*] *šarrani aḫ-ḫu-tum ṭa-bu-tum ša-li-mu ù a-ma-tum* [*ba-ni-tum*], "Among the kings are brotherhood, goodwill, peace, and [good] relations" (EA 11.22'; cf. also EA 4.15, 17); [*aḫi-ia*]*el a-bi-šu ra-'a-mu-ta*[*ù*] *a*[*ḫu-u*]*t-ta 10-šu li-te-it-te-ir-an-ni*, "May [my brother] treat me with ten times greater love and brotherliness than his father did" (EA 29.166);

- *aḫu* → *na*[*p-*]*ḫu-u-ri-*[*i*]*a-ma aḫi-ia i-na libbi*^{bi}*-ni ša nira-'a-a-mu* [*am-mi-tum i-na-an-na e*]*l ni-im-mu-*[*u-*]*ri-ia a-bi-i-šu* [*1*]*o-šu*, "Napḫureya is my brother. That we love, that is in our hearts. It is going to be ten times greater than what there was with Nimureya, his father" (EA 29.65–67);

- *ardu* → *be-lí i-na aš-ri an-ni-im a-na-ku šu-ú-tú* ^{amêlu}*arduka*, "My lord, I am your servant in this place" (EA 55.4–5);

- *ardûtu* → *ù e-pu-uš ardu-da a-na šarri bêli-ka ù bal-ṭa-da*, "So perform service for your lord the king and you will live" (EA 162.39);

- *atterūtu* → *ma-ni-e amêl šipri-šu ša aḫi-ia it-ta-*[*l*]*a-ka a-*[*n*]*a at-te-ru-ti a-na-aššati-šu ša aḫi-ia*, "in view of 'friendly relations,'[23] Mane, my brother's messenger, came to take my brother's wife" (EA 20.8–9); [*i*]*-na bi-r*[*i-*]*ni at-te-ru-ut-*[*t*]*a ni-ip-pu-*[*u*]*š-mi*, "let us make friendly relations with each other" (EA 41.9); *undu abuka u anāku atterūta ni-pu-šu u ana aḫḫē ṭābūti nitūru*, "when your father and I established good relations and became good brothers" (*KUB* 3 72:7); *Hatti u Kizzuwatna lu šummuḫu atterūtu ina*

---

20. Murnane, "Egypt," 104–5.
21. Meier, "Diplomacy," 166. Mangano examines the rhetorical peculiarities of the Amarna correspondence in his dissertation ("Amarna").
22. See Steymans, *Deuteronomium*, 1–4.
23. This is Moran's translation (*Amarna*, 47). Knudtzon translates as a temporal adverb (*abermals*); *CAD* A/2.511 labels *atterūtu* a "foreign word."

birīšunu lu i-teni-ip-pu-šu, "Hatti and Kizzuwatna are united; friendly relations have been established between them" (*KBo* 1.5.3.6)[24];

- ***izirtu*** → *a-na-ku-me ip-ša-ti i-zir-t[a] a-n[a]* ^{alu}*ṣur-ri*, "I have brought security to Tyre" (*EA* 89.17–18);[25]

- ***kittu*** → *ù lu-[ú en-ni]-pu-uš ki-it-tu i-na bi-[ri-]ku-ni*, "So let us make an alliance between us" (*EA* 34.42); *i-pu-ša a-na-ku ki-ta it-ti abdi-a-ši-ir-ta . . . bal-ṭati ša-ni-tu*, "Send back word to me or I will make an alliance with Abdi-Aširta . . . and stay alive" (*EA* 83.25); ^{iṣ}*elippē-šu-nu a-ṣa ki-ma ki-ta iš-tu* ^{matu}*mi-iṣri*, "their ships, by an agreement, left Egypt" (*EA* 105.20–21); *a-na ma-ni i-pu-šu ki-ta*, "Why should I make an alliance?" (*EA* 125.39); *at-ta ki-ta it-[ti] abdi-a-ši-ir-ta . . .*," "If you make an alliance with Abdi-Aširta . . ." (*EA* 132.33–34); *ù ni-pu[-uš ki]-tu* "and we ma[de an al]liance" (*EA* 138.53); *ki-it-me ša-li-me u ki-it-me it-[t]a-me*, "Is the alliance at peace or is the alliance destroyed?" (*EA* 252.10);[26] *inanna iš-ku-nu ki-it-ta ina berīšunu*, "Inanna made a treaty with (the hungry) among them" (*RS* 17.123.6); *iškunu kitta ina berīšunu ki-i-ma da-ri-i-ti*, "They established a treaty between them as of old" (*RS* 17.123.7);

- ***mamîtu*** → *e-te-pu-uš [m]a-mi-ta [it-]ti amêli [š]a* ^{alu}*ku-ub-liki ù it-ti a[mêli] š[a* ^{alu} *] [ù] gab-bu* ^{amēlūtu}*ḫal-zu-uḫ-lu-ti ša mâti-ka [ù* ^d*] it-ti-šu iṭîbu-nim*, "He made an [o]ath-treaty [wi]th the ruler of Gubla and with the ruler of . . . and] all the military officers in your land . . . [. .] became friendly with him" (*EA* 67.13); *i-pu-uš nu-kur-tum la-a it-te-ir ma-mi-ta*, "He has created enmity—has he not broken the oath-treaty?" (*EA* 148.37); *šiṭirtu ša māmīti ša šarru rabû . . . i-pu-ša-anni*, "the text of the oath-treaty which the great king has made"(*KBo* 1.24.9´; see also *KBo* 1.23.3–4);

- ***parṣu*** → *parṣū ša dārīti ša* ^dUD *u* ^dIM *i-pu-šu*, "It is an 'eternal order'[27] established by the sun god [of Egypt] and the storm god [of Hatti]" (*KBo* 1.7.24);

- ***qīštu*** → *qi-i-ša-a-ti*^{meš} *ša aḫi-ia-u[l]-te-e-bi-la-am-ma*, "the (peace-)gifts which my brother sent to me" (*EA* 29.83); *ia-di-na qišta a-na ar-di-šu ù ti-da-ga-lu* ^{amēlūtu}*a-ia-bu-nu ù ti-ka-lu ipra*, "May he grant a (peace-)gift to his servant(s) so our enemies will see (this) and eat dirt" (*EA* 100.33);

24. *CAD* E.204 notes that the word appears *passim* in the Boğazköy texts.

25. Lit., "made help for Tyre." Moran: "I made connubium with Tyre"; Knudtzon: "Ich habe Tyrus Hilfe verschafft."

26. Knudtson: "Ist der Treue unversehrt oder ist der Treue zerstört worden?" Moran: "When I had sworn my peace—and when I swore, the magnate swore with me—the city, along with my god, was seized."

27. Lit., "order which is of old." *CAD* D.114: "treaty, written in Egypt."

- **ra'âmu/ raḫâmu** → be-lí ki-i-me-e a-na-ku a-na šarri be-lí-i[a] a-ra-aḫ-am ù ki-ia-am šar ^{mātu}nu-ḫa-aš-še, "My lord, just as I love the king, my lord, so too the king of Nuḫašše"[28] (EA 53.41); [m]i-ia i-ra-mu ù a-mu-[t]a, "Who will be 'loyal'[29] if I die?" (EA 114.68); [šum-]ma i-ra-am šarr[u^{ru} bêl]^{ili} arad ki-t[i-šu ù] uš-ši-ra [3]d amêla ù ib-lu-ta, "[I]f the ki[ng], my [lor]d, loves [his] loya[l] servant, [then] send (back) the [3] men that I may live" (EA 123.23; cf. also EA 121.61); š[u]m[-m]a šar[ru bê]l-[i-i]a la i-ra-am-an-ni u i-ṣi-i-ra-a[n]-[ni] ù a-na-ku mi-na-am l[u-ù] aḳ-[b]i, "[I]f the king, my lord, does not love me and rejects me, then what a[m] I to s[a]y?" (EA 158.36);

- **riksu** → be-lí tuppa^{pa}-te^{meš} ù ri-ik-[sa-te . .] ù a-na ša šar ^{mātu}mi-iṣ-ri, "My lord, [I have rejected] the (offer of) tr[eaty]-tablets, and [am (still) a servant of] the king of Egypt" (EA 51.4'-6')[30];

- **šalāmu** → ka-li $^{amēlū[tu}$bêl alāni] šal-mu a-na abdi-a-[ši-ir-ta], "all the [mayors] are at peace with ʿAbdi-A[širta]"[31] (EA 90.27-28); gab-bu i-na ^{mātu}a-mur-ri šal-mu-šu-nu, "Everyone in the land of Amurru is at peace with them"[32] (EA 114.14); gab-bi ^{amēlūtu}ḫa-za-nu-tum šal-mu-šu, "All the mayors are at peace with him"[33] (EA 126.10-11); a-li-ik-mi arki mar-abdi-a-ši-ir-ta ù ni-pu-uš šal-ma bi-ri-nu, "Ally yourself with the son of ʿAbdi-aširta so we can make peace between us"[34] (EA 136.11-13); ip-pu-uš-ti nu-kur-te šal-ma-at a-na ia-ti-ia šu-terat ^{ali}ki-ia, "I waged war, but it[35] is now at peace with me. My city is restored to me" (EA 280.13);

- **šiṭirtu** → mi-ḫi-ir ṣitirti ša DN e-pu-šu ina birīt miṣri u ina birīt ḫatti, "copy of the 'treaty'[36] made by the god Tešup[37] between Egypt and Hatti" (KBo

---

28. "Rich" territories (Akk. nuḫāšu, "to be prosperous") between Hamath and Aleppo, the Euphrates and the Orontes (Bryce, Hittites, 179–80).

29. Lit., "love."

30. Von Soden lists numerous references from Alalakh, Boğazköy, and Ugarit (AHw 984–85; cf. rikiltu in other ANE texts).

31. Moran: "all the [mayors] are at peace with ʿAbdi-A[širta]," restoring ḫa-za-nu for Knudtzon's suggested bêl alāni, ("lords of the cities").

32. Knudtzon: "Alle in Amurri sind mit ihnen einig."

33. Knudtzon: "alle Regenten mit ihm einig sind."

34. Knudtzon: "Gehe hinter dem Sohn Abdi-Aširtas her, und lasset uns unterein-ander Frieden stiften."

35. I.e., the village of aluki-el-te ("Qeltu," EA 280.11; i.e., קעילה, "Keilah," Josh 15:44).

36. Lit. "inscription."

37. Hurrian storm-deity from the upper Tigris.

1.23.1);[38] *ši-ṭe-er-du ša māmīti ša šarru rabû . . . īpušanni*, "the sworn written agreement which the great king made" (*KBo* 1.23.3–4);

- *šulmanu* → "From the time my ancestors and your ancestors 'made'[39] a mutual declaration of 'friendship' (*ṭa-bu-ta*), they sent 'beautiful greeting-gifts' (*šu-ul-ma-na ba-na-a*) to each other and refused no request for anything beautiful. My brother has now sent me 2 minas of gold as 'my greeting-gift' (*šu-ul-ma-ni-ia*). Now, if gold is plentiful, send me as much as your ancestors did. Why have you sent me 2 minas of gold? At the moment, my work on a 'temple' (*bît ili*) is extensive, and I am quite busy with carrying it out. Send me much gold. And you, for your part, whatever you want from my country, write me so that it may be brought to you" (*EA* 9.6–18);

- *šulmu* → *šulma ittišunuma lu i-pa-aš*, "let me make peace with them" (*RS* 17.286.12); *ana e-bi-ši šulmi adi ūmi anni*, "to keep the peace until this day" (*KBo* 1.7.26);

- *tappûtu* → PN *u* PN2 *ša ina* GN *tappûtam i-pu-šu*, "PN and PN2, who entered into a partnership in Isin" (*KBo* 1.7.26);

- *ṭābūtu* → ("friendship alliance") // *aḫḫutum* ("brotherhood," *EA* 4.15, 17) // *aḫḫutum, šalimu* (*EA* 11.22′); *a-na-ku i-pu-ma-am ṭâbûta \Tu.Ka\ it-ti-šu ša am-mu-ni-ra ù al-ka-ti biti-šu as-sum e-pu-uš ṭâbûti*, "'Come, I must make a friendship alliance with Ammunira.' So I went to his house in order to make a friendship alliance" (*EA* 136.27–29);

- *ṭemu* → *ṭema* SIG5 *ša šarra raba ša Miṣri i-pu-šu ittiša* [Hatti], "the good relations which the great king, the king of Egypt, established with the king of Hatti" (*KBo* 1.24.10)[40];

- *ṭuppu* → *ṭuppa ša rikilti ana* RN . . . *abua* . . . *e-pu-ša-aš-šu*, "my father drew up a treaty-tablet for RN" (*KBo* 1.6.4 and *passim* in Boghazköy documents).

TREATY TERMINOLOGY IN THE AMARNA CORRESPONDENCE

Four of the most common contributors to this semantic grid are "love," "brother(hood)," "peace (-gifts)," and "treaty/alliance/covenant."

---

38. See *CAD* E.221.
39. Akk *dabābu* ("to speak").
40. See *KUB* 3.65.9; *KBo* 1.7.12.

"Love"

In *EA* 53, Akizzi of Qatna complains to Pharaoh[41] that the king of Hatti has sent one of his vassals, Aitukama, to harrass and, if possible, pull him away from the Egyptian alliance.[42] The purpose of this letter is to report the problem to Amenhotep and assure him that Akizzi has no intention whatsoever of abandoning his "love" (*raʾâmu*) for him. In line 13, he even replays for Pharaoh his indignant response to Aitukama: "I said, 'How could I go to the king of Hatti? I am a servant of the king, my lord, the king of Egypt.'" Then he recommits himself to Pharaoh, pledging not only his "love" but also the love of colleagues in four neighboring cities: "My lord, just as I love the king, my lord, so too the king of Nuḫasse, the king of Nii, the king of Zinzar, and the king of Tunanab—all of these kings are my lord's servants." As Moran notes, "love" and "servanthood" often stand in parallel in the Amarna correspondence, so whether this language is genuine or artificial,[43] the parallel itself is significant. In line 24, however, Akizzi delicately informs Pharaoh how much this "love" is going to cost him in light of the fact that Aitukama has already launched a military campaign against Egyptian vassals in the region: "My lord, Aitukama came and he sent Upu,[44] the land of my lord, up in flames. He took the ruler's house . . . and he took one disk . . . from the house of Birwaza." In addition, he reports, Aitukama has launched a subversive propaganda campaign designed to undermine Akizzi's faith in the Egyptians' "love." For example, when Aitukama taunts him by saying, "The king, my lord, will not come forth," this taunt sounds much like Sennacherib's taunt of Hezekiah: "Do not let Hezekiah deceive you, for he will not be able to deliver you from my hand."[45] In spite of these taunts, however, Akizzi reiterates his loyalty to Egypt as well as the loyalty of his colleagues, suggesting that, if Pharaoh were to "name his price," each of these colleagues would immediately respond. All Akizzi asks in return is that Pharaoh send troops to intervene in this crisis and put a stop to Aitukama's shenanigans.

In *EA* 41, the Hittite king Šuppiluliuma writes to Pharaoh to remind him of the "friendly relations" (*atterūtu*)[46] previously enjoyed between

---

41. Amenhotep III (d. 1382 BCE). Qaṭna is modern Tell el-Mišrife, located on the Wadi il-Aswad, a tributary of the Orontes.

42. In this era Hittite commanders regularly badger the vassal city-states of Syria-Palestine in the hope of pulling them away from Egyptian control; see Avruch ("Amarna," 154–64); Bryce (*Hittites*, 189–90).

43. Meier, "Diplomacy," 165–73.

44. The region from which Damascus originates (Burns, *Damascus*, 4–6).

45. 2 Kings 18:29.

46. This term often stands in close parallel to *raḥâmu* in the Amarna correspondence.

their two countries. In fact, in light of this history he finds it difficult to understand why Pharaoh would renege on his father's promise to deliver two male-shaped statues of gold (one standing, one sitting) and two female-shaped statues of silver, along with several pounds of lapis lazuli. Each of these letters, one from the vassal correspondence and one from the international correspondence,[47] illustrates well the pervasive use of "love" and "friendship" as primary components in idealistic depictions of ANE international relations.

"Peace (-Gifts)"

In *EA* 136, Rib-Hadda,[48] Pharaoh's most prolific (and annoying) correspondent, writes as an old man in exile. Languishing in Beirut, he frets anxiously as his wife and servants urge him to "make peace" with Aziru, the son of his hated nemesis, Abdi-Aširta.[49] Hoping against hope that Pharaoh will send a squadron of archers to rescue him, part of him begins to wonder whether he should not take their advice and "make an alliance" with the mayor of Beirut, Ammunira—just in case Pharaoh does not send aid. Often in the Amarna correspondence disputants talk of "making peace" with their enemies even as they try to "stay at peace" with their friends. In *EA* 90, for example, a much younger Rib-Hadda complains to Pharaoh that Egypt has abandoned the cities around Byblos to the aforementioned Abdi-Aširta. Things are so bad, he reports, not only have the cities of Batruna, Mittana, and Šigata fallen to him, but Rib-Hadda himself has had to sell all of his belongings just to survive. On top of this, "all the (neighboring) [mayors] have made peace with Abdi-Aširta," a line which in the context of the letter looks to be the proverbial "last straw." Alone and afraid, he knows that his only remaining ally now is Pharaoh, a "patron" who lives hundreds of miles away.

In *EA* 114, Rib-Hadda worries that "everyone in the land of Amurru is at peace with" Tyre, Beirut, and Sidon, and further, that this situation will force him, by staying loyal to Pharaoh, to become an "enemy" of this new coalition. Pharaoh's garrison has deserted Siumur, and the townspeople of Byblos—his own people—are considering doing the same. In *EA* 126, Rib-Hadda informs Pharaoh that he will not be able to fill his order for an exotic species of wood because the neighboring mayors, having "made peace" with

---

47. On this genre distinction see Liverani ("Contrasti," 1–18).

48. Mayor of Byblos, a Canaanite seaport with close ties to Egypt (Roth, "Gebal," 922–23).

49. A rogue leader of possible royal descent from one of the coastal cities of Amurru; see Altman ("Abdi-Ashirta," 1–11); Singer ("Amurru," 141).

Aziru, are blockading the port cities of Salḫi and Ugarit. Syro-Palestinian neighbors, like all neighbors, cement "peace" (*šulmu*) via the giving and receiving of "peace-gifts" (*šulmanū*).[50] From an anthropological perspective, this reciprocation of gifts—particularly the gifts of women and land and gold—is often the first stage of what can become a lengthy negotiation process.[51] Anyone who has ever haggled with a carpet vendor in Ankara or a jeweler in Aleppo understands how the process works. The vendor's initial "gift" of hot tea, for example, looks at first glance to be a token of Middle Eastern hospitality, but in reality it's the opening salvo of a negotiation process intended to hook a recipient into becoming a client. Reciprocal gift-giving characterizes almost all of the peer relationships in the Amarna texts. In *EA* 9, for example, the Kassite king Burnaburiaš begins by reminding Pharaoh of their countries' peaceful history,[52] a history in which their ancestors make mutual declarations of "friendship" and send to each other many "peace-gifts."[53] The objective of this history lesson soon becomes clear when Burnaburiaš begins complaining to Pharaoh about his most recent gift: a mere 2 minas of gold.[54] Obviously disappointed, he offers Pharaoh a face-saving way out of his *faux pas*. Should gold no longer be as plentiful as it once was, he politely suggests, then perhaps Burnabariaš will accept, say, one-half the amount originally expected. Whatever Pharaoh sends, however, must come quickly because (a) Burnaburiaš is building a temple and needs "much gold" to complete it, and (b) Burnaburiaš has learned that some of his Assyrian vassals have made a clandestine trip to Egypt without his permission. Thus, after a bit more lecturing, he concludes with a warning: "If you 'love' me (*ta-ra-aḫ-ma-a-ni*), do not allow them to conduct any business. Send them back to me empty-handed." Should Pharaoh entertain this request, Burnaburiaš promises to send him yet another "peace-gift" (*šulmanu*) of lapis-lazuli and war-chariots.

50. See Nam, *Economic*, 72.

51. Moore, *WealthWatch*, 54–55; Godelier, *Enigma*, 205–7.

52. The Kassites, a militant people from NW Iran speaking an Indo-European language, rule Mesopotamia c. 1531–1155 BCE.

53. Moran thinks this letter is addressed either to Amenhotep IV (Akhenaton) or Tutankhamun (*Amarna*, 18).

54. Approx. 2.5 lbs.

"Brother(hood)"

A few texts from Boğazköy document not only that terms for "friendly relations" (*atterūtu*) can and do appear in discussions of treaties,[55] but that terms for "friendly relations" and "brother(hood)" (*aḫḫû[tu]*) can and do appear in parallel.[56] At Amarna, "brother(hood)" is one of the more important terms in the international correspondence between members of what Mario Liverani calls the "Great Powers Club."[57] In *EA* 29, for example, Tušratta of Mitanni[58] writes a long letter to Amenhotep IV (Akhenaton) practically *exuding* the language of "brother(hood)." Like Hiram with Solomon, Tušratta wants to make sure that his relationship with the new Pharaoh can pick up where the old one leaves off, baptized in "brotherhood" and liberated from "distress" (*marṣu*).

About halfway through the letter, however, Tušratta subtly makes clear to his reader why "brother(hood)" is so important to him—because he thinks it's being tested on two fronts. The *first* is the ever-sensitive problem of international political marriage. For all his "love" for Pharaoh, Tušratta feels that Egypt is not treating him fairly in this important area of "exchange." Following Lévi-Strauss, Kevin Avruch points out that the exchange of women between social groups is "the fundamental, indeed (the) primordial (means of) social exchange" in the ANE.[59] Thus, what we may be seeing in *EA* 29 is not egalitarian reciprocity, but a "generalized exchange" in which one group (Mitanni) "gives" its daughters and sisters, while another group (Egypt) "takes" them. For several reasons (many ably discussed by Betsy Bryan in an incisive study),[60] Egypt seems content with this arrangement. Mitanni, however, is not. From Tušratta's perspective Egypt does not want to reciprocate the gift he has already given them (viz., his daughter Tadu-Ḫeba). *Question:* Why does Egypt prefer generalized exchange over egalitarian reciprocation? Is it because Pharaoh considers Egyptian women to be superior to all others, including Hurrian women? Is it because Egypt considers Mitanni to be a vassal state in which women are merely "tribute," not "gifts?"[61] Is it because Egyptian inheritance rights are so fragile,

---

55. *KBo* 15.3.6.
56. E.g., *KUB* 3.72.7.
57. Liverani, "Club," 15–27.
58. A confederation of Hurrian states located in north Mesopotamia and Syria in the second half of the 2nd millennium (Morrison, "Mitanni," 874–76).
59. Avruch, "Reciprocity," 163 (cf. Lévi-Strauss, *Kinship*, 459–98).
60. Bryan, "Egyptian," 80–83.
61. "Clearly, in the vassal correspondence, Pharaoh asks for women as tribute, along with timber, glass, and so on" (Avruch, "Reciprocity," 163).

they need to be protected from "outsiders?"⁶² Or is it because the Egyptians intentionally slant the whole process to their own advantage, so ingrained are they in their own self-centeredness?⁶³ Whatever the reasons, Pharaoh balks at the idea of sending Egyptian women to Mitanni, and this bothers Tušratta enough to write several letters to him about it, *EA* 29 being the most extensive.

Second, Tušratta is worried that, to paraphrase a phrase from Torah, "a new Pharaoh has arisen who knows not Tušratta."⁶⁴ Constantly he reminds Pharaoh that international relations with his father, Amenhotep III, were very good. Constantly he challenges him to check with the queen mother, Teye, to verify this claim. Constantly he suggests, in his ingratiating way, that the stress now building between their two governments is of recent, not ancient origin. In short, Tušratta does not want the inevitable disruption of dynastic succession to tear down the diplomatic work of their ancestors. He wants to strengthen the peace between Mitanni and Egypt, though not at the expense of Mitanni or its needs, particularly the need to secure his western flank from Hittite expansionism.

"Treaty/Alliance/Covenant"

Opinions are divided over the precise nature of the relationship between Egypt and its "asiatic" provinces.⁶⁵ William Murnane thinks that, in the absence of treaty-tablets, the question of whether or not Pharaoh concludes actual "treaties" with Byblos, Qidšu, Qaṭna, or Tyre should remain open, and further, that fealty oaths, if taken at all, should be viewed only as unilateral promises, not "treaties."⁶⁶ Raymond Westbrook acknowledges these difficulties as well, but questions whether the existence of formal treaties should be considered a "prerequisite" for understanding the reality of "vassalage."⁶⁷ Mario Liverani goes in a slightly different direction, suggesting that questions of historicity, important as they are, are often irresolvable

---

62. Bryan, "Egyptian," 82.
63. Philo, *Agr.*, 61–62.
64. Exod 1:8.
65. Egypt's love-hate relationship with the *retenu*—the Egyptian term often trans. 'asiatics' (i.e., Hittite/Syro-Palestinian foreigners)—is well known (see Murnane, "Egypt," 700). The Akk equivalent to Egyptian *retenu* is ḫupšu (*EA* 117:90; 118:23; 125:27; cf. *CAD* P.37–49; Moore, *WealthWatch*, 122–24).
66. Murnane, "Imperial," 104–5.
67. "In contrast to modern law, (ANE) treaties do not have to be in written form" (Westbrook, "Amarna," 38).

and too often eclipse ideological questions. Thus, he argues, "the problem is not to sift away ideology in order to discover the 'real facts,' but on the contrary, to appreciate ideology better through an evaluation of its factual basis."[68]

Applying Liverani's approach to the Amarna texts, we see that in *EA* 83 Rib-Hadda whines to Pharaoh that he has not yet heard back from his previous letter, prompting him to ask, "Why are you so negligent that you allow your land to be taken?" Afraid that the ḫapiru[69] will take over Byblos, he warns Pharaoh that, to "stay alive," he may have to "make an alliance" (*i-pu-ša a-na-ku ki-ta*) with his hated enemy Abdi-Aširta. Noting that his neighbors Yapaḫ-Adda and Zimrida have already made alliances with this enemy, he tells Pharaoh that he may have to follow their lead. In *EA* 105, he reports that the village of Sumur is trapped "like a bird in a cage."[70] The sons of Abdi-Aširta have blockaded it by land and Arwada's men have blockaded it by sea, the latter having "made an alliance" with other maritime states. So strong is this alliance, Rib-Hadda cannot break through and rescue Sumur. In *EA* 125, Rib-Hadda takes off the gloves and tells Pharaoh what he *really* thinks. The Egyptian garrison has completely abandoned him. He has sold all his possessions for food and supplies. The townspeople of Byblos are leaving the city to look for food wherever they can find it, and his enemy Aziru wants him to "make an alliance" against Egypt. In a similar vein Lab'ayu, the mayor of Shechem, later reports that, despite the fact that his enemies have broken a previously-sworn "treaty" (*kittu*),[71] he will nevertheless obey Pharaoh and hold these men captive.

THE SOLOMON-HIRAM TREATY

In light of this socioliterary context, several problems immediately confront us in the Solomon-Hiram treaty-encounter, problems which, when taken together, militate against any sort of facile comparison between the Amarna texts and the biblical book of Kings. *First*, these are very different types of literature. Evidence about the Solomon-Hiram treaty does not come down to us on unedited clay tablets but through a thoroughly edited religious

---

68. Liverani, *International*, 119.

69. "The emergence of ḫapiru influence ... lends support to the idea that in a tribal society the ḫapiru probably also include elements of the detribalized since, in effect, it is they who constitute the economically and socially uprooted" (Green, "Social," 199).

70. Sennacherib uses the same idiom to describe the fate of Jerusalem (*ANET* 288).

71. *EA* 252.10–15.

document driven by a distinctive ideological agenda.[72] *Second*, the historical gap between the Amarna period and the Solomonic kingdom is significant, even if we refuse to question, as is fashionable in some circles, the possibility of Solomon's historical existence in the tenth century (BCE).[73] Yet even if we *do* assume a tenth-century Solomonic kingdom, the historical gap between these texts speaks little to the question of covenant ideology. *Third*, the relationship between Hiram and Solomon, in part because of the nature and character of the Dtr literature, looks rather ambiguous when compared with the international relationships in the Amarna texts. Neither of these kings, for example, is a member of the "Great Powers Club,"[74] and this makes it difficult to imagine their relationship as anything like that between Egypt and Mitanni, or even that between Byblos and Qaṭna.

So how are we to view the Solomon-Hiram relationship? Is their alliance predominantly political or economic?[75] Are we to view these rulers as vassals dependent on a superpower (if so, which one?), or as more-or-less independent sovereigns?[76] Certainly DtrH would lead us to imagine the latter, but this may be due primarily to the fact that Dtr, as a rule, tends to shy away from international politics. If we follow Liverani, however, and pursue these questions along ideological rather than sociopolitical lines, several parallels come immediately to mind, some more focused than others.

First, the language of "love" and "friendship" is pervasive in both the Amarna correspondence and the Hebrew book of Kings. Just as Tušratta's "love" for Amenhotep III drives him to reaffirm "friendly relations" with his son, Amenhotep IV (Akhenaton), so Hiram's "love" (אהב)[77] for David drives him to reaffirm "friendly relations" with *his* son, Solomon. Even to notice that Hiram has "love" for David "all his days" reminds us of Tušratta's claim that his "love" for Pharaoh's father is not haphazard. Leaders in the Amarna texts constantly write to each other to express a desire for peace. Similarly Hiram tells Solomon that his "love" for his father David lasted "all his days."[78]

---

72. Moore, *WealthWatch*, 13.
73. See, e.g., Lemche, *History*, 143-46.
74. Liverani, "Club," 15-27.
75. Fensham sees elements of both ("Tyrians," 74).
76. In Eupolemus' history, Hiram addresses Solomon as βασιλεὺς μέγας ("great king"), implying a higher status (Holladay, *Fragments*, 1.122). Holladay (1.146) ascribes the use of this title "to Hellenistic practice," but Mendels (*Israel*, 134) sees a Hebrew parallel in Ezra 5:11 (מלך לישראל רב, "a great king in Israel").
77. 1 Kings 5:15 (ET 5:1).
78. כל־הימים, 1 Kings 5:15 (ET 5:1).

Second, in addition to the fact that ברית formally signifies the existence of a "treaty" between Solomon and Hiram, Dtr relies on an interesting idiom to describe it: עשׂה חפץ (lit., "to do/accomplish a desire"). Hiram assures Solomon, "I will do all your desire,"[79] if Solomon will appropriately reciprocate; i.e., *if* "you will do my desire."[80] In light of similar usage of *ḥpṣ* in the Old Aramaic treaty between Matʿiʾel of Arpad and Birgaʾyah of KTK,[81] its usage here looks suspiciously technical, especially in light of the cognate *ḥpṣ* at Sefire alongside the terms *rḥm* ("love") and *šlm* ("peace"):

> "With regard to any of the kings with whom I have trading relations or any who is my 'friend' (*rḥm*), when I send my envoy to him to ask about his 'peace' (*šlm*), or anything else pertaining to 'my desire' (*ḥpṣy*) . . . the road shall remain open to me."[82]

More to the syntactic point, this Hebrew idiom, עשׂה חפץ, like the Akkadian idioms *epēšu atterūtu* ("to make friendly relations"), *epēšu izirtu* ("to make help"), *epēšu kittu* ("to make an alliance"), *epēšu mamîtu* ("to make an oath"), *epēšu parṣu* ("to make an [eternal] order"), *epēšu šulmu* ("to make peace"), *epēšu šiṭirtu* ("to make a treaty"), *epēšu tappûtu* ("to make a partnership"), *epēšu ṭābūtu* ("to make a friendship alliance"), *epēšu ṭēmu* ("to make good relations"), and *epēšu ṭuppu* ("to make a treaty-tablet"), certainly conveys more about the treaty binding Solomon to Hiram than simply, "I will meet your needs" (NRSV) or "I will do all you want" (NIV).

Third, at the sociohistorical heart of this exchange stands the question of reciprocity.[83] As Victor Matthews points out, obligatory gift-giving carries with it both a means of gaining honor as well as a means of imposing shame. When a balanced exchange occurs, both the donor and the recipient occupy "honorable" positions. When an unequal exchange occurs, however,[84] this creates a social tension which can easily lead to enmity and conflict. Is this not what happens in the Cabul incident?[85] When Solomon makes treaties with neighboring states, some of his interests lie southward, for sure, but primarily his interests lie northward, and from the Amarna correspondence we now see that the northern villages of Acco, Shechem, and Megiddo distinguish themselves by little else than a penchant for bickering. Constantly

---

79. אני אעשׂה את־כל חפצך, 1 Kings 5:22 (ET 5:8).
80. אתה תעשׂה את־חפצי, 1 Kings 5:23 (ET 5:9).
81. See Fitzmyer, *Sefire*, 96.
82. *KAI* 224.8–9.
83. Matthews, "Gift," 91–104.
84. E.g., Jacob and Esau (Gen 33:8–17).
85. 1 Kgs 9:13 (see Naʿaman, "Sources," 67–69).

they fight with each other. Constantly they beg Pharaoh for troops and food and horses and soldiers. Some of the Pharaohs of this period, particularly Amenhotep III (d. 1349 BCE) and Amenhotep IV (Akhenaten, d. 1334 BCE) respond directly to these requests, but more often than not they just let these small-town mayors fight it out.

SUMMARY AND CONCLUSION

In other words, the cities given to Hiram already have a troubled history long before Solomon succeeds David. Abimilku of Tyre sends letters to Pharaoh which very much resemble those exchanged between Solomon and Hiram.[86] Just as Abimilku writes to Pharaoh to request cattle fodder and troops, so Solomon writes to Hiram to ask for cedarwood, both kings listing their needs in measurable units.[87] Just as Abimilku complains that he needs at least twenty palace attendants, so Hiram complains that the twenty cities received from Solomon are terribly inadequate.[88] Jerusalem's treaty with Tyre therefore leads to much more than a new temple for Israel's deity. Architecturally, Hiram builds Solomon a religious sanctuary based on Canaanite/Phoenician prototypes.[89] Socioeconomically, Hiram invites Solomon to participate in a booming economy at a time when the Mediterranean is one big Phoenician lake.[90] Ideologically, Dtr relates these events to his readers dispassionately, even while condemning Solomon for worshiping the gods of Pharaoh's daughter, his wife by political marriage.[91]

---

86. See Na'aman, "Amarna," 174–81.
87. See *EA* 148.12–14; 151.15, 46; 154.5–19; and 1 Kings 5:10–11.
88. See *EA* 149.40–176 and 1 Kings 9:12–14.
89. Dever, *Discoveries*, 111–15.
90. Aubet, *Phoenicians*, 43–46.
91. 1 Kings 11:1–13 (see Moore, *Faith*, 72–79).

10

SEARCHING IN SHEBA
The Desire for "Biblical Literacy"*

THE STORY OF THE Queen of Sheba[1] is one of the great stories of antiquity, a text inspiring sages,[2] prophets,[3] mystics,[4] poets,[5] novelists,[6] and artists of

---

* Revised from a paper read to the students and faculty of St. Petersburg Christian University in St. Petersburg, Russia, subsequently published in *ResQ* 44 (2002) 33–42.

1. 1 Kgs 10:1–13. Ancient opinion divides over whether שבא refers to Ethiopia/Egypt (Jos. *A.J.* 8.165) or Yemen. Q 27.22 reads من سبإ ("from Saba") and Q 34 is commonly entitled "Saba."

2. Lassner's survey is broad, if not comprehensive (*Sheba*).

3. Besides Tanak, perhaps no other text does more to color the global imagination than Qur'an, which claims that the purpose of the queen's visit is to give Solomon the opportunity to bring her into مسلمين ("submission," Q 27.31), i.e., convert her from paganism to Islam (Q 27.24). Qur'an's understanding of this encounter basically follows the legendary retelling in *Targum Sheni* (*Tg. Esth.* 2.3.1–3).

4. Ephraem the Syrian (d. 373 CE): "The Queen of Sheba was a sheep who came into a den of wolves, but Solomon gave her the lamp of truth and married her when he fell away" (*Pearl* 3.3; see Conti, *Kings*, 68–70).

5. Medieval Persian poet Ganjavi (d. 1202 CE) draws several parallels between the "romance" of Solomon and Bilqis (the queen's name in Arab-Iranian legend) and the romance between the Sassanid king Chosrou and the Armenian princess Shirin (*Ganjavi*). Contemporary poets Angelou (*Sheba*) and Freeman (*Balkis*) interact with themes in the story as well.

6. Liptzin notes several thematic parallels in the novels of de Nerval, Flaubert, and Dos Passos ("Sheba," 172–86).

every stripe.⁷ Something about it simply captures the imagination, whether attention focuses on the mystery enshrouding this foreign queen, or the behavior of this Hebrew king, or even the elusive deity hovering behind the scenes. Legends of all sorts grow up around this text like weeds on a sidewalk, making the task of interpretation as challenging as it is fascinating.⁸

The first line is interesting, if a bit problematic. Most English translations have the Sabean visiting Jerusalem at her own initiative to learn about the "fame of Solomon and his relation to the name of the LORD."⁹ This translation, however, is less than certain. The earliest versions vary considerably,¹⁰ and few contemporary translations adequately reflect the subtle nuances in the context, particularly the alliterative recurrence of שמע ("to hear/obey") and שם ("name").¹¹ Should more attention be allotted to this and the appearance of שמע in Yahweh's second appearance to the king,¹² the opening line might well be translated "When the Sabean queen heard of Solomon's 'obedience' to Yahweh's name."¹³ At any rate, whether the focal point is Solomon's "fame" or Solomon's "obedience," little doubt exists over whether the narrative shifts attention *away* from the Hebrew *toward* the Sabean monarch.¹⁴ Solomon's "fame" (Vg) and "listening heart,"¹⁵ important as they are, have little impact on the dynamics of this episode. Here the Arab is the center of attention, not the Hebrew. The primary action takes place in *her*, not him.¹⁶

---

7. Handel's (d. 1759) oratorio *Solomon* is one of the more famous musical compositions, and della Francesca's (d. 1492) painting is one of the more famous visual compositions.

8. Improbable-to-ridiculous are the theoretical reconstructions of Budge (*Sheba*) and Velikovsky (*Chaos*).

9. NIV, NRSV. MT: ומלכת־שבא שמעת את־שמע שלמה לשם יהוה. In Qur'an it is not *her* idea to visit Solomon; instead *he* commands her to come to *him* (Q 27.29).

10. In OG she hears τὸ ὄνομα Σαλωμων καὶ τὸ ὄνομα κυρίου ("the name of Solomon and the name of the Lord"). Vg has her hearing *fama Salomonis in nomine Domini* ("the fame of Solomon in the name of the Lord"). Syr has her hearing ܫܡܗ ܕܫܠܡܘܢ ܘܫܡܗ ܕܡܪܝܐ ("the report of Solomon and the report of the Lord").

11. The root שמע appears no less than six times in 1 Kings 10:1–13.

12. שמעתי ("I have heard," 1 Kings 9:3; see Moore, *Faith*, 275–79).

13. 1 Kings 10:1, revocalizing MT *šēmaʿ* to *šĕmaʿ*.

14. This is not the only time Tanak embeds a story about a heroine into one about a hero; N.B. Gen 38 (the Tamar story) in Gen 37–45 (the Joseph novella; see Trible, *Terror*, 37–64).

15. לב שמע (1 Kings 3:9; see Moore, *Faith*, 72–79).

16. See Moore, "Foreigners," 209–10.

Like this queen, ANE rulers constantly hear "reports" about their neighbors,[17] but seldom do they motivate them to go on long, expensive, dangerous journeys. The usual suspects are war and trade, not rumors of wisdom. Granted, this narrative completely depends on the perspective of a Hebrew narrator, but something must stand out in this particular "report" (שמע). What is it that so grabs this queen's attention? Does she see in Solomon a potential military rival?[18] Does she see in him a potential trading partner?[19] Does she see in him, as later legend so luridly speculates, a potential lover/mate?[20] Does the narrator simply use her as a mouthpiece to trumpet Solomon's achievements?[21] Or does this queen, as the narrative takes great pains to emphasize, make the arduous journey to Jerusalem because of an unquenchable "desire" (חפץ, v. 13) to "ask questions" (שאל, v. 13) about the "Name" (שם, v. 1)? Regardless of how later readers interpret her, this dimension of her character ought not simply be ignored. Whatever might be her motives (and our interpretations often "say more about us ... than about the story itself"),[22] there seems no valid reason to ignore the story's emphasis on her educational experience. In fact, as the text makes clear, this experience breaks down into three identifiable stages: *interrogation, perceptional shift,* and *affirmation*.

INTERROGATION

First, she "tests" Solomon with "hard questions" (lit., "riddles").[23] The use of this verb (נסה) is unusual, but not necessarily because a woman is "testing" a man.[24] The peculiarity rather stems from the fact that the creator,

17. The Amarna correspondence alone bears witness to this reality (Na`aman, "Amarna," 174–81).

18. Shalmeneser III reports having to face in battle a cavalry of one thousand camels from Arabia (*ANET* 279).

19. Gray argues this position (*Kings*, 241).

20. OG and Syr change the wording in v. 8 from "Happy are your 'men' (אנשים)" to "Happy are your 'wives'" (OG γυναῖκες; Syr ܢܫܝܟ), but later Jewish, Arab and Ethiopian tradition depicts her enacting a variety or roles, from "seductive temptress" to "hairy (Lilith) demon" (see Ogden Bellis, "Sheba," 17–28).

21. "The story as told has as its aim to exemplify Solomon's paradigmatic virtues of wisdom and wealth" (De Vries, *Kings*, 138; see Nelson, *Kings*, 65–67).

22. Ogden Bellis, "Sheba," 28.

23. MT לנסתו בחידות ("to test him with riddles"; see OG πειράσαι αὐτὸν ἐν αἰνίγμασιν; Vg *temptare eum in enigmatibus*); Syr ܠܡܢܣܝܘܬܗ ܒܐܘܚܕܬܐ ("to test him with riddle-telling"). Heb נסה ("to test") appears 36 times and in all three divisions of Tanak.

24. Where the Testament of Solomon imagines the Sabean as a "sorceress" (γόης)

not the creature, is the usual exam-giver, the proctor who tests people (a) to see what kind of "health care" they want,[25] (b) to see if they will follow his instructions,[26] (c) to instill in them a healthy fear,[27] (d) to distinguish them from others,[28] (e) to humble and examine their hearts,[29] (f) to prepare them for the "good life,"[30] and (g) to find out whether their "love" is, in fact, authentic and genuine.[31] Only rarely do human beings "test" God. When Gideon, for example, repeatedly lays out fleece before Yahweh, the deity's response is quiet patience mixed with unfettered grace.[32] But when the test comes from Israelites determined to abandon their covenant promises, this elicits a very different divine response.[33] *Conclusion*: spiritual behavior to a great extent determines divine response.[34] Mature believers generally understand this, both experientially and by faith. In light of the alternatives, most disciples are truly thankful, as Forsyth once put it, to have a God who "cares enough . . . to get angry."[35]

Question: How does this student "test" *her* teacher? *Answer*: By interrogating him with "hard questions."[36] What, exactly, do these "hard questions" look like? No one knows, really, though one medieval rabbi suggests a possible example:

> *Sabean Queen*: "What is an enclosure with ten doors—when one is open, nine are shut, and when nine are open, one is shut?"
> *Israelite King*: "The enclosure is the womb, and the ten doors are the ten orifices of a person, namely the eyes, the ears, the nostrils, the mouth, the apertures for discharge of excreta and

---

filled with "arrogance" (φρόνησις, *TSol* 19.3), R. Samuel ben Naḥmani steers his students away from the encounter's sexual dynamics: "Whoever says that the מלכת of Sheba is a woman is in error; the word מלכת here means 'kingdom' of Sheba" (i.e., not "queen," *b. Meṣiʿa* 59a).

25. Exod 15:25-26.
26. Exod 16:4.
27. Exod 20:20.
28. Deut 4:34.
29. Deut 8:2.
30. Deut 8:16 (נסתך להטיבך, "testing you to cause you good"). See *GE* 1.226-33 (Moore, *WealthWatch*, 64).
31. אהב, Deut 13:3 (this root appears 21 times in Deuteronomy).
32. Judg 6:36-40. Amit remembers "two . . . trials in which Gideon tests God—the scene of the fleece soaked with dew and that of the dry fleece" (*Judges*, 227).
33. Exod 17:7; Deut 6:16; Matt 16:1.
34. Gen 22:1; Ps 26:2; Heb 2:18. See Seitz, *Character*, 17-27.
35. See Escott, *Forsyth*, 113; see also McCarter, "Temper," 78-91.
36. חדות, "riddles" (1 Kings 10:1).

urine, and the navel. When the child is still in its mother's womb, the navel is open, but all the other apertures are shut. But when the child issues from the womb, the navel closes and the other orifices open up."[37]

What we *do* know is that the ancients regard riddle-telling as a highly prized skill. Not only are they used to entertain party guests,[38] but teachers use them constantly to entice students into thinking more deeply, thoroughly, and carefully. Riddles—old and new, aural and visual—are an important educational tool designed to distinguish students who truly want to learn from those who only want "to pass the course."[39] James Crenshaw unnecessarily moralizes this when he suggests that "riddles conceal valuable information from the unworthy while divulging important facts to those deserving them."[40] Sometimes this is true ("unless you eat my flesh and drink my blood"),[41] but more often than not riddles simply operate as pedagogical "test balloons."

The story before us is a case in point. The Sabean tests the Hebrew not necessarily to examine his "moral worthiness," but to find out (a) what kind of teacher he is, and (b) whether his teaching has the ability to quench her "desire." She has "hard questions" about the contours and content of "wisdom."[42] When she discovers this wisdom, her perceptions change, much like the perceptions of "all Israel" change after the "competing prostitutes" incident.[43] As Solomon does there, here he passes an important "test." More than this, the Sabean quickly realizes from her interrogations how difficult it is to "conceal" anything from her new teacher.[44]

37. *Midr. ha-Ḥefeṣ* (cited in Rappoport, *Myth* 3.128).

38. Greek and Roman guests who fail to solve after-dinner riddles are sometimes "punished" by being "forced" to drink salted wine (see sources cited in Crenshaw, "Riddles," 723).

39. Scurlock (*Sourcebook*, 337) observes how Mesopotamian teachers regularly "separate the poor student, whose commentary carefully belabors the obvious and skips over the difficult . . . from the truly expert"; i.e., the one who endeavors to "grasp the deeper meanings . . . behind (the) apparently ordinary."

40. Crenshaw, "Riddles," 721.

41. John 6:53. Scott (*Parable*, 7–62) discusses the relationship between parables and riddles in GNT.

42. חכמה, 1 Kings 10:8. See Weitzman, *Solomon*, 133–48.

43. "All Israel 'heard' (שמע, see above) of the judgment rendered by the king and 'stood in awe' of him (ירא, "to fear"; OG φοβέομαι, "to fear"; Syr ܕܚܠ, "to fear") because they perceived that divine wisdom was in him" (1 Kings 3:28; see Moore, *Faith*, 33–37).

44. NIV translates נעלם in 1 Kings 10:3 as "too hard," but this is not what the word means. עלם refers to things which are "hidden" (like חכמה) and only difficultly "dug up" (Job 28:21). In Arabic a "learned" person is علم.

PERCEPTIONAL SHIFT

What happens next is what happens in every educational experience. Her perceptions indeed change—about Israel, about Israel's government, about Israelite culture—about everything in her life. In fact, as the text implies, what she comes to "believe"[45] is the direct result of what she comes to *learn*. Not only does she discover the linkage between religion and politics, economics and ethics, art and spirit,[46] but she also learns how to engage the hidden force(s) responsible for producing the evidence which can be seen by "my own eyes."[47] The narrator's description of this response via the idiomatic expression ולא היה בה עוד רוח,[48] looks a lot like Job's response to Yahweh at the end of their conversation.[49] Even as Job finally falls on his face, stunned and shocked by the Power cyclonically exploding before *his* eyes, so also *this* "foreigner" finds herself gasping for breath. Responses like these are not uncommon among "foreigners" in Tanak.[50] Someone who has never experienced the famine of knowledge will never understand this, having never suffered the bitter loneliness of intellectual exile.

Put simply, what the Sabean queen experiences is the transformative power of learning.[51] To have all one's questions no longer ignored, no longer trivialized, no longer ridiculed, but straightforwardly *addressed*—well, that can be a "knock-the-wind-out-of-you" experience. Not only does the heart fill with gratitude, but the mind roars with new energy, like a computer upgraded to a higher speed. Granted, there can be social side-effects (i.e., the "wanting to belong and not belong at one and the same time"),[52] but the boundary between indoctrination and education is not fuzzy. Indoctrinated students never leave the "comfort zone." Educated students regularly move from the "comfort zone" to the "faith zone."[53]

---

45. אמן, 1 Kings 10:7.

46. This is the import of the casual descriptions listed in 1 Kings 10:4–5.

47. ותראינה עיני ("my eyes have seen," 1 Kings 10:7). OG ἑωράκασιν (perfect tense of ὁράω) emphasizes the life-changing nature of this perceptional shift.

48. Lit., "and not is in her any more spirit/breath" (1 Kings 10:5). Comparably idiomatic is the English expression "to have the wind knocked out."

49. Job 38:1–42:6.

50. See Moore, "Foreigners," 203–17.

51. For students like the Sabean, "theological learning and popular piety conjoin in pious response" (Sweetman, "Learning," 18). See Kang & Feldman, "Learning," 365–77.

52. Warner, "Sheba," 163.

53. See the essays in Snook, *Indoctrination*.

AFFIRMATION

Worship is the usual human response to discovering truth. Like other "foreigners"—Melchizedek, Tamar, Jethro, Balaam, Ruth, Nebuchadnezzar[54]—this grateful Sabean "blesses" God.[55] This behavior, however, does not *precede* her educational experience; it *succeeds* it. Obviously the Hebrew narrator has a vested interest in highlighting the *result* instead of the *process*, but to ignore the process is to enjoy the icing without the cake underneath. If this story teaches anything, it's that worship follows the discovery of truth—*not* vice versa.[56] *Question:* Can one truly worship the God of Israel apart from some (trans)formative educational experience leading to a true understanding of his character and being? Yeshu`a of Nazareth's conversation with a Samaritan woman squarely addresses this question. What the Father seeks, he says to another "foreign woman," are "true worshippers" willing to worship holistically (i.e., in both spirit and truth).[57] Does this not encapsulate what the Sabean does? She worships Solomon's God because in the process of learning about "wisdom" she discovers a significant measure of "truth."[58] Her desire for truth is what fuels this search. Her desire for truth is what drives her to make the journey to Jerusalem. Truth is what she most "desires" (חפץ).[59] Indeed, truth is what most people most desire. As Polonius puts it to Claudius, "If circumstances lead me, I will find where truth is hid, though it were hid indeed within the centre."[60]

Because she finds truth in Solomon's words and actions, she concludes that Yahweh must "take delight" in him (חפץ, same verb).[61] Put simply, she links her experience with her teacher to her experience with her teacher's God. She blesses *both* Solomon *and* Yahweh. Apparently she concludes that the synergy generated by the covenant between the king and his divine patron is the primary factor responsible for making the subjects of Jeru-

---

54. אנה נבוכדנצר משבח ומרומם ומהדר למלך שמיא כען, "Now I, Nebuchadnezzar, praise and exalt and honor the king of heaven" (Dan 4:34 [ET 4:37]).

55. ברוך (1 Kings 10:9).

56. Understanding this sequence would go a long way toward addressing the problems now causing the embarrassingly adolescent "worship wars" plaguing North American Christianity. See Dawn (*Wars*, ix-xv); Byars (*Wars*, 1-20); and Pinson (*Worship*, 1-17).

57. John 4:21-24 (see Thettayil, *Truth*, 123-65). Paffenroth ("Testing," 142-43) parallels the testing of Jesus with the testing of Solomon, but the Sabean/Samaritan parallel is closer.

58. אמת (1 Kings 10:6).

59. 1 Kings 10:13.

60. Shakespeare, *Hamlet* 1.5.157.

61. 1 Kings 10:9.

salem "happy" (אשרי), and she wants to experience this for herself. Is this surprising? No. As the narrator makes clear in his summary, this 3-stage process is the one by which "the whole world" comes to know "wisdom."[62]

APPLICATION

The Queen of Sheba story speaks to the education crisis in at least two ways. *First,* this encounter shows that not everyone is interested in learning about truth, but for those who are, there is a process to follow. I can speak to this issue with some expertise because for several decades my wife and I have been teaching classes in adult education programs of local congregations, and what we have discovered from this experience is that too many folks are willing to accept "crippled" methods and "diseased" curricula.[63] Too many are willing to ignore the "hard sayings."[64] *Question:* How many today are willing to follow the Sabean queen's example and ask the "hard questions?"

Second, this story warns us about the dangers of a counterfeit education, or, to state it more positively, celebrate the benefits of an authentic one. Rather than rely on secondhand "reports" about Solomon's wisdom, the Sabean student journeys all the way to Jerusalem to see with "my own eyes." She refuses, in other words, to settle for *secondary* sources, but instead chooses to expend the energy necessary to investigate the *primary* sources. Would that more students would follow her example! Although many take the process seriously in the disciplines of medicine, business, or law, it's rare to find it in the disciplines of theology, biblical studies, and pastoral care— the very disciplines necessary for supplying and renewing the lifeblood of the Faith.

Example: In 1990 two authors, one a poet and the other an English professor, published *The Book of J*,[65] a volume claiming to have translated the oldest "document" in Torah.[66] Reviewers gushed over it when it first came out, praising it as "a great book ... a superb piece of translation," a work of "erudition" filled with "poetic leaps of the imagination."[67] Richard

62. 1 Kings 10:24 (see Job 28:1–28; Jones, *Rumors*, 1–21).

63. See Mal 1:6–14.

64. Σκληρός ἐστιν ὁ λόγος οὗτος, "This is a hard saying" (John 6:60; cf. Kaiser, *Hard*).

65. Rosenberg & Bloom, *Book of J*.

66. Adherents of the nineteenth-century "documentary hypothesis" believe that Torah is the product of several documentary sources contributing bits and pieces over several centuries (see, e.g., Friedman, *Bible*, 246–60).

67. These comments, from the *Village Voice Literary Supplement* and the *Washington Post Book World*, appear as blurbs on the bookjacket.

Friedman, however, was not impressed—in fact, he was outraged. This is not a book filled with "erudition," he observed. Neither of these authors truly commands the language of the text (Classical Hebrew), nor is there evidence of appreciation for the literary, historical, and sociological worlds from which it originates.[68] *The Book of J* (not to be too critical, but clear) is little more than a piece of airport eye-candy, a blatant attempt to market a "spiritual" product to consumers who *style* themselves "students of the Hebrew Scriptures," but who, in fact, are biblically illiterate.[69] As any observant student will attest, this illiteracy is crippling the confidence of religious leaders everywhere. Fayette Breaux Veverka dares to ask the *truly* disturbing question: Does religious education any longer play a role in North American culture at all? From her careful social-scientific investigation, the answer is "no." Why? Because too many religious leaders attend only to the "safe" biblical passages, unwilling even to *ask* the "hard questions," much less engage them seriously.[70]

CONCLUSIONS

"Worship," however intricate or simple, however exciting or jejune, however classic or contemporary, is not identical to "education." These are not synonymous terms. *Worship* is the celebration which takes place whenever truth is discovered and/or affirmed. *Education*, however, is a *process*. Education is fundamentally about training oneself to work hard and labor well in the search for truth—wherever it is, however it sounds, in whomever it breathes. The goal is not to segregate one from the other, but to find responsible ways to integrate one into the other. The Sabean's story clearly illustrates this sequence. Later interpreters invite us to read it in differing ways from differing angles. When ישוע דנזרת reads it,[71] he reads it intertextually alongside the story of Jonah to order to indict "this wicked generation" for their biblical illiteracy.[72] Amazed at their complacency, he shares with them two analogies. If even Gentiles like the Ninevites and the Sabean queen, he asks, know how and where to search for truth, then what is the problem with "this generation?" Why does it so self-centeredly fritter away its opportunities and squander its gifts? So deep is this blindness, he warns, "this

---

68. Friedman, "Expert." See Klein (*Interpretation*); Tate (*Interpretation*); and Jonker (*Exclusivity*).

69. See Smart (*Silence*, 141–63), Blair (*Bible*, 1–6), and Wray (*Literacy*, 1–8).

70. Veverka, "Education," 77–90.

71. "Jesus of Nazareth" (Aram).

72. Luke 11:29–32.

generation" may eventually come to the point where it will not be able even to *recognize* the one in its midst who is "greater than Solomon," much less pledge its allegiance to him.

Charles Spurgeon, a nineteenth-century Englishman, draws from this story a plea which he unapologetically aims at the hearts of *his* generation:

> I want you tonight to come to Him, just as the Queen of Sheba came to Solomon, only for weightier reasons. You do not want to learn anything about architecture or navigation, agriculture or anatomy. You want only to know how you shall be built up into a spiritual house, and how you shall cross those dangerous seas which lie between this land and the celestial city.[73]

Spurgeon's age is different from "this generation," of course. Nineteenth-century preachers can make a number of assumptions about their audiences which, unfortunately, no longer hold true. Preachers to postmoderns must deal with the thorny problems of biblical illiteracy, resurgent racism, the worship wars, stubborn paternalism, angry feminism, and pagan spiritualities of various sorts—just to name a few. Yet with Luther we can still pursue *oratio, meditatio,* and *tentatio*.[74] With Denise Lardner Carmody, we can still open our eyes wide enough to see how "the right-wing ... groups who want to police lectures and articles, reading everywhere violations of orthodoxy" are "but ironic and painful counterparts to the leftist groups who monitor political correctness."[75] With Spurgeon we can still plead, "You have heard the report. Now, like the Queen of Sheba, go and see for yourself."[76]

---

73. Spurgeon, "Solomon," 3.248.
74. "I pray, I reflect, I test" (*LW* 34.286; *WA* 50.60.1–4).
75. Lardner Carmody, *Education*, 204–5.
76. Spurgeon, "Solomon," 3.255.

11

RESURRECTION AND IMMORTALITY
Two Motifs Navigating Confluent Theological Streams in Dan 12:1–4*

> O we can wait no longer / We too take ship, O soul / Joyous we too launch out on trackless seas / Fearless for unknown shores on waves of ecstasy to sail / Amid the wafting winds / (Thou pressing me to thee, I thee to me, O soul) / Caroling free, singing our song of God.

WHEN WALT WHITMAN WRITES these lines in his *Passage to India*,[1] he lives in a time when the Christian doctrines of resurrection and immortality are widely accepted.[2] In Tanak, however, the mood is a bit more somber. Not until relatively late in Hebrew history does a hope of an afterlife begin to

---

* Revised from an essay first published in *TZ* 39 (1983) 17–34.

1. Whitman, "Passage," 346.

2. According to Kuebrich ("Religion," 197), "Whitman insists that *Leaves of Grass* is a religious text"; i.e., an effort to create the "sacred text" necessary to empower a "post-Christian faith appropriate for America's emerging scientific and democratic culture."

take shape,³ and even then the breadth of its scope is less than clear.⁴ What are the factors responsible for this development? What role(s) do Hebrew thinkers assign to prophetic motifs focused on Israel's eschatological destiny? What role(s) do they assign to sapiential motifs hinting suggestively at the possibility of an afterlife?⁵ *Question:* What is the nature of the literary relationship between prophetic resurrection motifs and sapiential motifs referencing the possibility of an afterlife in the Hebrew Bible?

THESIS, PRESUMPTIONS, DELIMITATIONS AND METHOD

Hebrew motifs about resurrection and immortality are like ships in the night, each sailing in the same basic direction, but on confluent theological streams.⁶ Fragments of a resurrection hope float along the stream of prophecy, driven primarily by eschatological questions about the sovereignty of Yahweh over the universe (i.e., including the realm of death).⁷ Resurrection is the response formulated to these questions. Belief in immortality, however, though often ascribed only to Hellenistic sources,⁸ is also a Hebrew

---

3. Kellermann points out that both cultural hemispheres, occidental as well as oriental, begin formulating solutions to the problem of death very early, but Israel "at the end of its faith-history" ("Auferstehungsglauben," 261–62).

4. Wright (*Resurrection*, 83–108) summarizes the consensus view that Israel's only "hope" outside of that proclaimed in Dan 12:1–4 is for deliverance from premature death and life-threatening affliction.

5. Collins states the sages' dilemma: "Since the phenomenon of death cannot be avoided in the tradition which affirms wisdom as a principle of cosmic order, that tradition has to cope with the problem of death in such a way that its other assumptions about reality will not be undermined" ("Immortality," 178).

6. Use of the "multiple streams" metaphor follows the methodological lead of Odil Hannes Steck ("Streams," 183–214).

7. Ezekiel articulates the ANE belief in a netherworld via the expression ארץ תחתי(ו)ת ("netherworld"; lit. "land below," Ezek 26:20; 31:14, 16, 18; 32:18, 24). Cf. the cognate Akk expression *erṣetu šaplītu* (*CAD* Š.476). Daniel imagines the dead rising up from the אדמת עפר ("land of dust," Dan 12:2).

8. "Immortality," as defined here, is not to be confused with later Hellenistic belief in the immortality of the individual soul; i.e., as something *independent* of Yahweh as the Giver and Sustainer of all life, as Martin-Achard is quick to point out (*Résurrection*, 17). To argue, however, that Tanak "rejects the belief in the immortality of the soul" (Ibid., 17) is little more than a polemical reaction to extremist elements within the *religionsgeschichtliche* school. The Hebrews are not nihilists, nor are their ANE neighbors. "Immortality" here thus denotes *their* conception of the afterlife, a belief which later develops (under admittedly Hellenistic influence) into a fully-formed doctrine (Wis 2:21–23). Further, in the Wisdom of Solomon "immortality" roots itself in the Hebraic notion that "righteousness is immortal" (δικαιοσύνη γὰρ ἀθάνατός ἐστιν, Wis

motif,[9] driven primarily by the sages' questions about suffering and loss. Hope for an afterlife becomes one of the responses they eventually formulate to *their* questions.[10] Apocalyptic is a hybrid literary genre in which these two streams coalesce and converge into something altogether new, yet formally distinctive.[11] Many theological motifs flowing along these streams during the historical crises giving rise to Jewish apocalyptic might therefore be expected to interface with each other in some rather novel ways as each navigates familiar, yet strange and exciting waters. Dan 12:1-4 represents the delicate convergence of two of these motif-bearing streams before the powerful waters of Hellenism threaten to submerge all indigenous Hebrew ideas about afterlife under an alien doctrine of the immortality of the individual soul.[12]

The following delimitations draw this study into focus:

1:15), *not* the Platonic notion of the soul's immortal "essence." As Grabbe puts it, "it is often asserted in modern theology that the resurrection of the dead is the characteristic Jewish form of eschatology, whereas the immortality of the soul is Greek. The Wisdom of Solomon hardly recognizes this distinction! The origin of both the immortality of the soul and the resurrection of the dead in Judaism are the subject of debate, but the concept of the soul which survives the death of the individual appears as early as the concept of resurrection, as far as extant Jewish literature is concerned" (*Wisdom*, 53).

9. The most obvious text illustrating this is 1 Sam 28:3-25, where the בעלת אוב mediating the encounter between Saul and Samuel calls the latter individual אלהים (OG θεούς; Syr ܐܠܗܐ; Vg *deos*). OG's pl. reading contrasts with the sg. readings of Syr and Vg, thereby showing that early as well as contemporary commentators disagree on how to read אלהים. Kleiner (*Wahrsagung*, 135) translates it in the pl., identifying it with "the (spirits of) dead ancestors revered as 'protector-deities' within the tribal community."

10. García Martínez (*Wisdom*, xxvii) points out that Qumran wisdom texts "entertain hope in immortality, although not in the Platonic idea of the immortality of the soul, but rather the idea that righteous humans can be elevated to share the life of the angelic host to which the righteous on earth are closely associated."

11. *Contra* Barton (*Oracles*, 198-202) Chester thinks it "justifiable" to call a "moratorium" on the use of the terms "apocalyptic" and "proto-apocalyptic" when describing Tanak material outside of Daniel, but that "similar calls for abandoning these categories completely (that is, for the non-biblical material as well) should certainly be resisted" (*Future*, 90).

12. Willi-Plein ("Geheimnis," 62-63) asks whether apocalyptic should be defined as a literary phenomenon, an ideological phenomenon, or a theological phenomenon. To these options may be added the attempts of Hanson (*Dawn*, 29) and Millar (*Isaiah*, 103-32), following Plöger (*Theocracy*, 108-12), to establish for apocalyptic a firm sociological matrix. Though all of these questions need to be asked, they cannot all be asked here. Following Koch (*Ratlos*, 24) and Gammie ("Daniel," 192-93), the following essay will focus on *literary* questions, even while recognizing that literary criticism alone cannot define, in and of itself, a phenomenon as complex as apocalyptic.

1. Attention here will be given to Tanak passages from both tradition-streams, even though the ultimate focus will be the material in Dan 12:1-4.
2. The subtitle of this essay in no way precludes the existence of other tradition-streams. Priestly motifs about the cult, for example, flow along their own theological stream.[13] Tested by the pervasiveness of ANE mourning rituals,[14] sacrificial offerings for the dead,[15] and necromantic practices,[16] Hebrew cult (like all cults) tends to be more preservative than innovative.[17] Consequently this essay will have little to say about the cult, other than to recognize that funerary ritual goes a long way toward keeping Hebrew hopes of an afterlife alive.[18]
3. Foreign influences also contribute to Israel's religiocultural development, though it's probably more accurate to imagine early ANE sources (Sumerian, Egyptian, Akkadian, Hittite, Canaanite) as primeval clouds raining on Israel's headwaters, and later foreign influence (Babylonian, Persian, Hellenistic) as storm clouds thundering and pelting Israel's tradition-streams at critical bends in their development. At any rate, a full investigation of this process, admittedly vital to a complete understanding of Hebrew ideas about the afterlife, cannot be attempted here.[19]
4. To argue that apocalyptic is a composite literary genre in which two theological streams converge is not to generalize this phenomenon to be the same with regard to every motif in Hebrew apocalyptic, nor does it limit this confluence only to Hebrew teaching about the afterlife. It is simply an attempt to reconstruct

---

13. Steck, "Streams," 183-214.

14. Lev 19:28; 21:5; Deut 14:1. On ANE mourning ritual, see Shipp, *Dirges*, 47-66.

15. Deut 26:14; Jer 16:7; Ps 106:28; also Sir 30:18; Tob 4:17.

16. Tropper's definition of necromancy is too broad (*Nekromantie*, 27-46) and Schmidt's is too narrow (*Necromancy*, 141). See Moore, *Balaam*, 53-55.

17. Gillihan, e.g., defines the ideology embedded in the Rule scrolls (1QS, 1QSa and 1QSb) as a reactionary response to "Hasmonean state civic ideology" (*Ideology*, xvii).

18. Frankfort (*Kingship*, vii-ix) cautions against uncritical acceptance of views which, in his opinion, attach undue importance to the myth of the dying-rising deity, but Mettinger warns against hypercritical overreaction (*Resurrection*, 221).

19. Betz's ("Apokalyptik," 393) criticism of Rowley's (*Apocalyptic*, 37-39) oversimplification of this interrelationship is well-taken: "This in itself correct assessment becomes false because Rowley employs it as a methodological principle." Birkeland ("Resurrection," 62-63) labels extreme *any* view which would position the origin and/or development of this or any other motif wholly *inside* or wholly *outside* Hebraic sources.

a balanced interpretation of the recognizedly apocalyptic text of Dan 12:1–4.

5. Nor is this reconstruction intended to reopen debate about the "origins of apocalyptic." Clements' position seems closer than most: "Only in the course of its development does apocalyptic adopt more and more features from wisdom. In essence apocalyptic is a late and distinctive, yet nonetheless legitimate, form of prophecy."[20] Thus, since Dan 12:1–4 is widely considered to be "late," the metaphor of confluent streams seems solid-enough-yet-fluid-enough to provide a workable framework for analysis without leading off into tangential fiery lakes of incessant debate over *gradations* of influence.

6. Few subjects in Tanak studies are as divisive as the dating of the book of Daniel. The present critical consensus is that parts of the book, especially the stories in chapters 1–6, are quite old, but that the material in chapters 7–12 is an imaginative response to the persecution of Antiochus IV Epiphanes (d. 164 BCE).[21] Some will disagree with this chronology, but this is not the best place to rehearse this debate.[22]

7. Finally, this essay presumes, with von Rad and others, that there are serious limitations to the historico-critical method generally, and that history possesses a transcendent dimension with which historico-critical methods alone cannot fully engage.[23]

The methodology here may be described as a fusion of two approaches: (a) the *diachronic* approach, in which attention focuses on the

---

20. Clements, *Prophecy*, 11. This approximates the basic presumption of the present study, yet with the realization that the debate is far from closed. Smith ("Wisdom," 86), e.g., argues that "apocalypticism is Wisdom lacking a royal court and patron, and therefore it surfaces during the period of late antiquity not as a response to religious persecution, but as an expression of the trauma of the cessation of native kingship. Apocalypticism is a learned rather than a popular religious phenomenon" (because both scribal *literati* and apocalypticists prize the preservation of "*Listenwissenschaft*"). On the whole, however, von der Osten-Sacken's original objections (*Apokalyptik*, 18–34) to von Rad's "wisdom < apocalyptic" thesis (*Theology* 2.301–7) await convincing refutation.

21. See Moore, "Maccabees," 1055–71.

22. See Moore, "Daniel," 128–30. Collins ("Daniel," 2) reports a "broad consensus" that "the visions in chapters 7–12 are composed by persons . . . in the Maccabean era."

23. "For Israel, history consists only of Yahweh's self-revelation by word and action. And on this point conflict with the modern view is sooner or later inevitable, for the latter finds it perfectly possible to construct a picture of history without God" (von Rad, *Theology* 2.418). Kitchen takes a harsher view of what he calls "late-period minimalism's bizarre frolics" (*Reliability*, 485).

chronological development of ancient traditions over time; and (b) the *polyphonic* approach, which seeks to preserve the creative tension between variegated traditions.[24] Piloted by the foregoing presumptions, delimitations, and methodology, the purpose of this essay is to define as precisely as possible the nature of the relationship between the motifs of "resurrection" and "immortality" in Dan 12:1-4.

THE PROBLEM OF DEATH

To define with empirical precision exactly what death means is not an easy task. As Martin-Achard observes, death is "a mysterious phenomenon creating complex and contradictory reactions, and it is an error to try and integrate them at all costs."[25] Apparently early on in their history the Hebrews simply accept the reality of death as an essential part of human existence.[26] To die "old and full of years" is natural, almost peaceful,[27] but to die a premature death,[28] or to perish away from one's ancestral homeland is always tragic.[29] Contemporaneous with these notions (or perhaps later in Israel's development), death becomes something genuinely feared[30] because (a) it causes despair;[31] (b) it causes mournfulness;[32] and (c) it destroys the creature's life-giving relationship to its Creator.[33]

Residual mythological elements occasionally surface in various other efforts to define the origins of evil and death, but Tanak tends to redefine these issues in moral terms, relying particularly on the dynamics of human sin and guilt, elements conspicuously marginal in the myths of Israel's neighbors. In one area, however, Israelite beliefs are practically identical to

---

24. See Newsom, "Polyphonic," 3-31.

25. Martin-Achard, *Résurrection*, 16. "Careful investigation of death, as the laments and thanksgivings understand it, has had the unexpected result of showing that Israel holds a highly comprehensive and complex concept of it not at all easy to define" (von Rad, *Theology* 1.387).

26. Gen 27:2; 48:21; 50:24; 2 Sam 19:38. This survey, in line with the polyphonic methodology stated above, focuses longitudinally on the development of Hebrew beliefs, though Martin-Achard's criticism (*Résurrection*, 18) of Lods' (*Croyance* 1.43-75) over-reliance on this approach is well taken.

27. Gen 25:8; 35:29; Job 42:17; 1 Chron 23:1; 29:29.

28. Isa 38:10-13.

29. Jer 20:6; 22:11-12; 42:16-17; Ezek 12:13; 17:16; Amos 7:17.

30. Gen 20:8; 26:7; 32:12; 1 Kings 19:3.

31. Gen 37:35; 42:38; 44:31; 1 Sam 15:32; 2 Sam 19:1.

32. 2 Sam 1:19-27; 3:33-35; Jer 22:18.

33. Isa 38:10-13; Ps 6:6; 30:10; 88:11; 115:17.

those of her neighbors—their common belief in a netherworld. The solution Israel proposes to the finality of the Pit,[34] however, is very different from that found in the *Descent of Ishtar*[35] or the *Disappearance of Ba'al*.[36] Neighboring religious cultures habitually gravitate to ritual solutions organically linked to the cycle of the seasons when faced with the problem of death, but Israel goes in a different direction.

PROPOSED SOLUTIONS

Prophetic Eschatological Hope

Hos 6:1-3; 13:14—At first glance the prophet Hosea seems to place in the mouths of penitent Ephraimites a genuine confession of sin designed to enable the restoration of a revitalized covenant relationship with their Sovereign Lord Yahweh. Closer examination of this "confession," however, shows it to be more satirical than straightforward, at least in tone.[37] Its cultic language might well be intended to palliate Yahweh's wrath as one would appease any other capricious deity, an interpretation supported by the fact that the very next verses show Yahweh's prophet vocalizing frustration over Ephraim's adolescent syncretism, ridiculing their vegetation-cycle mentality like he would that of any other Ba'alist.[38] In 13:14, though, Hosea boldly addresses the question to which Ezekiel and Deutero-Isaiah give such direct attention later: "Where, O Death, are your plagues? Where, O Sheol, is your destruction?"[39]

Ezek 37:1-14—The national despair confronting Ezekiel seems terminal: "Our bones are dried up and our hope is lost; we are clean cut off."[40]

---

34. Particularly vivid is the imagery in Ps 69:16 (ET 69:15): ‏אל־תבלעני מצולה ואל־תאטר־עלי באר פיה‎, "Do not let the deep swallow me up; Do not let the pit close its jaws (lit. "mouth") over me."

35. Dalley, *Myths*, 154–62.

36. *UNP* 81–176.

37. See Barré, "Light," 129–41.

38. Hos 2:8. See Smith (*Ba'al*, 79–81); Moscati (*Orient*, 210); and Hayes (*Riches*, 287–96).

39. Continuing the 1st pers. of the previous couplet, MT reads ‏אהי דבריך מות אהי קטבך שאול‎, "I am your plagues, O Death; I am your destruction O Sheol." Vg follows, but OG and Syr read (or arbitrarily insert) interrogative pronouns. With many others, del Olmo Lete ("Deber," 232) reads these epithets as personifications of demonic power.

40. Olyan ("Nuances," 44, 46) sees this text applying not simply to dead Hebrews, but to "the state of exiled Judah's covenant relationship with Yhwh"; i.e., "not only does Yhwh no longer remember the dead, a striking claim in and of itself; he does nothing for them. They are cut off from his hand, which seems to mean that they exist in a realm

Lamenting Yahweh's "injustice,"⁴¹ some Hebrew exiles complain that the tragedy of losing their homeland is just too much to bear,⁴² forcing them to cry out, "How can we now live?"⁴³ Responding to this proverb, Yahweh projects before Ezekiel's eyes a fantastic vision—that of an entire nation's defiled skeletal remains miraculously coming back to life, vigorously reanimated by the divine רוח ("spirit"/"breath"). Yet for all the drama and spectacle of this "resurrection," it does not occur for *their* sake primarily, but "for the sake of my holy name."⁴⁴ Its *raison d'être* is to prove to all doubters that Yahweh of Hosts is indeed Lord of the *entire* universe—including the netherworld. Whereas Wisdom is the predominant vehicle for the theodical and later, retributional questions about human existence,⁴⁵ Ezekiel's main concern is to vindicate the Name before all pretenders, detractors, and critics.

Isa 53:10b-12—The suffering Servant of Yahweh, like the exiles he symbolically represents, experiences premature death, a (possible) debilitating disease (an intrusion of death's power),⁴⁶ and even the disgrace of having to be laid in the tomb of a wicked man. Yet in spite of all this Yahweh prolongs his days, gives him posterity, and allots him a portion with the great, making it clear that the operant force in the Servant's ability to extend Yahweh's צדק ("justice") to others is his דעת ("knowledge").⁴⁷ Some argue that in this last Servant song the streams of wisdom and prophecy already converge.⁴⁸

---

beyond the bounds of his activity and, perhaps, of his power."

41. Ezek 33:17.

42. Rautenburg ("Tobit," 101) argues that Tobit, like most diaspora tales, "clothes" itself "in a geographical setting . . . outside the motherland" in order to help struggling refugees keep their restoration hopes alive.

43. Ezek 33:10. Joyce (*Ezekiel*, 191) sees a sapiential nuance in this response: "Perhaps Heb פשעינו וחטאתינו in v. 10 should be taken to refer not to (acknowledged) sins, but rather to (undeserved) punishments," so that "the words of 33:10 would then amount to the same as the 'sour grapes' proverb of 18:2."

44. Ezek 43:22. Following de Vaux ("Yahvé," 221), Keck reasonably argues that "The Name formula . . . simply declares Yahweh's possession without attempting to revolutionize the nature of his presence at the sanctuary" ("Glory," 14).

45. Job 14; Qoh 9:1–6; Sir 41:1–13. Apparently Hasel disagrees ("Resurrection," 283).

46. Ch. Barth (*Tode*, 93) defines death not simply as the loss of temporal life, but as the loss of free movement, the loss of community, and the loss of natural nourishment due to sickness, misfortune or calamity. "The determinative thing is not that one still lives, but that one has ventured too close to the realm of the dead."

47. Isa 53:11. "The Servant who has the task of bringing forth redemptive justice (Isa 42:1, 3, 4) carries that task through by a knowledge (53:11, דעת) which is the praxis of his sufferings and thereby his participation in the work and play of redemptive wisdom" (Janzen, *Job*, 121).

48. Hilber identifies several parallels with Ps 91 (*Prophecy*, 208).

Certainly there are sapiential elements in this prophetic text: emphasis on a prosperous, healthy life,[49] "eternal" life through healthy posterity, and "eternal" life through the remembrance of one's good name."[50] Even though there is no explicit reference here to (a) the prophetic eschatological hope depicted elsewhere in Nevi'im (e.g., the phrase "on that day"),[51] or (b) the Servant's "resurrection,"[52] Martin-Achard is correct to point out that the emphasis here is on the glorious reward Yahweh's Servant receives for his vicarious atoning work.[53]

Isa 26:19—Within the Isa 24–27 "booklet" the prophetic eschatological hope rings loud and clear.[54] Whereas Ezekiel proclaims this hope to vindicate the Name, this text posits a polarity between the "ancestral dead"[55] and "Yahweh's dead."[56] Logically speaking, if the raising of Yahweh's "dead" is simply an Ezekiel-like metaphor for national restoration, then the "ancestral dead" must only be *metaphorically* "dead." But if the "ancestral dead" are, in fact the dead shades inhabiting Sheol, then must not Isaiah be promising to "your (Yahweh's) dead" the gift of resurrection? Of interest here also is the growing emphasis on Yahweh's universal reign. While one finds elements of retribution, the weight of the passage rests on Yahweh's kingship and glory. Later, in the fully apocalyptic text of Dan 12:1–4, these and other, more retributional motifs come into their fullest form in Tanak, though the Wisdom of Solomon in the Greek Bible speaks directly to (a) the ultimate destinies of the righteous and the wicked, as well as (b) the theological reasons for their different fates.[57]

---

49. See parallels in *SAA* 3.13.18, 24; 9.9.9, 16, 20–21, 1'–3'.

50. Brendsel, *Isaiah*, 141–42. Kellermann ("Auferstehungsglauben," 266–67) recognizes these motifs as in all likelihood developed by *Wisdom* to address the problem of death.

51. See Delcor, "Temps," 97–134.

52. Like many others, Levenson cannot decide on whether or not the Fourth Servant Song actually speaks of "resurrection" (*Resurrection*, 188).

53. Martin-Achard, *Résurrection*, 109.

54. See van der Woude, "Resurrection," 143–64.

55. MT רפאים; OG τῶν ἀσεβῶν; Vg *gigantum* (see Day, "Dependence," 360).

56. MT מתיך ("your dead"). Vg follows (*mortui tui*), but OG sidesteps this distinction (ἀναστήσονται οἱ νεκροί, "the dead will be resurrected"). Smith summarizes ("Rephaim," 675): "The Ugaritic view of the Rephaim as a dead group broadens in the biblical texts describing the Rephaim as the dead in general."

57. Wis 2:22; 3:1–13; 5:1–2, 15. Eichrodt (*Theology* 2.510) recognizes that "it is not primarily the idea of retribution which leads to the postulate of the resurrection of the dead. At least in the Isaiah Apocalypse hope of a revelation of God's glory plays an incomparably more important part." Linebaugh (*Solomon*, 32) adds that the Wisdom of Solomon delays this retribution so that "the symmetrical justice of deuteronomic

Wisdom Teaching

Whereas traditional "prophetic" circles[58] tend to deal with the problem of death by proclaiming against it the irrevocability of Yahweh's sovereignty, the vindication of his holy Name, and the coming of a "day"[59] when the faithful remnant of Israel will rise from the "dust," the sages deal with the problem quite differently. Like the prophets, they accept the existence of a netherworld, yet often voice bewilderment over why Yahweh so completely segregates himself from it.[60] Job even tentatively raises the possibility most abhorrent to the prophets; viz., that Sheol may be a place where one can actually *hide* from Yahweh.[61] Taken to its logical conclusion, this kind of thinking leads to theological dualism. Eliphaz thus condemns Job's speculation by voicing what he feels to be his *real* problem—Job's unwillingness to accept the need for retributional law.[62] To Eliphaz, as to Israelite Wisdom generally,[63] Job's agonized speech amounts to "unprofitable talk."[64] Consequently, if Yahweh's power *does* in fact extend to Sheol, does not the power to kill or make alive, to disestablish or reestablish any sort of relationship to this deity reside solely in Yahweh's hands? "Can death be conquered for *me*?" is the question preoccupying Job. The Hebrew sages wrestling with this question hardly lack concern for the fate of their nation. They simply choose to focus more on the plight of its suffering people.

Ps 90:13–17—Were it not for these five verses, this psalm would stand as a gloomy lament on the brevity of human life lived out under the consuming wrath of a vengeful deity, a fate for which the only valid response is quiet resignation. The sudden change of tone in vv. 13–17 leads many to wonder whether these final verses might not be the remnant of a lately-appended folksong.[65] Whatever its history of formation, however, the psalm's

---

theology is preserved by being postponed."

58. Defined here as those bands of Hebrew scribes most responsible for gathering, preserving, and reshaping earlier, classically written (and often oral) prophetic pronouncements into a living, flowing stream of tradition (see Knight, *Traditions*, 165–220).

59. See Moore, "Day," 193–208.

60. E.g., Job 14:20–22.

61. Job 14:13.

62. Job 15:20–26.

63. Von Rad (*Wisdom*, 304–6) temperately points out that Wisdom is to a great extent limited by human mortality (Prov 16:1). In his intensely personal confrontation with Death, Job soon finds himself running out of "acceptable" answers.

64. See Moore, "Terror," 670–73.

65. See discussion in Curtis, "Moses," 89–99.

final form represents, if only in embryo, an attempt to engage Job's question: "Resignation before death is *not* the final answer; there has to be more to 'life' than this."

Ps 22:29–31—Ps 22, another individual lament, replicates several of the motifs articulated in Job 14. It begins with the cry made famous centuries later in the Nazarene passion narrative, "My God, my God, why have you forsaken me?"[66] The solution offered here to the problem of death is more satisfying than the one in Ps 90. Gruesomely describing his sufferings, the psalmist urges Yahweh to linger until he can declare, in a sweeping crescendo of praise, how "all the proud of the earth shall bow down to him . . ., all who sink down into the dust, even those who cannot keep themselves alive."[67] To Job's question the psalmist replies that the relationship between creator and creature cannot only be reestablished, but that the dead can and will *praise* him, an activity from which even those yet unborn will someday profit. This is not resurrection in the prophetic sense, but it does represent faith in death's ultimate transcendence, even if reserved only for those who bask in the divine Presence.[68]

Pss 49:15 & 73:23–38—These wisdom-psalms distinguish between two groups: the righteous poor and the wicked rich—doubtless a polarity reflecting the type of sociological situation which is charted in the pioneering work of Plöger, Hanson, and Millar. Here the spectre of death is launched out into the broad mainstream of sapiential preoccupation with theodical retribution. Job 14 formulates this problem in the shape of a cry for rehabilitation. Qohelet preemptively dismisses it as הבל ("meaningless").[69] And Sirach characteristically advises his students not to worry about its implications.[70] These wisdom psalms, however, in contrast to Qohelet's portrayal of death as the great *leveller*, depict it as the great *divider*.[71] In Ps 49 Yahweh

---

66. Matt 25:46.

67. Though ignored by the versions, N.B. the clear priestly parallel between כל יורדי עפר ("all who sink into the dust") and כל דשני ארץ, "all the greasy ashes (left on) the earth"; i.e., after an animal sacrifice (Ps 22:30).

68. See Moore, "Presence," 166–70.

69. כי החיים יודעים שימתו והמתים אינם יודעים מאומה ואין עוד להם שכר כי נשכח זכרם, "For the living know that they will die, but the dead know nothing; they have no more reward, and even their memory is forgotten" (Qoh 9:5).

70. אל תפחד ממות חקך זכר קדמון ואחרון עמד זה קץ כל ב[שר, "Do not fear death, your 'destiny' (lit., 'statute'); remember your people—those who come before and those who come after you. This is the end of all fl[esh]" (Sir 41:3–4a).

71. "Death is encountered here not, as in the skepticism of Qohelet, as the great *leveler*, but as the great *divider*" (Kellermann, "Auferstehungsglauben," 275).

graciously does for the righteous what the wicked cannot do; viz., "ransom my soul" and "receive me (to glory)."[72]

Job 19:25-27—Though the text is difficult and the date uncertain,[73] here a similar hope appears for a גואל redeemer like the one promised in Pss 49 and 73; i.e., a redeemer who delights in making it possible for suffering, dying individuals to reexperience their relationship with the Living God.[74]

THE APOCALYPTIC TEXT OF DAN 12:1-4

The scribe responsible for shaping this passage fuses together elements from both prophetic and sapiential streams into an explicit statement about the resurrection of the dead and the immortality of the righteous. Prophetic notions provide the eschatological framework,[75] which consists of a strong belief in the absolute sovereignty of God, challenged so arrogantly by the heathen king, yet here reaffirmed through Michael the great prince who "stands over" God's elect.[76] Employing many of the same motifs heretofore traced to the prophetic stream of tradition in Tanak, the Danielic scribe boldly voices a now-mature, dynamic faith in the resurrection of God's righteous elect from the dead. The *extent* of this resurrection may be debatable,[77] but not its *provenance*.

---

72. אך אלהים יפדה נפשי מיד שאול כי יקחני, "Surely God will ransom my soul from the power of Sheol, for he will receive me" (Ps 49:16).

73. See Moore, "Terror," 665-66.

74. In Brichto's schema ("Afterlife," 21), the גואל-redeemer is "not merely a close kinsman obligated to blood vengeance or privileged to redeem property," but the one "who redeems the dead from the danger to his afterlife by continuing his line."

75. N.B. the references to specific dates and phrases like "at this time" and "in those days" in Dan 10:1-2, 14; 11:7, 14, 27, 29, 35, 40; 12:1 (עת four times), 12:4 (again עת), 7, 9, 11, 13. De Vries ("Observations," 273-74) sees in the later sections of Daniel a sharpened particularism and dualism, cosmic speculation, and the radical periodization of time—all elements of a heightened prophetic eschatology.

76. See parallels in Jub 17.15-18.12; 48.9-19; 1 Enoch 89.70-77; 90.17; 11QMelch. "The occurrence of the term עמד . . . suggests that Michael's defense of Israel is not only military, but also judicial" (Nickelsburg, *Resurrection*, 14).

77. Discussion centers on the word רבים (Dan 12:2). Does it mean "many" or "all"? The first interpretation ("many") leads some to argue that only righteous martyrs will be raised from the dead (see Charles, *Daniel*, 140; Mowinckel, *Cometh*, 173; Porteous, *Daniel*, 20, 170). The second interpretation ("all") leads others to argue that both pious and impious will be raised alike (see Meinhold, *Daniel*, 336; König, *Jenseitsvorstellungen*, 241). A third view is that general resurrection applies to all Israel; see Davidson (*Theology*, 528); von Gall (*Eschatologie*, 307); Goettsburger (*Daniel*, 237); Snaith (*Ideas*, 89); Dexinger (*Daniel*, 69); Plöger (*Daniel*, 171).

Wisdom contributes most of the content within this prophetic framework. The "book" (of life) is a very old motif[78] originating either from a prophetic eschatological recasting[79] or from the anguished cry of *a* man fearful of falling into the Pit, seeking a redeemer, seeking retribution against his enemies, and asking that their names be blotted out of "the book of the living."[80] Even stronger retributional promises flow from the pen of the Danielic scribe when writing not only about restoring the righteous dead to life, but also when predicting the eternal fate of the wicked after *their* resurrection (unlike Pss 49 and 73).[81] A much discussed motif in sapiential circles,[82] this recasting opens the door for even more explicit prediction about the fate of the wicked "in these last days."[83]

Perhaps the most obvious sign of sapiential influence comes in the explicit identification of "the wise"[84] who "shine like the brightness of the firmament." Scattered throughout the book of Daniel this root שׂכל appears no less than ten times. In almost every instance it describes Daniel or his Hebrew colleagues.[85] In the opening story, for example, Daniel and his colleagues are "wise in all wisdom,"[86] as those to whom God gives "knowledge and skill in every aspect of literature and wisdom."[87] In his prayer of supplication, Daniel laments that even after all the calamities they have suffered, his people Israel still seem unwilling "to understand your truth."[88] In response to this prayer, Gabriel comes to Daniel "to give you wisdom and

---

78. Exod 32:32-33.

79. Isa 4:3; Jer 22:30; Ezek 13:9.

80. Ps 69:15, 18, 22-27, 29. Kellermann ("Auferstehungsglauben," 263) stoutly maintains that the problem of human (esp. individual) suffering is *wisdom*'s task. Nickelsburg (*Resurrection*, 15-16) posits several parallels between Dan 12:1 and 4QDibHam, a "Qumran prayer manuscript almost contemporary with the writing of Daniel."

81. 2 Bar 49-51 elaborates in some detail (see Harrington, "Afterlife," 21-34).

82. Wis 3:1-13; 4:16-20.

83. 4 Macc 9:8, 32; 10:11, 15; 12:19; 13:15; 18:5, 22; Matt 18:8-9; Mark 9:48; Luke 12:4-5.

84. המשׂכלים (Dan 12:3). Martin-Achard's analysis sidesteps the close connections here with the sapiential terms חכמה, בינה, and דעת (*Résurrection*, 109). It is pure conjecture to translate ישׂכיל as "he will be exalted" in Isa 52:13.

85. The exception occurs in Dan 8:25, describing the "wisdom/cunning" (שׂכל) of the "king of bold countenance" (8:23 // מבין חידות, lit. "skilled with riddles").

86. משׂכלים בכל חכמה (Dan 1:4).

87. מדע והשׂכל בכל ספר וחכמה (Dan 1:17).

88. להשׂכיל באמתך (Dan 9:13).

understanding,"[89] urging him to "know and understand" what the future holds.[90]

CONCLUSIONS

In the Epiphanian persecution only the Danielic "wise ones" will be able to guide people through "the time of trouble, such as never has been since a nation existed."[91] Like the Suffering Servant before them, who through his knowledge makes many to be accounted righteous (accounting himself as "wise" in the process), these "wise ones" learn that even though many of them will suffer cruel deaths, this is *not* the end. The wicked will never understand what "life" truly means, but the "wise" eventually will. Returning to his prophetic eschatological framework, the Danielic scribe concludes by insisting that even though this knowledge increases (now made privy to the wise), the final outcome will not and cannot change. Daniel is thus to "shut up the words and seal the book" until all the divine promises are fulfilled.

---

89. להשכילך בינה (Dan 9:22).
90. תדע ותשכיל (Dan 9:25).
91. עת צרה אשר לא נהיתה מהיות גוי (Dan 12:1).

PART 3: WISDOM AND OTHER WRITINGS

12

RUTH THE MOABITE AND THE BLESSING OF FOREIGNERS*

THE BOOK OF RUTH preserves in written form one of the most compelling stories ever told. Not only does it represent the "perfect example of the art of telling a story,"[1] it also raises profound questions about human destiny and divine purpose. No other short story[2] so subtly ponders the phenomenon of female functionality in androcentric culture, or so gingerly contemplates the paradox of familial love in a creation corrupted by generations of ethnic "cleansing."[3] Contemporary literary analysis follows two main approaches: one synchronic,[4] the other increasingly structuralist.[5] Historical analysis often leads to theories about where the book "best fits," i.e., within a premonarchic,[6] monarchic,[7] or postmonarchic context[8] (or

---

* Revised from an essay published in *CBQ* 60 (1998) 203–17.
1. Trible, "Ruth," 842.
2. "Typically the short story combines fairytale, legendary, heroic, or mythic elements with a history-like orientation to daily affairs in some recognizable sphere of life.... Ruth is easily the most charming and exquisite of the ... biblical short stories" (Gottwald, *Introduction*, 314, 316).
3. Fewell & Gunn exploit these and other conflicts in the story, though often to unwarranted extremes (*Ruth*, 11–19).
4. See, e.g., Witzenrath (*Rut*); Sacon ("Ruth," 3–22).
5. See, e.g., Bertman ("Ruth," 165–68); Porten ("Ruth," 23–49); Korpel (*Ruth*, 218–24).
6. According to Talmud, Samuel is the author of Ruth (*b. B. Bat.* 14b).
7. Harrison (*Introduction*, 1062); Campbell (*Ruth*, 24); Hubbard (*Ruth*, 35).
8. Vesco, "Ruth," 245–47; Lacocque, "Ruth," 588–89.

some variation thereof).⁹ This essay will not engage these issues directly,¹⁰ but will instead examine the ברוך blessings in Ruth from a traditio-historical perspective. To anticipate my conclusions, I will argue that the blessings of Boaz (3:10) and the Bethlehemite women (4:14–15) operate within a particular subset of Tanak blessing traditions here designated the *Aussensegen* trajectory.¹¹ Evidence for this comes from a traditio-historical examination of (a) the *Aussensegen* trajectory against the backdrop of Tanak blessing traditions, (b) the contribution of the aforementioned blessings in Ruth to this *Aussensegen* trajectory, and (c) reactions to this trajectory in two early Jewish sources, *Tg. Ruth* and *b. Yebamot*.

BLESSING TRADITIONS IN TANAK

In 1929 Albrecht Alt investigates the tension in Torah between the promise of many descendants and the promise of a homeland. Relying on a rather atomistic, yet academically fashionable analysis of Gen 15, he decides that the promise of descendants must be older than the promise of land.¹² Many of his colleagues agree with this identification, yet challenge his chronology. Walther Zimmerli, for example, thinks that the promise of land is no less important than the promise of descendants, and disagrees with Alt's decision to date it later.¹³ Jacob Hoftijzer simply views these promises as sequential, the promise of a homeland being Abraham's immediate reward for trusting in the promise of many descendants.¹⁴ Gerhard Von Rad and Martin Noth take a different tack altogether, arguing that because the promise of land so powerfully energizes the "promise-fulfillment" construct knitting Torah's traditions altogether,¹⁵ it must be the more significant of the two, regardless of its chronological standing in the history of tradition.¹⁶

---

9. See, e.g., Glanzman, "Ruth," 201–7. Lemaire's attempt ("Ruth," 124–29) to link Phoen גאולה (attested on the seventh-century-BCE inscription from Cebel Ires Daği) to the Hebrew institution of גאולה (Ruth 4:7; Lev 25:29) Lipiński finds "a bit far-fetched" (*Phoenicia*, 129).

10. Korpel provides a thorough history of research (*Ruth*, 5–30).

11. "Blessing-of/by-foreigners."

12. Alt, "Fathers," 3–86.

13. Zimmerli, "Promise," 89–122.

14. Hoftijzer, *Verheissungen*, 6–25.

15. I.e., ancestral saga + exodus from captivity + Sinai covenant + guidance into arable land.

16. Von Rad, "Promised," 79–102; Noth, *Traditions*, 54–58.

It is Hans Walter Wolff, however, who finally recognizes a fundamental sociohistorical distinction between these two promises.¹⁷ Gen 15 confirms the promise of a homeland via an *oath* while the promise of descendants is validated by the phenomenon of divine *blessing*.¹⁸ Blessing is the essential element in the creator's desire to reclaim his creation, and does not in any way depend on human activity or behavior. Each promise, in other words, arises from a different *Sitz im Leben*, and these two *Sitze* cannot be confused if authentic interpretation is to occur. Moving the discussion about the ancestral promises to a new plane, Wolff thus achieves two results. *First*, he successfully applies contemporary form criticism to Torah by focusing attention on the variegated *Sitze im Leben* out of which each promise arises (regardless of chronology). *Second*, by so doing he moves discussion about these promises away from simplistic typological schemas and uncertain chronological speculation, thereby opening up more specific questions about the nature, function and purpose of the Hebrew blessing traditions.¹⁹

THE AUSSENSEGEN TRAJECTORY

Now we might pause right here, and without further ado examine the book of Ruth from the perspective of these ancestral promises because one of the book's main goals is to "replenish"²⁰ Israel's hope in the promise for descendants. Most students of Ruth agree that the תולדות genealogy sits at the end of the book (regardless of how or when it gets there)²¹ in order to catalyze reflection on the ancestral promise of descendants first enunciated in Torah, particularly since one of these descendants, David son of Jesse, proves to be a great blessing to the Hebrews,²² and from a Christian perspective, to the rest of creation as well.²³ Yet the book of Ruth is much more than a messianic preamble. Fundamentally it tells the story of a Moabite נכריה²⁴

---

17. Wolff, "Kerygma," 41–66.
18. Gen 12:1–4. See Westermann, "Blessing," 85–117.
19. See Westermann (*Promises*, 95–163); Boorer (*Promise*, 1–128); and Baden (*Promise*, 9–10).
20. Many see the heroine's name, רות, as deriving from the root רוה, "to replenish."
21. Nielsen argues that the תולדות ("genealogy") is what inspires the writing of the rest of the book as a "final ancestral narrative" ("Ruth," 81–93).
22. "R. Ḥunya says, 'It is as a result of the blessings of those women that the line of David is not entirely cut off in the days of Athaliah'" (*Ruth Rab.* 7.15).
23. Matt 12:22–23; 20:29; Acts 4:25; 2 Tim 2:8. See Hatina, "David," 130–32.
24. Heb "foreigner" (Ruth 2:10; see *HAL* 661–62).

extending and receiving a blessing from southern Hebrews.²⁵ To understand *this* dimension of the story, however, we must read it from an angle committed to ascertaining whether and/or how much the blessings in Ruth resonate with those in other international encounters. We must try to find out how these *Aussensegen* blessings fit into the larger story of Hebrew redemption, and if possible, assess them within a recognizable socioliterary grid.²⁶

The Blessing of Melchizedek

The first of Tanak's international encounters occurs near the beginning of Genesis in Melchizedek's blessing of Abraham:²⁷

Blessed be Abram before El Elyon	ברוך אברם לאל עליון
Creator of heaven and earth	קנה שמים וארץ
And blessed be El Elyon	וברוך אל עליון
Who delivers your adversaries into your hand	אשר מגן צריך בידך

As is well known, the historicity of this encounter is disputed. Maximalists vehemently argue for an historical kernel here, while minimalists relegate the entire Melchizedek tradition to the realm of literary legend.²⁸ It's tempting to jump into this discussion, only this would only lead us away from the task at hand. What can be said about *this* text? *First*, these parallel bicola have a regular metrical structure (8+8+8+8) similar to that found in other *Aussensegen* texts (e.g., Num 24:3–9). *Second*, the twice-repeated DN in Melchizedek's blessing, אל עליון, is clearly attested elsewhere.²⁹ *Third*, active participles govern each mention of this divine name to emphasize the beneficent power³⁰ of the ANE deity responsible for authorizing this blessing.³¹

---

25. Prinsloo ("Ruth," 341) intuitively understands this, speaking of "an additional level of meaning" in Ruth "in that the blessings of Yahweh are shown not to be confined to a single family, but to extend much further."

26. See Moore, "Ruth," 293–99.

27. Gen 14:19–20. See Horton, *Melchizedek*, 12–53.

28. See Provan, "Ideologies," 585–606. Lehmann may be right to call the "maximalist-minimalist" labels "facile and misleading" ("Jerusalem," 117), but no other terms more precisely describe this polarity.

29. See *CAT* 1.16.3.6 and *KAI* 222.A.11. Lack argues ("Elyon," 44–64) that עליון is an early epithet for אל, then later, as the storm-god's influence progresses, for בעלשמין (Ba'alšamayin, "Ba'al of the heavens," *KAI* 202.3).

30. "The benefits of the blessing are interpreted through its verbs" (Nitzan, *Prayer*, 146).

31. Sarna sees מגן as a catchword linking Gen 14:20 with 15:1, thereby stitching together two major sections of the Abraham cycle (*Genesis*, 121–22).

In short, Melchizedek's blessing consists of a rather typical ברוך-formula pronounced over a Hebrew leader by a foreign priest in a southern locale at a cultic occasion specially arranged for this purpose.

The Blessing of Jethro

Soon after Israel's foray into the wilderness another foreign priest pronounces another *Aussensegen* blessing over yet another Hebrew leader:[32]

Blessed be Yahweh who delivers you	ברוך יהוה אשר הציל אתכם
From the hand of Egypt and the hand of Pharaoh	מיד מצרים ומיד פרעה
Who delivers the people	אשר הציל את העם
From the suffocating hand of Egypt	מתחת יד מצרים
Now I know that Yahweh is greater	עתה ידעתי כי גדול יהוה
Than all the gods	מכל האלהים
Because of the moment	כי הדבר
When they defamed them	אשר זדו עליהם.

Someone reworks this blessing to fit into the surrounding prose narrative,[33] yet without eliminating altogether its poetic elements. The verb נצל, for example, appears twice in practically identical parallel clauses. Phrases involving the word יד ("hand/power") repeat three times,[34] certainly for poetic emphasis, yet doubtless also to assure the blessing's recipient of the deity's approval. Note also the nice concluding rhyme with אלהים and עליהם. The *first* main difference between this blessing and Melchizedek's blessing is the mention of Egyptian attempts to "defame" (זיד) Israel, evidently a "matter" (דבר) Yahweh takes very seriously. The *second*, of course, is that Yahweh is the deity upon whom the foreign priest calls, not El Elyon. Thus this ברוך blessing, like Melchizedek's, highlights the victory of Israel over a determined adversary, and likewise comes from a southern priest in a neighboring tribe. The content unabashedly revels in the power of Yahweh to conquer, and like the blessing of Melchizedek, probably occurs at a cultic ceremony.[35]

---

32. Exod 18:10–11. "The text seems unwilling to admit Jethro fully into the community, to assimilate him and thereby eliminate his otherness.... His value and credibility inhere specifically within his alien identity" (Shoulson, *Conversion*, 48).

33. The final line looks rather awkward, however, particularly in its use of דבר, here translated "moment" to effect better English flow.

34. See Roberts, "Hand," 244–51; *HAL* 369–71.

35. "The act of blessing Yahweh is a cultic form of praise ... uncommon in the Pentateuch" (Dozeman, *Exodus*, 403).

The Blessing of Balaam

A third blessing appears in the fourth oracle of Balaam:[36]

How pleasant are your tents, O Jacob	מה טבו אהליך יעקב
Your pavilions, O Israel	משכנתיך ישראל
Like wadis, they branch out	כנחלים נטיו
Like orchards beside a river	כגנת עלי נהר
Like aloes Yahweh has planted	כאהלים נטע יהוה
Like cedars beside the water	כארזים עלי מים
He pours out water from his buckets	יזל מים מדליו
His seed over "many waters"[37]	וזרעו במים רבים
He exalts his king(ship) higher than Gog[38]	וירם מאגג מלכו
His kingdom is exalted	ותנשא מלכתו
El leads him out of Egypt	אל מוציאו ממצרים
His glory is like that of a wild ox	כתועפת ראם לו
He devours the nations hostile to him	יאכל גוים צריו
He gnaws their bones, strikes with his arrows	ועצמתיהם יגרם וחציו ימחץ
Like a lion he lies down and sleeps	כרע שכב כארי
And just as with any lion, who will disturb him?	וכלביא מי יקימנו
Blessed be those who bless you	מברכיך ברוך
And cursed be those who curse you	וארריך ארור.

This magnificent poem, with its vivid imagery and powerful metaphors, is one of the most energetic contributors to the *Aussensegen* trajectory. Its unabashed celebration of Hebrew power emphasizes a theme already present in the blessings of Melchizedek and Jethro. Yet note the differences. Most obviously, the metaphors of "conquest" are more elaborate, and the language in which they appear more ebullient. Balaam does not see just one tent; he

---

36. Num 24:5–9. Rouillard puts the final redaction of this poem in the (post)exilic period (*Balaam*, 1–35).

37. See May, "Cosmic," 9–21.

38. MT Num 24:7 reads אגג (Syr ܐܓܓ), but OG reads Γωγ ("Gog"), as does Sam, Th, and OL. Gog, of course, is the mythical name of a foreign deity in Ezek 38–39, and is likely paralleled by Ωγ in OG Num 24:23 (see Tooman, *Gog*, 141). Rouillard (*Balaam*, 371) is inclined to see here the historical Agag (1 Sam 15:32–33), even though "Agag becomes here almost symbolic, even mythical, and this intuition leads the versions to prefer 'Gog.'"

sees a pavilion of tents. He does not see one stream; he sees a network of streams, all branching out into the desert.³⁹ The poet's point seems to be that Abraham's family has now grown into a tribe no longer confined to the loins of weary old men or the wombs of barren old women. This "seed" is now a force so powerful, it has to be carted about in buckets. In short, Balaam's blessing is another ברוך blessing pronounced by another foreign priest in another southern locale in yet another cultic setting.⁴⁰

The Blessing of the Sabean Queen

The Sabean queen's blessing occurs outside of Torah in Nevi'im:⁴¹

Happy are your wives⁴²	אשרי אנשיך
Happy are these your servants	אשרי עבדיך אלה
Who stand before you continually	העמדים לפניך תמיד
Who listen to your wisdom	השמעים את חכמתך
Blessed be Yahweh your God!	יהי יהוה אלהיך ברוך.

The historicity of this international encounter, like those attested above, is hotly disputed. Minimalists like Würthwein and Davies challenge it,⁴³ while maximalists like de Vaux, Gray, and Provan do not.⁴⁴ I am of the opinion that at the core of this narrative stands an original poetic blessing which, like the Balaam and Jethro blessings, only slightly changes at the hands of scribes later preoccupied with (a) magnifying Solomon's כבוד, and (b) highlighting Solomon's חכמה.⁴⁵ At any rate, this "parade example of international adulation"⁴⁶ occurs (again) in a southern locale (Jerusalem), and while not explicitly stated, the Temple may well be where it is pronounced,⁴⁷ since

---

39. Compare Ezekiel's vision in 47:1–12.

40. For a fuller description of this cultic context, see Moore, *Balaam*, 97–109.

41. 1 Kings 10:8–9. I am indebted to Prof. Claus Westermann for reading this essay in an earlier draft and suggesting (in personal correspondence) that I consider this blessing as part of the *Aussensegen* trajectory.

42. Reading with OG (γυναῖκές σου) and Syr (ܐܢܬܬܟ) against MT (אנשיך) and Vg (*viri tui*); see van Keulen, *Solomon*, 108–9.

43. Würthwein, *Könige*, 121; Davies, *Israel*, 29.

44. De Vaux, *Rois*, 71; Gray, *Kings*, 240–42; Provan, *Kings*, 86–87.

45. Whereas *TSol* 19.3 portrays the queen of Sheba as a *foil* to Solomon (Morray-Jones, *Illusion*, 265), 1 Kings 10 portrays her as a student willing to travel great distances to learn from a respected חכמה-professor (see Moore, "Sheba," 33–42).

46. Knoppers, *Solomon*, 131.

47. *TSol* 21.2 depicts the Sabean actually entering the דביר ("holy of holies").

the text *does* say that the Sabean "sees" the "holocaust offering"[48] sacrificed by Solomon at the בית יהוה.[49] Also, since Solomon's dedicatory prayer for the Temple explicitly pleads for Yahweh to listen to the prayer of the "foreigner" (נכרי),[50] I am inclined to see here the inclusion of a blessing which is organic, not secondary, to this text, one which, like the blessings in Ruth, expressly links a Davidic messiah to the *Aussensegen* trajectory.[51]

THE BLESSINGS IN THE BOOK OF RUTH

The first blessing in Ruth occurs when a Hebrew farmer (Boaz) blesses a Moabite widow (Ruth):[52]

May you be blessed by Yahweh, my daughter[53]	ברכה את ליהוה בתי
Your second kindness is better than the first	היטבת חסדך האחרון מן הראשון
For you have not gone after the young men	לבלתי לכת אחרי הבחורים
Whether poor or rich	אם דל ואם עשיר.

The second comes from the Bethlehemite women blessing Naomi:

Blessed be Yahweh who does not leave you today without a redeemer

ברוך יהוה אשר לא השבית לך גאל היום

May his name become famous in Israel	ויקרא שמו בישראל
May he be a lifesaver for you	והיה לך למשיב נפש
To sustain your grey head	ולכלכל את שיבתך
For your daughter-in-law, who loves you, has begotten him	כי כלתך אשר אהבתך ילדתו

---

48. ותרא מלכת שבא . . . עלתו אשר יעלה, "The Queen of Sheba saw . . . his עלה (OG ὁλοκαύτωσιν; Vg *holocausta*) which he offered," (1 Kings 10:4).

49. Heb "house of Yahweh," 1 Kings 10:4–5.

50. 1 Kings 8:41–43.

51. See Pomykala, *Messianism*; Roberts, "Messianic," 39–51; Chester, *Messiah*, 205–29.

52. Ruth 3:10. N.B. that Boaz earlier shares a ברוך blessing with his employees, the קוצרים ("harvesters," Ruth 2:4; // נערים in 2:9), men whose ethnicity is not specified.

53. The designation בתי ("my daughter"), combined with Boaz's clear admission that he is not one of the בחורים ("choice young men," 3:10) leads many early readers to conclude that he must be older than this young widow. Talmud imagines him as the father of sixty sons when Ruth enters his life, thus inspiring the proverb, "Of what use to you are the sixty you have already begotten? Marry again, and beget one 'stronger' (זריז) than these sixty" (*b. B. Bat.* 91a).

| She who is better for you than seven sons | אשר היא טובה משבעה בנים.[54] |

Vestigial poetic elements remain visible beneath the prose surface, even if we do not posit, with Jacob Myers, an original "epic poem."[55] At any rate, these international encounters share several characteristics with other *Aussensegen*; e.g., the comparative מ here occurs also in the blessings of Jethro and Balaam. In Jethro's blessing the comparison comes between Yahweh and "all the gods." In Balaam's blessing, it comes between Israel and Moab (and their neighbors). In the Bethlehemite women's blessing, the comparison comes between a Moabite girl and "seven sons," of whom this Hebrew mother-in-law can only now dream. Here in Ruth the locale is again southern, but lacking a foreign priest or a cultic setting. Instead we see a simpler, yet no less profound international encounter between a Hebrew man and a Moabite woman. Some rabbis identify him as Ibzan, mentioned in Judges 12:8 as a Bethlehemite שופט who rules briefly before the rise of the monarchy.[56] Yet even if this identification cannot be sustained, the man pronouncing the blessing over Ruth is *not* a priest.

Further, the content changes along with the form. The blessings in Ruth focus more on marital than martial "conquest." In fact, the nature of the Boaz-Ruth encounter is so subtly understated, at least when compared with other *Aussensegen* encounters, that the narrator seems to want readers to ask, "Who is 'conquering' whom?" The Hebrews or the Moabites? In other words, the *Aussensegen* trajectory is transforming.[57] Some of its elements remain intact (the meeting of Hebrew and Gentile; the use of ברוך; the southern locale), yet both form and content adapt considerably. Now the scope looks more familial than national, the tone less xenophobic and triumphalist. As the *Aussensegen* trajectory helps clarify, the emphasis here shifts from the glory of conquest to the struggle for survival. Distant echoes of these possibilities lie deep beneath the Jethro, Melchizedek, and Balaam encounters, yet here they define the very landscape of Ruth. In fact, in the blessing of the Bethlehemite women one gets the distinct impression that Naomi herself has become something of a "foreigner." Having taken on a different name (Mara) and different status (childless widow), she seems almost unrecognizable to her old friends ("Is this Naomi?"). Yet still they bless

---

54. Ruth 4:14–15. Doubtless Talmud's hyperbolic comparison (*b. B. Bat.* 91a) is inspired by this one.

55. Myers (*Ruth*, 34–36), challenged by Sasson (*Ruth*, 222) and Korpel (*Ruth*, 6), but supported by Porten ("Ruth," 23–49). De Moor cannot decide whether Ruth is prose with poetic insertions or "narrative poetry" ("Ruth," 16–41).

56. *Tg. Ruth* 1.6, followed by *b. B. Bat.* 91a.

57. See the essays in Halpern & Levenson, *Transformation*.

her as though she is as fruitful as their common ancestor, Tamar.[58] They bless her in the hope that the son produced by her Moabite daughter-in-law will eventually become her "lifesaver" (משיב נפש)[59] and redeemer (גואל).[60] It is this hope, this desire to fulfill the ancestral promise-for-descendants which the concluding תולדות makes explicit.

RABBINIC ENCOUNTERS WITH THE TRAJECTORY

As rabbinic thinkers start reading the Ruth scroll some begin to wonder whether the "replenishing" going on in Elimelek's family might not symbolically parallel the "replenishing" of Israel itself, even though they struggle with why Yahweh would choose to provide this replenishment through a נכריה.[61] Many derive the Moabite's name, רות, from the semitic root רוה, "to replenish,"[62] but do not argue with as much vitriolic energy over Ruth as over other foreigners like Melchizedek, Jethro, Job, and Balaam.[63] Most see her as a "good person," and the book of Ruth as "beautiful literature," yet wrestle hard with the questions it raises, wondering how this story might connect to issues involving national identity,[64] and struggling to figure out how its universalist ethic might actually work in a world so often and so determinedly anti-semitic.[65]

---

58. Gen 38:1–30. Whether or not Tamar is ethnically Hebrew is not clearly stated (see Menn, *Tamar*, 54).

59. Lit., "returner of soul."

60. See Moore, "Gyroscope," 27–35.

61. "There is a sense in which ... the birth of each child (is) the birth of another member of Israel ... which signifies a projection toward the future in terms of messianism .... Thus we arrive at the religio-ethical significance of fecundity" (Katz, *Levinas*, 88).

62. See esp. روٰل (WCA 369) According to Saxegaard (*Ruth*, 106), "philologically associated suggestions are 'to see,' 'to tremble,' 'to satiate' ... or 'to replenish.'" Because all these etymological connections are so loose, Block (*Ruth*, 587) describes them as "wishful thinking."

63. See Baskin, *Pharaoh*, 1–17.

64. See Goodblatt, *Nationalism*, 28–48.

65. See Beattie, *Exegesis*, 2–7. Maccoby (*Antisemitism*, 9) challenges the notion that "the Jewish sense of being a chosen people" is "a narrow insularism rather than a sense of universal vocation," arguing that "if this were true it would be most puzzling that the Judaism following the teaching of Ezra believes strongly in proselytism and gives canonical status to the books of Ruth, Jonah, and Job."

Targum Ruth

Tg. Ruth begins with a preamble in which the Aramaic translator states his opinion on why the book's opening famine drives Elimelech from Palestine: "Ten severe famines are decreed from heaven . . . from the day eternity was created until the coming of the messianic kingdom to reprove (the nations) . . . for polluting the earth."⁶⁶ Then he lists these famines in chronological order. The first nine occur in the days of Adam, Lamech, Abraham, Isaac, Jacob, Boaz, David, Elijah and Elisha. The tenth is to occur in the future, and is to be by far the worst of the lot. In its wake will arise a tremendous hunger not only for literal food, but for "the prophetic decree of God," i.e., a "famine of knowledge."⁶⁷ In other words, one of the earliest commentaries on Ruth reads it not as part of the *Aussensegen* trajectory, but as a xenophobic diatribe aimed at the enemies of Israel, real or imagined. From this translator's perspective, God sends the famine in the days of Ibzan/Boaz to test Israel and punish everyone else. Elimelek's tragedy thus sits on a *famine* trajectory, not a blessing trajectory, much less one interested in the blessing of *foreigners*.

Examples: Whereas Mahlon and Chilion simply "take Moabite wives" in MT Ruth 1:4,⁶⁸ the Aramaic commentator argues that by so doing "they transgress the decree of Yahweh."⁶⁹ Again, whereas MT Ruth 1:4 states that the second wife's name is "Ruth," the Aramaic commentator, far from mentioning that her name might signify "replenishing," crudely defames her and the "liberal" attitude she represents, identifying her as a "daughter of Eglon, king of Moab"⁷⁰ (the infamous fat chieftain killed by the שופט Ehud).⁷¹ Again, whereas Mahlon and Chilion simply "die" in Ruth 1:5,⁷² the Aramaic commentator argues that they die because they "transgress the decree of Yahweh and connect themselves to foreign peoples."⁷³ All of this takes place in Moab, a land this rabbi habitually calls "polluted"⁷⁴ in spite of the fact

---

66. *Tg. Ruth* 1.1 (Aramaic text cited from Sperber's edition).

67. The Hasmoneans speak of a time when prophets no longer prophesy (1 Macc 4:46).

68. וישאו להם נשים מאביות (Ruth 1:4).

69. ועברו על גזירת מימרא דיהוה (*Tg. Ruth* 1.4).

70. בת עגלון מלכא דמואב (*Tg. Ruth* 1.4), echoed in *b. Nazir* 23b. Similar defamation tactics are applied to Balaam (*b. Sanh.* 105).

71. Judg 3:22. "In this satirization of Ehud we see a theme developing whereby foreign kingship is exposed as an unworthy institution" (Guest, "Judges," 191).

72. וימותו גם שניהם מחלון וכליון (Ruth 1:5).

73. ועל דעברו על גזירת מימרא דיהוה ואתחתנו בעממין נוכראין (*Tg. Ruth* 1.5).

74. ארעא מסאבתא (*Tg. Ruth* 1.5).

that, after all, Moabite food grown in Moabite soil is what saves the life of David's great-grandmother.⁷⁵

Again, MT Ruth 1:6 has Naomi returning to Bethlehem after learning that the famine in Judah is over, and, in a rare reference to deity, the narrator states that she hears that Yahweh has visited his people "to give them bread."⁷⁶ The Aramaic translator, however, puts a very different spin on these events. For him, Naomi goes back to Judah not because of what Yahweh has done, but "because of her plea to Ibzan the prince and her prayers which she prayed before Yahweh."⁷⁷ In other words, she returns not because of divine grace, but because of her meritorious religious behavior. The translator also insinuates that when Naomi's Moabite daughters-in-law try to return with her to Judah, Naomi's rationale for rejecting their offer is mercenary: "May Yahweh give you wages of peace for the goodness you have given me—and it is a wage."⁷⁸ The journey cannot even be considered, however, until Ruth and Orpah admit they are willing to "convert"⁷⁹ to Yahwism, a scenario nowhere mentioned in MT or the versions, but one upon which the commentator staunchly insists. This is embellished by having them *refuse* to say, "Let us return to our people and our religion," even though Naomi clearly tells Ruth to follow Orpah back to "her gods."⁸⁰ This religious ambiguity deepens when Ruth says "Your God is my God," but only after Naomi says, "I am commanded by God not to practice foreign worship."⁸¹ The Aramaic commentator finally tries to resolve the "conversion question" by having Ruth say to Naomi, "If you return (to Judah) I will convert."⁸² Many more examples might be cited, but these should suffice. In short, the Targum of Ruth consistently "converts" one of Tanak's most beautiful narratives about

---

75. "The 'Moabite women' in Numbers and 'Ruth the Moabite' may be polar opposites on the approval-disapproval, disaster-delight, angelic-demonic scale, but they have more in common than might seem apparent" (Frymer-Kensky, *Women*, 258).

76. לתת להם לחם (Ruth 1:6). Sasson ("Ruth," 322) stands in a long line of readers recognizing and appreciating this alliteration.

77. בגין זכותיה דאבצן נגידא ובצלותיה דצלי קדם יהוה (*Tg. Ruth* 1.6).

78. יהב יהוה לכון אגר שלים על טיבותא די עבדתון לי ובההוא אגר (*Tg. Ruth* 1.9). Aram אגר can also mean "reward" (*DTTML* 14).

79. אתגיירא (*Tg. Ruth* 1.16).

80. אלהיה (Ruth 1:15). While Naomi might conceivably have the sg. term "god" in mind (i.e., Ruth's personal deity; see Di Vito, *Personal*, 260), the language of the Moabite Stone makes this highly unlikely (*KAI* 181).

81. אתפקידנה דלא למפלח פולחנא נוכראה אמרת רות אלהיך הוא אלהי (*Tg. Ruth* 1.16).

82. ארום תאכה אנא לאתגיירא (*Tg. Ruth* 1.16).

religious tolerance into a manifesto for ethnoreligious puritanism, thereby ignoring the *Aussensegen* trajectory upon which it canonically sits.[83]

Talmud

In Talmud the tradition continues to transform. One of the best places to see this is the famous rabbinic debate over the interpretation of Deut 23:4-7, a Torah passage which clearly states that Moabites and Ammonites are prohibited from entering Yahweh's קהל ("assembly") for at least ten generations, a span of time Mishnah equates with "forever" (לעולם).[84] Talmud, however, is not so rigid. In *Yebamot* the rabbis approach this question by staging a mock debate between "Saul," "Abner," and "Doeg the Edomite." "Doeg" plays the role of prosecuting attorney while "Abner" plays that of "defense attorney." "Doeg" opens the discussion by questioning whether the Torah prohibition excluding Moabites and Ammonites has been faithfully followed. Angrily he attacks the legitimacy of every Jew guilty of relaxing Torah on this point. Then he attacks David, arguing that "instead of inquiring whether (David) is fit to be king, inquire rather whether he is fit to enter into the assembly ... because he descends from Ruth the Moabitess."[85] To this "Abner" responds with a well-known *halakah*: "We learned: 'An Ammonite, but not an Ammonitess; a Moabite, but not a Moabitess.'"[86]

This does little to pacify "Doeg," who demands that "Abner" explain this *halakah* to his satisfaction. Responding to this request, "Abner" offers the following five-part explanation:[87] (a) Since Tanak gives a specific reason for the prohibition of Moabites and Ammonites ("because they did not meet you 'on the way' with food and water"),[88] and (b) since respectable women in antiquity would never walk on a public highway, one must conclude (c) that no Ammonite or Moabite *woman* can fairly be held responsible for the behavior of their brethren,[89] which means (d) that Moabite and Ammonite *women* cannot be prohibited from Yahweh's assembly; thus (e) Ruth is a le-

---

83. For a fuller discussion see Beattie, "Targum," 222-29.
84. *M. Yeb.* 8.3.
85. *b. Yeb.* 76b.
86. Ibid. This *halakah* appears often in Talmud (*b. Yeb.* 69a; *b. Ket.* 7b; *b. Qidd.* 75a), and is hermeneutically explained in *b. Yeb.* 6a.
87. *b. Yeb.* 77a.
88. בדרך (Deut 23:5).
89. Deut 23:5. Support for this position is drawn from Ps 45:14, "all glorious is the princess within," in which the adverb פנימה ("within") is taken, in classic rabbinic fashion, to mean that a respectable woman always stays "within" (i.e., indoors), defined by the psalmist as כבודה (the sphere of "her glory").

gitimate ancestor of David, and accusations like "Doeg's" should be thrown out. In this way Talmud attempts to show readers how to guide their thinking back to a view of foreigners influenced more by covenant ideology than nativistic fear. The method used to accomplish this goal in this particular passage resembles little more than a legal technicality, but the message is hardly unclear. Nativistic fear simply cannot be allowed to dictate the parameters of international relations.[90]

CONCLUDING REFLECTIONS

Far from disparaging the Talmudic tradition, the remarks in this essay hope to buttress it by suggesting that the *Aussensegen* trajectory offers a much firmer framework for identifying the message of Ruth than the reactionary puritanism in *Tg. Ruth*. That this trajectory needs to be (re)identified becomes clear from even a cursory glance at *Tg. Ruth*, not to mention other puritanical texts of the era.[91] Puritan ethnocentrism and nativistic nationalism are problems deeply embedded in the collective psyches of many proud peoples,[92] not just ancient Israel, and something more than legal acrobatics and semantic rescue operations is needed if the message of Ruth is to be allowed to speak. This novella is a beautiful example of what Hermann Gunkel calls the "heroism of faith,"[93] a powerful statement about one refugee's persistent desire to recover her faith.[94] Ruth bears witness to the power of human love itself—the love of two women bound together by common sorrow, the love of an older man for a younger woman, the love of a born-again community welcoming home one of its daughters, however battered and bruised.[95] Read as part of the *Aussensegen* trajectory, however, Ruth bears powerful witness to a God who keeps his promises when no one else does, a גואל-redeemer who will use any means—any people, any tradition, any *person*—to replenish his creation.[96]

90. Baumgarten tends to deemphasize and gloss over the nationalistic elements of the rabbinic tradition ("Ruth," 11–15). On the persistence and consequences of nativism generally, see Moore ("Monocultural," 39–53).

91. In addition to the Moabite and the Ammonite, e.g., one Qumran fragment excludes from Yahweh's assembly the בן נכר ("foreigner"), the ממזר ("bastard"), and the גר ("proselyte," 4Q174 frags. 1–3.4).

92. Lewis discusses the power of ethnicity to shape values generally (*Values*, 86–97).

93. Gunkel, "Ruth," 76.

94. See Moore, "Naomi," 151–63.

95. On each of these perspectives see the essays edited by Brenner-Idan (*Feminist*).

96. I am thus in basic agreement with Rudolph (*Ruth*, 32) that the primary thrust of the book is "to speak not of human things, but of God."

13

TO KING OR NOT TO KING
A Canonical-Historical Approach to Ruth*

> One day the trees went out to anoint for themselves a king. They said to the olive tree, "Be our king." But the olive tree answered, "Should I give up my oil, by which both gods and men are honored, to hold sway over the trees?" So the trees said to the fig tree, "Come and be our king." But the fig tree replied, "Should I give up my fruit, so good and sweet, to 'hold sway'[1] over the trees?" So the trees said to the vine, "Come and be our king." But the vine answered, "Should I give up my wine, which cheers both gods and men, to hold sway over the trees?" Finally all the trees said to the bramble, "Come and be our king." The bramble said, "If you really want to anoint me king over you, come and take refuge in my shade; but if not, then let fire shoot forth from the bramble and consume Lebanon's cedars!"[2]

---

* Revised from an essay first published in *BuBR* 11 (2001) 27–41. Many thanks to Tom Parker, Eric Elnes, and Bob Hubbard for their help on earlier drafts.

1. Whatever the meaning of נוע in Judg 9:9 ("to dominate?" *HAL* 644), the structure of the parable makes it difficult to translate apart from the parallel term מלך in 9:8 ("to reign").

2. Judg 9:8–15. Schipper believes that Jotham's parable "sets the tone for the use of parables throughout the Hebrew Bible" (*Parables*, 38). See Bartelmus ("Jothamfabel," 97–120) and Ruprecht (*Jothamfabel*, 9–25).

AFTER SHECHEM CROWNS ABIMELECH their first "king,"[3] a man named Jotham, apparently the sole survivor of Abimelech's "royal purge," climbs to the top of Mt. Gerizim at the coronation ceremony and barks out the words of this "tree parable," doubtless to some pretty puzzled party guests. Scholarly puzzlement continues to the present day, much of it focused around the question of leadership. Does this parable, as Martin Buber argues, contain "the strongest anti-monarchic poetry of world literature?"[4] Or does it merely intend to *critique* the monarchy, not *condemn* it?[5] Is this text even about "monarchy" *per se*, or is it more broadly about "leadership?"[6] Are there deep theological questions here or merely political sour grapes?[7] Should we read this text intertextually alongside the texts about Saul, David, Solomon, Ahab and Jehoiakim, and interpret it as part of an identifiable Hebrew invective against slavery?[8] Or do such readings tend to ignore the canonical-historical context; i.e., "the days when the judges judged?"[9]

The book of Judges is a dour book preoccupied with grainy questions about politics and power. The last section of the book (Judg 17–21) is a grim collection of vignettes all tangled together into one gruesome *mêlée* loosely designed to illustrate what the narrator believes to be *the* reason for Israel's political, social, and spiritual chaos: "In those days there was no king in Israel."[10] This sweeping observation, repeated no less than four times in five

3. וימליכו את־אבימלך למלך, "and they made Abimelech king" (Judg 9:6); also ותמליכו את־אבימלך, "when you made Abimelech king" (9:16).

4. Buber, *Königtum*, 29.

5. Lindars ("Jotham," 355–66) thinks it is an overreaction to view this parable as a protest against monarchy *per se*.

6. Maly ("Jotham," 299–305) sees the original fable directed not against kingship *per se*, but against those who refuse, for whatever reasons, the responsibility of civic leadership. Thus, since the original fable offers no general condemnation of kingship, neither does the biblical adaptation.

7. McKee ("Politics," 598–607) sees in the "trees-vs.-bramble" polarity two things: (a) an idealistic approach to politics ("trees") which grounds itself in an overly optimistic view of human nature, and (b) a realistic approach ("bramble") which recognizes the first approach to be rather pollyannish. The shortcoming in "tree" politicians is the danger of self-righteousness, while the danger in "bramble" politicians is cynicism. Each is needed to correct the shortcomings of the other.

8. Wolff, "Masters," 269–72.

9. Ruth 1:1.

10. Campbell (*Ruth*, 36) sees only Judg 19–21 as a unit, but Satterthwaite ("King," 75–88) offers substantive reasons for viewing all of Judg 17–21 as a coherent narrative unit. Wilson ("Idolatry," 73–85) thinks that Judg 17–18 forms a logical sequel to the material in Judg 1–16; i.e., where Judg 1–16 depicts the incorrigibility of Israel with respect to idolatry, Judg 17–18 describes, via carefully crafted dialogue, the inner psychology of this idolatry. Bal thinks that attempts to relegate these chapters to a later date

chapters,[11] summarily repositions these vignettes under a single ideological umbrella. To the narrator of Judges the absence of monarchy is not *a* factor, it is *the* factor responsible for Israel's slide into moral apathy, religious apostasy, and criminal violence. Extending Jotham's metaphor, each story in this section explores a different aspect of Abimelech's "exploding bramble."[12] In chapter 17, an Ephraimite named Micah hires an unemployed Levite to establish an idiosyncratic priesthood, literally in his own backyard.[13] Why? Because "there is no king in Israel" to stop him. In chapter 18, a gang of Danites convinces this same Levite to abandon Micah and bless their guerilla wars.[14] Why? Because "there is no king in Israel" to stop them. In chapter 19, another Ephraimite hides in a stranger's house as a gang of Benjaminites rapes and murders his concubine outside, publicly, in the streets of Gibeah.[15] Why? Because "there is no king in Israel" to stop them. With each episode the argument gains momentum. Only kings have the power to police "apostate" cults. Only kings have the authority to enforce the law. Only kings have the ability to punish criminal violence. Tribal authority is too weak. Israel *needs* a king. What can anyone say to such an "obvious" conclusion?

CANONICAL-HISTORICAL CONTEXT

At first, the narrator of Ruth seems to concur. A famine ravages Judah. A father dies. Survivors remain childless. A firstborn son dies. A remaining son dies. Widows grieve. Within the span of five verses a world comes miserably into focus, looking every bit as anguished, every bit as dark, and every bit as hopeless as the world depicted at the end of Judges. But looking more closely, something seems different about this world. Difficult to see at first,

---

inappropriately prioritize the motifs of political nationalism and military accomplishment (*Death*, 9–16); see also Yee, "Body," 146–69.

11. Judg 17:6; 18:1; 19:1; and 21:25.

12. Judg 9:15.

13. Amit sees a "hidden polemic" here against the Bethel cult ("Polemic," 18–19), but Frolov (*Judges*, 299) sees the juxtaposition of two narratives, one about the creation of a local shrine (Judg 17:1–6), another about the creation of a royal shrine (17:7–18:31) much like the shrine at Bethel (1 Kings 12:31–13:9; Amos 7:13).

14. "The Danites steal Micah's idol. Theoretically they can melt it down for silver. But instead they maintain Micah's idolatrous worship (Judg 18:30–31). Thus the idolatry of one man becomes the idolatry of an entire tribe. What is more, according to v. 30, Moses' grandson and great-grandsons serve as the Danites' priesthood.... What could be more ludicrous than the descendents of Moses presiding over an overtly idolatrous cult?" (McCann, *Judges*, 124).

15. Lasine ("Guest," 52) views the inclusion of so much grisly detail as a not-so-subtle attempt to generate outrage against Benjamin.

only gradually does it become clear as the story unfolds. In Judges 17–21 each character balks in the face of challenge. In Ruth, they persevere. In Judges, priests, landowners, husbands, wives, and warriors all abandon their responsibilities. In Ruth, people shoulder their responsibilities, however burdensome. In Judges, men treat women insensitively, shamefully, even violently. In Ruth, men treat women as partners on a common mission. And there is no king *here*, either. No king appears in *either* text.

Having been led by the last segment of Judges to wonder whether the one and only source of Israel's pain is kinglessness, Ruth is something of a surprise. Thus, to read the Judges 17–Ruth 4 narrative *as a narrative* raises the following question: If kinglessness is not the reason for Israel's chaos, then what *is* responsible? This is a *canonical-historical* question—*canonical*, because MT is not the only, nor in many cases the preferable witness to the book of Ruth;[16] *historical*, because the book itself claims to come from the "days in which the judges judged."[17] Certainly Ruth can be fruitfully explored from a variety of angles. Historical interpretations engage questions about dating and authorship and ANE context. Literary interpretations show this to be a beautiful novella of timeless impact. Broader canonical

---

16. MT places Ruth in the third section of Tanak called כתובים ("Writings") as one of the five מגלות ("little scrolls"), the other four being Canticles, Qoheleth, Lamentations, and Esther. Doubtless the book finds a home here because of an eventual need to connect Scripture more intentionally with the liturgical calendar; i.e., just as Esther is read at Purim, and Canticles at Passover, so Ruth is read at חג שבעת, the Feast of Weeks (Exod 34:22). The scribal tradition of placing it in כתובים, however, is fluid and indeterminate. OG, one of several Greek translations based on a Hebrew text-tradition predating "by several hundred years the complete manuscript on which our Hebrew Bible is based" (Peters, "Septuagint," 1102), situates it after Judges, in the section of Scripture called נביאים (N.B. the phrase הנביאים הראשנים, "former prophets," in Zech 1:4). Though there will always be some who argue for the priority of MT's canonical order, such discussions tend to ignore the results of newer research on "text types" and "text families" generated by the discovery and publication of all the known Dead Sea Scrolls. Knowing what we now know about the fluidity and flexibility of the Qumran canon, "it is . . . no longer possible to posit that Ruth was moved to the Prophets by hellenized Jews whose canon is reflected in LXX . . . . Different arrangements of the Prophets and the Writings arise among different elements of the Jewish community and exist side-by-side until the time of Jerome" (Bush, *Ruth*, 8–9). Therefore, taking all four of these factors into account (ascription of the book to the historical period of *the judges*, antiquity of OG, witness of Talmud, and canonical fluidity), we must conclude that there is no longer any convincing reason for reading Ruth solely against the ahistorical background provided by its inclusion in מגלות. Practically speaking, what this means is that all the old arguments for the *priority* of one canonical context (MT) over all others are antiquated. On the contrary, OG's canonical order is just as legitimate, just as authoritative, and just as interesting as that preserved in MT.

17. Ruth 1:1.

interpretations invite us to consider the book's intentions within the context of Tanak as a whole. Each approach brings with it certain advantages.

Yet to read Ruth in canonical-historical context is to read it with some of its earliest interpreters. Talmud, for example, preserves a chronological tradition in which Ruth (written by Samuel) is followed by Psalms (written by David), then Proverbs (written by Solomon).[18] Rab Ḥanina wonders whether Ruth herself descends from Eglon, the obese Moabite sheikh assassinated by the שופט Ehud.[19] Augustine sees Ruth as an extensive introduction to the book of Kings.[20] Reading the book from this angle also opens up another window into its internal structure. Judges 17–21 and Ruth 1–4, for example, both end in climactic courtroom scenes, an observation which, though it seems obvious, is hardly ever highlighted by contemporary observers,[21] even though comparison of these courtroom scenes goes a long way toward clarifying the primary motifs in each.

At Mizpah, for example, an Israelite tribal council wrestles over what to do with the Benjaminites, a tribe in trouble because of its refusal to hand over the Gibeonite murderers of the Levite's concubine.[22] This resistance generates a major crisis, yet no one on the council seems to know what to do. Mizpah's eventual response, its "crisis management strategy," if you will, is so poorly conceived and so clumsily implemented, a civil war breaks out driving the whole tribe of Benjamin to the brink of annihilation.[23] Not so in Ruth. In Bethlehem, another council convenes to deal with another potentially troublesome problem—what to do with Elimelech's inheritance.[24] Particularly delicate is how, exactly, to incorporate Ruth the Moabite into that inheritance. Yet the solution reached here is markedly different from the one reached in Mizpah. The social, legal, and political factors here are in

---

18. *b. B. Bat.* 14b.

19. *b. Naz.* 23b (see Judg 3:12–25).

20. Augustine, *Doctr. chr.* 2.8.13.

21. Following Buber (*Kingship*, 70–78), e.g., Olson lays out a different possibility: "Several details within Judges 17–21 echo places and events in Saul's life and thus implicitly associate Saul with all the negative events that occur in Israel's social and religious meltdown at the end of Judges" ("Buber," 201).

22. Judg 20:1–11. Miller identifies ancient Gibeah with the contemporary village of Jabaʿ ("Geba/Gibeah," 151–62), but Finkelstein identifies it with Tell en-Nasbeh (*Archaeology*, 52–55).

23. Instead of Benjamin's "salvation," O'Connell sees "the whole of Judg 19–21 portraying a situation involving national abandonment of YHWH's standards of justice for the sake of one tribe" (*Rhetoric*, 263). Amit, however, views these chapters "as an attack against the tribe of Benjamin in general, and the town of Gibeah in particular" (*Judges*, 342).

24. Ruth 4:1–12.

many ways just as flammable as those in Mizpah, yet the Bethlehem council's decision leads to restoration and healing, not violence and war. Why? How can these two councils deal with situations so similar, yet come up with such radically different responses?[25]

The only way to answer this question is to examine Ruth against its canonical-historical context. True, Ruth can be profitably read as a romantic novella,[26] as a human comedy,[27] as a response to nativistic fear about intermarriage,[28] as a messianic preamble,[29] or as a Yahwistic response to ANE fertility myth.[30] Each approach bears legitimate exegetical fruit, yet all remain inadequate—not because they are mistaken or misguided, but because they simply cannot address the questions just posed.

SOCIAL CONTEXT

One of the most pertinent advantages of reading Ruth through a canonical-historical lens is the insight it helps bring to our paltry understanding of Hebrew society at a volatile time in Syro-Palestinian history. Historians are thoroughly investigating this era, yet the focus so far centers predominantly on *macrodiachronic* concerns; e.g., whether there are twelve actual "tribes" in premonarchic Israel, whether these "tribes" are organized into one tribal "league," and/or whether Israel's sociopolitical shift from "judges" to "kings" is best described as *progressive* or *regressive*.[31]

Contemporary readers are more interested in *microsynchronic* interpretation,[32] and this paradigm shift has proven itself to have an enormous impact on Ruth research.[33] Recent interest in the book's depiction of gender roles, for example, is rather unexplainable apart from some understanding of this tectonic shift. Today in many circles gender is not simply

---

25. The Bethlehem council scene does not just parallel its counterpart in Mizpah, it contests it, quietly but firmly challenging the integrity of its procedures, the purpose for its convening, the motives of its participants, and the wisdom of its decision-making (see Moore, "Ruth, 359–66").

26. Gunkel, "Ruth," 65–92.

27. Trible, *Rhetoric*, 195.

28. Vesco, "Ruth," 235–47.

29. See *Ruth Rab.* 7.15.

30. Staples, "Ruth," 145–57. The medieval work *HaNe'elam* (Englander & Basser, *Ruth*) imagines the characters and events in Ruth as veiled allusions to divine realities.

31. See Gottwald, *Introduction*, 104–34.

32. Dobbs-Alsopp thoughtfully searches for common ground upon which both synchronic and diachronic interpreters can stand ("Rethinking," 35–71).

33. See Holbert ("Ruth," 130–35) and Perdue (*Collapse*, 7–11).

an issue, it is *the* issue around which everything else in the book orbits, and not simply because the book boasts two heroines. In many circles today the most pressing interpretive concern is the sociopolitical climate in which many postmodern readers themselves live.[34] Older scholarship says practically nothing about gender issues. Contemporary scholarship, however, is honestly (in some cases, courageously) attempting to read the book with an eye to new sociological realities.[35] Two major obstacles, however, stand in the way of progress. *First*, too many interpreters, regardless of their presumptions about gender and sexuality,[36] fail to employ critically defensible research methods in their approach to the Ruth novella. *Second*, too many ignore the book's canonical-historical context. The result, in many cases, is shallow politicization instead of serious interpretation. Too often the air over Ruth is breezy and speculative, whether the discussion focuses on Ruth's alleged sociopolitical beliefs,[37] or the author's "strategy" for deconstructing "traditional" gender roles,[38] or even the alleged "sexual orientation" of its main characters.[39]

Interpretations divorced from historical, literary, and canonical controls, however, tend to be embarrassingly narcissistic.[40] Tikva Frymer-Kensky, in a definitive study of ANE goddess religion, makes this point quite forcefully, reminding her readers that "in some areas the Bible does not offer extensive discussion of matters that people need to consider."[41] In other words, we still know very little about ANE gender roles, especially in Syria-Palestine, and this dearth of information ought to inspire more circumspection and less speculation, not only about gender roles, but about

---

34. I.e., the stratospheric popularity of "reader-response" criticism (see McKnight, "Reader," 230–52).

35. See, e.g., Heine (*Goddesses*), Frymer-Kensky (*Goddesses*), and Brenner-Idan (*Ruth*).

36. See Grenz (*Welcoming*) and Moore (*Welcoming*, 143–46).

37. Ljung, *Silence*, 22–26.

38. Berquist, "Ruth," 23–37.

39. Bollinger, "Models," 363–401; Alpert, "Ruth," 91–96. Greenberg (*Construction*, 487) reminds us that the contemporary Western notion of homosexuality as a static, biologically based "orientation" is "the product of a constellation of ideas in our society, and not the transcultural reality proponents assume it is."

40. The classic example of this tendency is Wellhausen's application (*Prolegomena*) of an absolutist evolutionary paradigm—the dominant paradigm of nineteenth-century Continental scholarship—to his reconstruction of Israelite history. Following Perlitt (*Vatke*, 61–63), Halpern (*Historians*, 19–24) shows how Wellhausen simplistically applies to Tanak the paradigmatic presumptions of Mommsen (*Geschichte*) and Burckhardt (*Geschichte*).

41. Frymer-Kensky, *Goddesses*, 213.

the sociopolitical character of the entire book.⁴² Yet given these limitations, it is still possible to observe how *particular* women function in *particular* texts, then try to formulate from these comparisons specific questions. Here the canonical-historical approach can be of great value. Take, for example, the roles enacted by the Levite's concubine vs. those enacted by the Moabite Ruth. The Levite's wife is a "concubine" (פלגש).⁴³ Ruth, however, is a "female foreigner" (נכריה),⁴⁴ a Moabite widow who eventually becomes the "wife" (אשה)⁴⁵ of an Israelite "gentleman" (גבור חיל).⁴⁶ What do these terms mean? What roles do they signify? One does not need to know Classical Hebrew to see the terminological distinctions here, and since anthropologists insist that kinship terms be read on dynamic continuums rather than in static categories, one of the least speculative observations we can make is that "concubine" and "female foreigner" likely denote gender roles relatively close together on the same societal continuum; i.e., somewhere between the extreme poles of "female slave" (שפחה) and "(Hebrew) wife" (אשה).⁴⁷

Why is it important to recognize this? Because the similarities on the *social* continuum are what make the dissimilarities on the *moral* continuum stand out so sharply. Each of these women lives in the same geographical area (Bethlehem) and enacts a number of roles relatively close together on the same societal continuum. Yet each experiences a vastly different fate. One follows an unprepared, foolish man on an ill-conceived journey only to be raped, murdered, chopped into pieces, and mailed (!) to tribal leaders.⁴⁸

---

42. Perdue's warning is well-taken: "To attempt to transplant gender roles, the roles of parents and children, polygamy, monogamy, celibacy, and a host of other specific features of the Israelite family into contemporary cultures would be naïve" ("Household," 254).

43. Judg 19:1. Probably a non-semitic loanword (Ellenbogen, *Foreign*, 162), the term פלגש ("concubine") "reflects a system of marriage and sexual relations in which a man can legitimately have more than one woman as ongoing or permanent sexual partners, and that these women do not always fill the same role or hold the same status" (Stone, "Marriage," 179). Engelken uniformly translates פלגש as "secondary wife" (*Frauen*, passim).

44. Ruth 2:10. Bal (*Lethal*, 80) emphasizes that נכריה never casts a fully positive shadow in Tanak (see, e.g., Prov 2:16; 5:20; 6:24; 7:5—all references to the "foreign/strange/loose" woman).

45. Ruth 4:10.

46. Ruth 2:1. Burrows ("Marriage," 452) assumes that "Mr. So-and-So" (פלני אלמני, Ruth 4:1) and Boaz are both married fathers, but "if Boaz is single and without an heir, this situation holds the greatest 'absolute risk' for him" (Lau, *Ruth*, 80).

47. Pressler ("Wives," 161) insists that while she may enjoy a less restrictive role-set than פלגש or נכריה, the אשה ("wife") still enjoys "no independent legal status."

48. Rab Ḥisda puts it bluntly: "The concubine of Gibeah? Her husband 'terrorizes' her" (הטיל עליה, lit. "perpetrates injury against her," *b. Git.* 6b).

The other accompanies her Hebrew mother-in-law back to her homeland, and unexpectedly finds there a Hebrew gentleman who protects her, marries her, and restores through her the heritage of her dead Hebrew husband.

THEOLOGICAL REFLECTIONS

Interpreted in its canonical-historical context, then, the book of Ruth is a masterfully crafted response to the dark politics of despair blanketing the grisly stories in Judges 17–21. Its short-story format makes it the perfect vehicle for communicating this subversive response. No prophetic oracle, priestly torah, or psalmic lyric can match the short-story for subtlety, ambiguity, and memorability.[49] Character by character, episode by episode, Ruth is a well-crafted, entertaining story, but *in context* it is much more. *In context* it is a sharp chisel in the hands of a master sculptor, methodically chipping away at Israel's pain and despair until a marvelous theology of hope begins to emerge. The parameters of this theology remain hidden and covert, never becoming as visible as, say, the theology of hope in Isaiah or Ezekiel. Yet Ruth does contain a theological message,[50] and one of the easiest ways to identify it is to filter its contents through the following polarized lenses: the *wandering-restoration* lens, the *religion-ethics* lens, and the *chaos-kindness* lens.

Wandering-Restoration

Hebrews are wanderers. In fact, the very word "Hebrew" (עברי) means "wanderer."[51] This "wandering" begins with Abraham's trek out of Ur and climaxes with Moses' exodus out of Egypt.[52] It echoes in David's escape from Saul and climaxes again in the deportations to Assyria, Babylon, and Persia.[53] For tannaitic Jews this trajectory continues on into Talmud, where various rabbis discuss, among other things, the final destinies of those who choose

---

49. "One of the great contributions of the Hebrew Bible to world literature (is) the . . . short-story" (Collins, *Introduction*, 547). Ogden Bellis emphasizes Ruth's "subversive" character (*Helpmates*, 10–24).

50. Many follow Hals in seeing the "hidden hand of God" behind the events in this short-story (*Ruth*, 12).

51. The noun עברי derives from the verb עבר ("to cross over, wander"; see *HAL* 735–40).

52. Gen 12:1–4; Num 10:11–36:13.

53. Jer 2:1–3; Ezek 20:33–38.

to "wander" with "Moses" through the "wilderness/diaspora."⁵⁴ For Christians it transforms into something universally inclusive in the NT treatise *To the Hebrews*. All believers in the One God, this author claims, are "strangers and exiles upon the earth,"⁵⁵ and "Israel," the "one who wrestles with God" (whether person or nation or universal faith-community), is an organism forever on the move, constantly traversing spatial, temporal, ethnic, social, political, religious, theological, and spiritual boundaries. "Wandering" is thus a profoundly important motif in both the Jewish *and* Christian Bibles. Every wanderer tends to ask the same questions: Is it my fate to wander forever? Am I ever going to find my way home? What does "home" look like?⁵⁶

Powerful echoes of this motif resonate in Judges 17-Ruth 4. Three Bethlehemites find themselves forced to "wander." A Levite wanders north to find work.⁵⁷ A concubine wanders north to find "home."⁵⁸ An Ephrathite wanders east to find food.⁵⁹ All three have to make painful decisions about when and where to pull up stakes. All three have to cope with life on the road, packing and unpacking, stopping and starting *ad infinitum*.

Wanderer #1 sets out, as the text puts it, "to wander to whatever (place) he might find."⁶⁰ The path he chooses, however, leads to territory as morally ambiguous as it is religiously uncharted. Quickly dissatisfied, he throws in his lot with a gang of Danites, enticed away by offers of more money and prestige. Nowhere does he pray or make inquiries of God/the gods before making these decisions, even though this is his purported function as a religious leader. Never does he find his way "home."⁶¹

Wanderer #2 sets out to follow her new husband to a new land and a new life. Soon, however, the marriage fails and she returns to her father's house. Four months later, her husband arrives in Bethlehem to take her "home" to Ephraim. Three times her father begs them not to go, sensing

---

54. *b. Sanh.* 110b.

55. ξένοι καὶ παρεπίδημοί εἰσιν ἐπὶ τῆς γῆς (Heb 11:13). Polybius records a time when the Roman senate expels all Macedonians "sojourning" (παρεπιδημοῦντες) in the city (*Hist.* 27.6.3).

56. See Ackroyd (*Exile*, 237-56), Clines (*Pentateuch*, 17-21), and Brueggemann (*Cadences*, 1-14).

57. Judg 17:8-9.

58. Judg 19:1.

59. Ruth 1:1. Saxegaard posits אפרתה to be a "clan name" (*Ruth*, 62), but more likely it references the *region* in which Bethlehem is located (Gen 35:19; Mic 5:1; Ps 132:6).

60. לגור באשר ימצא (Judg 17:8).

61. "Levites are wandering holy men who bring good luck with them ... quintessential mediators between God and humans (with) divinatory abilities" (Niditch, *Judges*, 182).

something ominous on the road north. But the Levite ignores his warnings, and this leads to one of the most grisly horror stories ever told, a terrifying tale about cowardice and rape and murder and war. No one here even comes close to making it "home."[62]

Wanderer #3 leaves home to save his family from the scourge of famine. Elimelech the Ephrathite makes a painful decision to leave his ancestral inheritance. The text says little about this "exile," but like Jacob's in Padan-Aram[63] and Joseph's in Egypt,[64] it soon proves to be difficult. Unlike *Wanderers #1* and *#2*, however, *Wanderer #3* eventually does make his way "home," or at least his name does.[65] Even though every male in the family dies in a foreign land, two of the surviving three widows stubbornly refuse to let death have the last word. Ruth and Naomi set out to make sure that the family name is "not cut off from his brothers and from the gate of his place."[66] Playing on the Hebrew word for "return/restore" (שׁוּב), the narrator guides us step-by-step through their journey "home."[67] Naomi decides to "return" to Judah. She pressures her daughters-in-law to "return" to Moab, but they deflect her command: "No, we will 'return' to your people."[68] A second time she insists that they "return," then a third.[69] Finally Orpah *does* "return," and Naomi seizes on her decision to pressure Ruth into doing the same.[70] Her strategy fails. Ruth refuses to give in to her mother-in-law's depression, deciding instead to take her across the Jordan to the land of her ancestors, the land of Judah. Arriving in Bethlehem, Naomi updates her old friends, "I went away full, but Yahweh has 'returned' me empty."[71] Ruth's new co-workers soon begin to call her "the returnee."[72] Finally, after the birth of

---

62. Brown ("Judges," 275–76) suggests that OG Judg 19:2 ὠργίσθη ("became angry") may be preferable to MT זנה ("prostituted herself") because OG may be reading a homonym, זנה, "to become angry" (*HAL* 264; cf. Akk *zenû*, *CAD* Z.85–86).

63. Gen 28:5–31:55.

64. Gen 39:1–40:23.

65. Ruth 4:10. Japhet recognizes that שׁם ("name") here denotes a designated legal claim ("Proposal," 69–80).

66. ולא יכרת שם־המת מעם אחיו ומשער מקומו (Ruth 4:10).

67. Ruth 1:7. Holladay's monograph (*Testament*) is still the seminal analysis of this Heb verb.

68. Ruth 1:10.

69. Ruth 1:11–12.

70. Ruth 1:15.

71. אני מלאה הלכתי וריקם השבני יהוה (Ruth 1:21).

72. השבה (Ruth 2:6).

Obed, the people of Bethlehem describe Naomi's long-awaited grandson as the "soul-returner."[73]

Religion-Ethics

For all their gloom and doom, the stories in Judges 17–21 are quite religious. Compared to Ruth, this might not seem to be the case, but even a cursory reading of the text confirms this. In Judges 17, for example, a man named Micah builds a shrine, stocks it with an assortment of religious icons, then hires a Levite to maintain it, both as כהן ("priest") and as אב ("father").[74] Why does he build this shrine? Because he wants to secure Yahweh's "favor."[75] Overtly calling these icons "my gods,"[76] Micah uses a common, yet ambiguous term. In Judges 17-Ruth 4 אלהים usually refers to the One God, but sometimes (as here) it refers to the world of unseen "daemons" much like those inhabiting the earliest layers of the Balaam traditions, the dialogues of Job, and other ANE texts.[77] Micah believes this Levite will help him stay in touch with the Unseen World.[78] Soon afterwards, the Danites ask him to divine the future, and he manipulates the אלהים to satisfy their request.[79] Divination occurs not only here but later, when the warriors from the non-Benjaminite tribes go up to Bethel to inquire of Yahweh, "Which of us shall go up first to fight against Benjamin?" Yahweh's reply—"Judah shall go up first"—is likely ascertained via the same divinatory techniques as those practiced by Micah's Levite.[80]

This type of religious activity never occurs in Ruth. No one divines the future. No one bargains for priests. No one steals אלהים-icons from desperate landlords, much less divines the future with them. This is one of the greatest contrasts between these two books. In place of Micah's hollow religiosity stands Boaz's humble integrity. In place of the tribal elders' divinatory

---

73. משיב נפש (Ruth 4:15).

74. Hendel ("Aniconic," 381) thinks that Micah's desire for religious icons illustrates the ambivalence among early Hebrews for a king/god.

75. עתה ידעתי כי ייטיב יהוה לי, "Now I know that Yahweh will make it good for me" (Judg 17:13).

76. אלהי (Judg 18:24). KJV and NRSV translate "my gods"; NIV translates simply "gods." N.B. that Jotham's fable uses אלהים twice (Judg 9:9, 13).

77. See Tigay (*Gods*, 7–20), Lewis ("Ancestral," 602–3), van der Toorn ("Teraphim," 210–11), Handy ("Pantheon," 27–44).

78. Judg 17:13.

79. Judg 18:15.

80. Judg 20:18. See Huffmon ("Divination," 355–59), Jeffers (*Magic*, 58–60), and Nougayrol ("La divination," 65).

speculation stands Naomi's Yahwistic faith. In place of the Danites' cruelty to the residents of Laish stands Ruth's compassion for Naomi and her family. Doubtless some form of traditional Yahwism stands behind all these distinctions, yet the narrator of Ruth never identifies it.[81] On the one hand, Ruth epitomizes the best of Yahwism, quietly radiating a message of inclusion in a world divided by artificial barriers and prejudicial hatred. Every Hebrew in Bethlehem accepts Ruth for who she is—a נכריה. Yet tolerance for "foreigners" never translates into abandonment of responsibility, particularly family responsibility. The book of Ruth may *begin* with a Moabite's compassion, but it *ends* with the restoration of a Hebrew family—not a Moabite one.

The canonical-historical approach makes it easier for us to see the loyalty of Ruth's characters over against the fickleness of those in Judges. Micah's Levite abandons his employer without batting an eye—yet one cannot imagine Ruth doing such a thing.[82] The concubine's husband drags her foolishly and needlessly into harm's way—yet one cannot imagine Boaz doing such a thing.[83] The Levite abandons his concubine to a violent mob, yet Ruth absolutely refuses to abandon Naomi.[84] In short, the book of Ruth quietly subverts the hollow religiosity so prominently displayed in its canonical-historical context, thus showing it to be much more than "the loveliest little composition."[85] Instead, *in its context*, Ruth is an "autonomous text" refusing to "allow itself to be absorbed" into a callous world.[86] Indeed, this book, like no other, challenges Israel to rethink the depth of its character, the goals of its mission, and the character of its אלהים.

Chaos-Kindness

Perhaps the most overlooked contrast between the two books is the way each depicts the notion of "kindness." The term in Ruth (חסד) is justifiably hailed by interpreters everywhere as one of its most important concepts.[87] The parallel term in Judges, however (חן), is virtually ignored. No one, to my knowledge, systematically compares these synonyms for "kindness" within

---

81. Hals, *Ruth*, 12.
82. Judg 17:11; 18:20; Ruth 3:11–13.
83. Judg 19:9–22; Ruth 2:8–9.
84. Judg 19:2; Ruth 1:16–18.
85. Goethe, *Werke* 21.231 ("das lieblichste kleine Ganze," cited in Gunkel, "Ruth," 65).
86. Van Wolde, "Ruth," 7.
87. See Glueck (*Wort*, 1–32), Clark (*Bible*, 15–34), Andersen ("Kind," 41–88), and Sakenfeld (*Meaning*, 108–9).

their canonical-historical context. In Judges 21, Israel drives Benjamin to the brink of extinction. Not only this, but the rest of Israel, succumbing to tribal vengeance, issues a ban against any Hebrew taking a Benjaminite wife. Mercifully, this mistake is soon realized (must Benjaminites now take spouses from their uncircumcised neighbors?), and Mizpah's tribal council backpedals hard to correct it. Hastily drafting an "exception clause," they permit the Benjaminites to seize four hundred virgins from the border town of Jabesh Gilead. However, since this number is not nearly enough, they have to backpedal again and permit the Benjaminites to seize more brides away from nearby Shiloh. The people of Jabesh-Gilead say nothing about this "legal-rape" policy, but the Shilonites protest it, thereby forcing Mizpah to issue the following rationale:

> "Do us a kindness" (חנונו) by helping them, because we did not get wives for them during the war, but you are innocent, since you did not give your daughters to them.[88]

In short, "kindness" at Mizpah is not a trait rooted in personal character or moral example. "Kindness" is rather a poker chip, a necessary political evil imposed on innocent bystanders after not one but hundreds of their citizens have been institutionally raped.[89]

In Ruth, the family of Elimelech also teeters on the brink of extinction. Famine, death, and depression have taken a huge toll. Things are so bad that Elimelech's widow actually talks of changing her name from Naomi ("sweet") to Mara ("bitter"). So depressed does she become, her daughter-in-law feels it necessary to challenge her.[90] Yet as soon as Boaz enters the picture, Naomi dares to do something never attempted by any character in Judges 17–21. She dares to trust in Yahweh—*not* manipulate the אלהים! She dares to imagine, even before anything is planned or dreamed or attempted, a different future for her family, saying,

> May he (Boaz) be blessed by Yahweh, who does not abandon his "kindness" (חסד) to the living or the dead."[91]

---

88. Judg 21:22.

89. Rubin (*Israel*, 48) jocularly speaks of these abductions as "the world's oldest singles gathering," but such description reveals an embarrassing lack of understanding, not to mention empathy.

90. Ruth 1:16–17. Many view Ruth's words here as a "pledge of allegiance" (Lau, *Ruth*, 92–95), but from a socioliterary perspective they challenge the validity of Naomi's complaints (see Moore, "Naomi," 156).

91. Ruth 2:20.

In other words, "kindness" for Naomi is not a poker chip easily cashed in at the first sign of tribal trouble.[92] No, kindness is a gift rooted in the promises of Yahweh, the God of her ancestors, the God to whom she now (re)turns with chastened heart and renewed hope.[93] Only after reopening her heart to this God do things start changing in her life. The narrator wants readers to recognize this clearly. It is only after her faith "returns" (שׁוּב) to her that a plan begins to form in her mind to help Boaz do what a גֹּאֵל ("redeemer") is supposed to do—raise up heirs for deceased male relatives. Restored by *Yahweh's* kindness, Naomi dares to dream of a different life months before Obed is born, decades before David is born, centuries before Yeshu`a is born.

SUMMARY

In short, Ruth is less a romantic novella than a compelling drama, less a messianic preamble than a pastoral gift. *In context* Ruth's major themes—the yearning for "home" in the midst of homelessness, the hunger for conviction in the midst of hypocrisy, the celebration of kindness in a world of unspeakable cruelty—all come into much clearer focus, projecting a much sharper image. Ruth is a bright light in a dark world.

Changing the metaphor, Ruth is a challenge to hear as well as see. Not only does each character bring a different "voice" to the "performance," each listener brings a different ear to the symphonic "score."[94] One reader hears the "soprano line" of a broken woman trying to find her way "home." Another resonates to the "alto line" sung by her loyal daughter-in-law. Another gravitates to the "bass line" sung by the benevolent patriarch. This trio soon joins a larger orchestra in which the countermelodies of justice and compassion blend and blur into grander harmonies where discerning listeners soon discover that Ruth is a quiet place where "Maras" of all sorts can find the strength to become "Naomi" again, where discerning leaders can learn how to tell the difference between "political gamesmanship" and "servant leadership," and where "wanderers" everywhere can find reasons to keep searching for "home."[95]

---

92. "'Ethnic cleansing' implies an ideal state of tribal purity—cleanliness—that is sullied by alien people. It demands restoration, the undoing of those wrongs that corrupt the tribe" (Morrow, "Purity," 245).

93. See Moore, "Naomi," 158–59.

94. See Young, *Performance*, 45.

95. Wolff, "Masters," 272. Gerleman (*Ruth,* 10) characteristically cuts to the point: "Behind this desacralized narrative stands a different conception of reality.... The divine leader is first and foremost the leader of the human heart."

14

JOB'S TEXTS OF TERROR*

ANCIENT NEAR EASTERN PEOPLES fear less the prospect of their going to hell than that of hell's coming to them. Anatolians fear demons with names like "The Fear before the Lion," "The Terror before the Snake," and "The Thing which Sticks to the Mouth."[1] Mesopotamians fear numerous demons. In the Amarna version of *Nergal and Ereshkigal*, for example, no fewer than fourteen of them accompany the netherworld deity Nergal, holding ominous-sounding names like "The Driver," "The Seizer," "The Decayer," and "The One Who Brings up the Void."[2] According to the portal amulets from Arslan Tash, Syro-Palestinians chant incantations to demons called "the Strangler" and "the Splatterer."[3] Alongside the broadly generic term *ēl*, the more specific root used to describe these chthonic beings is the term *šēd*. In Akkadian, *šēdu* appears with or without the determinative for deity, and denotes protector daemons as well as devouring demons.[4]

---

* Revised from a paper read to the SBL Hebrew and Cognate Literature section in Kansas City, Missouri on November 21, 1991, subsequently published in *CBQ* 55 (1993) 662–75.

1. Hit. *dam-me-in-ku-wa-ar* (see Haas & Thiel, *Allaituraḫḫi*, 104.4–6; 146–47–48); see Friedrich, "Angst," 148.

2. Akk ^{d}*ṭi-ri-id*, ^{d}*ṣi-i-da-na*, ^{d}*mi-ki-it*, and ^{d}*mu-ta-ab-ri-qá* (EA 357.68–71); see Abusch, *Witchcraft*, 3–27; Hutter, *Unterwelt*, 70–73. The pioneering study is Thompson, *Devils*.

3. KAI 27.4 (*ḥnqt*); cf. *iltm ḥnqtm* ("two strangling goddesses," CAT 1.102.13). See *lḥšt lmzh* ("incantation against the Splatterer," SSI 3.24.1; Cross, "Leaves," 488).

4. In one instance both denotations occur right next to each other in the same Assyrian prayer: ^{d}*šêdu ḫa-a-a-ṭu al-lu-ḫap-pu ḫab-bi-lu gal-lu-u râbiṣu ilu limnu* ("the *Šêdu*, the 'Lookout,' the 'Snatching Net,' the *Gallu*, the *Rabiṣu*, the evil god," KAR

In Classical Hebrew שדים are the demons before whom Hebrews sacrifice their own children in the wilderness.[5] Imperial Aramaic inscriptions from Parthia and Palmyra preserve an emphatic plural (שדיא)[6] while the plural שידין appears on a number of terra-cotta incantation bowls "from Sasanian Babylonia before and after 600 (CE)."[7]

To this already extensive evidence must now be added the appearance of the term *šdyn* on the plaster texts discovered in Transjordan at Tell Deir ʿAllā.[8] Like the שטן-adversary in Job, the *šdyn* in these texts "take a stand" (*nṣb*) in a divine "council" (*mwʿd*) to accuse mortals of wrongdoing.[9] Before this council they command, "Sew up the bolts of heaven with your cloud. Ordain darkness, not light; gloom, not radiance."[10] Interpreters of this text continue to disagree over the identity and intentions of these *šdyn*.[11] I have argued that the language of this Transjordanian inscription substantively and stylistically echoes the cadences of the ANE priestly incantation literature.[12] The "bolts-of-heaven" motif, for example, often appears in this literature[13] because one of an exorcist's primary tasks is to ensure that the heavenly doors remain open (i.e., "unbolted") so that the *ilāni rabûti* (the

---

2.58.42) . . . ^{d}*šêdu na-ṣi-ru ilu mu-šal-li-mu* ("the protecting *šêdu*, the healing god," *KAR* 2.58.47). N.B. that the שדי//אל word-pair occurs repeatedly in the Joban dialogues (Job 5:17; 6:4; 8:3; 13:3; 22:17, 26; 27:10; 31:2, 35).

5. ויזבחו את־בניהם ואת־בנותיהם לשדים, "they sacrificed their sons and their daughters to the *šēdîm*" (Ps 106:37; Syr ܠܫܐܕܐ "to the demons"; OG τοῖς δαιμονίοις; Vg *daimonibus*). Torah specifies that although the שדים are אלהים are of an unknown type, they are definitely *not* equivalent to אלה (Deut 32:17).

6. See texts cited in *DNWSI* 1111.

7. Gordon, *Adventures*, 161. See Isbell, *Aramaic* 3.14; 7.17; 47.2; 48.1.

8. The *editio princeps* is published by Hoftijzer & van der Kooij. Hackett (*Balaam*, 88) claims that "Akkadian *šēdu* is generally a protective spirit, and only means 'demon' with the addition of *lemnu*," but this is inaccurate. N.B., e.g., that neither *lemnu* nor a comparable synonym occurs in the following series of *Maqlû* chants: ^{d}*šêdê^{meš} li-ba-ʾ-ki utukke^{meš} liš-te-ʾ-u-ki eṭimme^{meš} lis-saḫ-ru-u-ki*, "May the *šēdu*-demons seek after you. May the *utukku*-demons stare you down. May the spirits of the dead surround you" (*Maq* 2.210–12; see Abusch, *Maqlû*, 66–67).

9. *wnṣbw šdyn mwʿd wʾmrw*, "the *šdyn* took a stand in the divine council and said . . ." (*DAT* 1.6). Cf. ויבאו בני האלהים להתיצב על יהוה ויבא גם השטן בתוכם, "the sons of God entered to take a stand before Yahweh, and the Adversary also entered into their midst" (Job 1:6).

10. *trpy skry šmyn bʿbky šm ḥšk wʾl ngh ʿṭm wʾl smr* (*DAT* 1.6–7), trans. ʿṭm as "gloom" with Hoftijzer & van der Kooij (*Aramaic*, 106) on epigraphic grounds, and Wolters on literary grounds ("Literary," 295).

11. See the sample of opinion in Hoftijzer & van der Kooij, *Re-Evaluated*.

12. Moore, *Balaam*, 66–96.

13. Recognized by Hoftijzer & van der Kooij (*Aramaic*, 193–94), Kaufman (Review, 73), Dahood (Review, 125), and M. & H. Weippert ("Bileam," 92).

"great gods" living on the other side of these doors) might easily access the world of mortals, especially to protect them from demonic attack.[14] Like benevolent parents, the *ilāni rabûti* leave the bedroom door open and the night-light on, so to speak, for their frightened children. The *šdyn* at Deir ʿAllā, however, like demons everywhere, want only to lock the door and blow out the light. So, whatever else the Deir ʿAllā texts might teach us—and they have already taught us a lot—they shed new light on a variety of texts. The purpose of this essay is to ascertain whether or not they illuminate a problematic text in Job.[15]

As is well known, the book of Job sustains very little contact with the primary components of Hebrew historical tradition.[16] The dialogues of chapters 3–31, in particular, are certainly pre- or non-Yahwistic, regardless of the way one interprets the book's final form or assesses its contribution to the history of religion.[17] Because of this, interpreters tend to look beyond Tanak for hints and clues to the identities of the Leviathan,[18] the "king of terrors,"[19] "death's firstborn,"[20] "the night flyers,"[21] and "the Adversary."[22] Emboldened by the Deir ʿAllā texts, Baruch Levine suggests that the Joban dialogues, along with several other texts, originate from what he calls an "El repertoire," and further, that the sanctuary excavated by H. J. Franken at Deir ʿAllā looks to be one of its depositories.[23] So the question persists. If in fact an "El repertoire" exists, and even if we resist delimiting its scope to the

---

14. An Assyrian chant against pestilence begins *šu-ḫa-ru-ur ṣi-e-ru pa-ar-ka* $^{iš}dalatu^{meš}.tu$ . . . *na-du-u ši-ga-ru šu-qam-mu-mu il[âni ša irṣiti] pa-ta-a-ma abullâte^{meš} ša šamê ra-[ap-šu-ti]*, "Quiet are the steppes, bolted are the doors . . . silent are the gods of the earth, fully open are the doors of the heavens" (*TuL* 34.8–10).

15. Job is catalogued among the "wisdom literature" in older taxonomies, but more and more are beginning to recognize, with Pope, that "there is no single classification appropriate to the literary form of the book of Job" (*Job*, xxxi).

16. Roberts ("Job," 107–14); Maillot ("Job," 567–76).

17. Cross ("Apocalyptic," 344) views Job as a major corrective to the enfranchised priestly and deuteronomistic schools of Hebrew religious tradition. Janzen (*Job*, 9–14) sees more affinities between Job and these schools than do Cross or Roberts.

18. לויתן (Job 40:25; cf. Isa 27:1; Ps 74:14; Ug *ltn*, *CAT* 1.5.1.1–3). See Rowold ("Leviathan," 104–9); Diewert ("Job," 203–15); and Janzen ("Watch," 109–16).

19. מלך בלהות (Job 18:14). See Irwin ("Redeemer," 217–29) and Sarna ("Background," 315–18).

20. בכור מות (Job 18:13). See Burns ("Death," 362–64); Wyatt ("Mythological," 207–16); and Michel ("Death," 5–20).

21. עיפתה (Job 10:22). See Torczyner, "Incantation," 20.

22. השטן (Job 1:6; 2:1). See Day, *Adversary*, 69–106 (see Moore, Review of *Adversary*, 508–10). On the advantages and disadvantages of comparative analysis, see Albertson ("Job," 213–30), Albertz ("Hiobbuch," 349–72) and Smick ("Job," 213–28).

23. Levine, "Aspects," 326–39, and "General," 58–72.

Canaanite deity El,[24] how *are* we to explain the strikingly non-Yahwistic cast of the Joban dialogues? More to the point, what can we learn about the *šdy* texts embedded in these dialogues—Job's "texts of terror," if you will[25]—if we were to examine them carefully against the relevant incantation texts?

שדין IN JOB 19:29

The foremost observation we want to make in this regard is that the plural term *šdyn* in *DA* 1.6 appears also in Job 19:29. The context of this *hapax* in Tanak is the famous "Redeemer" speech in which Job laments his illness, his loneliness, and the pain inflicted on him by his oppressors, both divine and human.[26] Defensive and angry, he demands that a גואל-redeemer come forward to plead his case,[27] and further, that a written record be made of the dispute he has had to endure from his three "friends." Finally, he issues the following warning:

If you continue to say	כי תאמרו
"How shall we persecute him?"	מה נרדף לו
and "How[28] is the root of the problem to be found in him?"[29]	ושרש דבר נמצא בי
Then beware of the fever[30]	גורו לכם מפני חרב
For wrath's punishment[31] is fever	כי חמה עונות חרב

---

24. Herrmann, "El," 274–80.

25. The title of this essay derives from Phyllis Trible's ground-breaking study, *Texts of Terror*, first published in 1984.

26. Westermann reads Job's speeches predominantly as laments (*Hiob*, 55–56).

27. Gordis thinks the גואל in Job 19:25 refers to God (*Job*, 526). Habel sees it referring to a heavenly being like the celestial "witness" (עד, Job 16:19) or "arbiter" (מוכיח, 9:33) for whom Job longs in his early speeches (*Job*, 306–7).

28. Interrogative pronoun מה in the first question extends to the second one (*GKC* §137).

29. MT בי (1st pers.) does not match לו (3rd pers.) in the previous question (cf. OG ἐν αὐτῷ, "in him").

30. MT חרב occurs twice in Job 19:29. Syr ܣܝܦ and Vg *gladius* can be translated "sword," but OG studiously avoids this semantic choice. Since Heb חרב (and Syr ܣܝܦ) denote "heat/dryness," the trans. "fever" seems most appropriate (see Job 30:30; Isa 25:4–5; *HAL* 336), especially since, as Fohrer points out, the fever of illness is widely believed to be demonic in origin ("Krankheit," 172–87).

31. MT עונות is pl. of עון, but see *HAL* 756.

So,³² you (too) will come to know the *šdyn*.³³ למען תדעון שדין.

The versions read שדין in several ways. The Greek Codex Alexandrinus apparently reads the term as a derivative of שדד ("to overpower, destroy"),³⁴ given the fact that it offers ἰσχύς as a translation.³⁵ In the Latin tradition, Vg reads שדין as *iudicium*, a composite term probably reflecting an original relative particle שׁ prefixed to the noun דין ("judgment").³⁶ In the Aramaic tradition the lacuna in 11QtgJob makes it impossible to read the translation of Job 19:29, but Syr reads ܫܐܕܐ, a sg. term used in Syr Job 8:3 to translate MT שדי.³⁷

In light of the Deir ʿAllā evidence, and in light of the appearance of שדין in Job 19:29, it seems obvious that this term refers to "demons" in both texts. Deciding whether each text comes from an "El-repertoire" obviously requires more scrutiny of a great deal more evidence than is presently available, but is it only a coincidence that each of these texts uses the same term within what appears to be a practically identical juridical context? Re-read in light of this newer evidence, Job thus seems to be pleading at the end of his "Redeemer" speech not only for a גאל-redeemer to protect *him* from divine wrath, but Eliphaz, Bildad and Zophar as well. Instead of looking for the "root of the problem" in him, he suggests, perhaps they should prepare for the day when *they* will need a benevolent גאל to protect *them* from the same malevolent forces which now threaten *him*.

ELIPHAZ'S DEBATE WITH JOB

Intertextually, the appearance of שדין in Job's "Redeemer" speech, coupled with the multiple appearances of שדי throughout the Joban dialogues, casts the DN שדי in a whole new light. The etymological relationship between שדי and שדין may forever remain obscure,³⁸ but the mysterious identity of

32. MT למען ("so that," *HAL* 581; Syr ܡܛܠ followed by ܕ; see *PSD* 267). OG reads εἰ ... τότε ("if... then"; see Job 19:28–29; *LSJ* 1808).

33. MT *ketiv* שדי; *qere* שדין. Whether *qere* is proposed for stylistic or ideological reasons is unclear (see Tov, *Textual*, 56–59).

34. *HAL* 1318.

35. *LSJ* 844. See Rahlfs, *Septuaginta* 2.303. The usual translations of שדי in OG Job are κύριος and παντοκράτωρ.

36. Rowley (*Job*, 140) lists Klostermann, Budde, Gray and Fohrer as proponents of this interpretation.

37. Working from the Ug evidence, Fisher ("ŠDYN," 342–43) proposes that שדין be read as an archaic variant of שדי.

38. Listing no fewer than eight etymological possibilities, Koch ("Šaddaj," 308–9) concludes that "whichever theory one chooses, it offers little help for interpreting the

Šadday seems, in light of this newer evidence, to be a bit less foggy. In point of fact, Šadday now looks to be standing at the vortex of a fierce debate between Job and Eliphaz over the nature of good vs. evil.[39] Attending closely to this debate may therefore help us understand better whether Job's texts of terror intend to communicate something other than mere psychological terror.[40]

Eliphaz vs. Job on Šadday's Intentions

Eliphaz fires the first salvo in this debate by confidently affirming Šadday's ability to rescue Job from seven terrors if only Job will knuckle under and accept divine "discipline."[41] These terrors include famine, death, war, the sword, the tongue, destruction, and the beasts of the earth.[42] Eliphaz even hints at the possibility of corralling these terrors via a "covenant," though without specifying what particular type.[43] This is neither the first nor the only time in Tanak that seven terrors run together in a pack. Moses, for example, threatens the unleashing of seven terrors if and when Israel's covenant with Yahweh goes awry: consumption, fever,[44] inflammation, fiery heat, the sword, blight, and mildew.[45] Similarly, seven attendants of Lord Yahweh come together in Ezekiel to mark out the righteous remnant of Jerusalem for salvation while the rest are executed.[46]

Outside of Tanak, however, the closest parallel is the angry gang of demons unleashed by the chthonic deity Erra in his bid to terrorize the

---

OT texts."

39. See the anthology of essays recently published by Nesselrath & Wilk.

40. Psycho-social pain is difficult, of course, but Trible's insistence that it generates the worst kind of pain imaginable (*Terror*, 2), while politically popular, is hopelessly materialistic (see Moore, "Text," 39–42).

41. מוסר שדי אל־תמאס, "Do not reject the discipline of Šadday" (Job 5:17).

42. (In order) שוט לשון, ידי חרב, מלחמה, מות, רעב (cf. שוט in Job 1:7; 2:1), שוד, חית הארץ (Job 5:20–23).

43. כי עם אבני השדה בריתך, "for with the stones of the field is your covenant" (Job 5:23).

44. One of the terms for "fever" here (קדחת) is not the same as that found in Job 19:29 (חרב), but to translate חרב as "fever" (19:29) hardly precludes translating חרב as "sword" here or in 5:21.

45. (In order) חרב, חרחר, דלקת, קדחת, שחפת (cf. same term in Job 19:29), שדפון, ירקון (Deut 28:22).

46. Ezek 9:1–11. Zimmerli (*Ezekiel* 1.246) links these terrors to the משחית ("destroyer") in Exod 12:23, but May ("Glory," 320), Frankena (*Ezechiël*, 18–19), and Bodi (*Erra*, 97–99) link them to the Babylonian Seven.

"dark-headed people,"[47] a gang Kabti-ilāni-marduk simply calls "the Seven."[48] Like Nergal, Erra is a feared underworld deity in charge of demonic lackeys only tenuously subordinated to his control. The Seven, however, have their own personality and history. They can act alone or in concert with other chthonic creatures.[49] In Anatolia an "old woman" can protect her clients by setting out goblets of alcohol to distract the Seven.[50] One Assyrian ritual begins with a list of foods prepared for their consumption, after which the exorcist pleads, "Accept it, O Seven . . . Accept it!"[51] How they originate is a bit murky, of course. According to *Erra*, the old high god Anu impregnates Earth, who then spawns the Seven like a pack of dogs.[52] Anu then assigns them roles: the first "spreads terror"; the second "burns like fire"; the third "takes the form of a lion"; the fourth "flattens mountains to the ground"; the fifth "blows like a wind"; the sixth "strikes upwards and downwards"; and the seventh "kills everything with viper venom."[53] The guardian entrusted with the difficult job of controlling the Seven is Erra's steward Išum, significantly called "a door bolted before them."[54] Even as (formerly) hostile parties invoke the power of the gods to enforce covenant stipulations in international treaties,[55] so also do priestly exorcists attempt to neutralize the demonic forces (potentially) harming their clients. At Arslan Tash, for example, priestly exorcists expel demons via a "covenant" (*'lt*) made between "all the sons of the gods" (*kl bn 'lm*) and "all the holy ones" (*kl qdšm*) under the watchful eye of Assur and/or El.[56] Presumably this covenant guarantees the peace and protection of everyone living behind the door over which this portal plaque hangs.

---

47. *ṣalmāt qaqqadi*, Erra 1.43 (see *CAD* Ṣ, 75).

48. *Erra* 1.23–44. Kabti-ilāni-marduk is the author of the Babylonian poem of *Erra* (see *Erra* 5.42).

49. Roberts, *Pantheon*, 115. One of their most terrifying alliances is with the soul-stealing demon Lamaštu, as illustrated on the plaque published by Farber (*Lamaštu*, 2).

50. *[kezz-iy]a 7* DUG^{GAL} *isqāri [kezz-iy]a 7* DUG^{GAL} *isqāri*, "on one side she sets 7 goblets, and on the other side she sets seven goblets" (*VBoT* 24.1.45–46).

51. *m]u-uḫ-ra* ^{d}*sebet-bi* . . . *mu-uḫ-ra-ma* (*BBR* 26.2.28).

52. *Erra* 1.28–29.

53. (In order) *[ta-a]n-di-ru-ma, kīma* ^{d}*Girri ku-bu-um-ma, zi-im la-bi, a-na na-še-e* ^{giš}*kakke*^{meš}*-ka ez-zu-ti šadû li-tab-bit, iq-ta-bi ki-ma šari, e-liš u šap-liš ba-'a-ma, i-mat ba-áš-me i-ṣe-en-šu-ma šum-qí-ta napištata* (*Erra* 1.32–38)

54. ^{d}*i-šum dal-tum-ma e-dil pa-nu-[uš-šu]n* (*Erra* 1.27); see Lambert, "Etana," 83.

55. See, e.g., the treaty of Birga'yah with Mat`i'el (*KAI* 222–24).

56. *KAI* 27.8–12. Cross & Saley read *šr* as the goddess Asherah and *'lm* as "the Eternal One," a common epithet of El in northwest semitic ("Incantations," 45). Zevit reads *šr* as the god Aššur ("Inscription," 115).

Eliphaz, in other words, appears to draw from two well-known traditions in his first speech to Job: (a) that evil runs in packs, and (b) that these packs can be corralled by the cutting of covenants, either with the pack itself, or with the deity in charge of the pack. Where Eliphaz presumes a distinction between Šadday and these שדין, however, Job does not. He, too, is familiar with traditional chthonic motifs, and chooses one of the most graphic to launch his lament:

| The arrows of Šadday are within me | חצי שדי עמדי |
| My spirit drinks their venom. | חמתם שתה רוחי |

Alongside the fact that one of the Seven kills via "viper venom,"[57] the "divine archer" metaphor is a common motif with which Eliphaz and Job are evidently quite familiar.[58] In Canaan, for example, the deity Rešep is sometimes called *b'l ḥẓ*, "lord of the arrow."[59] In Assyria, Nergal is "lord of the bow, the arrow, and the quiver,"[60] and Asalluḫi, "exorcist of the gods,"[61] habitually drives away the "oath of the lance and the arrow"[62] (i.e., the demonic curses which threaten his clients). In the *Erra Epic*, one of Erra's "arrows" successfully penetrates the "inner wall" of Babylon.[63] Mortally wounded, the wall itself—a personalized being in Babylonian myth—cries out, "Ah, my heart!"[64] Much like Rešep and Nergal, Šadday is therefore a foreboding, menacing figure in Job's eyes, a "divine archer" who takes great delight in targeting defenseless mortals.[65]

---

57. *i-mat ba-aš-me* (Erra 1.38).

58. וירם אלהים חץ, "God will shoot an arrow at them" (Ps 63:8).

59. *CAT* 1.82.3 (*b'l ḥẓ ršp*). "Undoubtedly Resheph . . . is a heavenly archer" (Münnich, *Resheph*, 130). Note also Anat's fondness for the bow and arrow (*CAT* 1.17.6.13, 25).

60. *[bē]l* ^{iš}*qašti u-ṣu u iš-pat* (AGH 116.4).

61. *maš-maš* DINGIR^{MEŠ} (Šur 3.2).

62. *ma-mit* ^{giš}*as-ma-re-e u til-pa-nu* (Šur 3.29). Akk *tilpānu* is probably more accurately translated "throwstick" (see *GE* 12.17–18; George, *Gilgamesh*, 729).

63. The city-wall surrounding Babylon includes Nemet-Enlil (the name of the outer wall, meaning "seat of Enlil") and Imgur-Enlil (the name of the inner wall, meaning "Enlil's envelope").

64. *u-ù'-a lib-bi* (Erra 4.16).

65. Elsewhere Job complains that "my adversary" (צרי) "sets me up for his target" (יקימני לו למטרה) where "his archers surround me" (יסבו עלי רביו), Job 16:9, 12–13).

Eliphaz vs. Job on the Fate of the Wicked

In his second speech, Eliphaz responds to Job by agreeing with him: mortals often *are* forced to drink deeply of evil's poison. Yet the source of this evil cannot be Šadday—at least not the Šadday to whom Eliphaz prays. For Eliphaz, evil must ultimately come from somewhere else. He readily admits that a "divine council" (סוד אלוה) exists in the heavens, but he remains firm in his resolve that Šadday is too wise to put all his trust in "his holy ones."[66] Eliphaz has no difficulty recognizing the reality of evil. What he rejects is the fatalistic mentality which always tries to eliminate the element of human choice. Instead, he argues, the wicked *are* wicked because they *choose* to be so, thereby justifiably leading to "the sound of terrors in their ears."[67] Because of their wickedness they deserve to die by the sword. Because of their wickedness they deserve to suffer from hunger after their crops have died from drought, blight and fire. Justifiably they deserve to live in the fear that a "day of darkness" will soon descend upon them, a darkness from which they can never escape.[68] Because they persist in deluding themselves into thinking that they cannot be held responsible for their choices, the "Destroyer"[69] will sneak up on them at a time they least expect, even as they bask in the trappings of "peaceful calm."[70] All these consequences, Eliphaz argues, will occur because the wicked "have stretched forth their hand against El and vaunted themselves against Šadday."[71]

Eliphaz crudely recycles many of the traditional evils listed in his first speech into the second one. Against so simple a dichotomy between good and evil, however, Job wisely asks why there seem to be so many "exceptions." Why, for example, do so many wicked people live in safehouses free from danger? Why is it that the "rod of Eloah" rarely seems to fall upon *them*? Why are their families and herds so happy and productive? Why does an allegedly all-powerful deity like Šadday allow them to ridicule him, blasphemously demanding, "Who is Šadday that we might serve him?" and "What is our 'profit' in approaching him?"[72] Frustrated by Eliphaz's shallow orthodoxy, Job nonetheless agrees with him: the wicked do indeed deserve to suffer for their crimes. But why the *innocent*? Returning to the "divine

---

66. קדשיו (Job 15:15).
67. קול פחדים באזניו (Job 15:21).
68. יום־חשך (Job 15:23). See Moore, "Day," 193–208.
69. שודד, not שדי (Job 15:21).
70. שלום (Job 15:21). See Olyan, "Considerations," 652–68.
71. כי־נטה אל־אל ואל שדי יתגבר (Job 15:25).
72. Job 21:15. Heb יעל ("to profit") almost always appears in contexts ridiculing the worship of foreign gods (e.g., Isa 44:9; 47:12; 57:12; Jer 2:8, 11; 16:9).

archer" metaphor, he paints another judgmental portrait: "In his anger he lays out snares ... Let their eyes see his snare! Let them drink of Šadday's wrath!"[73] Snare imagery, like archery imagery, is also quite common in ANE incantation literature. In Anatolia, particularly, the breeding and ensnaring of exotic birds for ritualistic consumption is a peculiar task entrusted to a specialist called the ^{LÚ}MUŠEN.DÙ priest.[74] As many of the Boğazköy texts attest, the denizens of the Hittite netherworld have an insatiable craving for "bird flesh."[75]

Several Mesopotamian texts show demonic beings ensnaring human beings like gullible birds. In one poem, for example, a tormented sufferer laments that in spite of all his efforts to keep the Seven away, they still ensnare him:[76]

My eyes stare, but do not see	pal-ṣa-a-ma ul i-na-aṭ-ṭal i-na-a-a
My ears open, but do not hear	pe-ta-a-ma ul i-šem-ma-a uz-na-a-a
Numbness seizes my whole body	kal pag-ri-ia i-ta-ḫaz ri-mu-tú
Paralysis falls upon my flesh	mi-šit-tu im-ta-qut UGU UZU^{MEŠ}-ia ...
A snare covers my mouth	ina pi-ia na-aḫ-ba-lu na-di-ma
A bolt locks my lips	nap-ra-ku se-ki-ir šap-ti-ia ...
All my country says, "How trapped he is!"	kal ma-ti-ia ki-i ḫa-bíl iq-bu-ni.[77]

Since two nominal forms of Akk ḫabālu occur here in a context of "entrapment," the use of the Heb cognate חבל in Job hardly seems coincidental, especially when Job warns the wicked that "their destruction will come upon them" when Šadday "lays out 'snares' (חבלים)."[78] For Job, then, Šadday is not only a "divine archer," but also a "divine fowler."

---

73. Job 21: 17, 20.

74. One ritual features an "augur" (^{LÚ}MUŠEN.DÙ) named Ḫuwarlu conducting a ritual to protect his client from a "frightening bird" (ḫatugauš, KBo 4.2; see Ünal, "Augures," 31).

75. Further examples cited in Haas & Wilhelm, Kizzuwatna, 50–59, 137–43.

76. ik-ṣu-ru-nim-ma ri-kis se-bet i-lat-su-un, "The gang of Seven organize their pack" (Lud 1.65).

77. Lud 2.73–76, 84–85, 116.

78. Job 21:17. The nearest antecedent subject of יחלק ("to lay out, apportion") in 21:17 is שדי in 21:15.

Eliphaz vs. Job on Job's Personal Fate

As students of Job well know, Eliphaz really "takes off the gloves" in his third and final speech.[79] Frustrated to the breaking point, he genuinely abhors Job's insistence that Šadday is the source of all his suffering. To hold such a position strikes him as unwarranted and unproven, even blasphemous.[80] In his final speech he thus virtually explodes at Job, throwing aside all third-person gentility and shooting straight for the jugular. Misguided by anger, he misquotes Job horribly. Even though Job has made it plain in his previous speech that he holds the *wicked* responsible for critical questions like "What is Šadday, that we might serve him?"[81] and "What do we 'profit' if we draw near to him?,"[82] Eliphaz rips these questions out of context, treating them as if they are *Job's* questions. "Can a man be 'profitable' to El?" he snorts.[83] "Is it 'surplus booty' for Šadday if your way is blameless?"[84] For Eliphaz, simply to *ask* such questions is blasphemous, and Job must be held accountable for his "arrogance." Maybe Job *deserves* to be "ensnared," paralyzed by "sudden terror," and "covered with darkness."[85]

Should the writer of Job be aware of the *šdyn* at Deir ʿAllā, he may well be playing on two *Leitwörten* here. Putting words in Job's mouth, he has him chant the bipolar mantra of the depressed agnostic: "They say to El, 'Leave him alone!' and What can Šadday do for him?'"[86] Two of the words in this mantra appear in Balaam's *DA* oracle to his people: "Let me tell you what the *šd[yn* have done]. Come see the doings of the gods"[87]—i.e., the noun *šdy(n)* and the verb *pʿl*. Whereas Balaam bluntly warns his *DA* audience to

---

79. Job 22:1–30. "The graduated and sophisticated fashioning of the figure of Eliphaz" appears "not merely as background to the figure of Job, but as his antithesis" (Hoffman, *Blemished*, 139).

80. "Once he begins to engage in sophisticated formulations of discredited theories, he is in the final analysis forced to distort and falsify reality" (Ibid., 139).

81. מה שדי כי נעבדנו (Job 21:15).

82. מה נועיל כי נפגע בו (Job 21:15; for יעל OG reads ὠφέλεια). Job makes it clear that he wants absolutely nothing to do with the עצת רשעים ("counsel of the wicked," Job 21:16).

83. הלאל יסכן־גבר (Job 22:2).

84. לשדי... אם־בצע כי־תתם דרכי (Job 22:3; for בצע OG again reads ὠφέλεια; see Moore, *WealthWatch*, 141, 193–94, 199–201).

85. Job 22:10–11. "Eliphaz's inconsistency or incoherence . . ., like his attempts to invent failures Job must be guilty of, is a sign that he is flailing in his attempt to make theological sense of what has happened to Job" (Goldingay, *Job*, 113).

86. האמרים לאל סור ממנו ומה יפעל שדי למו (Job 22:17).

87. *ḥwkm mh šd[yn pʿlw] wlkw rʾw pʿlt ʾlhn* (DA 1.5), restoring *šd[yn pʿlw]* with Hackett (*Balaam*, 25).

beware of the malevolent "doings" (*p ʿlt*) of the *šdyn*, Eliphaz uses these same terms to mock the despondent nihilism of those "wicked" souls who, like Job, believe Šadday to be powerless to "do" anything.

At any rate, Job's response to Eliphaz's final onslaught is filled with despair:

El makes my heart faint	אל הרך לבי
Šadday terrifies me	שדי הבהילני[88]
Here is my mark	הן תוי
Let Šadday answer me	שדי יענני.[89]

If an intertextual play on *šdy(n)* and *p ʿl* seems tenuous, the appearance of the word תו ("mark") does not. As in the earlier "Redeemer" speech, Job again pleads for something to be written down on his behalf.[90] But here at the end of his debate with Eliphaz he appears to have another kind of writing in mind. Instead of a written record of his dispute with Šadday, he asks instead that a תו-mark be written over his forehead, much like the one written over the foreheads of the righteous[91] to protect them from Jerusalem's seven "executioners" in Ezekiel.[92]

CONCLUSIONS

In the end, Job no longer pleads a case for his integrity. No longer does he seek to engage in theological debate. No longer does he plead for a גואל-redeemer to intervene on his behalf. Battered and bludgeoned, he simply reverts to the same magical instinct so predominant among his contemporaries—that primordial, deeply-ingrained instinct to hide in a safe place until "things blow over," when the door to healing can again be unlocked and the light to salvation can again be illuminated.[93] It goes without saying that we desperately need to uncover and analyze more inscriptional evidence before anything truly substantive can be said about the extent to which the priestly incantation literature influences the book of Job.[94] So we must be

---

88. Job 23:16.
89. Job 31:35.
90. Job 19:23–24.
91. Ezek 9:4 (again, תו).
92. פקדות העיר (Ezek 9:1; see Bodi, *Ezekiel*, 95–110).
93. Analysis of this magico-religious worldview appears in Jeffers (*Magic*, 1–24), Frantz-Szabó ("Magic," 2007–19), Farber ("Magic," 1895–1909), and Moore (*Balaam*, 20–96).
94. Though out-of-date in many ways, Pope's 1965 commentary on Job remains the

careful and cautious in our final reflections, content merely to point out a few of the more obvious possibilities.

First, the terror facing Job in the dialogues is fundamentally plural, unlike the singular term שטן initiating the action in the prologue.⁹⁵ Use of the Aramaized plural term שדין in 19:29 overtly underlines this contrast and the continuous appearance of the PN שדי covertly highlights it. Both Eliphaz and Job presume this plurality over the course of an increasingly caustic conversation. *Second*, the dispute between Eliphaz and Job over the character of Šadday is never resolved. From first to last Eliphaz views the world as a relatively secure cosmos under Šadday's protection, whereas Job views it as an unstable chaos operating under no single protector. Eliphaz holds the pervasive forces of evil responsible for Job's suffering. Job, however, holds Šadday responsible. Eliphaz sees Šadday's intentions as essentially benevolent. Job sees them as essentially malevolent. It may go without saying, but interpreters need to avoid the temptation to resolve conflicts in Job left unresolved in the text itself.⁹⁶

Third, in light of the sociohistorical context, suddenly made more visible by the discovery of the *DA* texts, we need to investigate more thoroughly the potential sources of non-Yahwistic material deeply embedded in the Joban dialogues. The Deir ʿAllā and other texts preserve a number of terms and motifs quite similar, if not identical, to those found throughout these dialogues—parallels which need to be examined and tested, not marginalized or ignored. Much more evidence needs to come to light before anything truly definitive can be said about the existence or practical function of an "El repertoire," but it may yet turn out that Levine and others are on the right track. At the very least we now know enough to state unequivocally that El religion coexists alongside Yahwism as a matter of historical record.⁹⁷ So, if the comparative approach contributes anything, it is that the book of Job shows no real evidence of Job "repenting" of any "sin." To hold such a position is to identify too closely with Eliphaz's rigid theology of

---

most thorough comparative analysis.

95. Like OG (ὁ διάβολος, "the devil"), Syr (ܣܛܢܐ, "the saṭan"), Vg ("Satan"), *TJob* ("Saṭan"), and Qurʾan (الشيطن, "The Šayṭan," Q 38.41) personalize השטן ("the Adversary") prosecuting Job in the prologue (Job 1:6; 2:1; see Day, *Adversary*, 69–106).

96. "Job's conflict with his friends remains unresolved" (Habel, *Job*, 34).

97. "There is no evidence that El is in decline during the Israelite period. On the other hand, there are a number of indications that throughout the time in which the Hebrew Bible is being formed, there is periodic contact with El traditions which continue to be alive outside of Israel" (L'Heureux, *Canaanite*, 67). See de Moor (*Yahwism*, 42–100) and Smith (*Yahweh*, 145–60).

retribution.⁹⁸ Yet neither can we say that Job, upset by his plight as innocent sufferer, simply repudiates Šadday altogether. To hold *this* position is to ignore the fact that the book of Job now sits in a canon edited by Hebrew tradents fully devoted to Yahweh as the one true God.⁹⁹ Both positions are extremist because both fail to take seriously the book's sociohistorical context.

---

98. *Contra* Newell, "Job," 298–316. Simundson (*Job*, 13–45) recognizes the kind of havoc Eliphaz's theology can create, yet still believes that Job eventually "repents" of "sin" (Job 42:6, mistranslating נחם).

99. *Contra* Curtis, "Yahweh," 497–511. Muenchow plausibly argues that Job's response in 42:6 is less a confession of repentance than an ANE expression of shame before an acknowledged superior ("Dust," 610).

15

HUMAN SUFFERING IN LAMENTATIONS*

AMONG CRITICAL STUDIES OF Lamentations the approaches of Norman Gottwald and Bertil Albrektson have dominated discussion.[1] It is Gottwald's view, first of all, that (a) a "single key" to the theology of Lamentations can be found—a problematic presumption from the outset—and (b) that this "key" emerges from the tension between deuteronomic faith and the tragic events of history to which these poems bear awful witness.[2] During the Josianic reform many older, more conservative beliefs reassert themselves among some Israelites attempting to think through the problem of evil. The deuteronomic solution, however, short-circuits this process because it positions itself behind the simplistic polarity that sin *always* brings punishment while faith *always* brings vindication. To this *faux* solution, however, reality quickly invades via several unexplainable tragedies. Josiah, the righteous reformer, dies in battle (609 BCE). King Jehoiachin and his cabinet are dragged off into Babylonian captivity (597 BCE). Jerusalem suffers the ignobilities of besiegement, starvation, defeat, exile, and slavery (587 BCE). To Gottwald, Lamentations is therefore a serious theological

---

* Revised from an essay first published in *RB* 90 (1983) 534–55.

1. Gottwald, *Lamentations*, 47–49; Albrektson, *Lamentations*, 214–16.

2. Curiously, few of the reviewers identify this problem. See McDonnell (*Lamentations*, 517–18), Mauchline (*Lamentations*, 230), Gailey (*Lamentations*, 471–72), Thomas (*Lamentations*, 262–65), Dowd (*Lamentations*, 282). Albrektson, however, observes that "it (is) debatable . . . whether one can speak at all of 'the key' in the singular" (*Lamentations*, 238).

manifesto designed to address the crucial theodical question, "Why do the righteous suffer alongside the wicked?" It represents the first time in history that a sensitive Hebrew poet has to face this question stripped of all the old symbols of Yahweh's favor—the city, the temple, the people, the torah. Here the בת ירושלים ("daughter of Jerusalem")[3] has to deal directly with יהוה צבאות ("Yahweh of Hosts") as the prophetic warnings so long ignored come suddenly to fulfillment, imploding in the process all the shallow presumptions of the so-called "deuteronomic school."[4]

Albrektson goes straight to the heart of this hypothesis, however, by asking whether *any* evidence exists of a recognizable tension between *deuteronomic* faith and history. Accepting with Gottwald that Lamentations seeks to explain the hideous events of 587 within the framework of a faith-vs.-history polarity, he nonetheless rejects the notion that a pristine *deuteronomic* faith ever commands Judah's full attention. More likely, he submits, the people living in and around Jerusalem have simply allowed themselves to be lulled to sleep by the hundreds of feel-good sermons extolling, *ad absurdum*, the beauty, sanctity, and impregnable inviolability of Zion.[5] Thus, when Zion falls, so does their faith. Albrektson thus views Lamentations as a poetic collection designed to lead Judah back to a *person* instead of a *place*. In fact, he insists, Gottwald's thesis makes sense only if deuteronomic faith is universally (or at least quasi-universally) revered by a majority of the populace. Since this cannot be proven, he reluctantly rejects any attempt to build a theology of Lamentations on such a presumption, however attractive.[6]

The problem with these hypotheses is that each presumes, *a priori*, (a) that one theological motif somehow dominates this entire poetic collection, and (b) that all other motifs must therefore be secondary. This kind of methodology is often suspect in studies where authorship, time, and place of composition are identifiable. It is *highly* suspect when applied to a diffuse collection of poems like the "books" of Psalms or Lamentations. Accordingly it is important to question it critically, based as it is on so many unproven (and unprovable) presumptions and correlations. It seems to me that one might go so far as to concede that deuteronomic and Zion traditions serve as traditional sources contributing to the development of Lamentations'

3. See Häusl & König, "Weg," 18–21.

4. Weinfeld, *Deuteronomy*, 1–9.

5. הדם רגליו ("his footstool," Lam 2:1; see Ps 99:5; 132:7; 1 Chron 28:2).

6. This does not mean that Albrektson dismisses Gottwald altogether. In fact, he even tries at the end of his essay to synthesize their two theses, a process later picked up by Ackroyd in his attempt to explain the significance of the exile (*Exile*, 45–46; see Smith-Christopher, *Exile*, 30–32).

impact. But to claim more than this seems wrongheaded for the following reasons:

(1) To posit a single theological focus presumes the adoption of some kind of unity theory framing all five chapters. As will be shown below, neither Gottwald nor Albrektson are the first to suggest this (theological focus + unity of form/content), even though neither expressly links the two.

(2) To posit a single theological focus most likely implies that the poet(s) responsible for this collection of laments is calculatedly conscious of "doing theology" in the modern sense; i.e., that he feels a crying need to go beyond Israel's "grief work" to the formation of a rational theological "treatise." But is this what Lamentations sets out to do? Or is it any more than what it claims to be—a poetic dirge over the fall of a great city?[7] Doubtless the author(s) stand(s) within a peculiar theological framework (deuteronomic? Zionistic?), but is he *consciously* and *methodically* employing stock symbols, epithets, and word-pairs[8] for any other purpose than to facilitate communal lament?[9] I am more inclined to think that the hard theologizing comes later.[10] Tragedies of this magnitude need time to be absorbed. How many soundly-reasoned books on the massacre at Wounded Knee are written (by the Lakota) before the end of the nineteenth century?[11] How many analyses of the European holocaust are written (by Jews) within the first decade after Dachau, Buchenwald or Auschwitz?[12] How many films about Vietnam are made (by Americans) in the first decade after the fall of

---

7. Dobbs-Allsopp, *Lamentations*, 7–10; see also *Weep*, 4–13.

8. Watters is succinct: "While formula criticism is not the final solution to all the questions about Hebrew poetry, it nevertheless goes a long way toward helping us repair and relate texts. And it alone just might be the key to a better understanding of the meter" (*Formula*, 146–47). Critical of Watters' approach, Scharbert nevertheless finds insightful his understanding of poetic word-pairs and how they operate in Classical Hebrew (*Formula*, 289).

9. Albrektson concedes that "elements from different traditions can be found in the same author or the same work, but this does not in itself mean that any real synthesis has been established" (*Lamentations*, 215, 238).

10. As Gottwald puts it, Lamentations "presupposes and contains, though embryonically, the tensions of later theology" (*Lamentations*, 71); see Rudolph, *Klagelieder*, 194.

11. The massacre at Wounded Knee occurs on Dec 29, 1890 (Brown, *Wounded*).

12. "A person had to summon all his wits, and focus entirely on the present. One had to learn the rules and search for the signals that told how things were done in the new situation, to find out what the dangers were, whom to trust, what resources to count on. In a new situation there was no place for yesterday's problems. It was only when he was much older that he took to brooding. And he did take to it. He had the brooder's memory, the passion for details, the tireless capacity for rage" (Rabinowitz, *Holocaust*, 222).

Saigon?[13] Persistent uncertainties among interpreters as to whether Lamentations focuses on a single theological theme make it seem much more likely that these laments, composed and collected as they are so close to the horrifying events of 587,[14] simply set out to lament the city's destruction; i.e., put forward a tender first step toward picking up the emotional pieces by articulating the anger, guilt, despair, and stubborn hopes of a nation too shell-shocked to begin this "grief work" without help.[15] This is not to deny that significant theological motifs resurface here and there throughout the collection, but it is to affirm that the historical context in which they operate precludes the kinds of theological discussions more fully engaged in books like Isaiah and Ezekiel.

(3) To posit a single theological focus tends in the final analysis to reduce and constrict the variegated impact of Lamentations' broad theological thrust. It tends to marginalize motifs and themes peremptorily rendered "secondary." One might well seize on the question H. H. Schmid raises to pentateuchal research and apply it to Lamentations:

> Has the text been more often adjusted to our hypotheses than our hypotheses to the text?[16]

The present essay is an attempt to shed more light on one of these "secondary" themes in order to engage it seriously without distorting the theological intentionality of the book as a whole. I suggest that *one* of the themes in Lamentations is the theme of human suffering. This seems to be such an obvious conclusion from even a cursory reading, yet few interpreters assign to this theme much more than a footnote. This is unfortunate, because careful study of the metaphorical as well as historical passages in these poems dealing with human suffering—from the starving of infants to the abandonment of the aged—not only points the way toward illuminating a major theme in the Bible, it also opens the door a bit wider to the kind of biblical interpretation which speaks more clearly to the contemporary needs of a broken world. What is God saying here about his relationship to suffering humanity? What is this poet(s) trying to accomplish? What theological (and even psychological) value might the book of Lamentations have should the light of interpretation be more intentionally focused on this theme?

---

13. Saigon falls on Apr 30, 1975. Michael Cimino's *The Deer Hunter* appears in 1978, but Oliver Stone's *Platoon* does not appear until 1986.

14. With Rudolph (*Klagelieder*, 193) and Cannon ("Lamentations," 43–44), I presume these poems to be eyewitness accounts (*contra* Wiesmann, "Augenzeuge," 84).

15. See Kübler-Ross (*Death*); Bowlby (*Bonds*); Worden (*Grief*).

16. Schmid, *Jahwist*, 12.

LITERARY "UNITY"?

The issue of literary unity within Lamentations is multi-layered and complex. Many nineteenth-century readers profoundly doubt whether Lamentations can be characterized as a "unified" document in any sense of that term (i.e., formally *or* substantively). Others promote what they believe to be a conscious attempt on the part of "the author" (sg.) to create a unified structure.[17] Some seek a middle solution; i.e., that these five poems are individually composed, but that a later redactor arranges and modifies them according to *his* singular intentions. Hermann Wiesmann, for example, champions the inner, *theological* unity of the book, yet Gottwald and Albrektson hastily dismiss his approach, calling it unsophisticated and "primitivist."[18] Doubtless Wiesmann's later work (particularly his 1954 commentary, *Die Klagelieder*) goes far enough to merit such opprobrium, but not his 1926 essay, "Der planmässige Aufbau der Klagelieder des Jeremias."[19] Here he stakes out a carefully balanced position, vigorously distinguishing it from some of the more radical "unity" theories in his immediate context. Granted, his approach is almost purely descriptive (i.e., not formally tied to form-, literary-, or traditio-historical methods), yet within it one finds few of the exegetical excesses decried by critical readers like Rudolph (though not in a description of Wiesmann *per se*).[20] Instead this 1926 essay initiates what can only be described as the beginning of the modern theological discussion.

Several of Wiesmann's contemporaries reject outright the book's "unity," yet others do not, often because so many are preoccupied with protecting its "Jeremianic authorship" from critical attack. W. M. L. de Wette, for example, argues that the book lays out the destruction of the city in recognizable stages from a pre-established outline.[21] Wiesmann rejects this "gradational" approach, however, because he finds no evidence to sustain it from the poems themselves. Each poem rather presumes, explicitly or implicitly,

---

17. Most nineteenth- and early-twentieth-century readers follow Talmud's assumption of Jeremianic authorship (*b. Mo'ed Qaṭ* 26a).

18. Albrektson, *Lamentations*, 215. Gottwald's reading is magnanimous— "Wiesmann (is) the only scholar known to the present writer who has made a close scrutiny of the theology" (*Lamentations*, 52). Similarly Rudolph (*Klagelieder*, 193), after criticizing Wiesmann's attempts to date the book, commends his understanding of the book's internal unity.

19. *Bib* 7 (1926) 146–61.

20. Rudolph, *Klagelieder*, 195.

21. De Wette, *Lehrbuch*, §273.

the city's destruction (even chapter 1, *contra* Rudolph).²² Heinrich Ewald argues that the author/editor molds five independent laments into one anthology.²³ Carl Friedrich Keil accepts this theory with the *proviso* that the author/editor does not work from a predetermined theological focus (e.g., the "hope motif" in 3:22-33), yet still operates from a "well-thought-out plan."²⁴ Wiesmann immediately sees through this inconsistency, however, wryly noting that Keil conspicuously fails to specify any of the details of this "well-thought-out plan."²⁵

He saves his strongest critique, however, for the detailed hypothesis put forward by Eduard Nägelsbach. Nägelsbach takes this developing line of approach (i.e., the attempts of de Wette, Ewald, and Keil to build a portrait of unity based on *external* factors) and summarily frames it around the "hope motif" in 3:22-33, picking out this passage as the "culmination point of the whole book."²⁶ Like the peak of a mountain, everything in the preceding verses leads up to it, while everything in the succeeding verses leads back down. Chapters 1, 2, 4 and 5 represent the night of misery after the fall of the city. For Nägelsbach these chapters only serve to bracket the book's dominant thrust. Chapters 1 and 2 are crescendo; chapters 4 and 5 decrescendo. Chapter 3 itself also breaks down into similarly recognizable sections: (a) 3:1-21 represents the night of doubt (3:1-18), followed by the dawn of hope (3:19-21); (b) this hope then bursts forth like the rays of the sun (3:22-40) as heavenly trust is rekindled and divine love reaffirmed; (c) this paroxysm then subsides back into twilight (3:40-42), after which the night of anguish returns (3:43-66). To support this interpretation Nägelsbach argues that the poetic intensity of chapters 1 and 2 builds to a high point in chapter 3, but that chapters 4 and 5 are not artistically comparable to the poetry in chapters 1 and 2. The three-line acrostic in chapters 1 and 2 intensifies in chapter 3 where every line has to be chosen with care, but chapter 4 abandons this style for a 2-line acrostic, and chapter 5 abandons the acrostic altogether.

Without even pausing to salute the literary ingenuity of this hypothesis, Wiesmann curtly dismisses it because if Lamentations truly intends to articulate a theology of hope, then why lead readers into the "light of day" only to lead them back into "the darkness?"²⁷ To Wiesmann this makes

---

22. Wiesmann ("Planmässige," 155); Rudolph (*Klagelieder*, 194).
23. Ewald, *Dichter*, 323.
24. Keil, *Klagelieder*, 546.
25. Wiesmann, "Planmässige," 155-56.
26. Nägelsbach, *Klagelieder*, vii-ix.
27. Wiesmann, "Planmässige," 156-57.

no sense—in fact, one might even characterize it as a cruel joke. Further, though the imagery shifts from "night" to "day" in a literary sense, does this imply that suffering is somehow proof that God still cares? Does it mean that the more one suffers under God's discipline, the more one can expect to experience his chastening concern? Against Nägelsbach, Wiesmann rather argues that the point of chapter 3 is to state unequivocally that the one who stands in the midst of suffering should not give up hope on the reality of divine love, *especially* when it seems so well hidden.[28] In fact, Wiesmann argues (*contra* Karl Budde),[29] the misery of the people appears in an individual lament in chapter 3 not merely to intensify things, but to give suffering people a tangible model of dignified behavior in the midst of horrid realities like war, slavery, famine, and cannibalism.[30]

So, what kind of unity *does* Wiesmann see in Lamentations? One of the first to reject the placement of an artificially-constructed *external* schema over these lament-poems, Wiesmann insists that the book's *internal* characteristics reflect a coherent unity designed to articulate an identifiable theological intentionality:

> Our five songs do picture a unity, and indeed, not merely from external considerations (because they are unified in a collection like some of the Psalms), but also on inner grounds. Therefore (a) they are first of all composed around a similar situation: all set forth the destruction of Jerusalem and the misfortune which thereby comes over the people. Further, (b) they collectively draw these mournful events into the realm of their concern and place them opposite similar situations: there resounds within all of them a lament over the terrible fall of the kingdom (as well as) the voices of profoundest pity for its unfortunate inhabitants. (c) The same basic views are then drawn through all the fragments: concerning the reasons for this fate, the results of the affliction, the instruments of punishment, etc. (d) All follow, further, the

---

28. McCarter ("Temper," 87–88) argues that because so many Canaanite myths go out of their way to equate divine anger with divine "sickness," Yahweh's anger might be interpreted as "a hypostatic or quasi-independent entity" which, in spite of his "beneficent regard for people, can be provoked into destructive activity by certain forbidden human activities, especially . . . cultic violations." Bordt ("Zorn," 152) similarly argues that that while *mercy* can be a "character-trait," *wrath* cannot (because it is simply an "emotion"). This distinction is important because even though Plato can on occasion refer to the "wrath of the gods" (*Leg.* 880e8–881a1; *Phdr.* 244d6), this in no way implies that he considers wrath to be a divine "character trait." Bordt rather believes that both attributes are simply primitive analogues for what "can more clearly and better be expressed through philosophical or perhaps even *naturwissenschaftlicher* terminology."

29. Budde, "Klagelied," 1–2.

30. Wiesmann, "Planmässige," 157.

same goal: the consolation of the people and their return to the Lord.[31]

The advantages of Wiesmann's approach are several. *First*, it rests on the text itself, not a superimposed literary schema (Nägelsbach), a hypothetical explanation for the book's ideological framework (Gottwald, Albrektson), a cultic hypothesis anchored in the unprovable presumption that these laments (particularly the mixture of individual and communal laments in chapter 3) are originally composed to be sung by an individual + a chorus (Kraus),[32] nor a complex theory of compositional stages (several years, same author—Rudolph;[33] chapters, in order of composition, 4, 1, 2, 3 over a 27-day period—Brunet).[34] Whatever else might be said about Wiesmann, it's hard to find fault with him here. Granted, he sometimes gets carried away, as, for example, when he asserts that all five chapters describe Yahweh's righteousness,[35] or when he overreacts to the theses of Budde and Nägelsbach and neglects to point out the genuine lexical and historical points-of-contact between chapter 3 and the rest of the book.[36] Still, his basic desire to let the text interpret itself is refreshing.

Second, this *internal* unity hypothesis may be unpalatable to form-critics interested predominantly in artistic purity (Jahnow),[37] or source-critics interested predominantly in finding evidence for multiple authorship (Löhr),[38] but it has largely proven itself acceptable to many readers because of its flexibility. One can accept it and still remain consistent to positions either for or against Jeremianic authorship, Babylonian or Palestinian *Sitze im Leben*, deuteronomic or Zionistic background, oral or written composition, or any number of still-unresolved *external* issues. This needs to be underscored, especially to anyone truly interested in uncovering its theology (see Lam 3:44!). The alternative is to suggest that neither the poet (assuming individual authorship) nor the poets/redactor(s) are at all interested in

---

31. Wiesmann, "Planmässige," 155–56. Ironically, Rudolph fundamentally misunderstands what Wiesmann is trying to say when he lumps him into the same category as Ewald, Keil, and Nägelsbach (*Klagelieder*, 196).

32. Kraus, *Klagelieder*, 12–15.

33. Rudolph, *Klagelieder*, 193.

34. Brunet, *Lamentations*, 1–7.

35. Wiesmann, "Planmässige," 150–51. Neither chapter 4 nor 5 explicitly ascribe righteousness to Yahweh.

36. Ibid., 156.

37. Jahnow, *Leichenlied*, 14–18.

38. Löhr, "Threni," 1–16.

conveying an intelligible message at a time when Judah most needs to hear a word from God.

Third, this emphasis on *internal* unity effectually opens the way for further investigation into the several themes articulated throughout the book as well as the ways in which these themes resonate and interface. Moreover, it also helps open up clearer avenues for exposition, interpretation and contemporary application.[39] Application of a process hermeneutic, for example, to the themes of human suffering or divine consolation might yield fruitful results, if responsibly administered.[40] The same might be said for structuralist analysis.[41] The following discussion, in fact, will attempt to interpret the theme of human suffering in Lamentations from a quasi-structuralist approach restricted by the following guidelines:

(1) The intention here is to set aside, for a moment, the book's historical problems and focus solely on matters of literary structure. The risk inherent in this approach, of course, is that the meaning of the text can easily be distorted. This risk will be monitored carefully. I have no wish to follow in the footsteps of Nägelsbach or de Wette. Further, the objection might be raised that this type of approach applies only to material self-consciously written as literature. In Lamentations' case the presence of the acrostic literary form ought to quell any objections from this quarter.[42]

(2) The intention here is to focus on deep structures lying underneath the surface of the text rather than surface structures like words, lines, and stanzas.[43] This should prove particularly fruitful for a document like Lamentations, since the poetry here is filled with such deep human emotion and longing. One initially needs to deal with words and lines, of course, but the *intention* here, so long as it can be justified, is to try and dig deeper into

---

39. See esp. Parry, *Lamentations*, 159–82. I fail to grasp (a) why Wiesmann chooses to emphasize only the themes of *lament* and *punishment* in his concluding remarks, and (b) why he returns to a quasi-external structure in his conceptualization of the interplay between these two themes, esp. since he carefully avoids, even criticizes this approach in the preceding pages ("Planmässige," 160–61).

40. "Postmodernism cautions us that all theology is concrete, situational, and time-bound . . . . Process theologians affirm that people can still tell a universal story but, along with postmodernism, they also recognize that this story is grounded in experience and perspective, and must be open-ended and liberating if it is to be of value to twenty-first century persons" (Epperly, *Process*, 1–2). Coats attempts to apply this approach to the Balaam cycle in Num 22–24 ("Balaam," 53–79).

41. See Barthes ("Introduction," 79–124), Richter (*Exegese*, 72–125), Fokkelman (*Narrative*, 20–45).

42. Even Watters, in a study primarily focused on the characteristics of oral poetry, recognizes that Lamentations is "written poetry from the beginning" (*Formula*, 133).

43. See Zholkovsy & Shchlegov, "Poetics," 175–92.

the mind and heart of the poet(s) responsible for composing this series of laments over Zion. I am consciously attempting to construct a theological statement about the book in the tradition of Wiesmann. The major difference is that I am making use of contemporary hermeneutical tools Wiesmann either cannot or chooses not to employ. Moreover, since it is highly doubtful that the Hebrew poet(s) is trying to construct a theology in the modern sense, it seems to me that eventually one *has* to adopt some sort of internal approach to get at the full meaning of these texts. I have no illusions that this approach will enable us to "map the mind" of the author(s) of Lamentations, the sour impression often left by practitioners of this approach.[44] The goal here is rather to focus attention upon one (and only one) of the book's major themes, not offer an exhaustive Theology of Lamentations.

METAPHORS AND EPITHETS

Delbert Hillers, in the Introduction to his Anchor Bible commentary, notes the unusually large number of metaphorical epithets scattered throughout these poems. The phrase בת-*x* or בתלת-בת-*x* appears no less than 20 times, whereas in Tanak as a whole it occurs only 45 times.[45] Hillers suggests two reasons for this prevalence: (a) a need for flexible literary units able to expand and contract according to metrical need; and (b) a desire to "help make explicit the personification of the people or city as a woman."[46] This second explanation raises pointed questions: Why does the poet(s) seek to personify the misery of Judah like this? What does this imply about his theological worldview?

Concordial analysis of these poems reveals an astonishingly complete spectrum of epithets referencing nearly every age, sex, and class of humanity. Babes, sucklings, children, boys, young men, young women, mothers, fathers and old men suffer varying degrees of trauma. Slaves, priests, prophets, widows, orphans, princes, and kings suffer, too. In fact, because so many social groupings are included, the following analysis is restricted to the societal continuum governed mainly by gender and age.

---

44. See the classic critique of Smith ("Territory," 289–309); also Jeanrond, "Interpretation," 442.
45. The majority of the other occurrences are in Jeremiah.
46. Hillers, *Lamentations*, xxxviii.

Metaphorical Usage

Metaphorical Epithets

- בת ציון (1:6; 2:1, 4, 8, 10, 13, 18; 4:22; cf. בתולת בת ציון in 2:13; בני ציון in 4:2);
- בת יהודה (1:14; 2:2, 5; cf. בתולת בת יהודה in 1:15);
- בת ירושלם (2:13, 15);
- בת עמי (2:11; 3:48; 4:3, 6, 10; cf. בנות עמי behind OG 4:3);
- בת אדום (4:21);
- בנות עירי (3:51)

Single Metaphors

מחמדיהם ("their precious ones," 1:11; cf. מחמדי עין, "those precious to the eye," 2:4)[47]

Historical Usage

Infant Children

- Fainting from hunger (2:11–12, 19; 4:3–5);
- Sold by parents for food (1:11);
- Murdered/seized by the enemy (1:5; 2:22);
- Eaten by starving parents (2:20; 4:10)

Adolescent Boys

- נער וזקן lie in the streets, felled by the sword (2:21);
- נערים stumble with wood (5:13);
- it is good for a גבר to bear the yoke בנעוריו ("in his youth," 3:27)

---

47. N.B. the PN "Muhammad" (محمد, lit., "the one who is precious") comes from the Arab cognate of this semitic root.

Young Men and Women

- בתולותיה נוגות, "her virgins suffer" (1:4);
- the Lord rejects כל אבירי ("all my warriors," 1:15);
- the Lord decrees a time to crush בחורי ("my young men," 1:15);
- בתולתי and בחורי go into captivity (1:18);
- בתולת ירשלם bow their heads to the ground (2:10);
- בתולתי and בחורי fall by the sword (2:15);
- בתלת and נשים are "afflicted"[48] by נכרים ("foreigners," 5:10, 2);
- בחורים must carry their own grinding stones (5:13);
- בחורים have stopped making music (5:14)

Parents

- לאמתם the children cry, "Where is bread and wine?" (2:12);
- the children's lives expire on the laps of אמתם ("their mother," 2:12);
- אמתינו כאלמנות, "our mothers are like widows" (5:3);
- the hands of נשים רחמניות cook their own children ("compassionate women," 4:10);
- we are orphans אין אב, ("without a father," 5:3);
- אבותנו חטאו, "our fathers have sinned" (5:7)

Old Men

- זקני perish in the city (1:19);
- זקני בת ציון sit silently on the ground (2:10);
- נער וזקן lie on the ground in the streets (2:21);
- זקנים receive no "favor" (חנן, 4:16);
- זקנים receive no "honor" (הדר, 5:12);
- זקנים stop sitting in the city gate (5:14)

---

48. On the polysemantic possibilities of ענה, see Moore, "Anomalies," 235–38.

Historical and/or Metaphorical Usage

עלל

- עלליה led away captive ("her children," 1:5);
- עולל and יונק faint on the city streets (2:11);
- lift your hands for the נפש עולליך (2:19);
- should women eat the פרים עללי טפחים ("fruit of the children they have borne," 2:20);
- עוללים beg for food (4:4)

בן -בני are desolate ("my sons," 1:16)

טפח—my enemy has destroyed the ones טפחתי ורביתי ("I cherished and nurtured," 2:22)

יתום—we have become יתומים ("orphans," 5:3)

אלמנה—our mothers are like אלמנות ("widows," 5:3; see also 1:1)

DEEP STRUCTURE

Looking at this mass of data, some striking structural angles become visible as soon as we try to understand *how* everything goes together. Gottwald is doubtless correct to argue that the poet(s) is much more interested in conveying an intelligible message than he is in achieving artistic purity. In particular, his response to Jahnow's assertion (i.e., that the free mixture of types and images in the first four poems arises from the lack of "the powerful originality of a unitary artistic conception")[49] lands right on target: (a) were the poet to focus only upon the figure of "mother Zion," the collection would lack concreteness; plus (b) were he to focus only upon the actual scenes of the dead, the collection would lack communal appeal. For Gottwald, this poet(s) refuses to "sacrifice a realistic lament in order to achieve artistry."[50]

Debates over literary types, however, offer little help to the expositor interested in probing deeper. Agreement with the contention that theological intentionality overrides artistic design does not necessarily mean that the book is somehow astructural. The question is, What *type* of structure? Surface structure or deep structure? Debate over acrostic and lament forms focuses on surface structure. A closer reading of these poems, however,

---

49. Jahnow, *Leichenlied*, 172.
50. Gottwald, *Lamentations*, 36.

reveals an interesting pattern—a pattern repeatedly referring the reader to the pain of human suffering.

Chapter 1

Four times in this chapter there is a sudden shift in perspective. In three of these occurrences[51] the poet turns to prayer (1:11), lament (1:16),[52] and admonition (1:18) in particularly noteworthy contexts. In 1:11 he employs a metaphorical term for "their precious ones" (מחמדיהם) reprising the word מחמדיה ("her precious things") in the previous verse; i.e., it is one thing for the enemy to invade the sanctuary compound and steal what is "precious" (1:10), but the thought of "precious ones" having to be sold for food wrenches out of him the exclamation, "Look, Yahweh, and behold!" Similarly, in 1:16 the perspectival shift comes not after a complaint about the enemy's activities (1:14), but after he truly realizes the depth of the human tragedy.[53] The 1st person admonition in 1:19 elaborates the description of מכאבי ("my pain") in v. 18 with mourning over the captivity of בתולתי ובחורי as the worst imaginable pain, followed by yet another prayer asking Yahweh to attend to the poet in his distress.[54]

Chapter 2

The first ten verses of chapter 2 read like a 3rd person laundry-list of metaphorical images all attempting to describe the depth and breadth of Yahweh's destructive power. Significantly, however, it is not until the images of the זקני ציון בת and the בתולת ירשלם flash across the poet's mind in 2:10 that a perspectival shift occurs. In 2:11 the poet elaborates the reasons for this lament by specifying what it is that so moves him to tears—the sight of עלל and יונק starving to death in their mothers' arms.[55] Here he sets the metaphorical epithet (בת עמי) in parallel with the historical term(s) (עלל ויונק) in a type of

---

51. The shift in 1:9c seems premature because (a) only 3 f s suffixes occur elsewhere in the verse; (b) the 3 f s suffix returns in vv 10–11b; and (c) Bohairic and Ambrose read עניה for MT עניי in 1:9c.

52. Granted, the shift here is not from 3rd to 1st person, but analysis of the usage of אני indicates that this verse contains one of only four occurrences in Lamentations (and here // ממני; see 1:21; 3:1, 63).

53. N.B. בחורי and בתולת בת יהודה in 1:15; בני in 1:16.

54. Lam 1:20–22.

55. See Moore, "Siege," 148–49.

literary parallel which occurs often in this collection.[56] This heartbreaking sight then leads him to a short sequence of rhetorical questions underlining his sense of helpless agony (2:13). The intervening 2nd person material then coughs out seven imperative verbs: שפכי, רני, קומי, אל תתני, הורידי, צעקי,[57] and שאי.[58] As the last of these ever louder hammer-blows strikes the page, his thoughts stubbornly return to the "life of your children."[59] This drags out of him another concluding prayer in which he begs Yahweh not to look away from what *he* sees: starving mothers eating their own children, young men and women dying violently by the sword, enemy soldiers annihilating "those whom I cherished and nurtured."

Chapter 3

Saturated as this chapter is with the 1st person format of the individual lament,[60] no dramatic perspectival shifts occur. Overt personalization of the poet's agony, more communally expressed in the other four poems, inhibits his concern for the suffering of the various social groupings in and around Jerusalem. The focus here is personal, not societal. Accordingly no terms appear for suffering humanity, with the brief exception of two epithets in 3:48 and 3:51.[61] The 1st person plural contexts within which these epithets occur switch smoothly to the 1st person singular after the mention of בת עמי and the parallel בנות עירי, after which several frenzied statements lead up to the vocative prayer-plea in v. 55.

Chapter 4

In chapter 4 the first ten verses orbit around three comparisons, each anchored by the epithet בת עמי. Verse 3 depicts jackals as creatures always

---

56 See בת יהודי // בחורי ... אבירי // בתולת בת יהודה // שריה (1:6); בת ציון // (1:15); יענים (4:3); בת עמי // (3:48, 51); בנות עירי // העיר // בת ירשלם (2:15); בת עמי // ישראל (2:5); סדם // בת עמי (4:6).

57. Reading with Ewald, *Dichter*, 335.

58. See Lam 2:18–19.

59. נפש עלליך, Lam 2:19.

60. Previous debate centers on the "problem" of genre; i.e., individual vs. communal lament (see summary in Löhr, "Threni," 2–14). Gottwald (*Lamentations*, 41) doubts whether the poet(s), steeped in the milieu of "corporate personality," ever truly wrestles with genre as a "problem," and cautions readers not to become bound by "ironclad rules" orchestrated by "sheer arbitrariness."

61. בת עמי, 3:48; בנות עירי, 3:51.

able to remember, even under stress, to feed their young ... but בת עמי has forgotten to do so. The second comparison follows up on this ominous beginning with a pathetic description of starving children (who once had so much to eat, such nice clothes to wear), comparing the present holocaust to the well-known judgment inflicted upon Sodom ... except that the present holocaust is much, much worse (v. 6). Verse 10 stands as one of the most poignant passages of the entire book. Compassionate women, no longer able to stand the sight of their little ones in agony, and realizing that even death by the sword is preferable to the slow, lingering pain of starvation,[62] mercifully kill and cook their children for food.[63] Each comparison slides deeper into the poet's horror-numbed mind as the memories of these atrocities rush over him afresh. The second half of the chapter rehearses yet another laundry-list of the afflicted, keying off the word-pairs כוהן/נביא[64] and זקן/כוהן.[65] The term זקן, however, has a deeper meaning in Lamentations. Of its six occurrences, four appear in rather standard word-pairs.[66] Twice, however, the word broadly refers to the aged men of the city, not just the sociopolitical leadership. At any rate, the shift from 3rd to 1st person occurs right here in v. 17 after the word זקנים. It's difficult to comment on the intentionality of this shift, particularly when the term's other nuance may also be floating through the poet's mind.

Chapter 5

This final chapter, relegated by so many to a later date and different place,[67] admirably recapitulates the "suffering humanity" theme resonating throughout the previous chapters. This 1st person communal lament, a prayer from start to finish, comes stocked with references to a large segment of the human groupings heretofore buried beneath the surface:

- orphans (5:3);

---

62. According to Josephus, the zealot Eleazar convinces his compatriots to kill themselves rather than let the Romans capture and torture them at Masada (*Wars* 7.323–36).

63. J. J. M. Roberts (private correspondence) thinks that "the point is not that they *mercifully* kill, but that hunger drives these women to lose their compassionate character and eat their own children to still their own tormenting hunger."

64. Lam 4:13; see 2:20; Isa 28:7; Jer 2:8, 26; 4:9; 5:31.

65. Lam 4:16; see 1:19; Jer 19:1; 29:1; Ezek 7:26.

66. Watters, *Formula*, 212–13.

67. See discussions in Hillers (Lamentations, ii-xxiii), Eissfeldt (*Introduction*, 500–505), and Childs (*Introduction*, 590–97).

- mothers (5:3);
- fathers (5:7);
- women (5:11);
- virgins (5:11);
- princes (5:12);
- elders (5:12);
- young men (5:13);
- young boys (5:13);
- old men (5:14);
- young men (5:14).

Some occur in standard word-pairs, but not all. Some appear with differing connotations. Some appear for the first time in the book. The semantic weight here, however, seems to lay more upon what these people used to *do* than upon who they *are* or even how much they have suffered. So many distinctly *human* activities have been silenced. So many distinctly *human* institutions have been battered and bludgeoned. So many distinctly *human* freedoms have been violently taken away. The aftermath of human carnage is calmly sketched out in chiaroscuro shades of grey and brown. Life now limps along without direction or zest. The sparkling colors which used to animate this world no longer radiate. Yahweh's wrath has burned them all away.

SUMMARY AND CONCLUSION

Patrick Miller's insight into Hebrew lament holds particular relevance here at the conclusion of this essay.

> The interpretive task is not tied to the search for a single explanation for a particular lament, but can center in opening up through different stories and moments examples of the human plight that may be articulated through the richly figurative but stereotypical language of the laments.[68]

Miller is responding to (a) rather slavish attempts to identify precisely who the "enemies" in a particular lament might be,[69] and (b) the debate over the exact historical sequencing of Jeremiah's laments and the psalms of lament

---

68. Miller, "Trouble," 45.
69. See the seminal structural analysis of Westermann ("Struktur," 44–80).

by (c) relocating given laments more closely to their historical contexts. But the implications of his observation go much deeper. I heartily agree with him that there needs to be more flexibility in contemporary analyses of lament-forms. In fact, the brief review of research on Lamentations here only confirms his concern, particularly when so many interpreters presume (a) a single "key" to the theology of this collection, and (b) that this "key" magically "unlocks" a singular theological message as if the author *intended* for it to be found.

Hermann Wiesmann is one of the first modern interpreters to reject this "solution." That is why he focuses on internal rather than external structural concerns. Not surprisingly, his approach does not endear him to critics, even though so many of his original insights are now recognized, elaborated, and synthesized in their own theologies of Lamentations. Because so much uncertainty still exists with regard to external structure, this continues to make Wiesmann's approach attractive—even though it, too, should be engaged critically. His insistence that God's compassion *and* judgment stand in tension within all five poems points the way toward a balanced theological blueprint able to guide further investigation. "Atomizing" approaches are of no more value than "single key" approaches, and Wiesmann manages to avoid both extremes in his earlier work. A critically adapted, carefully constructed restructuring of his approach now makes it possible to fashion a relevant, balanced theology on any one of Lamentations' long-neglected "secondary" themes, as long as readers steadfastly guard against the temptation to make such analyses new "keys" to the Theology of Lamentations.

With the aid of some newer hermeneutical tools the deeper structures of the book might now be made a bit more accessible to the expositor's eye. The brief analysis offered here attempts to show that a preeminent concern of the poet(s) is to portray the horrifying scope of human suffering witnessed with his own eyes (could a redactor really have captured this?). Subtle shifts of perspective as well as macabre word-plays[70] most often appear in immediate contexts of human suffering as the poet(s) pours out the condensed pain stored up in the depths of his heart. Though his thoughts often turn to God, his feelings just as often turn to his beloved עמי. Like a survivor from a concentration camp, he has suppressed some grisly, nauseating memories. Wisely, he decides not to repress these memories, but give them artistic expression. Lamentations, the result of this "grief-work," itself becomes a focal point for the grief work of a nation, and indeed, of an entire

---

70. נידה appears in 1:8 because it can mean either "unclean" *or* "object of scorn"; זוללה can mean either "despised" *or* "gluttonous." In 1:10–11 מחמד can refer to precious *things* or precious *children*. Perhaps the most menacing example is the root עלל, esp. the macabre way it flits between nominal and verbal forms (see 1:12, 22; 2:20; 3:51).

religion. Its psychological insights profoundly stimulate survivors to grieve the loss of loved ones. Its theological underpinnings, however, insure that this grieving process remains therapeutic. Properly read, Lamentations continues to provide the essential, fundamental element every survivor needs to go on—hope.

16

BATHSHEBA'S SILENCE*

BATHSHEBA PLAYS A PIVOTAL role in Israel's first successful dynasty, but the contours of her character remain blurry and indefinite.[1] Certainly one of the roles she enacts in the Bible is that of *mediator*,[2] but the Hebrew text's reticence to provide details about it thoroughly frustrates interpreters.[3] With Nicol we might examine all the chapters in the Bathsheba tradition and wonder about the source(s) of this ambiguity.[4] Yet we might also marvel at the "deep aesthetic qualities" lying behind this ambiguity and wonder whether contemporary scholarship fully grasps its possibilities.[5] Because

---

* Revised from a paper read to the Hebrew and Cognate Literature section at the 2003 SBL meeting in Atlanta, Georgia, subsequently published in *Inspired Speech: Prophecy in the Ancient Near East: Essays Presented to Herbert B. Huffmon*, edited by J. Kaltner & L. Stulman, 336–46 (New York: Continuum, 2004).

1. For a sampling of interpretations from widely different perspectives, see Levenson & Halpern ("David," 507–18); Augustin ("Frau," 145–54); Bal (*Lethal*, 23); Yee ("Ambiguity," 240–53); Nicol ("Bathsheba," 360–63); Exum (*Fragmented*, 171–76); Ogden Bellis (*Helpmates*, 130–33); Berlin (*Poetics*, 25–30); Moore ("Trajectory," 87–103); and Stone (*History*, 95–100).

2. Margalit (*Aqhat*, 476–85) notes that female characters often enact roles as initiators in Syro-Palestinian stories.

3. Ambiguity is characteristic of biblical narrative. Only rarely will a biblical narrator explicitly expose a character's inner thinking—what Hopper calls "inscaping" ("Sonnets," 63).

4. Nicol, "Bathsheba," 360–63.

5. Gunkel, *Legends*, 2. There is no need to assume that attention to literary themes and characters automatically precludes, dismisses, or even speaks to historical issues and concerns.

the episode where she exits is the final episode of the "throne succession narrative" (2 Sam 11—1 Kings 2),[6] Bathsheba appears at a critical moment in Hebrew history, not to mention a critical moment in the history of Hebrew *literature*. For this reason alone we can ill afford to ignore this text, regardless of whether we read it as a unified composition[7] or as a lately edited amalgamation.[8] Historical, literary, and even ideological approaches tell us much about Bathsheba, but we still know little about the socioliterary context framing her mediatorial activity.

In an effort to surface more possibilities, the following essay reads the story of Bathsheba alongside another, similar story from its Syro-Palestinian context, the Canaanite legend of Aqhat.[9] The primary goal is to tease out of this intertextual comparison some of the most obvious (dis)similarities in order to explain Bathsheba's character more fully. By so doing we hope to demonstrate the enduring value of comparative intertextual analysis in which historical and literary methods work together, not against, each other.[10]

Whether or not we read, with Rost, the throne succession narrative as a unified composition,[11] it still tells us little about Bathsheba. We can, by suturing two passages together, conclude that she is (a) the daughter of a man named Eliam,[12] and (b) that a man named Eliam is the son of Ahithophel, one of David's most influential counselors.[13] But whether these Eliams are one and the same person is impossible to say, and the fact that her name later changes to "Bathshua" only complicates the matter.[14] Bathsheba re-

---

6. See Ishida (*History*, 102–74); Seiler (*Thronfolge*, 3–26).

7. Rost, *Succession*, 115.

8. Wurthwein, *Thronfolge*, 46–58. Seiler (*Thronfolge*, 3–26) succinctly summarizes the debate since Rost.

9. CAT 1.17–19.

10. Over thirty years ago my *Doktorvater* pointed out (Huffmon, "Israel," 66–77) that the decision to read Tanak through parochial instead of holistic lenses leads in many cases to some rather horrifying sociological, theological, and political consequences. Nazis and Zionists, however, are not the only ideologically-driven groups desperate to make the Bible say what they want. Many newer groups are busily engaged in the same practice, succumbing to what Herb calls "the temptation of being the Old Israel" (p. 72).

11. Rost, *Succession*, 115. Seiler (*Thronfolge*, 326) prefers Rost's analysis to Würthwein's.

12. 2 Sam 11:3.

13. 2 Sam 23:34.

14. בת־שׁוּעַ ("Bathshua"—"daughter of error," 1 Chron 3:5) is defamatory for בת־שׁבע ("Bathsheba"—"daughter number 7") in the same way בית־אוֶן ("house of nothing") is defamatory for בית־אל ("house of God," Hos 4:15; 5:8; 10:5).

mains swathed behind a veil of mystery, and because of this some readers are tempted to "fill in the gaps" and colorize her character.[15] Alice Ogden Bellis, for example, portrays her as "an innocent victim of lust," even though the text itself is conspicuously silent.[16] Levenson and Halpern imagine her not as a victim, but as a politician shrewd enough to entrap David sexually and replace him with the fruit of this entrapment, Solomon.[17] Ben Naḥmani argues that technically, David never commits adultery at all because (he suggests) every soldier in David's army is required to write a "bill of divorce" before going into battle. Torah says nothing about this "law," however, so Naḥmani's attempt to beatify David quickly joins the ranks of other failed attempts.[18]

Roger Whybray condescendingly labels Bathsheba "a good-natured, rather stupid woman who was a natural prey to more passionate and cleverer men,"[19] but this observation does little more than enrage feminists. Elizabeth Wurtzel, for example, insists that Bathsheba is a prime example of "those sexually compelling Bible women" (like Jael and Delilah) who represent the kind of sexual independence which frightens men.[20] Esther Fuchs paints with darker colors. Explaining Bathsheba's silence after David's "rape," she argues that such is to be expected from a book (the Bible) which customarily portrays *all* women—as a "class"—as slaves.[21] Cheryl Exum pushes this line of thinking a step further, accusing the Tanak narrator of deliberately "withholding (Bathsheba's) point of view" because he likes "disrobing her" as much as David does. Calling this behavior a "crime," Exum then labels as "criminal" the interpretations of all contemporary (predominantly male) commentators who "perpetuate" this opinion.[22]

Adele Berlin's reading, however, relies less on political ideology than literary insight. With Levenson and Halpern she too sees a shrewdness in

---

15. "Gap-filling" is not in itself inappropriate until or unless it becomes a subjective counterfeit for holistic interpretation (see Sternberg, *Poetics*, 186–229).

16. Ogden Bellis, however, distinguishes the "flat" character in Samuel from the "developed" character in Kings (*Helpmates*, 149).

17. Levenson & Halpern, "David," 507–18.

18. Brueggemann (*David*, 8–13) documents some of these attempts to "rescue" David's reputation, and van Seters ("David," 244) observes that "some (rabbis) attempt to exonerate (David), but those who find him guilty of wrongdoing see a divine purpose in the events; namely that David is to be an example of contrition and repentance to give hope and encouragement to Israel when it sins."

19. Whybray, *Succession*, 40.

20. Wurtzel, *Women*, 43.

21. Fuchs, *Politics*, 14–16.

22. Exum, *Women*, 173–74.

the older Bathsheba, whereas the younger woman in Samuel operates only as a "flat" character (Berlin calls her an "agent").[23] In Samuel her function is simply (a) to be a married woman and (b) to have adulterous sex with David. Later, when Abishag enters the picture, Bathsheba's character becomes more complex, a development Berlin traces to the literary irony triggered by the second mention of Abishag.[24] In short, "Bathsheba, who was once young and attractive like Abishag, is herself now aging, and has been, in a sense, replaced with Abishag, just as she comes for the purpose of replacing David with Solomon."[25] Later, when Adonijah asks for Abishag's hand (doubtless as his own "agent" for winning back the throne), Berlin notes the ambiguity in Bathsheba's response, but refrains from offering an explanation. *Questions:* Is Bathsheba feigning naïveté before Adonijah's request? Or does she still fear this Davidic prince and the potential harm he might do to her son? Or does she plan, like Medea,[26] to *use* Adonijah to wreak revenge against a philandering husband?[27]

Unfortunately few interpreters examine Bathsheba's behavior against that of other ANE female mediators, even though this approach has great potential. Jack Sasson recognizes the potential of comparative literary analysis in his classic study of Ruth, recognizing that in its place many fall prey to "a pervasive tendency to rely too much on a *deus ex machina* . . . to unravel the plot of the tale."[28] Neal Walls also recognizes the potential of the comparative approach, employing it effectively to identify the character of the Canaanite deity Anat against several other "virgin goddesses,"[29] thereby leading him to a deeper understanding of "the enigmatic quality of her (Anat's) symbolic identity" within "the complexities of ancient myths and mythic characters."[30] Both approaches have merit, though Walls' study

---

23. Berlin, *Poetics*, 28.

24. 1 Kings 1:15.

25. Berlin, *Poetics*, 28.

26. Like Bathsheba, Medea makes sure that her protector (Aegeus, king of Athens) takes an oath: "Dear woman . . . if you come to my country, I shall in justice try to act as your protector . . . . (this) I swear by Earth, by the holy light of Helios, and by all the gods" (Euripides, *Medea* 719–53). Unlike Medea, however, Bathsheba does not sacrifice her child in a fit of rage on the pretense that "this will sting my husband the most" (817).

27. Commentators are divided. Berlin (*Poetics*, 29) sees Bathsheba as "cunning" and "jealous," but Gunn (*David*, 137) sharply disagrees. Fokkelman (*Narrative*, 394) characteristically looks for a mediating position.

28. Sasson, *Ruth*, viii.

29. Walls, *Anat*, 23–28.

30. Ibid., 2.

is hailed by reviewers as "original," full of "common sense,"[31] and a "model" for research.[32]

On the fourth column of the third tablet of Aqhat a heroic character named Daniel (Nathan) "empowers"[33] a female character named Pağit (Bathsheba) to use deception[34] in her response to a terrible injustice, one with which her father El (David) passively refuses to get involved.[35] Avenging this injustice, she hires an assassin named Yatpan (Joab) to attack Daniel's son Aqhat (Solomon)[36] and steal his "bow" (the throne).[37] While it may not seem obvious at first glance, the primary elements of this Canaanite legend resonate deeply with the primary elements of the Bathsheba story. Both traditions use similar characters, manipulate similar plotlines, and highlight strikingly similar themes in order to address the same problem—the problem of genetic dynastic succession. The following chart breaks these parallels down into three subcategories: *characterization, plot,* and *theme*.[38]

SUCCEEDING DAVID (1 KINGS 1-2) // SUCCEEDING DANIEL (*CAT* 1.17-19)

Characterization

- David // El;
- Nathan // Daniel;
- Solomon // Aqhat;
- Bathsheba // Anat/Pağit;
- Abishag/(Adonijah) // Anat/Pağit;

31. Pardee, *Anat,* 505.

32. Parker, *Anat,* 139-40. To list another example, I argue from a reading of the Anat // Jehu traditions that the latter is a prophetic parody of the former ("Jehu," 97-114).

33. Ug *mrr* (*CAT* 1.19.4.33).

34. *CAT* 1.19.4.18-61.

35. *CAT* 1.18.1.1-19. Clifford ("Proverbs," 300) speaks of the "David-like charms of Ba'al in the heavenly court," but the elderly David looks more like El than Ba'al.

36. Is she attacking Aqhat to defend Ba'al in the same way she attacks Mot (*CAT* 1.6.2.30-37)?

37. That Aqhat's bow represents his virility is a logical conclusion as long as we recognize the broader implications of this mytheme (Hillers, "Aqhat," 71-80). Virility is only one of the requirements for effective leadership (Stone, *History,* 102-7).

38. This study proceeds, as does my study of the Jehu tradition ("Jehu," 97-114), on the presumption that most Syro-Palestinians are at least nominally aware of these characters, plots, and themes.

- Benaiah // Yaṭpan

Plot

- David is impotent // Daniel is impotent;
- Solomon is "longed-for" // Aqhat is "longed-for";
- Solomon rides David's mule // Aqhat receives the divine bow;
- Abishag replaces Bathsheba // Anat steals the bow;
- Adonijah steals the throne // Anat steals the bow;
- Nathan employs Bathsheba // Daniel employs Paǧit;
- Bathsheba defers to David // Anat defers to El;
- Bathsheba impugns David's integrity // Aqhat impugns Anat's integrity;
- Bathsheba impugns Adonijah before David // Anat impugns Aqhat before El;
- David impugns Joab before Solomon // Anat impugns El;
- Bathsheba "deceives" Adonijah // Anat "deceives" Aqhat;
- Solomon's reign becomes plagued // Aqhat's bow becomes "lost";
- Solomon warns Adonijah // Anat warns Aqhat;
- Solomon gives Adonijah options // Aqhat gives Anat options;
- Bathsheba resists threat to Solomon // Paǧit resists threat to Aqhat;
- Solomon lives // Aqhat lives;
- David curses his enemies // Daniel curses cities near Aqhat's grave.

Themes

- dynastic ambition is universal // dynastic ambition is universal;
- old age and death are inevitable // old age and death are inevitable;
- throne/power/virility is temporal // "bow"/power/virility is temporal;
- female mediation is complex // female mediation is complex;
- female mediation is necessary // female mediation is necessary.

CHARACTERIZATION

Like the Aqhat legend, the throne succession narrative in Samuel-Kings works with a stock cast of characters, what Vladimir Propp calls the *dramatis personae*.[39] Leadership vacuums, whether in the divine (El) or human realms (David), cannot exist indefinitely. The world has to go on and the people in this world have to be competently shepherded. Malevolent forces are always anxious to fill up these vacuums. Ambitious usurpers always stand waiting in the wings to seize power and take control. Thus impotent leaders, for all their experience and wisdom, eventually become a problem, and how this problem is resolved becomes the stuff of succession narrative.

Like Naomi in the book of Ruth, the characters of Daniel in Aqhat and Nathan in Kings serve as "dispatchers,"[40] individuals whose function is to react to the perennial crisis of impotence/aging/death. They *must* arise because the potential successor—the character Propp calls the "sought-for person" (Aqhat in Aqhat; Solomon in Kings; Obed in Ruth)—stands in dire need of help. Not having any power of his own, he stands in a very liminal, precarious situation. When leadership vacuums lead to leadership conflicts (Adonijah vs. Solomon; Abishag vs. Bathsheba; Anat vs. Aqhat), wise heroes must therefore fill these vacuums, especially when the crisis is driven by "villainy" (Anat; Adonijah; Joab). Often these roles become fluidly interchangeable as the characters in the *dramatis personae* interact with each other and narrators become creative, sometimes splitting roles in half or using several characters in the same role.[41] To varying extents these ancient tales always work with a stock cast of characters, and it is in the defining of the phrase "varying extent" that effective characterization replaces ineffective characterization, genius replaces mediocrity, and pan-cultural celebration replaces localized memory.[42]

PLOT

Plots are interesting only when they make effective use of surprise and suspense and lead to authentically satisfying conclusions. Without these elements a plotline becomes lifeless and slow, and therefore easily forgotten.

---

39. Propp, *Folktale*, 21–23.

40. Sasson, *Ruth*, 201.

41. de Moor ("Studies," 170–71) and Taylor ("Deborah," 99–108) note this phenomenon in the "twin" Canaanite goddesses Anat and Athirat, and Taylor points to similarities in the portrayals of Deborah and Jael in the Hebrew book of Judges.

42. See Card, *Characters*, 19–31.

With a good story, though, plotting the points of the action is like connecting the dots on a map.[43] Sometimes the shortest distance is not necessarily the best one. Sometimes it's more important to take the long way around to build suspense, or introduce a subplot, or test a character's mettle. In Aqhat, for example, El is not *genuinely* impotent,[44] but Daniel is, and so is David (and Kirta and Abraham).[45] David's impending death, like Elimelech's in Ruth, is the engine driving the plot forward, the catalyst for creating the narrative itself. The crisis of Daniel's impotence is what drives everything in Aqhat, however twisted or violent or strange or bizarre things eventually become. Everything in these plotlines begins with an initial crisis, the "childless patriarch" being one of the most common in androcentric cultures.[46] One cannot imagine David's sons fighting for the throne under the watchful eye of an engaged David; neither can one imagine Anat taking advantage of Aqhat apart from El's *laissez faire* aloofness.[47]

Watching the potential successors square off (Amnon vs. Absalom, Adonijah vs. Solomon, Anat vs. Aqhat), the "succession dilemma" comes clearly into focus. The very existence of succession narratives reminds us that dynastic succession is painfully difficult. It's easy for postmodern Westerners to overlook this, but ANE stories like these, so universal, so ubiquitous, testify (a) to the difficulty of the problem as well as (b) the persistence of the ancients in dealing with it. Zadok anoints Solomon only after the shedding of much royal blood.[48] Aqhat arrives as El's gift to Daniel only after much fervent prayer and priestly ritual.[49] Pağit goes to reclaim her brother in the same spirit that Isis goes to reclaim her brother Osiris,[50] or Anat goes to reclaim Ba'al.[51] That these conflicts can and must involve both heaven and earth is never doubted because the ancients do not segregate the cosmos into neatly stacked cubicles. Anat's attack against Aqhat is an attack on

---

43. "We might think of plot as the logic or perhaps the syntax of a certain kind of discourse, one that develops its propositions only through temporal sequence and progression . . . . Plot is the principle ordering force of those meanings that we try to wrest from human temporality" (Brooks, *Plot*, xi).

44. Reacting to El's behavior in *CAT* 1.23.33–34, Olyan states the obvious (*Asherah*, 42): "It is certainly clear that El is not impotent."

45. *CAT* 1.14–16; Gen 12–22 (see Moore, "Abraham," 2–3).

46. See Bauckham ("Ruth," 29–45); McAfee ("Patriarch," 246).

47. See Cross, "'El," 13–43.

48. 1 Kings 1:38–40 (see Moore, *Faith*, 59–64).

49. *CAT* 1.17.2.24–46. The literature on Ugaritic ritual is growing; see de Tarragon (*Culte*); Wright (*Ritual*); Merlo & Xella ("Cultic," 287–304); and Pardee (*Ritual*).

50. Griffiths, *Osiris*, 25–28.

51. *CAT* 1.5.6.25.

El because it savagely assaults his protégé Daniel, the mortal whose name means "El is my judge." Anat attacks Aqhat for the same reasons Adonijah attacks Solomon—not just because she wants power, but because conflict is necessary to advance the plot. This attack must sufficiently motivate a response from the *dramatis personae*.

Whether power is symbolized by a "bow" (Ug *qšt*)[52] or a "beautiful girl" (נערה יפה)[53] or a "ring"[54] is inconsequential. What is important is that this power be symbolically portrayed in such a way that would-be usurpers truly "long" for it—like Anat "longs" (Ug *ṣb*) for Aqhat's bow,[55] like Amnon "longs" for Tamar.[56] Whether this symbol is manipulated or stolen by this or that anti-hero is irrelevant. What is important is that the language grabs the soul of the audience and squeezes hard. It has to drive people to their knees in terror before lifting them to their feet in hope. Whether the "longed-for" successor eventually survives or not is peripheral. What is important is that peace be restored to the cosmos, basically in any way possible. Whether this attack is from clearly benevolent or clearly malevolent sources is also peripheral. What is important is that it sufficiently motivate a "dispatcher" to arise and empower a "mediator." Even whether the method used by this "mediator" is "ethical" or not is secondary. What's important is that equilibrium be restored by the mediator's actions. Thus Bathsheba uses deception just as surely as Pağit deceives Yaṭpan, or Jael deceives Sisera, or Tamar deceives Judah.[57]

In fact, it is in the execution of this deception that female mediators really show off their skill-sets.[58] In the apocryphal book of Judith, for example, the narrator takes great pains to show off Judith's ability to deceive Holofernes.[59] In Ruth, Naomi takes great pains to adorn Ruth before sending her off to Boaz to convince him to help save Elimelech's name from

---

52. Hillers' thesis is appropriate as long as the focus remains on Anat's desire for sexual *power* over Aqhat, not just sexual intercourse ("Aqhat," 72–74). Walls seems to miss this point when he limits her motivations only to sexual drive vs. confused sexual identity (*Anat*, 190).

53. 1 Kings 1:3.

54. Tolkien, *Fellowship*, 49.

55 CAT 1.17.6.13.

56 2 Sam 13:2.

57 CAT 1.19.4.41–61; Judg 4:17–22; Gen 38:12–18.

58 See Thompson (*Motif-Index*, s.v. "deceptions") and Williams (*Deception*, 1–2).

59 Jdt 11:1–13:10. Craven (*Artistry*, 121) thinks that "only the book of Ruth offers a parallel" to Judith's behavior, but this does not take into account the Ugaritic evidence.

extinction.⁶⁰ In Aqhat, Paġit takes great pains to deceive the murderer of her brother, Yaṭpan:

- She puts a hero's outfit (underneath) // t[ḥt] tlbš npṣ ġzr ;
- She places the knife in her belt // tšt ḥ[lpn] bnšgh ;
- She places the sword in its scabbard // ḥrb tšt bt ʻr[th] ;
- And over (it) she puts a woman's outfit // w ʻl tlbš npṣ att.⁶¹

So effective is this ruse, the men in Yaṭpan's camp confuse her with "the woman who hired us," an obvious reference to Anat as the androgynous deity who earlier employs them to assassinate Aqhat. What Paġit does after this preparation is unclear because the tablet breaks off, but doubtless she does what all mediators do. She restores equilibrium to an imbalanced situation by any means at her disposal. Deception is not a secondary role in the repertoire of female mediators. Even "old women" priestesses in Anatolia use it on occasion.⁶² The whole point of homeopathic ritual is to create a likeness of something or someone in order to deceive one's attackers into going after the likeness instead of the person imitated by the likeness. That Bathsheba does the same thing by planting the "likeness" of a promise in David's compliant mind can be concluded from two simple facts: (a) there is no textual evidence for such a Davidic promise, and (b) female mediators habitually use deception in such situations. Bathsheba's deception may look muted when compared to, say, the deceptions of Paġit or Judith or Anat or Esther, but this is probably due to the fact that the narrator does not want to portray David as a total "dupe."⁶³

THEMES

From this brief look at characterization and plot we might now list some of the predominant themes scattered throughout these parallel texts. One of the reasons for preserving succession narratives is to assure future generations that succession crises, no matter how difficult, are not the end of the world. If managed appropriately they can eventually be weathered, scars and all. Dynastic ambition is never going to go away because the longing for power is a universal human desire. Jeroboam wants just as desperately to sire a dynasty as does David or Daniel—that's why Ahijah's condemnation is

60. Ruth 3:1–6 (see Moore, "Ruth," 347–53).

61. *CAT* 1.19.4.43–46. On Anat's androgyny see de Moor (*Anthology*, 264) and Walls (*Anat*, 154–59).

62. See sources cited in Moore, *Balaam*, 20–29.

63. *Pace* Marcus, "David," 163–71.

not simply of *him*, but of his entire *house*.⁶⁴ Ba`al, too wants his own "house," just as David wants his own "house."⁶⁵ Leaders everywhere, when confronted by their mortality, become highly motivated to think about the legacy they will leave for the next generation. In succession narratives it is the *realization* of this mortality which so often drives aged leaders into action, however passive or reticent they may be to relinquish power to a successor.

Yet power itself is fleeting and David dies just as certainly as Aqhat's bow becomes lost and Gilgamesh's "special plant" falls into the sea.⁶⁶ In some situations these leaders are divinely punished for clinging to power too long and/or withholding it from legitimate successors.⁶⁷ In others it has to be pried out of their "cold, dead fingers." In the story of David, Bathsheba succeeds in loosening David's grip by "reminding" him of a promise he probably never makes, but perhaps one he wanted to or should have. Female mediation is one of the most traditional, most common, and most effective ways to force the issue with recalcitrant, desperate, and aging leaders.

CONCLUSION

Marvin Pope says of Anat that she "embodies the tensions and paradoxes of feminine power in an androcentric world."⁶⁸ The same might be said for Bathsheba. In rabbinic legend the David-Bathsheba-Uriah triad becomes a symbol for Adam, Eve, and the serpent, but this sort of "interpretation" does little to explain who she is or what she does.⁶⁹ Neither do contemporary analyses determined to read her character through ideological lenses determined to ignore the ancient literary context to which this story owes its basic shape. Doubtless the foregoing suggestions will not answer every question about her character, but at least they attempt to situate it in a plausible socioliterary context. Apart from some understanding of this context the temptation to colorize, marginalize, and/or ignore her character will remain too strong to resist, and Bathsheba will continue to remain silent.

---

64. 1 Kings 14:10 (see Moore, *Faith*, 242–48).
65. *CAT* 1.3–4; 2 Sam 7:1–16.
66. *GE* 12.295 (Akk *šammu nikitti*). N. B. that Utnapishtim's *wife* is the "agent" responsible for offering Gilgamesh the *šammu nikitti* (*GE* 12.273–86).
67. Hanson, "Deviance," 11–25.
68. Pope, *Anat*, 350.
69. Stern, "Afterlife," 120–24.

17

"WISE WOMEN" OR "WISDOM WOMAN?"

A Biblical Study of Gender Roles*

READERS REMAIN DIVIDED OVER the origin and identity of the Wisdom Woman in Proverbs 1–9. Many roads run back to her door through mythological,[1] sapiential,[2] apocalyptic,[3] rabbinic,[4] and early Christian

---

* Revised from an essay read to the Hebrew and Cognate Literature Section of the SBL on Nov 21, 1992 in San Francisco, California, subsequently published in *ResQ* 35 (1993) 147–58.

1. The myth of the Sybil at Cumae, an "old woman" who speaks in ecstatic utterances, animates pagan (Ovid, *Metam.* 14.132) and early Christian sources (Herm. *Vis.* 1.2.2–2.4.1). At Nag Hammadi, Sophia appears as a demi-goddess in *Ap. John* 8.20; 9.25–10.19; 23.21–35; 28.11–21; *Hyp. Arch.* 94.29–34; 95.18–31; *Orig. World* 98.13; 112.1–9; *Gos. Eg.* 57.1–4; 69.3; *Eugnostos* 77.4–6 (divine consort); 81.23–83.1; 88.6; *Soph. Jes. Chr.* 101.16; 102.13; 114.15 ("mother of the universe"). See Perkins, "Sophia," 96–112.

2. See *Sir* 1:4–20; 4:11–19; 6:18–31; 24:1–22; *Wis* 6:12–16; 7:7–14, 25–29; 8:1–21; 9:9–11; 10:1–21; see also *Jdt* 8:29; 11:20–23. See Goulder ("Sophia," 516–34) and Lampe ("Wisdom," 111–31).

3. See *Sib. Or.* Prologue 30–49; 2.1–5; 3.1–7, 809–29; 7.150–62; 11.315–24; *Herm Vis.* 2.4.1 (where ἡ σίβυλλα becomes ἡ ἐκκλησία). At Nag Hammadi, see 1 Apoc. Jas. 35.7; 36.6–8; *Great Pow.* 44.19–20.

4. See *b. B. Bat.* 123a; *Lam. Rab.* 24. See Umansky ("Sisters," 20–26).

channels.⁵ Attempts to pursue her prior to the book of Proverbs remain difficult, however—a problem for which at least four solutions are routinely proposed. *First*, some claim to see an indigenously Hebrew goddess lurking beneath the surface of Proverbs 1–9, hypothesizing her to be a regional minor deity in a Canaanite pantheon.⁶ More than mere observer at creation, she acts as a veritable "Co-Creator"⁷—a "mediatrix," in Samuel Terrien's words, of the "divine presence."⁸ Eventually demythologized by monotheistic Hebrews, she survives in Tanak only as a shadow of her former self.

Second, some agree with the essentials of this "goddess" hypothesis, but look outside Israel for her origins, usually to Egypt,⁹ Canaan,¹⁰ or Mesopotamia.¹¹ Proponents of this theory compare the Wisdom Woman in Proverbs to Inanna in Sumer,¹² Ma'at in Egypt,¹³ Asherah in Canaan,¹⁴ and even Athena in Greece.¹⁵ Muted indications of a polytheized Yahwism in ninth-century Sinai¹⁶ and fifth-century Egypt¹⁷ are often cited as corroborating

---

5. On the cult of Mary, see Maunder (*Mary*), Warner (*Alone*), Ashe (*Virgin*), and van den Hengel ("Miriam," 130–46).

6. As Lang puts it, "the wisdom goddess Ḥokma . . . belongs among the children of this god (El Elyon)" (*Hebrew*, 29).

7. O'Connor, *Wisdom*, 83.

8. Terrien, *Presence*, 357. See Moore, "Presence," 166–70.

9. See Donner ("Ürsprunge," 8–18), Kayatz (*Proverbien*, 98–102), von Rad (*Wisdom*, 153–55), and Kloppenborg ("Isis," 57–84).

10. See CAT 1.4.6.46; Albright ("Canaanite-Phoenician," 1–45); Day ("Asherah," 387).

11. See Albright ("Goddess," 258–94) and Boström (*Proverbiastudien*, 161–73).

12. See Wolkstein and Kramer (*Inanna*, 11–27).

13. "The understanding of Ma'at as an *interrelated order of rightness* in the course of its development in Kemetic intellectual history evolves from the conception of Ma'at as a constitutive part of creation itself, both as a goddess or divine spirit and as a conceptual personification of order, rightness, truth (and) justice" (Karenga, *Ma'at*, 7–8). See Bryce, *Legacy*, 87–89.

14. See Clifford, "Ugaritic," 305.

15. Hengel reports this and other possible Greek parallels (*Judaism*, 153–54).

16. The inscription on one of the pithos-jars unearthed by Meshel ("Consort," 30) at Kuntillet ʽAjrud reads brkt.ʼtkm.lyhwh.šmrn.wlʼšrth ("I bless you by Yahweh of Samaria and his A/asherah"). The problem, of course, centers on whether or not to capitalize "A/asherah." Neither Olyan (*Asherah*, 28) nor Hadley (*Asherah*, 121) capitalize the term, but among most critics theirs is the minority position.

17. N.B. the compound Aramaic name ענתיהו in a fifth-century affidavit from Egypt ("Anat-Yahu," CAP 44.3). In *Aḥiq* 7.95 Camp (*Wisdom*, 293) questions whether the entity designated יקירה ("precious") to the gods and נשא ("exalted") by the בעל קדשן ("lord of holiness") refers to חכמה ("wisdom") in the previous column (*Aḥiq* 6.92), but it's difficult to imagine any other antecedent.

evidence. Intramural debates within this camp tend to focus on whether the relationship of this goddess to the Wisdom Woman in Proverbs is organic and close, or inorganic and distant.[18] *Third*, many believe her to be an extension (hypostasis) of the one true God, much like the Shekinah, the Meṭaṭron, or the Memra in early Judaism.[19] For many this view stubbornly resists all critical challenges to the antiquity, plausibility, and homogeneity of Hebrew monotheism in 1st millennium Palestine (BCE).[20] *Fourth*, questions about origins are for many at least subsidiary, and at most irrelevant to questions of semiotic functionality.[21] That is, many see in the Wisdom Woman a personification, or more technically, a metaphorical symbol for the wisdom tradition itself, brilliantly conceived and structurally woven into the "book" of Proverbs for the purpose of unifying its disparate independent segments into a coherent whole.[22]

As debates go, this one seems more productive than most. Proponents of these various "goddess" hypotheses are at the very least forcing interpreters to reassess the reality of Israelite religion in both its official and popular forms,[23] while recent advances in literary criticism enable the reading of משלים ("Proverbs") as something other than a jumbled assortment of disconnected sentences.[24] More to the point, this change of methodological scenery now exercises enormous influence on contemporary discussions about gender roles in the Bible. As the ancient texts make clear, ANE "wise women" enact diverse roles as socioculturally important as they are identifiably diverse.[25] The Prologue to the Sybilline Oracles, e.g., lists no less than ten sybils by name—"wise women" whose identities run deep into the soil

---

18. See de Moor (*Yahwism*, 42–100), Smith (*Yahweh*, 145–60), Frymer-Kensky (*Goddesses*, 179–83) and Day (*Yahweh*, 42–67).

19. On Shekinah (שכינה) see *m. 'Abot*. 3.2; *b. Yoma* 9b; *b. Ber*. 6a; *b. B. Bat*. 25a; Goldberg (*Schekhinah*, 531–38). On Memra (מימרא) see *m. Sanh*. 6.4; Moore ("Memra," 52–59). On Meṭaṭron (מטטרון) see *3 En*. 1.4; 3.1–2; Orlov (*Enoch-Meṭaṭron*, 92–97).

20. See Ringgren (*Word*, 132–34), Hengel (*Judaism*, 153–56), Lang (*Wisdom*, 137–40), Camp (*Wisdom*, 34–36). In Q 43.63 Isa says, "Now I have come to you with 'Wisdom' (حكمة) in order to make clear to you some of the points on which you disagree." Whether or not W/wisdom should be capitalized is sharply debated by Islamic scholars (see Fakhry, "Islam," 77).

21. See Miles, *Wise*, 88–101.

22. See Camp (*Wisdom*, 71–77, 179–222), Yee ("Analysis," 58–66).

23. On the need to distinguish carefully between official and popular religion in ancient Israel, see Lewis, *Cults*, 5–34.

24. Camp's *Wisdom and the Feminine* is a major step forward.

25. See Haas & Thiel (*Allaituraḫḫi*, 22–23) and the comprehensive essays in Chavalas (*Women*).

of ancient belief and practice.[26] Hittitologist Oliver Gurney, for example, recognizes no less than thirteen (and perhaps as many as thirty-two) names in the Anatolian texts.[27]

Rather than simply rehearse these findings, the purpose here is to reflect briefly on the (dis)similarities between the portrayals of actual Anatolian/Syro-Palestinian "wise women" vs. the idealistic portrayal preserved in the book of Proverbs. *Questions:* (a) What functional roles do "wise women" play in ancient Anatolia, the culture for which we presently have the most written evidence? (b) What functional roles do "wise women" play in ancient Israel, the culture with which most contemporary readers of the Bible are most interested? and (c) What affinities, if any, exist between the roles enacted by "wise women" in the imaginary world of literature vs. the real world of magico-religious praxis?

WISE WOMEN IN ANATOLIA

The Anatolian "wise woman"[28] enacts a variety of roles. Her presence is required at most *rites de passage* and other, unexpected points of crisis—like plague, war, illness, and various other calamities. As *exorcist* she is the specialist culturally responsible for freeing clients from the chthonic power of sorcery and demonic curse. This is one of her most important roles. The wise woman Allaiturahhi of Mukis (northern Syria), e.g., lists several of these demons by name:

- "the spell which is called 'paralysis'";
- "the thing which sticks to the mouth";
- "the fear before the lion";
- "the terror before the snake."[29]

As *purification-priestess* she is responsible for cleansing clients from all kinds of defilement, whether caused by sin against the gods, or from illicit contact with defiled substances,[30] or from the diabolical spells of evil sorcerers.[31]

---

26. *Sib. Or.* Prologue 30–49; Parke (*Sibyls*, 81–94); Collins (*Sybils*, 181–238).

27. Gurney, *Religion*, 45.

28. The usual cuneiform designation in the Hittite texts is ^{SAL}ŠU.GI.

29. Haas & Thiel, *Allaiturahhi* 104.4′-5′; 146.47-48. Haas & Wegner (*Beschwörerinnen* 78.19′) list the names of several other Hittite demons.

30. See, e.g., the "ritual of the red heifer" (Num 19:1–22).

31. "If 'warlocks' (*kaššāpū*) bewitch you, I will break their bond; if 'witches' (*kaššāpātu*) bewitch you, I will break their bond" (*Maq* 7.94–95). Cf. Heb cognate כשף ("to practice sorcery," 2 Chron 33:6; Exod 7:11; Deut 18:10; Mal 3:5). See Abusch,

She does this by washing her clients with "pure" water, anointing them with healing salves, and/or releasing them from demonic curse through the construction and destruction of homeopathic images.³² As *incantation-reciter* she interprets and applies the myths of antiquity to the needs of her clients. Often she accomplishes this by weaving mythopoeic motifs and themes into the fabric of her purification rituals, making it difficult, at times, to tell whether she speaks about the "release" of a god or hero in the imaginary world of myth, or the "release" of a suffering client in the world of history.³³

Often these rituals can be rather complex. Maštikka, a ᴿᴬᴸŠU.GI from Kizzuwatna,³⁴ for example, manipulates both animate and inanimate homeopathic images in a ritual designed to heal conflicts dividing "father and son, husband and wife, or brother and sister."³⁵ To identify this evil she takes soft wax and molds it into the shape of human tongues. Then she ritually transfers the evil out of her clients into these wax images through a series of carefully-sequenced incantations. After this she burns the contaminated wax images to release her clients from the "evil of the tongue." Finally, just to be safe, she brings in a sacrificial animal, has the disputing parties spit into its mouth, and slaughters it in a "failsafe" effort to make sure the evil is fully expunged.³⁶ Thus, by means of both substitutionary and expulsionary magic, she resolves the problem afflicting her clients.³⁷

Two points need to be underlined before turning to Tanak. *First*, the Anatolian "wise woman" enacts many roles for many reasons, but fundamentally she acts as a priestly *mediator*, a culturally recognized expert in the art of conflict resolution.³⁸ Beyond all the strange rituals and repetitive chants, the reason why kings and commoners come to her is because of her proven track-record as a conflict-resolver. *Second*, homeopathic (or

---

Witchcraft, 3–26.

32. Haas & Thiel, *Allaiturahhi*, 140. Joines succinctly defines homeopathic magic as "the belief that the fate of an object or person can be governed by the manipulation of its exact image" ("Serpent," 251).

33. E.g., the "wise woman" Malli of Arzawa chants, [nu-kiš-a]n te-e-ez-zi ku-iš-wa-ra-an ḫar-ga-nu-uš-ki-it [. . .-ḫi-eš-]ki-it ki-nu-un-na-aš-ši-kán ḪUL- u-wa da-a[š-ki-mi], ["Then] she (the 'wise woman') chants: 'Whoever made him white . . . [and] whoever made him . . . now [I] take the evil away from him (the client)'" (*KUB* 41.1.1.12–13). See Vieyra, "Sorcier," 105–06.

34. Kizzuwatna encompasses an area contiguous to the SE coast of modern Turkey.

35. *KBo* 39.8.1.1–3.

36. It's common in ANE purification rituals to use "failsafe backups" (e.g., the use of *two* goats in Lev 16:1–22—one to kill, one to send away).

37. See explanation and discussion in Strauss, *Reinungsrituale*, 16–148.

38. "The priest is *ipso facto* a mediator, for the priesthood is an institution of mediation" (de Vaux, *Israel*, 357).

sympathetic) magic is fundamentally based on the concept of *parallelism*. If an invisible evil can be transferred into a visible image of clay or wax or leather or cloth, then the action taken to deal with the visible image can simultaneously deal with the invisible evil "tricked" into inhabiting it. To destroy, expel, or curse a visible homeopathic image is thus to destroy, expel, or curse the invisible evil inside it. Parallelism is the defining characteristic of homeopathic ritual.

WISE WOMEN IN ISRAEL

The Hebrew Bible preserves four stories in which "wise women" play major roles. In two of these stories the protagonist is expressly called אשת חכמה ("wise woman"): the אשת חכמה of Tekoa[39] and the אשת חכמה of Abel.[40] In 1 Samuel 25 Abigail enacts the "wise mediator" role-set in the dispute between David and her husband Nabal, though the narrator never pretends to call her אשת חכמה,[41] and in 1 Samuel 28 a "medium" from Endor,[42] familiar with the ins-and-outs of Syro-Palestinian necromancy, resolves a thorny dispute between Saul and Samuel—no small task inasmuch as one of the parties to this dispute is already dead.[43]

In 2 Samuel 14 the family of David sits on an explosive crisis of staggering proportions. Amnon, David's son by Ahinoam (an Ephraimite), has thoughtlessly raped his half-sister Tamar, David's daughter by Maacah (an Aramean),[44] and Absalom, Tamar's full-brother, has murdered him in retaliation. After this several years go by in which nothing is done to resolve the conflict festering between David and his son. When Joab, David's military commander, realizes how bad the situation has become, he decides to take action not only because the conflict between them has the potential to paralyze a family, but because left unresolved it has the power to paralyze an

---

39. 2 Sam 14:2.

40. 2 Sam 20:16.

41. McCarter (*2 Samuel*, 245) thinks the peculiarities of her behavior are strong enough to read her story intertextually with that of the Tekoite woman in 2 Sam 14.

42. I.e., a בעלת אוב (lit., "lady of the bag/pit," 1 Sam 28:7).

43. See Kleiner, *Saul*, 57–134. Caquot ("Divination," 100) thinks a conservative censor intentionally sanitizes the story in 1 Sam 28 of its "original" homeopathic elements.

44. Trible entitles this story "the royal rape of Wisdom" (*Terror*, 37–63).

entire nation.⁴⁵ He does what any other ANE leader would do in a situation like this. He hires a "wise woman" to resolve it.⁴⁶

A comparative intertextual reading of this text proves fruitful on at least two levels. *First*, it is not insignificant that the אשת חכמה hired by Joab to help David chooses to work with a type of literary device Ulrich Simon calls a "juridical parable."⁴⁷ Where parables in general compare situations in the real world with situations in the imaginary world,⁴⁸ juridical parables focus specifically on situations involving egregious injustice. In 2 Samuel 20, e.g., Nathan the prophet uses a juridical parable about a "little ewe lamb" to alert David to Yahweh's anger over his involvement in the murder of Uriah the Hittite.⁴⁹ Like all parables, juridical parables operate on the principle of analogical parallelism.⁵⁰ When those who hear a משל attempt to resolve the conflict it identifies, the intention is to promote genuine conflict resolution. To put it another way, any action taken on the listener's part to deal with the imaginary situation in the משל has an immediate effect on the real situation, however (c)overt. In short, juridical parables are literary homeopathic images crafted by professional mediators to resolve conflicts between real people in the real world.

Second, the משל related to David by the אשת חכמה from Tekoa is a classic example. Disguising herself as a mourning widow, she tells David the fictional story of a family, her family, which has recently become the victim of tragedy. One of her sons has killed the other in a violent dispute. This in itself is tragic, of course, yet the evil unleashed by this violence has now escalated as the woman's clan demands from her that her surviving son be handed over to the גואל הדם ("avenger of blood").⁵¹ Their specific demands

---

45. After all, with Amnon dead Absalom becomes the new crown prince (see Moore, "Teenagers," 49–60).

46. Whybray (*Succession*, 59) thinks this story is more about Joab than the אשת חכמה. Hoftijzer ("David," 444) believes her to be "capable," but of no particular sociocultural status, while Camp ("Model," 14–15) allots to her considerably more status.

47. Simon, "Parable," 208.

48. In Schipper's opinion (*Parables*, 4), parables should not be primarily defined by how "they function primarily to change their addressees' ways. Instead, the parables help create, intensify, and justify judgments and hostile actions against their addressees."

49. Following an offhand remark by Timo Veijola, Halpern speculates that Solomon's true father is Uriah, not David (*Demons*, 403–06).

50. Linguistically this is immediately evident from the verbal root of the Heb noun usually translated into English as "parable"—משל can mean either "to compare" or "to rule" (see Eissfeldt, *Maschal*, 29–44). Haas & Wegner summarily describe the incantations of the ˢᴬᴸŠU.GI as "analogical sayings" (*Beschwörerinnen*, 3).

51. Num 35:19–27. Stackert rigorously compares the (dis)similarities between the tribal asylum laws in Exod 21:12–14, Deut 19:1–13, and Num 35:9–34 (*Torah*, 31–112).

are terrifying: (a) that the נפש ("lifebreath") of the living son be handed over in exchange for the נפש of the dead son; otherwise (b) that they be allowed not only to "cause his death" (מות), but to "annihilate" (שמד)[52] the remaining son (and with him the name of her husband) from the face of the earth.[53] In other words, they demand that the evil in their midst be expunged by both substitutionary *and* expulsionary means.

To communicate the fullness of her dilemma, the אשת חכמה employs a revealing metaphor: "quench my surviving ember."[54] Assyriologist Rykle Borger points out that this phrase resembles a Babylonian text in which an unmarried man is described as someone "whose brazier has been quenched."[55] Based on this parallel, it thus seems hardly coincidental that the Heb term גחלת ("ember") occurs elsewhere in a prophetic satire of the "embers" (גחלת) in Babylonian rituals,[56] or that the Akk word for "brazier" (*kanūnu*) repeatedly occurs in Assyrian ritual texts underlining the cosmic peculiarities of "cultic fire."[57] At any rate, the "wise woman" helps David resolve his conflict with Absalom by leading him through a sequence of maneuvers. Like her sisters in Anatolia, success depends on her ability to secure her client's attention without alienating him, even while helping him make a decision he *thinks* he is making *alone*, without anyone's help. To do this she covertly introduces the problem in David's life by constructing a literary homeopathic image of it in the imaginary world; viz., the aforesaid juridical parable. David's response to the telling of this parable is noncommittal. He tells the "widow" to go away, weakly promising that he will look into her situation at a later time. Her response to this brush-off, however, is pointedly immediate: "Upon me, my lord and king, be 'the sin' (העון)[58] ... but let the king and his throne remain innocent."[59] Given the context of this crisis, this is the first time anyone mentions "the sin" (העון), much

---

52. 2 Sam 14:7. This term occurs repeatedly in Esther when describing Haman's intention to "annihilate" Jews (שמד, Esth 3:6, 13).

53. The Tekoite's story reflects a family crisis starkly similar to that precipitating the family crisis in Ruth 1:1–5.

54. וכבו את־גחלתי אשר נשארה (2 Sam 14:7).

55. *ālik idija ša kinunšu bi-lu-ú* ("my assistant whose brazier has been quenched," *CAD* B 73). Borger privately communicates this Akk parallel to Hoftijzer ("David," 422).

56. אין גחלת לחמם ("there is no ember with which to warm oneself," Isa 47:14).

57. See the texts cited in Reiner (*Šurpu*, 23), Meier (*Maqlû*, 29), and *CAD* K 393–95. The *kind* of fire used in ANE cultic ritual is never left to chance; cf., e.g., the אש זרה ("strange fire") in Lev 10:1.

58. Abigail uses the same articulated noun (העון) in her "confession" (1 Sam 25:24).

59. 2 Sam 14:9.

less associates it with the behavior of the royal family. The "wise woman" introduces "the sin" in the imaginary world of the parable because it is far too sensitive a subject to discuss in the real world—at least, not yet. Relying on her experience, she maneuvers David in a way bold enough to elicit his cooperation, yet subtle enough to avoid direct confrontation. She does not overtly say who might be responsible for "the sin"; she simply notes its existence. Yet by overtly offering to take personal responsibility for it she covertly communicates to David the seriousness of *his* dilemma.

Accepting her invitation to enter this imaginary world, David responds with a stereotypical promise of royal assurance: "If anyone says anything to you, bring him to me and he will not touch you again."[60] Paralleling the words דבר ("to speak") and נגע ("to touch"), the king subtly signals that he, too, understands the connection between the imaginary world of words and the gritty world of politics. He knows that the threatening words of the tribe cannot simply be dismissed, but he also knows that the word of the king is final. So he cracks open a door to the possibility that he might be willing to exercise this royal power, though without yet committing to anything concrete. This reaction encourages the אשת חכמה to take a final, crucial step. She asks the king to speak a certain *kind* of word on her behalf—a royal oath, a word with enough power to protect her son's נפש from the גואל הדם. Finally, David officially responds, pronouncing an oath of protection over her fictitious son in the name of Yahweh. In this way the "wise woman" of Tekoa successfully leads David to decide whether the "lifebreath" of her remaining son is more important than the clan's need to maintain tribal equilibrium.

Having accomplished this, she moves swiftly to apply David's decision in the imaginary world to the unresolved conflict still plaguing his family. *First*, she warns David of the consequences of indecision. By refusing to return "his banished one"[61] from exile, he is in reality preventing Absalom from enacting his responsibilities as crown prince. Indeed, this indecision is fueling a climate in which Absalom is reduced to little more than a "guilt offering" for Amnon.[62] David needs to realize how dangerous this passive-aggressive course of action is, and make the decision to bring his son home. *Second*, the longer David waits to make this decision, the more likely he is to lose his kingdom. Just as the death of the son in the imaginary world leads to potential disaster, so the banishment of Absalom holds the same potential.

60. 2 Sam 14:10. Had David said this to Tamar after the rape, this probably would have stopped the conflict from escalating so far out of control.

61. נדחו (2 Sam 14:13).

62. Revocalizing MT אשם (*'āšēm*) as *'āšām* ("guilt offering," Lev 5:6).

The אשת חכמה warns the king about this through another revealing metaphor depicting Israel's fate as "water poured out on the ground, so that it cannot be retrieved."[63] This metaphor, like her earlier one about "quenched embers," resonates deeply with other metaphors in the incantation literature. A close parallel occurs in the Canaanite legend where Kirta the king becomes ill, summons his son Ilḥu, and urges him not to mourn. This task he gives to his daughter, Thitmanat, because in her he finds someone more qualified to put "her water in the field, the extensions of her lifebreath on the heights."[64] Most Ugaritic ritual texts are sparsely detailed, yet death here appears in images not dissimilar to those used to motivate King David.

In short, this text shows us a master mediator at work. When the אשת חכמה accepts Joab's request to mediate the David-Absalom dispute, when she fashions a juridical parable, when she embellishes this parable with specific metaphors and symbols, when she invites her royal client into an imaginary world to make it easier for him to resolve a conflict which has hitherto paralyzed him, she stands squarely in the shadow of other ANE "wise women." To be sure, there is no trace of actual homeopathic magic in this monotheistic Hebrew text, just as there is none to be found in the story of the encounter of Saul and Samuel in 1 Sam 28. Yet the role of *mediator* resonates loudly in both narratives as both women deal with the complexities of human conflict.

WISE WOMEN AND WISDOM WOMAN

What, therefore, can we say about the nature of the relationship between the roles enacted by ANE "wise women" and the Wisdom Woman of Prov 1–9? Space restrictions prevent full-blown analysis, but a close reading of this sapiential poetry reveals an idealized character as baroquely stylized as she is socially complex. In Prov 1:20–33 the Wisdom Woman is an *angry prophet* who rails against her audience for rejecting her words and choosing panic, anguish, and calamity in their stead. She is not in a mediatorial mood. Instead she is indignant and judgmental, inflicting her audience with language much more at home in the Day-of-Yahweh prophecies than the relatively placid world of scribal academics.

Another facet of her personality surfaces in Prov 8:1–21. Here the Wisdom Woman is in a didactic mood, a *tenured professor* dropping wisdom sayings from her lips like polished pearls, dispassionately offering her message and herself to an eager audience of attentive male students. Prov.

---

63. 2 Sam 14:14.
64. *CAT* 1.16.1.34–35.

8:22–36 embellishes this role so brilliantly, she looks to be towering like a "goddess" over her "devotees." There is no trace of a mediatorial role here, either.

In Prov 9:1–18 the confrontation between the Wisdom Woman and the Strange Woman depicts these two women as *spiritual, ideological, and moral enemies*. The Strange Woman slavishly and diabolically imitates the message and demeanor of the Wisdom Woman in a concentrated attempt to lure away gullible students. But nowhere does she attempt to mediate a resolution to the conflict which so completely separates them. Instead, the book of Proverbs portrays this polarity as an ancient, inevitable, and irresolvable conflict between cosmic good and cosmic evil. Only those destined for Sheol fail to recognize it as such.

CONCLUSIONS

To be blunt, there seem to be very few affinities between the actual roles enacted by ANE "wise women" and the idealized roles ascribed to the Wisdom Woman in Proverbs. *First*, in the real world of priestly ritual both Anatolian and Hebrew "wise women" use parallelistic techniques of various types to help clients resolve conflicts. Whether one is comfortable calling these techniques "homeopathic" or "sympathetic," they are certainly "parallelistic." In the imaginary world of Proverbs the Wisdom Woman speaks prophetically, didactically, and cosmically to an all-male audience of future diplomats and scribes, but there is no parallelism here, no parables (juridical or otherwise), and certainly no trace of homeopathic praxis.

Second, Anatolian and Hebrew "wise women" are cautious and conservative in their behavior. As experienced professionals they understand well the need for indirection, caution, and discretion when dealing with complex disputes, as well as the unseen demonic forces universally believed to be driving them. By contrast, the Wisdom Woman is direct and forthright, whether enacting a prophetic role upbraiding the foolish, a professorial role enlightening the ignorant, or a divine role recounting the mysteries of the universe.

Third, there seems to be no real crisis pulsating at the center of Prov 1–9, no thorny conflict, no (potentially) bloody dispute. This is perhaps the greatest difference. "Wise women" in the real world are seasoned professionals hired by desperate clients to help mediate and resolve the most difficult, messy conflicts. Theirs is the world of human vanity and ambition. The Wisdom Woman, on the other hand, lives in a placid imaginary world in which dispute is marginal and conflict mercurial. Hers is a world of scribes and sages, not kings and warriors. In her world, "wisdom" is less a real person than a timeless ideal. Consequently those who would look to Tanak for contemporary insight into the possibilities and boundaries of gender roles would be better served by looking to the roles "wise women" play in the real world of history *as well as* the idealistic world of sapiential Israel. Whether one or the other of these portrayals is the primary influence behind the gender-specific statements attributed to the Apostle Paul[65] is another question altogether.[66]

---

65. See Rom 16:1–2; 1 Tim 2:8–15; 1 Cor 11:2–16, and 14:34–36.
66. See Osburn, *Essays*.

BIBLIOGRAPHY

Abba, R. "Priests and Levites." In *IDB* 3.876–89.
Abegg, Martin. "Who Ascended to Heaven? 4Q491, 4Q427 and the Teacher of Righteousness." In *Eschatology, Messianism, and the Dead Sea Scrolls*, edited by C. Evans and P. Flint, 61–73. Grand Rapids: Eerdmans, 1998.
Abusch, I. Tzvi. *Mesopotamian Witchcraft: Toward a History and Understanding of Babylonian Witchcraft Beliefs and Literature*. Leiden: Brill, 2002.
———. *The Witchcraft Series Maqlû*. Atlanta: SBL, 2015.
Ackroyd, Peter R. *Exile and Restoration*. Philadelphia: Westminster, 1968.
Adelman, Rachel. "Jonah's Sojourn in the Netherworld." In *The Return of the Repressed: Pirqe De-Rabbi Eliezer and the Pseudepigrapha*, 211–58. Leiden: Brill, 2009.
Ahlström, Gösta W. "King Jehu—A Prophet's Mistake." In *Scripture and History in Theology: FS J. Coert Rylaarsdam*, edited by A. L. Merrill and T. W. Overholt, 47–69. Pittsburgh: Pickwick, 1977.
Ahuis, Ferdinand. *Der klagende Gerichtsprophet. Studien zur Klage in der Überlieferung von den alttestamentlichen Gerichtspropheten*. Stuttgart: Calwer, 1982.
Albertson, Robert G. "Job and the Ancient Near Eastern Wisdom Literature." In *Scripture and Context 2: More Essays on the Comparative Method*, edited by W. Hallo et al., 213–30. Winona Lake, IN: Eisenbrauns, 1983.
Albertz, Rainer. "Der sozialgeschichtliche Hintergrund des Hiobbuches und der 'Babylonischen Theodizee' (*ludlul bēl nēmeqi*)." In *Die Botschaft und die Boten. FS für Hans Walter Wolff zum 70 Geburtstag*, edited by J. Jeremias & L. Perlitt, 349–72. Neikirchen-Vluyn: Neukirchener, 1981.
Albrektson, Bertil. *Studies in the Text and Theology of the Book of Lamentations*. Lund: CWK Gleerup, 1963.
Albright, William Foxwell. "The Goddess of Life and Wisdom." *AJSL* 36 (1919–20) 258–94.
———. "The Oracles of Balaam." *JBL* 63 (1944) 207–33.
———. "Some Canaanite-Phoenician Sources of Hebrew Wisdom." *VTSup* 3 (1955) 1–45.
Alexander, Philip S. "Bavli Berakhot 55a–57b: The Talmudic Dreambook in Context." *JJS* 46 (1995) 230–48.
Alford, C. Fred. *Whistleblowers: Broken Lives and Organizational Power*. Ithaca, NY: Cornell University Press, 2001.

Alpert, Rebecca T. "Finding Our Past: A Lesbian Interpretation of the Book of Ruth." In *Reading Ruth*, edited by J. Kates and G. Twersky Reimer, 91–96. New York: Ballantine, 1994.

Alt, Albrecht. "The God of the Fathers." 1929. Translated by by R. A. Wilson. In *Essays on Old Testament History and Religion*, 3–86. Oxford: Blackwell, 1966.

Alter, Robert. "Characterization and the Art of Reticence." In *The Art of Biblical Narrative*, 114–30. New York: Basic, 1981.

———. "How Important Are the Dead Sea Scrolls?" *Commentary* 93 (1992) 34–42.

Altmann, Alexander. "The Fate of Abdi-Ashirta." *UF* 9 (1977) 1–11.

Amit, Yaira. *The Book of Judges: The Art of Editing*. Leiden: Brill, 1998.

———. "Hidden Polemic in the Conquest of Dan: Judges 17–18." *VT* 40 (1990) 4–20.

Andersen, Francis I. *Habakkuk: A New Translation with Introduction and Commentary*. New York: Doubleday, 2001.

———. "Yahweh, the Kind and Sensitive God." In *God Who Is Rich in Mercy: Essays Presented to Dr. D. B. Knox*, edited by P. T. O'Brien and D. G. Peterson, 41–88. Homebush West, Australia: Lancer, 1986.

Anderson, Gary A. *Sacrifices and Offerings in Ancient Israel: Studies in Their Social and Political Importance*. Atlanta: Scholars, 1987.

Angelou, Maya. *Now Sheba Sings the Song*. New York: Dutton/Dial, 1987.

Anor, Netanel. *Reading the Oil Omens: A Study of Practice and Record of Mesopotamian Lecanomancy*. Jerusalem: Hebrew University, 2010.

Anthonioz, Stéphanie. *Le prophétisme biblique: De l'idéal à la réalité*. Paris: Les Éditions du Cerf, 2013.

Arnaud, Daniel. *Recherches au pays d'Aštata: Emar (Mission archéologique de Meskéné-Emar)*. Paris: Editions Recherche sur les civilizations, 1985.

Aro, Jean. "Remarks on the Practice of Extispicy in the Time of Esarhaddon and Assurbanipal." In *La divination en mesopotamie ancienne et dans les régions voisines. XIVe rencontre assyriologique internationale*, 109–17. Paris: Presses universitaires de France, 1966.

Ashe, Geoffrey. *The Virgin*. London: Routledge & Kegan Paul, 1976.

Athas, George. *The Tel Dan Inscription: A Reappraisal and a New Interpretation*. London: T. & T. Clark, 2003.

Atran, Scott. *In Gods We Trust: The Evolutionary Landscape of Religion*. New York: Oxford University Press, 2002.

Aubet, Maria Eugenia. *The Phoenicians and the West: Politics, Colonies, and Trade*. Cambridge: Cambridge University Press, 2001.

Audet, Jean-Paul. "Origines comparées de la double tradition de la loi et de la sagesse dans le prôche-orient ancien." *International Congress of Orientalists* 1 (Moskow, 1960) 352–57.

Augustin, Matthias. "Die Inbesitznahme der schönen Frau aus der unterschiedlichen Sicht der Schwachen und der Mächtigen." *BZ* 27 (1983) 145–54.

Aune, David E. *Prophecy in Early Christianity and the Ancient Mediterranean World*. Grand Rapids: Eerdmans, 1983.

Avigad, Na'aman. "Baruch the Scribe and Jeraḥmeel the King's Son." *IEJ* 28 (1978) 52–56.

Avis, Paul D. L. *God and the Creative Imagination: Metaphor, Symbol and Myth in Religion and Theology*. London: Routledge, 1999.

Avruch, Kevin. "Reciprocity, Equality, and Status-Anxiety in the Amarna Letters." In *Amarna Diplomacy*, edited by R. Cohen and R. Westbrook, 154–64. Baltimore: Johns Hopkins, 2000.

Axelrod, Alan. *Little Known Wars of Great and Lasting Impact*. Beverly, MA: Fair Winds, 2009.

Babuts, Nicolae. *Memory, Metaphors, and Meaning: Reading Literary Texts*. New Brunswick, NJ: Transaction, 2009.

Baden, Joel S. *The Composition of the Pentateuch: Renewing the Documentary Hypothesis*. New Haven: Yale, 2012.

———. *The Promise to the Patriarchs*. New York: Oxford University Press, 2013.

Bakhtin, Mikhail. *Problems of Dostoevsky's Poetics*. Minneapolis: University of Minnesota Press, 1984.

Bal, Mieke. *Death and Dissymmetry: The Politics of Coherence in the Book of Judges*. Chicago: University of Chicago Press, 1988.

———. *Lethal Love: Feminist Literary Readings of Biblical Love Stories*. Bloomington, IN: Indiana University Press, 1987.

Balentine, Samuel E. *Leviticus*. Louisville, KY: Westminster John Knox, 2002.

———. *Prayer in the Hebrew Bible: the Drama of Divine-Human Dialogue*. Minneapolis: Augsburg Fortress, 1993.

Baltzer, Klaus. *Deutero-Isaiah: A Commentary*. Minneapolis: Fortress, 2001.

Banton, Michael, ed. *Anthropological Approaches to the Study of Religion*. London: Tavistock, 1978.

Bardtke, Hans. "Considérations sur les cantiques de Qûmran." *RB* 63 (1956) 220–33.

Barker, Joel D. "Day of the Lord." In *DOTPr* 132–43.

Barr, James. *Old and New in Interpretation: A Study of the Two Testaments*. London: SCM, 1966.

———. *The Semantics of Biblical Language*. London: Oxford University Press, 1961.

———. "Some Semantic Notes on the Covenant." In *Beiträge zur alttestamentlichen Theologie: FS fur Walther Zimmerli zum 70 Geburtstag*, edited by H. Donner et al., 23–38. Göttingen: Vandenhoeck & Ruprecht, 1977.

———. "The Theological Case against Biblical Theology." In *Canon, Theology, and Old Testament Interpretation*, edited by G. M. Tucker, 3–19. Philadelphia: Fortress, 1988.

———. "Theophany and Anthropomorphism in the Old Testament." *VT* 9 (1960) 31–38.

Barré, Michael. "New Light on Hos 6:2." *VT* 28 (1978) 129–41.

———. "Treaties in the Ancient Near East." In *ABD* 6.653–56.

Barstad, Hans M. *History and the Hebrew Bible*. Tübingen: Mohr Siebeck, 2008.

———. *The Religious Polemics of Amos: Studies in the Preaching of Amos*. Leiden: Brill, 1984.

Bartelmus, R. "Die sogenannte Jothamfabel: Eine politisch-religiöse Parabeldichtung." *TZ* 41 (1985) 97–120.

Barth, Christoph. *Die Errettung vom Tode in den individuellen Klage- und Dankliedern des Alten Testaments*. Zürich: Theologischer Verlag, 1997.

Barth, Karl. "The Need and Promise of Christian Preaching." In *The Word of God and the Word of Man*, 97–135. New York: Harper & Row, 1928.

Barthes, Roland. "Introduction to the Structural Analysis of Narratives." Translated by S. Heath, 1966. In *Image, Music, Text*, edited by S. Heath, 79–124. New York: Hill & Wang, 1977.
Barton, John. *Oracles of God: Perceptions of Ancient Prophecy in Israel After the Exile*. New York: Oxford University Press, 2007.
Baskin, Judith R. *Pharaoh's Counselors: Job, Jethro and Balaam in Rabbinic and Patristic Tradition*. Chico, CA: Scholars, 1983.
Basson, Alec. *Divine Metaphors in Selected Hebrew Psalms of Lamentation*. Tübingen: Mohr Siebeck, 2006.
Bauckham, Richard. "The Book of Ruth and the Possibility of a Feminist Canonical Hermeneutic." *BibInt* 5 (1997) 29–45.
Baumer, Franklin L. *Religion and the Rise of Scepticism*. New York: Harcourt, Brace, 1960.
Baumgarten, Albert. "A Note on the Book of Ruth." *JANESCU* 5 (1973) 11–15.
Baumgartner, Walter. *Die Klagegedichte des Jeremia*. Berlin: Töpelmann, 1917.
Bautch, Richard J. *Developments in Genre Between Post-Exilic Penitential Prayers and the Psalms of Communal Lament*. Atlanta: Society of Biblical Literature, 2003.
Beattie, D. R. G. *Jewish Exegesis of the Book of Ruth*. Sheffield, UK: JSOT, 1977.
———. "The Targum of Ruth—A Sectarian Composition?" *JJS* 36 (1985) 222–29.
Beckman, Gary. *Hittite Birth Rituals*. Wiesbaden: Harrassowitz, 1983.
———. "Blood in Hittite Ritual." *JCS* 63 (2011) 95–102.
Behler, Gebhard Maria. *Les confessions de Jérémie*. Tournai: Éditions de Maredsous, 1959.
Beiser, Frederick C. "Hegel and Ranke: A Re-examination." In *A Companion to Hegel*, edited by S. Houlgate and M. Baur, 332–50. Malden, MA: Wiley, 2011.
Bell, Catherine. *Ritual Theory, Ritual Practice*. New York: Oxford, 1992.
Berger, Peter. "Different Gospels: The Social Sources of Apostasy." In *American Apostasy: The Triumph of "Other" Gospels*, edited by R. J. Neuhaus, 1–14. Grand Rapids: Eerdmans, 1989.
Berlin, Adele. "Characterization in Biblical Narrative: David's Wives." *JSOT* 23 (1982) 69–85.
———. *Poetics and Interpretation of Biblical Narrative*. Winona Lake, IN: Eisenbrauns, 1994.
Berman, Joshua. *Created Equal: How the Bible Broke with Ancient Political Thought*. New York: Oxford University Press, 2008.
Berquist, Jon. "Role Dedifferentiation in the Book of Ruth." *JSOT* 57 (1993) 23–37.
Berridge, John M. Review of *Der klagende Gerichtsprophet*, by F. Ahuis. *JBL* 103 (1984) 452–53.
Bertman, Stephen. "Symmetrical Design in the Book of Ruth." *JBL* 86 (1965) 165–68.
Betz, Hans Dieter. "Zum Problem des religionsgeschichtliche Verständnisses der Apokalyptik." *ZTK* 63 (1966) 391–409.
Biale, David. *Blood and Belief: The Circulation of a Symbol between Jews and Christians*. Berkeley: University of California Press, 2007.
Biddle, Bruce J. *Role Theory: Expectations, Identities and Behaviors*. New York: Academic, 1979.
Biddle, Mark E. *Polyphony and Symphony in Prophetic Literature: Re-reading Jeremiah 7–20*. Macon, GA: Mercer University Press, 1996.

Bidmead, Julye. *The Akītu Festival: Religious Continuity and Royal Legitimation in Mesopotamia*. Piscataway, NJ: Gorgias, 2004.
Birkeland, H. "The Belief in the Resurrection of the Dead in the OT." *ST* 3 (1950) 60–78.
Black, Max. *Models and Metaphors: Studies in Language and Philosophy*. Ithaca, NY: Cornell University Press, 1976.
Blair, Christine Eaton. *The Art of Teaching the Bible: A Practical Guide for Adults*. Louisville, KY: Geneva, 2001.
Blank, Sheldon H. "The Confessions of Jeremiah and the Meaning of Prayer." *HUCA* 21 (1948) 331–54.
Blenkinsopp, Joseph. *A History of Prophecy in Israel*. Louisville, KY: Westminster John Knox, 1983.
———. *The Pentateuch: An Introduction to the First Five Books of the Bible*. New York: Doubleday, 1992.
Bloch, René. *Judische Drehbühnen: Biblische Varationen im antiken Judentum*. Tübingen: Mohr Siebeck, 2013.
Block, Daniel I. *Judges, Ruth*. Nashville: Broadman, 1999.
Blum, Erhard. *Studien zur Komposition des Pentateuch*. Berlin: De Gruyter, 1990.
———. "Die Kombination I der Wandinschrift von Tell Deir 'Allā: Vorschläge zur Reconstruktion mit historisch-kritischen Anmerkungen." In *Berührungspunkte: Studien zur Sozial- und Religionsgeschichte Israels und seiner Umwelt. Festschrift für Rainer Albertz zu seinem 65. Geburtstag*, edited by I. Kottsieper et al., 573–601. Münster: Ugarit-Verlag, 2008.
Bodi, Daniel. *The Book of Ezekiel and the Poem of Erra*. Göttingen: Vandenhoeck & Ruprecht, 1991.
Bogel, Frederic V. *The Difference Satire Makes: Rhetoric and Reading from Jonson to Byron*. Ithaca, NY: Cornell University, 2001.
Bohak, Gideon. *Ancient Jewish Magic: A History*. Cambridge: University Press, 2008.
Bollinger, Laurel. "Models for Female Loyalty: The Biblical Ruth in Jeanette Winterson's *Oranges Are Not the Only Fruit*." *Tulsa Studies in Women's Literature* 13 (Fall 1993) 363–401.
Boman, Thorleif. *Hebrew Thought Compared with Greek*, 1952. Translated by J. L. Moreau. Philadelphia: Westminster, 1960.
Boorer, Suzanne. *The Promise of the Land as Oath: A Key to the Formation of the Pentateuch*. Berlin: De Gruyter, 1992.
Bordt, Michael. "Platon über Gottes Zorn und seine Barmherzigkeit." In *Divine Wrath and Divine Mercy in the World of Antiquity*, edited by R. Kratz and H. Spieckermann, 143–52. Tübingen: Mohr Siebeck, 2008.
Boström, Gustav. *Proverbiastudien. Die Weisheit und das fremde Weib in Sprüche 1–9*. Lund: Gleerup, 1935.
Bottéro, Jean. *Le problème des Ḫabiru à la 4e Rencontre assyriologique internationale*. Paris: Impremerie nationale, 1954.
Botterweck, G. J. "חפץ." *TDOT* 5.92–106.
Bourke, J. "Le jour de Jahvé dans Joel." *RB* 66 (1959) 5–31, 191–212.
Bowlby, James. *The Making and Breaking of Affectional Bonds*. London: Tavistock, 1979.
Brendsel, Daniel J. *"Isaiah Saw His Glory": The Use of Isaiah 52–53 in John 12*. Berlin: De Gruyter, 2014.
Brenner-Idan, Athalya, ed. *A Feminist Companion to Ruth*. Sheffield, UK: Sheffield Academic Press, 2001.

Brettler, Marc. "Redaction, History, and Redaction-History of Amos in Recent Scholarship." In *Israel's Prophets and Israel's Past: Essays on the Relationship of Prophetic Texts and Israelite History in Honor of John H. Hayes*, edited by B. E. Kelle and M. B. Moore, 103–12. London: T. & T. Clark, 2006.
Brichto, Herbert Chanan. "Kin, Cult, Land, and Afterlife—A Biblical Complex." *HUCA* 44 (1973) 1–54.
Bright, John. *A History of Israel*, 4th ed. Louisville, KY: Westminster John Knox, 2000.
———. *Jeremiah*. Garden City, NY: Doubleday, 1965.
Brooks, Peter. *Reading for the Plot: Design and Intention in Narrative*. New York: Knopf, 1984.
Brown, Callum G., and Michael F. Snape, eds. *Secularisation in the Christian World*. Farnham, UK: Ashgate, 2010.
Brown, Cheryl A. "Judges." In *Joshua, Judges, Ruth*, by J. G. Harris, C. A. Brown, and M. S. Moore, 123–289. Grand Rapids: Baker, 2000.
Brown, Dee. *Bury My Heart at Wounded Knee*. New York: Holt, Rinehart, Winston, 1971.
Brown, Peter. "Sorcery, Demons, and the Rise of Christianity: From Late Antiquity into the Middle Ages." In *Religion and Society in the Age of Saint Augustine*, 119–46. London: Faber & Faber, 1972.
Brown, William P. *Seeing the Psalms: A Theology of Metaphor*. Louisville, KY: Westminster John Knox, 2002.
Brueggemann, Walter. *Cadences of Home: Preaching among Exiles*. Louisville, KY: Westminster John Knox, 1997.
———. *A Commentary on Jeremiah: Exile and Homecoming*. Grand Rapids: Eerdmans, 1998.
———. *David's Truth in Israel's Imagination and Memory*. Philadelphia: Fortress, 1985.
———. *Deep Memory, Exuberant Hope: Contested Truth in a Post-Christian World*. Minneapolis: Fortress, 2000.
———. "Priests for the Kingdom: Two Priesthoods for Two Regimes." In *The Bible as a Human Witness to Divine Revelation: Hearing the Word of God through Historically Dissimilar Traditions*, edited by R. Heskett et al., 3–14. London: T. & T. Clark, 2010.
———. *Theology of the Old Testament: Testimony, Dispute, Advocacy*. Minneapolis: Fortress, 1997.
Brunet, Gilbert. *Les lamentations contre Jérémie. Réinterprétation des quatre premières lamentations*. Paris: Presses universitaires de France, 1968.
Bruns, Gerald L. "Allegory and Satire: A Rhetorical Mediation." *New Literary History* 11 (1979–80) 121–32.
Bryan, Betsy M. "The Egyptian Perspective on Mitanni." In *Amarna Diplomacy*, edited by R. Cohen and R. Westbrook, 71–84. Baltimore: Johns Hopkins University, 2000.
Bryce, Glendon. *A Legacy of Wisdom: Egyptian Contribution to the Wisdom of Israel*. Lewisburg, PA: Bucknell University Press, 1979.
Bryce, Trevor. *The Kingdom of the Hittites*. New York: Oxford, 1998.
———. *Life and Society in the Hittite World*. Oxford: Oxford University Press, 2004.
Buber, Martin. *Kingship of God*, 1932. Reprint. London: Allen & Unwin, 1967.
———. *Königtum Gottes*. Berlin: Schocken Verlag, 1932.
Buchwalter, Andrew. "Is Hegel's Philosophy of History Eurocentric?" In *Hegel and History*, edited by Will Dudley, 87–110. Albany, NY: SUNY, 2009.

Budde, Karl Ferdinand Reinhardt. "Das hebraische Klagelied." *ZAW* 2 (1882) 1–52.
Budge, E. A. Wallis. *The Queen of Sheba and her Only Son Menyelek*. London: Hopkinson, 1922.
Bultmann, Christoph. "A Prophet in Desperation? The Confessions of Jeremiah." In *The Elusive Prophet: The Prophet as a Historical Person, Literary Character, and Anonymous Artist*, edited by J. C. de Moor, 83–93. Leiden: Brill, 2001.
Burckhardt, Jacob. *Über das Studium der Geschichte: Der Text der "Weltgeschichtlichen Betrachtungen" nach der Handschriften herausgegeben*. 1871. Reprint edited by P. Ganz. Munich: Beck, 1982.
Burns, John Barclay. "The Identity of Death's First-Born (Job 18:13)." *VT* 37 (1987) 362–64.
Burns, Ross. *Damascus: A History*. New York: Routledge, 2005.
Burrows, Millar. "The Marriage of Boaz and Ruth." *JBL* 59 (1940) 445–54.
———. *More Light on the Dead Sea Scrolls*. New York: Viking, 1958.
Bush, Frederic. *Ruth, Esther*. Dallas: Word, 1996.
Buss, Martin J. "The Social Psychology of Prophecy." In *Prophecy: Festschrift Georg Fohrer*, edited by J. Emerton, 1–11. Berlin: De Gruyter, 1980.
Byars, Ronald P. *The Future of Protestant Worship: Beyond the Worship Wars*. Louisville, KY: Westminster John Knox, 2002.
Cagni, Luigi. *L'epopea di Erra*. Roma: Istituto di Studi del Vicino Oriente, Universita di Roma, 1969.
Callaway, Mary. "The Lamenting Prophet and the Modern Self: On the Origins of Contemporary Readings of Jeremiah." In *Inspired Speech: Prophecy in the Ancient Near East: Essays Presented to Herbert B. Huffmon*, edited by J. Kaltner and L. Stulman, 48–62. New York: Continuum, 2007.
Camp, Claudia. *Wisdom and the Feminine in the Book of Proverbs*. Sheffield, UK: Almond, 1985.
———. "The Wise Women of 2 Samuel: A Role Model for Women in Early Israel?" *CBQ* 43 (1981) 14–29.
Campbell, Edward F. *Ruth: A New Translation and Commentary*. Garden City, NY: Doubleday, 1975.
Cannon, William W. "The Authorship of Lamentations." *BSac* 81 (1924) 42–58.
Caplice, Richard. *The Akkadian Namburbi Texts*. Los Angeles, Undena, 1974.
Caquot, André. "La divination dans l'ancien Israel." In *La divination*, edited by A. Caquot and M. Leibovici, 87–110. Paris: Presses Universitaires de France, 1968.
———. "Les songes et leur interpretation selon Canaan et Israel." In *Les songes et leur interprétation*, edited by A.-M. Esnoud et al., 99–124. Paris: Editions du Seuil, 1959.
Caquot, André, and André Lemaire. "Les textes araméenes de Deir 'Allā." *Syria* 54 (1977) 189–208.
Card, Orson Scott. *Characters and Viewpoint*. Cincinnati: F+W Media, 2010.
Carr, David M. *The Formation of the Hebrew Bible: A New Reconstruction*. New York: Oxford, 2011.
Carroll, Robert P. *From Chaos to Covenant: Prophecy in the Book of Jeremiah*. New York: Crossroad, 1981.
———. "Is Humour Also Among the Prophets?" In *On Humour and the Comic in the Hebrew Bible*, edited by Y. T. Radday and A. Brenner, 169–90. Louisville, KY: Westminster John Knox, 1992.

Cathcart, Kevin J. "Day of Yahweh." In *ABD* 2.84–85.
Černý, Ladislav. *The Day of Yahweh and Some Relevant Problems*. Praze: Nákladem Filosofické Fakulty University Karlovy, 1948.
Charles, Robert Henry. *A Critical and Exegetical Commentary on the Book of Daniel*. Oxford: Oxford University Press, 1929.
Chavalas, Mark W., ed. *Women in the Ancient Near East: A Sourcebook*. London: Routledge, 2013.
Chazon, Esther G. "Scripture and Prayer in 'The Words of the Luminaries.'" In *Prayers That Cite Scripture*, edited by J. L. Kugel, 25–41. Cambridge: Harvard University Press, 2006.
Chester, Andrew. *Future Hope and Present Reality: Eschatology and Transformation in the Hebrew Bible*. Tübingen: Mohr Siebeck, 2012.
———. *Messiah and Exaltation*. Tübingen: Mohr Siebeck, 2007.
Chesterton, G. K. *Heretics*, 1905. Reprint. London: Catholic Way Publishing, 2014.
Childs, Brevard S. *Biblical Theology in Crisis*. Philadelphia: Westminster, 1970.
———. *Biblical Theology of the Old and New Testaments: Theological Reflection on the Christian Bible*. Minneapolis: Fortress, 1992.
———. *Introduction to the Old Testament as Scripture*. Philadelphia: Fortress, 1979.
———. *Isaiah and the Assyrian Crisis*. London: SCM, 1967.
Christensen, Duane. *Prophecy and War in Ancient Israel: Studies in the Oracles against the Nations in Old Testament Prophecy*. Berkeley, CA: BIBAL, 1989.
Clark, Gordon R. *The Word חסד in the Hebrew Bible*. Sheffield, UK: JSOT, 1993.
Clarke, Ernest G., et al., eds. *Targum Pseudo-Jonathan of the Pentateuch: Text and Concordance*. Hoboken, NJ: KTAV, 1984.
Clements, Ronald E. *Jeremiah*. Atlanta: John Knox, 1988.
———. *Prophecy and Tradition*. Atlanta: John Knox, 1975.
Clifford, Richard. "Proverbs IX: A Suggested Ugaritic Parallel." *VT* 25 (1975) 298–306.
Clines, David J. M. *The Theme of the Pentateuch*. Sheffield, UK: JSOT, 1982.
Clines, David J. M., and David M. Gunn. "'You Tried to Persuade Me' and 'Violence! Outrage!' in Jeremiah 20.7–8." *VT* 28 (1978) 20–27.
Coats, George W. "The Way of Obedience: Traditio-Historical and Hermeneutical Reflections on the Balaam Story." *Sem* 24 (1982) 53–79.
Cody, Aelred. "An Excursus on Priesthood in Israel." In *Ezekiel: With an Excursus on Old Testament Priesthood*, 256–63. Wilmington, DE: Glazier, 1984.
Cogan, Mordechai, and Hayim Tadmor. *2 Kings*. New York: Doubleday, 1988.
Cohen, Raymond. "All In The Family: Ancient Near Eastern Diplomacy." *International Negotiation* 1 (1996) 11–28.
Cohen, Shaye J. D. *The Beginnings of Jewishness: Boundaries, Varieties, Uncertainties*. Berkeley, CA: University of California Press, 1999.
Cohn, Stephen Martin. *The Whistleblower's Handbook: A Step-by-Step Guide to Doing What's Right and Protecting Yourself*. Guilford, CT: Lyons Press, 2011.
Collins, Billie Jean. "Ḫuwarlu's Ritual (CTH 398)." In *Hittite Rituals from Arzawa and the Lower Land*. Atlanta: Scholars, forthcoming.
Collins, John J. "Current Issues in the Study of Daniel." In *The Book of Daniel: Composition and Reception*, edited by J. Collins and P. Flint, 1–15. Leiden: Brill, 2001.
———. *The Dead Sea Scrolls: A Biography*. Princeton: Princeton University Press, 2013.
———. *Introduction to the Hebrew Bible*. Minneapolis: Fortress, 2014.

———. "The Root of Immortality: Death in the Context of Jewish Wisdom." *HTR* 71 (1978) 177–92.
———. *The Scepter and the Star: The Messiahs of the Dead Sea Scrolls and Other Ancient Literature*. New York: Doubleday, 1995.
———. *Seers, Sybils, and Sages in Hellenistic-Roman Judaism*. Leiden Brill, 1997.
Conradie, Ernst M. *Saving the Earth? The Legacy of Reformed Views on "Re-Creation."* Zurich: LIT Verlag, 2013.
Conti, Marco, ed. *Ancient Christian Commentary on Scripture Vol. 5: 1-2 Kings, 1-2 Chronicles, Ezra, Nehemiah, Esther*. Downers Grove, IL: IVP, 2008.
Conzelmann, Hans. *The Theology of St. Luke*. 1954. Translated by G. Buswell. New York: Harper and Brothers, 1960.
Copenhaver, Brian. "Astrology and Magic." In *The Cambridge History of Renaissance Philosophy*, edited by C. B. Schmitt and Q. Skinner, 264–300. Cambridge: Cambridge University Press, 1988.
Coppens, Joseph. *Le messianisme royal: Ses origins, son développement, son accomplissement*. Paris: Les Editions du Cerf, 1968.
———. "Les oracles de Bileam: leur origine littéraire et leur portée prophétique." In *Mélanges Eugène Tisserant*, 67–80. Citta del Vaticano: Biblioteca Apostolica Vaticano, 1964.
Cornell, Vincent J. *Voices of Islam*. Westport, CT. Praeger, 2007.
Craigie, Peter. "Deborah and Anat: A Study of Poetic Imagery (Judges 5)." *ZAW* 90 (1978) 174–81.
Craven, Toni. *Artistry and Faith in the Book of Judith*. Chico, CA: Scholars, 1983.
Creach, Jerome F. D. *Yahweh as Refuge and the Editing of the Hebrew Psalter*. Sheffield, UK: Sheffield Academic Press, 1996.
Crenshaw, James. *Old Testament Wisdom: An Introduction*. Louisville, KY: Westminster John Knox, 2010.
———. "Riddles." In *ABD* 5.721–23.
———. "Seduction and Rape: The Confessions of Jeremiah." In *A Whirlpool of Torment: Israelite Traditions on God as an Oppressive Force*, 31–56. Philadelphia: Fortress, 1984.
Cross, Frank Moore. "The Council of Yahweh in Second Isaiah." *JNES* 12 (1953) 274–77.
———. "The Divine Warrior." In *Canaanite Myth and Hebrew Epic*, 91–111. Cambridge: Harvard University, 1973.
———. "'El and the God of the Fathers." In *Canaanite Myth and Hebrew Epic*, 13–43. Cambridge: Harvard University Press, 1973.
———. "Kinship and Covenant in Ancient Israel." In *From Epic to Canon: History and Literature in Ancient Israel*, 3–22. Baltimore: Johns Hopkins University Press, 1998.
———. "Leaves from an Epigraphist's Notebook." *CBQ* 36 (1974) 486–94.
———. "Notes on a Canaanite Psalm in the Old Testament." *BASOR* 117 (1950) 19–21.
———. "A Note on Apocalyptic Origins." In *Canaanite Myth and Hebrew Epic*, 343–46. Cambridge: Harvard University Press, 1973.
———. "A Note on the Study of Apocalyptic Origins." In *Canaanite Myth and Hebrew Epic*, 343–46. Cambridge: Harvard University Press, 1973.
———. "The Origin and Early Development of the Alphabet." *EI* 8 (1967) 8–24.

———. "The Priestly Houses of Early Israel." In *Canaanite Myth and Hebrew Epic*, 195–215. Cambridge: Harvard University Press, 1973.

———. "Reuben, Firstborn of Jacob." In *From Epic to Canon: History and Literature in Ancient Israel*, 53–70. Baltimore: Johns Hopkins University Press, 1998.

———. "The Themes of the Book of Kings and the Structure of the Deuteronomistic History." In *Canaanite Myth and Hebrew Epic*, 274–89. Cambridge: Harvard University Press, 1973.

———. "Yahweh and Ba`l." In *Canaanite Myth and Hebrew Epic*, 147–94. Cambridge: Harvard University Press, 1973.

Cross, Frank Moore, and Richard Saley. "Phoenician Incantations on a Plaque of the Seventh Century BC from Arslan Tash in Upper Syria." *BASOR* 197 (1970) 42–49.

Cryer, Frederick. *Divination in Ancient Israel and Its Ancient Near Eastern Environment: A Sociohistorical Investigation*. Sheffield, UK: JSOT, 1994.

Culley, Robert C. "The Confessions of Jeremiah and Traditional Discourse." In *A Wise and Discerning Mind: Essays in Honor of Burke O. Long*, edited by S. Olyan and R. Culley, 69–81. Providence: Brown Judaic Studies, 2000.

Curtis, Adrian. "Moses in the Psalms, with Special Reference to Psalm 90." In *La construction de la figure de Moïse*, edited by T. Römer, 89–99. Paris: Gabalda, 2007.

Curtis, John B. "On Job's Response to Yahweh." *JBL* 98 (1979) 497–511.

Curtiss, Samuel I. *The Levitical Priests: A Contribution to the Criticism of the Pentateuch*. Edinburgh: T. & T. Clark, 1877.

Dahood, Mitchell. *Psalms*. 3 vols. Garden City, NY: Doubleday, 1966–70.

———. Review of *Aramaic Texts from Deir `Allā*, by J. Hoftijzer and G. van der Kooij. *Bib* 62 (1981) 124–27.

Daiches, Samuel. "Balaam: A Babylonian *bārû*." In *Assyrologische und archaeologische Studien Herman von Hilprecht gewidmet*, 60–70. Leipzig: Hinrichs'sche, 1909.

Dalley, Stephanie. *Myths from Mesopotamia*. New York: Oxford University Press, 2000.

Davidson, Andrew Bruce. *The Theology of the Old Testament*. New York: Scribner, 1907.

Davidson, Robert. *The Courage to Doubt: Exploring an Old Testament Theme*. London: SCM, 1983.

Davies, Philip. *In Search of "Ancient Israel."* Sheffield, UK: JSOT, 1992.

Dawn, Marva J. *How Shall We Worship? Biblical Guidelines for the Worship Wars*. Carol Stream, IL: Tyndale House, 2003.

Day, John. "Asherah in the Hebrew Bible and Northwest Semitic Literature." *JBL* 105 (1986) 385–408.

———. "The Dependence of Isa 26:13—27:11 on Hos 13:4—14:10 and Its Relevance to Some Theories of the Redaction of the 'Isaiah Apocalypse.'" In *Writing and Reading the Scroll of Isaiah: Studies of an Interpretive Tradition*, edited by C. Broyles and C. Evans, 357–68. Leiden: Brill, 1997.

———. *Yahweh and the Gods and Goddesses of Canaan*. Sheffield, UK: JSOT, 2000.

Delcor, Mathias. "Le passage du temps prophétique au temps apocalyptique." In *Salvacion en la Palabra: Targum—Derash—Berith; en memoria del professor Alejandro Díez Macho*, edited by D. M. Léon, 97–134. Madrid: Ediciones Cristiandad, 1986.

del Olmo Lete, Gregorio. "Deber." In *DDD* 231–32.

de Moor, Johannes C. *An Anthology of Religious Texts from Ugarit*. Leiden: Brill, 1987.

———. "The Poetry of the Book of Ruth." *Or* 53 (1984) 262–83; 55 (1986) 16–41.

———. *The Rise of Yahwism: The Roots of Israelite Monotheism*. Leuven: Peeters, 1990.

———. "Studies in the New Alphabetic Texts from Ras Shamra I." *UF* 1 (1969) 170–71.
de Moor, Johannes C., and Klaus Spronk. "More on Demons in Ugarit (*CAT* 1.82)." *UF* 16 (1984) 237–50.
Dempster, Stephen G. "Mythology and History in the Song of Deborah." *WTJ* 41 (1978) 33–53.
DeRoche, Michael. "Jeremiah 2:2–3 and Israel's Love for God during the Wilderness Wanderings." *CBQ* 45 (1983) 364–76.
de Tarragon, Jean-Michel. *Le culte à Ugarit d'après les textes de la pratique en cunéiformes alphabétiques*. Paris: Gabalda, 1980.
———."Witchcraft, Magic, and Divination in Ancient Israel." In *CANE* 3.2071–81.
de Troyer, Kristen. "Blood: A Threat to Holiness or Toward (Another) Holiness?" In *Wholly Woman, Holy Blood: A Feminist Critique of Purity and Impurity*, edited by K. de Troyer et al., 45–64. Harrisburg, PA: Trinity, 2003.
de Vaulx, Jules. *Les nombres*. Paris: Gabalda, 1972.
de Vaux, Roland. *Ancient Israel: Its Life and Institutions*, 1958. Translated by J. McHugh. New York: McGraw-Hill, 1961.
———. "Le lieu que Yahvé a choisi pour y etablir son nom." In *Das ferne und das nahe Wort: FS Leonhard Rost*, edited by F. Maas, 219–28. Berlin: De Gruyter, 1967.
———. *Les livres de Rois*. Paris: Cerf, 1958.
Dever, William G. *Recent Archaeological Discoveries and Biblical Research*. Seattle: University of Washington Press, 1990.
de Vries, Simon. *1 Kings*. Waco, TX: Word, 1985.
———. "Observations on Quantitative and Qualitative Time in Wisdom and Apocalyptic." In *Israelite Wisdom: Theological and Literary Essays in Honor of Samuel Terrien*, edited by J. Gammie et al., 263–76. Missoula: Scholars, 1978.
de Waal Malefijt, Annemarie. *Religion and Culture: An Introduction to Anthropology of Religion*. New York, MacMillan, 1968.
de Wette, Wilhelm Martin Lebericht. *Lehrbuch der historisch-kritischen Einleitung in die kanonischen und apocryphischen Bücher des alten Testaments*. Berlin: G. Reimer, 1845.
Dexinger, Ferdinand. *Das Buch Daniel und seine Probleme*. Stuttgart: Verlag Katholisches Bibelwerk, 1969.
Diamond, A. R. ("Pete"). *The Confessions of Jeremiah in Context: Scenes of Prophetic Drama*. Sheffield, UK: JSOT, 1987.
Dietrich, Manfred. "Das Einsetzungsritual der *entu* von Emar (*Emar* VI/3, 369)." *UF* 21 (1989) 47–100.
Diewert, David A. "Job 7:12: *Yam, Tannin*, and the Surveillance of Job." *JBL* 106 (1987) 203–15.
Diez Macho, Alejandro, ed. *Neophyti I: Targum Palestinense MS de la Biblioteca Vaticana, Vol. IV Numeros*. Madrid: Consejo Superior de Investigaciones Cientificas, 1974.
Dijkstra, Meindert. "Is Balaam Also Among the Prophets?" *JBL* 114 (1995) 43–64.
Di Vito, Robert A. *Studies in Third Millenium Sumerian and Akkadian Personal Names: The Designation and Conception of the Personal God*. Roma: Editrice Pontificio Istituto Biblico, 1993.
Dobbs-Alsopp, F. W. *Lamentations*. Louisville, KY: Westminster John Knox, 2002.
———. "Rethinking Historical Criticism." *BibInt* 7 (1999) 35–71.
———. *Weep, O Daughter of Zion: A Study of the City-Lament Genre in the Hebrew Bible*. Rome: Pontifical Biblical Institute, 1993.

Dong, Hyun Bak. *Klagender Gott—klagender Menschen. Studien zur Klage im Jeremiabuch*. Berlin: De Gruyter, 1990.

Donner, Herbert. "Balaam Pseudopropheta." In *Beiträge zur alttestamentlichen Theologie. Festschrift für Walther Zimmerli*, edited by H. Donner et al., 112–23. Göttingen: Vandenhoeck & Ruprecht, 1977.

———. "The Confessions of Jeremiah—Their Form and Significance for the Prophet's Biography." *OTWSA* 24 (1981) 55–66.

———. "Die religionsgeschichtlichen Ursprunge von Prov. Sal. 8, 22–31." *ZÄS* 82 (1957) 8–18.

Donner, Herbert, and W. Röllig, eds. *Kanaanäische und aramäische Inschriften*. Wiesbaden: Harrassowitz, 1962–64.

Douglas, Mary. *In the Wilderness: The Doctrine of Defilement in the Book of Numbers*. Oxford: University Press, 2001.

———. *Purity and Danger: Analysis of Concepts of Pollution and Taboo*. 1966. Reprint. London: Routledge, 2003.

Douglas, Michael C. "Power and Praise in the *Hodayot*: A Literary-Critical Study of 1QH 9.1—18.14." PhD diss., University of Chicago, 1998.

———. "The Teacher Hymn Hypothesis Revisited: New Data for an Old Crux." *DSD* 6 (1999) 239–66.

Dowd, William A. Review of *Lamentations*, by N. Gottwald. *TS* 16 (1955) 282.

Dozeman, Thomas B. *Exodus*. Grand Rapids: Eerdmans, 2009.

Draffkorn-Kilmer, Anne E. "*Ilāni/Elohim*." *JBL* 76 (1957) 216–24.

Drazin, Israel, and Stanley M. Wagner, eds. *Onkelos on the Torah: Bamidbar*. Jerusalem: Geffen, 2009.

Duhm, Bernhard. *Das Buch Jeremia*. Tübingen: Mohr (Siebeck), 1901.

Durkheim, Emile. *The Elementary Forms of the Religious Life*, 1912. Translated by Joseph Ward Swain. New York: Collier, 1915.

Dussaud, René. *Les découvertes de Ras Shamra (Ugarit) et l'Ancien Testament*. Paris: Geuthner, 1941.

Eagleton, Terry. *An Introduction to Literary Theory*. Minneapolis: University of Minnesota Press, 2008.

Ebeling, Erich. *Die akkadische Gebetsserie "Handerhebung."* Berlin: Akademie-Verlag, 1953.

———. "Keilschrifttexte aus Assur religiösen Inhalts 1–2." *WVDOG* 28 & 34. Leipzig: J. C. Hinrichs, 1915–19 and 1920–23.

———. *Tod und Leben nach den Vorstellung der Babylonier*. Berlin: De Gruyter, 1931.

Eberstadt, Mary. *How the West Really Lost God: A New Theory of Secularization*. West Conschocken, PA: Templeton Press, 2013.

Eco, Umberto. *The Limits of Interpretation*. Bloomington, IN: Indiana University Press, 1990.

Edzard, Dietz Otto. *Gudea and His Dynasty*. Toronto: University of Toronto, 1997.

Eichler, Ulrike. "Der klagende Jeremia. Eine Untersuchung zu den Klagen Jeremias und ihrer Bedeutung zum Verstehen seines Leidens." PhD diss., University of Heidelberg, 1978.

Eichrodt, Walther. *Theology of the Old Testament*. 1964. Translated by John Baker. Philadelphia: Westminster, 1967.

Eissfeldt, Otto. *Der Maschal im Alten Testament*. Giessen: Töpelmann, 1913.

———. *The Old Testament: An Introduction*. 1934. Translated by P. Ackroyd. New York: Harper & Row, 1965.
Eliade, Mircea. *The Sacred and the Profane*. New York: Harcourt, Brace, Jovanovich, 1959.
———. *Shamanism: Archaic Techniques of Ecstasy*, 1951. Reprint. New York: Penguin, 1964.
Ellenbogen, Maximilian. *Foreign Words in the Old Testament: Their Origin and Etymology*. London: Luzac, 1962.
Elliger, Karl. *Leviticus*. Tübingen: Mohr Siebeck, 1966.
———. *Das Buch der zwölf kleinen Propheten: Vol. 25, Die Propheten Nahum, Habakuk, Zephanja, Haggai, Sacharja und Malachi*. Göttingen: Vandenhoeck & Ruprecht, 1967.
Elliott, Kimberly Ann, ed. *Corruption and the Global Economy*. Washington, DC: Institute of International Economics, 1997.
Elwolde, John. "The Hodayot's Use of the Psalter: Text-Critical Contributions (Book 2: Pss 42–72)." In *The Dead Sea Scrolls in Context: Integrating the Dead Sea Scrolls in the Study of Ancient Texts, Languages and Cultures*, edited by A. Lange et al., 79–100. Leiden: Brill, 2011.
Engelken, Karen. *Frauen im Alten Israel: Eine begriffsgeschichtliche und sozialrechtliche Studie zur Stellung der Frau im Alten Testament*. Stuttgart: Kohlhammer, 1990.
Englander, Lawrence A., and Herbert W. Basser, eds. *The Mystical Study of Ruth: Midrash HaNe'elam of the Zohar to the Book of Ruth*. Atlanta: Scholars, 1993.
Ephraem the Syrian. *The Pearl: Seven Hymns on the Faith*. Translated and Introduction by Kathleen M. McVey. New York: Paulist Press, 1989.
Epperly, Bruce G. *Process Theology: A Guide for the Perplexed*. London: T. & T. Clark, 2011.
Escott, H, ed. *The Cure of Souls: An Anthology of P. T. Forsyth's Practical Writings*. Grand Rapids: Eerdmans, 1971.
Esler, Philip F., and Anselm C. Hagedorn. "Social-Scientific Analysis of the Old Testament: A Brief History and Overview." In *Ancient Israel: The Old Testament in Its Social Context*, edited by P. F. Esler, 15–32. Minneapolis: Augsburg Fortress, 2006.
Evans, Carl D. "Naram-Sin and Jeroboam: The Archetypal *Unheilsherrscher* in Mesopotamian and Biblical Historiography." In *Scripture in Context II: More Essays on the Comparative Method*, edited by W. W. Hallo et al., 97–125. Winona Lake, IN: Eisenbrauns, 1983.
Everson, A. J. "The Days of Yahweh." *JBL* 93 (1974) 329–37.
Everstadt, Mary. *How the West Really Lost God: A New Theory of Secularization*. West Conshocken, PA: Templeton, 2013.
Ewald, Heinrich. *Die Dichter des alten Bundes*. Göttingen: Vandenhoeck & Ruprecht, 1866.
———. *Die Propheten des alten Testaments, Vol. 2: Jeremja und Hezeqiel mit ihren Zeitgenossen*. Göttingen: Vandenhoeck & Ruprecht, 1868.
Exum, J. Cheryl. *Fragmented Women: Feminist (Sub)Versions of Biblical Narratives*. Sheffield, UK: JSOT, 1993.
Fakhry, Majid. "Islam." In *Routledge Companion to Philosophy of Religion*, edited by C. Meister and P. Copan, 76–86. London: Routledge, 2007.

Farber, Walter. *Lamaštu: An Edition of the Canonical Series of Lamaštu Incantations and Rituals and Related Texts from the Second and First Millenia B.C.* Winona Lake, IN: Eisenbrauns, 2014.

———. "Witchcraft, Magic, and Divination in Ancient Mesopotamia." In *CANE* 1895–1909.

Feder, Yitzhaq. *Blood Expiation in Hittite and Biblical Ritual: Origins, Context and Meaning.* Atlanta: SBL, 2011.

Feliu, Lluís. *The God Dagan in Bronze Age Syria.* Translated by W. G. E. Watson. Leiden: Brill, 2003.

Fensham, Frank Charles. "A Possible Origin of the Concept of the Day of the Lord." In *Biblical Essays*, edited by A. van Zyl, 90–97. Potschefstroom: Herald, 1966.

———. "The Treaty between the Israelites and Tyrians." *VTSup* 17 (1969) 71–87.

———. "The Treaty between Solomon and Hiram and the Alalakh Tablets." *JBL* 79 (1960) 59–60.

Fewell, Danna Nolan, and David M. Gunn. *Compromising Redemption: Relating Characters in the Book of Ruth.* Louisville, KY: Westminster John Knox, 1990.

Fields, Weston W. *Sodom and Gomorrah: History and Motif in Biblical Narrative.* Sheffield, UK: Sheffield Academic, 1997.

Finet, A. "Le port d'Emar sur l'Euphrate, entre le royaume de Mari et le pays de Canaan." In *The Land of Israel: Crossroads of Civilizations*, edited by E. Lipiński, 27–38. Leuven: Peeters, 1985.

Finkel, Irving L. "Necromancy in Ancient Mesopotamia." *AfO* 29 (1983) 1–17.

Finkelstein, Israel. *The Archaeology of the Period of the Settlement and Judges.* Tel Aviv: Hakibbutz Hameuchad, 1986.

Fischoff, Ephraim. "Translator's Preface" to *The Sociology of Religion*, by Max Weber, xix–xxix. 1963. Reprint. Boston: Beacon, 1993.

Fisher, Loren R. "ŠDYN in Job xix 29." *VT* 11 (1961) 342–43.

Fitzmyer, Joseph A. *The Aramaic Inscriptions of Sefîre.* Rome: Pontifical Biblical Institute, 1967.

Fleming, Daniel E. *The Installation of Ba'al's High Priestess at Emar: A Window on Ancient Syrian Religion.* Atlanta: Scholars, 1992.

———. *Time at Emar: The Cultic Calendar and the Rituals from the Diviner's Archive.* Winona Lake, IN: Eisenbrauns, 2000.

Fohrer, Georg. *History of Israelite Religion.* 1969. Translated by David A. Green. Nashville: Abingdon, 1972.

———. "Krankheit im Lichte des alten Testaments." In *Studien zu alttestamentlichen Texte und Themen*, 172–87. Berlin: De Gruyter, 1981.

Fokkelman, Jan P. *Narrative Art and Poetry in the Books of Samuel.* Assen: Van Gorcum, 1981.

———. *Reading Biblical Narrative: An Introductory Guide.* Leiden: Deo, 1999.

Forster, Edward Morgan. *Aspects of the Novel.* London: Arnold, 1927.

Foster, Benjamin. "In Search of Akkadian Literature." In *Before the Muses: An Anthology of Akkadian Literature*, 1–47. Bethesda, MD: CDL, 2005.

Frankena, Rintje. *Kanttekeningen van een Asyrioloog bij Ezechiël.* Leiden: Brill, 1965.

Frankfort, Henri. *Kingship and the Gods.* Chicago: University of Chicago, 1948.

Frantz-Szabó, Gabriella. "Hittite Witchcraft, Magic and Divination." In *CANE* 2007–19.

Frazer, James. *Folk-lore in the Old Testament.* London: McMillan, 1919.

———. *The Golden Bough.* New York: MacMillan, 1922.

Freedman, David Noel. *Pottery, Poetry and Prophecy: Studies in Early Hebrew Poetry*. Winona Lake, IN: Eisenbrauns, 1980.
Freeman, John. *Solomon and Balkis*. London: MacMillan, 1926.
Fretheim, Terence. *First and Second Kings*. Louisville, KY: Westminster John Knox, 1999.
Fried, Lisbeth. *Ezra and the Law in History and Tradition*. Columbia, SC: University of South Carolina Press, 2014.
Friedman, Richard Elliott. "Tabernacle." In *ABD* 6.292–300.
———. "Is Everybody a Bible Expert? Not the Authors of *The Book of J*." *Bible Review* 7 (1991) 16–18, 50–51.
———. *Who Wrote the Bible*? New York: Simon & Schuster, 1987.
Friedrich, Johannes. "'Angst' und 'Schrecken' als niedere Gottheiten bei Griechen und Hethitern." *AfO* 17 (1954–55) 148, 156.
———. *Hethitisches Elementarbuch*. Heidelberg: Winter, 1967.
Frolov, Serge. *Judges*. Grand Rapids: Eerdmans, 2013.
Frye, Northrop. *Anatomy of Criticism*. Princeton: Princeton University Press, 1971.
Frymer-Kensky, Tikva. *In the Wake of the Goddesses: Women, Culture, and the Biblical Transformation of Pagan Myth*. New York: Free, 1992.
———. *Reading the Women of the Bible: A New Interpretation of Their Stories*. New York: Schocken, 2002.
Fuchs, Esther. *Sexual Politics in the Biblical Narrative: Reading the Hebrew Bible as a Woman*. Sheffield, UK: Sheffield Academic Press, 2000.
Gaddy, C. Welton. *Soul under Siege: Surviving Clergy Depression*. Louisville, KY: Westminster John Knox, 1991.
Gailey, James H. Review of *Lamentations*, by N. Gottwald. *Int* 9 (1955) 471–72.
Gaines, Janet Howe. *Forgiveness in a Wounded World: Jonah's Dilemma*. Leiden: Brill, 2003.
Galling, Kurt. "Kohelet Studien." *ZAW* 50 (1932) 276–99.
Gammie, John G. "The Classification, Stages of Growth, and Changing Intentions in the Book of Daniel." *JBL* 95 (1976) 191–204.
Ganjavī, Nizāmī. *Kullīyāt-i Khamsa-yi Hakīm Nizāmī Ganjavī*, 1331. Reprint. Tehran: ʿAli Akbar ʿIlmi, 1952.
García Martínez, Florentino. *Wisdom and Apocalypticism in the Dead Sea Scrolls and in the Biblical Tradition*. Leuven: Peeters, 2003.
Garcia-Treto, Francisco. "The Fall of the House: A Carnivalesque Reading of 2 Kings 9 and 10." *JSOT* 46 (1990) 47–65.
Garr, W. Randall. *Dialect Geography of Syria-Palestine, 1000–586 B.C.E.* Philadelphia: University of Pennsylvania, 1985.
Gaster, Theodor Herzl. *Myth, Legend and Custom in the Old Testament*. New York: Harper & Row, 1969.
Geller, Markham J. *Ancient Babylonian Medicine: Theory and Practice*. Malden, MA: Wiley-Blackwell, 2010.
———. "Incipits and Rubrics." In *Wisdom, Gods, and Literature: Studies in Assyriology in Honour of W. G. Lambert*, edited by A. R. George and L. L. Finkel, 225–58. Winona Lake, IN: Eisenbrauns, 2000.
George, Andrew R. *Babylonian Topographical Texts*. Leuven: Peeters, 1992.
———. *The Babylonian Gilgamesh Epic: Introduction, Critical Edition and Cuneiform Texts*. Oxford: Oxford University Press, 2003.

Gerleman, Gillis. *Ruth, Das Hohe Lied*. Neukirchen-Vluyn: Neukirchener Verlag, 1981.
Gerstenberger, Erhard S. *Israel in the Persian Period: The Fifth and Fourth Centuries B.C.E.*, 2005. Translated by S. Schatzmann. Atlanta: SBL, 2011.
———. "Jeremiah's Complaints: Observations on Jer. 15:10–21." *JBL* 82 (1963) 393–408.
———. *Wesen und Herkunft des "apodiktisches Rechts."* Neukirchen-Vluyn: Neukirchener, 1965.
Gese, Hartmut. "Komposition bei Amos." *VTSup* 32 (1981) 74–95.
Ghantous, Hadi. *The Elisha-Hazael Paradigm and the Kingdom of Israel: The Politics of God in Ancient Syria-Palestine*. New York: Routledge, 2014.
Gilders, William K. *Blood Ritual in the Hebrew Bible: Meaning and Power*. Baltimore: Johns Hopkins, 2004.
Gillihan, Yonder M. *Civic Ideology, Organization, and Law in the Rule Scrolls: A Comparative Study of the Covenanters' Sect and Contemporary Voluntary Associations in Political Context*. Leiden: Brill, 2012.
Giovino, Mariana. *The Assyrian Sacred Tree: A History of Interpretations*. Göttingen: Vandenhoeck & Ruprecht, 2007.
Glanzman, George. "The Origin and Date of the Book of Ruth." *CBQ* 21 (1959) 201–7.
Glazer, Myron P., and Penina M. Glazer. *The Whistleblowers: Exposing Corruption in Government and Industry*. New York: Basic, 1991.
Glazov, Gregory Yuri. *The Bridling of the Tongue and the Opening of the Mouth in Biblical Prophecy*. Sheffield, UK: Sheffield Academic Press, 2001.
Glueck, Nelson. *Das Wort חסד im alttestamentlichen Sprachgebrauche als menschliche und gottliche gemeinschaftgemasse Verhaltungsweise*. Giessen: Töpelmann, 1927.
Gnuse, Robert K. "Dreams in the Ancient World." In *Dreams and Dream-Reports in the Writings of Josephus: A Traditio-Historical Analysis*, 34–128. Leiden: Brill, 1996.
Godelier, Maurice. *The Enigma of the Gift*. Chicago: University of Chicago Press, 1999.
Goethe, Johann Wolfgang von. *Goethe's Werke*. Vol. 21/23. Edited by C. Schüddekopf. Weimar: Böhlau, 1898.
———. *Wisdom and Experience*. Translated by H. H. Weigand. New York: Pantheon, 1949.
Goettsberger, Johann. *Das Buch Daniel*. Bonn: Hanstein, 1928.
Goetze, Albrecht. *Kulturgeschichte Kleinasiens*. München: Beck'sche, 1957.
———, ed. *Verstreute Boghazöi-Texte*. Marburg: Lahn, 1930.
Gogarten, Friedrich. *Verhängnis und Hoffnung der Neuzeit. Die Säkularisierung als theologisches Problem*. Stuttgart: Kohlhammer, 1953.
Goldberg, Arnold M. *Untersuchungen über die Vorstellung von der Schekhinah in der frühen rabbinischen Literatur*. Berlin: De Gruyter, 1969.
Goldingay, John. *Job for Everyone*. Louisville, KY: Westminster John Knox, 2013.
———. *Models for Interpretation of Scripture*. Grand Rapids: Eerdmans, 1995.
———. *Theological Diversity and the Authority of the Old Testament*. Grand Rapids: Eerdmans, 1987.
———, ed. *Uprooting and Planting: Essays on Jeremiah for Leslie Allen*. London: T. & T. Clark, 2007.
Goldziher, Ignaz. *Abhandlungen zur arabischen Philologie. Erster Teil*. Leiden: Brill, 1896.
Goodblatt, David M. *Elements of Ancient Jewish Nationalism*. Cambridge: Cambridge University Press, 2006.

Goodenough, W. R. "Rethinking 'Status' and 'Role': Toward a General Model of the Cultural Organization of Social Relationships." In *The Relevance of Models for Social Anthropology*, edited by M. Banton, 1–24. London: Tavistock, 1965.

Goodnick-Westenholz, Joan. "Emar: The City and Its God." In *Languages and Cultures in Contact: At the Crossroads of Civilizations in the Syro-Mesopotamian Realm*, edited by K. van Lerberghe and G. Voet, 145–68. Leuven: Peeters, 1999.

Gordis, Robert. *The Book of Job*. New York: Jewish Theological Seminary of America, 1978.

———. *Poets, Prophets and Sages: Essays in Biblical Interpretation*. Bloomington, IN: Indiana University Press, 1971.

Gordon, Cyrus H. *Adventures in the Nearest East*. London: Phoenix House, 1957.

Gorman, Frank H., Jr. *The Ideology of Ritual: Space, Time and Status in the Priestly Theology*. Sheffield, UK: JSOT, 1990.

———. "Ritual Studies and Biblical Studies: Assessment of the Past, Prospects for the Future." *Sem* 67 (1994) 13–36.

Gottwald, Norman K. *The Hebrew Bible: A Brief Socio-Literary Introduction*. Minneapolis: Fortress, 2009.

———. *The Politics of Ancient Israel*. Louisville, KY: Westminster John Knox, 2001.

———. *Studies in the Book of Lamentations*. London: SCM, 1954.

Goulder, Michael. "Sophia in 1 Corinthians." *NTS* 37 (1991) 516–34.

Grabbe, Lester L., ed. *Ahab Agonistes: The Rise and Fall of the Omri Dynasty*. London: T. & T. Clark, 2007.

———. *Priests, Prophets, Diviners, Sages: A Socio-Historical Study of Religious Specialists in Ancient Israel*. Valley Forge, PA: Trinity, 1995.

———. *Wisdom of Solomon*, 1997. Reprint. London: T. & T. Clark, 2003.

Gray, George Buchanan. *A Critical and Exegetical Commentary on the Book of Numbers*. Edinburgh: T. & T. Clark, 1903.

Gray, John B. *1 & 2 Kings*. Philadelphia, Westminster, 1970.

———. "The Blood Bath of the Goddess Anat in the Ras Shamra Texts." *UF* 11 (1979) 315–24.

———. *The Legacy of Canaan: The Ras Shamra Texts and Their Relevance to the Old Testament*. Leiden: Brill, 1957.

Grayson, A. Kirk. *Assyrian Rulers of the Early First Millennium BC, II*. Toronto: University of Toronto Press, 1996.

Green, Alberto R. W. "Social Stratification and Cultural Continuity at Alalakh." In *The Quest for the Kingdom of God: Studies in Honor of George E. Mendenhall*, edited by H. B. Huffmon et al., 181–204. Winona Lake, IN: Eisenbrauns, 1983.

Greenberg, David F. *The Construction of Homosexuality*. Chicago: University of Chicago Press, 1988.

Greenfield, Jonas C. "Hadad." In *DDD* 377–82.

Greengus, Samuel. "Biblical and Ancient Near Eastern Law." In *ABD* 4.242–52.

Greenstein, Edward L. "Jeremiah as an Inspiration to the Poet Job." In *Inspired Speech: Prophecy in the Ancient Near East: Essays Presented to Herbert B. Huffmon*, edited by J. Kaltner & L. Stulman, 98–110. New York: Continuum, 2004.

Grenz, Stanley J. *Welcoming, But Not Affirming: An Evangelical Response to Homosexuality*. Louisville, KY: Westminster John Knox, 1998.

Gressmann, Hugo. *Der Ursprung der israelitische-jüdischen Eschatologie*. Göttingen: Vandenhoeck & Ruprecht, 1905.

Grieshammer, Reinhard. "Altes Testament." In *Lexicon der Ägyptologie*, edited by W. Helck and E. Otto, 163–66. Wiesbaden: Harrassowitz, 1972–73.

Griffin, Dustin H. *Satire: A Critical Reintroduction*. Lexington, KY: University of Kentucky Press, 1994.

Griffiths, John Gwyn. *The Origins of Osiris and His Cult*. Leiden: Brill, 1980.

Gross, Walther. *Bileam. Literar- und formkritische Untersuchung der Prosa in Num 22–24*. München, Kösel, 1974.

Grossfeld, Bernard. *The Two Targums of Esther: Translated, with Apparatus and Notes*. Collegeville, MN: Liturgical Press, 1991.

Gross Schaeffer, Arthur and Steve Jacobsen. "Understanding Clergy Burnout: A Guide for Spiritual Directors Working with Religious Leaders." *Presence: An International Journal of Spiritual Direction* 2 (2009) 20–30.

———. "Surviving Clergy Burnout." *Encounter* 70 (2009) 37–66.

Gruenwald, Ithamar. תעשה: *Rituals and Ritual Theory in Ancient Israel*. Leiden: Brill, 2010.

Guest, Deryn. "Judges." In *ECB* 190–207.

Guilhamet, Leon. *Satire and the Transformation of Genre*. Philadelphia: University of Pennsylvania, 1987.

Gunkel, Hermann. *Einleitung in die Psalmen*, 2nd ed. Göttingen: Vandenhoeck & Ruprecht, 1966.

———. *Israel and Babylon: The Babylonian Influence on Israelite Religion*. 1902. Reprint. Translated and edited by K. C. Hanson. Eugene, OR: Cascade, 2009.

———. *The Legends of Genesis*. Translated by W. H. Carruth. Chicago: Open Court, 1901.

———. "Ruth." In *Rede und Aufsätze*, 65–92. Göttingen: Vandenhoeck & Ruprecht, 1913.

Gunn, David M. *The Story of King David: Genre and Interpretation*. Sheffield, UK: JSOT, 1978.

Gurney, Oliver R. "The Babylonians and Hittites." In *Oracles and Divination*, edited by M. Loewe and C. Blacker, 142–73. Boulder, CO: Shambhala, 1981.

———. *Some Aspects of Hittite Religion*. Oxford: University Press, 1977.

Guthrie, Stewart. "Religion as Anthropomorphism." In *Faces in the Clouds: A New Theory of Religion*. Oxford: University Press, 1993.

Haag, Herbert. "Gad und Nathan." In *Archäologie und Altes Testament: Festschrift für Kurt Galling*, edited by A. Kuschke and E. Kutsch, 135–43. Tübingen: Mohr (Siebeck), 1970.

Haak, Robert D. *Habakkuk*. Leiden: Brill, 1992.

Haas, Volker. *Hethitische Orakel, Vorzeichen und Abwehrstrategien*. Berlin: De Gruyter, 2008.

Haas, Volker, and Gernot Wilhelm. *Hurritisch und luwische Riten aus Kizzuwatna*. Kevelaer: Butzon & Bercker, 1974.

Haas, Volker, and H. J. Thiel. *Die Beschwörungsrituale der Allaituraḫḫi und verwandte Texte*. Kevelaer: Butzon & Bercker, 1978.

Haas, Volker, and I. Wegner. *Die Rituale der Beschwörerinnen* ^{SAL}ŠU.GI. *I: Die Texte*. Roma: Multigrafica Editrice, 1988.

Habel, Norman C. *The Book of Job: A Commentary*. Philadelphia: Westminster, 1985.

Hackett, Jo Ann. *The Balaam Text from Deir ʿAllā*. Chico, CA: Scholars, 1980.

Hadley, Judith M. *The Cult of Asherah in Ancient Israel and Judah: Evidence for a Hebrew Goddess*. Cambridge: Cambridge University Press, 2000.
Haldar, Alfred Ossian. *Associations of Cult Prophets Among the Ancient Semites*. Uppsala: Almqvist & Wiksells, 1945.
Hallo, William W. "New Viewpoints on Cuneiform Literature." *IEJ* 12 (1962) 13–26.
Halpern, Baruch. *David's Secret Demons: Messiah, Murderer, Traitor, King*. Grand Rapids: Eerdmans, 2001.
———. "Dialect Distribution in Canaan and the Deir ʿAllā Inscriptions." In *Working with No Data: Semitic and Egyptian Studies Presented to Thomas O. Lambdin*, edited by D. M. Golomb and S. T. Hollis, 119–40. Winona Lake, IN: Eisenbrauns, 1987.
———. *The First Historians: The Hebrew Bible and History*. San Francisco: Harper & Row, 1988.
———."Yaua, Son of Omri, Yet Again." *BASOR* 265 (1987) 81–85.
Halpern, Baruch, and Jon D. Levenson, eds. *Traditions in Transformation: Turning Points in Biblical Faith*. Winona Lake, IL: Eisenbrauns, 1981.
Hals, Ronald. *The Theology of the Book of Ruth*. Philadelphia: Fortress, 1969.
Hamilton, Gordon J. Review of *The Balaam Traditions: Their Character and Development*, by M. S. Moore. *JBL* 110 (1991) 703–6.
Handy, Lowell K. "The Appearance of Pantheon in Judah." In *The Triumph of Elohim: From Yahwisms to Judaisms*, edited by D. V. Edelman, 27–44. Kampen: Kok Pharos, 1995.
Hanson, K. C. "When the King Crosses the Line: Royal Deviance and Restitution in Levantine Ideologies." *BTB* 26 (1996) 11–25.
Hanson, Paul. *The Dawn of Apocalyptic: The Historical and Sociological Roots of Jewish Apocalyptic Eschatology*. Philadelphia: Fortress, 1979.
———. *The People Called: The Growth of Community in the Bible*, 1986. Reprint. Louisville, KY: Westminster John Knox, 2001.
Haran, Menachem. *Temples and Temple Service in Ancient Israel: An Inquiry into Biblical Cult Phenomena and the Historical Setting of the Priestly School*. Winona Lake, IN: Eisenbrauns, 1985.
Harding, James E. "The Silent Goddess and the Gendering of Divine Speech in Jeremiah 44." In *Prophecy and Power: Jeremiah in Feminist and Postcolonial Perspective*, edited by C. Mayer and C. Sharp, 208–23. New York: Bloomsbury, 2013.
Harkins, Angela Kim. "Observations on the Editorial Shaping of the So-Called Community Hymns from 1QH^a and 4QH^a (4Q427)." *DSD* 12 (2005) 233–56.
———. *Reading with an "I" to the Heavens: Looking at the Qumran Hodayot Through a Visionary Lens*. Berlin: De Gruyter, 2012.
Harnisch, Sebastian, "Role Theory: Operationalization of Key Concepts." In *Role Theory in International Relations: Approaches and Analyses*, edited by S. Harnisch et al., 1–17. London: Routledge, 2012.
Harper, Robert F. *Assyrian and Babylonian Letters belonging to the Kouyunjik Collection of the British Museum*, 1892–1914. Reprint. New York: N & N, 1977.
Harrington, Daniel J. "Afterlife Expectations in Pseudo-Philo, 4 Ezra and 2 Baruch, and their Implications for the New Testament." In *Resurrection in the New Testament: FS J. Lambrecht*, edited by R. Bieringer et al., 21–34. Leuven: Peeters, 2002.
———. *Pseudo-Philon, Les Antiquités bibliques 1: Introduction et texte critique*. Translated by J. Cazeaux. Paris: Editions du Cerf, 1976.

Harrison, Roland K. *Introduction to the Old Testament*. Grand Rapids: Eerdmans, 1969.
Hasel, Gerhard F. *Old Testament Theology: Basic Issues in the Current Debate*. Grand Rapids: Eerdmans, 1991.
———. "Resurrection in the Theology of OT Apocalyptic." *ZAW* 92 (1980) 267–83.
Hatina, Thomas R. "David." In *EOHJ* 130–32.
Hauerwas, Stanley, and William H. Willimon. *Resident Aliens: Life in the Christian Colony*. 1989. Reprint. Nashville: Abingdon, 2014.
Häusl, Maria, and Hildegard König. "Auf dem Weg." In *Tochter Zion auf dem Weg zum himmlischen Jerusalem. Rezeptionslinien der "Stadtfrau Jerusalem" von den späten alttestamentlichen Texten bis zu den Werken der Kirchenväter*, edited by M. Häusl, 11–49. Leipzig: Leipziger Universitätsverlag, 2011.
Hayes, Christopher B. *Hidden Riches: A Sourcebook for the Comparative Study of the Hebrew Bible and the Ancient Near East*. Louisville, KY: Westminster John Knox, 2014.
Hayter, Mary. *The New Eve in Christ: The Use and Abuse of the Bible in the Debate about Women in the Church*. Grand Rapids: Eerdmans, 1987.
Hegel, Georg Wilhelm Friedrich. "Systemfragment von 1800." In *Hegels theologische Jugendschriften*, edited by H. Nohl, 343–51. Tübingen: Mohr, 1907.
Heidelberger, Michael. "From Mill via von Kries to Max Weber: Causality, Explanation and Understanding." In *Historical Perspectives on Erklären und Verstehen*, edited by U. Feest, 241–66. New York: Springer, 2010.
Heimpel, Wolfgang. *Letters to the King of Mari: A New Translation, with Historical Introduction, Notes, and Commentary*. Winona Lake, IN: Eisenbrauns, 2003.
Heine, Suzanne. *Christianity and the Goddesses*. London: SCM, 1988.
Heinrich, Ernst. *Die Tempel und Heiligtümer im alten Mesopotamien*. Berlin: De Gruyter, 1982.
Heintz, Jean-Georges. "Aux origines d'un expression biblique: *ūmūšû qerbū* in *ARM*, X/6, 8′?" *VT* 21 (1971) 528–40.
———. "Oracles prophetiques et 'guerre sainte' selon les archives royales de Mari et l'Ancien Testament." *VTSup* 17 (1969) 112–38.
———. "Royal Traits and Messianic Figures: A Thematic and Iconographical Approach." In *The Messiah: Developments in Earliest Judaism and Christianity*, edited by J. A. Charlesworth, 52–66. Minneapolis: Fortress, 1992.
Hendel, Ronald S. Review of *Sodom and Gomorrha*, by Weston W. Fields. *JBL* 118 (1999) 126–28.
———. "The Social Origins of the Aniconic Tradition in Early Israel." *CBQ* 50 (1988) 365–82.
Hengel, Martin. *Judaism and Hellenism: Studies in Their Encounter in Palestine during the Early Hellenistic Period*. 1973. Translated by John Bowden. Philadelphia: Fortress, 1974.
Herrmann, Siegfried. *A History of Israel in Old Testament Times*. 1973. Translated by J. Bowden. Reprint. Philadelphia: Fortress, 1981.
Herrmann, Wolfgang. "El." In *DDD* 274–80.
Heschel, Abraham. *The Sabbath: Its Meaning for Modern Man*. New York: Farrar, Strauss & Young, 1951.
Heschel, Susannah. *The Aryan Jesus: Christian Theologians and the Bible in Nazi Germany*. Princeton: Princeton University Press, 2008.
Hess, Richard S. *Amarna Personal Names*. Winona Lake, IN: Eisenbrauns, 1993.

Hiebert, Theodore. "Theophany in the Old Testament." *ABD* 6.505–11.
Hiers, Richard H. "Day of the Lord." In *ABD* 2.82–83.
Hilber, John W. *Cultic Prophecy in the Psalms.* Berlin: De Gruyter, 2005.
Hillers, Delbert R. "The Bow of Aqhat." In *Orient and Occident*, edited by H. Hoffner, 71–80. Kevelaer: Butzon & Bercker, 1973.
———. *Lamentations: A New Translation with Introduction and Commentary.* Garden City, NY: Doubleday, 1972.
Himmelfarb, Martha. *A Kingdom of Priests: Ancestry and Merit in Ancient Judaism.* Philadelphia: University of Pennsylvania, 2006.
Hofman, Abel. *Jeremia 23,16–32 (Falsche Propheten).* Norderstedt: GRIN Verlag, 2010.
Hoffman, Georg. "Versuch zu Amos." *ZAW* 3 (1883) 87–126.
Hoffmann, Hans-Detlef. *Reform und Reformen: Untersuchungen zu einem Grundthema der deuteronomistischen Geschichtsschreibung.* Zurich: Theologischer Verlag, 1980.
Hoffman, Yair. *A Blemished Perfection: The Book of Job in Context.* Sheffield, UK: Academic Press, 1996.
Hoffner, Harry A. "בית." In *TDOT* 2.107–16.
Hoftijzer, Jacob. "David and the Tekoite Woman." *VT* 20 (1970) 419–44.
———. *Die Verheissungen an die drei Erzväter.* Leiden: Brill, 1956.
Hoftijzer, Jacob, and Gerrit van der Kooij, eds. *Aramaic Texts from Deir ʿAllā.* Leiden: Brill, 1976.
Hoftijzer, Jacob, and Geritt van der Kooij, eds. *The Balaam Text from Deir ʿAllā Re-Evaluated.* Leiden: Brill, 1991.
Holbert, John C. "The Bible Becomes Literature: An Encounter with Ruth." *WW* 13 (1993) 130–35.
———. "Keren-Happuch." In *ABD* 4.24.
———. "'The Skies Will Uncover His Iniquity': Satire in the Second Speech of Zophar (Job XX)." *VT* 31 (1981) 171–79.
Holladay, Carl R. *Fragments from Hellenistic Jewish Authors, Volume 1: Historians.* Chico, CA: Scholars, 1983.
Holladay, William S. *Jeremiah 1: A Commentary on the Book of Jeremiah, Chapters 1–25.* Philadelphia: Fortress, 1986.
———. "A Fresh Look at 'Source B' and 'Source C' in Jeremiah." *VT* 25 (1975) 402–8.
———. *The Root* שוב *in the Old Testament.* Leiden: Brill, 1959.
Holm-Nielsen, Svend. *Hodayot: Psalms from Qumran.* Leiden: Brill, 1960.
Hölscher, Gustav. *Die Ürsprunge der jüdischen Eschatologie.* Berlin: Töpelmann, 1925.
Hopkins, David S. "Between Promise and Fulfillment: Von Rad and the 'Sacrifice of Abraham.'" *BZ* 24 (1980) 180–93.
Hopkins, Denise Dombrowski. "The Qumran Community and 1QHodayot: A Reassessment." *RevQ* 10 (1981) 323–64.
Hopper, Stanley R. "The 'Terrible Sonnets' of Gerard Manley Hopkins and the 'Confessions' of Jeremiah." *Sem* 13 (1978) 29–73.
Horsley, Richard A. *Covenant Economics: A Biblical Vision of Justice for All.* Louisville, KY: Westminster John Knox, 2009.
Horster, Marietta, and Anna Klöckner, eds. *Civic Priests: Cult Personnel in Athens from the Hellenistic Period to Late Antiquity.* Berlin: De Gruyter, 2011.
Horton, Fred L. *The Melchizedek Tradition: A Critical Examination of the Sources to the Fifth Century A.D. and in the Epistle to the Hebrews.* Cambridge: Cambridge University Press, 1976.

Hubbard, Robert L. *The Book of Ruth*. Grand Rapids: Eerdmans, 1988.
Hubmann, Franz. "Jer 18:18-23 im Zusammenhang der Konfessionen." In *Le Livre de Jérémie*, edited by P.-M. Bogaert, 280-93. Leuven: University Press, 1981.
Huey, F. B., Jr. *Jeremiah, Lamentations*. Nashville: Broadman, 1993.
Huffmon, Herbert Bardwell. "The Covenant Lawsuit in the Prophets." *JBL* 78 (1959) 285-95.
———. "Israel of God." *Int* 23 (1969) 66-77.
———. "Priestly Divination in Israel." In *The Word of the Lord Shall Go Forth: Essays in Honor of David Noel Freedman*, edited by C. L. Meyers and M. O'Connor, 355-59. Winona Lake, IN: Eisenbrauns, 1983.
———. "Prophecy, Ancient Near Eastern." In *ABD* 5.477-82.
Hughes, Julie A. *Scriptural Allusions and Exegesis in the Hodayot*. Leiden: Brill, 2006.
Hundley, Michael. *Gods in Dwellings: Temples and Divine Presence in the Ancient Near East*. Atlanta: SBL, 2013.
Hunter, Austin Vanlier. *Seek the Lord! A Study of the Meaning and Function of the Exhortations in Amos, Hosea, Isaiah, Micah, and Zephaniah*. Baltimore: St. Mary's Seminary and University, 1982.
Hutter, Manfred. *Altorientalische Vorstellungen von der Unterwelt: Literar- und religionsgeschichtliche Überlegungen zu "Nergal und Ereškigal."* Göttingen: Vandenhoeck & Ruprecht, 1985.
Hyatt, J. Philip. *Jeremiah*. Nashville: Abingdon, 1956.
———. "Torah in the Book of Jeremiah." *JBL* 60 (1941)
Irsigler, Hubert. *Gottesgericht und Jahwetag. Die Komposition Zef 1,1 -2,3, untersucht auf der Grundlage der Literarkritik des Zefanjabuches*. St. Ottilien: EOS Verlag, 1977.
Irwin, William A. "Job's Redeemer." *JBL* 81 (1962) 217-29.
Isbell, Charles D. *Corpus of the Aramaic Incantation Bowls*. Missoula: Scholars Press, 1975.
Ishida, Tomoo. *History and Historical Writing in Ancient Israel: Studies in Biblical Historiography*. Leiden: Brill, 1999.
Irvine, Stuart. "The Threat of Jezreel (Hosea 1:4-5)." *CBQ* 57 (1995) 494-503.
Ittmann, Norbert. *Die Konfessionen Jeremias. Ihre Bedeutung für die Verkündigung des Propheten*. Neukirchen-Vluyn: Neukirchener, 1981.
Iwry, Samuel. "New Evidence for Belomancy in Ancient Palestine and Phoenicia." *JAOS* 81 (1961) 27-34.
Jacobsen, Thorkild, and Kirsten Nielsen. "Cursing the Day." *SJOT* 6 (1992) 187-204.
Jagersma, Hendrik. "ישׂיח in 1 Könige xviii 27." *VT* 25 (1975) 674-76.
Jahnow, Hedwig. *Das hebräische Leichenlied im Rahmen der Völkerdichtung*. Giessen: Töpelmann, 1923.
Janzen, J. Gerald. "Another Look at God's Watch Over Job." *JBL* 108 (1989) 109-16.
———. *Job*. Louisville, KY: Westminster John Knox, 1985.
———. *Studies in the Text of Jeremiah*. Cambridge: Harvard, 1973.
Japhet, Sara. "ושׁם יד (Isa 56:5)—A Different Proposal." *Maarav* 8 (1992) 69-80.
Jeanrond, Werner G. "Interpretation, History of." In *ABD* 3.433-43.
Jeffers, Ann. *Magic and Divination in Ancient Palestine and Syria*. Leiden: Brill, 1996.
Jellicoe, Sidney. *The Septuagint and Modern Study*. Oxford: Oxford University Press, 1968.

Jemielity, Thomas. *Satire and the Hebrew Prophets*. Louisville, KY: Westminster John Knox, 1992.
Jeremias, Joachim. *Der Lehrer der Gerechtigkeit*. Göttingen: Vandenhoeck & Ruprecht, 1963.
Jeremias, Jörg. *Theophanie. Die Geschichte einer alttestamentlichen Gattung*. Neukirchen-Vluyn: Neukirchener, 1965.
Joas, Hans, and Klaus Wiegandt, eds. *Secularization and the World Religions*. Liverpool: Liverpool University Press, 2009.
Joines, Karen. "The Bronze Serpent in the Israelite Cult." *JBL* 87 (1968) 245–56.
Jones, Scott C. *Rumors of Wisdom: Job 28 as Poetry*. New York: De Gruyter, 2009.
Jonker, Louis C. *Exclusivity and Variety: Perspectives on Multidimensional Exegesis*. Kampen: Kok Pharos, 1996.
Joyce, Paul M. *Ezekiel: A Commentary*. London: T. & T. Clark, 2009.
Kaiser, Walter C. *Hard Sayings of the Bible*. Downers Grove, IL: InterVarsity, 1996.
Kalisch, Marcus M. *Bible Studies, Part I: The Prophecies of Balaam*. London: Longmans, Green and Co., 1877.
Kammenhuber, Annelies. *Orakelpraxis, Träume, und Vorzeichenschau bei den Hethitern*. Heidelberg: Carl Winter, 1976.
Kang, S. Steve, and Michael Feldman. "Transformed by the Transfiguration: Reflections on a Biblical Understanding of Transformation and Its Implications for Christian Education." *CEJ* 9 (2013) 365–77.
Kapelrud, Arvid S. *The Message of the Prophet Zephaniah*. Oslo: Universitetsvorlaget, 1975.
Karenga, Maulana. *Maat, the Moral Ideal in Ancient Egypt: A Study in Classical African Ethics*. New York: Routledge, 2004.
Katz, Claire Elise. *Levinas, Judaism, and the Feminine: The Silent Footsteps of Rebecca*. Bloomington, IN: Indiana University Press, 2003.
Kaufman, Stephen A. Review of *Aramaic Texts from Deir 'Allā*, by J. Hoftijzer and G. van der Kooij. *BASOR* 239 (1980) 71–74.
Kaufmann, Yeḥezkel. *Golah ve Nekhar I-IV: An Historical-Sociological Study Concerning the Fate of the Jewish People from Antiquity to the Modern Period*. Tel-Aviv: Dvir, 1929–32.
———. *The Religion of Israel: From Its Beginnings to the Babylonian Exile*, 1935. Translated by M. Greenberg. Chicago: University of Chicago Press, 1960.
Kayatz, Christa. *Studien zu Proverbien 1–9. Eine form und motivgeschichtliche Untersuchung*. Neukirchen-Vluyn: Neukirchener, 1966.
Keane, Catherine. *Figuring Genre in Roman Satire*. New York: Oxford University Press, 2006.
Keck, Elizabeth. "The Glory of Yahweh, Name Theology, and Ezekiel's Understanding of Divine Presence." PhD diss., Boston College, 2011.
Keesing, Roger M. "Toward a Model of Role Analysis." In *A Handbook of Method in Cultural Anthropology*, edited by R. Naroll and R. Cohen, 423–53. New York: Natural History, 1971.
Keil, Carl Friedrich. *Biblischer Commentar über den propheten Jeremia und die Klagelieder*. Leipzig: Dörffling & Franke, 1872.
Keller, Carl, and René Vuilleumier. *Michée, Nahoum, Habacuc et Sophonie*. Paris: Delachaux et Niestlé, 1971.

Kellermann, Ulrich. "Überwindung des Todesgeschicks in der alttestamentlichen Frömmigkeit vor und neben dem Auferstehungsglauben." *ZTK* 73 (1976) 259–82.

Kille, D. Andrew. *Psychological Biblical Criticism*. Minneapolis: Augsburg Fortress, 2001.

Kim, Koowon. *Incubation as a Type-Scene in the Aqhatu, Kirta, and Hannah Stories: A Form-Critical and Narratological Study of CAT 1.14.1—1.15.3, 1.17.1–2, and 1 Samuel 1:1—2:11*. Leiden: Brill, 2011.

King, Leonard W. *Babylonian Magic and Sorcery, being "The Prayers of the Lifting of the Hand."* 1896. Reprint. Boston: Red Wheel/Weiser, 2000.

Kitchen, Kenneth A. *On the Reliability of the Old Testament*. Grand Rapids: Eerdmans, 2003.

Kittel, Bonnie Pedrotti. *The Hymns of Qumran: Translation and Commentary*. Atlanta: Scholars Press, 1981.

Kitz, Anne Marie. "The Plural Form of *'ûrîm* and *tummîm*." *JBL* 116 (1997) 401–10.

———. "Prophecy as Divination." *CBQ* 65 (2003) 22–42.

Kiuchi, Nobuyoshi. *The Purification Offering in the Priestly Literature*. Sheffield, UK: JSOT, 1987.

Klawans, Jonathan. *Purity, Sacrifice and the Temple: Symbolism and Supersessionism in the Study of Ancient Judaism*. New York: Oxford, 2006.

Klein, Michael L. *The Fragment Targums of the Pentateuch*. Rome: Biblical Institute Press, 1980.

Klein, William W., et al. *Introduction to Biblical Interpretation*. Nashville: Thomas Nelson, 2004.

Kleiner, Michael. *Saul in En-Dor—Wahrsagung oder Totenbeschwörung? Eine synchrone und diachrone Untersuchung zu 1 Sam 28*. Leipzig: Benno, 1995.

Klingbeil, Gerald A. *Bridging the Gap: Ritual and Ritual Texts in the Bible*. Winona Lake, IN: Eisenbrauns, 2007.

———. *A Comparative Study of the Ritual of Ordination as Found in Leviticus 8 and Emar 369*. New York: Mellen, 1998.

Klinger, Jörg. *Untersuchungen zur Rekonstruktion des hattischen Kultschicht*. Wiesbaden: Harrassowitz, 1996.

Kloppenborg, John S. "Isis and Sophia in the Book of Wisdom." *HTR* 75 (1982) 57–84.

Knauf, Ernst A. Review of *The Balaam Text from Deir ʿAllā*, by Jo Ann Hackett. *ZDPV* 101 (1985) 191.

Knibb, Michael. *The Qumran Community*. Cambridge: Cambridge University Press, 1987.

Knierim, Rolf. *The Task of Old Testament Theology: Substance, Method and Cases*. Grand Rapids: Eerdmans, 1999.

Knight, Douglas A. *Rediscovering the Traditions of Israel*. Atlanta: Society of Biblical Literature, 2006.

Knohl, Israel. *The Sanctuary of Silence: The Priestly Torah and the Holiness School*. Minneapolis: Augsburg Fortress, 1995.

Knoppers, Gary N. *Two Nations Under God: The Deuteronomistic History of Solomon and the Dual Monarchies I: The Reign of Solomon and the Rise of Jeroboam*. Atlanta: Scholars, 1993.

Knudtzon, Johannes A. *Assyrische Gebete an den Sonnengott*. Leipzig, Pfeiffer, 1893.

———. *Die El Amarna Tafeln*. 1915. Reprint. Aalen, Germany: Zeller, 1964.

Koch, Klaus. "אהל." In *TDOT* 1.118–30.

———. *Ratlos vor der Apokalyptik*. Gütersloh: Gütersloher Verlag, 1970.

———. "Šaddaj: Zum Verhältnis zwischen israelitischer Monolatrie und nordwestsemitischem Polytheismus." *VT* 26 (1976) 299–332.

Kofoed, Jens Bruun. *Text and History: Historiography and the Study of the Biblical Text*. Winona Lake, IN: Eisenbrauns, 2005.

Kohn, Stephen M. *The Whistleblower's Handbook*. Guilford, CT: Globe Pequot, 2011.

König, Franz. *Zarathustras Jenseitsvorstellungen und das alte Testament*. Wien: Herder, 1964.

Korpel, Marjo. *The Structure of the Book of Ruth*. Assen: Van Gorcum, 2001.

Kratz, Reinhard G. *Die Komposition der erzählenden Bücher der Alten Testaments: Grundwissen der Bibelkritik*. Göttingen: Vandenhoeck & Ruprecht, 2000.

Kraus, Hans Joachim. "Gilgal. Ein Beitrag zur Kulturgeschichte Israels." *VT* 1 (1951) 181–99.

———. *Klagelieder*. Neukirchen-Vluyn: Neukirchener, 1968.

Krinetzki, Günter. *Zefanjastudien: Motiv- und Traditionskritik + Kompositions- und Redaktionskritik*. Frankfurt: Lang, 1977.

Kuan, Jeffrey K. "Jehu." In *EDB* 682–84.

Kübler-Ross, Elisabeth. *On Death and Dying*. New York: Scribner, 1969.

Kuebrich, David. "Religion and the Poet-Prophet." In *A Companion to Walt Whitman*, edited by D. Kummings, 197–215. London: Blackwell, 2006.

Kuenen, Abraham. "Bijdragen tot de Critiek van Pentateuch en Josua. X. Bileam." *TT* 18 (1884) 497–540.

———. *The Pentateuch and Book of Joshua Critically Examined*. London: Longman, Roberts & Green, 1865.

Kugel, James L. *The Great Poems of the Bible*. New York: Free, 1999.

———. *The Idea of Biblical Poetry: Parallelism and Its History*. Baltimore: Johns Hopkins University Press, 1998.

Kühne, Cord. *Die Chronologie der internationalen Korrespondenz von El-Amarna*. Neukirchen- Vluyn: Neukirchener, 1973.

Kunin, Seth. *The Logic of Incest: A Structuralist Analysis of Hebrew Mythology*. London: Bloomsbury, 1995.

Kuntz, J. Kenneth. "The Canonical Wisdom Psalms of Ancient Israel—Their Rhetorical, Thematic, and Formal Dimensions." In *Rhetorical Criticism: Essays in Honor of James Muilenberg*, edited by J. Jackson & M. Kessler, 186–222. Pittsburgh: Pickwick, 1974.

Kutsch, Ernst. *Verheissung und Gesetz: Untersuchungen zum sogenannte Bund im Alten Testament*. Berlin: De Gruyter, 1973.

———. "Weisheitsspruch und Prophetenwort: Zur Traditionsgeschichte des Spruches Jer 9:22–23." *BZ* 25 (1981) 161–79.

LaBarbera, Robert. "The Man of War and the Man of God: Social Satire in 2 Kings 6:8—7:20." *CBQ* 46 (1984) 637–51.

Labat, René. *Traité akkadien de diagnostics et prognostics médicaux*. Leiden: Brill, 1951.

Laberge, Leo. "Le Dramé de la Fidélité chez Jérémie." *EgT* 11 (1980) 9–31.

Lack, Rémi. "Les origins de Elyon, le Très-Haut, dans le tradition culturelle d'Israël." *CBQ* 24 (1962) 44–64.

Lacocque, André. "Date et milieu du livre de Ruth." *RHPR* 59 (1979) 583–93.

Laessøe, Jørgen. *Studies on the Assyrian Ritual and Series* bît rimki. Copenhagen: Munksgaard, 1955.

Lakoff, George, & Mark Turner. *More Than Cool Reason: A Field Guide to Metaphor*. Chicago: University of Chicago Press, 1989.

Lalleman, Hetty. *Jeremiah and Lamentations*. Downers Grove, IL: IVP, 2013.

Lambert, Wilfrid G. *Babylonian Creation Myths*. Winona Lake, IN: Eisenbrauns, 2013.

———. "Line 10 of the Old Babylonian Etana Legend." *JCS* 32 (1980) 81–85.

Lampe, Peter. "Theological Wisdom and the 'Word About the Cross': The Rhetorical Scheme in 1 Cor 1–4." *Int* 44 (1990) 111–31.

Lang, Bernhard. *The Hebrew God: Portrait of an Ancient Deity*. New Haven: Yale University Press, 2002.

———. *Wisdom and the Book of Proverbs: An Israelite Goddess Redefined*. New York: Pilgrim, 1986.

Lange, Armin. "Reading the Decline of Prophecy." In *Reading the Present in the Qumran Library: The Perception of the Contemporary by Means of Scriptural Interpretations*, edited by K. de Troyer and A. Lange, 181–94. Atlanta: Society of Biblical Literature, 2005.

Lardner Carmody, Denise. *Organizing a Theological Mind: A Theology of Higher Education*. Valley Forge, PA: Trinity, 1996.

Largement, René. "Les oracles de Bile'am et la mantique suméro-akkadienne." In *Memorial du cinquantenaire, 1914–1964*, 37–50. Paris: Travaux de l'Institut de Paris, 1964.

Lasine, Stuart. "Guest and Host in Judges 19: Lot's Hospitality in an Inverted World." *JSOT* 29 (1984) 37–59.

———. "Jehoram and the Cannibal Mothers." *JSOT* 50 (1991) 27–53.

———. *Knowing Kings: Knowledge, Power and Narcissism in the Hebrew Bible*. Atlanta: SBL, 2001.

LaSor, William S., David Allan Hubbard, and Frederick W. Bush. *Old Testament Survey*, 2nd ed. Grand Rapids: Eerdmans, 1996.

Lassner, Jacob. *Demonizing the Queen of Sheba: Boundaries of Gender and Culture in Postbiblical Judaism and Medieval Islam*. Chicago: University of Chicago Press, 1993.

Lau, Peter Hon Wan. *Identity and Ethics in the Book of Ruth: A Social Identity Approach*. Berlin: De Gruyter, 2011.

Lauha, Aarre. *Kohelet*. Neukirchen-Vluyn: Neukirchener, 1978.

Leach, Edmund. *Culture and Communication*. Cambridge: Cambridge University Press, 1976.

Lehmann, Gunnar. "The United Monarchy in the Countryside: Jerusalem, Judah, and the Shephelah in the Tenth Century B.C.E." In *Jerusalem in Bible and Archaeology: The First Temple Period*, edited by A. Vaughan and A. Killebrew, 117–62. Atlanta: SBL, 2003.

Lemaire, André. "Une inscription phénicienne découverte récemment et le mariage de Ruth la Moabite." *EI* 20 (1989) 124–29.

Lemche, Niels Peter. "The Greek 'Amphictyony': Could It be a Prototype for the Israelite Society in the Period of the Judges?" *JSOT* 4 (1976) 48–59.

———. *The Old Testament between Theology and History: A Critical Survey*. Louisville, KY: Westminster John Knox, 2008.

Lenzi, Alan. *Secrecy and the Gods: Secret Knowledge in Ancient Mesopotamia and Biblical Israel*. Helsinki: Neo-Assyrian Text Corpus Project, Institute for Asian and African Studies, 2008.

Leuchter, Mark. *The Polemics of Exile in Jeremiah 26–45*. Cambridge: Cambridge University Press, 2008.

Levenson, Jon. *Resurrection and the Restoration of Israel: The Ultimate Victory of the God of Life*. New Haven: Yale University Press, 2006.

Levenson, Jon, and Baruch Halpern. "Political Import of David's Marriages." *JBL* 99 (1980) 507–18.

Levine, Baruch A. "The Balaam Inscription: Historical Aspects." In *Biblical Archaeology Today*, edited by J. Amitai, 326–39. Jerusalem: Israel Exploration Society, 1985.

———. "The Deir ʿAlla Plaster Inscriptions." *JAOS* 101 (1981) 195–205.

———. "The Descriptive Ritual Texts from Ugarit." In *The Word of the Lord Shall Go Forth: Essays in Honor of David Noel Freedman*, edited by C. L. Meyers and M. L. O'Connor, 467–75. Winona Lake, IN: Eisenbrauns, 1983.

———. "The Descriptive Tabernacle Texts of the Pentateuch." *JAOS* 85 (1965) 307–18.

———. *In the Presence of the Lord: A Study of Cult and Some Cultic Terms in Ancient Israel*. Leiden: Brill, 1974.

———. *Numbers 21–36*. New York: Doubleday, 2000.

———. "The Plaster Inscriptions from Deir ʿAllā: General Interpretation." In *The Balaam Text from Deir ʿAllā Re-Evaluated*, edited by J. Hoftijzer and G. van der Kooij, 58–72. Leiden: Brill, 1991.

Lévi-Strauss, Claude. *The Elementary Structures of Kinship*, 1949. Translated by J. H. Bell *et al*. Boston: Beacon, 1969.

———. *Structural Anthropology*. 1958. Translated by C. Jacobson. New York: Basic, 1963.

Lévy-Bruhl, Lucien. *La mentalité primitive*. Paris: Alcan, 1922.

Lewis, Hunter. *A Question of Values: Six Ways We Make the Personal Choices that Shape Our Lives*. San Francisco: Harper & Row, 1990.

Lewis, Ioan M. *Ecstatic Religion: An Anthropological Study of Spirit Possession and Shamanism*. Baltimore: Penguin, 1971.

Lewis, Jack P. "'A Prophet's Son' (Amos 7:14) Reconsidered." *ResQ* 49 (2007) 229–40.

Lewis, Theodore J. "The Ancestral Estate (נחלת אלהים) in 2 Samuel 14:16." *JBL* 110 (1991) 597–612.

———. *Cults of the Dead in Ancient Israel and Ugarit*. Atlanta: Scholars, 1989.

———. "Teraphim." In *DDD* 844–50.

Lewis-Williams, J. D. and T. A. Dowson. "The Signs of All Times: Entoptic Phenomena in Upper Paleolithic Art." *CA* 29 (1988) 201–45.

L'Heureux, Conrad E. *Rank among the Canaanite Gods El, Baʿal and the Rephaʾim*. Missoula: Scholars, 1979.

Limburg, James. "The Root ריב and the Prophetic Lawsuit Speeches." *JBL* 88 (1969) 291–304.

Lindars, Barnabas. "Jotham's Fable: A New Form-Critical Analysis." *JTS* 24 (1973) 355–66.

Lindblom, Johannes. *Prophecy in Ancient Israel*. Oxford: Blackwell, 1962.

———. "Wisdom in the Old Testament Prophets." In *Wisdom in Israel and in the Ancient Near East: Presented to Professor Henry Harold Rowley in Celebration of his Sixty-Fifth Birthday*, edited by M. Noth and D. W. Thomas, 192–204. Leiden: Brill, 1955.

Linebaugh, Jonathan A. *God, Grace and Righteousness in Wisdom of Solomon and Paul's Letter to the Romans: A Conversation*. Leiden: Brill, 2013.

Lipiński, Edward. *Itineraria Phoenicia*. Leuven: Peeters, 2004.
———. "Shemesh." In *DDD* 764–68.
Liptzin, Shulamit. "Solomon and the Queen of Sheba." *Dor Le Dor* 7 (1979) 172–86.
Liver, Y. "The Image of Balaam in Biblical Tradition." *EI* 3 (1954) 97–100.
Liverani, Mario. "Contrasti e confluenze de consezioni politiche nell' età di El-Amarna." *RA* 61 (1967) 1–18.
———. "The Great Powers Club." In *Amarna Diplomacy*, edited by R. Cohen & R. Westbrook, 15–27. Baltimore: Johns Hopkins, 2000.
———. *International Relations in the Ancient Near East, 1600–1100 BC*. New York: Palgrave MacMillan, 2001.
Livesey, Nina E. *Circumcision as a Malleable Symbol*. Tübingen: Mohr Siebeck, 2010.
Ljung, Inger. *Silence or Suppression: Attitudes towards Women in the Old Testament*. Stockholm: Almqvist, 1989.
Lloyd, Jeffery B. "Anat and the 'Double Massacre' of *KTU* 1.3.2." In *Ugarit, Religion, and Culture: Essays in Honour of J. C. L. Gibson*, edited by N. Wyatt et al., 151–65. Münster: Ugarit-Verlag, 1996.
Loader, James Alfred. "Creating New Contexts: On the Possibilities of Biblical Studies in Contexts Generated by the Dead Sea Scrolls." In *The Dead Sea Scrolls in Context: Integrating the Dead Sea Scrolls in the Study of Texts, Languages and Cultures*, edited by A. Lange et al., 27–46. Leiden: Brill, 2011.
Lods, Adolphe. *La croyance à la vie future et le culte de morts dans l'antiquité Israélite*. Paris: Fischbacher, 1906.
Löhr, Max. "Threni III und die jeremianische Autorschraft des Buches der Klagelieder." *ZAW* 24 (1904) 1–16.
Long, Burke O. "Social Dimensions of Prophetic Conflict." *Sem* 21 (1982) 31–53.
Long, Thomas G. *The Witness of Preaching*. Louisville, KY: Westminster/John Knox, 1989.
Luhrmann, Tanya M. *Persuasions of the Witch's Craft: Ritual Magic in Contemporary England*. Cambridge: Harvard University Press, 1989.
Lundbom, Jack. *Writing Up Jeremiah: The Prophet and the Book*. Eugene, OR: Cascade, 2013.
Maccoby, Hyam. *Antisemitism and Modernity: Innovation and Continuity*. New York: Routledge, 2006.
Maier, Christl. *Jeremia als Lehrer der Tora: Soziale Gebote des Deuteronomiums in Fortschreibungen des Jeremiabuches*. Göttingen: Vandenhoeck & Ruprecht, 2002.
Maillot, Alphonse. "L'apologétique du livre de Job." *RHPR* 59 (1979) 567–76.
Malamat, Abraham. "Prophetic Revelations in New Documents from Mari and the Bible." *EI* (1966) 207–27.
Malinowski, Bruno. *Magic, Science, and Religion and Other Essays*, 1925. Reprint. Garden City, NY: Doubleday, 1954.
Maly, Eugene H. "The Jotham Fable: Anti-monarchical?" *CBQ* 22 (1960) 299–305.
Mangano, Mark. "Rhetorical Content in the Amarna Correspondence from the Levant (Egypt)." PhD diss., Hebrew Union College—Jewish Institute of Religion, 1990.
Marcus, David. "David the Deceiver and David the Dupe." *Prooftexts* 6 (1986) 163–71.
———. *From Balaam to Jonah: Anti-Prophetic Satire in the Hebrew Bible*. Atlanta: Scholars, 1995.
Margalit, Baruch. *The Ugaritic Poem of Aqhat: Text, Translation, Commentary*. Berlin: De Gruyter, 1989.

Markter, Florian. *Transformationen. Zur Anthropologie des Propheten Ezechiel unter besonderer Berücksichtigung des Motivs "Herz."* Würzburg: Echter, 2013.
Marsman, Hennie J. *Women in Ugarit and Israel: Their Social and Religious Position in the Context of the Ancient Near East.* Leiden: Brill, 2003.
Martin-Achard, Raymond. *De la Mort à la Résurrection d'après l'Ancien Testament.* Paris: Neuchatel, Delachaux & Niestlé, 1956.
Matthews, Victor H. "The Unwanted Gift: Implications of Obligatory Gift-Giving in Ancient Israel." *Sem* 87 (1999) 91–104.
Mauchline, John. Review of *Lamentations*, by N. Gottwald. *ExpTim* 66 (1954–55) 230.
Maunder, Chris. *Origins of the Cult of Mary.* New York: Bloomsbury Academic, 2008.
May, Herbert G. "The Departure of the Glory of Yahweh." *JBL* 56 (1937) 309–21.
———. "Some Cosmic Connotations of מים רבים." *JBL* 74 (1955) 9–21.
Mayer, Werner. *Untersuchungen zur Formensprache der babylonische "Gebetsbeschwörungen."* Rome: Biblical Institute, 1976.
McAfee, Eugene Clifford. "The Patriarch's Longed-for Son: Biological and Social Reproduction in Ugaritic and Hebrew Epic." PhD diss., Harvard University, 1996.
McCann, J. Clinton. *Judges.* Louisville, KY: Westminster John Knox, 2011.
McCarter, P. Kyle. *2 Samuel: A New Translation with Introduction, Notes and Commentary.* Garden City, NY: Doubleday, 1984.
———. "When the Gods Lose Their Temper: Divine Rage in Ugaritic Myth and the Hypostasis of Anger in Iron Age Religion." In *Divine Wrath and Divine Mercy in the World of Antiquity*, edited by R. Kratz and H. Spieckermann, 78–91. Tübingen: Mohr Siebeck, 2008.
———. "Yaw, Son of Omri: A Philological Note on Israelite Chronology." *BASOR* 216 (1974) 5–7.
McCarthy, Dennis. *Treaty and Covenant.* Rome: Pontifical Biblical Institute, 1978.
McComiskey, Thomas. "Prophetic Irony in Hos 1:4: A Study of the Collocation פקד על and its Implications for the Fall of the Jehu Dynasty." *JSOT* 58 (1993) 93–101.
McCumber, John. "Hegel and the Logics of History." In *Hegel and History*, edited by Will Dudley, 69–86. Albany, NY: SUNY, 2009.
McDonnell, John F. Review of *Lamentations*, by N. Gottwald. *CBQ* 17 (1955) 517–18.
McKane, William. *Prophets and Wise Men.* London: SCM, 1965.
McKee, Donald K. "The Role of Self-Interest in Politics: The Biblical Fable of the Trees and the Bramble." *Religion in Life* 29 (1960) 598–607.
McKnight, Edgar V. "Reader-Response Criticism." In *To Each Its Own Meaning: An Introduction to Biblical Criticisms and Their Application*, edited by Steven L. McKenzie and Stephen R. Haynes, 230–52. Louisville, KY: Westminster John Knox, 1999.
Meier, Gerhard. *Die assyrische Beschwörungssammlung Maqlû.* 1937. Reprint. Osnabruck: Biblio-Verlag, 1967.
Meier, Samuel A. "Diplomacy and International Marriages." In *Amarna Diplomacy: The Beginnings of International Relations*, edited by R. Cohen and R. Westbrook, 165–73. Baltimore: Johns Hopkins University, 2000.
Meinhold, Johannes. *Die Composition des Buches Daniel.* Greifswald: Abel, 1884.
Meletinsky, Eleazar M. *The Poetics of Myth.* 1998. Reprint. London: Routledge, 2013.
Mendels, Doron. *The Land of Israel as a Political Concept in Hasmonean Literature.* Tübingen: Mohr Siebeck, 1987.
Mendenhall, George E. *The Tenth Generation.* Baltimore: Johns Hopkins, 1973.

Menn, Esther Marie. *Judah and Tamar (Genesis 38) in Ancient Jewish Exegesis: Studies in Literary Form and Hermeneutics*. Leiden: Brill, 1997.

Merlo, Paolo, and Paolo Xella. "The Ugaritic Cultic Texts: The Rituals." In *Handbook of Ugaritic Studies*, edited by W. G. E. Watson and N. Wyatt, 287–304. Leiden: Brill, 1999.

Merton, R. K. "The Role-Set: Problems in Sociological Theory." *BJS* 8 (1957) 106–20.

Meshel, Ze'ev. "Did Yahweh Have a Consort?" *BAR* 5.2 (1979) 24–34.

Mettinger, Tryggve N. D. *The Riddle of Resurrection: "Dying and Rising Gods" in the Ancient Near East*. Stockholm: Almqvist & Wiksell, 2001.

Meyer, Ivo. *Jeremia und die falsche Propheten*. Göttingen: Vandenhoeck & Ruprecht, 1977.

Meyers, Carol. "Ephod." In *ABD* 2.550–51.

Michel, W. L. "צלמות: 'Deep Darkness' or 'Shadow of Death?'" *BR* 29 (1984) 5–20.

Mihalic, Joseph L. "Dialogue with God: A Study of Some of Jeremiah's Confessions." *Int* 14 (1960) 43–50.

Miles, Johnny. *Wise King, Royal Fool: Semiotics, Satire, and Proverbs 1–9*. London: T. & T. Clark, 2004.

Milgrom, Jacob. *Leviticus 1–16*. New York: Doubleday, 1991.

———. *Leviticus 17–22*. New York: Doubleday, 2000.

———. *Leviticus 23–27*. New York: Doubleday, 2001.

———. "Numbers, Book of." *ABD* 4.1146–55.

Milik, Józef T. "An Unpublished Arrowhead with Phoenician Inscription of the 11th–10th Century B.C." *BASOR* 143 (1956) 3–6.

Millar, William R. *Isaiah 24–27 and the Origin of Apocalyptic*. Missoula: Scholars, 1976.

Miller, J. Maxwell. "Geba/Gibeah of Benjamin." *VT* 25 (1975) 145–66.

Miller, Patrick D. "Divine Council and the Prophetic Call to War." *VT* 18 (1968) 100–107.

———. "Trouble and Woe: Interpreting the Biblical Laments." *Int* 37 (1983) 32–45.

Momigliano, Arnaldo. *Essays on Ancient and Modern Judaism*. Chicago: University of Chicago Press, 1994.

Mommsen, Theodor. *Römische Geschichte*. Berlin: Reimer, 1856.

Moore, George Foot. "Intermediaries in Jewish Theology: Memra, Shekinah, Metatron." *HTR* 15 (1922) 41–85.

Moore, Megan, and Brad Kelle. *Biblical History and Israel's Past: The Changing Study of the Bible and History*. Grand Rapids: Eerdmans, 2011.

Moore, Michael S. "הגואל: The Cultural Gyroscope of Ancient Hebrew Society." *ResQ* 23 (1980) 27–35.

———. "1–2 Maccabees." In *The Old Testament and Apocrypha. Fortress Commentary on the Bible*, edited by G. Yee et al., 1055–71. Minneapolis: Fortress, 2014.

———. "Abraham." In *EOHJ* 2–3.

———. "America's Monocultural Heritage." *FH* 15 (1982) 39–53.

———. "Are Our Wounds Incurable (Mic 1:9)?" In *Today Hear His Voice: The Minor Prophets Speak*, edited by D. Shackleford, 313–24. Searcy, AR: Harding University, 1993.

———. *The Balaam Traditions: Their Character and Development*. Atlanta: Scholars, 1990.

———. "Balaam the Prophet?" *ResQ* 39 (1997) 101–06.

———. "Daniel." In *EOHJ* 128–30.

———. "David and His Teenagers." In *Reconciliation: A Study of Biblical Families in Conflict*, 49–60. Joplin, MO: College, 1994.
———. "Divine Presence." In *DOTPr* 166–70.
———. *Faith Under Pressure: A Study of Biblical Leaders in Conflict*. Siloam Springs, AR: Leafwood, 2003.
———. "Jehu's Coronation and Purge of Israel." *VT* 53 (2003) 97–114.
———. "Jeremiah's Progressive Paradox." *RB* 93 (1986) 386–414.
———. "Job's Texts of Terror." *CBQ* 55 (1993) 662–75.
———. "Job's Text of Terror." *Leaven: A Journal of Christian Ministry* 4 (2012) 39–42.
———. "Naomi's Journey." In *Reconciliation: A Study of Biblical Families in Conflict*, 151–61. Joplin, MO: College, 1994.
———. "Resurrection and Immortality: Two Motifs Navigating Confluent Theological Streams in the Old Testament (Dan 12.1–4)." *TZ* 39 (1983) 17–34.
———. Review of *An Adversary in Heaven: שטן in the Hebrew Bible*, by Peggy Day, *JBL* 109 (1990) 508–10.
———. Review of *Psalms*, by Mitchell Dahood. *HS* 22 (1981) 35–38.
———. Review of *Old Testament Wisdom: An Introduction*, by James Crenshaw. *HS* 24 (1983) 185–88.
———. Review of *Welcoming, But Not Affirming*, by Stan Grenz. *BuBR* 10 (2000) 143–46.
———. "Role Preemption in the Israelite Priesthood." *VT* 46 (1996) 316–29.
———. "Ruth the Moabite and the Blessing of Foreigners." *CBQ* 60 (1998) 203–17.
———. "Ruth." In *Joshua, Judges, Ruth*, by J. G. Harris, C. Brown, and M. S. Moore, 293–383. Grand Rapids: Baker, 2000.
———. "Searching in Sheba: The Goal of Christian Education." *ResQ* 44 (2002) 33–42.
———. "To King or Not to King: A Canonical-Historical Approach to Ruth." *BuBR* 11 (2001) 27–41.
———. "Two Textual Anomalies in Ruth." *CBQ* 59 (1997) 234–43.
———. "Under Siege." In *Faith Under Pressure: A Study of Biblical Leaders in Conflict*, 148–52. Siloam Springs, AR: Leafwood, 2003.
———. *WealthWatch: A Study of Socioeconomic Conflict in the Bible*. Eugene, OR: Pickwick, 2011.
———. "Wise Women in the Bible: Identifying a Trajectory." In *Essays on Women in Earliest Christianity. Vol. 2*, edited by C. D. Osburn, 87–103. Joplin, MO: College, 1995.
———. "Yahweh's Day." *ResQ* 29 (1987) 193–208.
Moran, William L. "Ancient Near Eastern Background of the Love of God in Deuteronomy." *CBQ* 25 (1963) 77–87.
———. *The Amarna Letters*. Baltimore: Johns Hopkins University, 1992.
———. "New Evidence from Mari on the History of Prophecy." *Bib* 50 (1969) 15–56.
Morawe, Günter. *Aufbau und Abgrenzung der Loblieder von Qumran. Studien zur gattungsgeschichtlichen Einordnung der Hodajoth*. Berlin: Evangelische Verlagsanstalt, 1961.
Morray-Jones, Christopher R. A. *A Transparent Illusion. The Dangerous Vision of Water in Hekhalot Mysticism: A Source-Critical and Tradition-Historical Inquiry*. Leiden: Brill, 2002.
Morris, Brian. *Anthropological Studies of Religion: An Introductory Text*. Cambridge: Cambridge University Press, 1987.

Morrison, Martha A. "Mitanni." In *ABD* 4.874–76.
Morrow, Lance. "The Quest for Purity." In *Evil: An Investigation*, 245–50. New York: Basic, 2003.
Moscati, Sabatino. *Comparative Grammar of the Semitic Languages*. Wiesbaden: Harrassowitz, 1980.
———. *The Face of the Ancient Orient: Near Eastern Civilization in Pre-Classical Times*. London: Routledge & Kegan Paul, 1960.
Mottu, Henri. *Les "confessions" de Jérémie: une protestation contre la souffrance*. Genève: Labor et Fides, 1985.
Mouton, Alice. *Rêves Hittites. Contribution à une histoire et une anthropologie du rêve en Anatolie ancienne*. Leiden: Brill, 2007.
Mouton, Alice, and Ian Rutherford. "Luwian Religion, A Research Project: The Case of 'Hittite' Augury." In *Luwian Identities: Culture, Language, and Religion between Anatolia and the Aegean*, edited by A. Mouton et al., 329–44. Leiden: Brill, 2013.
Mowinckel, Sigmund. *He That Cometh: The Messiah Concept in the Old Testament and Later Judaism*. 1951. Translated by G. W. Anderson. Grand Rapids: Eerdmans, 2005.
———. *Psalmenstudien II: Das Thronbesteigungsfest Jahwäs und der Ursprung der Eschatologie*. Oslo: Dybwad, 1922.
———. *Psalmenstudien III: Kultprophetie und prophetische Psalmen*. Oslo: Dybwad, 1923.
———. "Der Ursprung der Bil`amsage." *ZAW* 48 (1930) 233–71.
———. "Psalms and Wisdom." In *Wisdom in Israel and in the Ancient Near East: Presented to Professor Henry Harold Rowley in Celebration of his Sixty-Fifth Birthday*, edited by M. Noth and D. W. Thomas, 205–24. Leiden: Brill, 1955.
———. *Zur Komposition des Buches Jeremia*. Kristiana: Dybwad, 1914.
Muenchow, Charles. "Dust and Dirt in Job 42:6." *JBL* 108 (1989) 597–611.
Mullen, E. Theodore. *The Assembly of the Gods: The Divine Council in Canaanite and Early Hebrew Literature*. Chico, CA: Scholars, 1980.
———. "The Royal Dynastic Grant to Jehu and the Structure of the Books of Kings." *JBL* 107 (1988) 193–206.
Müller, Hans Peter. "Die aramäischen Inschrift von Deir `Allā und die älteren Bileamsprüche." *ZAW* 94 (1982) 214–44.
———. "Einige alttestamentliche Probleme zur aramäischen Inschrift von Dēr `Allā." *ZDPV* 94 (1978) 56–67.
Munch, Peter A. *The Expression* ביום ההוא: *Is It an Eschatological Terminus Technicus?* Oslo: Dybwad, 1936.
Münnich, Maciej M. *The God Resheph in the Ancient Near East*. Tübingen: Mohr Siebeck, 2013.
Murnane, William J. "The History of Ancient Egypt: An Overview." In *CANE* 691–717.
———. "Imperial Egypt and the Limits of Power." In *Amarna Diplomacy: The Beginnings of International Relations*, edited by R. Cohen and R. Westbrook, 101–11. Baltimore: Johns Hopkins University, 2000.
———. *Texts from the Amarna Period in Egypt*. Atlanta: SBL, 1995.
Murphy Roland E. "The Use of Proverbial Sayings in Sirach." In *Treasures of Wisdom: Studies in Ben Sira and the Book of Wisdom (FS M. Gilbert)*, edited by N. Calduch-Benages and J. Vermeylen, 31–40. Leuven: Peeters, 1999.
Myers, Jacob. *The Linguistic and Literary Form of the Book of Ruth*. Leiden: Brill, 1955.

Na'aman, Nadav. "Amarna Letters." In *ABD* 1.174–81.
———. "The Political Disposition and Historical Developments of Eretz Israel according to the Amarna Letters." Ph.D. diss., Tel Aviv University, 1973.
———. "Sources and Composition in the History of Solomon." In *The Age of Solomon: Scholarship at the Turn of the Millenium*, edited by L. K. Handy, 57–80. Leiden: Brill, 1997.
———. "Three Notes on the Aramaic Inscription from Tel Dan. *IEJ* 50 (2000) 92–104.
Nägelsbach, Carl Wilhelm Eduard. *Die Klagelieder.* Leipzig: Belhagen & Klasing, 1868.
Nam, Roger S. *Portrayals of Economic Exchange in the Book of Kings.* Leiden: Brill, 2012.
Nauta, Rein. "Flight from Ministry." In *Religious Leadership and Christian Identity*, edited by D. Nauer et al., 211–23. Münster: LIT Verlag, 2004.
Nelson, Richard D. *1 & 2 Kings.* Louisville, KY: John Knox, 1987.
Nesselrath, Heinz-Günther, and Florian Wilk, eds. *Gut und Böse in Mensch und Welt: Philosophische und religiöse Konzeptionen vom Alten Orient bis zum frühen Islam.* Tübingen: Mohr Siebeck, 2013.
Newell, B. Lynne. "Job: Repentant or Rebellious?" *WTJ* 46 (1984) 298–316.
Newsom, Carol A. "The Book of Job as a Polyphonic Text." In *The Book of Job: A Contest of Moral Imaginations*, 3–31. New York: Oxford, 2003.
Nicholson, Ernest. "Deuteronomy 18:9–22, the Prophets, and Scripture." In *Prophecy and the Prophets in Ancient Israel*, edited by John Day, 151–71. London: T. & T. Clark, 2010.
Nickelsburg, George W. *Resurrection, Immortality, and Eternal Life in Intertestamental Judaism.* Cambridge: Cambridge University Press, 1972.
Nicol, George G. "The Alleged Rape of Bathsheba: Some Observations on Ambiguity in Biblical Narrative." *JSOT* 73 (1997) 43–54.
———. "Bathsheba, A Clever Woman?" *ExpTim* 99 (1988) 360–63.
Niditch, Susan. *Judges: A Commentary.* Louisville, KY: Westminster John Knox, 2008.
Niehaus, Jeffrey J. *Ancient Near Eastern Themes in Biblical Theology.* Grand Rapids: Kregel, 2008.
Nielsen, Kirsten. "Stamtavle of fortaelling i Ruths bog." *DTT* 57 (1994) 81–93.
Nissinen, Martti, et al., trans. *Prophets and Prophecy in the Ancient Near East.* Atlanta: Society of Biblical Literature, 2003.
Nitzan, Bilha. *Qumran Prayer and Religious Poetry.* Leiden: Brill, 1994.
Noegel, Scott B. "Dreams and Dream Interpreters in Mesopotamia and the Hebrew Bible." In *Dreams: A Reader on Religious, Cultural, and Psychological Dimensions of Dreaming*, edited by K. Bulkeley, 45–71. New York: Palgrave MacMillan, 2001.
———. "Greek Religion and the Ancient Near East." In *A Companion to Greek Religion*, edited by D. Ogden, 21–38. Malden, MA: Wiley Blackwell, 2010.
Noort, Edward. *Untersuchungen zum Gottesbescheid in Mari.* Neukirchen-Vluyn: Neukirchener, 1977.
Noth, Martin. *A History of Israel.* 1950. Translated by P. R. Ackroyd. New York: Harper and Row, 1960.
———. *A History of Pentateuchal Traditions.* 1948. Translated by Bernhard W. Anderson. Englewood Cliffs, NJ: Prentice-Hall, 1972.
———. *Das System der zwölf Stämme Israels.* Stuttgart: Kohlhammer, 1930.
———. *Überlieferungsgeschichtliche Studien.* Tübingen: Niemeyer, 1943.
Nötscher, Friedrich. "šumma ālu." *Or* 51–54 (1930) 150–90.

Nougayrol, Jean. "La divination babylonienne." In *La Divination*, edited by A. Caquot and M. Leibovici, 25–81. Paris: Presses universitaires de France, 1968.

———. "'Oiseau' ou Oiseau?" *RA* 6 (1967) 23–38.

Nougayrol, Jean, et al., eds. *Ugaritica V: Nouveaux texts accadiens, hourrites et ugaritiques des archives et bibliothèques privées d'Ugarit*. Paris: Imprimerie Nationale/Librairie, 1968.

Nunn, Astrid. "Bildhaftigkeit und Bildlosigkeit im Alten Orient: Ein Widerspruch?" In *Von Göttern und Menschen: Beiträge zu Literatur und Geschichte des Alter Orients. Festschrift für Brigitte Groneberg*, edited by D. Shahata et al., 131–68. Leiden: Brill, 2010.

O'Brien, Julia. *Priest and Levite in Malachi*. Atlanta: Scholars, 1990.

O'Brien, Mark A. *The Deuteronomistic History Hypothesis: A Reassessment*. Göttingen: Vandenhoeck & Ruprecht, 1989.

O'Connell, Robert H. *The Rhetoric of the Book of Judges*. Leiden: Brill, 1996.

O'Connor, Kathleen M. *The Confessions of Jeremiah: Their Interpretation and Role in Chapters 1–25*. Atlanta: Scholars, 1988.

———. Review of *Prophecy and Ideology in Jeremiah. Struggles for Authority in the Deutero-Jeremianic Prose*, by Carolyn J. Sharp. *RBL* 2004 (bookreviews.org/pdf/3315_3706.pdf).

———. *The Wisdom Literature*. Wilmington, DE: Glazier, 1988.

Odell, Margaret S. "You Are What You Eat: Ezekiel and the Scroll." *JBL* 117 (1998) 229–48.

Ogden-Bellis, Alice. *Helpmates, Harlots, Heroes: Women's Stories in the Hebrew Bible*. Louisville, KY: Westminster John Knox, 1994.

———. "The Queen of Sheba: A Gender-Sensitive Reading." *JRT* 51 (1996) 17–28.

Olfman, Sharna, ed. *The Sexualization of Childhood*. Westport, CT: Greenwood, 2009.

Ollenburger, Ben C. *Zion, the City of the Great King: A Theological Symbol of the Jerusalem Cult*. Sheffield, UK: Academic, 1987.

Olson, Dennis T. "Buber, Kingship, and the Book of Judges." In *David and Zion: Biblical Studies in Honor of J. J. M. Roberts*, edited by B. Batto and K. Roberts, 199–218. Winona Lake, IN: Eisenbrauns, 2004.

Olyan, Saul M. "השלום: Some Literary Considerations of 2 Kings 9." *CBQ* 46 (1984) 652–68.

———. *Asherah and the Cult of Yahweh in Israel*. Atlanta: Scholars, 1988.

———. "Honor, Shame, and Covenant Relations in Ancient Israel." *JBL* 115 (1996) 201–18.

———. *Social Inequality in the World of the Text: The Significance of Ritual and Social Distinctions in the Hebrew Bible*. Göttingen: Vandenhoeck & Ruprecht, 2011.

———. "'We Are Utterly Cut Off': Some Possible Nuances of נגזרנו לנו in Ezek 37:11." *CBQ* 65 (2003) 43–51.

———. "What Do Shaving Rights Accomplish and What Do They Signal in Biblical Ritual Texts?" *JBL* 117 (1998) 611–22.

Oppenheim, A. Leo. *The Interpretation of Dreams in the Ancient Near East, with a Translation of an Assyrian Dreambook*. Philadelphia: American Philosophical Society, 1956.

Orlov, Andrei A. *The Enoch-Metatron Tradition*. Tübingen: Mohr Siebeck, 2005.

Orton, David E., ed. *Poetry in the Hebrew Bible: Selected Studies from Vetus Testamentum*. Leiden: Brill, 2002.

Osburn, Carroll D. *Essays on Women in Earliest Christianity*, 2 vols. 1993–95. Reprint. Eugene, OR: Wipf & Stock, 2007.

Oshima, Takayoshi. *Babylonian Prayers to Marduk*. Tübingen: Mohr Siebeck, 2011.

Otten, Heinrich. *Hethitisches Totenrituale*. Berlin: Akademie-Verlag, 1958.

Otto, Eckhart. *Krieg und Frieden in der Hebräischen Bibel und im Alten Orient. Aspekte fur eine Friedensordnung in der Moderne*. Stuttgart: Kohlhammer, 1999.

Overholt, Thomas. "Jeremiah 2 and the Problem of 'Audience Reaction.'" *CBQ* 41 (1979) 262–73.

Paffenroth, Kim. "The Testing of the Sage: 1 Kings 10:1–13 and Q 4.1–13 (Luke 4:1–13)." *ExpTim* 107 (1996) 142–43.

Pardee, Dennis. "The Baʿalu Myth." In *The Context of Scripture: Canonical Compositions from the Biblical World*, edited by W. W. Hallo and K. L. Younger, 241–74. Leiden: Brill, 1997.

———. Review of *The Goddess Anat in Ugaritic Myth*, by Neal Walls. *JBL* 113 (1994) 505–6.

———. *Ritual and Cult at Ugarit*. Atlanta: Society of Biblical Literature, 2002.

Parekh, Sûrya. "Hegel's New World: History, Freedom and Race." In *Hegel and History*, edited by Will Dudley, 111–34. Albany, NY: SUNY, 2009.

Parke, Herbert W. *Sibyls and Sibylline Prophecy in Classical Antiquity*. London: Routledge, 1988.

Parker, Simon B. Review of *The Goddess Anat in Ugaritic Myth*, by Neal Walls. *RSR* 20 (1994) 139–40.

Parrinder, Geoffrey. "Exorcism." In *ER* 5.225.

Parrot, André, and Georges Dossin, eds. *Archives royales de Mari*. Paris: Geuthner, 1950–.

Parry, Robin A. *Lamentations*. Grand Rapids: Eerdmans, 2010.

Payne, Robin. "The Prophet Jonah: Reluctant Messenger and Intercessor." *ExpTim* 100 (1989) 131–34.

Pedersen, Johannes. *Israel: Its Life and Culture*. London: Milford, 1926–40.

Perdue, Leo G. *The Collapse of History: Reconstructing Old Testament Theology*. Minneapolis: Augsburg Fortress, 1994.

———. "The Household, Old Testament Theology, and Contemporary Hermeneutics." In *Families in Ancient Israel*, edited by L. Perdue et al., 223–58. Louisville, KY: Westminster John Knox, 1997.

Perkins, Pheme. "Sophia as Goddess in the Nag Hammadi Codices." In *Images of the Feminine in Gnosticism*, edited by K. L. King, 96–112. Philadelphia: Fortress, 1988.

Perlitt, Lothar. *Bundestheologie im Alten Testament*. Neukirchen-Vluyn: Neukirchener Verlag, 1969.

———. *Vatke und Wellhausen*. Berlin: Töpelmann, 1965.

Peters, Melvin K. H. "Septuagint." In *ABD* 5.1093–1104.

Petersen, David L. *The Roles of Israel's Prophets*. Sheffield, UK: JSOT, 1981.

———. *Interpreting Hebrew Poetry*. Minneapolis: Augsburg Fortress, 1992.

Peterson, Eugene. *Run with the Horses: The Quest for Life at Its Best*. Downers Grove, IL: IVP, 2009.

Pinson, J. Matthew, ed. *Perspectives on Christian Worship: Five Views*. Nashville: Broadman & Holman, 2009.

Pittmann, S. P. "The Essentials of a Better Ministry." *Gospel Advocate* 59 (1919) 828.

Plant, Robin J. R. *Good Figs, Bad Figs: Judicial Differentiation in the Book of Jeremiah.* London: T. & T. Clark, 2008.
Plöger, Otto. *Das Buch Daniel.* Gütersloh: Gütersloher Verlagshaus G. Mohn, 1965.
———. *Theocracy and Eschatology.* 1959. Translated by S. Rudman. Oxford: Blackwell, 1968.
Pohlmann, Karl-Friedrich. *Die Ferne Gottes. Studien zum Jeremiabuch: Beiträge zu den "Konfessionen" im Jeremiabuch und ein Versuch zur Frage nach den Anfängen der Jeremiatradition.* Berlin: De Gruyter, 1989.
Polk, Timothy. *The Prophetic Persona: Jeremiah and the Language of the Self.* Sheffield, UK: JSOT, 1984.
Polner, Murray. *Rabbi: The American Experience.* New York: Holt, Rinehart & Winston, 1977.
Pomykala, Kenneth E. *The Davidic Dynasty Tradition in Early Judaism: Its History and Significance for Messianism.* Atlanta: Scholars, 1995.
Pope, Marvin. *Job.* Garden City, NY: Doubleday, 1965.
———. *Song of Songs.* Garden City, NY: Doubleday, 1977.
———. Review of *The Goddess Anat in Ugaritic Myth*, by Neal Walls. *CBQ* 56 (1992) 349–51.
Popitz, H. *Der Begriff der sozialen Rollen als Element der sozialischen Theorie.* Tübingen: Mohr, 1967.
Porteous, Norman W. *Daniel: A Commentary.* Philadelphia: Westminster, 1965.
Porten, Bezalel. "The Scroll of Ruth: A Rhetorical Study." *GCA* 7 (1978) 23–49.
Porter, Richard A. "Following a Fallen Pastor: Recovering from Docetism." *Faith and Mission* 5 (1988) 42–57.
Poser, Ruth. *Das Ezechielbuch als Trauma-Literatur.* Leiden: Brill, 2012.
Pressler, Carolyn. "Wives and Daughters, Bond and Free: Views of Women in the Slave Laws of Exodus 21:2–11." In *Gender and Law in the Hebrew Bible and the Ancient Near East*, edited by V. Matthews et al., 147–72. London: T. & T. Clark, 1998.
Priest, John. "The Covenant of Brothers." *JBL* 84 (1965) 400–406.
Prinsloo, W. S. "The Theology of the Book of Ruth." *VT* 30 (1980) 330–41.
Propp, Vladimir. *Morphology of the Folktale.* Austin: University of Texas Press, 1968.
Provan, Ian. *1 & 2 Kings.* Peabody, MA: Hendrickson, 1995.
———. "Ideologies, Literary and Critical: Reflections on Recent Writing on the History of Israel." *JBL* 114 (1995) 585–606.
Puech, Emile. "Hodayot." In *EDSS* 365–69.
Quintero, Ruben, ed. *A Companion to Satire: Ancient and Modern.* Oxford: Blackwell, 2007.
Rabinowitz, Dorothy. *New Lives: Survivors of the Holocaust Living in America.* New York: Knopf, 1976.
Radcliffe-Brown, Alfred. *Structure and Function in Primitive Society.* London: Cohen & West, 1952.
Rahlfs, Alfred. *Septuaginta.* 2 Vols. Stuttgart: Württembergische Bibelanstalt, 1935.
Rainey, Anson F. *Canaanite in the Amarna Tablets: A Linguistic Analysis of the Mixed Dialect used by Scribes from Canaan.* 4 vols. Leiden: Brill, 1996.
———. *El AmarnaTablets 359–379: Supplement to J. A. Knudtzon, Die El-Amarna Tafeln.* Kevalaer: Butzon & Bercker, 1970.
Rappoport, Angelo Solomon. *Myth and Legend in Ancient Israel.* New York: KTAV, 1966.

Rappaport, Roy A. *Ritual and Religion in the Making of Humanity*. Cambridge: Cambridge University Press, 1999.
Rautenburg, Johanna. "Die Stadtfrau Jerusalem und ihre Kinder—Zur Bedeutung der Stadt Jerusalem in Gemeinschaftskonzept des Buches Tobit." In *Tochter Zion auf dem Wege zum himmlischen Jerusalem*, edited by M. Häusl, 51–101. Leipzig: Leipziger Universitätsverlag, 2011.
Rayburn, Carole, et al. "Religious Professionals and Clergy Spouses: Stress among Religious Leaders." *JPC* 23 (1988) 1–71.
Ready, Jonathan L. *Character, Narrator and Simile in the Iliad*. New York: Cambridge University Press, 2011.
Rediger, G. Lloyd. *Beyond the Scandals: A Guide to Healthy Clergy Sexuality*. Minneapolis: Augsburg Fortress, 2003.
Reiner, Erica. "Die akkadische Literatur." In *Neues Handbuch der Literatur-Wissenschaft: Altorientalische Literaturen*, edited by Wolfgang Röllig, 1.151–210. Wiesbaden: Athenaion, 1978.
———. "La magie babylonienne." In *Le monde du sorcier*, edited by D. Bernot, et al., 67–98. Paris: Editions du Seuil, 1959.
———. Review of *Studies on the Assyrian Ritual and Series* bît rimki, by Jørgen Laessøe. *JNES* 17 (1958) 204–7.
———. *Šurpu: A Collection of Sumerian and Akkadian Incantations*. 1958. Reprint. Osnabruck: Biblio Verlag, 1970.
Rendtorff, Rolf. *Das überlieferungsgeschichtliche Problem des Pentateuch*. Berlin: De Gruyter, 1977.
Renger, Johannes. "Heilige Hochzeit." In *RlA* 4.255.
———. "Untersuchungen zum Priestertum in der altbabylonischen Zeit." *ZA* 58 (1967) 110–88; 59 (1969) 104–230.
Reventlow, Henning Graf. *Liturgie und prophetisches Ich bei Jeremia*. Gütersloh: Gern Mohn, 1963.
Rich, Phil. *Understanding, Assessing, and Rehabilitating Juvenile Sexual Offenders*. Hoboken, NJ: Wiley, 2011.
Richards, Igor A. *The Philosophy of Rhetoric*. Oxford: Oxford University, 1936.
Richter, Wolgang. *Exegese als Literaturwissenschaft. Entwurf einer alttestamentlichen Literaturtheorie und Methodologie*. Göttingen: Vandenhoeck & Ruprecht, 1971.
Ricoeur, Paul. "La métaphore et le problème central de l'herméneutique." *RPL* 70 (1972) 93–112.
———. *The Rule of Metaphor*. Toronto: University of Toronto, 1977.
Rieger, Gabriel A. *Sex and Satiric Tragedy in Early Modern England: Penetrating Wit*. Burlington, VT: Ashgate, 2009.
Riley, Jason L. "Does Yhwh Get His Hands Dirty? Reading Isaiah 63:1–6 in Light of Depictions of Divine Postbattle Purification." In *Warfare, Ritual and Symbol in Biblical and Modern Contexts*, edited by B. Kelle et al., 243–70. Atlanta: SBL, 2014.
Ringgren, Helmer. "The Impact of the Ancient Near East on Israelite Tradition." In *Tradition and Theology in the Old Testament*, edited by D. F. Knight, 31–46. Philadelphia: Fortress, 1977.
———. *Word and Wisdom: Studies in the Hypostatization of Divine Qualities and Functions in the Ancient Near East*. Lund: Haken Ohlssons Boktryckeri, 1947.
Ritter, E. K. "Magical Expert (=*āšipu*) and Physician (=*asû*): Notes on Two Complementary Professions in Babylonian Medicine." In *Studies in Honor of*

Benno Landsberger on his 75th Birthday, edited by H. Güterbock and T. Jakobsen, 299–321. Chicago: University of Chicago Press, 1965.

Roberts, Jimmy Jack McBee. "The Ancient Near Eastern Environment." In *The Hebrew Bible and Its Modern Interpreters*, edited by D. A. Knight and G. M. Tucker, 75–121. Chico, CA: Scholars, 1985.

———. *The Earliest Semitic Pantheon*. Baltimore: Johns Hopkins, 1972.

———. "The Hand of Yahweh." *VT* 21 (1971) 244–51.

———. "Job and the Israelite Religious Tradition." *ZAW* 89 (1977) 107–14.

———. "The Mari Prophetic Texts in Transliteration and English Translation." In *The Bible and the Ancient Near East*, 157–253. Winona Lake: Eisenbrauns, 2002.

———. "Mowinckel's Enthronement Festival: A Review." In *The Book of Psalms: Composition and Reception*, edited by P. W. Flint & P. D. Miller, 97–115. Leiden: Brill, 2005.

———. *Nahum, Habakkuk, and Zephaniah: A Commentary*. Louisville, KY: Westminster/John Knox, 1991.

———. "The Old Testament's Contribution to Messianic Expectations." In *The Messiah: Developments in Early Judaism and Christianity*, edited by J. H. Charlesworth, 39–51. Minneapolis: Fortress, 1992.

———. Review of *Chaos and Covenant: Prophecy in the Book of Jeremiah*, by Robert Carroll. *PSB* 4 (1983) 126–27.

Robinson, H. Wheeler. "The Council of Yahweh." *JTS* 45 (1944) 151–57.

Robinson, James M. "The Historicality of Biblical Language." In *The Old Testament and Christian Faith: A Theological Discussion*, edited by B. Anderson, 124–58. Freiburg: Herder & Herder, 1969.

———, and Helmut Koester. *Trajectories through Early Christianity*. Philadelphia: Fortress, 1971.

Robker, Jonathan Miles. *The Jehu Revolution: A Royal Tradition of the Northern Kingdom and Its Ramifications*. Berlin: De Gruyter, 2012.

Robson, Eleanor. "Reading the Libraries of Assyria and Babylonia." In *Ancient Libraries*, edited by J. König et al., 38–56. Cambridge: University Press, 2013.

Rofé, Alexander. ספר בלעם: *The Book of Balaam (Num 22:2—24:25)*. Jerusalem, Simor, 1979.

———. *The Prophetical Stories: The Narratives about the Prophets in the Bible, Their Literary Types and History*. Jerusalem: Simor, 1982.

Römer, Thomas. *The So-Called Deuteronomistic History: A Sociological, Historical, and Literary Introduction*. London: Bloomsbury, 2007.

Rooker, Mark F. *Leviticus*. Nashville: Broadman & Holman, 2000.

Rosenberg, David, and Harold Bloom. *The Book of J*. New York: Grove, 1990.

Rosenthal, Franz. "Notes on the Third Aramaic Inscription from Sefire-Sûjîn." *BASOR* 158 (1960) 28–31.

Rost, Leonhard. "Fragen um Bileam." In *Beiträge zur alttestamentlichen Theologie. Festschrift für Walther Zimmerli*, edited by H. Donner et al., 377–87. Göttingen: Vandenhoeck & Ruprecht, 1977.

———. *The Succession to the Throne of David*. 1926. Translated by M. D. Rutter and D. M. Gunn. Sheffield, UK: Almond, 1982.

Rost, Liane. "Ein hethitisches Ritual gegen Familienzwist." *MIO* 1 (1953) 345–79.

Roth, Ray L. "Gebal." In *ABD* 2.922–23.

Rothbell, Gladys. "Just a Housewife: Role-Image and the Stigma of the Single Role." In *Social Roles and Social Institutions: Essays in Honor of Rose Laub Coser*, edited by J. Blau et al., 21–36. New Brunswick, NJ: Transaction, 1995.

Rothstein, J. W. *Das Buch Jeremia*. 4th ed. Tübingen: Mohr/Siebeck, 1922.

Rouillard, Hedwige. *Le péricope de Balaam (Nombres 22–24): la prose et les "oracles."* Paris: Gabalda, 1985.

Rowold, Henry. "*Mî hû'?Lî hû'!* Leviathan and Job in Job 41:2–3." *JBL* 105 (1986) 104–9.

Rowley, Harold H. *Job: A Commentary*. London: Nelson, 1970.

———. *The Relevance of Apocalyptic*. London: Athlone, 1944.

Rubin, David. *God, Israel, and Shiloh: Returning to the Land*. Jerusalem: Mazo, 2007.

Rudolph, Wilhelm. *Das Buch Ruth, das Hohe Lied, die Klagelieder*. Gütersloh: Mohn, 1962.

———. *Der "Elohist" von Exodus bis Josua*. Berlin: Töpelmann, 1938.

———. *Jeremia*. 3rd ed. Tübingen: Mohr/Siebeck, 1968.

———. *Micha, Nahum, Habakuk, Zephanja*. Gerd Mohn: Gütersloher, 1975.

Ruether, Rosemary Radford. *Goddesses and the Divine Feminine: A History of Western Religion*. Berkeley: University of California, 2005.

Ruprecht, Eberhard. *Die Jothamfabel und ausserisraelitischen Parallelen*. Göttingen: Vandenhoeck & Ruprecht, 2003.

Rutz, Matthew. *Bodies of Knowledge in Ancient Mesopotamia: The Diviners of Late Bronze Age Emar and Their Table Collection*. Leiden: Brill, 2013.

Sabottka, Liudger. *Zephanjah. Versuch einer Neuübersetzung mit philologischem Kommentar*. Roma: Biblical Institute Press, 1972.

Sabourin, Leopold. *Priesthood: A Comparative Study*. Leiden: Brill, 1973.

Sacon, Kiyoshi K. "The Book of Ruth: Its Literary Structure and Theme." *AJBI* 4 (1978) 3–22.

Sakenfeld, Katharine D. *The Meaning of* חסד *in the Hebrew Bible: A New Inquiry*. Missoula: Scholars, 1978.

Sanders, James A. "Intertextuality and Dialogue." *BTB* 29 (1999) 35–44.

———. Review of *The Hymns of Qumran*, by Bonnie Pedrotti Kittel. *JBL* 102 (1983) 330–32.

Sapin, J. "Quelques systèmes socio-politiques en Syrie au 2e millenaire avant J.-C. et leur évolution historique d'après des documents religieux (légendes, rituels, sanctuaries)." *UF* 15 (1983) 157–90.

Sarbin, Theodore R., and V. L. Allen. "Role Theory." In *The Handbook of Social Psychology*, edited by G. Lindzey and E. Aronson, 488–567. Reading, MA: Addison-Wesley, 1968.

Sarna, Nahum M. "The Mythological Background of Job 18." *JBL* 82 (1963) 315–18.

———. *Understanding Genesis*. New York: Jewish Theological Seminary of America, 1966.

Sasson, Jack M. *Ruth: A New Translation with a Philological Commentary and a Formalist- Folklorist Interpretation*. Sheffield, UK: Sheffield Academic Press, 1989.

———. "Ruth." In *A Literary Guide to the Bible*, edited by R. Alter and F. Kermode, 320–28. Cambridge: Belknap Press of Harvard University, 1987.

Satterthwaite, Philip. "'No King in Israel': Narrative Criticism and Judges 17–21." *TynBul* 44 (1993) 75–88.

Savran, George W. *Encountering the Divine: Theophany in Biblical Narrative*. London: T. & T. Clark, 2005.

Saxegaard, Kristen M. *Character Complexity in the Book of Ruth.* Tübingen: Mohr Siebeck, 2010.
Scharbert, J. Review of *Formula Criticism and the Poetry of the Old Testament,* by W. Watters. *BZ* 22 (1978) 289.
Schifferdecker, Kathryn M. "Out of the Whirlwind: Creation Theology in the Book of Job." ThD diss., Harvard University, 2005.
Schiffman, Lawrence. "The מלאים Ceremony in the Temple Scroll." In *New Qumran Texts and Studies,* edited by G. J. Brooke, 255–72. Leiden: Brill, 1994.
———. "Origin and Early History of the Qumran Sect." *BA* 58 (1995) 37–48.
Schipper, Jeremy. *Parables and Conflict in the Hebrew Bible.* Cambridge: Cambridge University Press, 2009.
Schmid, Hans Heinrich. "Canaanite Magic vs. Israelite Religion: Deuteronomy 18 and the Taxonomy of Taboo." In *Magic and Ritual in the Ancient World,* edited by P. Mirecki and M. Meyer, 243–62. Leiden: Brill, 2001.
———. *Der sogenannte Jahwist.* Zurich: Theologischer Verlag, 1976.
———. *Wesen und Geschichte der Weisheit.* Berlin: De Gruyter, 1966.
Schmidt, Brian B. *Israel's Beneficent Dead: Ancestor Cult and Necromancy in Ancient Israelite Religion and Tradition.* Tübingen: Mohr, 1995.
Schmidt, Ludwig. "Die alttestamentliche Bileamüberlieferung." *BZ* 23 (1979) 234–61.
Schmitt, Armin. *Prophetischer Gottesbescheid in Mari und Israel. Eine Strukturuntersuchung.* Stuttgart: Kohlhammer, 1982.
Schmitt, John J. "Preexilic Hebrew Prophecy." In *ABD* 5.482–89.
Schmitt, Rudiger. *Magie im Alten Testament.* Münster: Ugarit-Verlag, 2004.
———. "The Problem of Magic and Monotheism in the Book of Leviticus." *JHS* 8 (2008) art. 11.
Schneider, Tammi J. "Rethinking Jehu." *Bib* 77 (1996) 100–107.
Schniedewind, William M. "History and Interpretation: The Religion of Ahab and Manasseh in the Book of Kings." *CBQ* 55 (1993) 649–61.
———. "Tel Dan Stela: New Light on Aramaic and Jehu's Revolt." *BASOR* 302 (1996) 75–90.
———. *The Word of God in Transition: From Prophet to Exegete in the Second Temple Period.* Sheffield, UK: Sheffield Academic Press, 1995.
Schreiner, Josef. "Jer 9:22–23 als Hintergrund des paulinischen 'Sich-Rühmens.'" In *Neues Testament und Kirche: FS Rudolf Schnackenburg,* edited by J. Gnilka, 530–42. Freiburg: Herder, 1974.
Schuller, Eileen M. *Qumran Cave 4 XX: Poetical and Liturgical Texts, Part 2.* Oxford: Clarendon, 1999.
Schuller, Eileen M., and Carol A. Newsom. *The Hodayot (Thanksgiving Psalms): A Study Edition of 1QH^a.* Atlanta: Society of Biblical Literature, 2012.
Schulte, Hannelis. "The End of the Omride Dynasty: Social-Ethical Observations on the Subject of Power and Violence." *Sem* 66 (1995) 133–48.
Schulz, Hermann. *Leviten im vorstaatliche Israel und im mittleren Osten.* München: Chr. Kaiser, 1987.
Schunk, K. D. "Strukturlinien in der Entwicklung der Vorstellung vom Tag Jahwes." *VT* 14 (1964) 319–30.
Schweitzer, Steven. *Reading Utopia in Chronicles.* London: T. & T. Clark, 2007.

Schwemer, Daniel. *Die Wettergottgestalten Mesopotamiens und Nordsyriens im Zeitalter der Keilschriftkulteren. Materielen und Studien nach den schriftlichen Quellen.* Wiesbaden: Harrassowitz, 2001.
Scott, Bernard Brandon. *Hear Then the Parable: A Commentary on the Parables of Jesus.* Minneapolis: Fortress, 1989.
Scurlock, JoAnn. *Diagnoses in Assyrian and Babylonian Medicine: Ancient Sources, Translations, and Modern Medical Analyses.* Champaign, IL: University of Illinois Press, 2005.
———. "KAR 267 // BMS 53: A Ghostly Light on *bît rimki*?" JAOS 108 (1988) 203–9.
———. *Sourcebook for Ancient Mesopotamian Medicine.* Atlanta: SBL, 2014.
Sebba, Mark. "Societal Bilingualism." In *The Sage Handbook of Sociolinguistics*, edited by R. Wodak et al., 445–60. London: Sage, 2011.
Seibert, Eric. *The Violence of Scripture: Overcoming the Old Testament's Troubling Legacy.* Minneapolis: Fortress, 2012.
Seiler, Stefan. *Die Geschichte von der Thronfolge Davids [2 Sam. 9–20; 1 Kgs. 1–2]: Untersuchungen zur Literarkritik und Tendenz.* Berlin: De Gruyter, 1998.
Seitz, Christopher. *The Character of Christian Scripture: The Significance of a Two-Testament Bible.* Grand Rapids: Baker, 2011.
Sellin, Ernst. *Der alttestamentliche Prophetismus.* Leipzig: Deichert, 1912.
Sharp, Carolyn J. *Irony and Meaning in the Hebrew Bible.* Bloomington, IN: Indiana University Press, 2009.
———. *Prophecy and Ideology in Jeremiah: Struggles for Authority in the Deutero-Jeremianic Prose.* New York: Continuum, 2003.
Sherwood, Yvonne. *A Biblical Text and Its Afterlives: The Survival of Jonah in Western Culture.* Cambridge: Cambridge University Press, 2000.
Shields, Martin A. *The End of Wisdom: A Reappraisal of the Historical and Canonical Function of Ecclesiastes.* Winona Lake, IN: Eisenbrauns, 2006.
Shipp, R. Mark. *Of Dead Kings and Dirges: Myth and Meaning in Isaiah 14:4b–21.* Leiden: Brill, 2003.
Shoulson, Jeffrey S. *Fictions of Conversion: Jews, Christians, and Cultures of Change in Early Modern England.* Philadelphia: University of Pennsylvania Press, 2013.
Simon, Ulrich. "The Poor Man's Ewe Lamb: An Example of a Juridical Parable." Bib 48 (1967) 207–42.
Simundson, Daniel. *The Message of Job: A Theological Commentary.* Minneapolis: Augsburg Fortress, 1986.
Singer, Itamar. "A Concise History of Amurru." In S. Izre'el, *Amurru Akkadian: A Linguistic Study*, 141–48. Atlanta: Scholars, 1991.
———. *Hittite Prayers.* Atlanta: SBL, 2002.
Skinner, John. *Prophecy and Religion: Studies in the Life of Jeremiah.* Cambridge: Cambridge University Press, 1930.
Smart, James D. *The Past, Present, and Future of Biblical Theology.* Philadelphia: Westminster, 1979.
———. *The Strange Silence of the Bible in the Church: A Study in Hermeneutics.* Philadelphia: Westminster, 1970.
Smend, Rudolf. *Jahwekrieg und Stämmebund.* Göttingen: Vandenhoeck & Ruprecht, 1963.
Smick, Elmer. "Another Look at the Mythological Elements in the Book of Job." WTJ 40 (1978) 213–28.

Smith, Jonathan Z. "Map Is Not Territory." In *Map Is Not Territory: Studies in the Histories of Religions*, 289–309. Chicago: University of Chicago Press, 1978.

———. "Wisdom and Apocalyptic." In *Map Is Not Territory: Studies in the Histories of Religions*, 67–87. Chicago: University of Chicago Press, 1978.

Smith Mark S. *The Early History of God: Yahweh and the Other Deities in Ancient Israel*. Grand Rapids: Eerdmans, 2002.

———. *The Laments of Jeremiah and Their Contexts: A Literary and Redactional Study of Jeremiah 11–20*. Atlanta: Scholars, 1990.

———. *The Memoirs of God: History, Memory, and the Experience of the Divine in Ancient Israel*. Minneapolis: Augsburg Fortress, 2004.

———. "Rephaim." In *ABD* 5.675–76.

———. *The Ugaritic Ba'al Cycle, Volume 1: Introduction with Text, Translation and Commentary of CAT 1.1–1.2*. Leiden: Brill, 1994.

Smith, Sidney. *The Statue of Idri-mi*. London: British Institute of Archaeology, 1949.

Smith-Christopher, Daniel L. *A Biblical Theology of Exile*. Minneapolis: Augsburg Fortress, 2002.

———. "Reading the Christian Old Testament in the Contemporary World." In *The Old Testament and Apocrypha. Fortress Commentary on the Bible*, edited by G. A. Yee et al., 43–66. Minneapolis: Fortress, 2014.

Snaith, Norman H. *The Distinctive Ideas of the Old Testament*. London: Epworth, 1947.

Snell, Daniel C. *Flight and Freedom in the Ancient Near East*. Leiden: Brill, 2001.

Snijders, Lambertus A. "מלא." In *TDOT* 8.297–307.

Snook, Ivan A., ed. *Concepts of Indoctrination: Philosophical Essays*. London: Routledge, 2010.

Snyder, Graydon F. "Sayings on the Delay of the End." *BR* 20 (1975) 19–35.

Soderlund, Sven. *The Greek Text of Jeremiah Revisited*. Sheffield, UK: JSOT, 1985.

Soggin, J. A. "Gilgal, Passah und Landnahme . . ." *VTSup* 15 (1966) 263–77.

Sommer, Benjamin. "New Light on the Composition of Jeremiah." *CBQ* 61 (1999) 646–66.

Soskice, Janet Martin. *Metaphor and Religious Language*. Oxford, Clarendon, 1985.

Sparks, Kenton L. *God's Word in Human Words: An Evangelical Appropriation of Critical Biblical Scholarship*. Grand Rapids: Baker, 2008.

Spencer, Herbert. *Principles of Sociology, Vol. 1*. London: Williams & Norgate, 1871.

Sperber, Alexander. *The Bible in Aramaic 4A: Hagiographa*. Leiden: Brill, 1968.

Spurgeon, Charles H. "A Greater than Solomon." 1881. In *The Spurgeon Sermon Collection*. 4 Vols. Portland, OR: Ages Software, 1997.

Stackert, Jeffrey. *Rewriting the Torah*. Tübingen: Mohr Siebeck, 2007.

Staples, W. "The Book of Ruth." *AJSL* 53 (1936–37) 145–57.

Starr, Ivan. *The Rituals of the Diviner*. Malibu, CA: Undena, 1983.

Steck, Odil Hannes. "Theological Streams of Tradition." In *Tradition and Theology in the Old Testament*, edited by D. A. Knight, 183–214. 1977. Reprint. Sheffield, UK: JSOT, 1990.

Stern, David. "Afterlife: Jewish Concepts." In *ER* 1.120–24.

Stern, Philip. "The 'Bloodbath of Anat' and Psalm xxiii." *VT* 44 (1994) 120–25.

Sternberg, Meir. *The Poetics of Biblical Narrative*. Bloomington, IN: Indiana University, 1985.

Steymans, Hans-Ulrich. *Deuteronomium 28 und die* adê *zur Thronfolgeregelung Asarhaddons. Segen und Fluch im Alten Orient und in Israel.* Göttingen: Vandenhoeck & Ruprecht, 1996.

Stienstra, Nelly. *YHWH is the Husband of his People: Analysis of a Biblical Metaphor with Special Reference to Translation.* Kampen: Kok Pharos, 1993.

Stökl, Jonathan. *Prophecy in the Ancient Near East. A Philological and Sociological Comparison.* Leiden: Brill, 2012.

Stone, Ken. "Marriage and Sexual Relations in the World of the Hebrew Bible." In *The Oxford Handbook of Theology, Sexuality, and Gender*, edited by A. Thatcher, 173–88. New York: Oxford University Press, 2014.

———. *Sex, Honor and Power in the Deuteronomistic History.* Sheffield, UK: Academic Press, 1996.

Strauss, Rita. *Die Reinungsrituale aus Kizzuwatna: Ein Beitrag zur Erforschung hethitischer Ritualtradition und Kulturgeschichte.* Berlin: De Gruyter, 2006.

Stuart, Douglas. "Sovereign's Day of Conquest." *BASOR* 221 (1976) 159–64.

Stulman, Louis. *Jeremiah.* Nashville: Abingdon, 2005.

Sturtevant, Edgar H. "A Hittite Text on the Duties of Priests and Temple Servants." *JAOS* 54 (1934) 363–406.

Sukenik, Eleazar L. *The Dead Sea Scrolls of the Hebrew University.* Jerusalem: Magnes, 1956.

Suriano, Matthew James. "The Formulaic Epilogue for a King in the Book of Kings in Light of Royal Funerary Rights in Ancient Israel and the Levant." PhD diss., University of California at Los Angeles, 2008.

Swatos, William H., Jr., and Daniel V. A. Olson, eds. *The Secularization Debate.* Lanham, MD: Rowman & Littlefield, 2000.

Sweetman, Robert S. "When Popular Piety and Theological Learning Conjoin: St. Bonaventure on Demonic Powers and the Christian Soul." *Fides et Historia* 23 (1991) 4–18.

Tadmor, Ḥayim. "The Inscriptions of Nabunaid: Historical Arrangement." In *Studies in Honor of Benno Landsberger*, edited by H. G. Güterbock & T. Jacobsen, 351–64. Chicago: Oriental Institute, 1965.

Talmon, Shemaryahu. "The Comparative Method in Biblical Studies: Principles and Problems." *VTSup* 29 (1977) 320–56.

———. "Literary Motifs and Speculative Thought in the Hebrew Bible." *HUSLA* 16 (1988) 150–68.

Tanzer, Sarah J. "Biblical Interpretation in the Hodayot." In *A Companion to Biblical Interpretation in Early Judaism*, edited by M. Henze, 255–78. Grand Rapids: Eerdmans, 2012.

Tate, W. Randolph. *Biblical Interpretation: An Integrated Approach.* Peabody, MA: Hendrickson, 2008.

Taubmann, Paul. *Textanalyse zu Friedrich Gogarten, "Verhängnis und Hoffnung der Neuzeit. Die Säkularisierung als theologisches Problem."* Norderstedt: GRIN Verlag, 2008.

Taylor, J. Glen. "The Song of Deborah and Two Canaanite Goddesses." *JSOT* 23 (1982) 99–108.

Teichman, Milton. "How Writers Fought Back: Literature from the Nazi Ghettos and Camps." *Judaism* 47 (1998) 338–50.

Terrien, Samuel. Review of *Psalms II*, by Mitchell Dahood. *USQR* 23 (1968) 391.

———. *The Elusive Presence: Toward a New Biblical Theology.* New York: Harper & Row, 1978.

Thettayil, Benny. *In Spirit and Truth: An Exegetical Study of John 4:19–26 and a Theological Investigation of the Replacement Theme in the Fourth Gospel.* Leuven: Peeters, 2007.

Thiel, Winfried. *Die deuteronomistische Redaktion von Jeremia 1–25.* Neukirchen-Vluyn: Neukirchener, 1973.

Thielicke, Helmut. *Nihilism: Its Origin and Nature—with a Christian Answer.* London: Routledge & Kegan Paul, 1961.

Thomas, David Winton. Review of *Lamentations,* by N. Gottwald. *JTS* 6 (1955) 262–65.

Thompson, John Arthur. *The Book of Jeremiah.* Grand Rapids: Eerdmans, 1980.

Thompson, Reginald Campbell. *The Devils and Evil Spirits of Babylonia.* 1903. Reprint. Whitefish, MT: Kessinger, 2010.

Thompson, Stith. *Motif-Index of Folk Literature,* 1932–36. Reprint. Bloomfield, IN: Indiana University Press, 1955–58.

Thureau-Dangin, F. *Rituels accadiens.* 1921. Reprint. Osnabruck: Otto Zeller, 1975.

Tigay, Jeffrey H. *You Shall Have No Other Gods: Israelite Religion in the Light of Hebrew Inscriptions.* Atlanta: Scholars, 1986.

Tigchelaar, Eibert J. C. "The Addressees of 4QInstruction." In *Sapiential, Liturgical and Poetic Texts from Qumran: FS Maurice Baillet,* edited by D. Falk et al., 62–78. Leiden: Brill, 1999.

Tolkien, J. R. R. *The Fellowship of the Ring.* London: Allen and Unwin, 1954.

Tooman, William A. *Gog of Magog: Reuse of Scripture and Compositional Technique in Ezekiel 38–39.* Tübingen: Mohr Siebeck, 2011.

Torczyner, H. "A Hebrew Incantation against Night-Demons from Biblical Times." *JNES* 6 (1947) 18–29.

Tov, Emanuel. *Textual Criticism of the Hebrew Bible.* Minneapolis: Fortress, 2012.

Trachtenberg, Joshua. *Jewish Magic and Superstition.* 1939. Reprint. Philadelphia: University of Pennsylvania Press, 2004.

Trible, Phyllis. *God and the Rhetoric of Sexuality.* Philadelphia: Fortress, 1978.

———. "Ruth." In *ABD* 5.842–47.

———. *Texts of Terror: Literary-Feminist Readings of Biblical Narratives.* Philadelphia: Fortress, 1984.

Tropper, J. *Nekromantie. Totenbefragung im Alten Orient und im Alten Testament.* Neukirchen-Vluyn: Neukirchener, 1989.

Turner, Ralph H. "Role Theory." In *Handbook of Sociological Theory,* edited by Jonathan H. Turner, 233–54. New York: Springer, 2006.

Turner, Victor W. *Dramas, Fields and Metaphors: Symbolic Action in Human Society.* Ithaca, NY: Cornell University Press, 1975.

Tylor, Edward B. *Primitive Culture: Researches into the Development of Mythology, Philosophy, Religion, Art and Custom.* London: John Murray, 1871.

Udoekpo, Michael Ufok. *Re-Thinking the Day of YHWH and Restoration of Fortunes in the Prophet Zephaniah.* Bern: Lang, 2010.

Uehlinger, Christoph. "Nimrod." In *DDD* 627–30.

Umansky, Ellen. "Between Sisters." In *Chapters of the Heart: Jewish Women Sharing the Torah of Our Lives,* edited by S. L. Elwell and N. Fuchs Kreimer, 20–26. Eugene, OR: Cascade, 2013.

Ünal, Ahmet. "Zum Status der 'Augures' bei den Hethitern." *RHA* 31 (1973) 27–56.

van Dam, Cornelis. *The Urim and Thummim: A Means of Revelation in Ancient Israel.* Winona Lake, IN: Eisenbrauns, 1997.
van den Hengel, John. "Miriam of Nazareth: Between Symbol and History." In *A Feminist Companion to Mariology*, edited by Amy-Jill Levine, 130–46. London: T. & T. Clark, 2005.
VanderKam, James. "2 Maccabees 6:7a and Calendrical Change in Jerusalem." *JSJ* 12 (1981) 52–74.
VanderKam, James, and Peter Flint. *The Meaning of the Dead Sea Scrolls: Their Significance for Understanding the Bible, Judaism, Jesus, and Christianity.* London: T. & T. Clark, 2002.
van der Toorn, Karel. "Anat-Yahu, Some Other Deities, and the Jews of Elephantine." *Numen* 39 (1992) 80–101.
———. "From the Mouth of the Prophet: The Literary Function of Jeremiah's Prophecies in the Context of the Ancient Near East." In *Inspired Speech: Prophecy in the Ancient Near East: Essays Presented to Herbert B. Huffmon*, edited by J. Kaltner and L. Stulman, 191–202. New York: Continuum, 2007.
———. "The Nature of the Biblical Teraphim in the Light of the Cuneiform Evidence." *CBQ* 52 (1990) 203–22.
van der Woude, Annemarieke. "Resurrection or Transformation? Concepts of Death in Isaiah 24–27." In *Formation and Intertextuality in Isaiah 24–27*, edited by J. T. Hibbard and H. C. Paul, 143–64. Atlanta: Society of Biblical Literature, 2013.
van Driel, G. *The Cult of Aššur.* Assen: Van Gorcum, 1969.
van Gelder, Geert Jan. *The Bad and the Ugly: Attitudes Toward Invective Poetry* (Hijā') *in Classical Arabic Literature.* Leiden: Brill, 1988.
van Keulen, Percy S. F. *Two Versions of the Solomon Narrative: An Inquiry into the Relationship between MT 1 Kgs. 2–11 and LXX 3 Reg. 2–11.* Leiden: Brill, 2005.
van Seters, John. "David." In *ER* 4.242–44.
van Wolde, Ellen. "Texts in Dialogue with Texts: Intertextuality in the Ruth and Tamar Narratives." *BibInt* 5 (1997) 1–28.
Velikovsky, Immanuel. *Ages in Chaos.* Garden City, NY: Doubleday, 1952.
Vesco, Jean-Luc. "La date du livre de Ruth." *RB* 74 (1967) 235–47.
Veverka, Fayette Breaux. "Congregational Education: Shaping the Culture of the Local Church." *RelEd* 92 (1997) 77–90.
Vetter, Dieter. *Seherspruch und Segensschilderung.* Stuttgart: Calwer, 1974.
Vieyra, Marcel. "Le sorcier hittite." In *Le monde du sorcier*, edited by D. Bernot et al., 101–25. Paris: Editions du Seuil, 1959.
Virolleaud, Charles. "Anat et la génisse." *Syria* 17 (1936) 150–73.
———. "La déesse Anat: Poème de Ras Shamra." *Syria* 18 (1937) 85–102.
Volz, Paul. *Das Neujahrsfest Jahwes: Laubhüttenfest.* Tübingen: Mohr, 1912.
———. *Der Prophet Jeremia.* Leipzig: Deichert, 1928.
———. *Studien zum Text des Jeremia.* Leipzig: Deichert, 1920.
Von der Osten-Sacken, Peter. *Die Apokalyptik in ihrem Verhaltnis zu Prophetie und Weisheit.* Munich: Kaiser, 1969.
von Gall, August Freiherr. βασιλεία τοῦ θεοῦ: *Eine religionsgeschichtliche Studie zur vorkirchlichen Eschatologie.* Heidelberg: Winter, 1926.
———. *Der hebräische Pentateuch der Samaritaner.* Giessen: Töpelmann, 1918.

von Pákozdy, Ladislaus M. "Theologische Redaktionsarbeit in der Bileam-Perikope." In *Von Ugarit nach Qumran. Festschrift für Otto Eissfeldt*, edited by J. Hempel and L. Rost, 161–76. Berlin: Töpelmann, 1958.

von Rad, Gerhard. *Holy War in Ancient Israel*. 1951. Translated by B. C. Ollenburger. Grand Rapids: Eerdmans, 1991.

———. "Die Konfessionen Jeremias." *EvT* 3 (1936) 265–96.

———. "The Origin of the Concept of the Day of Yahweh." *JSS* 4 (1959) 97–108

———. *Old Testament Theology*. 2 Vols., 1957–60. Translated by D. M. G. Stalker. New York: Harper & Row, 1962–65.

———. "Promised Land and Yahweh's Land." 1943. Translated by E. W. Trueman Dicken. In *The Problem of the Hexateuch and Other Essays*, 79–102. Edinburgh: Oliver & Boyd, 1966.

———. *Wisdom in Israel*, 1970. Translated by James D. Martin. Nashville: Abingdon, 1972.

von Ranke, Leopold. *Geschichten der romanischen und germanischen Völker von 1494 bis 1514*. Leipzig: Duncker & Humblot, 1824.

von Weiher, E. *Spätbabylonischen Texte aus Uruk, II*. Mainz am Rhein: P. von Zabern, 1983.

Vyse, Stuart. *Believing in Magic: The Psychology of Superstition*. Oxford: University Press, 2014.

Wagar, W. Warren. "Introduction." In *The Secular Mind: Transformations of Faith in Modern Europe*, edited by W. Wagar, 1–12. New York: Holmes & Meier, 1982.

Waldrop, M. Mitchell. *The Emerging Science at the Edge of Order and Chaos*. New York: Simon & Schuster, 1992.

Walker, Christopher, and Michael Dick. *The Induction of the Cult Image in Ancient Mesopotamia: The Mesopotamian Mīs Pî Ritual*. Helsinki: Helsinki University, 2001.

Walls, Neal H. *The Goddess Anat in Ugaritic Myth*. Atlanta: Scholars, 1992.

Walton, John, et al. *The IVP Bible Background Commentary: Old Testament*. Downers Grove, IL: IVP, 2000.

Ward, William A. "Egyptian Relations with Canaan." In *ABD* 2.399–408.

Warner, Marina. *Alone of All Her Sex: The Myth and the Cult of the Virgin Mary*. New York: Random House, 1976.

———. "In and Out of the Fold: Wisdom, Danger and Glamour in the Tale of the Queen of Sheba." In *Out of the Garden: Women Writers on the Bible*, edited by C. Büchmann and C. Spiegel, 154–63. New York: Fawcett Columbine, 1994.

Warning, Wilfried. *Literary Artistry in Leviticus*. Leiden: Brill, 1998.

Watson, Wilfred G. E. *Classical Hebrew Poetry: A Guide to Its Techniques*. 2nd ed. Sheffield, UK: JSOT, 1986.

Watters, William R. *Formula Criticism and the Poetry of the Old Testament*. Berlin: De Gruyter, 1976.

Weber, Max. *The Sociology of Religion*, 1922. Translated by E. Fischoff. Boston: Beacon, 1993.

Weidner, Ernst Friedrich. "Aus den Tagen eines assyrischen Schattenkönigs." *AfO* 10 (1935–36) 1–52.

Weigel, Sigrid. "The Role of Lamentation for Scholem's Theory of Poetry and Language." In *Lament in Jewish Thought: Philosophical, Theological, and Literary Perspectives*, edited by I. Ferber and P. Schwebel, 185–204. Berlin: De Gruyter, 2014.

Weinfeld, Moshe. *Deuteronomy and the Deuteronomic School*. Oxford: Oxford University Press, 1972.
Weippert, Manfred. "Heilige Krieg in Israel und Assyrien." *ZAW* 84 (1972) 460–93.
———. "*Jau(a) mār Ḫumri*: Joram oder Jehu von Israel?" *VT* 28 (1978) 81–85.
Weippert, Manfred, and Helga Weippert. "Die 'Bileam'-Inschrift von Tell Dēr ʿAllā." *ZDPV* 98 (1982) 77–103.
Weir, Jack. "Amphictyony/Confederacy." *MDB* 27.
Weiser, Artur. *Das Buch Jeremia. Kap. 1–25:14*. 6th ed. Göttingen: Vandenhoeck & Ruprecht, 1969.
Weisman, Ze'ev. *Political Satire in the Bible*. Atlanta: Scholars, 1998.
Weiss, Meir. "The Origin of the 'Day of the Lord'—Reconsidered." *HUCA* 37 (1966) 29–60.
Weitzman, Steven. *Solomon: The Lure of Wisdom*. New Haven: Yale University Press, 2011.
Wellhausen, Julius. *Die Composition des Hexateuchs und der historischen Bücher des alten Testaments*. Berlin: Goschen'sche, 1899.
———. *Israelitische und jüdische Geschichte*. 9th ed. Berlin: De Gruyter, 1958.
———. *Prolegomena zur Geschichte Israels*. Berlin: Reimer, 1883.
———. *Reste Arabischen Heidentums*. 1887. Berlin: De Gruyter, 1961.
Wesley, John. "Sermon 39: Catholic Spirit." In *The Complete Works of John Wesley, Vol. 5: Biography and Sermons 1–39*, edited by E. Sugden, 567–79. Nashville: Abingdon, 1983.
Westbrook, Raymond. "International Law in the Amarna Age." In *Amarna Diplomacy: The Beginnings of International Relations*, edited by R. Cohen and R. Westbrook, 28–41. Baltimore: Johns Hopkins University, 2000.
Westermann, Claus. *Der Aufbau des Buches Hiob*. Tübingen: Mohr, 1956.
———. "The Blessing God and Creation." 1978. Translated by D. W. Stott. In *Elements of Old Testament Theology*, 85–117. Atlanta: John Knox, 1982.
———. *Praise and Lament in the Psalms*. 1977. Translated by K. Crim and R. Soulen. Atlanta: John Knox, 1981.
———. *The Promises to the Fathers: Studies on the Patriarchal Narratives*. 1976. Translated by D. E. Green. Philadelphia: Fortress, 1979.
———. "Struktur und Geschichte der Klage im alten Testament." *ZAW* 66 (1954) 44–80.
Weyde, Karl William. *The Appointed Festivals of YHWH*. Tübingen: Mohr Siebeck, 2004.
Wheeler, Brannon M. *Moses in the Qur'an and Islamic Exegesis*. New York: Routledge Curzon, 2002.
White, Marsha. "Naboth's Vineyard and the Legitimation of a Dynastic Extermination." *VT* 44 (1994) 66–76.
Whitelam, Keith W. "Hiram." In *ABD* 3.203–5.
Whitman, Walt. "A Passage to India." In *Leaves of Grass*, 340–48. 1855. Reprint. New York: Bantam Dell, 2004.
Whittaker, David J. *Conflict and Reconciliation in the Contemporary World*. London: Routledge, 1999.
Whybray, Roger N. *The Succession Narrative*. London: SCM, 1968.
———. *The Intellectual Tradition in the Old Testament*. Berlin: De Gruyter, 1974.

Wickman, Charles A. *Pastors at Risk: Protecting Your Future, Guarding Your Present*. New York: Morgan James, 2014.
Wiesmann, Hermann. *Die Klagelieder, übersetzt und erklart*. Frankfurt: Philosophisch-theologische Hochschule Sankt George, 1954.
———. "Der planmässige Aufbau der Klagelieder des Jeremias." *Bib* 7 (1926) 146–61.
———. "Der Verfasser des Büchleins der Klagelieder ein Augenzeuge der behandelten Ereignisse?" *Bib* 17 (1936) 71–84.
Wightman, Gregory J. *Sacred Spaces: Religious Architecture in the Ancient World*. Leuven: Peeters, 2007.
Williams, Michael J. *Deception in Genesis: An Investigation into the Morality of a Unique Biblical Phenomenon*. New York: Lang, 2001.
Willi-Plein, I. "Das Geheimnis der Apokalyptik." *VT* 27 (1977) 62–81.
Wilson, Michael K. "As You Like It: The Idolatry of Micah and the Danites." *Reformed Theological Review* 54 (1995) 73–85.
Wilson, Robert R. *Prophecy and Society in Ancient Israel*. Philadelphia, Fortress, 1980.
Wimmer, Donald. "The Sociology of Knowledge and the Confessions of Jeremiah." In *SBLSP* 1, edited by P. Achtemeier, 393–406. Missoula: Scholars, 1978.
Wiseman, Donald. *The Alalaḫ Tablets*. London: British Institute of Archaeology at Ankara, 1953.
Witt, Lance. *Replenish: Leading from a Healthy Soul*. Grand Rapids: Baker, 2011.
Witte, Henk. "Profession and Ministry in Conflict?" In *Religious Leadership and Christian Identity*, edited by D. Nauer et al., 168–80. Münster: LIT Verlag, 2004.
Witzenrath, Hagia Hildegard. *Das Buch Rut. Eine literaturwissenschaftliche Untersuchung*. Munich: Kösel, 1975.
Wöhrle, Jacob. *Die frühen Sammlungen des Zwölfprophetenenbuches: Entstehung und Komposition*. Berlin: De Gruyter, 2006.
Wolff, Hans Walter. *Joel and Amos*. Philadelphia, Fortress, 1977.
———. "The Kerygma of the Yahwist." 1964. Translated by W. A. Benware. In *The Vitality of Old Testament Traditions*, edited by W. Brueggemann and H. W. Wolff, 41–66. Atlanta: John Knox, 1982.
———. "Masters and Slaves: On Overcoming Class Struggle in the Old Testament." *Int* 27 (1973) 259–72.
Wolkstein, Diane, and Samuel Noah Kramer. *Inanna, Queen of Heaven and Earth: Her Stories and Hymns from Sumer*. New York: Harper & Row, 1983.
Wolters, Al. "Aspects of the Literary Structure of Combination I." In *The Balaam Text from Deir ʿAllā Re-Evaluated*, edited by J. Hoftijzer and G. van der Kooij, 294–304. Leiden: Brill, 1991.
———. "The Balaamites of Tell Deir ʿAllā as Aramean Deportees." *HUCA* 59 (1988) 101–13.
Worden, James W. *Grief Counseling and Grief Therapy: A Handbook for the Mental Health Professional*. London: Routledge, 1991.
Worthington, Ian. *Alexander the Great: Man and God*. London: Routledge, 2014.
Wray, T. J. *What the Bible Really Tells Us: The Essential Guide to Biblical Literacy*. Lanham, MD: Rowman and Littlefield, 2011.
Wright, David P. *The Disposal of Impurity: Elimination Rites in the Bible and in Hittite and Mesopotamian Literature*. Atlanta: Scholars, 1987.
———. *Ritual in Narrative: The Dynamics of Feasting, Mourning, and Retaliation Rites in the Ugaritic Tale of Aqhat*. Winona Lake, IN: Eisenbrauns, 2001.

Wright, N. T. *The Resurrection of the Son of God*. London: SPCK, 2003.
Wu, Kuang-Ming. *On Metaphoring: A Cultural Hermeneutic*. Leiden: Brill, 2001.
Würthwein, Ernst. *Das Erste Buch der Könige, Kapitel 1–16*. Göttingen: Vandenhoeck & Ruprecht, 1977.
———. *Die Erzählung von der Thronfolge Davids. Theologisch oder politische Geschichtsschreibung?* Zurich: Theologischer Verlag, 1974.
Wurtzel, Elizabeth. *Bitch: In Praise of Difficult Women*. New York: Doubleday, 2000.
Wyatt, Nicolas. "The Expression בכור מות in Job 18:13 and Its Mythological Background." *VT* 40 (1990) 207–16.
Yee, Gale A. "An Analysis of Prov. 8:22–31 according to Style and Structure." *ZAW* 94 (1982) 58–66.
———. "The Anatomy of Biblical Parody: The Dirge Form in 2 Samuel 1 and Isaiah 14." *CBQ* 50 (1988) 565–86.
———. "Fraught with Background: Literary Ambiguity in 2 Samuel 11." *Int* 42 (1988) 240–53.
———. "Ideological Criticism: Judges 17–21 and the Dismembered Body." In *Judges and Method: New Approaches in Biblical Studies*, edited by G. A. Yee, 146–69. Minneapolis: Augsburg Fortress, 1995.
———. "'I Have Perfumed My Bed with Myrrh': the Foreign Woman (אשה זרה) in Prov. 1–9." *JSOT* 43 (1989) 53–68.
Yon, Marguerite. *The City of Ugarit at Tell Ras Shamra*. Winona Lake, IN: Eisenbrauns, 2006.
Young, Frances M. *The Art of Performance: Towards a Theology of Holy Scripture*. London: Darton, Longman and Todd, 1990.
Youngblood, Ronald. "The Amarna Correspondence of Rib-Haddi, Prince of Byblos." PhD diss., Dropsie College, 1961.
Zaccagnini, Carlos. *Lo scambo dei doni del Vicino Oriente durante i secoli XV—XVIII*. Rome: Centro per le antichita e la storia dell'arte del Vicino Oriente, 1973.
Zevit, Ziony. "A Phoenician Inscription and Biblical Covenant Theology." *IEJ* 27 (1977) 110–18.
———. *The Religions of Ancient Israel: A Synthesis of Parallactic Approaches*. New York: Continuum, 2001.
Zholkovsy, Alexander K., and Yuri Shchlegov. "Structural Poetics is a Generative Poetics." In *Soviet Semiotics*, edited by D. Lucid, 175–92. Baltimore: Johns Hopkins University Press, 1978.
Zimmerli, Walther. *Ezechiel*. Neukirchen-Vluyn: Neukirchener, 1969.
———. "Promise and Fulfillment." 1953. Translated by J. L. Mays. In *Essays on Old Testament Hermeneutics*, edited by C. Westermann, 89–122. Richmond, VA: John Knox, 1963.
Zimmermann, Ruben. "Nuptial Imagery in the Revelation of John." *Bib* 84 (2003) 153–83.
Zimmern, Heinrich. *Beiträge zur Kenntnis des babylonischen Religion. Die Beschwörungstafeln* Šurpu. *Ritualtafeln für den Wahrsager, Beschwörer, und Sanger*. Leipzig: Hinrichs'sche, 1896–1901.
———. "Zu den 'Keilschrifttexte aus Assur religiösen Inhalts.'" *ZA* 30 (1915–16) 206–13.

Author Index

Abusch, I. T., 29, 212, 213, 259, 269
Alt, A., 184, 270
Anthonioz, S., 4, 7, 20, 270

Barr, J., 47, 49, 53–54, 140, 142, 271
Beckman, G., 12, 36, 272
Berlin, A., 245, 247–48, 272
Blenkinsopp, J., 15, 26, 37, 273
Brueggemann, W., 47, 55, 57, 89, 95, 119, 206, 247, 274

Caquot, A., 4, 10–11, 13–14, 17, 126, 261, 275, 302
Childs, B. S., 47, 49, 86, 241, 276
Collins, J. J., 94, 113, 167, 170, 205, 259, 276
Crenshaw, J., 58, 59, 60, 64, 96, 160, 277, 299
Cross, F. M., 10, 11, 26, 36, 53–55, 71, 123, 136, 140–41, 212, 214, 218, 252, 277–78

Douglas, M., 6, 26, 280

Eliade, M., 47, 281
Freedman, D. N., 96, 101, 283, 290, 295
Friedman, R. E., 22, 27, 39, 163, 283
Frymer-Kensky, T., 35, 194, 203, 258, 283

George, A. R., 28, 219, 283
Goldingay, J., 94, 99, 222, 284

Gottwald, N., 6, 26, 48, 122, 183, 202, 226–28, 230, 233, 238, 240, 280, 283, 285, 297, 312
Gunkel, H., 27, 49, 60, 196, 209, 286
Gurney, O. R., 8, 9, 259, 286

Hackett, J., 4, 13, 16, 17, 18, 213, 222, 286, 292
Hallo, W., 6, 269, 281, 287, 303
Halpern, B., 5, 125, 191, 203, 245, 247, 262, 287, 295
Hanson, K. C., 286, 287
Hoftijzer, J., 3, 4, 26, 71, 184, 213, 262, 263, 278, 289, 291, 295, 316
Huffmon, H. B., 10–11, 61, 208, 245–46, 275, 285, 290, 313

Ittmann, N., 60–64, 77, 89, 92, 95, 290
Janzen, J. G., 67, 173, 214, 290

Kammenhuber, A., 9, 12, 291
Kaufmann, Y., 26, 33, 37, 40, 291
Kittel, B. P., 99, 100, 102, 120, 292, 307
Knoppers, G. N., 189, 292
Knudtzon, J. A., 8, 142–45, 292, 304

Laessøe, J., 8, 28, 293, 305
Lambert, W.,
Lasine, S., 127, 137, 294
Lemaire, A., 4, 14, 17, 184, 275, 294
Levenson, J., 174, 191, 245, 247, 287, 295
Levine, B. A., 4, 13, 16, 26, 32, 214, 224, 295
Lévi-Strauss, C., 33, 150, 295

AUTHOR INDEX

Lloyd, J. B., 130, 131, 133, 296

McCarter, P. K., 16, 46, 125, 159, 232, 261, 297
Mendenhall, G., 5, 18, 19, 285, 297
Milgrom, J., 18, 26, 31, 32, 33, 35, 40, 298
Moore, M. S., 3–5, 7–9, 12, 14, 16–17, 19–21, 23, 27, 33, 35, 37, 38–39, 45, 51, 59, 70–72, 76, 85–89, 95–96, 109, 112, 115, 117–18, 126, 129, 134–37, 149, 151, 153, 155, 157, 159–61, 169–70, 175–77, 186, 189, 192, 196, 202–3, 210–11, 213–14, 217, 220, 222–23, 237, 239, 245, 252, 254, 255, 257, 262, 274, 287, 298
Moran, W., 52, 142–45, 147, 149, 299
Mowinckel, S., 5, 17, 48, 49, 50, 55, 56, 59, 62, 64, 69, 87, 96, 177, 300, 306

Noegel, S. B., 10, 301
Noth, M., 5, 21, 22, 49, 122, 124, 184, 295, 300, 301

Olyan, S. M., 26, 135, 142, 220, 252, 257, 278, 302
Oppenheim, A. L., 7, 8, 10, 302
Otto, E., 137, 303

Pardee, D., 130, 131, 249, 252, 303
Parry, R. A., 234, 303
Pope, M., 5, 214, 223, 255, 304
Reiner, E., 16, 28, 102, 263, 305
Rendtorff, R., 22, 37, 305
Ricoeur, P., 100, 305

Roberts, J. J. M., 47, 50, 51, 187, 190, 214, 241, 302, 306
Rofé, A., 3–5, 14, 124, 128, 306
Rudolph, W., 5, 46, 56, 63, 68–69, 73–75, 196, 228–31, 233, 307

Sasson, J. M., 191, 194, 248, 307
Schiffman, L., 35, 136, 308
Schniedewind, W. M., 123, 125, 308
Scurlock, J., 28, 29, 309
Smith, M. S., 30, 34, 60–61, 96, 130–31, 134–35, 172, 174, 224, 258, 310

Terrien, S., 51, 57, 88, 257, 279, 311
Trible, P., 157, 215, 217, 312

van der Toorn, K., 96, 131, 208, 313
von Rad, G., 21, 45, 46, 48–53, 55, 59–60, 63–64, 75, 79, 85, 87, 89, 95, 122, 124, 170–71, 175, 184, 257, 289, 314

Weber, M., 7, 282, 288, 314
Wellhausen, J., 5, 22, 26–27, 36–38, 40, 63, 140–41, 203, 303, 315
Westbrook, R., 142, 151, 271, 274, 296–97, 300, 315
Westermann, C., 62, 185, 189, 215, 242, 315, 317
Wilson, R. R., 6, 10, 62, 316
Wolff, H. W., 49, 53–56, 185, 198, 211, 269, 316

Yee, G. A., , 127–28, 139, 199, 245, 258, 298, 310, 317

Zevit, Z., 41, 218, 317

Subject Index

Aaron, 26-27, 32-36, 38-39
Abiathar, 36
Abraham, 34, 184, 186, 189, 193, 205, 252, 289, 298
Addu-dūri, 11
Ahab, 70, 123-24, 126, 128-29, 135, 136, 139, 198, 285, 308
Akk(adian), 7, 27-28, 50, 52, 145, 151, 154, 167, 169, 207, 212-13, 219, 221, 255, 263, 275, 279-80, 282, 293-94, 305, 309
Alalaḫ, 10, 316
Aleppo, 29, 145, 149
Alla, 35
Allaiturah(h)i, 9, 15, 212, 258-60, 286
Amarna, 10, 136, 141-43, 146-55, 158, 212, 271, 274, 293, 296, 297, 299-301, 305, 315, 317
Amman, 3
amphictyon(ic), 49, 294, 315
Anat, 125, 130-39, 219, 248-55, 257, 277, 285, 296, 303-4, 311, 313-14
Anathoth, 61, 65, 78, 90, 96, 115, 121
Anatolia, 5, 9, 12, 15, 17-18, 29, 36, 212, 218, 221, 254, 259-60, 263, 266, 300
Annunitum, 51
angel(ic), 3, 91, 168, 194
anthropology, 6, 14-16, 19, 23-24, 26-28, 31, 33, 141, 149, 204, 271, 279, 285, 291, 295, 297, 300
apocalyptic, 33, 43, 55, 56, 59, 99, 113, 117, 168-70, 174, 177, 214, 256, 277, 279, 283, 287-88, 298, 307, 310
Aqhat, 10, 245-46, 249, 250-255, 289, 292, 297, 317
Arabic, 5, 32, 34, 36, 128, 156, 157-58, 160, 236, 284, 313, 315
Aramaic, 9, 11, 13, 16-17, 34, 69, 71, 75, 126, 154, 164, 193-94, 207, 213, 216, 224, 257, 261, 275, 278, 280, 282, 289-91, 300, 301, 306, 308, 310, 316
archaeology, 3, 5, 29, 41, 201, 278, 279, 282, 294, 295, 310, 316
Aristophanes, 127
Aristotle, 22
Assyria, 7, 14, 15-17, 19, 22, 28-29, 33-36, 39, 56, 73, 86, 122, 124-26, 149, 205, 212, 214, 218-19, 263, 270, 273, 276, 278, 283-85, 287, 292, 294-95, 297, 303, 305-6, 309, 315
Aššurbanipal, 28, 32, 270
augury, 9, 13, 221, 300, 313
Azazel, 34

Ba`al, 11, 30, 46, 108, 122, 124-26, 130-39, 172, 186, 249, 252, 255, 282, 295, 303
Babylon, 8, 15, 21, 27, 29, 45, 49, 50-52, 56, 68, 75, 84, 86-89, 91, 122, 128, 136, 169, 205, 213, 217-19, 226, 233, 263, 269, 278, 280, 283-, 284, 286, 287, 291-92, 294, 297, 302-3, 305-6, 309, 312, 314, 318

SUBJECT INDEX

Balaam, 3–9, 11–24, 33, 37–39, 41, 91, 96, 127–28, 162, 169, 188–89, 191, 193, 208, 213, 222–23, 234, 254, 269, 272, 276–80, 286–87, 289, 291–93, 295–97, 299–300, 306–8, 314–16
Baruch, 64, 96, 270, 287
Beowulf, 51
Bibl(ical), 3, 6, 13, 15, 18, 20–22, 25–27, 33–34, 37, 39, 41, 47, 59, 72, 75, 76, 81, 84, 90, 94, 97, 99, 101, 118, 124, 139–41, 152, 156, 163–68, 174, 183, 197, 198, 200. 203, 205–6, 209, 224, 229, 235, 245, 247, 256, 258–59, 261, 270–279, 281–85, 287–99, 301–17
Bildad, 4, 216
bît rimki, 8, 16, 28, 29, 31, 39, 294, 305, 309
bless(ing), 5, 8, 13, 34, 47, 55–56, 98, 111–12, 162, 183–93, 195, 199, 210, 257, 299, 315
Boğazköy, 9, 143, 144, 154, 150, 221
Book of the Twelve, 57
bribe, 86

Canaan(ite), 122, 124–25, 130–31, 133–39, 142, 148, 155, 169, 215, 219, 224, 232, 246, 248–49, 251, 257, 265, 269, 275, 277, 278, 280, 282, 285, 287, 295, 300, 305, 308, 312, 314
Christian, 35, 57, 81, 84, 141, 156, 162, 166, 185, 206, 256, 270–72, 274, 276–77, 288–89, 291, 299, 301, 303–4, 306, 309–13, 316
church, 57, 81, 82, 83, 92, 93, 288, 310, 313
complexity theory, 41
consume(rism), 41, 46, 93, 164, 175, 197, 217, 218, 221
continuum, 6–9, 11, 18, 39, 40, 59, 204, 235
corruption, 84, 87, 116, 281, 284
covenant, 12, 48, 57, 78, 83, 87, 88–89, 98, 104–5, 108, 116–18, 121, 124, 132, 137, 138, 140–42, 146, 151, 153, 159, 162, 172, 184, 196, 217–19, 271, 277, 284, 289, 290, 297, 302, 304, 306, 317
creation, 26, 35, 50, 59, 77, 90, 183, 185, 196, 199, 257, 277, 294, 308, 315
(oc)cult(ic), 4–6, 13, 18, 27, 30, 35, 38, 40, 45, 46–48, 50–52, 54–55, 57, 62, 64, 73, 75, 77–78, 131, 169, 172, 187, 189, 191, 199, 232–33, 252, 257–58, 263, 274, 279, 282, 286–87, 289, 291, 295–98, 302–3, 308, 313, 314
curs(ing), 5–6, 8, 9, 13, 15, 50, 55, 56, 95, 188

Daniel, 10, 167–68, 170, 177–79, 249–54, 276, 279, 283–84, 297, 299, 304
Dan(ites), 38–39, 123, 126, 199, 206, 208–9, 270, 301, 308, 316
David, 11, 124, 153, 155, 185, 190, 193–96, 198, 201, 205, 211, 245, 246–52, 254–55, 261–65, 272, 274, 286–89, 295–96, 299, 302, 304, 307, 309, 313, 317
d(a)emon, 8–9, 11, 16–17, 28, 31, 39, 85, 92, 158, 172, 194, 208, 212–19, 221, 259–60, 262, 266, 274, 279, 287, 294, 311–12
deception, 118, 249, 253–54, 316
deuteronom/istic, 21, 59, 96–97, 174, 214, 226, 228, 233, 278, 289, 292, 296, 302, 306, 311, 312, 315
divination, 4, 7–8, 10, 12–16, 18, 22, 26, 29, 33, 35, 36, 38, 39, 86, 206, 208, 261, 270, 275, 278–79, 282, 285–86, 290, 292, 302, 307, 310
divine council, 4, 11, 35, 46, 213, 220, 298, 300
documentary hypothesis, 163, 271
dream(s), 7–8, 10–13, 46, 71, 75, 87, 141, 143, 145, 147, 149, 151, 153, 155, 191, 210–211, 269, 284, 300–301, 303

SUBJECT INDEX

economics, 22, 84–85, 89, 92, 129, 149, 152–53, 155, 161, 281, 289, 299, 301
Egypt(ian), 50, 55, 67, 84, 128–29, 131, 136, 143–53, 156, 169, 187–88, 205, 207, 257, 274, 287, 291, 296, 300, 301, 314
Eliphaz, 4, 175, 216–17, 219–20, 222–25
Emar, 26, 29, 30–35, 39, 41, 270, 279, 282, 285, 292, 307
Ephraim, 38, 40, 76, 78, 172, 199, 206, 261
Erra, 28, 217–19, 273, 275
eschatology, 46, 48–49, 56–57, 84, 167–68, 172, 174, 177–79, 269, 276, 286, 287, 289, 300, 304, 314
Euphrates, 29, 145, 282
exorcism, 8, 9, 11, 15, 16, 18, 213, 218–19, 259, 303
Ezra, 21, 22, 46, 153, 192, 277, 283, 287

foreign(er), 15, 22, 45–46, 52, 57, 59, 129, 138, 143, 151, 157, 161–62, 169, 183–85, 187–94, 196, 204, 207, 209, 220, 237, 281, 299, 317

gender, 202–4, 235, 256, 258, 267, 287, 294, 302, 304, 311
genre, 142, 148, 168–69, 240, 272, 279, 286, 291
Gilgal, 54, 55, 293, 310
Gilgamesh, 71, 219, 255, 284
Greek, 4, 49, 59, 64, 68, 168, 174, 200, 216, 257, 273, 294, 301, 310

Hadad, 29, 30, 31, 35, 70, 280
Hebrew, 3, 5, 6, 10, 12–15, 21–27, 31, 33–36, 38–40, 47–48, 50, 52–54, 56, 59, 61, 62, 67, 75, 85, 97, 102, 120, 122, 124, 125, 127, 133–34, 137, 140, 142, 153–54, 157–58, 160, 162, 164, 166–69, 171-, 173, 175, 178, 184–88, 190–92, 197–98, 200, 202, 204–10, 212–14, 224–25, 227–28, 235, 242, 245–46, 251, 256–58, 261,
265–66, 269–73, 275–79, 283–85, 287–88, 290–291, 293–94, 296–304, 306–9, 311–12, 314
Hellenist(ic), 54, 57, 62, 153, 167, 168, 169, 200, 277, 288–89
Herakles, 47, 127
Hezekiah, 110, 147
histor(ical), 4, 5, 12–15, 17, 21–25, 27, 31, 36–38, 40–41, 46–49, 55–58, 61, 63-, 64, 68, 73, 79, 85–86, 89, 97, 120, 122–25, 129, 135–41, 148–49, 151, 153–55, 164, 166–68, 170–71, 175, 183–86, 188–89, 197–205, 209–10, 214, 218, 224–27, 229–30, 233–34, 236, 238–39, 242–43, 245–46, 249, 257, 260, 267, 269, 270–271, 273, 279, 281–85, 287–95, 297–304, 306–11, 313, 315
Hittite, 8, 9, 26, 30, 33, 50, 75, 145, 147, 151, 169, 221, 259, 262, 272, 274, 276, 282–83, 286, 291, 300, 303, 307, 309, 311, 313, 317
holiness, 33, 35, 46, 49–53, 55–57, 76, 81, 105, 110, 173, 175, 189, 206, 218, 220, 248, 257, 279, 292, 314, 317
homosexual, 51, 203, 285
hypostasis, 258, 297

Idri-mi, 10, 12, 310
immortal(ity), 166–68, 169, 171, 173, 175, 177, 179, 277, 299, 301
Inanna, 51, 128, 144, 257, 316
incubation, 11, 292
inscaping, 85, 89, 245
intellectual(ist), 25, 41, 59, 68, 69, 72, 75, 78, 81, 87, 90, 101, 142, 161, 257, 316
intertextual(ity), 21, 23–24, 31, 36, 40, 47, 49, 57, 77, 94–95, 101, 118, 125, 127, 130–31, 139, 164, 198, 216, 223, 246, 261–62, 307, 313
incantation, 9, 11, 13–14, 28–29, 52, 212–15, 218, 221, 223, 260, 262, 265, 278, 282, 290, 305, 312
Islam, 25, 36, 156, 258, 277, 281, 294, 301, 315

Israel(ite), 25–27, 33–34, 36–38, 40–41, 46–50, 52, 54, 56, 58–59, 71, 84, 122, 126, 128–29, 131, 133–35, 137, 139–42, 153, 155, 159–62, 167, 169–72, 175, 177–78, 185, 187–93, 196, 198–206, 209–10, 217, 224, 226, 228, 245–47, 257–61, 265, 267, 270, 272–82, 284–88, 290–317

Jacob, 12, 140, 154, 188, 193, 207, 278
Jeroboam, 123–24, 129, 254, 281, 292
Jerusalem, 21, 45, 54, 56–57, 59, 64–65, 67, 72–73, 75–78, 80, 87, 89, 136, 142, 152, 155, 157–58, 162–63, 186, 189, 217, 223, 226–27, 232, 240, 288, 294, 302, 305, 313
Job, 4, 11, 28, 39, 50, 59–60, 79–80, 89–90, 95–96, 114, 128, 160–61, 163, 171, 173, 175–77, 192, 208, 212–17, 219–25, 269, 272, 275, 278–79, 282, 284–86, 289–91, 296, 299–301, 304, 306–10, 315, 317
Jonah, 22, 128, 164, 192, 269, 283, 297, 303, 309
Jordan, 3, 5, 14, 17, 19, 84, 207, 213
Joseph, 12, 157, 207
Josephus, 4, 241, 284
Judah(ite), 12, 46, 48, 56, 64, 69, 75, 78, 84–89, 93, 95, 119, 122, 126, 133, 172, 194, 199, 207, 208, 227, 234–35, 253, 287, 294, 298
Judaism/Jew(ish), 3, 4, 12, 22, 97, 158, 168, 184, 192, 195, 200, 205–6, 228, 257-, 258, 263, 272–73, 276–77, 285, 287–89, 291–92, 294, 298, 300–301, 304, 306, 309, 311–13, 315
judg(ment), 45, 57, 60, 87, 105–6, 108, 113–15, 117, 119, 124–25, 136, 160, 198, 200, 202, 216, 221, 241, 243, 253, 262, 265

Kirta, 10, 71, 252, 265, 292

lament, 10, 23, 49, 59–62, 68, 78–80, 84–85, 90–91, 94–103, 107, 109, 111, 113, 115–17, 119, 121, 126, 129, 171, 173, 175–76, 178, 215, 219, 221, 228–29, 231–35, 238–43, 272, 275, 279, 280, 298, 310, 315
Lamentations, 21, 59, 200, 226–35, 237–41, 243–44, 269, 271, 274, 275, 279–80, 283, 285, 289–91, 293, 294, 296, 297, 301, 303, 307, 312, 316
law(suit), 12, 15, 21, 39–40, 60–61, 90, 103, 105, 108, 113, 118–19, 137, 141, 151, 163, 190–92, 194, 199, 205, 207, 210–11, 247, 262, 283–85, 290, 295, 304, 315
legend, 71, 126, 156, 157–58, 183, 186, 246, 249, 251, 255, 265, 283, 286, 294, 304, 307
levite, 36, 38–40, 199, 201, 204, 206–9, 269, 302, 308

magic(ian), 6–11, 13–15, 17–20, 23–24, 26, 38–40, 75, 128, 208, 223, 243, 259, 261, 265, 273, 277, 279, 282, 290, 292, 296, 306, 308, 312, 314
Marduk, 49, 50, 136, 303
Mari, 11, 50–52, 56, 143, 282, 288, 296, 299, 301, 303, 306, 308
marriage, 21, 22, 29, 31, 82, 129, 150, 155, 202, 204, 206, 275, 295, 297, 311
medic(al), 8, 28, 163, 283, 293, 306, 309
Meskene, 29, 270
Mesopotamia, 5, 7–9, 14, 17, 26, 28, 30, 35, 129, 149, 150, 160, 212, 221, 257, 269–70, 273, 278, 281–82, 285, 295, 301, 307, 309, 314, 317
messia(nic), 33, 47, 113, 126, 129, 185, 190, 192–93, 202, 211, 269, 276–77, 287–88, 300, 304, 306
metaphor, 21, 46, 90, 94, 95, 99–102, 113–14, 116–21, 130, 167, 170, 174, 188, 199, 211, 219, 221, 229,

235–36, 238–39, 258, 263, 265, 270–74, 294, 305, 310, 311–12, 317
meter/metrical, 55, 67, 68, 69, 186, 228, 235
Micah, 3, 12, 27, 36, 38–40, 56, 86, 199, 208, 209, 290, 316
Moab, 3, 15–17, 76, 129, 131, 183, 185, 187, 189–96, 201, 204, 207, 209, 294, 299
monarch(y)/king(dom), 5, 6, 9–11, 14, 16–22, 28–29, 46, 48–51, 55, 60, 71–73, 81–82, 86–87, 89, 122–26, 128–29, 133–34, 136–37, 140, 143–47, 149, 153–57, 159–60, 162, 169–70, 174, 177–78, 183, 188, 191, 193, 195, 197, 198–203, 205, 207–9, 211, 214, 226, 232, 235, 248, 260, 263–67, 269–70, 274, 282, 284–89, 292, 294, 296, 298–99, 302, 306, 308–9, 311
monotheism, 34, 39, 257, 258, 265, 278, 308
Moses/Mosaic, 4, 10, 13, 25, 32–34, 36, 47, 49, 60, 78, 88, 175, 199, 205–6, 217, 278, 315
motif, 45, 47–57, 61, 78–79, 87, 95, 113–14, 116, 166–69, 171, 174, 176–78, 199, 201, 206, 213, 219, 224, 227, 229, 231, 253, 260, 282, 299, 311, 312
myth(ical/ological/opoeic), 14, 33, 50, 55, 125, 136–37, 171, 183, 188, 213, 248, 256–57, 260, 279, 293, 307, 310, 313, 317

Nathan, 11, 249, 250, 251, 262, 286
Nazarene, 35, 57, 162, 164, 176, 313
Nazi(s), 86, 138, 246, 289, 312
netherworld/chthonic, 39, 128, 167, 172, 173, 175, 212, 217, 218, 219, 221, 259, 269
Nineveh, 28, 31, 33, 39, 143, 164

Palestin(ian), 7, 9, 21, 140, 147, 149, 151, 193, 202–3, 212, 233, 245–46, 249, 258–59, 261, 279, 283, 284, 288, 290
Pannamuwa, 73
parable, 262, 263, 264, 265, 266, 271, 308, 309
Passover, 28, 200
Persia(n), 22, 31, 40, 46, 59, 62, 64, 97, 141, 156, 169, 205, 284
Philo, 13, 151
philolog(ical), 5, 7, 18, 23, 33, 41, 54, 128, 141, 192, 284, 297, 307–8, 311
philosoph(ical), 23, 36, 40, 89, 120, 232, 273–74, 277, 281, 301–2, 305, 310, 313, 315–16
Phoenicia(n), 9, 17, 155, 184, 257, 269–70, 278, 290, 296, 298, 317
poet(ry/ical), 5, 22, 51, 55, 68–69, 74, 87, 94–102, 114–21, 134, 138, 156, 163, 187, 189, 191, 198, 227–29, 231, 233–35, 238–41, 243, 245, 247–48, 265, 271–72, 277–78, 282–83, 285, 291, 293, 298, 301, 303, 308, 311–15, 317
polyphonic, 22, 142, 171, 272, 301
polytheis(tic), 14, 34, 293
pray(er), 16, 22, 28–29, 59, 61, 75, 88, 93, 95, 165, 178, 186, 190, 194, 206, 212, 220, 239, 240–41, 252, 271–73, 276, 292, 301, 303, 309
preach, 11, 56, 78–79, 81, 84, 88, 91, 92, 96, 116, 118, 134, 165, 271, 274, 296
priest, 6–10, 13–14, 16–18, 25–41, 45, 48–50, 55, 57, 61–63, 65, 74–75, 86–, 88, 121, 128, 132, 136, 137, 169, 176, 187, 189, 191, 199–200, 205, 208, 213–14, 218, 221, 223, 235, 252, 254, 259–60, 266, 269, 274, 276, 278, 282, 285, 287, 289–90, 292, 299, 302, 304–5, 307, 311
promise, 91, 93, 124, 139, 141, 143, 145, 147–49, 151, 153, 155, 159, 177, 179, 184–85, 192, 196, 211, 254–55, 264, 271, 273, 289, 314–15, 317

prophecy, 4–7, 10–12, 15, 20–24, 33, 38, 45–48, 50–53, 55–65, 69, 71–75, 77, 80, 84–90, 95–97, 107, 115, 118, 121–22, 124, 126–29, 132, 135, 137–39, 156, 167, 170, 172–79, 193, 200, 205, 227, 235, 245, 249, 262–63, 265–66, 269–70, 272–81, 283–85, 287–306, 308–9, 311, 313–14, 316
proverbs, 74, 77–79, 201, 249, 256–59, 266, 275–76, 294, 298
psalms, 50–51, 60, 62, 70–71, 77, 94, 99, 175–76, 195, 201, 205, 227, 232, 242, 272, 274, 277–78, 286, 289, 293, 299–300, 306, 308, 311–12, 315
psycholog(ical), 37, 63, 83–85, 133, 198, 217, 229, 244, 275, 292, 301, 307, 314
purif(ication)

Qur'an, 4, 25, 30, 156–57, 224, 315
rabbi(nic), 3, 4, 25, 86, 124, 159, 191–93, 195–96, 205, 247, 255–56, 269, 272, 284, 304

Ras Shamra, 29, 125, 279, 280, 285, 313, 317
religi(ous), 4, 6–25, 28–29, 33, 37–41, 47, 55, 58, 63, 69, 75, 82, 85, 123–25, 127–29, 135–39, 141, 152, 155, 161, 164, 166–67, 170, 172, 192, 194–95, 199, 201, 203, 205–6, 208–9, 214, 223–24, 244, 258–59, 270–274, 279–82, 285–86, 290–291, 293, 295–97, 300–301, 305–10, 312–18
rephaim, 56, 174, 310
resurrection, 47, 81, 166–69, 171, 173–74, 176–78, 273, 287–88, 295, 297, 299, 301, 313, 317
ritual, 4, 5, 9, 11–19, 25–29, 31–37, 41, 48–50, 54–55, 57, 126, 129, 130, 136, 169, 172, 218, 221, 252, 254, 259, 262–63, 265–66, 272, 276, 279, 282, 284, 286, 292, 294–96, 298, 302–3, 305, 307–8, 310–11, 314, 317–18

role (theory), 4, 6–13, 15–20, 22–24, 27, 29, 35–41, 61, 64, 77, 83, 117, 133–34, 151, 158, 164, 167, 195, 202–4, 218, 245, 251, 254, 256, 258, 259–61, 265–67, 272, 275, 285, 287, 291, 297, 298–99, 302–3, 307, 312, 315

sacred, 14, 29–32, 46–47, 166, 211, 281, 284, 316
sacrific(ial), 10, 13, 16, 17, 29–32, 34, 46, 48, 131, 169, 176, 190, 213, 238, 248, 260, 270, 289, 292
Samari(tan), 125, 126, 127, 133, 135, 162, 257, 314
Šamaš, 28, 71
Samuel, 128, 133, 168, 183, 201, 247–48, 251, 261–62, 265, 275, 283, 292, 295, 297, 317
satir(ize), 3, 5, 12, 21, 23, 67–68, 76, 79, 87, 89, 125–29, 131, 133–35, 138-, 139, 172, 193, 263, 273–74, 286, 289, 291, 293, 297–98, 304-, 305, 315
Saul, 12, 118, 168, 195, 198, 201, 205, 261, 265, 292
sceptic(ism), 48, 58–60, 62–64, 77–79, 89–91, 176, 272
secular(ization), 47, 82, 84, 124, 274, 281, 289, 291, 311, 314
seer, 3, 4, 8, 10, 11, 12, 18, 22, 38, 69, 86, 277
Sefire, 73, 75, 143, 154, 282, 306
Sibitti/the Seven, 8, 16–17, 28, 32, 35, 139, 217–19, 221, 223, 240
Shiloh, 36, 210, 307
Simon the sorcerer, 11
Sinai, 47, 48, 54, 137, 184, 257
sociolog(ical), 60, 63, 84, 123, 141, 164, 168, 176, 203, 246, 282, 287, 291, 298, 306, 310–12, 315–16
Solomon, 126, 137, 140–42, 150, 152–58, 160, 162–63, 165, 167–68, 174, 189–90, 198, 201, 247–53, 262, 282, 283, 285, 292, 295, 296, 301, 310, 313, 315
sorcer(er), 8–9, 11–15, 22, 158, 259, 274, 292

suffer(ing), 59, 60, 63, 78–79, 86, 90–91, 101, 118, 129, 161, 168, 173, 175, 177, 179, 220–22, 224–27, 229, 231–35, 237, 239–43, 260
Sumer(ian), 50, 169, 257, 279, 294, 305, 316
Syria(n), 5, 9, 12, 15, 18–19, 29, 51–52, 123, 126, 147, 150, 156, 203, 259, 278, 281–84, 290

Talmud, 4, 5, 12, 124, 136, 159, 183–84, 190–91, 193, 195–96, 200–201, 204–6, 230, 256, 258, 269
targum(s), 4, 16, 18, 24, 156, 184, 191, 193–96, 272, 276, 278–79, 286, 292
Tel Dan, 126, 270, 301, 308
Tel Deir 'Allā, 3, 4, 6, 13–14, 16–20, 23, 26, 41, 213–14, 216, 222, 224, 273, 275, 278, 287, 289, 291, 292, 295, 300, 316
temple, 19, 27, 28, 29, 33, 37, 50, 82
terror(ism), 8–9, 19, 39, 86, 108, 114–15, 122, 129, 157, 175, 177, 204, 212, 214–15, 217, 218, 220, 222, 224, 253, 259, 261, 299, 312
theolog(ical), 4, 6, 10, 13–15, 20–21, 23, 40, 45, 48–50, 53, 56, 58–59, 64, 75, 79, 84, 90, 95, 97, 119, 122, 124, 135, 138–39, 141–42, 161, 163, 166–71, 174–75, 177, 198, 205, 222–35, 238, 243–44, 246, 269–71, 274, 276–81, 284–85, 287–89, 291–92, 294, 298–99, 301–4, 306–12, 314–17
theophany, 45–46, 52–57, 71, 271, 289, 291, 308
Tiamat, 50
Torah, 5, 15, 31–33, 48, 65–66, 68–69, 74–75, 78, 81, 86–88, 123, 128, 151, 163, 184–85, 189, 195, 205, 213, 227, 247, 262, 280, 290, 292, 310, 312

Ugarit(ic), 9, 11, 28–29, 46, 51, 125–26, 130, 138, 143, 145, 149, 174, 252–53, 257, 265, 273, 276, 278–80, 295–98, 302–4, 308, 310, 314, 316, 317
Urim & Thummim, 10, 33, 292, 313
Uruk, 28, 71, 314

victim(ology), 34, 127, 133, 137, 138, 247, 262
violence, 12, 47, 86, 109–10, 118–19, 122–23, 129, 134, 137–38, 199–200, 202, 209, 240, 242, 252, 262, 276, 308–9

war(rior), 12, 18, 37, 46–57, 71, 73, 79, 86, 91, 126, 130–31, 133–34, 141, 145, 149, 158, 162, 165, 199–202, 207, 210, 217, 232, 237, 241, 259, 267, 271, 275–78, 293, 298, 305, 314
wealth, 22, 37, 70–71, 86–87, 137, 149, 151, 153, 158–59, 299
West(ern), 25, 99, 203, 252, 270, 280, 281, 307, 309
wisdom, 23, 55, 58–59, 66–67, 69–70, 72–73, 77, 79, 87, 89, 93, 158, 160, 162–63, 167–68, 170, 173–76, 178, 189, 202, 214, 251, 256, 258, 261, 265–67, 269, 274–75, 277, 279, 283–84, 285, 291, 295, 299–300, 302, 305, 309–10, 314–15
wise men, 8, 58, 61, 66, 87–89, 95, 297
wise woman, 259–64
word-pair, 12, 68–69, 79, 213, 228, 241–42

Yahw(istic), 3–5, 11–13, 15–16, 21, 32–34, 39–40, 45–57, 59–60, 62, 64–66, 69, 70–77, 79–80, 84–85, 87, 89–91, 93, 96, 102, 105, 107, 110, 112–13, 119, 122–24, 126, 128, 129, 131, 133, 135, 137, 138–39, 208–11, 213–15, 217, 224–25, 227, 232–33, 239–40, 242, 257–58, 262, 264–65, 270, 276–78, 281, 287, 291, 297–99, 302, 306, 310, 314, 316

Zadok, 36, 128, 252
Zakkur, 11
Zinjirli, 69, 73

Zion, 57, 72–73, 76, 227–28, 233, 235, 238, 246, 279, 288, 296, 302, 305, 317
Zophar, 4, 128, 216, 289

Textual Index

AKKADIAN TEXTS

ABL
539.21	143

AGH
116.4	219
132.47	18

ANET
166.2	15
184.A.47	15
279	158
288	152

ARM
9.22.14	11
10.4.35	60
10.6.3'-8'	51
10.6.8'	51, 52, 288
10.50.23–26	60
13.23.6	11

AT
281	10

BBR
1–20.8	8
1–20.18	14
24.9	10
26	36
26.1.11	18
26.1.19	28
26.1.20	10
26.2.2	28
26.2.25	17
26.2.28	218
26.3.19	28
26.3.20–21	28
26.3.20	28
52.2	17
79–82.21–22	8

BWL
60.101	30

Dreambook
221–25	7
221	8

EA
4.15	143, 146
4.17	143, 146
9	149
9.6–18	146
11.22'	143, 146

EA (continued)

20.8-9	143
29	150, 151
29.33	144
29.65-67	143
29.166	143
34.42	144
35.26	10
41	147
41.9	143
51.4'-6'	145
53	147
53.41	145
55.4-5	143
67.13	144
83	152
83.25	144
89.17-18	144
90	148
90.27-28	145
100.33	144
105	152
105.20-21	144
114.14	145
114	148
114.68	145
117.90	151
118.23	151
121.61	145
123.23	145
125	152
125.27	151
125.39	144
126	148
126.10-11	145
132.33-34	144
136	148
136.11-13	145
136.27-29	146
138.53	144
148.12-14	155
148.37	144
149.40-76	155
151.15	155
151.46	155
154.5-19	155
158.36	145
162.39	143
252.10-15	152
280.11	145
280.13	145
357.68-71	212

Ee

4	50
4:28	50

Erra

1.23-44	28, 218
1.27	218
1.28-29	218
1.32-38	218
1.38	219
1.43	218
4.16	219
5.42	218

GE

3.2	71
12.17-18	219
12.273-86	255
12.295	255

Idr

28-29	10, 12

KAR

2.58.42	213
2.58.47	213
25.2.22	16
267	309

Maq

2.124	8
2.210-12	213
2.210	8
4.110-11	12
7.94-95	259
9.22	17

Racc

44.1–5	17

RS

17.123.6	144
17.123.7	144
17.286.12	146

šā

79.35	12
79.36	12

Šur

1.1–3	14
1.2	17
1.3	17
3.2	219
3.29	219

TuL

7.26	14
17.20	17
34.8–10	214
74.4	8
74.5–6	12
117.3	17

EGYPTIAN TEXTS

ANET

443	60

HITTITE TEXTS

ANET

195.170	15
350–51	9

HT

32.9–14	8
58.3—60.7	9
66.1—68.36	9
66.1	17
66.10	17
66.20	17

KBo

1.5.3.6	144
1.6.4	146
1.7.12	146
1.7.24	30, 144
1.7.26	146
1.23.1	146
1.23.3–4	144, 146
1.24.9'	144
1.24.10	146
4.2	9, 221
15.3.6	150
39.8.1.1–3	260

KUB

3.65.9	146
3.72.7	143, 150
5.1	33
7.5.4.1–10	12
7.60	9, 15
18.5.4	9
18.5.12	8
22.15.1.1–14	8
24.1–4	13
24.3.2.42	12
41.1.1.12–13	150

UGARITIC TEXTS (CAT)

1.1–1.2	310
1.3–4	255
1.3.1–3	125, 131
1.3.1	136
1.3.2	136
1.3.1.2–11	46

UGARITIC TEXTS
(CAT) (continued)

1.3.1.15	136
1.3.2.4	135
1.3.2.5	135
1.3.2.18	135
1.3.2.19	135
1.3.2.29–30	135
1.3.2.34–35	134
1.3.2.41	130
1.3.3.4–8	139
1.3.3.38–42	139
1.4.5.58—7.29	127
1.4.6.46	257
1.4.7.46	11
1.5.1.1–3	214
1.5.5–6	126
1.5.6.25	252
1.6.2.27	130
1.6.2.30–37	249
1.14–16	252
1.14.1–1.15.3	292
1.14.3.154–155	71
1.15.3.46–51	10
1.16.1.34–35	265
1.16.3.6	186
1.16.5.26	11
1.16.6.8	8, 10
1.17–19	246, 249
1.17.1–2	292
1.17.2.24–46	252
1.17.6.13	219, 253
1.17.6.25	219
1.18.1.1–19	249
1.18.4.6	130
1.18.4.24	34
1.19.3.2–4	10
1.19.3.10	10
1.19.3.24	10
1.19.3.32–33	10
1.19.3.38	10
1.19.4.18–61	249
1.19.4.33	249
1.19.4.41–61	253
1.19.4.43–46	254
1.23.33–37	12
1.23.33–34	252
1.82	279
1.82.3	11, 219
1.100.5	11
1.102.13	212
1.108.7	130

CANAANITE TEXTS
(KAI)

26A.6	5
27.4	212
27.8–12	218
181	194
181.19	16

HEBREW TEXTS

Genesis

12–22	252
14:20	186
15	184, 185
15:1	186
22:10	34
26:9	66
31	39
31:10–12	12
33:8–17	154
35:19	206
37–45	157
38	157, 298
38:12–18	253
40:8	12
41:17	12
44:4–5	12
44:14–17	8

Exodus

4:20	10
6	31
6:12	118
6:30	118
7:11	259
12:22	28
12:23	217

15	55	17:23	12
15:1–18	50, 54	19:1–22	259
15:3	54	21–36	295
19–23	48	22–24	3, 5, 12, 13, 24, 234, 286, 306
21:2–11	304		
21:12–14	262	22	16
22:17	8	22:5	13
22:18	15	22:6	16
28:30	10	22:8–20	11, 19
29	31, 33	22:21–35	128
34	48	22:41	16
34:22	200	23–24	128
		23:7	5, 24
		23:14	16

Leviticus

		23:18	5
1–16	298	23:28	16
5:6	264	24:1	16
7:37	35	24:3–9	186
8	292	24:3	5
8–9	27, 31, 32, 38	24:5	39
8:1–2	33	24:7	188
8:7–8	33	24:9	8
8:22	32	24:15	5
8:22–27	32	24:23	188
8:23	32	31:16	5, 13, 24
8:27	32	35:9–34	262
8:31	32		
8:33	35, 38, 136		

Deuteronomy

9	31		
9:8	34	4:34	159
9:22–24	34	6:16	159
10	40	8:2	159
10:1	263	8:15	106
10:1–3	32	8:16	159
16:1–22	260	10:16	118
16:21	18	13:3	159
16:26	34	14:1	169
16:32	35	16:13	50
17–22	298	18	308
19:26	11	18:9–22	60
23–27	298	18:10	8, 11, 15, 259
23:34	35	18:11	11
25:29	184	19:1–13	262
		23:4–7	3, 195

Numbers

		23:5	195
		26:14	169
10:11—36:13	205	27–28	87
12:6	10		

Deuteronomy (continued)

27:15	38
28	311
28:22	217
32:17	213
33:2–3	54
34:10	4

Joshua

3–5	55
13:21–22	3
13:22	22
15:44	145
24	48
24:9–10	3

Judges

1–16	198
3:12–25	201
3:22	193
4:6	130
4:17–22	253
5	277
5:1–31	130
5:4–5	54
5:20	130
5:21	130
5:30	130
6:36–40	159
7	56
9:6	198
9:8–15	197
9:9	197, 208
9:13	208
9:15	199
9:16	198
16:15	66
16:21	17
17–21	198, 200, 201, 205, 208, 210, 307, 317
17–18	27, 38, 198, 270
17	36, 206, 208
17:1–13	36
17:1–6	199
17:3	38
17:6	199
17:8–9	206
17:8	206
17:11	209
17:12	38, 136
17:13	208
18:1	199
18:15	208
18:20	209
18:24	38, 208
18:30–31	199
19–21	198, 201
19	294
19:1	199, 204, 206
19:2	207, 209
19:9–22	209
19:29	34
20:1–11	201
20:18	208
21	210
21:22	210
21:25	199

Ruth

1–4	201
1:1–5	263
1:1	206
1:4	193
1:5	193
1:6	194
1:7	207
1:10	207
1:11–12	207
1:15	194, 207
1:16–18	209
1:21	207
2:4	190
2:6	207
2:8–9	209
2:9	190
2:10	185, 204
3:9	129
3:11–13	209
4	200, 206, 208
4:7	184
4:10	204, 207
4:15	208

1 Samuel

1-3	36
1:1—2:11	292
5:5	47
9:9	10
9:12-24	10
15:32-33	188
15:32	171
17:18	46
18:22	73
25	261
25:24	263
28	13, 261, 265, 292
28:3-25	168
28:6-7	12
28:7	261

2 Samuel

1	317
1:19-27	171
3:33-35	171
5:20-25	56
7:1-16	255
7:4-5	12
7:11	138
9-20	309
11	246, 317
11:3	246
13:2	253
14	261
14:2	261
14:7	263
14:9	263
14:10	264
14:14	265
14:16	295
19:1	171
19:38	171
20	262
20:16	261
22:20	73
23:34	246
24:13	11

1 Kings

1-2	249
1:3	253
1:15	248
1:38-40	252
2	246
3-11	72
3:4-5	10
3:9	157
3:28	160
5:10-11	155
5:10	69
5:14	69
5:15-32	141
5:15	153
5:24	142
8:14-53	137
8:41-43	190
9:3	157
9:12-14	155
10	189
10:1-13	157, 303
10:1	157, 159
10:3	160
10:4-5	161, 190
10:4	69, 190
10:5	161
10:6	162
10:7	161
10:8-9	189
10:9	73, 162
10:13	162
10:18	124
10:19	124
10:24	163
10:31	124
11:1-13	155
12:31—13:9	199
13	128
14:10	255
16:15-20	134
16:35	135
18:1-40	126
18:27	126
19:3	171
19:16	126
21	125

2 Kings

2:23–25	128
3:27	17
6:1–23	126
6:8—7:20	293
6:24—7:20	126
7:2	126
7:19	126
8:7–15	126
9–10	125, 131, 283
9	125, 302
9:1—10:31	122
9:1–10	129
9:1	128
9:11	129, 135
9:17	135
9:18	135
9:20	135
9:21	135
9:22	135
9:24	136
9:26	139
9:31	135
9:34—10:17	136
10:6–10	133
10:15	135
10:18–28	135
10:30	123, 139
10:31	123, 124
17:7–40	137
18:29	147

1 Chronicles

3:5	246
16:27	72
16:29	72
16:40	75
23:1	171
28:2	227
29:29	171

2 Chronicles

8:13	75
20:21	72
23:18	75
30:5	75
33:6	259
35:25	59

Ezra

5:11	153
9–10	21
9:1	22, 46
10	22

Nehemiah

2:17	76
8:1	45
13:1–2	3

Esther

3:6	263
3:13	263

Job

1:6	213, 214, 224
1:7	28, 217
2:1	214, 217, 224
3:1–12	80
3:1–10	50
5:17	213, 217
5:20–23	217
5:23	217
6:4	213
7:12	279
8:3	213, 216
10:22	214
13:3	213
14	173, 176
14:13	175
14:20–22	175
15:8	11
15:15	220
15:17	11
15:20–26	175
15:21	220
15:23	220
15:25	220
16:9	219
16:12–13	219
16:14	79

16:16	79	24	50
16:19	215	24:7–10	54
18	307	26:2	159
18:13	214, 275, 317	29	50
18:14	214	29:2	72, 71
19:23–24	223	29:4	72
19:25–27	177	33	50
19:28–29	216	45:4	72
19:29	215, 216, 217, 282	45:5	72
20	289	45:14	195
20:1–29	128	46	50
21:15	220, 221, 222	47	50
21:16	222	48	50
21:17	221	49	176, 177, 178
21:20	221	49:7	70, 77
22:1–30	222	49:15	76
22:2	222	49:16	177
22:3	222	58:6	11
22:10–11	222	63:8	219
22:17	213, 222	66	50
22:26	213	66:5	11
23:16	223	69:15	178
27:10	213	69:16	172
28	291	69:18	178
28:1–28	163	69:22–27	178
28:21	160	69:29	178
30:30	215	73	70, 177, 178
31:2	213	73:23–38	176
31:35	213, 223	74:14	214
38–42	90	75	50
38:1—42:6	161	76	50
40:25	214	81	50
41:2–3	307	82	50
42:6	300	84	50
42:17	171	87	50
		90	176, 278
		90:13–17	175

Psalms

		90:16	72
6:6	171	91	173
8	50	93	50
11:1	66	93:1	50
15	50	95	50
21:6	72	96	50
22	176	96:6	72
22:9	73	96:9	72
22:29–31	176	96:10	50
22:30	176	97	50
23	130, 135, 310	97:1	50

Psalms (continued)

98	50
99	50
99:5	227
100	50
104:1	72
106:28	169
106:37	213
110:3	72
111:3	72
114	50
118	50
132	50
132:1–18	54
132:6	206
132:7	227
140:12	75
145:5	72
145:12	72
149	50

Proverbs

1–9	256, 257, 265, 266, 273, 291, 298, 317
1:20–33	265
2:16	204
5:20	204
6:24	204
7:5	204
8:1–21	265
8:22–31	280, 317
8:22–36	266
9	276
9:1–18	266
11:31	78
13:13	78
14:28	72
16:1	175
25:6	72
30:9	74, 75, 77

Qohelet/Ecclesiastes

	200
9:1–6	173
9:5	176
10:11	75

Canticles/Song of Songs

	200

Isaiah

1:11	73
2:3	76
2:5	76
2:6–22	56
2:10	72
2:19	72
2:21	72
3:3	11
4:3	178
5:14	72
5:24	77
8:16–18	60
9:3	56
10:5–7	122
11:1	17, 113
13	45, 53
13:6–22	53
13:6–13	47
13:6	45, 51
14	317
14:4–23	128
14:4–21	309
19:11	66, 67, 77
22:1–14	53
22:18	17
24–27	174, 298, 313
24:18	126
25:4–5	215
26:13—27:11	278
26:16	46
26:19	174
27:1	214
28:7	241
28:21	56
29:14	69
30:21	76
30:33	17
33:6	68
34:1–17	53
34:2–6	46
35:2	72
38:10–13	171
38:17	104

42:1	173	5:31	88, 241
42:3	173	6:9–12	65
42:4	173	6:10	118
44:9	220	6:12	65
47:9	11	6:13–15	65
47:12	11, 220	6:13	88
47:14	263	6:17–18	65
49:4	67	6:19	74, 76
52–53	273	7:3–7	75
52:13	178	7:9	67
53:4	67	7:29	94
53:10–12	173	8	89
53:11	173	8:1	87
55:11	73	8:4–9	65, 96
56:4	73	8:4–6	65
57:4	76	8:4–5	70
57:12	220	8:4	78
63:1–6	305	8:6–7	65
63:1	72	8:8–9	59, 64, 65, 72, 74, 77, 78, 85, 96
65:12	73	8:8	67, 72, 74, 75, 76, 77, 87
66:4	73	8:9	67, 68, 72, 77, 79
		8:10–12	65
		8:10	65, 88

Jeremiah

1–25	289, 302, 312, 315	8:17	11
1:5	64	9	89
1:8	77	9:9	94
1:14	86	9:11	64
1:17	68	9:12	74
2	303	9:16	64
2:1–3	205	9:19	94
2:2–3	279	9:22–23	59, 64, 69, 70, 73, 74, 77, 78, 85, 96, 293, 308
2:2	21, 72	9:22	69, 72, 77
2:8–9	65	9:23–24	70
2:8	69, 74, 75, 77, 79, 86, 87, 88, 220, 241	9:23	70, 72, 77
2:9	69, 87	9:25	118
2:11	220	10:7	64
2:23	66, 67	10:14	68
2:26	241	11–20	61, 84, 310
3:20	67	11–15	90
3:23	67	11	61
4:1–2	70	11:18—12:6	60, 84, 94
4:1	70	11:18–23	90
4:9	87, 241	11:18	103, 104, 119
4:22	64	11:19	78, 103, 104, 108, 109, 119
5:2	67	11:20	60, 78, 102, 103, 105, 106, 117, 119
5:13–14	65		

Jeremiah *(continued)*

11:21–22	65
11:21	85, 103, 104
11:22	105
11:23	111
12	61
12:1–6	90
12:1–4	79
12:1–2	62
12:1	60, 78, 79, 89, 105, 110, 119
12:2	78, 105, 106, 110, 114, 117
12:3	102, 104, 112, 119
12:4	78, 102, 103, 105, 109, 114
12:5	79
12:6	78
13:13–14	87
14:9	71
14:14–15	65
14:18	88
15:10–21	60, 84, 94, 284
15:10–14	91
15:10–12	62
15:10	60, 61, 105
15:14	104
15:15–21	91
15:15–19	65
15:15	85, 103, 104, 105, 107, 112, 119, 120
15:16	107, 111, 112
15:17–20	61
15:17	109, 119
15:18	66, 79, 85, 89, 106, 108, 114, 115
15:19	78
16:5–7	61
16:5	5
16:7	169
16:9	220
16:11	74
16:16	112
16:18	112
17–20	90
17:14–18	60, 84, 94
17:14	104, 105, 112, 114, 115
17:15	79, 89, 107
17:16–18	117
17:16	104, 110, 111, 117, 119
17:17	78, 108, 112, 115
17:18	68, 78, 79, 102, 103
18	61, 76
18:8	77
18:11	77
18:12	77
18:18–23	60, 74, 84, 94, 290
18:18	59, 61, 62, 64, 74, 77, 78, 85, 87, 96
18:19	60, 78, 106
18:20	74, 78, 89, 103, 106, 111, 116
18:22	78, 104, 109, 111, 116
18:23	78, 104, 107, 110, 113, 116, 119
19:1	241
20:1–6	85, 88
20:1–3	88
20:6	171
20:7–18	60, 62, 84, 94
20:7–8	276
20:7	61, 90, 104, 105, 111, 117, 118
20:8	103, 107, 112, 115
20:9	80, 103, 112, 118
20:10	105
20:11	71, 78, 79, 102, 104, 116
20:12	60, 78, 102, 110
20:14–18	80
20:18	78
22:3	73
22:11–12	171
22:15	73
22:18	171
22:30	178
23:1–4	87
23:5	73
23:8	11
23:9–32	87
23:9–22	85
23:16–32	289
23:18	11, 35
23:22	88
23:34–38	65
26–45	295
26:4	74
26:10–11	85
26:19	110
27:16–22	88
28	88

29	87	1:12	243
29:1-23	87	1:14	239
29:1	241	1:15	239, 240
29:6	21	1:16	239
29:26	88, 129	1:18	239
29:31	61	1:19	239, 241
30-31	64	1:20-22	239
31:33	74	1:21	239
32:18	71	1:22	243
32:23	74	2:1-10	239
34:19	87	2:1	227
35:1-11	136	2:5	240
35:6-16	135	2:10	239
38:6	89, 116	2:11	239
38:28	68	2:13	240
42:16-17	171	2:15	240
43:2	87	2:18-19	240
44	287	2:19	240
44:10	74	2:20	241, 243
44:15-30	131	3	232
44:23	74	3:1	239
46:1-12	53	3:14	109
46:10	46	3:44	233
48:1	68	3:48	240
48:2	76	3:51	240, 243
48:14	66, 67	3:55	240
48:41	68	3:63	239
49:7	64	4:3	240
50-51	87	4:6	240, 241
50:2	68	4:13	241
50:9	68	4:16	241
50:24	68	4:17	241
50:35	64	5:3	241, 242
50:36	71	5:7	242
51:1-14	86	5:11	242
51:31	68	5:12	242
51:41	68	5:13	242
51:56	68	5:14	242
51:57	64, 71		

Lamentations

Ezekiel

1:6	72, 240	1:1	86
1:8	243	3:15	86
1:9	239	3:23	86
1:10-11	239, 243	7:1-27	53
1:10	239	7:19	75
1:11	239	7:26-27	86
		7:26	75, 241

Ezekiel (continued)

9	28
9:1	223
10:15	86
10:20	86
10:22	86
12:13	171
13:5	56
13:9	178
16:36	11
17:16	171
18:2	173
20:33–38	21, 205
24:5	17
24:9	17
26:20	167
30:1–9	53
31:14	167
31:16	167
31:18	167
32:18	167
32:24	167
33:10	173
33:17	173
33:30–33	60
34:12	56
37:1–14	172
37:11	302
38–39	56, 188, 312
43:22	173
47:1–12	189

Daniel

1:4	178
1:17	178
1:20	68
2:2	11
2:10	11
2:27	11
4:4	11
4:34	162
4:37	162
8:23	178
8:25	178
8:26	14
9:13	178
9:22	179
9:25	179
10:1–2	177
10:14	177
11:7	177
11:14	177
11:27	177
11:29	177
11:35	177
11:40	177
12:1–4	166, 167, 168, 169, 170, 171, 174, 177, 299
12:1	177, 178, 179
12:2	167, 177
12:3	178
12:4	177
12:7	177
12:9	177
12:11	177
12:13	177

Hosea

1:4–5	124, 290
1:4	123, 125, 297
4:12	10
4:15	246
5:8	246
6:1–3	172
6:1	76
6:2	271
9:7	129
10:5	246
13:14—14:10	278
13:14	172

Joel

1–4	56
1	53
1:15	51
2	53
3	53
4	53
4:14	51

Amos

4:16–23	128

5:6	128
5:14–15	128
5:16–17	49
5:18–20	49, 56
6:7	5
7:10–17	88
7:13	199
7:14	295
7:17	171

Obadiah

	53
15	51

Jonah

2:1–10	128
2:6	104

Micah

1:4	108
1:8	60
1:9	298
3:5–12	86
4:2	76
5:1	206
6:3–5	3
6:5	12, 22
7:1–4	60
7:18	73

Nahum

1:14	38

Habakkuk

1:2–4	60
1:13	59
3:5	11
3:13–16	122

Zephaniah

1:2–6	45
1:7—2:14	56
1:7—2:4	53
1:7–16	47
1:7–15	56
1:7	46, 51
1:8	45, 46
1:9	47
1:14–18	46
1:14	47
3:7	67

Zechariah

1:4	200
2:17	45
14	53, 55
15	56

Malachi

1:6–14	163
2:17	73
3:5	259
3:10	126
3:16	120

1QpHab

1.13	97, 136
2.2	97
5.10	97
7.4	97, 98
8.3	97
9.9–10	97
11.5	97

1QHodayot

4.20	110, 111
5.3	109
5.5	107, 112
5.9	103, 117
5.24	107
5.25	107
6.4	117
6.12	104, 119
6.15	110
6.17	104, 119
6.24	106
7.15	104, 119
7.20	112

1QHodayot (continued)

7.25	104, 119
7.28	104
8.17	110
8.19	110
8.23	104
8.26	106
9.1—20.6	98
9.1—18.14	280
9.2	103
9.17	105
9.21	103, 104, 117, 119
9.23-24	120
9.23	108, 115
9.30-31	112
10.5-19	98
10.7	111, 118
10.9-10	107, 112
10.10-11	110
10.11	109, 111
10.12	110
10.13	102, 119
10.14	105, 119
10.17	103
10.20-30	98
10.21	103, 111, 116
10.22	109
10.23	104
10.28	108, 114
10.30	112
10.31	104, 107, 115
10.32	103
10.33-34	107
10.34	112
10.35	103, 104, 116
11.6-19	98
11.12	111, 116
11.16-17	111
11.16	116
11.18	110, 111, 116
11.19	104, 111, 115
11.20-37	98
11.20	103
11.21	109
11.26	109, 116
11.27-28	107
11.28	105, 113, 117
11.29	109
12.5—13.4	98
12.8-9	109
12.9-10	107
12.12-13	110
12.13	110
12.14-19	117
12.14	103, 106
12.15-16	107
12.15	104, 116
12.17	107
12.19	103, 104
12.22	104, 118
12.23	102
12.30	104, 119
12.31	110
12.34	108, 114
12.35-36	108
12.35	103, 107
12.36	103, 115
13.4	108
13.5-19	98
13.5-6	106
13.6	119
13.11-12	113, 117
13.12	106
13.13	104
13.20—15.5	98
13.22	105, 119
13.24	110
13.26	115
13.28	108, 115
13.29	103
13.30	105
13.35	102, 105, 108, 119
14.4	103, 106, 117
14.5	107, 109
14.6	103, 104, 119
14.11	109
14.15-17	114
14.15	105
14.16	106
14.19	105, 118
14.24	105
14.26	102, 119
14.29	113, 117
14.32	111
15.6-25	98
15.9	102, 119

15.17	108, 118	1QS erek	169
15.23	104		
15.34	109		
16.4—17.36	98		

CD (Damascus Document)

16.4	103, 114	1.11	97
16.6–9	109	20.32	97
16.6–7	106		
16.6	105		

11Q19 (Temple Scroll)

16.10	105, 110		
16.11	110	15.11	32
16.13	105, 110	15.14	35
16.20	110	15.15–16	136
16.23	106		
16.27–30	115		

11QMelchizedek

16.27	108, 118		177
16.28	115		
16.30	112, 118		
16.34	109, 116		

ARAMAIC TEXTS (*KAI*)

17.4	105		
17.9	119		
17.19	104	202.3	186
17.23	105	202.12–14	11
17.24–25	106, 115	202B.26	17
17.24	112	215.11	69, 72, 77
17.27	108	215.19	72
18.34–35	105	216.4	17
19.4–5	111	222–224	218
19.5	112, 118	222A.11	186
19.6	112	222A.26	17
19.7	108, 119	222A.28	17
19.8	107	222A.32	34
19.17	103, 117	224.8–9	154
19.19	102	224.17–21	76, 77
19.22	102		
19.23	112		
19.25	112		

DEIR ʿALLĀ TEXTS

DA

20.11	104, 119		
20.19	110		
20.22	113		
20.24	107	1	12, 19, 273
20.34	103, 117	1.1	4, 11, 16, 22
21.14	104	1.4	11
22.8	105, 118	1.5	11
22.16	104	1.7–9	12
23.9	108	1.7–8	12
25.13	105	1.8–9	12
25.14	107		
26.2	111		

DA (continued)

1.9	12
2	13, 14, 16, 17, 18, 19, 41
2.5	14, 17
2.7	14
2.12	14, 18
2.14	18
2.17	14

ARAMAIC TEXTS (TARGUMS)

Esth

2.3.1–3	156

Isa

37.26	18

Num

22.6	16
23.7	16, 24

Ruth

	184, 193, 196
1.1	193
1.4	193
1.5	193
1.6	191, 194
1.9	194
1.16	194

SYRIAC TEXTS (PESHITTA)

Lev

9:8	34

Num

22:5	13
24:7	188

1 Sam

28:13	168

1 Kings

3:28	160
10:1	157, 158
10:8	158, 189

Job

1:6	224
2:1	224
8:3	216
19:29	215, 216

Psa

106:37	213

Jer

5:2	67
18:18	76

Hos

13:14	172

GREEK TEXTS (LXX)

1 Macc

4:46	193

2 Macc

6:7	313

4 Macc

9:8	178

9:32	178
10:11	178
10:15	178
12:19	178
13:15	178
18:5	178
18:22	178

Jdt

8:29	256
11:1—13:10	253
11:20–23	256

Sir

1:4–20	256
4:11–19	256
6:18–31	256
24:1–22	256
30:18	169
41:1–13	173
41:3–4	176

Wis

1:15	168
2:21–23	167
2:22	174
3:1–13	174, 178
4:16–20	178
5:1–2	174
5:15	174
6:12–16	256
7:7–14	256
7:25–29	256
8:1–21	256
9:9–11	256
10:1–21	256

GREEK TEXTS (GNT)

Matt

12:22–23	185
16:1	159
18:8–9	178
20:29	185
24:27	57
24:37	57
24:39	57
25:46	176

Mark

9:48	178

Luke

4:1–13	303
12:4–5	178

John

4:19–26	312
4:21–24	162
6:53	160
6:60	163
12	273

Acts

1:6–7	57
2:38	35
4:25	185

Rom

16:1–2	267

1 Cor

1–4	294
7:26	93
11:2–16	267
14:34–36	267

Col

2:11	118

1 Tim

2:8–15	267

2 Tim

2:8	185

Heb

2:18	159
11:13	206

2 Pet

2:16	4

Jude

11	4

Rev

2:14	4

LATIN TEXTS (VULGATE)

Num

22:5	13

1 Sam

28:13	168

1 Kings

10:1	157, 158
10:4	190
10:8	189

Job

1:6	224
2:1	224
19:29	215, 216

Psa

106:37	213

Isa

26:19	174

Hos

13:14	172

www.ingramcontent.com/pod-product-compliance
Lightning Source LLC
Chambersburg PA
CBHW071149300426
44113CB00009B/1139